Certified Information System Security Professional (CISSP) exam objective map

D0841777

OBJECTIVE		
1.0	**ACCESS CONTROL**	
1.1	**Control access by applying the following concepts/methodologies/ tec...**	
1.1.1	Policies	1, 2, 4
1.1.2	Types of controls (preventive, detective, corrective, etc.)	2, 4, 5, 10
1.1.3	Techniques (e.g., non-discretionary, discretionary and mandatory)	2, 5
1.1.4	Identification and Authentication	2, 4, 7, 10
1.1.5	Decentralized/distributed access control techniques	2, 5, 7, 10
1.1.6	Authorization mechanisms	2, 3, 4, 5, 7, 10
1.1.7	Logging and monitoring	2, 4, 7, 9, 10
1.2	**Understand access control attacks**	2, 4, 9, 10
1.2.1	Threat modeling	2, 4, 5, 6, 7, 8, 9, 10
1.2.2	Asset valuation	2, 8
1.2.3	Vulnerability analysis	2, 3, 4, 5, 7, 8, 9, 10
1.2.4	Access aggregation	2, 10
1.3	**Assess effectiveness of access controls**	2, 4, 5, 6, 8, 9
1.3.1	User entitlement	1, 2, 4, 5, 6, 8, 10
1.3.2	Access review & audit	1, 2, 4, 5, 6, 7, 8, 9, 10
1.4	**Identity and access provisioning lifecycle (e.g., provisioning, review, revocation)**	1, 2, 4, 5, 10
2.0	**TELECOMMUNICATIONS AND NETWORK SECURITY**	
2.1	**Understand secure network architecture and design (e.g., IP & non-IP protocols, segmentation)**	5, 7, 8
2.1.1	OSI and TCP/IP models	7
2.1.2	IP networking	7
2.1.3	Implications of multi-layer protocols	7
2.2	**Securing network components**	4, 5, 7, 8, 10
2.2.1	Hardware (e.g., modems, switches, routers, wireless access points)	2, 4, 7, 8, 10
2.2.2	Transmission media (e.g., wired, wireless, fiber)	2, 3, 4, 7, 8, 10
2.2.3	Network access control devices (e.g., firewalls, proxies)	2, 4, 7, 8, 10
2.2.4	End-point security	2, 3, 4, 5, 7, 8, 10
2.3	**Establish secure communication channels (e.g., VPN, TLS/SSL, VLAN)**	3, 7
2.3.1	Voice (e.g., POTS, PBX, VoIP)	7
2.3.2	Multimedia collaboration (e.g., remote meeting technology, instant messaging)	7
2.3.3	Remote access (e.g., screen scraper, virtual application/desktop, telecommuting)	2, 7, 10
2.3.4	Data communications	2, 3, 5, 6, 7, 10
2.4	**Understand network attacks (e.g., DDoS, spoofing)**	3, 7, 8, 9, 10

Exam Objectives   The exam objectives listed here are current as of this book's publication date. Exam objectives are subject to change at any time without prior notice and at the sole discretion of ISC². Please visit the ISC² Certifications webpage for the most current listing of exam objectives at *https://www.isc2.org/cissp/default.aspx*.

OBJECTIVE		CHAPTER
3.0	**INFORMATION SECURITY GOVERNANCE & RISK MANAGEMENT**	
3.1	**Understand and align security function to goals, mission and objectives of the organization**	1, 8
3.2	**Understand and apply security governance**	1, 2, 4, 5, 6, 8, 9, 10
3.2.1	Organizational processes (e.g., acquisitions, divestitures, governance committees)	1, 6, 8
3.2.2	Security roles and responsibilities	1, 2, 4, 6, 8, 9, 10
3.2.3	Legislative and regulatory compliance	1, 5, 6, 8
3.2.4	Privacy requirements compliance	1, 5, 6, 8, 9
3.2.5	Control frameworks	1, 2, 5, 6, 9
3.2.6	Due care	1, 5, 6, 8
3.2.7	Due diligence	1, 5, 6, 8
3.3	**Understand and apply concepts of confidentiality, integrity and availability**	1, 2, 3, 4, 5, 7
3.4	**Develop and implement security policy**	1, 5, 6, 8, 10
3.4.1	Security policies	1, 5, 6, 8
3.4.2	Standards/baselines	1, 5, 6, 8
3.4.3	Procedures	1, 5, 6, 8
3.4.4	Guidelines	1, 5, 6, 8
3.4.5	Documentation	1, 5, 6, 8, 10
3.5	**Manage the information life cycle (e.g., classification, categorization, and ownership)**	1, 6, 8, 9, 10
3.6	**Manage third-party governance (e.g., on-site assessment, document exchange and review, process/policy review)**	1, 5, 6, 8, 9, 10
3.7	**Understand and apply risk management concepts**	1, 5, 6, 8, 9, 10
3.7.1	Identify threats and vulnerabilities	1, 2, 4, 5, 6, 7, 8, 9, 10
3.7.2	Risk assessment/analysis (qualitative, quantitative, hybrid)	1, 2, 4, 5, 6, 8, 10
3.7.3	Risk assignment/acceptance	1, 6, 8
3.7.4	Countermeasure selection	1, 2, 3, 4, 5, 6, 7, 8, 10
3.7.5	Tangible and intangible asset valuation	1, 8
3.8	**Manage personnel security**	1, 4, 8, 10
3.8.1	Employment candidate screening (e.g., reference checks, education verification)	1
3.8.2	Employment agreements and policies	1, 4, 6, 8
3.8.3	Employee termination processes	1
3.8.4	Vendor, consultant and contractor controls	1, 6, 8
3.9	**Develop and manage security education, training and awareness**	1, 2, 3, 4, 6, 7, 8, 10
3.10	**Manage the Security Function**	1, 4, 5, 6, 8, 9, 10
3.10.1	Budget	1, 4, 6, 8
3.10.2	Metrics	1, 4, 5, 6, 7, 8, 9, 10
3.10.3	Resources	1, 4, 5, 6, 7, 8, 9, 10
3.10.4	Develop and implement information security strategies	1, 2, 3, 4, 5, 6, 7, 8, 9, 10
3.10.5	Assess the completeness and effectiveness of the security program	1, 2, 3, 4, 5, 6, 7, 8, 9, 10
4.0	**SOFTWARE DEVELOPMENT SECURITY**	
4.1	**Understand and apply security in the software development life cycle**	9
4.1.1	Development Life Cycle	9
4.1.2	Maturity models	5, 9
4.1.3	Operation and maintenance	9, 10
4.1.4	Change management	9, 10
4.2	**Understand the environment and security controls**	2, 4, 5, 7, 8, 9, 10
4.2.1	Security of the software environment	2, 5, 7, 8, 9
4.2.2	Security issues of programming languages	9
4.2.3	Security issues in source code (e.g., buffer overflow, escalation of privilege, backdoor)	7, 8, 9, 10
4.2.4	Configuration management	4, 8, 9, 10
4.3	**Assess the effectiveness of software security**	7, 8, 9, 10

OBJECTIVE		CHAPTER
7.0	**OPERATIONS SECURITY**	
7.1	**Understand security operations concepts**	7, 8, 10
7.1.1	Need-to-know/least privilege	1, 2, 10
7.1.2	Separation of duties and responsibilities	1, 2, 9, 10
7.1.3	Monitor special privileges (e.g., operators, administrators)	1, 2, 10
7.1.4	Job rotation	1, 2, 10
7.1.5	Marking, handling, storing and destroying of sensitive information	1, 2, 7, 10
7.1.6	Record retention	1, 2, 10
7.2	**Employ resource protection**	2, 8, 9, 10
7.2.1	Media management	1, 2, 3, 7, 8, 9, 10
7.2.2	Asset management (e.g., equipment life cycle, software licensing)	1, 2, 5, 7, 8, 9, 10
7.3	**Manage incident response**	6, 8, 10
7.3.1	Detection	6, 8, 10
7.3.2	Response	6, 8, 10
7.3.3	Reporting	6, 8, 10
7.3.4	Recovery	6, 8, 10
7.3.5	Remediation and review (e.g., root cause analysis)	4, 6, 8, 10
7.4	**Implement preventative measures against attacks (e.g., malicious code, zero-day exploit, denial of service)**	1, 2, 3, 4, 5, 7, 8, 10
7.5	**Implement and support patch and vulnerability management**	9, 10
7.6	**Understand change and configuration management (e.g., versioning, base lining)**	4, 8, 9, 10
7.7	**Understand system resilience and fault tolerance requirements**	5, 7, 8, 10
8.0	**BUSINESS CONTINUITY & DISASTER RECOVERY PLANNING**	
8.1	**Understand business continuity requirements**	1, 4, 6, 8, 10
8.1.1	Develop and document project scope and plan	1, 8
8.2	**Conduct business impact analysis**	1, 8
8.2.1	Identify and prioritize critical business functions	8
8.2.2	Determine maximum tolerable downtime and other criteria	8
8.2.3	Assess exposure to outages (e.g., local, regional, global)	8
8.2.4	Define recovery objectives	8
8.3	**Develop a recovery strategy**	8
8.3.1	Implement a backup storage strategy (e.g., offsite storage, electronic vaulting, tape rotation)	4, 7, 8, 10
8.3.2	Recovery site strategies	4, 8, 10
8.4	**Understand disaster recovery process**	4, 8
8.4.1	Response	4, 8, 10
8.4.2	Personnel	4, 8, 10
8.4.3	Communications	4, 8, 10
8.4.4	Assessment	4, 8
8.4.5	Restoration	8, 10
8.4.6	Provide training	4, 8
8.5	**Exercise, assess and maintain the plan (e.g., version control, distribution)**	4, 8

OBJECTIVE		CHAPTER
9.0	**LEGAL, REGULATIONS, INVESTIGATIONS AND COMPLIANCE**	
9.1	**Understand legal issues that pertain to information security internationally**	1, 6, 8
9.1.1	Computer crime	6
9.1.2	Licensing and intellectual property (e.g., copyright, trademark)	6
9.1.3	Import/Export	6
9.1.4	Trans-border data flow	6, 7
9.1.5	Privacy	6
9.2	**Understand professional ethics**	1, 6
9.2.1	(ISC)² Code of Professional Ethics	1, 6
9.2.2	Support organization's code of ethics	1, 6
9.3	**Understand and support investigations**	6, 8
9.3.1	Policy, roles and responsibilities (e.g., rules of engagement, authorization, scope)	1, 4, 6, 8, 10
9.3.2	Incident handling and response	6, 8, 10
9.3.3	Evidence collection and handling (e.g., chain of custody, interviewing)	6, 8
9.3.4	Reporting and documenting	6, 8, 10
9.4	**Understand forensic procedures**	6, 8
9.4.1	Media analysis	6, 7
9.4.2	Network analysis	6, 7
9.4.3	Software analysis	6
9.4.4	Hardware/embedded device analysis	5, 6, 7
9.5	**Understand compliance requirements and procedures**	1, 2, 5, 6, 8
9.5.1	Regulatory environment	1, 4, 5, 6, 8
9.5.2	Audits	1, 5, 6, 8
9.5.3	Reporting	1, 5, 6, 8
9.6	**Ensure security in contractual agreements and procurement processes (e.g., cloud computing, outsourcing, vendor governance)**	1, 5, 6, 8
10.0	**PHYSICAL (ENVIRONMENTAL) SECURITY**	
10.1	**Understand site and facility design considerations**	2, 4, 8, 10
10.2	**Support the implementation and operation of perimeter security (e.g., physical access control and monitoring, audit trails/access logs)**	1, 2, 4, 8
10.3	**Support the implementation and operation of internal security (e.g., escort requirements/visitor control, keys and locks)**	2, 4, 8
10.4	**Support the implementation and operation of facilities security (e.g., technology convergence)**	2, 4, 6, 8, 10
10.4.1	Communications and server rooms	2, 4, 8
10.4.2	Restricted and work area security	2, 4, 6, 8
10.4.3	Data center security	2, 4, 8
10.4.4	Utilities and Heating, Ventilation and Air Conditioning (HVAC) considerations	4, 8
10.4.5	Water issues (e.g., leakage, flooding)	4, 8
10.4.6	Fire prevention, detection and suppression	4, 8
10.5	**Support the protection and securing of equipment**	2, 4, 8, 10
10.6	**Understand personnel privacy and safety (e.g., duress, travel, monitoring)**	1, 4, 8

CISSP Training Kit

David R. Miller

ISBN: 978-0-7356-5782-3

Third Printing June 2014

Printed and bound in the United States of America.

Microsoft Press books are available through booksellers and distributors worldwide. If you need support related to this book, email Microsoft Press Book Support at *mspinput@microsoft.com*. Please tell us what you think of this book at *http://www.microsoft.com/learning/booksurvey*.

Microsoft and the trademarks listed at *http://www.microsoft.com/about/legal/ en/us/IntellectualProperty/Trademarks/EN-US.aspx* are trademarks of the Microsoft group of companies. All other marks are property of their respective owners.

The example companies, organizations, products, domain names, email addresses, logos, people, places, and events depicted herein are fictitious. No association with any real company, organization, product, domain name, email address, logo, person, place, or event is intended or should be inferred.

This book expresses the author's views and opinions. The information contained in this book is provided without any express, statutory, or implied warranties. Neither the authors, Microsoft Corporation, nor its resellers, or distributors will be held liable for any damages caused or alleged to be caused either directly or indirectly by this book.

Acquisitions Editors: Ken Jones and Michael Bolinger
Developmental Editor: Box Twelve Communications
Production Editor: Kristen Brown
Editorial Production: Online Training Solutions, Inc.
Technical Reviewer: Michael Gregg
Copyeditor: Kerin Forsyth
Indexer: Bob Pfahler
Cover Design: Twist Creative • Seattle
Cover Composition: Ellie Volckhausen
Illustrator: Rebecca Demarest

I dedicate this work to Ms. Veronica Leigh Miller and to Mr. Ross Adam Maxwell Miller, sources of enduring warmth, happiness, and pride for me. Forever yours.

Further, I wish to express my deep regret over the loss of Mr. Harold (Hal) F. Tipton, who cofounded (ISC)², the International Information Systems Security Certification Consortium, in 1989. The (ISC)² established and maintains the Certified Information Systems Security Professional (CISSP) certification. Mr. Tipton passed away in March 2012 at the age of 89. This book is also dedicated to him for his vision and leadership in the information technology and IT security industry.

—David R. Miller

Contents at a glance

Contents

What do you think of this book? We want to hear from you!

Microsoft is interested in hearing your feedback so we can continually improve our
books and learning resources for you. To participate in a brief online survey, please visit:

www.microsoft.com/learning/booksurvey/

What do you think of this book? We want to hear from you!

Microsoft is interested in hearing your feedback so we can continually improve our
books and learning resources for you. To participate in a brief online survey, please visit:

www.microsoft.com/learning/booksurvey/

Chapter 5   Security architecture and design   303

Chapter 7   Telecommunications and network security   415

What do you think of this book? We want to hear from you!

Microsoft is interested in hearing your feedback so we can continually improve our
books and learning resources for you. To participate in a brief online survey, please visit:

www.microsoft.com/learning/booksurvey/

Introduction

This is a big book with a lot of pages and not many pictures. You must be serious about achieving this certification. That's good news. This book focuses directly on the security concepts, technologies, and processes that will help you prepare for the most recent edition of the Certified Information Systems Security Professional (CISSP) certification exam. This book presents the wide range of topics you need to know and understand to pass the CISSP exam. As you plow through these chapters, you will recognize how the individual chapters and topics tie together to form a complete and comprehensive framework of security and protection for the valuable information assets of the enterprise. Further, the information you learn from these pages will help you develop the skills and vision necessary to operate as a security professional, helping companies prepare for and defend themselves from the ever-growing array of threats to information systems and business continuity as a whole.

Cybercrime is becoming a more prevalent threat every day. The attacks are becoming more sophisticated and targeted. Financial institutions and governments are being attacked successfully, and the breaches cost companies millions and even billions of dollars in losses. Reports on the breach of Sony's PlayStation Network in April 2011 set the losses at $3.2 billion USD. In April 2012, more than 1.5 million credit cards were stolen in a breach at a card processing company in Atlanta, Georgia. In 2012, the number of breached customer records containing personally identifiable information (PII) tripled from 2011. Ponemon Institute estimates the average cost of the breach of customers' PII at $142 per record. In spite of the efforts of diligent network administrators and security professionals, the breaches continue to occur and seem to be much more targeted, sophisticated, and stealthy every day.

There are indications that corporations and even governments are sponsoring the development of attacks on computers and networks, developing new ways to replicate and spread malware, remain hidden, cover the tracks of the malicious presence and activities, and provide remote command and control to compromise any aspect of confidentiality, integrity, or availability at its master's choosing. This new breed of attack is called advanced persistent threat (APT) and is becoming the most challenging and destructive attack ever developed. The defenses of every IT system and network must be carefully considered, well understood, and implemented correctly to provide an appropriate level of protection. Developing this vision and understanding requires the development of skills in a broad range of areas—exactly the focus of the CISSP body of knowledge.

The CISSP certification is becoming an essential piece of the IT and security professional's résumé. Anyone who works in, or hopes to work in, the commercial world or within the government as an IT or security professional will benefit from the knowledge and vision preparing for the CISSP exam will provide. Improving your upward mobility in the organizational chart, hoping to land that new job, and, in some cases, keeping your existing job might require attaining this certification. For government workers, the Department of Defense (DoD) Directive 8570 has mandated security certifications for everyone at and above a specific pay grade.

> **NOTE DEPARTMENT OF DEFENSE DIRECTIVE 8570**
>
> From the (ISC)² website at *https://www.isc2.org/dod-fact-sheet.aspx*:
>
> This DoD-wide policy, made official in August 2004 and implemented according to the requirements of DoD 8570.1M Manual in December 2005, requires any full- or part-time military service member, contractor, or foreign employee with privileged access to a DoD information system, regardless of job or occupational series, to obtain a commercial information security credential accredited by ANSI or equivalent authorized body under the ANSI/ISO/IEC 17024 Standard. The Directive also requires that those same employees maintain their certified status with a certain number of hours of continuing professional education each year.

This book marches through the 10 domains outlined by the (ISC)²'s Common Body of Knowledge (CBK), providing the topics, concepts, and technologies needed to develop your skills as a security professional and to pass the very challenging CISSP certification exam. Each chapter contains exam tips and practice questions with answers and explanations. In addition, a large collection of questions, answers, and explanations help you become reacquainted with the testing process and identify areas of study requiring more attention.

The book includes the following:

- Information about the prerequisites for the certification
- Guidance on how to prepare for the exam
- Insights on how to analyze exam questions and answer sets on the exam
- A big-picture overview of the CISSP body of knowledge, tying it all together
- Guidance on how to register for the exam
- A 60-minute review of the major topics of the exam to help prepare yourself just before entering the exam center
- A description of the processes you'll witness on the day of the exam
- A description of the additional steps you must perform to become certified after passing the exam

> **NOTE DOWNLOAD THE REVIEW**
>
> Be sure to download the CISSP 60-minute review from *http://aka.ms/cisspTK/examples*.

The author, the editors, and the production team have worked hard to bring you a preparation tool worthy of your time. Take this challenge seriously, commit to the effort, become determined to pass the exam, and achieve certification to propel your career to new heights.

This training kit is designed for information technology (IT) professionals; IT security professional and business managers who support, plan to support, or are responsible for information systems information technologies; and those who plan to take the 2012 edition of the (ISC)^2 Certified Information Systems Security Professional (CISSP) exam or the SANS Institute Global Information Assurance Certified (GIAC) Information Security Professional (GISP) certification exam.

The material covered in this training kit describes the concepts and technologies targeted on the CISSP exam covering the 10 domains of the (ISC)^2 CISSP CBK. The topics in this training kit cover what you need to know for the exam as described on the (ISC)^2 website for the exam. The CISSP exam objectives are available at *https://www.isc2.org/cissp/default.aspx* and in the CISSP Candidate Information Bulletin (CIB) at *https://www.isc2.org/cib/default.aspx*.

By using this training kit, you learn test-worthy concepts and technologies in the following 10 domains of the CBK:

1. Information security governance and risk management

2. Access control

3. Cryptography

4. Physical (environmental) security

5. Security architecture and design

6. Legal, regulations, investigations and compliance

7. Telecommunications and network security

8. Business continuity and disaster recovery planning

9. Software development security

10. Operations security

The CISSP certification is one of the most sought-after requirements in information technology jobs in commercial enterprises and in the government sector. This certification is ideal for mid-level and top-level managers working in or seeking work as senior security engineers, chief information security officers (CISOs) or chief security officers (CSOs). It is assumed that before you begin using this kit, you have met the professional experience requirements for the CISSP certification: a minimum of five years of direct, full-time experience in two or more of the 10 domains of the (ISC)^2 CISSP CBK; or four years of direct, full-time experience in two or more of the 10 domains of the (ISC)^2 CISSP CBK plus a four-year degree. In addition, a CISSP certification candidate should have a foundation-level understanding of common business functions, operating systems, applications, and common Internet technologies.

Preparing for the exam

The CISSP exam covers a wide range of concepts and technologies that deal with securing information systems and protecting the enterprise from losses. Because the exam covers such a broad spectrum of concepts and technologies, the best approach to passing the exam is to study sufficiently to understand the concepts and technologies rather than trying to memorize sentences or strings of words.

Most candidates prepare for 6 to 12 months prior to scheduling and taking the exam. Reading a comprehensive book like this one is a key component of preparing for the exam. Poring over practice test questions is another. However, (ISC)^2 is very focused on protecting the secrecy of the questions in the exam, so don't consider the practice tests, any of them, worthy of memorizing. Nobody but (ISC)^2 knows the questions and answers on the actual exam. Recognize that the practice test questions are good for two primary targets:

- Getting used to the Q&A process because many of us haven't had to take an exam for years, since school. Studying accustoms you to taking information in. Practice tests accustom you to putting out information, as you have to do on the exam.

- Identifying areas of knowledge that might need additional reading and study if you might not be doing so well with answering the answers correctly.

There are many questions with answers and explanations in this book. Many more are available online, both free and for purchase. When using any free and even inexpensive resources, be a little leery of the declared correct answer, especially if you disagree with it for good cause. If you disagree with an answer to a question, do your homework and verify your understanding and don't cave in just because someone else, who may know substantially less than you, wrote and uploaded some misguided question and answer. If you can justify your answer, stick to your understanding and your answer. This is the sign of competence: trusting in your knowledge.

As indicated before, many candidates spend 6 to 12 months preparing by reading books and related documentation and reviewing hundreds of questions, answers, and explanations and then, within a month of actually sitting the exam, they attend a 5-day or 6-day CISSP class that is more like a boot camp. Attending a class like this is putting the polish on the apple. It brings a fresh perspective and provides a grasp of the big picture, pulling it all together for you just at the right time. Attending a class like this also provides a live person, usually highly skilled, rehearsed in the CISSP body of knowledge, and with security vision, to answer questions to clarify your understanding of some of those fuzzy areas. Try to take the exam relatively soon after sitting such a class. The information you need to pass the exam tends to diffuse over time as you become consumed once again by your real-world, daily activities.

Many students make the mistake of answering the questions based on their specific daily activities and procedures. Remember that these practice tests and this certification exam have been developed to encompass every type of enterprise, organization, business, and agency in the commercial world as well as in government and military IT environments. Many questions target the more generic, complete, and comprehensive answer that would apply to every type of computing environment. Because many exam questions include multiple potentially correct answers, don't add the phrase "on my job" to the question. The security structure and practices used daily in your specific environment are only one example or implementation of many types of appropriate security solutions and implementations. The larger, superset type answer that would apply to any IT environment is often the correct answer. On the exam, consider an international solution or recommendation first instead of a country-specific recommendation. Then verify that the international solution satisfies the nature of the issue in the question best. Consider the answer "Use a firewall" for improved LAN security, instead of "Use (some specific) firewall rule" unless the question is targeting the specific rule.

As the day of the exam draws near, focus more on the practice questions and less on trying to read new material. At this point, you probably know as much as you can cram into your head on this topic. The questions will accustom you to putting out information instead of absorbing information. At least one week before your exam, review Appendix B, "CISSP 60-minute review," (available at *http://aka.ms/cisspTK/examples*), and be familiar with every term on the list. The week before your exam, try to work through 250 to 400 questions in a single session to develop a sense of the endurance required on exam day.

Signing up for the exam

Details about registering for the CISSP certification exam can be found on the (ISC)[2] website at *https://www.isc2.org/certification-register-now.aspx*. A list of where and when the exams are provided is available on this site. Filter this list of scheduled exams by the exam type (CISSP), the state (optional), and country (optional). When the list appears, verify that the one(s) you are interested in are not sold out, private, or closed. As of June 1, 2012, (ISC)[2] exams are offered as computer-based exams through Pearson VUE testing centers, and the historic paper-based exams are rarely offered. You should be able to schedule the exam one day and take it the next day through Pearson VUE.

At some point, you'll need to create a login with (ISC)^2, agree to its terms and conditions, and complete the registration form. You must receive approval from (ISC)^2 before you are allowed to schedule a computer-based exam. The most recently published fees are as follows:

- For the Americas, Asia/Pacific, Africa, and Middle East nations: $599 USD
- For European nations: €520 EUR
- For the United Kingdom: £415 GBP

(ISC)^2's pricing can be found at *https://www.isc2.org/uploadedFiles/Certification_Programs/exam_pricing.pdf.*

If you qualify for special arrangements such as for disabilities, languages, or the necessary use of a translation dictionary, contact (ISC)^2 directly at Customer Support at +1-866-331-4722 (toll free in North America) or +1-727-785-0189 (outside North America). Requests may also be made by email to *registration@isc2.org* or by fax to +1-727-683-0785. Some details can be found at *https://www.isc2.org/cancel-policy.aspx.*

You should review and understand the somewhat strict cancellation/rescheduling/retake policy, which you can find at *https://www.isc2.org/cancel-policy.aspx.*

The exam itself

This will be one of the most difficult exams you have ever taken. The following list provides an overview of the exam, and Table 1 explains the retake policy.

- **Number of questions**   250
- **Type of question**   Multiple choice
- **Number of answer choices**   4 potential answers
- **Number of correct answers per question**   1 correct answer
- **Number of questions being graded**   225
- **Points per question**   Weighted, based on difficulty
- **Allotted time**   6 hours
- **Questions provided by**   Computer-based exam

TABLE 1 CISSP exam retake policy

Exam attempt	# of days before a candidate can retake the exam
Second	30 days
Third	90 days
Fourth	180 days

There are several versions of the exam so that no two adjacent candidates will have the same questions. The exam consists of 250 multiple-choice questions with 4 possible answers but only one correct one. Many questions are looking for the best answer of two or more answers that could be considered correct. Some questions seem to be looking for the best answer of four incorrect answers. In a few places on the exam, multiple questions (two or three) are based on a simple scenario described in the first question of the series. Many of these "best of the multiple correct or no correct answers" are based on the concepts of the superset and its subsets. For example, consider the following question:

1. As part of the security program, you must mitigate the likelihood and impact of a security breach. Which of the following should you perform?

   A. A physical inspection of the facility

   B. Risk assessment

   C. Risk management

   D. A review of the security policies of the organization

In this case, all four answers are good answers, each correct on its own. However, your challenge is to pick the one best answer. To do this, recognize that risk management includes a risk assessment. Risk management begins with the assessment so you understand where the risks are, but it also includes the development of proposed countermeasures and the implementation of approved countermeasures, when you are actually managing the risks. The risk assessment will likely require a physical inspection of the facility and a review of the organization's security policies. Risk management is the superset, and the risk assessment is a subset. Risk management is the bigger, more correct answer. As you are preparing for the exam, remember to identify these superset–subset relationships. During the exam, recognize these relationships in the answers and then verify the specific target of the question. The question will often be focusing on the larger, more comprehensive superset answer, but reconfirm this by rereading the question after you establish the superset–subset relationships in the answer set.

Only 225 questions of the 250 questions are counted against your grade, and these are weighted based on their level of difficulty. The other 25 questions are being qualified (or disqualified) as viable questions to be used in future exams. The candidate has six hours to complete all questions, so it is a long day in the exam center. Don't forget to breathe. Every now and again, sit back, relax, stretch, take another deep breath, and then hit the exam again, refreshed and confident in your knowledge.

Proceed through the exam one question after the other, in order. If taking the computer-based exam, (ISC)² currently reports that you can go back to earlier questions one at a time. Upon completion of the exam, after all 250 questions have been answered, you can jump directly to any question by number.

You will be required to perform one or more mathematical calculations. A calculator is provided on the computer-based exam. The calculations will be addition, subtraction, multiplication, and division, such as those you'll see when calculating the single loss expectancy (SLE) or the annualized loss expectancy (ALE) for some potential incident.

That sounds ugly enough already, but it is time now for the really ugly part. The questions and answers are filled with subtleties and ambiguity, making this exam one that requires excellent reading and comprehension skills. Some questions aim at solid, reasonably obvious or direct targets, but many questions aim at ancillary targets, not necessarily the key concepts of the technologies. Many questions are vague or difficult to understand what the question is really asking, and many answers mirror that ambiguity.

Overall, the exam seems designed not only to gauge the candidate's knowledge of the topic but also to confuse and demoralize him, degrading his confidence, as if trying to convince him that he has already suffered a defeat. After teaching the CISSP courses for about 10 years, I don't recall ever hearing a student describe feeling good about the exam after taking it. It seems no one is ever comfortable that she has passed; most feel that they probably have failed. This seems to be the desired outcome—wear the candidate down and convince him to concede. "Stop the pain. Just quit. You can always retake the test in six months or a year."

Although this makes the CISSP exam ugly, difficult at best, it is the norm. Get used to the idea that you will not enjoy taking this exam and that you must rise to the challenge and overcome. Remember that the penalty for conceding and giving up during the exam is that you will probably have to (or want to) retake the exam later on. Let the thought of having to retake the exam drive you onward aggressively, with determination to complete it with the best you have to put out. During the exam, when you bump into a question whose correct answer completely eludes you, pat yourself on the back and consider that you just ran into another one of the 25 questions that will not be graded. Do your best to answer these questions correctly but do not beat yourself up for having to guess at an answer. Have confidence in your knowledge. You have studied hard, and you know your stuff. March forward through all 250 questions with confidence and unflinching determination.

The day before the exam, try to spend several hours working practice test questions and reviewing this study kit along with your notes and additional resources, especially in areas that still might not be clear. Nevertheless, allocate your time so you have one or two hours to relax and get away from the work. Then get to bed early and get a good night's rest. You'll need to be up early on exam day. Set and recheck your alarm clock. Most paper-based exams begin candidate check-in at 8 A.M., with testing beginning at 9 A.M. You'll want to get there early to reduce the stress of running late to an important appointment and to provide time, approximately one hour, for a final review (included in Appendix B ,which you can download at *http://aka.ms/cisspTK/examples* or find on this book's practice CD). Consider the time necessary for getting ready, breakfast, traffic, roads, traveling distance, parking issues, and the hour for the review before the exam check-in time. With that list in mind, set your alarm clock appropriately.

Consider whether you want or need to take a snack with you to the exam center to survive the six-hour exam time.

Seeing the big picture of CISSP

The security structure of the organization should be designed to protect the *confidentiality*, *integrity*, and *availability* (CIA) of the organization's valuable information assets effectively. These are three distinct security objectives and often require different types of countermeasures for their protection. Some information assets need to be kept secret (confidentiality) like the recipe for grandma's secret sauce. Other information assets are public information but must remain highly accurate (integrity) like the trading prices of stocks. In most cases, the information must also remain accessible (availability) to business managers and workers when they need it so they can make the best business decisions to optimize the profits of the organization.

Many of the concepts presented within the CISSP CBK and tested on relate closely to prudent business management—aspects of running a business such as establishing a security program, defining the security program through policies, performing risk management, planning disaster recovery and business continuity, and managing compliance with relevant laws and industry regulations. Business management must perform due diligence and due care prudently to avoid being negligent and liable for preventable losses. Anonymous CISSP exam candidates have reported a high concentration of exam questions targeting the disaster recovery planning (DRP) and business continuity planning (BCP) processes. These concepts fall largely into the category of *administrative controls*.

Much of the exam is technology-centric, such as secure computer hardware design—secure operating system design, secure application development, networking technologies and architecture, and cryptography. These fall into the category of *technical* (also called *logical*) *controls*.

Still, a large piece of the exam focuses on physical security such as the location, design, and construction of the facility, security guards, physical access controls, and fire protection. These fall into the category of *physical controls*.

In addition to the recognition of superset–subset relationships, several key concepts permeate the bulk of the CBK. Keep these concepts in mind as you dissect and analyze the way-too-many questions on the exam.

- It might not be presented everywhere it is relevant, but remember that *human safety is always the top priority.*

- The most ethical answer will likely be the correct answer unless it causes injury or risk to people's safety.

- Senior management must drive the security program by requiring its development and assigning the appropriate level of responsibility, authority, and support to the security team.

- Although many topics include security in the government setting, the CISSP is largely focused on the commercial business. The primary goal is to *maximize the profits of the business* by avoiding losses (preventive controls), reducing losses when a breach does occur (disaster recovery), and never letting the company fail by going out of business due to some disaster (business continuity).

- Every security control must be cost justified, weighing the cost of the control against the financial benefits that the control will provide. Accurately performing this cost justification for every proposed control helps ensure satisfaction of the requirement to maximize profits.

- All decisions are made by management. Security professionals simply provide quality input, vision, understanding, options, and cost versus benefit analyses and then request approval from senior management before implementation or action.

- Implement every aspect of security by following the principle of least privilege, assigning just the barest minimum of privilege required for the user to perform her authorized duties. Review the assigned privileges for all users to avoid security-related conflicts of interest and defend against insider fraud.

- No single countermeasure or control will provide complete and adequate security. Multiple layers of security are required in every solution.

- The use of automated tools helps deal with the complexity of planning, assessments, audits, and recovery.

- Department managers must be the enforcers of the security policies. They operate in every facet of the organization. They know the people, the processes, and the detailed activities occurring within their area of responsibility in the organization on a daily basis.

- Users tend to be the weakest link in the security of ongoing daily operations. To mitigate this vulnerability, security awareness training is essential for every user. Users with increased access or privilege require specialized and more frequent security awareness training.

- The first tier of management, the tier closest to the workers, is responsible for the dogmatic and consistent monitoring and enforcement of policy. Failure to remain aware and enforce policy consistently is a recipe for negligence and discrimination lawsuits.

- Senior management must perform due diligence and due care and manage the enterprise prudently to mitigate risks and avoid being negligent, a critical component of litigation against the enterprise.

The information in the CBK is divided into 10 domains, but these domains have close relationships to one another. When you understand how these domains relate, the big picture becomes clearer. There might be some overlap in some of the topics, which are covered in more than one domain. This demonstrates that these 10 topics are related. Don't let the redundancy bother you. Gain a second perspective on the topic as it relates to the nature of the other domains. The order of the domains is also not something to be concerned about. This book covers all known areas of knowledge the CISSP certification exam requires and (hopefully) presents these concepts and technologies in a manner that allows a more linear and logical flow and progression of the information.

Domain 1, on information security governance and risk management, introduces the security program in the organization. The security program is defined by policies and other documentation. These policy documents establish the security posture of the organization and should include the specific and sometimes unique security concerns but must also include all the laws and regulations that are applicable to the organization. These laws and regulations are covered in Domain 6 on legal, regulations, investigations and compliance, so recognize that relationship. Domain 1 continues with risk management and the risk assessment. Risk assessment, with the inventory of information assets it is based on and the valuation of those information assets, will be useful later, in Domain 8 on business continuity and disaster recovery planning (BCP and DRP). This is the business or administrative side of CISSP.

Domain 2, on access control, introduces the three main control categories: administrative controls, technical controls, and physical controls.

Administrative controls define the policies concerning how workers are supposed to behave and make decisions. The rules are documented but are also well known by all users through security awareness training and consistently enforced by management.

Technical controls begin with the fundamental understanding that, today, our valuable information assets are stored on, transmitted between, and processed on computers and computer networks. Therefore, users must use computers, operating systems, and applications to access those assets. If we hope to implement prudent security controls to protect those assets, we must establish that the computer, its operating system, and its applications will not cause security violations. This level of trust in the technological equipment is addressed in Domain 5, on security architecture and design, and in Domain 9, on software development security, so that additional technical controls that can be implemented, such as cryptography

(Domain 3), networking technologies (Domain 7), and system fault tolerance and redundancy (Domain 10) in operations security can be effective.

The physical aspect of securing valuable information assets requires the facility to remain secure, reasonably well protected from natural threats such as tornados and fire; from human threats such as burglars, an internal thief, or a social engineer; and from failures in the supply system that keeps the physical environment safe and functional. Domains 4 and 10 address these types of physical threats and the related controls.

The day of the exam

The day of the exam has arrived. Be sure you don't oversleep. Wake up early enough to provide time for the following tasks, which you should perform before checking in for your exam.

- Get up, get ready, and be awake.

- Have something to eat. This will be a long day, and there isn't much of an opportunity for a real break until after you complete the exam, possibly six hours after entering the exam center. Put some food in your stomach and, if you're into caffeine, you'll want a healthy supply in your belly.

- Get your materials together before leaving the house. This includes a photo ID; a printout of your exam registration letter; address and directions to the testing center, including floor number and room number; your study notes; and this book for your final review. Bring your snack if you decided you want one.

- Figure out a secure place to keep things you might normally carry with you that won't be allowed in the testing center such as your purse, laptop, cell phone, suit case, pager, pens, pencils, iPod, headphones, and so on. It is kind of like going through security at the airport. Nothing in your pockets.

- Get to the testing center one and a half hours before the candidate check-in time. Use this time to review Appendix B, "CISSP 60-minute review." Spend approximately one minute per page reviewing the terms and recalling as many details as possible for each item on the list. Review any other notes you consider important to you.

- Leave all but your ID, exam registration letter, and snack someplace secure. Enter the testing center and get to the exam check-in location. Identify the location of the restrooms (and perhaps take a final pause because you won't want to step out of the potentially long check-in line later).

- Check in. This is typically a very rigid and formalized process, the continuation of the induced stress and demoralization that seems to permeate the CISSP testing process. After the check-in personnel carefully check your ID and your exam registration letter, they'll give you the once over, looking for contraband, anything that isn't required. Any identified items must be dispensed with, one way or another. Finally, they'll walk you into the testing room and place you in your preassigned seat. You must sit here quietly, patiently waiting until all have been checked in, inspected, escorted, and quietly seated.

- For paper-based testing, at or near the scheduled testing time, the proctoring team will pass out the various versions of the sealed exam booklet, the Scantron answer sheet, and one or two #2 pencils. The lead proctor (a local CISSP volunteer), will begin to explain how the exam is conducted—more formality and induced stress. Instructions will be provided on filling out the Scantron sheet with codes, names, dates, and so on. Paper-based exams are rarely issued but might still be used when computer-based testing is not an option.

- As soon as all the formalities (and stress) have been dumped on the candidates, the lead proctor will announce that you may break the seal on your copy of the exam booklet or begin the computer-based exam. The test has just begun. Take your time. The exam is not a race but keep your eye on the clock to be sure your pace allows you to answer all 250 questions in the six-hour timeslot. You must average 42 or more questions per hour to complete the exam in the allotted time.

- Try to avoid adding "in my job" to every question. Candidates preparing for this exam are often in this IT line of work already and are familiar with many of the concepts and technologies presented. The exam is not about your specific job but about general security concepts that apply to virtually every business. Some candidates must learn to dumb down a little in their areas of expertise and go with the more generic CISSP answer on the exam. This exam targets every business, not the one you are currently thinking of.

- Identify the discriminators that lead you to the one best answer and the distracters that deliberately add confusion to the question and might lead you to the wrong answer. References to specific industry niches, products, or vendors are usually distractors of this type. Evaluate whether these details have any relevance to the answers and ignore them when they don't.

- In some cases, there are multiple correct answers. Identify broader superset answers and the more specific subset answers. Many times, the test is looking for the best answer, which will probably be the broader, more comprehensive correct answer—the superset answer. After you identify the superset answer, reconfirm that it still matches all the discriminators in the question and then go with it. An example might be a question about designing secure communications between the headquarters and a branch office. Answers might include a VPN, an IPsec tunnel, an L2TP tunnel, and an SSH tunnel using public key/private key authentication. The VPN includes these other more specific VPN types, so it is the broader, more comprehensive, superset answer. Next, verify that there isn't anything in the question to cause the VPN superset answer to be incorrect, such as a requirement for symmetric keys and security associations. (Therefore, IPsec would be more correct.)

- In some cases, you might not find an answer you feel is correct in the four choices. Review the question and substitute similar words or phrases that might be more commonly used in the IT environment to make one of the answers correct. After exercising this technique for a minute, assume the most likely substitution is accurate and choose the correct answer.

- Remember to breathe. Every now and again, sit back and take a deep breath. It will help keep your head clear and minimize fatigue.

- Bathroom breaks are allowed, but typically, only one candidate may go at a time to avoid the potential for consorting and cheating. You must raise your hand, be recognized, carefully collect your testing materials, sign out, be escorted to the restroom and back, sign in, be escorted to your preassigned seat, and then allowed to resume your exam. The clock does not stop. The time you take on bathroom breaks is included in the six-hour time limit, so be brief about it.

- (ISC)² does allow the quiet consumption of snacks during the exam, but you must bring the items with you, leave the items in the back of the testing room, raise your hand and be escorted to your snacks, quietly consume the snack, and then be escorted back to your exam. The time you take on food is included in the six-hour time limit, so, again, be brief about it.

After completing the exam

When taking the computer-based exam, the results are typically available immediately after completion of the exam, or you might be required to see the testing center representative for your results. If your effort is successful, you will be informed that you passed the exam. Congratulations! Typically, passing scores are not provided. If you failed the exam, your score, and a breakdown by domain is provided. This helps guide your studies as you prepare for the second certification attempt. Paper-based exam results are provided to candidates by email. This process can take up to six weeks but often takes one or two weeks.

Upon successfully completing and passing the (ISC)² CISSP exam, the CISSP candidate must complete the certification requirements by answering several questions regarding criminal history and related background and complete the (ISC)² CISSP Candidate Agreement, describe the related experience, attest to the truthfulness of the affidavit, and commit to adhering to the (ISC)² Code of Ethics. Further, the (ISC)² CISSP candidate must acquire a signed endorsement from a holder of CISSP certification, attesting to the accuracy of the candidate's assertions regarding professional experience and good standing within the community to the best of that person's knowledge. (ISC)² randomly performs audits of about 10 percent of candidates on the claimed professional experience and criminal history.

> **NOTE CONTINUING PROFESSIONAL EDUCATION CREDITS**
>
> Upon certification, the CISSP must acquire and record 120 continuing professional education (CPE) points every three years, as outlined on the (ISC)^2 website at *https://www.isc2.org/maintaining-your-credential.aspx*.
>
> CISSPs must not have violated the (ISC)^2 Code of Ethics and must submit the annual maintenance fee of $85 USD.

Using the companion CD

A companion CD is included with this training kit and contains the following:

- **Practice tests** You can reinforce your understanding of the topics covered in this training kit by using electronic practice tests that you customize to meet your needs. You can practice for the CISSP certification exam by using tests created from a pool of 250 practice exam questions, which give you many practice exams to ensure that you are prepared.
- **Appendix B** An electronic version of the 60-Minute Review is included for you to study before you take the CISSP certification exam.

How to use the practice tests

To start the practice test software, follow these steps.

To install the practice test software for a training kit, open Program And Features in Control Panel.

1. Click Start, choose All Programs, and then select Microsoft Press Training Kit Exam Prep.

   A window appears that shows all the Microsoft Press training kit exam prep suites installed on your computer.

2. Double-click the practice test you want to use.

When you start a practice test, you choose whether to take the test in Certification Mode, Study Mode, or Custom Mode:

- **Certification Mode** Closely resembles the experience of taking a certification exam. The test has a set number of questions. It is timed, and you cannot pause and restart the timer.
- **Study Mode** Creates an untimed test during which you can review the correct answers and the explanations after you answer each question.
- **Custom Mode** Gives you full control over the test options so that you can customize them as you like.

In all modes, the user interface when you are taking the test is about the same but with different options enabled or disabled, depending on the mode.

When you review your answer to an individual practice test question, a "References" section is provided that lists where in the training kit you can find the information that relates to that question and provides links to other sources of information. After you click Test Results to score your entire practice test, you can click the Learning Plan tab to see a list of references for every objective.

How to uninstall the practice tests

To uninstall the practice test software for a training kit, open Program And Features in Control Panel.

Acknowledgments

The author's name appears on the cover of a book, but I am only one member of a much larger team. Each of my managers, editors, and reviewers contributed significantly to this book. I wish to thank them each, and I hope to work with them all in the future.

- **Michael Bolinger**   O'Reilly Media, Inc.
- **Dan Fauxsmith**   O'Reilly Media, Inc.
- **Kara Ebrahim**   O'Reilly Media, Inc.
- **Kristen Brown**   O'Reilly Media, Inc.
- **Jeff Riley**   Production, Box Twelve Communications
- **Michael Gregg**   Technical reviewer, Superior Solutions, Inc.
- **Kerin Forsyth**   Copy editor, Online Training Solutions, Inc. (OTSI)
- **Jaime Odell**   Project Manager, OTSI
- **Neil Salkind**   Literary Agent, Studio B

I'd also like to thank the following individuals for their initial work on the project:

- Ken Jones
- Carol Vu
- Susan McClung
- Kurt Meyer

I also wish to thank Ms. Shon Harris, a mentor, a professional associate, and a dear friend. You're the best, Shon.

Support and feedback

The following sections provide information on errata, book support, feedback, and contact information.

Errata

We've made every effort to ensure the accuracy of this book and its companion content. Any errors that have been reported since this book was published are listed at:

http://aka.ms/cisspTK/errata

If you find an error that is not already listed, you can report it to us through the same page.

If you need additional support, email Microsoft Press Book Support at:

mspinput@microsoft.com

Please note that product support for Microsoft software is not offered through the preceding addresses.

We want to hear from you

At Microsoft Press, your satisfaction is our top priority and your feedback our most valuable asset. Please tell us what you think of this book at:

http://www.microsoft.com/learning/booksurvey

The survey is short, and we read every one of your comments and ideas. Thanks in advance for your input!

Stay in touch

Let us keep the conversation going! We are on Twitter at *http://twitter.com/MicrosoftPress*.

Information security governance and risk management

This first chapter in your adventure of preparing for the CISSP exam is first for a good reason. It describes how an organization would begin to address the prudent management of a business (enterprise, organization, department, or agency). This chapter describes the foundational components management must have in place to understand the nature of the business it controls, the risks it faces and their severity, and then how to assemble a framework of controls to manage those risks prudently to minimize and avoid unnecessary losses and maximize profits.

Exam objectives in this chapter:

3.1   Understand and align security function to goals, mission and objectives of the organization

3.2   Understand and apply security governance

    3.2.1   Organizational processes (e.g., acquisitions, divestitures, governance committees)

    3.2.2   Security roles and responsibilities

    3.2.3   Legislative and regulatory compliance

    3.2.4   Privacy requirements compliance

    3.2.5   Control frameworks

    3.2.6   Due care

    3.2.7   Due diligence

3.3   Understand and apply concepts of confidentiality, integrity and availability

3.4   Develop and implement security policy

    3.4.1   Security policies

    3.4.2   Standards/baseline

Where do information security and risk management begin?

Consider a start-up business being built in the garage of one or two bright individuals with a bright idea. The goal of the business is to maximize its profits. At first, the bright individuals are scratching for their daily wages, and the production of anything they can sell is paramount. This is a business in its infancy; it is generally not well managed but, rather, running recklessly at full throttle to accomplish some level of completion that can begin to generate revenue. "We need a paycheck!"

As these two scramble to develop some product, they have little concern for rules and regulations. Whatever it takes, whatever shortcuts are required, they do that to make the product functional so it can be sold. If they are lucky, and if no disasters strike while they are operating without any protections, in time, a product is developed that they can sell.

With their first trickle of revenue, a little of the frantic level of pressure is released, and now they take a little time to fix some glaring mistakes they've noticed in their product and in their work environment.

Still, they are far from managing the business prudently. Still, they are fighting for the life of the business every day. However, their luck holds, and as the days go by, their product gets better, and they sell to more customers. The revenue increases, and more of the intense level of pressure is released.

At some point, as the pressure continues to decline and approaches a more normal, livable level, the entrepreneurs begin to notice that they've actually built something that has value. They become aware of the need to protect their product from harm. This is when your adventure begins, when the owners and now managers of the business become concerned with how to manage (govern) their valuable business. It is time to establish some rules to minimize the potential for losses and, in some cases, to avoid those losses altogether.

Therefore, the founders begin to document some of the rules they've figured out and agreed on to manage the workplace and keep some sense of order and control. They have experienced some mistakes that could have been avoided, so they write down some rules to avoid those mishaps. The framework of governance begins. They realize that this approach is haphazard; they are already aware of many vulnerabilities in their environment, threats to their assets, and holes in the rule base that could cost them in the future. Although their precautions seem enough for now, they realize they must develop a more complete vision of their environment to begin to deal with these costly issues in a proactive manner rather than solely in a reactive manner.

They gain the vision required to achieve this loss avoidance through an assessment of the business environment and an understanding of the risks the business faces, but this vision is woefully incomplete. Therefore, with the help of others who have better vision in this area, they perform a complete risk assessment to develop a picture of all the things that could harm the business and an appraisal of how much each would it hurt if it occurred.

Now that they see all the bad things that could negatively affect their growing business, and they see which bad things could hurt them the most, they must understand the countermeasures that could mitigate (reduce) the risks. They have to reduce the vulnerabilities in their systems and processes to diminish the likelihood of harm and the impact of damage if it does occur.

Management can now make effective business decisions about which risks to manage and how best to manage those risks through the implementation of a security program. It can now develop a much more complete collection of rules to establish the framework of governance by which to manage the business. This framework is documented in a collection of policies and further fleshed out in other documents such as lists of procedures and standards. As additional risks are identified, this collection of documents can be refined, revised, and added to as the enterprise maintains its position of control over foreseeable and, therefore, avoidable losses.

Driven by this now-rich collection of policies, effective governance can commence. Losses can be reduced to an acceptable level and even avoided completely in many cases. This framework will grow further and describe the implementation of additional practices to be performed regularly and consistently within the organization to drive down these unnecessary and avoidable losses.

This is the foundation for the governance of a well-managed enterprise and the foundation required for the development of plans to defend the organization against the collection of unforeseen disasters that could severely damage or even destroy the enterprise. These plans, which address disastrous or catastrophic events, called the disaster recovery plan and the business continuity plan, are the next stage of maturity for an organization. Chapter 8, "Business continuity and disaster recovery planning," discusses these potentially lifesaving plans.

It is generally accepted that management will take approximately three years to recognize the need to protect its assets and develop this framework for governance, perform its first full risk assessment, complete its collection of policy documentation, and implement its initial security structure to defend itself against avoidable losses.

Senior management must drive this program to its completion. It must support the effort by formally assigning responsibility and authority for the completion of this project. It must support it with vision, oversight, and a reasonable budget. However, senior management is too busy performing its senior management tasks to do all this work itself. This is where the security professional comes in. The security professional has the specialized skills to develop the proper vision on the current security status of the systems and processes, the business needs those systems and processes support, the risks those systems face, and the collection of potential countermeasures that could be implemented to mitigate the risks to those valuable assets. It is with these security-professional goggles that this complex picture achieves clarity, and with this clarity of vision, the security professional becomes a valuable asset to senior management. Your job as security professional is to achieve that clarity of vision, to recognize and summarize the risks the organization faces, and provide that cohesive vision to senior management in an efficient manner.

Now all that is needed is for senior management to make its choices of which countermeasures it feels is wise. By approving specific countermeasures, senior management galvanizes the security program (for at least the upcoming year). These choices define the security posture of the organization and identify management's level of tolerance for risk. It also establishes the budget for the security program. It defines the people who must be hired; the hardware and software that must be purchased; the training of personnel to implement, maintain, and administer these new security controls; the policy documents that must be written to govern the use of these systems; and the additional components required in the security awareness training program for users to include these new aspects of the workplace.

Further, the security program should identify goals and objectives for the security program at various stages in the future. These goals and objectives should be presented in plans and should include:

- **Operational goals**   These are daily goals and objectives. What can you do or should you be doing right now to support, maintain, and improve the security posture of the organization?
- **Tactical goals**   These are mid-term goals that might take weeks or months to accomplish.
- **Strategic goals**   These are long-term goals that might take months or even years to accomplish. As you get into Chapter 8 on business continuity planning, you will see that these plans look forward for decades into the future.

Security objectives and controls

The CISSP targets the protection of information systems and information assets. Please remember that although focused mainly on inanimate assets such as databases and file servers, the protection of human safety is always the top priority. With the people safe, you can turn your sights toward the protection of these valuable information assets.

The collection of valuable information assets includes all the data files stored on any of the computers the organization owns, on every database, every Microsoft Word document, and every spreadsheet. The assets also include everything required to make these assets available to the workers and business decision makers, such as the hard disk drives that store the files, the server computers that house the disk drives, the workstations where the end users enter, modify, and read the information, and the networking infrastructure that connects these devices and provides the access. Further, the valuable information assets you are commissioned to protect include the data center(s) that house the servers, the office space and environment that provides the functional workplace for the end users, and the building that houses the data center and the end user workplace. The valuable information assets include the heated, cooled, and filtered air; the stable and clean electricity that powers the computers and infrastructure, and everything else that makes the information systems functional and the workplace habitable to the end users.

These are the assets that security professionals are charged to protect. The next question is, "What does 'protection' mean?" In the context of the CISSP, protection has three objectives, called the *CIA triad*. The CIA triad includes the security goals of providing confidentiality, integrity, and availability of the valuable information assets.

- **Confidentiality**   *Confidentiality* is best described as keeping secrets secret. The enterprise will have many reasons to keep many pieces of information secret. You must keep these details secret because the enterprise will lose money if the secret is exposed. Whether it is some new invention or technology, some plan to buy or sell a division, some new marketing campaign, or to avoid breaking a privacy law or regulation, the secret must be kept.

- **Integrity**   *Integrity* is a characteristic of information that implies the information is known to be good; the information can be trusted as being complete, consistent, and accurate. Information with high integrity is information that has not been inappropriately altered or tampered with and that can be trusted to some acceptable extent. Accuracy of information implies that the information reflects reality and is truthful. Information is complete when all appropriate data is presented to the user at the time of need. For example, if 20 records in a database match your query, and you are authorized to view all records, you can view all 20 matching records. Fewer than all authorized and matching records would be a breach of completeness, a breach of integrity of the information. Providing anything less than all relevant information to business decision makers could lead to a bad business decision and could affect the revenue and profits of the enterprise negatively.

  Consistency of information comes into play when multiple copies exist of the data. Each copy of the data must be consistent with every other copy. Otherwise, information is missing or inaccurate. This consistency of data is referred to as knowledge consistency; when the data sets agree, usually through automated synchronization or replication processes, it is also known as convergence of the multiple and redundant data sets.

  As a security objective, integrity has two components: *integrity protection* and *integrity verification.*

  - **Integrity protection**   Disallowing the unauthorized alteration of your (known good) information is *integrity protection.* Access controls, like physical controls, permissions on files, and encryption, keep unauthorized people away from the information asset. If an unauthorized person cannot access or read the meaning of a message, that person cannot intelligently modify the meaning of the message, so the integrity of the message has been protected.

  - **Integrity verification**   The verification of integrity at time of use is essential to ensure that the information about to be used to make a business decision is accurate, complete, and consistent with the best known good information the enterprise has and has not been altered. *Integrity verification* is most commonly implemented by calculating a message digest (also called a hash value) of the information at time of its creation, when the integrity of the information is known to be good. This message digest acts as a fingerprint of the known good information. Then, at time of use, a new message digest is calculated. If these two digest values are identical, this proves that the information has not been altered since the creation of the message when the information was known to be good. The integrity of the information has been verified.

- **Availability**   Providing users access to the information at their time of need is *availability.* Availability means that the information systems provide the required networking services that allow the needed connectivity, that the systems provide sufficient fault tolerance and redundancy, and that the business has appropriate recovery plans and capabilities to overcome an outage or failure within an acceptable time frame. If a decision maker cannot access the information needed at the time of need, all the expense to develop, store, maintain, and protect the information might have been a waste. The decision makers need access to their information at critical times. A bad business decision could cost the business a fortune, so it is essential for the best possible information to be available to the decision maker at that time of need. It is the job of the security professional to anticipate the many ways this access can fail, to avoid those failures, and to recover from those failures in a timely manner.

 The terms "confidentiality," "integrity," and "availability" may also be referenced by the breaches to each of them. The terms commonly used to describe breaches to the confidentiality, integrity, and availability of the assets are *disclosure*, *alteration*, and *destruction* (*DAD*), respectively.

 The protection of these information assets has to be consistent at various times and in whatever state the information may be. Sometimes the objective is to protect sensitive (valuable) content from unauthorized persons while you store it for use at a later time (*data at rest*). Permissions on files, encryption, and physical access controls help protect data at rest. Examples might include the protection of a file that is stored on a file server and holds the secret sauce recipe for your top-selling product, the protection of a file that holds a collection of passwords in a password vault on a laptop computer, and the protection of the sensitive information printed on paper. Permissions are described in more detail in Chapter 5, "Security architecture and design." Encryption is described in more detail in Chapter 3, "Cryptography." User security awareness training on social engineering is described in more detail later in this chapter.

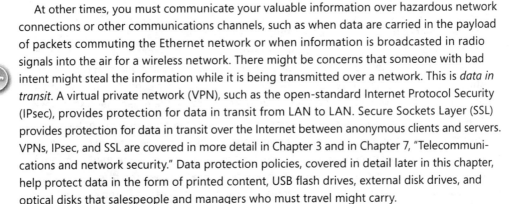 At other times, you must communicate your valuable information over hazardous network connections or other communications channels, such as when data are carried in the payload of packets commuting the Ethernet network or when information is broadcasted in radio signals into the air for a wireless network. There might be concerns that someone with bad intent might steal the information while it is being transmitted over a network. This is *data in transit*. A virtual private network (VPN), such as the open-standard Internet Protocol Security (IPsec), provides protection for data in transit from LAN to LAN. Secure Sockets Layer (SSL) provides protection for data in transit over the Internet between anonymous clients and servers. VPNs, IPsec, and SSL are covered in more detail in Chapter 3 and in Chapter 7, "Telecommunications and network security." Data protection policies, covered in detail later in this chapter, help protect data in the form of printed content, USB flash drives, external disk drives, and optical disks that salespeople and managers who must travel might carry.

 There is another area of protection of data. As the user is actively accessing and using the information, sensitive data might be presented on video displays or in printed reports. This is an example of *data in use*. Data in this state cannot be protected by cryptography because it must be in a human-readable form, so it must be protected by physical security measures, the user's awareness, and defenses against social engineering, described in the "Providing security awareness training" section later in this chapter.

Understanding risk modeling

Information systems are built on hardware computer systems and infrastructure devices. These systems run on software such as operating systems and applications. The systems require a stable supply of electricity and need to be kept cool enough to continue operation. From time to time, attackers try to compromise the confidentiality, integrity, and availability of the valuable information assets. In addition, Mother Nature occasionally throws her fury at the world and wreaks havoc on information systems as well.

When something bad happens to the valuable assets, the organization cannot remain as productive as before, and this means less product to sell. In addition, the damages must be repaired. Time must be spent on recovery and repair, and physical and soft assets might have to be purchased. All this takes away from the maximum profits an organization could have and should have accomplished. This is the nature of loss. Any reduction from the maximum potential profitability of the organization is *loss*. After the safety of people, the avoidance of loss is the top priority of the security professional.

In the context of information systems and information assets, losses occur when a *compromise* of the confidentiality, integrity, or availability of valuable information assets of the organization occurs. An information asset is compromised when a policy related to the protection of these assets is violated or breached, allowing the asset to be exposed, altered, or rendered inaccessible (usually) through some unauthorized activity. A compromise, also called an *exploit*, of any of these aspects of the valuable information assets of the organization reduces the profits of the organization due to the resulting losses.

The valuable information systems and information assets that you are supposed to protect have inherent weaknesses, called *vulnerabilities*, that could lead to a compromise of CIA and introduce losses. Because you manage these systems and assets, you have some control over the management of these vulnerabilities. Although you can eliminate some vulnerabilities completely by using various forms of protective controls, you can never eliminate all vulnerabilities. You might implement protective controls to eliminate or reduce one or more vulnerabilities. An existing vulnerability implies the absence of a protective control. This means that there is a potential for some sort of compromise that could cause the organization some losses.

A *threat* is the potential that someone or something will affect one or more of the vulnerabilities that exist within the valuable information assets. Threats come in many forms, such as a computer virus, destruction of the data center from a hurricane, or the theft of goods by an unscrupulous employee. The active component of a threat is called the *threat agent*. This is the malicious payload of the computer virus, the wind and rain of the hurricane itself, and the unscrupulous employee. Because threats and threat agents are not under your control, they are not necessarily easily managed. Threats require much more effort in your attempts to protect the organization from unnecessary losses. Threats to valuable information assets drive much of the protective controls the security program implements.

Threats can be from within the organization (*internal threats*) or outside the organization (*external threats*). You must consider both sources. When performing a threat analysis for each valuable information asset, consider threats from each of the following four categories:

- **Natural**   Natural threats are Mother Nature having her way with the world. They include earthquake, volcanic eruption, tornado, hurricane, tsunami, ice storm, snow storm, flood, and fire.

- **Human-made**   Human-made threats are the actions of humankind such as errors and omissions, litigation, theft, sabotage, riot, strike, malicious hacker attack, social engineering attacks, dumpster diving, fraud, assignment of too much privilege, lack of an incident response plan, and political action.

- **Technical**   Technical threats are the failings of technology such as a hard disk drive crash, a server failure, data corruption, and damages from a computer virus infection.

- **Supply system**   To remain functional, humans and computers need certain supplies. Humans need a habitable workplace, and the supplies that keep the workplace habitable are clean air; heating, ventilation, and air conditioning (HVAC); drinkable water; and a sewer system. Computers need a clean supply of electricity and typically require a certain amount of cooling.

In Chapter 8, you learn that the threats to the supply system extend to a somewhat extreme, and perhaps even bizarre, degree. When it comes to keeping the business operational for decades to come, threats to the supply system even include the availability of raw materials to produce whatever products the company produces.

Some vulnerabilities within the information systems and information assets might not have a real threat that could affect them, such as the destruction of the data center from a hurricane when the data center is in Montana. Hurricanes almost exclusively exist in warm tropical waters, and none of those is near enough to Montana to support a hurricane. Nevertheless, when a vulnerability such as the destruction of the data center has a matching threat, such as an

earthquake or volcanic eruption, *risk* exists. The risk is that the threat and its active ingredient, the threat agent, will exploit the vulnerability and cause losses to the organization.

Recognizing the presence of risk is a critical insight. However, risk is almost everywhere. Because it is impossible to eliminate every risk, how will you ever know which of the many risks to the valuable assets should be addressed? You must somehow quantify the level of risk for each threat to each valuable information asset. You can accomplish this by assessing the *likelihood* that the threat will be successful in exploiting the vulnerability of the valuable information asset and quantifying the *impact* (the losses that will result) of the compromise when it does occur. The determination of the likelihood and the impact of a compromise identifies which risks are greater and which risks might be negligible. If the secret sauce recipe (the valuable information asset) is documented only on paper and kept in a well-protected safe (the countermeasure), exposure of the secret by a hacker attack (the threat) is very unlikely (because the recipe is not stored in digital format on any computer system—the medium of the hacker). However, if the recipe is ever exposed, the impact to the enterprise could be costly, yielding an assessment of very low likelihood but high impact. In this example, because the likelihood of a hacker exposing the secret recipe is so low, this is an example of a threat to an asset with a low level of risk.

 Some risks will have a very high likelihood of occurrence but a very low impact. Other risks might have a very low likelihood of occurrence but a very high impact. Still other risks might have a high likelihood of occurrence and a very high impact. The greater these two attributes are, the greater the *attack surface*, also called the *exposure*, of the asset. The attack surface of an asset is the part of the asset that is vulnerable to exploit or compromise. A smaller exposure means that losses to this asset from this threat are less likely, and if it does happen, the losses will likely be smaller. A larger exposure means that a compromise is more likely and will be severe.

Understanding countermeasures and controls

 Risk can be recognized, and it can be quantified to identify the attack surface or exposure of an asset. The next step is to defend the organization from avoidable losses due to these risks. You accomplish this by introducing *countermeasures*, also called *controls*. A countermeasure is a tactic or a strategy that reduces or eliminates one or more of the vulnerabilities, reduces or eliminates the likelihood of occurrence, or reduces or eliminates the impact of the compromise. Countermeasures include laws and policies, encryption, permissions, authentication and authorization mechanisms, fences and locks, and security guards, to name a few.

 Countermeasures are typically required and applied in multiple layers because, usually, no one countermeasure can protect the assets from every type of threat. This is referred to as *defense in depth*. An example of defense in depth, also called *layered security*, is the building of a strong castle but, also, building a moat around the castle and assembling a quantity of weapons and trained soldiers to defend the castle if and when it is attacked. The different countermeasures work together (complementary controls) and tend to compensate for one or more weaknesses in the other countermeasures (compensating controls), collectively strengthening the overall security of the assets.

The cost of every proposed and implemented countermeasure must be carefully justified to ensure that the enterprise is protecting the information assets at an appropriate level. Too much security costs the company more than it should be spending, and too little security exposes the company to more risk than is desired or tolerable.

Figure 1-1 shows the relationships between most of these risk-related terms.

Risk Management Flowchart

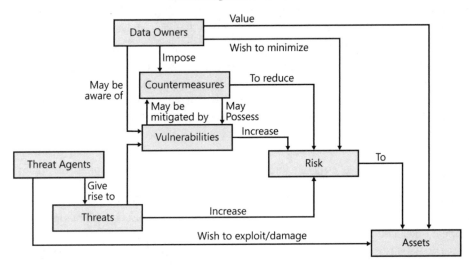

FIGURE 1-1 Risk management flowchart

EXAM TIP

It is important for you to understand the relationships among the following terms: loss, compromise, exploit, vulnerability, threat, threat agent, internal threats, external threats, risk, likelihood, impact, attack surface, exposure, countermeasure, control, defense in depth, and layered security.

The controls you choose come from the following three major categories:

- ***Administrative controls***   These controls are the policies, rules, and laws you must abide by. For these controls to be enforceable, they must first be formalized, typically in writing, the users in the environment must be educated about the existence of these controls with an expectation of compliance, and there must be some form of monitoring and enforcement, including the penalties paid in case of violation of the rules.

- ***Physical controls***   Generally speaking, if you can drop a control on your foot or bump your head on it, it must be a physical control. These are the walls, fences, and locks that establish security boundaries around your facilities. These are the signs that warn of electric shock or dog bites that might happen if you enter the wrong places. These are the server clusters, the security appliances, and the sensor devices that provide improved availability and protect and monitor the corporate network.

- ***Technical controls***   Technical controls are also called logical controls. These controls are almost always implemented in software, such as permissions on a file system; the encryption of digital content; asymmetric key pairs used on digital certificates; the rule base in a firewall; and the signature database used in intrusion detection systems.

Recognize that no one countermeasure or security control provides comprehensive protection for any of the valuable information assets. You will be required to implement defense in depth. That is multiple layers of security, often from more than one of the major categories, to protect these assets adequately.

 One control that should be used whenever possible to complement the aforementioned layers of security is *security through obscurity*, which describes the concept of simply not letting the bad guys know that valuable assets are to be had. If you can keep the existence or the location of the assets a secret, you reduce the likelihood that an attacker can compromise the CIA of the asset.

Reducing the risk of litigation

 One family of risks that every enterprise faces is the risk of litigation. Civil litigations are very often warranted because, from time to time, accidents happen and mistakes are made. When this happens, most court systems identify a *liability* to provide compensation for losses to the injured party. Liability is the legally required reimbursement of losses to the injured party. If *negligence* is involved, the penalties go up. Negligence is the failure to exercise reasonable care. If the *plaintiff* (the one asking for compensation for losses suffered) can show that the defendant was negligent, the financial penalties imposed on the defendant increase dramatically.

If an employee slips and falls while at work, the company is generally found liable for the losses the employee suffers. This would often include the payment of reasonable medical bills, the costs of any needed physical therapy, and perhaps payment of lost wages while injured. However, if the injured employee can show that the company was somehow negligent, and that negligence was a contributing factor to the incident, the lawyers and often the injured party sense the opportunity to become rich from this one event.

So, to avoid and minimize losses by reducing the risk of litigation, it is your job to:

1. Protect people from injuries.

2. Protect your business partners (including customers, vendors, the public, and so on) from suffering losses by the actions, mistakes, or shortcomings of the organization.

3. Ensure that the organization is not, and does not appear to be, negligent.

    The avoidance of negligence is accomplished by following these guidelines:

    - **Perform *due diligence***   Due diligence is the development of knowledge and awareness of the risks present in the workplace and in the marketplace. Due diligence continues with ongoing maintenance, monitoring, response, enforcement, training, and evaluation of the controls currently in place.

    - **Implement *due care***   With the vision developed from due diligence, due care is when you implement safety measures, countermeasures, and controls to protect people from harm (physically and financially). Due care continues with the monitoring enforcement, and with the maintenance of the safety measures, countermeasures, and controls as a prudent person would to assure the effectiveness of the controls.

The sensible implementation of due diligence and due care is the foundation of the avoidance of negligence. You must be able to show that these have been performed in a comprehensive manner. The plaintiff's attorney will present to the court that your efforts were incomplete and have fallen short of adequately protecting people; therefore, you are not only liable, you are also negligent, and, being negligent, you must pay a much higher penalty. The claim will be that your negligent action or failure to act (negligence) prior to an incident led to or resulted in the damages to the plaintiff. This is called *proximate causation*.

Although the plaintiff's attorney will demand that anything shy of perfection on your part is negligence, if you can show that you implemented the safety measures, countermeasures, and controls to protect people from harm as a *prudent person* would, then you are not negligent.

The prudent-person rule says that if you acted in a reasonable manner under the circumstances you were facing at the time of the incident, exhibiting good judgment as a prudent person would, in spite of the fact that your controls were not perfect protection, then you are not negligent. Although the organization might still be liable for the losses an injured party suffered, the organization is typically not found to be negligent, and therefore, the payment to the injured party will be less. This is often the best position the organization can achieve under circumstances like those described.

EXAM TIP

It is important for you to understand the significance of the impact of negligence on lawsuits and the techniques used to avoid being or appearing to be negligent.

✓ **Quick check**

1. What are the components of avoiding negligence?
2. What are the three primary targets for which to provide security?

Quick check answers

1. Due diligence, due care, and managing the environment prudently.
2. Protect the confidentiality, integrity, and availability (CIA) of the organization's assets.

Policies and frameworks

Senior management must actively pursue the formation of the framework for governance for the enterprise. The absence of this framework is likely to be perceived as negligence. As management develops vision and understanding of the controls required to manage (govern) the enterprise adequately, the collection of policy documents must be developed. The rules of acceptable use and behavior for the workers must be formalized to establish the basis of control. These documents become essentially contracts or agreements between management and the employees of the company. They become somewhat legalist and potentially binding, and should include the caveat that violation of any of the policy documents, failure to comply, is sufficient grounds for termination.

The fully implemented security program should address and include the following features:

- Provide a safe environment for employees, visitors, customers, vendors, and so on.
- Maximize profits.
- Mitigate and avoid losses.
- Support the business needs.
- Identify and defend the enterprise against threats specific to the business.
- Abide by applicable laws and regulations.
- Convey and implement senior management's vision and governance standards.
- Convey and implement senior management's desired ethical posture for the organization.
- Define roles and responsibilities.
- Define the risk management program.
- Define the disaster recovery and business continuity planning program.
- Define the data classification and protection program.
- Define privacy requirements.
- Define the auditing and monitoring to be performed.
- Define physical security.
- Define incident response.
- Define the security awareness training and enforcement program.
- Define configuration management and change control.
- Define the employee hiring and termination practices.
- Define the governance practices of third-party service providers.

This book addresses each of these topics to provide details and guidance.

The consistent enforcement of the rules in the formal framework that governs the workplace is critical. If management is lax in its enforcement of the policies, the workers will conclude that because management doesn't take the rules seriously, they do not need to take the rules seriously. Why apply the extra effort to comply if it doesn't really matter? Security and prudent management will suffer, and management could be viewed as negligent.

Further, if management is inconsistent with its enforcement of the policies, the company becomes potentially liable for discrimination lawsuits. By reprimanding one worker for a violation of policy and then not reprimanding another worker for a violation of policy, the appearance of discrimination becomes prevalent and likely a winnable lawsuit. According to a report by the United States Equal Opportunity Employment Commission (U.S. EEOC), more than 100,000 discrimination-related lawsuits were filed in 2011 in the United States.

To strengthen the efforts of management in the enterprise, to avoid losses and maximize profits, and to avoid litigation, all personnel must consistently adhere to and enforce all policies.

Policy documents

The standard of behavior and activity of the workers of the enterprise must be established in written form. These written documents become much like a legal contract or agreement between the enterprise and the employees. Five types of documents establish the framework of governance for an enterprise, and they are collectively referred to as policy documents. They include *policies*, *standards*, *procedures*, *baselines*, and *guidelines*.

- **Policy** This type of document describes the expected behavior of the employees (people) of the company. They set the tone for ethical behavior. They identify operational, tactical, and strategic goals, and they define the objective to adhere to legal and regulatory compliance requirements. Policies outline the high-level requirements for each of the security features described in the preceding bulleted list, and should remain nonspecific about how the high-level objectives should be accomplished. Those details live in the supporting document types.

    - **Organizational policy** This is a high-level, general, and overarching statement from senior management regarding the governance of the enterprise.

    - **Issue specific policies** These policies describe the company's expectations regarding specific issues such as being a nonsmoking environment, avoiding the use and distribution of objectionable or offensive materials, and observing rules regarding bringing weapons on the premises.

    - **System-specific policies** These describe the use of specific computer and infrastructure systems within the organization such as policies regarding the use of the company's email system for personal use, the installation of software from an approved list, maximum disk use quotas on the users' home folders, and the requirement for all remote access to be encrypted and require multi-factor authentication.

    Several of the most commonly implemented policies include:

    - Acceptable use policy
    - Monitoring policy

- Data classification and protection policy
- Hiring practices
- Termination practices

- **Standards**   Standards establish a definition of required compliance. Standards are high level and largely technical in nature and define the required encryption algorithm and key length for protecting sensitive content, the minimum password length for authenticating to your user account, and how information systems must be configured.

- **Baseline**   A baseline is a lower-level document that supports the details defined within standards. The baseline is an established reference point used to compare against over time or as an acceptable level. Baselines help establish metrics that allow you to evaluate changes in performance over time.

- **Procedure**   Procedures are step-by-step instructions on how to accomplish some task or activity that supports the policies. These would include how to make a hundred gallons of the secret sauce, how to install a server operating system, and how to configure the firewall rule base. The specific settings of the firewall rule base (like a rule to block all inbound ICMP traffic) would be defined in a standard or baseline. The procedure describes not what the setting must be but how to configure the setting.

- **Guideline**   The guideline is the only type of document in which compliance is not mandatory. Policies, standards, baselines, and procedures define how to act under established and predictable conditions. Guidelines are recommendations on how to manage under unusual and unpredictable conditions and whenever the other documents don't apply. If it is optional, it is a guideline.

EXAM TIP

It is important to understand the difference between these types of documents, which collectively build the framework of governance of the organization. Policies and standards are high-level documents. Procedures and baselines are lower-level documents. Policies and procedures target people and their activities. Standards and baselines target technologies. Guidelines describe the recommended behavior when the circumstances are not defined within policies, procedures, standards, and baselines.

Sources

The good news is that much of the structure of the collection of policy documents has already been developed in numerous control frameworks. Although every enterprise is unique in its specific collection of security concern, ethical posture, and tolerance for risk, you can begin with a generic set of policies and customize each one as necessary to fit the specific needs of the enterprise. There are numerous frameworks, standards, and recommended best practices already available to draw from as you pull together this integrated assembly of documents. In addition, recall that if the organization is subject to compliance with any laws and regulations, these requirements must also be included in their entirety within the policies of the organization. The established and recognized frameworks, standards, applicable laws and regulations, and recommended best practices include:

- **Health Insurance Portability and Accountability Act (HIPAA)**   Controls the flow medical information

- **Sarbanes-Oxley Act (SOX)**   Requires truth in reporting for publicly held companies

- **Gramm-Leach-Bliley Act (GLBA)**   Requires the protection of personally identifiable information of the customers of financial institutions (among other things)

- **Federal Information Security Management Act (FISMA**)   Requires the management and protection of information within government agencies

- **Payment Card Industry Data Security Standard (PCI DSS)**   Requires the protection of information related to credit card and debit card transactions (industry regulation, not a law)

- **Committee of Sponsoring Organizations of the Treadway Commission (COSO)**   An enterprise-level framework on governance and risk management released in 1985 by the National Commission on Fraudulent Financial Reporting

- **Control Objectives for Information and related Technology (COBIT)**   Describes the IT security subset of COSO by the Information Systems Audit and Control Association (ISACA), and the IT Governance Institute (ITGI)

- **Zachman Framework**   Provides an enterprise-level framework used to provide structure and vision to the enterprise by asking the questions, "What, where, when, why, who, and how"

- **Sherwood Applied Business Security Architecture (SABSA)**   Provides enterprise security architecture structured much like the Zachman Framework

- **International Organization for Standardization (ISO) and International Electrotechnical Commission (IEC) 27000 series**   Provides a collection of recommended standards and best practices on information security, including:

  - ISO / IEC 27001   Information Security Management System (ISMS) (from BS7799-2)

  - ISO / IEC 27002   Information Security Standard Code of Practice (was ISO 17799 from BS7799-1)

  - ISO / IEC 27003   Implementation of an ISMS

  - ISO / IEC 27004   Measurement and Metrics for ISMS

  - ISO / IEC 27005   Information Security Risk Management

  - ISO / IEC 27006   Certification and Accreditation of ISMS

  - ISO / IEC 27799   Protection of personal health information

- **National Institute of Standards and Technology (NIST) Special Publication (SP) 800 series**   Provides a collection of IT-related standards and recommended best practices

- **Hardware and software vendors**   Often provides best practices for configuring their software (such as operating systems and applications) and devices (such as firewall appliances, VPN concentrators, and load balancers)

> **MORE INFO   ASSEMBLING A FRAMEWORK**
>
> These frameworks, standards, laws, regulations, and recommended best practices can and perhaps should be used to build the framework for governance. They are covered in additional detail in Chapter 5.

Ethical standards

The policy documents and security awareness training should convey the essence of senior management's desired ethical posture for the organization. This ethical posture should permeate the entire corporate culture and strive to avoid strategies and activities that could lead to unethical behavior. Advising salespeople to get the order, no matter what it takes, or encouraging employees to try to obtain a competitor's trade secrets can entice workers to violate ethical standards.

ISC2, the certifying body for the CISSP certification, requires each CISSP candidate to agree to and adhere to the ISC2 Code of Ethics as part of his certification process. The ISC2 code of ethics includes this preamble:

> *Safety of the commonwealth, duty to our principals, and to each other requires that we adhere, and be seen to adhere, to the highest ethical standards of behavior. Therefore, strict adherence to this Code is a condition of certification.*

The ISC2 Code of Ethics includes four primary canons:

1. Protect society, the commonwealth, and the infrastructure.

2. Act honorably, honestly, justly, responsibly, and legally.

3. Provide diligent and competent service to principals.

4. Advance and protect the profession.

EXAM TIP

Know these four canons, in the proper order, for the exam. In case of an ethical conflict, the first canon takes priority over the lower three, the second canon takes priority over the lower two, and the third canon takes priority over the last one.

In essence, the first canon says to protect society, the second canon says be a good person, the third canon says to be a good CISSP, and the fourth canon says to help ISC2 sell more stuff.

Another source of ethical standards is the Internet Architecture Board (IAB), which oversees the Internet Engineering Task Force (IETF) and the Internet Research Task Force (IRTF). It has published its two-page Request for Comment (RFC) 1087 entitled "Ethics and the Internet." The IAB describes the nature of unethical behavior when using the Internet. These canons state that it is unethical to:

- Purposely seek to gain unauthorized access to the resources of the Internet.
- Compromise the privacy of users.
- Destroy the integrity of computer-based information.
- Disrupt the intended use of the Internet, waste resources (people, capacity, computer) through purposeful actions.
- Conduct Internet-wide experiments that might waste, degrade, or destroy resources.

One additional body to be aware of is the Computer Ethics Institute (CEI), a nonprofit organization based in Washington, D.C. The CEI has published the Ten Commandments of Computer Ethics, a "thou shalt . . ." list that includes:

1. Not use a computer to harm other people.

2. Not interfere with other people's computer work.

3. Not snoop around in other people's computer files.

4. Not use a computer to steal.

5. Not use a computer to bear false witness.

6. Not copy or use proprietary software for which you have not paid.

7. Not use other people's computer resources without authorization or proper compensation.

8. Not appropriate other people's intellectual output.

9. Think about the social consequences of the program you are writing or the system you are designing.

10. Always use a computer in ways that ensure consideration and respect for your fellow humans.

Certification and accreditation

In some cases, more commonly when dealing with government entities, the security status of an information system must be formally technically verified against a standard (certification), and the decision to allow information flow, processing, and storage on that system must be authorized by a specially appointed responsible party (accreditation) on behalf of management. The standard is developed to minimize risk and to identify clearly to management the level of residual risk.

In general, the certification (C) and accreditation (A) processes include:

- The definition of the standard of security for compliance purposes. This includes the overall information system (such as the networking environment, complete with servers, routers, switches, firewalls, monitoring systems, and so on), and specific standards for each individual component within that larger system.

- A definition of the roles and responsibilities for and selection of the people and organizations performing the C and A processes.

- The scope of the information system attempting C and A.

- A definition of who can accredit the system after proper certification.

- Test procedures used to verify compliance with the standards.

- The actual testing of the systems to verify compliance.

- A risk assessment to determine the total residual risk within the system.

- If the testing shows compliance with the standards, a recommendation for accreditation is submitted to the Designated Approving Authority (DAA).

- The DAA assigns their approval level on the information system:

    - Accredited

    - Granted interim approval to operate

    - Denied accreditation

As you can imagine, this is a time-consuming and costly process, so it is usually required and performed in the commercial world when a business must connect its computer networks to government computer networks and when the prospective revenue generated from this close and trusted relationship justifies the cost of the C and A process.

If the organization has the desire or the need to implement the C and A process, these details must also be fully documented within the collection of policy documents.

Awareness

The development of this collection of documents is a huge accomplishment for an organization. The good news is that the security professionals and senior management (who approve the documents) now know and understand the policies and the resulting technical and procedural requirements these documents impose on the environment. The bad news is that nobody else does, at least not until this information is pushed out to all employees through security awareness training. Management cannot expect to enforce policies unless all users have been trained on the policies, and awareness and enforcement are prevalently permeating the corporate culture and environment. The *security awareness training* program conveys this policy information to the workers and is described in detail in the section entitled "Providing security awareness training."

Revisions, updates, and change control

This collection of documents becomes a formalized component of the structure of the organization. It must be maintained over time as new features occur in the environment, as technology changes, and as the posture of the organization changes over time. These changes result in different iterations or versions of the updated policy document. They must be implemented through carefully described and strictly adhered-to policies and procedures themselves. Organizations must develop formal *change control* procedures that include thorough documentation and approvals prior to making any changes and verifications and reporting after changes are made to these documents. Change control is the formally defined process of documenting, approving, implementing, and verifying change requests to controlled documents, application code, and configurations. Change control must be managed relative to the policy documents; the business continuity plans; the disaster recovery plans; the software development process; and configuration management of information systems, appliances, operating systems, and applications. Change control is covered in more detail in Chapter 8; Chapter 9, "Software development security"; and Chapter 10, "Operations security."

✔ **Quick check**

1. What are the types of documents that form the governance framework?
2. What are the documents called from the ISO/IEC that describe information security?

Quick check answers

1. Policy documents, standards documents, baseline documents, procedure documents, and guideline documents.
2. They are the ISO/IEC 27000 series.

Risk assessment and management

A comprehensive appraisal within an organization that should be defined clearly and completely within the policy documents is the project of risk management. Virtually every enterprise should be performing a risk assessment and following it up with management of the identified risks. Because risk management has become identified as a standard of due care, any company that is not performing these functions is essentially negligent and faces increased exposure to negligence-related and liability-related litigation.

To manage risks, one must first become aware of and knowledgeable about the risks to be managed. The *risk assessment* is the development of knowledge and awareness of all the risks to all the assets of the organization. The risk assessment is all talk and paper and no action, the mechanism used to accomplish due diligence, described earlier in this chapter. After the risks present in an environment are identified, risk management countermeasures can be identified along with a cost justification for each countermeasure.

The risk assessment and the following implementation of risk managing countermeasures is part of that three-year project mentioned earlier for an enterprise as it matures from the mom-and-pop efforts in a garage toward becoming an industry leader. As a comprehensive, enterprise-wide effort that considers the risks to essentially every asset the enterprise owns, the risk assessment should be treated as a full-featured project, complete with senior management support and oversight, assigned roles and responsibilities for the members of the risk assessment team, a project plan and schedule of deliverables, and adequate tools (such as an automated risk assessment and risk management software application) to support the effort.

The primary deliverable is a report to management that succinctly identifies the greatest to the least risks presented to the enterprise in its current state and a selection of cost-justified countermeasures that help manage the identified risks with the preferences and recommendations identified. From this report, management can choose the countermeasures that satisfy the corporate budget as well as management's tolerance for risk. Management will choose countermeasures that mitigate (reduce) risks (by reducing or eliminating vulnerabilities, likelihood, and impact) or countermeasures that transfer risks (such as buying insurance or outsourcing some risky process) or countermeasures that help avoid risks (stop doing the risky things). It will choose various, cost-justified countermeasures from these three types until it has reduced risk to a level it can accept of the remaining risks. To summarize, management has *four* types of countermeasures to choose from. Those are:

- Mitigate risk
- Transfer risk
- Avoid risk
- Accept risk

Management will be spending money as it selects from options 1, 2, and 3 until the remaining risk is low enough to choose option 4. Accepting risk will also carry an associated cost, but that price must be paid only when the bad thing happens to the asset, and losses at the level of the residual and accepted risks occur. This level of acceptable risk is wholly defined by management and identifies its level of tolerance for risk.

As described earlier, management needs the security professional to use her specialized and skilled vision to develop this succinct vision and produce the summarizing report with proposed countermeasures. With this executive summary style of operation, management can quickly apply its specialized management skills and reach well-informed decisions that guide the enterprise as management should and establish the security posture that management desires and finds appropriate for the enterprise.

The list of approved countermeasures defines the structure and posture of the security program for the enterprise for the next year at least. It defines the hardware and software that must be purchased and the new employees who must be hired to implement and manage the new systems. It defines the training required for the administrators of the new technologies and the changes required to existing policies, procedures, standards, baselines, and guidelines. It identifies the collection of new policy documents required to implement and maintain the new technologies and procedures. Further, it defines the approved budget for the security program for (again, at least) the next year.

Starting the risk management project

Senior management must drive and support this project by defining it within the policy documentation for the enterprise. The project will include a budget, the formal assignment of responsibility, a definition of scope, the formation of a risk assessment team, and the provision of appropriate tools to accomplish the task. Senior management must also have some notion of its level of tolerance for risk, but this notion will likely be rewritten when you show it the actual risk posture of the organization and the costs to bring that level of risk down.

 Management defines the *scope of the assessment* and identifies which portion of the enterprise the assigned assessment is to be performed on. The scope might be a single department or a floor in a building. It might be an entire building, a campus of buildings, or the entire enterprise. A common problem to avoid on the project is that of *scope creep*, an unauthorized increase or addition to the scope of the assessment. If management defines the scope to be the facilities in Oshkosh but, for Oshkosh to stay functional, several items are required from the facilities in Schenectady each week, it is easy to consider and assume that the Schenectady facilities must also be within scope. This is how scope creep occurs. To manage scope creep, the team lead should identify the interface between Oshkosh and Schenectady and identify the assumption that these required items will be provided by Schenectady each week on schedule. Now the reliance on these items from Schenectady is clearly identified, and management can make a decision to add Schenectady to your scope or assign the risk assessment of Schenectady to another security professional to help ensure timely delivery of the critical items. The scope might also include limitations or inclusions of the nature of a specific set of assets or the protection of assets from a specific and limited set of threats.

Consider how you will gather information. The team members will need to interview people with specific knowledge of the assets within scope and their roles in the organization. The team members might issue surveys to be completed, and need to perform vulnerability and penetration testing to acquire an accurate appraisal of the security posture of the portion of the organization within the scope of the risk assessment.

The definition of the scope of the risk assessment identifies the team members required for the risk assessment project. The team will require senior management support, one or more security professionals (the ones with those security goggles that give them the proper security vision), and, typically, representation from the legal department, the human relations department, and the IT and network operations department. Beyond that core team, you need representation from each major facet of the organization within the defined scope of the assessment.

EXAM TIP

This is one of the several areas in which ISC2 likes the idea of the use of automated tools to assist with the management of large and complex projects. If the risk assessment part of the risk management project is your task, you will also like the use of the automated tools, in this case, a software application, to help you on this project.

Performing the risk assessment

Now that the project is defined, the budget has been allocated, the scope is defined, and the team and tools are in place, it is time to dive in and get some work done. This is the information-gathering phase. Again, this phase is all just talk and paper. The risk assessment is a large component of performing or demonstrating due diligence.

Inventory the assets

The first step is to complete an inventory of all assets the enterprise owns. This would include the files and databases that are used to make business decisions. It would include the servers that store, process, and transmit the information, the data center that houses and supports the servers, and the networking infrastructure systems that provide the connectivity to the information assets and the application servers. It includes the workstations and cubicles that provide the workplace for the workers, the building that houses the workplace, and the data center. Everything that has some potential value to the enterprise should go on this list.

At the first pass, brainstorm and add everything you can think of to the list, without a critical appraisal. On the second pass, begin to refine the list and remove any duplication and overlap. Be sure you have captured everything within the defined scope for the assessment.

Consider all *tangible assets*, which are physical assets that can be bumped into or dropped. Workers with specialized skills might be considered tangible assets. It isn't a good thing, but if a person in the organization provides a unique skill set (the only person who can accomplish some critical task) or provides a unique public presence such as a strong figurehead for an organization, the loss or absence of this person could introduce losses to the organization. Whenever these situations are recognized, the proper countermeasure (not part of the risk assessment but part of risk management) is to spread those skills and figurehead-like public presence around. Duplicate the unique skills. Duplicate the single points of failure. Duplicate whatever skills or knowledge or presence the one individual brings to the organization to eliminate the critical dependence on that individual.

 In addition, consider all the *intangible assets*. These are not the physical assets that can be bumped into or dropped. These are typically the information assets that are stored in some software format as binary bits on some computer storage device or system. This would include databases, customer lists, vendor lists, marketing plans and projections, production details, custom applications, and proprietary processes. Intangible assets would also include intellectual property such as copyrights, trademarks, patents, and trade secrets.

Another intangible asset that must be added to the list is the good reputation and positive name recognition the company has in the marketplace. Recognize that if some event or incident causes damage to the reputation of the company, consumers will be less likely to search out and preferentially purchase your company's products. They might even be repelled and actively search out your competition's products. This will translate into less revenue than before and is, in fact, a form of loss to the company—a loss of market share and a loss of revenue. It is the purpose of the risk assessment and risk management project to minimize losses and maximize profits. The company's good reputation is an asset worthy of protection. Put it on the list.

Assign a value to each asset

Now that the list of assets is complete, the next step is to assign each asset a value. This might be more complex than you first think. On the first level of approximation, the price that was paid for the asset is its value. That is clear-cut, direct, and not exactly wrong, but it is an incomplete appraisal. It begins with the price paid, but consider also the cost to deliver and install the asset. Although you paid a certain price for the asset two years ago, what is the purchase price if you had to buy one today? Consider the costs to develop, maintain, and protect the asset, such as a customer database that is built over time or a vendor list that has redundant suppliers for each required resource or supply. Consider the role the asset brings to the organization. A $4,000 server that controls a $1 million-a-day production line is worth $1 million per day in lost productivity. Consider delayed losses that would occur if the asset were compromised, such as lost orders even after the production line resumes full activity, because your customers were forced to find an alternate supplier and are still purchasing from that supplier instead. Consider any potential liabilities the company might face if the asset is compromised, such as late-delivery penalties or, worse, civil lawsuits claiming damages resulting from a breach. Consider the value your competition might have for the asset and might be willing to pay if it could steal the asset from you.

 Many of these aspects of value can be looked up on receipts or monthly reports. Values for which specific prices paid can be assigned are referred to as *quantitative values* when the quantity is known. These are typically the easy values to identify.

The more difficult, less tangible, opinion-based values to identify are referred to as *qualitative values*. Any time an event causes the enterprise losses, it has the distinct potential to affect productivity or become known to the public. If productivity is negatively affected, delivery schedules might slip, and your customers will not be happy. If knowledge of the loss event becomes public, the public and, more specifically, your customers, suppliers, and partners (and perhaps even the employees), will be unsure of the company's ability to manage itself. As the public recognizes the company's failure to manage itself and avoid unnecessary losses, it begins to have doubts about the company's ability to deliver as promised and pay its bills as promised and questions the company's ability to protect the sensitive information that customers, vendors, and partners might have shared with the now compromised company. In essence, the compromise or breach damages the reputation of the company, driving away business and opportunity. That translates into less revenue, which violates the basic premise for the enterprise and the security program of avoiding losses and maximizing profits.

It is commonly felt that an assessment could be performed using only qualitative assessment, but it is not possible to complete an assessment by using only a quantitative assessment. A hybrid approach would be to use both quantitative and qualitative assessment during the risk assessment process.

The determination of value of the company's good reputation is somewhat subjective, but it is certainly a valuable asset that needs protection and can be damaged by breaches of security. It is therefore a component of the risk assessment that must be quantified to establish an appropriate (cost-justified) level of protection. As each threat to each asset is identified and quantified, you must also determine any possible damage to the company's reputation for the threat-related breach and additionally quantify the potential losses due to the (qualitative) damage to the company's good reputation.

To accomplish this, begin by identifying the maximum possible loss (in the appropriate currency) resulting from damage to the company's reputation for any reason. For example, a certain product line might be generating $1 million in revenue per year. Estimate what portion of that $1 million in sales depends on the company's reputation. Imagine a certain demographic (or collection of demographics) of your customer base was completely offended and was willfully avoiding purchasing your products from this line altogether. You might conclude that number to be 65 percent, or $650,000.

Next, for a specific asset and threat relationship, you must determine the likelihood of the threat successfully compromising the asset. Identify this value on a scale of 1 to 10.

The third step is accomplished by surveying the appropriate people, your customers, suppliers, partners, and the employees; describe scenarios in which the asset is compromised by the threat and determine how severe the damage to the company's reputation is in the interviewee's opinion. You might want to begin with the threats that are most likely to occur. Have the interviewee rate this severity on a scale of 1 to 10. After surveying an acceptable number of candidates, determine the average value of severity.

Now plot this point on the diagram shown in Figure 1-2 to determine the significance of the event with regard to the company's reputation.

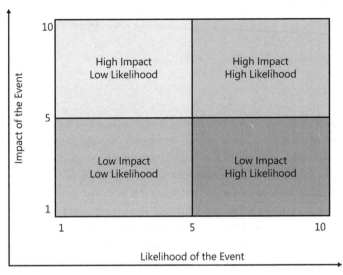

FIGURE 1-2 Likelihood versus impact of a qualitative loss event

Next, to quantify the reputation-damaging event, overlay Figure 1-3 on the diagram with the plotted point(s).

10	20	30	40	50	60	70	80	90	100
9	28	27	36	45	54	63	72	81	90
8	16	24	32	40	48	56	64	72	80
7	14	21	28	35	42	49	56	63	70
6	12	18	24	30	36	42	48	54	60
5	10	15	20	25	30	35	40	45	50
4	8	12	16	20	24	28	32	36	40
3	6	9	12	15	18	21	24	27	30
2	4	6	8	10	12	14	16	18	20
1	2	3	4	5	6	7	8	9	10

1-19%	Lowest Risk
20-39%	Medium Risk
40-59%	Increased Risk
60-100%	High Risk

FIGURE 1-3 Quantifying the qualitative loss event

If you determined that the likelihood of occurrence was 6 and the impact was 3, the resulting percentage would be 18 percent. Using the previously determined value identified as the maximum possible loss resulting from damage to the company's reputation for any reason, calculate the estimated losses from this asset or threat event by multiplying the number in the cell where your point is plotted, as a percentage, with the maximum possible loss value. Multiplying the earlier example of $650,000 maximum losses by the 18 percent for this specific loss event, the potential losses from this event would be $117,000.

This technique is used to quantify the losses from a qualitative loss event (damage to the company's reputation). This quantified value is needed to cost-justify appropriate countermeasures proposed to prevent or mitigate the qualitative loss event.

> **NOTE** **THE DELPHI METHOD**
>
> It has been discovered that during a survey, when the identity of the interviewee is known, the responses are often biased and therefore less accurate. People aren't willing to admit the truth in many cases because they don't want to admit doing the wrong things, because they want to inflate their self-worth, or because they are intimidated and fearful of repercussion when their identity is tied to their responses, to name a few reasons. To gather more information that is more accurate and less biased by fear or ego, interviewers should allow the interviewees to remain anonymous. This technique of allowing the interviewees to remain anonymous to gather the most accurate information is called the *Delphi Method*.

Using a combination of quantitative and qualitative valuation, determine a specific value for each asset, called the asset value (AV).

Classify assets

As you can imagine, there are many items in the inventory of assets, perhaps tens of thousands, or even hundreds of thousands of assets to protect. To simplify the protection strategy for the organization, define several categories or classifications to indicate the criticality (value) of the assets to the organization. Typically, four to six classifications are used.

By grouping similarly valued assets into a classification, you can establish several protective security levels and standards applied to the group of assets rather than developing specific requirements for each of the (too many) individual assets. By classifying the assets, you have now identified appropriate prioritizing for the protection of the assets. The assets with the highest value, in the top-most category, are the assets to analyze and protect first.

Identify threats

At this point, you have a complete inventory of every asset the organization owns. You have accurately identified the value of the asset to the organization, and you have arranged each into classification categories that identify from the most valuable group of assets to the least valuable.

Next, you must identify every bad thing you can imagine that could happen to each asset. Beginning with the assets in the most valuable classification category, list every vulnerability and related threat that could compromise the confidentiality, integrity, or availability of the asset.

Each threat category must be considered. As stated earlier in this chapter, the four threat categories are:

- Natural
- Human-made
- Technical
- Supply system

List the threats that could affect each asset negatively.

Calculate the annualized loss expectancy

Most companies, departments, agencies, and similar entities allocate their budgets on an annual basis. The security program will be an ongoing effort and likely will be subject to this annual proposed and approved budget structure. The *annual loss expectancy* (*ALE*) calculation for each asset identifies the anticipated losses due to the identified threats each year. The ALE is designed to provide the necessary information to build an appropriate annual budget proposal for approval.

The ALE is also beneficial as a mechanism to educate senior management in the current security posture of the organization, showing the assets with the highest expected losses and the overall expected losses for the upcoming year.

This calculation must be performed for each asset and each threat to the asset. Again, beginning with the most valuable asset and a related threat, determine what percentage of the asset will be lost or destroyed if the threat occurs. This is called the *exposure factor* (*EF*). For example, if the building is worth $1.2 million, and a flood is the threat, you might conclude that 30 percent of the asset will be destroyed. In this example, the exposure factor is 30 percent. The values determined for exposure factor can be developed from information provided by your insurance company or statistics from the Federal Emergency Management Agency (FEMA) or the National Oceanic Atmospheric Administration (NOAA). You might find calculations in published papers and news articles. This value will be speculative—you are predicting the future—but the value should be based on research, homework, and a well-considered and educated estimate.

Knowing the asset value (AV), and the exposure factor (EF), you can calculate the *single loss expectancy* (*SLE*), the loss you expect when the threat occurs.

$AV \times EF = SLE$

Run this calculation for every threat to each asset.

Next, determine how often this threat is likely to occur. You should research this parameter the same way you researched the exposure factor. Then you determine how many times each year the threat might occur to determine the *annualized rate of occurrence* (*ARO*). If the threat is likely to occur once every 8 years, the ARO is 1/8 or 0.125. If the threat is likely to occur once every 20 years, the ARO is 1/20 or 0.05. If the threat is likely to occur every month (12 times per year), the ARO is 12.

Using the previously calculated SLE and the ARO, you can determine the annualized loss expectancy (ALE) used to establish the annual security budget.

SLE × ARO = ALE

Table 1-1 shows some examples of these calculations. Remember that a calculation must be performed for each threat to each asset. Note the calculation when the loss is expected more than once per year.

TABLE 1-1 Examples of SLE and ALE calculations

Asset	Threat	Asset value $ (AV)	Exposure factor % (EF)	Single loss expectancy $ (SLE)	Annualized rate of occurrence (ARO)	Annualized loss expectancy $ (ALE)
Building	Flood	$1,000,000	28%	$280,000	1 each 20 years	$14,000
Building	Tornado	$1,000,000	62%	$620,000	1 each 10 years	$62,000
Server cluster	Disk failure	$180,000	10%	$18,000	1 each 4 years	$4,500
Database	Corruption	$250,000	5%	$12,500	Quarterly	$50,000
Database	Data theft by hacker	$250,000	100%	$250,000	1 each 10 years	$25,000
App server for remote users	Internet connectivity failure	$140,000	8%	$11,200	Twice per year	$22,400

EXAM TIP

Be prepared to perform these calculations on the exam. On the computer-based exams, a calculator is provided to assist with the basic math, but you must know the formulas.

The ALE identifies, in its current state, the (annualized) level of risk for the asset. This is the asset's current *residual risk*, which is the amount of loss that management is currently accepting (even when it was unaware of it) for this asset, relative to this threat, on an annual basis.

ALE = Residual Risk (per year)

If you divide the ALE by the asset value, you identify the part of the asset that is not protected by the controls (countermeasures). This is called the *control gap*, which is the gap in the controls that allows exposure of the asset.

ALE / AV = Control Gap

For example, if the asset is worth $25,000 and its ALE is $1,000, its control gap is

$1,000 / $25,000 = 0.04 or 4%

This ALE value defines the most that should be spent to protect the asset from the threat each year. If no action is taken, this value is what management should expect to lose each year on this asset to this threat. If you were to spend this amount each year to protect the asset from the specified threat, you have a break-even situation. Why go to the trouble? You need to develop countermeasures that cost less than this amount to avoid losses and maximize profits.

Identify cost-effective countermeasures

Countermeasures are controls that help prevent threats from affecting the assets of the organization, or they might mitigate the threat by reducing or eliminating the vulnerability, the likelihood, or the impact of the threat. For each threat, you identify a list of potentially effective countermeasures. Remember that countermeasures come from these three major categories, and each category should be examined for countermeasures for each threat to each asset.

- Administrative
- Technical
- Physical

Initially, this step is more of a brainstorming process, first adding every countermeasure to the list that might be a good choice, and then you qualify each countermeasure until you have summarized the countermeasures that are appropriate for your proposal to management. The qualification process involves determining the effectiveness of the countermeasure (how much will it improve the protection of the asset) and identifying the real cost of the countermeasure.

To determine the effectiveness of the countermeasure, identify what the expected new ALE would be after the countermeasure is in place. The countermeasure should certainly reduce the ALE. If it does not reduce the ALE, it is ineffective and should be removed from the proposal.

Next, identify the real cost of the countermeasure. Once again, you identify every aspect of the cost of the countermeasure as you did when identifying the value of an asset. You consider the tangible and intangible costs; the quantitative and qualitative costs, including the cost to purchase the control, to have it delivered, to install it; the service contract and maintenance costs; the cost to integrate it into the system; the cost to write the policies and procedures related to the control; the negative impact on productivity the control introduces; the potential damage to the company's reputation when the employees become frustrated from having to learn the system or device; and the additional tasks the control requires of them. Aggregate these costs to determine the real cost of the control to the organization.

Now you are ready to run the numbers and identify just how cost effective the countermeasure actually is. Subtract the cost of the countermeasure and the new ALE after the proposed countermeasure is installed from the current ALE.

Current ALE – Cost of countermeasure – New ALE = Increase in profits

Suppose an ALE for an asset is $100,000. Suppose further that you find a countermeasure that costs $15,000 and reduces the ALE to $10,000. This would avoid losses and produce an increase in profits by $75,000.

$100,000 – $15,000 – $10,000 = $75,000$

This is a worthy countermeasure to add to your risk assessment and security program proposed countermeasures.

If an ALE for an asset is $100,000 and you find a countermeasure that costs $50,000 and reduces the ALE to $60,000, this would avoid losses but would not produce an increase in profits. This countermeasure would actually be reducing the profits of the company an additional $10,000 each year.

$100,000 – $50,000 – $60,000 = ($10,000)$

You should keep this countermeasure in the documentation of the risk assessment so you know about it next year, but do not add this countermeasure to the security program proposal you present to management. Provide several proposed and cost-justified countermeasures for each threat to give management some options in its balance of cost versus residual risk considerations. Identify countermeasures that can or must work in combination with other countermeasures. (Remember defense in depth.) Each countermeasure has a different cost and offers a different level of effectiveness. This provides management with a spectrum of options to choose from so it can balance the costs with its tolerance for risk.

EXAM TIP

Understand the process of performing the cost justification for a countermeasure.

The four methods of managing risk

Based on the risk assessment and the ALE for each threat to each asset, the security professional identifies a spectrum of cost-justified countermeasures that:

1. **Mitigate**   Reduce the risk (losses), typically, by reducing or eliminating vulnerabilities in the assets, the likelihood of loss, and the impact of loss. This would include controls such as establishing a formal and routine patching process for operating systems and applications, implementing a VPN concentrator to secure communications with remote workers, and hiring a security company to patrol the property after hours. This is called *risk mitigation*.

2. **Transfer**   This is shifting the risk to another entity; you pay the other entity to handle the risk. This is often accomplished by purchasing insurance, so that the insurance company absorbs the losses, and the residual risk is the deductible. Another technique to transfer risk is to hire a third-party service provider, such as a credit card processing company. Your company must be able to accept and process credit cards, but this external credit card processing company is now handling all the risk associated with the sensitive credit card information. This is called *risk transference*.

3. **Avoid**   Cease the activity to avoid the risk or remove the asset that carries too much risk. If the activity or the asset is too risky, stop doing that! This is usually the choice when management was unaware of the risk. (That should never happen again after the first risk assessment.) This is a last choice when management is unwilling to spend more on countermeasures and is unwilling to accept the residual risk. This is called *risk avoidance.*

4. **Accept**   Management accepts the remaining residual risk. After management finishes choosing options from numbers 1, 2, and 3 (mitigating, transferring, and avoiding risk), management must accept whatever is left. This is called *risk acceptance.* If this residual risk is too great to accept, dive back into the choices in 1, 2, and 3 until the residual risk is low enough to accept. The risk assessors must give management enough options in 1, 2, and 3 to bring the residual risk down to a point that management can choose option 4.

EXAM TIP

Know the four methods of managing risk.

Manage speculation and uncertainty

The risk assessment is a snapshot in time of the current security posture of the organization. It is also forward looking, an educated guess about bad things that might happen, are likely to happen, or are certain to happen. Predicting the future is not a science, and there are few if any certainties. Estimates, assumptions, speculation, and uncertainty are all features of the risk assessment. Wherever this occurs, it is the responsibility of the security professional to cause management to recognize the absence of definable facts and the need to provide estimates, ones based on solid research and historic trends whenever possible.

Identify to management where, within the risk assessment, these educated estimates are due to lack of accurate and specific information so management has the opportunity to accept the estimated values or assign weighting based on its vision and notions. This provides proper balance to the assessment and, once again, places the real responsibility with management, where it should be.

Complete the assessment

The completed assessment is developed by security professionals (individuals usually with a high level of technical proficiency). However, the assessment has been designed to include concepts and language that senior management clearly understands: improving profits by spending in the right places. It isn't just a wish list of expensive hardware and software described in ultra-geek terms. The assessment describes the avoidance of losses and the maximization of profits, providing choices for management to support decisions on how much security is enough security, how much security the enterprise can justify and afford, and how much risk is acceptable to management.

This report and proposal enable management to develop a clear and comprehensive vision of the risks to the organization, to categorize risks, and to establish an appropriate budget for the security program. The proposed countermeasures must provide a balance between the need for access by authorized users and an appropriate level of protection for the asset.

Realize that this is still all within the risk assessment, the development of knowledge and awareness of the risks to the enterprise, and the collection of potential countermeasures that might be chosen to help manage those risks. Still, it is all just talk and paper, but it is the highly refined information and vision management needs to make the best business decision, made possible by the vision and skills of the security professional.

At this point, the risk assessment is complete and ready for presentation to management along with the collection of cost-justified countermeasures.

Implement the security program

As management reviews the presentation and develops its sense and vision of the state of security of the organization, it will begin to understand where it must act to defend the organization from the identified potential and, often, certain losses. It is its sole responsibility (not the security professional's) to approve specific countermeasures for implementation and not approve others, based on the budget, management's current vision, and management's tolerance for risk.

As management approves specific new countermeasures for implementation, it is galvanizing the security program, and it is approving the budget for the security program for the next year. Now formally approved are the new devices to purchase; new software to acquire; new people to hire; training requirements for the administrators; new policy documents to write, get approved, and implement; and the new security awareness training to push out to all users, with supplemental training of some. This all comes together as management reviews, understands, and approves.

Following the approval of countermeasures identified by the risk assessment, the approved countermeasures will be acquired, developed, and implemented in the enterprise workplace environment. This is risk management and the implementation or performance of due care.

After the initial risk assessment, the risk management project is generally performed each year to identify the organization's current risk level, assess the effectiveness of the current security program, and adjust the countermeasures as necessary to reduce the residual risk to an acceptable level as defined by management. The risk management project should also be performed any time there is any substantial change to the assets of the organization, such as the selling of a division, starting a new product line or division, or the acquisition of another company.

Quick check

1. What is the formula for determining the single loss expectancy?

2. What are the two types of assessments required to identify the value of an asset?

Quick check answers

1. Asset value x exposure factor = single loss expectancy

   $AV \times EF = SLE$

2. Quantitative and qualitative assessments

Implementing the security program

The process of implementing a security program all starts with senior management laying down a collection of relatively high-level statements in policy documents that initially define the governance structure for the organization. Then a risk assessment is performed to understand where the most critical assets are and where the most dangerous risks are. Acting on the information, more like the vision, developed from the risk assessment, administrative, technical, and physical security controls are selected by management to implement safety and security within the organization.

The ongoing implementation of that safety and security within the organization is the security program. Understood through ongoing assessments, security professionals propose an array of countermeasures to management for its selection and approval. When approved, the changes and additions to the control and governance of the organization are now budgeted for and are implemented in more detailed policy documents to define the structure in hardware and software, in personnel, and in the training of the existing and new personnel as well as through monitoring, auditing, and enforcement.

The countermeasures added to the enterprise from the risk assessment and risk management project become a standard part of the enterprise, elements of the routine and standard operating procedures, and become the definition of the security posture of the enterprise. The ongoing and prudent maintenance, monitoring, response, enforcement, training, and evaluation of the controls currently in place are the continuation of due diligence and are components of the ongoing security program.

This list was provided earlier within this chapter, but it is the foundation for the entire common book of knowledge, and for the CISSP certification, so it is worth repeating here. The fully implemented security program should address and include the following components:

- Provide a safe environment for employees, visitors, customers, vendors, and so on.

- Maximize profits.

- Mitigate and avoid losses.

- Support the business needs.
- Identify and defend the enterprise against threats specific to the business.
- Abide by applicable laws and regulations.
- Convey and implement senior management's vision and governance standards.
- Convey and implement senior management's desired ethical posture for the organization.
- Define roles and responsibilities.
- Define the risk management program.
- Define the disaster recovery and business continuity planning program.
- Define the data classification and protection program.
- Define privacy requirements.
- Define the auditing and monitoring.
- Define physical security.
- Define incident response.
- Define the security awareness training and enforcement program.
- Define configuration management and change control.
- Define the employee hiring and termination practices.
- Define the governance practices of third-party service providers.

EXAM TIP

Know the major components of the security program.

Understanding the new organization chart

Historically, security was often considered a firewall the network operations department implemented. The comprehensive platform most companies require today was virtually never implemented. To some extent, you can credit the increased maturity of business management to becoming smarter and better at what it does and wanting to do the right thing. What a lovely and complimentary notion. However, to the largest extent, this evolution toward protecting the assets of the organization is the product of relatively new laws and regulations that have been imposed on businesses because of massive fraud, deception, and negligence.

Some publicly held companies deliberately misled their investors, financial institutions were careless about protecting the private and sensitive information of their customers, and commercial businesses were unwilling to foot the bill for secure credit card transactions. Couple this lack of interest in protection with the continued improvements in technology and the skills of hackers and other cyber-criminals, and the losses become gigantic. Therefore, governments and industry leaders step in to protect the public and (try to) reduce and manage losses.

Historically, the security team and the auditing team were subordinate to production. They were there to assist production. However, production typically has a very different mentality about managing priorities than the security and auditing teams. Production typically has the mentality of "availability at all costs." If the production line is not running, the company is losing money. Keep the production line running, always, no matter what else might be happening.

Security has a diametrically opposed mentality of, "If it is not secure, shut it down. Pull the plug and pull it fast." If a breach is happening, the losses to the company could far exceed the losses of a little down time. Shut it down now.

If you subordinate security and auditing to production, the systems will usually err in favor of production, and security and auditing will be pushed aside and remain ineffective. As these laws and regulations took effect on organizations in the 1990s and in the first decade of the 2000s, management was forced to restructure the organization chart to avoid conflicts of interest. This required the security team and the auditing team no longer to be subordinate to production and to hold an equal position in the organization chart, as presented in Figure 1-4.

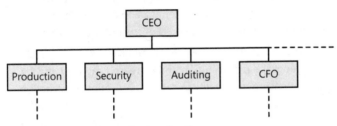

FIGURE 1-4 The new organization chart

Understanding the information life cycle

To protect information assets continuously and appropriately, you must recognize how the asset evolves in an enterprise. This is referred to as the information life cycle, and there are six elemental phases. They are:

- **Creation** The information asset is created by a human or an application and is usually produced in a digital form (residing on a computer or computer media). Information assets can also be created on paper.

- **Storage** This is data at rest. Information assets must be maintained or stored until needed. Again, the principal storage media types include hard disk drives, optical disks, flash memory, other magnetic media (such as backup tapes), and printed paper.

- **Distribution** This is data in transit. Information can be pushed from its source to intended recipients or pulled from a storage location by an authorized user at time of need. This implies connectivity between source and destination. That connectivity is most commonly the computer network, which might be the private corporate network or the public Internet. Other distribution mechanisms include physical mail (snail mail) and printed content made available for access (such as newspapers or advertising flyers). Distribution by video (such as cable television) is possible but is not a common form of corporate information distribution.

- **Use** This is data in use. This is where enterprises reap the benefits of their information assets. At time of need, users and computer programs access (read) information for processing and decision-making purposes. Often, at this point, the information can be modified, updated, duplicated, or transformed in some way, and then the data must be written to some storage media for future use or distribution to others.

- **Maintenance** This classically involves the protection of the confidentiality, integrity, and availability of the valuable information asset in whatever state the asset might be (rest, transit, or use).

  - Appropriate access controls (such as permissions or encryption) must be implemented and audited over time to ensure continuous and appropriate *confidentiality*.

  - The access controls also provide *integrity* protection. Integrity verification procedures can be performed to confirm the accuracy, completeness, and consistency of the information asset at time of use to provide a high level of trust of the information.

  - Multiple copies of the information assets (such as distributed databases and back-ups) are likely required for geographic distribution and increased capacity and for disaster recovery purposes to ensure *availability* in case of corruption, destruction, or system failure. These maintenance processes must occur continuously from the moment of creation until the data has lost its value, and its required retention period (if any) has expired.

- **Disposal** When the information asset has lost its value, and its required retention period has expired, as defined by corporate policy or laws and regulations, the information asset should be destroyed securely. Although the asset has no value to the enterprise, it might have value to others, such as your competition, or be usable to introduce some form of harm, damage, or loss to the enterprise, potentially damaging to the company's reputation, or used against the company in some future lawsuit. All information assets, unless already available to the public, should be securely destroyed at its time of disposal.

Classifying data

A strongly recommended, if not required, core component of every security program, and often required by laws and regulations, is the requirement for the classification of each information asset. When the asset is classified, a classification label is affixed to it, and a level of protection is defined for each classification to ensure the confidentiality, integrity, and availability of the classified assets at an appropriate level.

The initial data classification project and ongoing program must first be fully documented within the organization's policy documents. Then it must be deployed and implemented with ongoing training, awareness, enforcement, and maintenance. All users and applicable third-party service providers must participate and comply completely with the data classification requirements.

Assign roles and responsibilities

Several key roles must be defined and specifically assigned in the security program and within the data classification program. They are:

- **Data owner**   Often the business owner of the division, product line, or department. This person typically reports directly to senior management and is responsible for all aspects of a specific branch or facet of the company. Although this person probably will not be involved with the specific actions required, he must be held responsible for seeing that the data classification program is fully implemented and adhered to over time within his area of responsibility by delegating responsibilities and tasks to subordinates.

- **Data custodian**   The person (or persons) responsible for implementing the protection (CIA) of the data elements (files, databases). This includes the implementation of permissions and encryption and ensures that appropriate redundancy is provided, often in the form of distributed copies and routine data backups. Policies and procedures define the specifics of her (or their) tasks.

- **System custodian**   The person (or persons) responsible for the ongoing maintenance of the computer servers and the connecting network. Tasks include routine updating of the operating system and applications, server maintenance (power supply, disk drive space, system memory, and so on), firmware upgrades, and configuration of the networking infrastructure systems that provide user connectivity to the information assets.

- **Enforcer**   Typically the first tier of managers. Although all users are technically responsible for the enforcement of the data classification policies and requirements, the first tier of managers is responsible for the management of their subordinates within their department and are assigned the responsibility for providing oversight. This tier of management must be aware of any violations of policy, implement remediation to correct a breach (perhaps nothing more than reporting the breach to security operations), and implement the appropriate reprimand and remedial training for the user(s) who violate policy.

- **User**   The productive element in the picture. These are the people who actually use the information. They might be the creators or simply the readers of the data. They might be responsible for the manipulation, processing, and transformation of data.

They might store, duplicate, and distribute the data. All users must be trained in the relevant data protection policies with the expectation of compliance and must be kept aware, on an ongoing basis, of the requirements of strict compliance. Users might also provide oversight and initial remediation in case of violation or breach.

- **Auditor**   The person who performs inspections and evaluations to verify that all data elements are properly classified, that all security controls are being used as specified, and that all responsible parties are adhering to policy. The auditing function is often an in-house function but might often be an external, third-party function to ensure an unbiased appraisal. The auditor reports directly to senior management to avoid any conflicts of interest.

Define classification categories

Identify the classification labels that describe the value (also referred to as the level of sensitivity) of the information assets. In most cases, four or five classification categories are appropriate. If too few categories are used, the range of values of the assets within a category is too wide, and some assets will be protected too much, whereas others within the same category will be protected too little. If too many categories are used, the complexity and ambiguity can lead to misclassified content.

Examples of classification categories for government use include:

- **Top secret**   A breach introduces grave damage to national security.
- **Secret**   A breach introduces serious damage to national security.
- **Confidential**   A breach introduces damage to national security.
- **Sensitive but unclassified**   It is desirable to protect, but a breach will not affect national security (assets such as driver license number and Social Security number).
- **Unclassified**   Publicly available information.

Examples of classification categories in the private sector might include:

- Critical
- Confidential
- Internal
- Public

  or

- Red
- Orange
- Yellow
- Green

or

- Class I
- Class II
- Class III
- Class IV
- Class V

Define category criteria

Each category requires a specific definition of the level of sensitivity, or value, of the information assets it should contain. It is imperative for this classification criteria to be unambiguous, clearly defining one and only one category for each asset. The criteria are typically based on the losses to the organization that would occur if a breach of the confidentiality, integrity, or availability were to occur for the asset.

Define required protective controls for each category

Each classification category must include the specific requirements for the protection of the asset. This group of protective measures is chosen to be appropriately cost justified for the assets it is intended to protect. You shouldn't choose controls that cost $1 million to protect assets whose collective value is $100,000. The protective controls must also provide an appropriate level of access for authorized users. Some types of assets have specific protective requirements defined by laws and regulations. The types of protective controls described might include:

- **Labeling requirements and technologies**   The labels identify the value of the asset to the users and custodians who must access the content. Through training, users understand the protective requirements for handling the content.

  Media and systems must be clearly labeled with the classification of the asset with the highest value that the media or system holds. Labels must be applied within the documents as well, so that when the file is opened within an application, its classification is clearly identified to the authorized user. Through training, users understand the protective requirements for handling the content. This is often accomplished with labels embedded within the header of the document, the footer, and perhaps with a watermark, as shown in Figure 1-5.

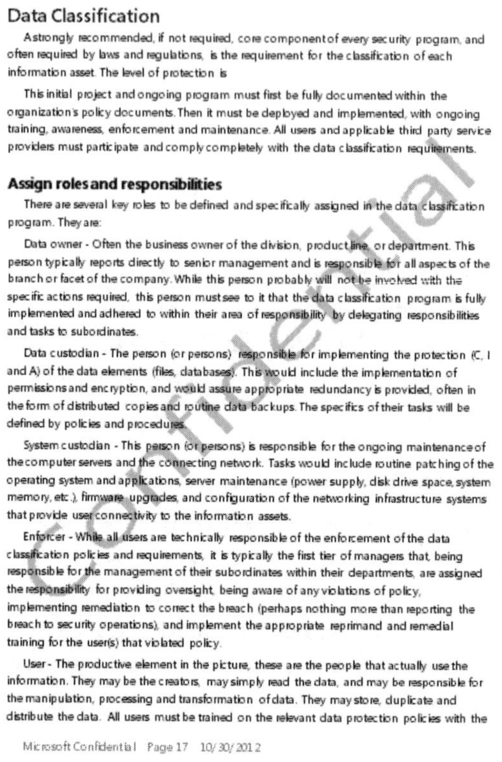

Data Classification

A strongly recommended, if not required, core component of every security program, and often required by laws and regulations, is the requirement for the classification of each information asset. The level of protection is

This initial project and ongoing program must first be fully documented within the organization's policy documents. Then it must be deployed and implemented, with ongoing training, awareness, enforcement and maintenance. All users and applicable third party service providers must participate and comply completely with the data classification requirements.

Assign roles and responsibilities

There are several key roles to be defined and specifically assigned in the data classification program. They are:

Data owner - Often the business owner of the division, product line, or department. This person typically reports directly to senior management and is responsible for all aspects of the branch or facet of the company. While this person probably will not be involved with the specific actions required, this person must see to it that the data classification program is fully implemented and adhered to within their area of responsibility by delegating responsibilities and tasks to subordinates.

Data custodian - The person (or persons) responsible for implementing the protection (C, I and A) of the data elements (files, databases). This would include the implementation of permissions and encryption, and would assure appropriate redundancy is provided, often in the form of distributed copies and routine data backups. The specifics of their tasks will be defined by policies and procedures.

System custodian - This person (or persons) is responsible for the ongoing maintenance of the computer servers and the connecting network. Tasks would include routine patching of the operating system and applications, server maintenance (power supply, disk drive space, system memory, etc.), firmware upgrades, and configuration of the networking infrastructure systems that provide user connectivity to the information assets.

Enforcer - While all users are technically responsible of the enforcement of the data classification policies and requirements, it is typically the first tier of managers that, being responsible for the management of their subordinates within their departments, are assigned the responsibility for providing oversight, being aware of any violations of policy, implementing remediation to correct the breach (perhaps nothing more than reporting the breach to security operations), and implement the appropriate reprimand and remedial training for the user(s) that violated policy.

User - The productive element in the picture, these are the people that actually use the information. They may be the creators, may simply read the data, and may be responsible for the manipulation, processing and transformation of data. They may store, duplicate and distribute the data. All users must be trained on the relevant data protection policies with the

FIGURE 1-5 Data classification watermark

- **Authorized personnel**   This might describe the types or groups of users the data is intended for—those who may be authorized for access—and might describe the types or groups of users the data is specifically not intended for—those who may not be authorized for access. For example, in a biochemical company, data classified as critical might only be provided to senior management and to the research and development department, where most of these types of information assets are created.

- **Distribution restrictions**   These are an extension of the authorized personnel controls and might declare that a certain type of information may not be sent to clients or vendors or is exclusively intended for the recipient's eyes only, not to be shared with an associate or secretary.

- **Access controls**   These are the physical controls, the technical controls, and the administrative controls that are mandated for each data classification category.

- **Encryption requirements**   To support the access controls, a description of the encryption requirements might be included for data at rest and when it is in transit over some network media.

- **Handling procedures and technologies**   These controls describe how content on removable media and printed copies must be handled, based on its classification. Examples might include the requirement for armored transport with armed guards for the most sensitive data and rules pertaining to encryption requirements for USB thumb drives and optical disks.

- **Retention period requirements**   Typically, companies want to retain their data for as long as the data holds some value to the company. If the company is subject to laws or regulatory compliance requirements, they might impose a required retention period for auditing and detective purposes. Recognize that holding data assets for longer than this period introduces additional costs to the company. In addition, to reduce potential liabilities, it is common for corporate lawyers to want the data to be destroyed securely as soon as the required retention period has been satisfied.

- **Secure disposal requirements**   All information assets should be securely destroyed when the retention period has expired. Secure destruction of digital data on hard disk drives requires overwriting the data with random bits, saving the now garbage data, and then deleting the data file. Secure destruction of printed content, optical disks, and even hard disk drives typically requires physical destruction of the objects. Magnetic media can be degaussed or overwritten to remove the data stored as magnetic impulses.

> **MORE INFO**   **WHERE TO FIND IT**
>
> The protective controls mentioned in the preceding section are described in more detail in various places throughout the book. Labeling, handling procedures, retention periods, and secure disposal are described in Chapter 10. Authorization, distribution restrictions, and access controls are covered in Chapter 2, "Access controls." Encryption is covered in Chapter 3.

Inventory the information assets (data elements)

Every information asset must be identified. This would include every file, database, and printed document. Even email messages must be classified. (This is typically accomplished by the end user after the data classification program has been introduced and training has been performed.) As you can imagine, this inventory list will become quite large.

Assign a value to each asset

The assignment of value for each data element is typically based on the losses to the organization that would occur if a breach of the confidentiality, integrity, or availability were to occur. This is subjective to some extent, but the policies should describe criteria to be used for the assignment of value. The assigned value aligns with a specific data classification category, which links the asset to the required and appropriate protective controls. It is also common to identify who is affected by the losses if a breach occurs.

Reappraise and adjust the classification of information assets

The value of data changes over time. A list of currently viable credit card numbers and account information has value today and perhaps for a few years to come, but in 5 or 10 years, this information has little or no value, and in 50 or 100 years, it will have no value at all. The secret details of a new product to be announced on Monday morning next week has potentially great value in its marketplace at this moment, but immediately after the announcement, the data is now public and holds no significant value. In the first example, the value of the data changed over time, whereas in the second example, the change in value occurs as a step function, happening instantaneously. The value of data can similarly increase over time as well.

Protecting data more strongly or longer than its value warrants costs and wastes money, which does not support the premise of maximizing the corporate profits. Protecting data more weakly than its value warrants, or not protecting it at all, exposes the company to undesirable risk and, likely, avoidable losses.

The classification of a data element, which dictates its value and its protection level, must first be appraised, reappraised on a regular basis, and adjusted as appropriate to provide the optimal level of protection for its current level of sensitivity and value. This periodic reappraisal and adjustment of the information asset's classification, including declassification, must be defined within the policies.

Provide security awareness training for all employees and applicable third parties

Every user must be educated in the data classification structure, labeling, and protection requirements. He must understand that full compliance is mandatory, that violations lead to breaches of security and introduce losses to the company, that violations are identified through ongoing and persistent monitoring, and that remedial actions follow when violations are detected.

Any third-party service providers that might gain access to the information assets of the organization must also be managed similarly. This typically must be a negotiated point at the onset of the relationship with the external entity and must be formalized in the contract with the external entity, complete with auditing and penalties identified, but must be managed by the hiring organization. Training the employee's third-party service provider might also be a requirement, with specific monitoring and enforcement responsibilities assigned by contract.

This training is typically performed for all employees during the initial deployment of the program and then again for every employee at least annually. All new hires must receive this security awareness training before they are authorized to access any sensitive content.

Assign enforcement responsibilities

All employees are expected to comply with the data classification and protection policies and to provide oversight wherever they may have the opportunity, but the managers of the first tier are the ones responsible for each end user who typically has the greatest access opportunities. It is this first tier of manager that typically is assigned the heaviest level of enforcement responsibility; they are held accountable for each subordinate employee. These managers must monitor their workers' activities and practices, identify any violations of policy, report the violations, and implement remediation procedures warranted by the violation, also defined within the data classification policies.

Managers become managers because of their recognition and acceptance of a higher level of responsibility. Although all workers always are expected to abide by all policies, managers are expected to be aware of, abide by, and enforce policies much more strictly than the typical worker. Managers of all levels are obligated to a higher level of performance relative to monitoring, detection of deviations, and enforcement (response) to any violation within their department or group of subordinates. Higher-tier managers become responsible for the enforcement of these policies for their subordinate, lower-tier managers, establishing a comprehensive chain of responsibility and enforcement.

With these pieces in place, it is time to implement the data classification program for the organization.

Implementing hiring practices

The employees of a company are the backbone of the company. They will be involved in every aspect of the activities of the organization. They must access the most valuable information assets. They must configure and monitor the security systems that protect those assets. They are expected to operate within the limits defined by policy, and they are expected to help enforce those policies.

This entire structure relies on a fundamental trust that management bestows on the employees. It becomes obvious that an organization must somehow develop this sense of trust in its employees. The development of trust of the employee begins with the hiring practices.

> *NOTE* **WORK WITH THE LEGAL DEPARTMENT**
>
> Before establishing and implementing any specific hiring and termination practices, be sure to have your local legal department review the proposed practices and, perhaps, the human resources department to avoid any possible violations of employee protection and labor laws and any other labor-related contracts that might be in place.

According to the American DataBank, results from a study that ran from 2008 to 2010 shows:

- In 72 percent of all negligent hiring lawsuits, the employers lose.
- Employee theft is blamed for as much as 30 percent of all business failures.
- As much as $20 billion annually is lost to fraud committed by employees in US. companies.
- As much as $120 billion is lost to workplace theft annually.
- 2 million criminal acts are reported in the workplace annually.

Before the company issues a job offer, it must develop an understanding of who the job candidate actually is. It must perform background checks on the prospective employee and is essentially negligent if it does not perform comprehensive checks on these candidates.

In many cases, this process begins with the candidate claiming knowledge and skills in the form of a résumé or certificate vitae (CV), also called a curriculum vitae.

According to the same study performed by the American DataBank, results from that study show:

- Approximately 6 percent of job applicants neglected to mention their criminal backgrounds.
- Approximately 55 percent of job applicants provided false information.
- Approximately 37.5 percent of job applicants have negative elements on their credit report history.
- Approximately 7.5 percent of job applicants receive negative reports from personal references the applicant provided.

Other studies show that from 1.8 percent to as many as 22 percent of candidates test positive for drug use during pre-employment drug screening. According to EBI Inc., a drug screening company, "drug-using employees are two times more likely to request early dismissal or time off, three times more likely to have absences of eight days or more, three times more likely to be late for work, four times more likely to be involved in a workplace accident, and five times more likely to file a workers' compensation claim."

It is imperative for all résumés to be verified and proper background checks to be completed for all prospective employees. Also, consider performing verification and background checks for all prospective contractors, vendors, and third-party service providers. These background checks should include:

- Education
- Job history
- Personal references
- Criminal background
- Drug screening
- Credit history

In addition, some companies are now reviewing information from social networks to qualify the background and character of prospective hires further.

If the background checks show that you can trust the individual at an acceptable level, and a desire or need to hire the individual exists, several other issues should be considered and possibly accomplished before actually extending a job offer. The prospective employee should be advised of the acceptable use policy, the monitoring policy, and any additional limiting documents such as confidentiality agreements, nondisclosure agreements, and noncompete agreements the organization requires. Making the candidate aware of these requirements and agreeing to them (by signature and date) before extending the job offer can strengthen the company's liability position in case of a future dispute or incident with the employee.

Implementing termination practices

When an employee quits or is terminated, a predefined procedure should be followed. You should consider that the outgoing employee might not have your best interest at heart and might even become violent. Involuntary termination presents the more critical concern and, therefore, the more defined and controlled process. Safety is your first priority, your own and that of the other workers at the facility.

The termination process should begin by following policy on the issue. This would include a procedure involving the manager of the employee, the human resources (HR) department, network operations, and possibly the legal department and the business owner where the employee works. This should be a coordinated effort to remove the worker from the workplace safely, securely, smoothly, and effectively.

At the planned time for the termination to occur, the worker should be invited into a meeting room. This meeting is the *exit interview*. Consider having a security guard and one or more witnesses present at the exit interview. An exit interview should be conducted for every outgoing worker.

At this time, all access should be shut off for the worker. The user's network user account should be disabled as well as all remote access and all physical access for the worker. In addition, any place the worker might represent the organization should be formally and traceably notified to disallow any further representation and authority to purchase, sell, order, or otherwise change any current ongoing activities. Change the recipient for any subscriptions, such as TechNet or other resource access the organization might have issued the worker. Monitor these accounts and access points for attempted unauthorized access.

In the exit interview, a summary of why the termination is occurring should be presented. If the termination is planned, this is easy. If the termination is involuntary and for some violation or breach, the specific incidents should be presented along with a quick review of the policies that were violated and the worker's awareness of and agreement to comply with the policies. Point out the statement in the policies that declare that violation presents sufficient grounds for termination. Review any prior remediation steps the company took in its attempt to resolve the issue with the worker. Advise the worker that all company-issued privileges, access, responsibility, and authority are hereby immediately revoked. Attempt to get the worker to sign a prepared statement declaring why she is being terminated. This might help during any litigation that might arise later in this regard.

Review any and every persistent agreement the worker might have signed. This would include confidentiality agreements, nondisclosure agreements, and noncompete agreements. Review the terms and the penalty clauses in these agreements.

Review a list of all the company-owned physical assets that are or might be in the possession of the worker. The goal is to have all company-owned assets returned. These assets would include:

- Identity or access badge
- Cell phone
- Laptop computer(s)
- Authentication tokens
- Smart cards, memory cards
- Keys
- Printed content
- Optical media
- USB flash drives
- Vehicle
- Tools
- Devices
- Samples
- Protective wear
- Other physical assets the company owns

It might be beneficial to offer something to the outgoing employee to get cooperation with the exit process and the return of the assets. Consider extending the medical coverage or increasing any severance package, providing vacation pay, or providing outgoing job placement assistance to obtain her full cooperation.

The worker should not be allowed to return to her desk or workplace. Someone should be clearing the worker's personal possessions from her workplace while the exit interview is underway. Toward the end of the exit interview, present the worker's personal possessions to her. Advise the worker that if she finds anything missing later on to let her former manager know, and the manager will search the terminated employee's workplace for the missing item or items.

The worker should be escorted off the property of the organization and should not be allowed to linger on the premises or speak with other workers at this time. While the exit interview is under way, or shortly thereafter, have management speak with the outgoing employee's coworkers to inform them of the termination. Consider any specific issues and instructions that should be addressed with the individual coworkers, especially those who worked more closely with the terminated employee or could provide the terminated employee access if he were unaware of the termination.

Providing security awareness training

If all goes well and the decision is made to hire the candidate, security awareness training should be provided before the new hire is authorized to perform any activities for the organization. Consider the need for supplemental training if the new hire has heightened privilege that increases the exposure of the organization, such as access to valuable assets, if the new hire will be issued a laptop computer, or he will be telecommuting to access corporate assets by the Internet. This training should be performed for every new hire, repeated at least annually, and adjusted and performed as the employee's access and privileges change. Remedial training should be performed for any employee who violates policy (assuming the violation doesn't trigger a termination).

This security awareness training should include a review of all the policy documents relevant to the worker's position and activities. The major components of the training include:

- The expectation of awareness and compliance with all policies of the organization
- The expectation of consistent enforcement of the policies
- Workplace behavior expectations, including tardiness, dress code, drug use, weapons, objectionable materials, and so on
- HR policies and procedures
- Acceptable use policy
- Password policy, including strong passwords
- Data classification and protection
- Monitoring policy—no expectation of privacy
- Technologies, concepts, and procedures required for compliance
- Supplemental training for users with heightened privileges
- Laptop security as applicable
- Remote-access security as applicable
- Incident response—what to do if some breach or incident occurs
- Additional agreements such as nondisclosure and noncompete as applicable
- Awareness that violation of any policy constitutes grounds for termination

You can include other topics as appropriate.

The primary security awareness training issues should be presented regularly to maintain continued and persistent awareness of security requirements and expectations to the users. These reminders can take the form of banners posted in common areas, logo banners, articles in periodic reports or newsletters, and, most important, through management's enforcement of policy in case of a violation of policy or a breach of security.

 EXAM TIP

Know the major components of the security awareness training program.

Managing third-party service providers

In many situations, a third party is responsible for providing services to the organization, especially as IT continues to move toward outsourcing services such as services provided in the *cloud* that include:

- **Infrastructure as a Service (IaaS)**   Cloud-based (usually) virtual machines, servers, firewalls, load balancers, storage
- **Platform as a Service (PaaS)**   Virtual servers (server operating system) with back-end application servers, software development execution environments, email servers, database systems, web servers
- **Software as a Service (SaaS)**   Virtual desktops (client operating system), applications made available to end users without ever installing any software on end-user systems other than perhaps a thin client application such as a browser
- **Security as a Service (SECaaS)**   Authentication, antivirus, intrusion detection, security information, and event management

Third-party service providers would include all cloud-related providers, all contractors and consultants, maintenance agreement service providers, payment card processors (payment card industry [PCI]–related), and other outsourced service providers. These relationships often mean that the third party not only has access to the valuable information assets, but it will often be in sole possession of those valuable information assets. From a management perspective, you are transferring some risk to the third party, but you are also accepting some risk the third party introduces. There must be a strong sense of trust between the organization and the service provider. That trust should be backed by contractual agreement and the imposition of your policies on the third party with the expectation of full compliance.

> **MORE INFO   PAYMENT CARD INDUSTRY DATA SECURITY STANDARD (PCI DSS)**
>
> PCI security requirements are covered in more detail later in this chapter and in Chapter 5.

Before turning the valuable information assets of the organization over to the third party, due diligence must be performed. Anything less would be negligence. This would include a risk assessment and verification of the third party's prudent and compliant management of those risks. The third party might very well need to be compliant with every law and regulation the organization is subject to when the assets being serviced or managed are within the scope of compliance. Moreover, the organization cannot simply ask a question and be satisfied with a simple answer. The formation of the relationship will likely require an initial, formal, and comprehensive external audit to ensure compliance and ongoing audits to verify continued compliance.

Consider whether you must impose your policies and security awareness training on the third party company to remain within compliance. To avoid negligence and increase likelihood of breach and litigation, these third-party entities typically must be trained, managed, and monitored, audited, and enforced at the same level and standard as the employees of the organization itself.

EXAM TIP

The governance of third-party service providers is a new component on the ISC2 CISSP exam objectives. You can expect to see a few questions on this topic. It will be discussed several more times within this book when it becomes relevant.

A darker side of cloud services that must be defended against is the energetic and technically progressive *Fraud as a Service (FaaS)*. Cyber criminals develop skills and tools and aggregate sensitive information on individuals and companies. These are the service providers in this case, but the services they offer are illegal and malicious in nature. The FaaS providers market their techniques, tools, and data to other cyber criminals. These FaaS providers typically operate their nefarious cloud services on underground, hidden, isolated, and guarded branches of the Internet called the *deep web*.

Armed with the desired techniques, tools, and sensitive data, the consumers of FaaS commit the actual theft from the victim, such as hacking into the corporate database to steal and resell trade secrets, stealing the credit card numbers and personally identifiable information of customers of a bank for extortion purposes, or electronically transferring all financial assets of the victim(s) to offshore accounts.

Monitoring and auditing

Monitoring the environment generally implies that there are recordings of events, and those recordings are likely being reviewed in near real time, (either real time or at least through daily reviews), and the recordings are typically stored for later review as might be required. Therefore, monitoring is typically a continuous evaluation of the environment of interest. Security cameras might be mounted inside and outside the facility and monitored in real time by security guards at a monitoring station. These videos can also be recorded on tape or on disk for later review. Event logs from network infrastructure systems, servers, and perhaps

even client workstations might be fed into a *security information and event management (SIEM)* system for real-time correlation and analysis. These same logs can also be aggregated and protected in a log repository for later review and a more detailed analysis. Legal and regulatory requirements often include specifications regarding the monitoring and archiving of information-system and security-related information like this.

Auditing is more of a periodic spot check, evaluating the status at a specific point in time. For example, auditing might occur on a quarterly basis to compare the current configuration of the VPN concentrator to the documented and authorized configuration standard to identify any deviations. Permissions assigned to user accounts might periodically be audited to identify and manage authorization creep when a user has aggregated more privilege over time than he currently requires. Legal and regulatory requirements often include specifications regarding the periodic spot-checking (auditing) of more specific information-system and security-related information like this. It is often the role of the auditor to perform this specialized review and analysis.

Unless management is paying attention to the activities of the employees, it cannot identify violations of policy and, therefore, cannot enforce policy. Not enforcing policy is negligent behavior that leads to unnecessary losses and likely to an increase in negligence-related lawsuits. In addition, if a worker commits a crime by using company resources, or while representing the company, or while on the company's property, very often litigation targets the company, implying that the criminal act was somehow the company's fault. The company often becomes the target of the civil lawsuit because the perpetrator of the crime usually does not have anywhere near the amount of money the company does, so settlements and judgments are likely be larger. Further, some area of perceived or apparent negligence on the company's part is often presented, whether the negligence is real or not. Very often, the company, not the individual(s) who committed the crime, becomes the responsible and liable party.

Monitoring and auditing can use a combination of automated systems and humans for detection of incidents, but the systems typically require human intervention as the response. Network monitoring includes capturing and reviewing the event logs of all systems of interest (routers, switches, firewalls, network access systems, authentication servers, resource servers, workstations, and so on), specific and targeted auditing of privileged users, alerts generated by intrusion detection and intrusion prevention systems (IDS and IPS), and alerts generated by other security systems. Monitoring the physical environment is required as well.

If the enterprise is subject to legal or regulatory compliance, a specific level of monitoring is likely to be mandated by the laws or regulations for systems and the physical environment within the scope of the laws and regulations. For example, in the *Payment Card Industry Data Security Standard (PCI DSS)*, an entire section of compliance is related to tracking (recording) and monitoring (at least in near real time) all access to network resources and cardholder (protected) data, and it includes requirements to:

- Be able to identify each network user uniquely and link the unique user account to network access activities, especially those activities performed using heightened privilege.
- Automatically record events in a manner that allows correlation to track a user's activities across multiple systems, including:
    - Access to cardholder data
    - Use of the highly privileged root (Linux) or administrator (Windows) accounts
    - Reading or modifying log files
    - Altering the logging processes
    - Failed logon attempts
    - Authentication attempts
    - Altering system-level objects

- All systems within the scope of compliance must record each event that occurs, and the records of what is being logged must include at least:
  - User identification
  - Type of event
  - Date and time
  - Success or failure indication
  - Origination of event
  - Identity or name of the affected data
  - System component or resource being accessed
- All systems within the scope of compliance must have their time clocks synchronized to support correlation, and that time configuration and information must be protected from alteration.
- The recorded logged data must be protected from deletion, destruction, and alteration.
- A security review must be performed on the logged data at least daily.
- Logged data must be retained for at least 1 year, with at least 3 months of data being immediately available.

Real-time monitoring is the most effective approach to knowing what is happening to the valuable assets. Typically, the sooner a breach can be identified and responded to, the lower the losses. Lower losses means maximized profits. With regard to information systems, if you only check the logs on a daily basis, the attacker could be helping himself to your assets for as much as 24 hours before you are even aware of the breach. Real-time monitoring can be quite expensive and typically requires a dedicated staff and some expensive hardware and software.

Newer SIEM systems are designed and configured to collect events from all systems of concern, usually those within the scope of compliance and others that might hold, transmit, or process critical information. The SIEM system then parses (reads) the events from the many source systems and correlates the types of events to identify potential malicious activity. Most SIEM systems use signature-based detection as well as behavior-based detection and often include analytical components considered to be artificial intelligence. Most SIEM can alert on defined rules. These rules would be produced to match the company's policies. When receiving 50 or 100 events per minute from 50, or 100, or 500 systems, no human could keep up, so when real-time monitoring is required, SIEM systems are often required.

Monitoring the physical environment is accomplished using different techniques. Cameras, displays, guards, and guard dogs are some of the tools you will consider for monitoring the physical environment. Motion detectors, fire detectors, contact switches on doors and windows, and electronic physical access systems (such as transponder authentication cards at locked doorways) that provide an audit trail can also be employed to help monitor the workplace. In some situations, radio frequency identification devices (RFID) and sensors at exits can be used. RFID chips are small and inexpensive and are often embedded within products for inventory control, pricing, and theft detection.

The metrics from these monitoring and auditing systems and processes should be recorded and analyzed over time to identify the effectiveness of the current security program and to show trends with regard to the security posture of the organization. A report of these metrics should be provided to senior management on a regular basis to keep management apprised of the security status of the enterprise and the changes in that status over time. Once again, if the organization is subject to legal or regulatory compliance, these recorded metrics and analysis are mandated.

 Quick check

1. What role within the security program performs periodic assessments of specific assets and users?
2. What are three of the things to look into before offering a job to a prospective employee?

Quick check answers

1. The auditor role
2. Verify the details of the résumé, including education and job history. Interview personal references. Perform drug screening, a criminal background check, and a credit history report (only within compliance of legal boundaries).

Exercises

In the following exercises, you apply what you've learned in this chapter. The answers for these exercises are located in the "Answers" section at the end of this chapter.

Exercise 1-1

Limiting the scope to a single laptop computer that you own, perform a risk assessment. Identify each asset but perform the assessment only on the computer hardware itself. Perform the ALE calculation for the threat of hard disk failure only. Assume the disk drive has a mean-time-between-failure rating of three years.

Exercise 1-2

Based on the results from the risk assessment performed in Exercise 1-1, list each policy document and a brief description of its contents that would help manage risks to the computer.

Chapter summary

- The prudent management of an enterprise is the responsibility of senior management. Human safety is always the highest priority. Ethical standards must be included within the framework of governance. Management must be the consistent enforcer of policy.

- The security program must support the (typically revenue-generating) needs of the business. Maximize profits and avoid losses by cost justifying all countermeasures. Protect the confidentiality, integrity, and availability of the valuable assets of the organization.

- Vulnerabilities and matching threats produce risk. Risk is quantified by its likelihood and its impact on the asset. Mitigate risk, transfer risk, and avoid risk until the level of residual risk is acceptable (risk acceptance).

- Access controls are physical, technical (logical), or administrative.

- Risk assessment is the development of knowledge and awareness of the potential losses that could affect the assets of the organization. Risk management includes the risk assessment but continues by implementing protective and mitigating controls in a sensible and cost-justified manner.

- Implement security awareness training for all employees at least annually. Implement supplemental security awareness training for highly privileged employees.

- Maintain ongoing metrics to evaluate the effectiveness of the current security controls, to identify the current state of security, and to identify trends in security.

Chapter review

Test your knowledge of the information in this chapter by answering these questions. The answers to these questions, and the explanations of why each answer choice is correct or incorrect, are located in the "Answers" section at the end of this chapter.

1. Which of the following accurately describes the risk management techniques?

    A. Risk acceptance, risk transference, risk avoidance, risk mitigation

    B. Risk acceptance, risk containment, risk avoidance, risk migration

    C. Risk acceptance, risk mitigation, risk containment, risk quantification

    D. Risk avoidance, risk migration, risk containment, risk quantification

2. Which of the following identifies a model that specifically targets security and not governance of an entire enterprise? (Choose all that apply.)

    A. The Zachman framework

    B. COBIT

    C. COSO

    D. SABSA

3. Which of the following terms enables management to be less than perfect and still avoid being negligent in lawsuits?

   A. Due care

   B. Prudency

   C. Due diligence

   D. Threat agent

4. Which of the following describes interviewing people anonymously?

   A. ISO/IEC 27001

   B. Qualitative valuation

   C. The Delphi method

   D. Quantitative valuation

5. Which of the following describes the appropriate standard for the governance of third-party providers?

   A. A nondisclosure agreement (NDA)

   B. An acceptable use policy

   C. The same level as employees

   D. The same level as defined by the ISC2 Code of Ethics

6. Which of the following terms identifies the anticipated cost of a loss event?

   A. Annualized loss expectancy (ALE)

   B. Exposure factor (EF)

   C. Asset value (AV)

   D. Single loss expectancy (SLE)

7. Why does an enterprise need to reevaluate the classification of data files and records on at least an annual basis?

   A. To comply with the requirements of the Internet Architecture Board

   B. Because the value of data changes over time

   C. Because new threats must be mitigated

   D. To protect the confidentiality of the data

8. Which of the following should be management's top priority when establishing the framework of governance?

   A. Maximizing profits

   B. Avoiding losses

   C. Supporting the business needs

   D. Safety

Answers

This section contains the answers to the exercises and the "Chapter review" section in this chapter.

Exercise 1-1

The asset inventory would include the computer as a tangible asset, and the data stored on the computer would be intangible assets. You would identify specific files and perhaps specific applications that have value. To simplify this, you might identify the directories and consider that the directory holding the files is the asset.

Assign a value to each asset, considering the many aspects of the asset's value. Considering only the computer hardware:

- **Quantitative value**   Hardware cost: $1,500; cost (time and software) to recover software, reconfigure settings, recover and re-create data: $4,000

- **Qualitative value** $10,000: employer's lost trust resulting lost promotion at $10,000 additional compensation per year

    Total value: $15,500

Order the assets based on their respective values. Identify threats to each asset. For the computer hardware, the threats include:

- **Natural**   Rain damage, nearby lightning strike
- **Human-made**   Theft, sabotage, hacker attack, owner drops computer, owner loses computer
- **Technical**   Hard disk failure, display failure, virus infection
- **Supply system**   Poor electrical supply, poor cooling

The following table identifies the likelihood and impact of each threat.

	Likelihood	Impact
Natural		
Rain damage	1%	5%
Nearby lightning strike	3%	75%
Man made		
Theft	10%	100%
Sabotage	1%	100%
Hacker attack	3%	35%
Owner drops computer	10%	50%

	Likelihood	Impact
Owner loses computer	10%	100%
Technical		
Hard disk failure	10%	60%
Display failure	2%	10%
Virus infection	15%	25%
Supply system		
Poor electrical supply	2%	3%
Poor cooling	1%	75%

AV x EF = SLE
$15,500 x 60% = $9,300

SLE x ARO = ALE
$9,300 x 1/3 = $3,100
ALE = $3,100

Proposed countermeasures and cost justification:

- Replace laptop every year (before the hard disk drive wears and fails)
  - **Cost**   Hardware: $1,500; software, configuration, and time: $4000
  - **Benefit**   ($3,700) Not a cost-effective plan. Do not propose.
- Reducing likelihood of failure from 10 percent to 1 percent reduces qualitative losses (to 1/10) from $10,000 to $1,000. New ALE:

  $6,500 x 60% = $3,900
  $3,900 x 1/3 = $1,300
  Current ALE – New ALE – Cost of Countermeasure = Benefit
  $3,100 – $1,300 – $5,500 = ($3,700)

- Back up the hard drive to another disk.
  - **Cost**   Hardware, software, and time: $200
  - **Benefit** $580
- Reduce time and software losses from $4,000 to $100 (Simple restore). New ALE:

  $11,600 x 60% = $6,960
  $6,960 x 1/3 = $2,320
  Current ALE – New ALE – Cost of countermeasure = Benefit
  $3,100 – $2,320 – $200 = $580

Exercise 1-2

Based on the results from the risk assessment performed in Exercise 1-1, list each policy document and a brief description of its contents that would help manage risks to the computer.

- **Data Backup Policy** Users will perform weekly, full backups and store the backups on enterprise servers.

- **Data Backup Guideline** Whenever possible, users will perform daily, full backups and store the backups on enterprise servers.

- **Data Backup Procedure** This is a step-by-step description of how to perform a full backup of the computer to enterprise servers.

- **Backup Data Protection Standard** All backups must be encrypted using AES 256.

Chapter review

1. **Correct answer:** A

   A. **Correct:** The four risk management techniques are risk mitigation, risk transference, risk avoidance, and risk acceptance.

   B. **Incorrect:** Risk containment and risk migration are not part of the four risk management techniques.

   C. **Incorrect:** Risk containment and risk quantification are not part of the four risk management techniques.

   D. **Incorrect:** Risk migration, risk containment, and risk quantification are not part of the four risk management techniques.

2. **Correct answers:** B and D

   A. **Incorrect:** The Zachman framework is an enterprise framework.

   B. **Correct:** COBIT—Control Objectives for Information-related Technologies—is a security (control) model.

   C. **Incorrect:** COSO—the Committee of Sponsoring Organizations of the Treadway Commission—is an enterprise framework.

   D. **Correct:** SABSA—the Sherwood Applied Business Security Architecture—is a security model.

3. **Correct answer:** B

   A. **Incorrect:** Due care is acting on the knowledge and awareness of the risks associated with the enterprise such as the implementation of countermeasures.

   B. **Correct:** Management must implement controls prudently to avoid being negligent. The controls do not need to be perfect but implemented as others (or a prudent person) would under those same circumstances.

   C. **Incorrect:** Due diligence is the development of knowledge and awareness of the risks associated with the enterprise and continues with the ongoing and prudent maintenance, monitoring, response, enforcement, training, and evaluation of the controls currently in place.

   D. **Incorrect:** The threat agent is the active component of an attack and is not directly related to the level of negligence of the enterprise.

4. **Correct answer:** C

   A. **Incorrect:** ISO/IEC 27001 describes the Information Security Management System (ISMS) and originates from BS7799-2.

   B. **Incorrect:** Qualitative valuation describes the value of the quality of an enterprise, essentially referring to the value of its good reputation.

   C. **Correct:** The Delphi method describes interviewing people anonymously.

   D. **Incorrect:** Quantitative valuation describes identifying numeric, direct values related to assets.

5. **Correct answer:** C

   A. **Incorrect:** A nondisclosure agreement (NDA) is a component of the appropriate governance of third-party service providers but only one of many required components.

   B. **Incorrect:** An acceptable use policy is a component of the appropriate governance of third-party service providers but only one of many required components.

   C. **Correct:** The appropriate standard for the governance of third-party providers is the same level as for employees, which includes all the policies, training, monitoring, and so on as would be performed internally.

   D. **Incorrect:** The ISC2 Code of Ethics is a component of the appropriate governance of third-party service providers but only one of many required components.

6. **Correct answer:** D

   A. Incorrect: The annualized loss expectancy (ALE) is the amount lost to the event but is also amortized (annualized) based on the expected frequency of the loss events.

   B. Incorrect: The exposure factor (EF) is the percentage of the asset that is expected to be lost, not the cost of the loss event. It must be multiplied by the asset value (AV) to identify the actual financial loss.

   C. Incorrect: The asset value (AV) must be multiplied by the exposure factor (EF) to identify the actual financial loss.

   D. Correct: The single-loss expectancy (SLE) identifies the anticipated cost of a loss event.

7. **Correct answer:** B

   A. Incorrect: The Internet Architecture Board describes unethical behavior when using the Internet.

   B. Correct: Because the value of data changes over time, it must be reappraised annually so that it is classified correctly and therefore protected appropriately.

   C. Incorrect: The value (sensitivity level) of the data drives the data classification. Threats to the data drive the potential countermeasures that protect the data.

   D. Incorrect: Confidentiality of the data is one of the three security goals, and although it is a component, the value (sensitivity level) of the data drives the data classification.

8. **Correct answer:** D

   A. Incorrect: Maximizing profits is one of the goals, but safety is always the primary goal.

   B. Incorrect: Avoiding losses is one of the goals, but safety is always the primary goal.

   C. Incorrect: Supporting the business needs is one of the goals, but safety is always the primary goal.

   D. Correct: Safety is always the primary goal when establishing the framework of governance.

CHAPTER 2

Access control

This chapter builds on the risk assessment discussion that was covered in Chapter 1, "Information security governance and risk management," and addresses the access control countermeasures that can be implemented to protect the safety of personnel and the confidentiality, integrity, and availability (CIA) of the valuable information assets of the enterprise. By implementing layers of cost-justified controls that target the vulnerabilities of the assets and the likelihood and impact of a successful exploit, the enterprise can mitigate and avoid losses and become better able to maximize profits.

Access control involves the implementation of security at some appropriate level as defined by senior management through policy and balanced with the need for access to accomplish the revenue-generating work of the business.

Exam objectives in this chapter:

1.1 Control access by applying the following concepts/methodologies/techniques

    1.1.1 Policies

    1.1.2 Types of controls (preventive, detective, corrective, etc.)

    1.1.3 Techniques (e.g., non-discretionary, discretionary and mandatory)

    1.1.4 Identification and Authentication

    1.1.5 Decentralized/distributed access control techniques

    1.1.6 Authorization mechanisms

    1.1.7 Logging and monitoring

1.2 Understand access control attacks

    1.2.1 Threat modeling

    1.2.2 Asset valuation

    1.2.3 Vulnerability analysis

    1.2.4 Access aggregation

Trusted path

Enterprises operate with a fundamental *expectation of trust* for their workers. They expect that after a worker is trained regarding the policies of the company, that worker tends to abide by the rules stated within the policies. The following statement is the basis for the interaction between the (relatively) trusted workers and the information systems:

- **Subjects access objects.**

    - The *subject* is the active entity that wants to interact with the information system. The subject is classically a user, a person, a worker, but can also loosely be considered a process.

    - The *object* is the repository of information, such as a file, a written document, or a record in a database.

    - The *access* implies a flow of information between the subject and the object. That flow has a direction. If the subject (the active entity) is reading information, the flow is from object to subject. If the subject is writing information, the flow is from subject to object.

NOTE **THE SUBJECT AS A PROCESS**

Most information systems provide access by first authenticating the user to establish some level of trust for the identity of the user. Permissions are granted on individual information assets (data elements) and other information system resources. When a user launches a word processor application, that user's identity, usually in the form of an access token, is bound to each process (programmatic tasks) spawned by the application. When the user attempts to open a file in the word processor, the file-open process, which carries the user's access token, is challenged by the file systems security mechanism, called the security reference monitor. The process feeds the user's access token to the security reference monitor, which compares the user's identity described in the access token to the access control list (ACL) on the file to identify what, if any, permissions have been granted to that user. Therefore, even though a process is performing the access function on the computer, it is actually a process acting as a delegate on behalf of a user. Even server services operate in this manner, by way of a service account—a user account that is granted privilege on resources and is automatically authenticated at the time of the service start-up.

To protect the information during this access function, the concept of the *trusted path* is required. Although the users are (relatively) trusted and can be trained in the rules governing the secure interaction with the valuable information assets, and the servers that hold, process, and transfer these information assets can be professionally secured, if the path between the subject and the object is not secure and cannot be trusted, the information system that provides the access simply cannot protect the information assets from compromise. The information systems must also provide a well-managed, secured, and trusted path between the subject and the objects that will be accessed.

To take this statement for the interaction between the trusted workers and the information systems to a more accurate, realistic, and contemporary level of complexity, it becomes:

- **Subjects use computers and applications to access objects.**

This statement is the basis for this chapter on access control, Chapter 5, "Security architecture and design" (computer security), and Chapter 9, "Software development security" (application security). Collectively, these chapters describe how to establish a trusted path.

Choices, choices, choices

In Chapter 1, senior management developed several high-level policies to establish a framework to manage or govern the enterprise in a prudent manner. Senior management initiated a risk management program to bring into focus the areas of greatest risk and to address and manage those risks by using cost-justified countermeasures. This chapter describes in more detail the various types of countermeasures (access controls) the security professional could choose from to implement that carefully administered security program.

> **NOTE COUNTERMEASURES VERSUS ACCESS CONTROLS**
>
> Access controls are a subset of countermeasures. All access controls will be countermeasures, but not all countermeasures are access controls. Countermeasures include the purchase of insurance and avoiding risky activities and processes, to name a few examples that are not access controls, but also include all types of access controls.

The risk management program began with a risk assessment and includes:

- An inventory of assets.
- Identification of the value (sensitivity) of those assets to the enterprise.
- A vulnerability and threat analysis for each of the assets (typically beginning with the most valuable assets).
- Analysis of the likelihood and impact of each threat on each asset.

- Calculation of the expected annual losses for each asset.

- Identification of a collection or list of applicable countermeasures that will save the enterprise more (by avoiding losses) than the countermeasure would cost.

- Approval of specific countermeasures by senior management that reduces the risks to a level senior management finds acceptable.

- Implementation and maintenance of those approved countermeasures.

This chapter takes a closer look at the many types of countermeasures that control access to the valuable assets of the enterprise and help mitigate and avoid losses to those assets. Further, this chapter shows how to implement multiple types of controls in combination to establish a more complete and cohesive defense against unauthorized access to those assets.

Remember that risk is created when a vulnerability (internal and more manageable) is met with a threat (external and less manageable) and that controls should mitigate or eliminate vulnerabilities, likelihood, and impact of a threat. The controls chosen are usually driven by the threat component and must always be cost justified.

Types of access controls

All access controls fall into these three major categories (a review from Chapter 1):

- **Administrative controls**   These controls are the policies, the rules, and the laws that users must abide by. For these controls to be enforceable, they must first be formalized, typically in writing; the users in the environment must be educated about the existence of these controls with an expectation of compliance; and there must be some form of monitoring and enforcement to detect and apply the penalties to be paid in the case of violation of the administrative controls.

- **Physical controls**   Generally speaking, if you can drop a control on your foot or bump your head on it, it must be a physical control. These are the walls, fences, and locks that establish security boundaries around our facilities. These are the signs that warn of electric shock, or the dog that bites if you enter the wrong places. These are the server clusters that provide improved availability and the security appliances and the sensor devices that protect and monitor the corporate network.

- **Technical controls**   Technical controls are also called *logical controls*. These controls are usually implemented in software, such as permissions on a file system, the encryption of digital content, asymmetric key pairs used with digital certificates, the rule base in a firewall, and the signature databases used in antivirus software and intrusion-detection systems.

The countermeasures and access controls will be chosen from these three primary types of controls and should perform a specific security function in the overall protection of the assets of the enterprise. Countermeasures should be effective at accomplishing one or more of the following security-related functions:

- **Deterrence**   A deterrent control introduces a psychological effect on the would-be attacker, *before the attack starts*, in the hope of convincing the attacker to change his mind and not attack. If you can deter the attacker successfully, you will avoid losses. Deterrents typically require the attacker's awareness of some potential harm to her if she proceeds with the attack and, therefore, are typically effective only against sentient beings, not technical threats, supply-system threats, and Mother Nature. Deterrent controls include signs that warn of guards; dogs that will capture and hurt the attacker; a strong and secure appearance indicating a mature, capable, and well-managed security structure; an employee's knowledge of the monitoring and auditing functions performed by the security staff; and the attacker's awareness of the bad things that could happen to him if he attacks.

- **Prevention**   A preventive control effectively stops, or tries to stop, an attack. Preventive controls are effective *during an attack*. If the preventive control is successful in preventing the attack, the attacker did attack, so any deterrent controls obviously have failed, but the attacker did not accomplish what he had hoped. A visible preventive control will also have a deterrent effect. Preventive controls include tall fences, strong locks on solid doors, encryption used on sensitive data, and effective security awareness training of all employees so they understand the policies of the organization and the punishments associated with any violations of policy.

  Even if the preventive control is effective, the enterprise might still suffer some, now minimized, losses. The security team and others had to spend time responding to the attack, reducing their revenue-generating opportunities. One or more security controls or systems might be damaged, so replacement parts and materials might need to be purchased. Productivity might be diminished until the repairs are complete, and someone will have to perform the repairs. All of these will cost the enterprise money and are losses, even though the breach was technically unsuccessful. Although these are losses, the losses are likely much less because of the effectiveness of the preventive control.

- **Delay**   If the deterrent controls don't work well enough and the attacker begins her attack, implement controls that will slow down the attack before a successful breach is achieved. Because the attacker is exposed for a longer period, this further deters the attacker, now committing the attack, and improves the ability of the security team to detect that an attack is underway. Delay controls are effective *during an attack*. Delay control types include tall and well-maintained fences with barbed wire angled toward the attacker, solid doors and locks that resist forcible entry, and the use of strong passwords and cryptography that are difficult to crack. Policies that require thorough background checks prior to hiring would also be a delay type of control.

- **Detection**   A detective control helps the security team during an attack to identify quickly that a breach or attempted breach is underway. Detective controls are effective *during and after an attack* to record and analyze the events of a breach to reveal the details of an attack such as the source and target of the attack, the vulnerability targeted, and the specific tools and methodology used to commit the attack. They can collect information to be used as evidence in case of prosecution. Detection controls monitor the technical and physical environment and include cameras, logging and auditing trails, intrusion detection sensors and systems, and rotation of duties such as using an external accountant to perform quarterly reviews of the finances of the enterprise. All levels of management are responsible for detecting breaches of administrative controls such as policies and laws.

- **Assess** The attack has started and has been detected. The next step is to assess the severity of the attack or breach. This is typically performed by a human but may also be performed by a program within a monitoring system. A guard dog doesn't necessarily know the difference between an authorized worker and an unauthorized attacker, and a fire detector (alone) can detect the presence of a fire, but without additional sensors, monitoring system and software, cannot identify the extent of the fire. The assessment of the severity of a breach is critical to the next phase of a breach, the appropriate response. If smoke is detected, without assessment, the sprinklers for the entire floor might open and cause substantial losses due to the water damage. However, if a person is alerted and can assess the severity of the fire, the person might just use a fire extinguisher to put out the small fire, greatly limiting the extent of the damage from the response. Alternatively, the human assessor might immediately call the fire department and describe a massive blaze, the need for many fire fighters and many fire trucks, and perhaps even medical assistance for injured people.

    An assessment control would be a security guard observing an unauthorized visitor to the facility and concluding that it is a sales representative from a vendor or an angry boyfriend attempting to commit physical violence. Another assessment control would be a system that monitors the fire detectors and, through a software program, can recognize when one versus multiple detectors have triggered and identify where the triggered detectors are located.

- **Respond** The response to an attack or breach is the attempt to mitigate and stop the losses and return the environment to a normal state. The response should be calibrated and based on the severity or extent of the losses being experienced (assessment). Smaller losses occurring would generally warrant a more subtle response. Greater losses occurring would generally warrant a more extreme response.

    The response to an attack or a breach will occur in two distinct phases. The initial response would be to stop the attack or breach or minimize losses, but it stops short of returning the environment to a fully normal state. Controls that work during this initial phase are called *corrective* controls and would include the security guard's first response to an intruder (sound the alarm, call additional guards), the use of a fire extinguisher to put out a fire, a cluster server failover function, and documenting and formalizing an incident response plan.

When the attack has been stopped, controls will be implemented to return the environment to a normal state. These are called *recovery* controls and would include a store of spare parts for the members of a cluster server, procedures and technology to restore a backup after a disk failure, and procedures for notifying law enforcement after an intruder has been subdued and detained.

- **Compensative**   Compensating controls are used in place of an otherwise specified control as an alternate. A law, regulation, or policy requirement might call for a specific control, but cost, conflicting technology, or business needs can preclude the use of the specified control. To satisfy the requirement without using the specified control, a compensating control must meet or exceed the intended level of security and protection. These types of controls must be tested and thoroughly documented in their performance and level of protection. They will likely come under scrutiny during audits because they are not the required control. Compensating controls include the use of iptables (a personal firewall used on Linux systems) on each server instead of an infrastructure-level firewall appliance, network isolation (air gapping) instead of the use of an encrypted-channel virtual private network (VPN), and strict physical controls that limit access to sensitive servers instead of the use of a specified multi-factor system authentication.

  Compensating controls are often implemented to maintain security even when another security control fails. These controls might operate in parallel with or in series with other controls. For example, by contracting with two Internet service providers (ISP) for the corporate Internet connectivity, the enterprise now has improved its availability through redundant and parallel Internet connections. If one ISP has an outage, the other ISP can continue to maintain Internet availability for the enterprise. In another example, most laws and regulations require a security system (firewall) to isolate the corporate network from the public Internet. By placing two firewalls in series and establishing a classic perimeter network (also known as demilitarized zone, DMZ, and screened subnet), the internal firewall acts as a compensating control to maintain the required isolation if the external firewall is compromised. The perimeter network is covered in more detail in Chapter 7, "Telecommunications and network security."

- **Directive**   Directive controls provide information, usually for the safety of personnel and visitors, and can also attempt to prevent unintended damage to systems. Directive controls would include signage that states, "Do not enter," procedures that describe the use of fire exits, directional arrows to indicate the appropriate path to some location, or a software control that governs the speed of some machinery. Notice the absence of any warning of danger or hazard. Signage or policy documents that carry any type of warning would be a deterrent, not a directive control.

EXAM TIP

Remember that these functional security objectives are embodied within access controls, and the access controls must be administrative, technical, or physical. Consider the following examples and be prepared to describe a combination of the nature of the control (administrative, technical, or physical) and the nature of the functional security objective described in the exam question:

Firewall appliance   Physical preventive

Firewall rule base   Technical preventive

Eight-foot tall fence with three strands of barbed wire   Physical preventive, physical deterrent, physical delay

Acceptable use policy   Administrative preventive

User awareness of the acceptable use policy   Administrative deterrent

Network logging and auditing   Technical detective, technical deterrent

Warning "Guard dogs on premises" signage   Physical deterrent

The provisioning life cycle

Provisioning describes administrative operations regarding the authentication, authorization, and auditing (called *triple A* or *AAA*) functions of its workers to provide appropriate access to the physical resources and to the information systems. It includes the creation, management, and removal of user accounts on access systems such as entryways and secure areas and on the information systems as well as the assignment of privileges that control the level of access of those entities on those systems. These three terms, authentication, authorization, and auditing, are covered in detail in the next section of this chapter, entitled "Authentication, authorization, and auditing."

> **NOTE**   **IS IT AUDITING AND ACCOUNTING, OR IS IT ACCOUNTABILITY?**
>
> The original use of the term "AAA" for information systems came from the use of modems and dial-up bulletin boards, largely predating the Internet as we know it. The business need was to authenticate the bulletin board's subscribers, identify and limit to the level of access the subscriber had paid for, and calculate the appropriate bill for the specific accesses of the inbound call. A bulletin board might have Gold-level subscriptions, Silver-level subscriptions, and Bronze-level subscriptions and then would charge a nickel or a dime per minute on the bulletin board, per kB uploaded or downloaded, or a combination thereof. Therefore, the original AAA included authentication, authorization and accounting services. Today, access control isn't so much about billing the client for another nickel but about tracking the activities of the users, so the third A in AAA becomes auditing. Don't be surprised to see either of the other terms used as well. (The requests for comment [RFCs] still commonly use the term "accounting.")

The procedures for the creation, management, maintenance, suspension, monitoring, and revocation of user accounts and privileges should be clearly defined within the policy documents. Account creation typically includes a summary of (requested) privileges for the new hire. The request should be initiated by a manager or the human resources (HR) department and should include approvals by several representatives that might include:

- The data owner (the business owner of the division or department the user was hired to work in)
- The direct manager of the new hire
- Human resources (HR)
- The security team (to review for excessive privilege, conflicts of interest, breaches of policy, and so on) and perhaps others as might be deemed appropriate.

After all the requisite approvals are in place, the approved request is typically sent to the network operations team for implementation. The user account is created, and the approved privileges are configured on the appropriate systems. As users transfer to different jobs or promote to higher positions, new privileges must be granted, but only through similar formalized request, review, and approval processes. Remember to provide access only for the user following the *principle of least privilege*. To carry that forward, a common mistake is to forget to remove any now-unneeded privileges when granting new privileges to users. This is called *authorization creep*, also known as *authorization aggregation*, the aggregation of too much privilege over time, a violation of the principle of least privilege.

Procedures should also be in place for the monitoring of users, more monitoring for the more privileged users and for the periodic auditing (targeted spot-checking) of privileges, and to identify vulnerabilities such as authorization creep. Monitoring and auditing of the users' activities is also a valuable tool to assess the effectiveness of the current access controls, identifying when violations are occurring and what unprotected or ineffectively protected vulnerabilities are allowing the violations to happen.

It might become necessary to lock down or otherwise disable user accounts. If a user, especially a highly privileged user, will be on vacation or sabbatical and away from work for some period of time, it might be appropriate to disable the account to minimize the attack surface of the enterprise and avoid the unauthorized access if the account is hacked.

When workers quit or are terminated, their user account should be at least disabled and have its password changed to revoke all access privileges for that user; at some point, the user account(s) should be removed from the systems. Again, these procedures should be described within the policy documents; system administrators should be trained and their procedures monitored and audited to ensure total compliance with the defined policies and procedures.

Managing fraud

Part of the provisioning process should always include a critical appraisal of whether the new privileges provide the user with too much access, enough access to entice the user to commit fraud and evade detection. *Fraud* commonly takes the form of an employee who can alter business records to steal money (or other assets) from the business without being detected for an extended period. The inappropriate or unauthorized alteration of data is a violation of the integrity of the data.

A collection of techniques has been used for decades to deter and detect fraud. The use of one control alone is rarely effective, so once again, you will find that security is stronger when the controls are deployed in depth.

The first control often used to deter and detect fraud is *separation of duties*, by which a worker is not given enough authority to complete an entire critical and vulnerable process for the enterprise. For example, an employee is assigned the responsibility to perform the purchasing tasks, to work the accounts payable, and to manage inventory control. This is too much authority and needs to be broken up. The worker with this much authority might recognize the felonious opportunity and could purchase 100 widgets (purchasing authority), pay for 100 widgets (accounts payable authority), but then alter the records to indicate the purchase of only for 50 widgets (inventory control authority) at the 100-widget price. Then the worker could steal 50 widgets and sell them at a flea market on the weekend, and their theft would go unnoticed for a long period, perhaps forever.

By separating these jobs (duties) across three people, for example, it is much less likely this theft would ever occur. All three people would have to agree to commit the theft and then would have to work together to commit the crime. When two or more come together to commit a theft of this nature, it is called *collusion*. Forcing the three to commit the crime through collusion reduces the likelihood that the crime will ever be committed. First, one worker must broach the subject and propose to commit a crime to the others. This might be enough to be fired or jailed, so separation of duties and forcing collusion acts as a deterrent.

In addition, carrying out the crime over time poses multiple hazards to the three in this example. Coordination might falter when the inventory control manager has altered the inventory records, but the purchasing agent has not yet been able to alter his related records, leading to an exposure of the crime. Alternatively, one of the three could become greedy, thinking she should get more of the cut than the others should. The teamwork falters, and the crime is detected. One user might be riddled with feelings of guilt and confess to the crime. Collusion implies that multiple workers are working together to steal from the business, generally considered to be a bad thing, but it is better to experience this state of collusion than to allow a single worker the authority to commit the crime alone.

Static separation of duties is a rigid rule that says worker A only ever performs a specific set of tasks, and worker B only ever performs a different specific set of tasks, as in a bank, where worker A receives a withdrawal request for $5,000 and must get approval from Worker B for this high-value withdrawal.

Dynamic separation of duties is less rigid and more practical in the commercial world. An example might be separation of duties that allows worker A to perform various sets of tasks but limits his authority under specific conditions, as in a bank where worker A receives a withdrawal request for $5,000 and must get approval from another teller for this high-value withdrawal. Worker A might be the teller who is working the counter and receives the withdrawal request and needs approval from worker B. If worker B were the teller who is working the counter and received the withdrawal request, worker A has the authority to approve the high-value $5,000 withdrawal request from worker B. Each worker can perform either task but never both tasks on the same transaction.

Separation of duties will help defend against fraud, but its effectiveness tends to erode over time. As workers work side by side over the years, they become friends and very comfortable with each other, and the risks to them associated with proposing a crime against the company shrink. Friendship grows and strengthens their bonds with one another, strengthening the potential collusion. A secondary control to implement in addition to separation

of duties is *job rotation*. For example, every 6 or 12 months, move a different person from a different location, or even a new hire, into critical positions. This new person is not so likely to dive right into committing crimes against her new employer and is likely to report anomalies in the books. Workers' knowledge and awareness of this practice of job rotation is also likely to deter them from entering into collusion and committing the crime in the first place. They know they'll be caught in a relatively short time. Job rotation can also be implemented through *mandatory vacations* for employees in critical roles.

Another mechanism to deter fraud is the use of *dual control*, when two (or more) are required to complete a critical function. It is common to require three of five managers with the appropriate authority to come together to recover the asymmetric private keys for users associated with digital certificates in a public key infrastructure (PKI). Private keys, digital certificates, and public key infrastructure (PKI) are covered in Chapter 3, "Cryptography."

The use of *auditing* detects the inappropriate or unauthorized alteration of the business records, and the workers' awareness of strict auditing practices act as a deterrent to committing fraud and altering the books. Knowing that someone else will be reviewing your records for accuracy tends to keep your numbers accurate instead of lending itself to the willful manipulation of those records for theft of the company's goods.

Finally, assigning the least privilege a worker requires to perform his assigned tasks is another routine practice that is effective in assisting with the management of fraud. Never give a worker more privilege than she needs to do her work. It only lends itself to increased exposure and risk and will likely result in increased losses.

Quick check

1. A policy that describes appropriate computer use and warns of repercussions is what type(s) of access control?

2. What is the term used to describe the notion of ensuring the security of information as it flows between the user and the information repository?

Quick check answers

1. Administrative preventive, administrative deterrent, administrative directive

2. Trusted path

Authentication, authorization, and auditing

In most workplaces, different workers perform different jobs, have different information access needs, and therefore require different privileges to manage their access requirements. Management must have some way to trust that only the authorized users are accessing only the content they are authorized to access. To maximize security, most information systems default to a state of no access and then only specifically grant Allow access permissions to provide access. Remember that this granting of allow permissions should always follow the principle of least privilege, allowing only the minimum level of privilege a user must have to perform his assigned work and no more privilege than that.

Before privileges can be assigned, the user accounts must be created, and some mechanism must be in place to identify and authenticate each authorized worker uniquely so that each worker is associated strictly with her intended privileges through her assigned user account. The process of managing access typically involves the following:

1. The worker's identity is verified by the system, and the system links the verified worker's identity to a user account (authentication).

2. The system manages or controls the level of access of the worker based on the associated user account and the privileges granted to that user account (authorization).

3. As the user performs his daily tasks on the system, his activities should be monitored and tracked on an ongoing basis (auditing).

This chain of processes for access control imposes three core components; authentication, authorization, and auditing. They have become the de facto access control mechanism most information systems use.

As stated previously, it is the worker (also called the subject or the user) who is the active entity in this process, so the user, the entity who desires access, initiates this identification mechanism by offering some form of identifying information that is unique to the individual user. This initial claim of identity by the user is called *identification*. The identification process or function is generally considered a subset of authentication. When the term "authentication" is presented, recognize that the subject most likely had to initiate the authentication process by first offering some claim of identity, so the identification process is typically included in the authentication process.

During the identification stage of the authentication process, the user is providing unique information to the authentication system. Some of the identification techniques that are commonly used include the user typing her name and password into a logon screen and then clicking a Login button or swiping a memory card and entering a personal identification number (PIN) or allowing a biometric system to perform a retina scan.

During the identification process, and before the completion of the authentication process, the subject might also be referred to as the claimant or as a supplicant. After the authentication process verifies the identity information provided, and the user's identity is now known and trusted, the worker is referred to as the authenticated user.

After the user has initiated the process by providing some unique information as his claim of identity, a back-end process, generically called the authentication service, attempts to verify the user's claim of identity. The authentication service is trusted by management and by the users of the system. The authentication service typically holds a repository of user account information in a user account database. *Authentication* is successful when the authentication service can verify that the unique information provided by the subject matches the unique information held within the user database for the related user's account. If the authentication system cannot match the identity information the subject supplies with its stored identity information, authentication fails, and the subject is typically denied access to any resources other than the authentication service. The authentication service usually runs on a domain controller (Windows), or a Kerberos Key Distribution Center (KDC).

EXAM TIP

Authentication may be described as "proving the veracity of a claim of identity."

When authentication is successful, the information system trusts the identity of the user, and the privileges granted to the associated user account can be enforced by the system. Providing the user controlled access to the approved resources within the information system is referred to as *authorization*, which is most commonly accomplished by assigning access permissions to user accounts to the appropriate data in a file system or application.

Auditing is the process of capturing, recording, and reviewing the various activities the users perform. Most systems have a logging function enabled by default, primarily for troubleshooting purposes. The level of detail the logging system records is usually adjustable and should be reviewed and adjusted to capture the level of detail required by policy, laws, and regulations. In addition to the relatively routine logging, a more targeted capturing of specific users' activities can usually be configured. This targeted capturing and recording of events is common for the more valuable information assets and for the more highly privileged users.

Although all this capturing and recording of events is a fine thing to accomplish, unless it is being reviewed and responded to, it is wasted effort. The term *monitoring* tends to imply the routine, ongoing review of these captured and recorded events, whereas auditing implies more of a periodic and targeted review of the captured event details, more like spot-checking.

As stated previously, this last A, auditing, can also be called accounting or accountability.

EXAM TIP

Have a clear distinction between the three components of the AAA services. The remainder of this chapter provides additional detail in this regard.

Identity management

Identity management (IdM) begins with user account and privilege provisioning but quickly grows past those basics. Systems used to perform the AAA services are developed and produced by many vendors and are based on many operating systems. In a large environment, a network might have AAA systems from three or five vendors but must somehow integrate these systems. This is the challenge of identity management. The goal is to allow the user to authenticate once but provide the user access to every asset within the enterprise-wide information system the user has been granted permissions to, no matter what the nature of the authentication and provisioning system is. Designing and implementing these diverse authentication systems to be interoperable in this manner is referred to as *federated identity management*.

Federated identity management is often accomplished through trust relationships, designed into directory services and into Kerberos, by which one realm (or domain) trusts the users from another realm (or domain). A competing technology that accomplishes federated identity management is the synchronization of user names (at creation) and passwords (at time of change) between the different user databases of the different authentication and authorization systems. Kerberos, realms, and domains are described in more detail in the "Kerberos" section later in this chapter.

The practices of user account and privilege provisioning, the ongoing monitoring and auditing of the users and the resources, and the development of mechanisms that support the integration of trust and access between both internal and external entities must be defined and guided by established policies and procedures.

Authentication

The mechanisms use to authenticate users fall into the following categories:

- **Something you know**   Such as passwords or personal identification numbers (PIN)
- **Something you have**   Such as smart cards, memory cards, or token devices
- **Something you are**   Biometrics, such as a fingerprint, voiceprint, or retina scan

Something you know

Passwords are the most commonly used authentication mechanism. They are inexpensive, fast, and well accepted by the users. However, they are also the weakest of the authentication mechanisms. Users routinely choose passwords that are easy for them to remember, but that very often makes their chosen passwords substantially more predictable and easy for the bad guys to guess. Users often write their passwords on notes in case they forget a password. Users often use the same password for everything that needs a password. If any one logon is compromised, everything the user accesses that is secured with the one password is now potentially compromised. Users might also share their passwords with a coworker or friend they trust, in violation of policy.

A technique that strengthens passwords is to set a password policy, an administrative control (the policy) often enforced by technical controls (software) within the information system, that requires longer and more complex passwords that are harder to guess. A generally accepted minimum standard for *password complexity* is:

- A minimum of eight characters. (Many companies increase this for stronger security.)
- At least one uppercase alpha character.
- At least one lowercase alpha character.
- At least one number character.
- At least one symbol character.

It is recommended to require users to change their passwords periodically. Many information systems require a new password every 90 days, and users may not use the same password for one or two years. Some users simply use the same password and change a number to the end to represent the month or quarter for that password. Although it might facilitate the user's ability to remember his passwords, this unfortunately is not satisfying the intended increase in security.

Users must be trained to protect their passwords, to choose passwords that are difficult to guess, not to share their passwords, not to reuse their passwords, and not to write down their passwords. Users must be taught to recognize when their passwords might have been exposed and to change any password immediately that might have been exposed.

Some administrators use applications called *password generators* to produce strong passwords. These generated passwords are often too complex for users to memorize. However, these can be used for the initial password set for a new user account, but the user should be required to change her password at her first logon. Increasing the required complexity of passwords also increases the likelihood that the users will write down their passwords, which increases the chances of exposure. Be careful of requiring passwords so strong and complex that your users cannot remember them.

Another control related to passwords is the account lockout feature provided by most operating systems, by which some number of failed logon attempts (wrong passwords) lock the user account for some period. This *account lockout* feature is implemented to slow down (delay) and deter an attacker trying to guess a user's password by brute force.

Some systems perform authentication by using *personal identification numbers (PIN)* in conjunction with the use of their issued credit or debit cards. PINs are typically four to eight characters long and include a lockout feature to defend against PIN guessing.

 A longer and stronger version of a password is called a *passphrase*. A passphrase may be 15 to 50 characters long. Generally speaking, a longer password is a stronger password. Users often choose a line from a song, movie, or poem as their passphrase and should alter several of the characters to defend against guessing attacks. Most systems convert the passphrase into a smaller, obfuscated, and unique representation of the passphrase, called the *virtual password*, for secure storage of the passphrase. The virtual password is often a *hash* (also called a *message digest*) of the original passphrase. Hashes and message digests are covered in detail in Chapter 3.

 EXAM TIP

Remember that a virtual password is a representation of a passphrase, usually produced for secure storage and to reduce the amount of data (versus the longer passphrase) to be stored.

 Cognitive passwords are the weakest of all passwords (with passwords already being the weakest form of authentication). Cognitive passwords are related to the user's life and history, so they are easy for users to remember. Answers to questions such as, "What is your favorite food, your least favorite animal, your second grade teacher's name, your father's middle name, your mother's maiden name," are all examples of cognitive passwords. Cognitive passwords are most often used when the user doesn't need to authenticate very often, perhaps once or twice a year. Banks and credit card companies use these to authenticate users when they call for account service or support. Cognitive passwords are so weak because much of the information that generates cognitive passwords is not very secret and might be readily available information to anyone. As social sites continue to boom, more of this type of information can be easily accessed, making these cognitive passwords less secure.

 The strongest of all passwords is the *one-time password*. This password is generated and used once, and then the password is changed. The password that was used is discarded and never used again. One-time passwords defend against the replay attack, by which the attacker captures a logon event and then, somewhat blindly, replays the user's portion back to the authentication server, hoping to trick the authentication server into believing the attacker is the legitimate user. Many token devices (that fall into the "Something you have" category) are used to generate one-time passwords.

Passwords, and the other forms of the "Something you know" authenticators, must be kept secret. If they become exposed, anyone can authenticate as the user with the exposed password, and the required element of trust in the access control systems fails. Users must not share their passwords, and if they must document them, the password information should remain securely encrypted when not required for authentication processes, such as in a secure password vault application.

Authentication systems must typically store users' passwords and usually secure the stored passwords through the use of *hashing algorithm*s, a one-way function that generates a *hash value*. The hash value, also called a message digest, acts like a fingerprint of the password, but the original password cannot be regenerated from this hash value. Again, hashing and message digests are covered in Chapter 3.

Resetting passwords

It is bound to happen, so password-based authentication systems must plan for and accommodate the need to reset a user's password when the user forgets his password. In the corporate environment, it is often the job of the help desk to field the call from the forgetful user, and after re-verifying the user's identity, the help desk resets the user's password. This is called the

assisted password reset. Policy, and sometimes technical controls, typically force the settings on the user account, so that the user must change her password at first logon after the password is reset. This is so that the help desk personnel never knows the user's actual password, just the temporary, one-time, reset password.

Another implementation of the password reset is called the *self-service password reset*. In some cases, when a user enrolls for a user account, he must identify a third-party email address. It is trusted that the third-party email account is secure, so that only the authorized user has access to it, and that the user will remember that email account username and password. Now if the user forgets his password, a Forgot Password? hyperlink is available. When the user clicks this link, he is prompted for his user name. The systems looks up the third-party email address and sends either the one-time password or a secure hyperlink to reset the password to that third-party email address.

Attacks on passwords

If an attacker can come up with your password, the attacker can authenticate as you and have the same access to whatever resources you have access to. The audit trail will show that you, not the attacker, committed the infractions. The system relies heavily on the expected secrecy of the passwords and cannot tell when an unauthorized user is using another's password. Gaining access to another user's password also provides some level of access to the legitimate user's secure key store as well.

THE BRUTE FORCE ATTACK

Because passwords are simply strings of characters (or binary bits), only a finite number of combinations can be generated from those characters. By trying every possible sequence of characters, an attacker can eventually reveal any password. This exhaustive attack is a brute force attack. It is guaranteed to reveal any password, but the attack takes a long time, often requiring weeks, months, or even years to achieve success. This is one of the reasons passwords are typically required to be longer and changed periodically. Longer passwords have more characters and can produce many more combinations that the attacker must attempt. In addition, the password should be changed before the attacker can figure it out.

THE DICTIONARY ATTACK

The dictionary attack is a subset of the brute force attack. This attack tries dictionary words as the password because most users choose passwords that are easy to remember, such as regular dictionary words. This attack is much faster, and is often successful, but is not a guaranteed success like the brute force attack is.

THE HYBRID ATTACK

The hybrid attack begins with the dictionary attack, but if and when that attack fails, the hybrid attack continues by performing character substitutions such as the exclamation mark (!) or 1 for the letter *i*, 5 or $ for the letter *s*, the number 3 for an *e*, and so on. The hybrid attack can also simply add random characters before, after, or before and after each dictionary word in its attempt to guess a user's password. The hybrid attack is not as fast as the dictionary attack, but it increases the likelihood of successfully revealing the password.

THE RAINBOW ATTACK

As described earlier, systems very often store a user's password in its hashed form. If an attacker can retrieve one or more of these stored (or even just temporarily cached) credentials in its hashed form, she can use the rainbow attack. The rainbow attack begins with the generation of the rainbow tables, which are generated from a brute force attack that tries every possible sequence of characters for a given length password, and records the hash value output for each combination of characters. The rainbow tables can also be downloaded from a number of websites (but can you trust the download). When the rainbow tables are in hand, if the hashed value of a user's password can be stolen from a compromised system, it is a simple lookup on the rainbow tables to reveal the original plaintext password for the user who produced the hash value.

The rainbow tables for longer passwords become quite large. One collection ranges from about 64 GB to approaching 1 TB, depending on the number of characters, the diversity of the character types (alpha, uppercase, and lowercase, numeric, and symbols), and the hashing function used. Numerous tools are available to perform the actual rainbow table lookup but, once again, be careful of what you download from the hacker sites. Fellow hackers are also potential targets—no honor among thieves.

The use of the rainbow tables for cracking passwords is viewed as a tradeoff between hard disk storage space and time. You consume large amounts of disk drive space, but if you are cracking passwords (shame on you), you will likely save time.

THE REPLAY ATTACK

The replay attack was described earlier, in the "Something you know" section. The attacker captures and records a legitimate user's logon activity over the network, typically using a sniffer, also called a protocol analyzer or network analyzer. The attacker extracts the user's packets to the authentication server from the capture and replays them to the authentication server. The replay attack doesn't reveal the user's password but might trick the authentication server into believing the attacker is the legitimate user.

SOCIAL ENGINEERING

This is typically considered the easiest and most often successful attack on passwords. The social engineer (attacker) tricks the user into revealing his password. The attacker might simply search the user's Facebook pages to uncover cognitive passwords or to establish the basis for likely dictionary passwords. The attacker might call the user and pretend to be the help desk trying to do the user a favor and solve some technical problem. Of course, in the process of solving the problem, the user is prompted to tell the help desk imposter his password. The social engineer might gain physical access to the user's workplace and look over a user's shoulder while the user is typing her password (called *shoulder surfing*) to observe and memorize the password or to search for written passwords under keyboards, posted on the display monitor, or stored conveniently in the top desk drawers. The attacker might request some assistance, relying on most people's desire to be helpful and, in the process, for some seemingly legitimate reason, need to use the legitimate user's password.

Something you have

The second category of authentication mechanisms relies on some component or device to be issued from the trusted authority (management or network administration) to the legitimate user. The device is associated with a user account and is issued to a worker. When the worker needs access, the worker uses the device to authenticate the user to the authentication system. The device-related authentication mechanisms are considered more secure than the use of passwords but also carry a higher price tag. Every user in the authentication system must be supplied a device (the "something they have"), and many of these types of devices require electronic reader devices at every location authentication of users is required. Although these devices tend to be relatively small and designed to be portable, users are generally a bit frustrated by having to carry around the device and keep track of it. "Hm ... now where did I leave my ID badge?"

A *photo ID badge* is commonplace for physical access control. It is relatively inexpensive and provides a visual authenticator to not just the security guards at the entryway but throughout the facility. Users should be trained to (safely) challenge anyone without a visible photo ID badge. These badges, unfortunately, cannot provide an audit trail of use and attempted (failed) use, and they rely on trusted and trained humans for the actual authentication function.

Many information systems use *memory cards* to authenticate users. A memory card simply stores some unique authenticator that proves the card was issued through the system and is linked to an authorized user account. Some memory cards use a magnetic tape to store their data. Other memory cards now are using integrated, nonvolatile memory circuits, such as flash memory, to store the authenticator data. Memory cards do not process any data; they just store data. This detail distinguishes the memory card from the smart card. The memory card functions from power provided by the electronic reader device.

A similar device, called a *smart card*, often looks just like the memory card but includes a processor embedded within the card. This makes the smart card more expensive. The smart card also contains memory for storage of data and for storage of one or more programs, usually encryption and decryption algorithms. When activated, the smart card actually reads its program from its storage into its embedded CPU, reads ts data from its storage, and executes the program(s) on the data by using the embedded CPU chip. Encrypting and decrypting the stored data on the card makes the smart card more versatile and more secure than the memory card. A high-end smart card is tamper-resistant, both electrically and physically, and if it detects tampering, it destroys the content stored in its memory to avoid potential exposure.

Memory cards and smart cards might require the card to be swiped or inserted in the electronic reader. These types of cards are *contact-oriented* cards. Other forms of these cards are *contactless* and only require physical proximity to an electronic reader device called a transponder. The *transponder* is a reader that emits a radio frequency (RF) signal in the proximity of the reader. This RF energy is received by the nearby contactless card and is converted into the energy that powers the circuits in the card. When energized in this manner, memory cards simply transmit what they have stored in memory back to the transponder; smart cards initiate processing their locally stored data by using their locally stored programs in the embedded CPU and then wirelessly transmit that processed information back to the transponder. These proximity-based cards are vulnerable to attack unless their data is encrypted. It is relatively easy to carry around a transponder and to record all the responses from nearby proximity cards for later attacks. The readers, transponders, and administrative systems (used to program the cards and administer the authentication system) increase the cost of using these types of cards.

Smart cards can use both contact-oriented and contactless components on one card, enabling these devices to be used in two authentication systems, perhaps the contactless for physical access, such as at otherwise locked doorways, and the contact-oriented for computer and network access. The *combi-card* contains both contact-oriented and contactless components but uses a single CPU chip for the processing. The *hybrid card* contains both contact-oriented and contactless components and uses two CPU chips for the processing. The hybrid card is more expensive because of the dual CPU chips but is more secure than the combi-card because an attacker would need to compromise separate circuits (CPUs) within the card to compromise both authentication systems whereas with the combi-card, the compromise of a single circuit (CPU) compromises both authentication systems.

A different family of "something you have" authentication mechanisms is the family of *token devices*. Once again, these devices are associated with a user account on the information system and are then issued to the authorized user by the trusted administration of the enterprise. Token devices are available in two primary types: synchronous and asynchronous.

The *synchronous token device*'s internal clock is synchronized with the clock on the authentication server, and both components are initialized with the same starting value, often called a salt, a seed, an initialization vector, or a nonce. A similar application on each end (the synchronous token device and the authentication server) generates a new derivative of the original value (salt) on a periodic basis. At any point in time from then on, both endpoints are holding exactly the same derivative value. This newly calculated derivative value is used as a one-time password (described earlier in this chapter) for the next one or two minutes between the user in possession of the token device and the backend authentication server.

One minute later (for example), both endpoints calculate the next derivative value from the original salt value. When the user wants to log on, he checks his token device and uses the displayed value as his one-time password to prove to the authentication server that the user is in possession of the authorized and enterprise-issued token device.

The *asynchronous token device* is not based on a synchronized clock for the generation of a user's password. When a user wants to log on, she enters her user name in the local system, and that user name is sent to the back-end Authentication service (AS). The AS generates a random and unique character string called *challenge text* and sends the challenge text to the user. The user enters the challenge text in the asynchronous token device to produce the one-time password for that logon event. This process is called a *challenge response* and is commonly used, in several ways, in various authentication systems.

Token devices can be a small device, such as a key fob, or simply an application installed on your smart phone, but it typically requires some form of user input capability.

Another type of token device plugs into the universal serial bus (USB) port on the computer to authenticate the user (in possession of the token device) to the system. These can be synchronous, asynchronous, or simply contain a single, static key that authenticates the user to the system. These can also require the use of a password or PIN to perform multi-factor authentication, strengthening the authentication mechanism. This is very similar to the way a memory card or smart card might be used, but it eliminates the need and cost for an additional reader on each computer by using existing hardware on the computer (the USB port) and a simple application installed on the computer to check for the presence of an authorized USB token.

The use of *digital certificates* is growing as a trusted form of authentication. This relies on a user proving his identity to a *registration authority* (RA) and the RA requesting the digital certificate from a trusted *certification authority* (CA) on behalf of the now-authenticated user. The CA then binds a cryptographic key (*asymmetric public key*) to the certificate along with the user's identity details provided to the CA by the RA, and then the CA digitally signs the digital certificate. The digital certificate is then issued to the user or might be installed on the user's computer or embedded in a smart card that is issued to the user. The user is authenticated when he presents the digital certificate (something he has) to the authentication system. The generation and prudent management of the digital certificates requires a *public key infrastructure* (PKI), which is covered in more detail in Chapter 3.

Drawbacks of authentication devices (something you have)

A drawback to the use of authentication devices (something you have) is the cost of the devices themselves, the cost of the enrollment system(s), and, in some cases, the additional cost of the readers at every location authentication is required.

Further, these devices present a serious vulnerability if they are lost or stolen. All an attacker has to do is find a user's proximity card in the parking lot or at a restaurant, and he instantly becomes a trusted user on the system providing access to whatever the legitimate user was authorized for. For this second reason, many of these systems require the use of an additional authentication mechanism, such as a password or PIN (something you know), to strengthen the authentication process. When used as part of a multi-factor authentication system, the attacker must also still guess the user's password (or PIN) associated with the user account. Nevertheless, by itself, without the requirement for a second factor of authentication, the "something you have" form of authentication mechanism is still relatively weak—stronger than passwords alone but not by much. When used in conjunction with a second form of authentication, such as "something you know," these authentication mechanisms become notably stronger.

Users who are issued a "something you have" authentication device must be trained in the proper use of the devices and the vulnerabilities related to their use. Users must understand the need to report lost or stolen authentication devices immediately so the missing devices can be disabled and tracked and a new device issued.

Something you are

The third primary authentication mechanism is called *biometrics*. This system scans a specific type of biological attribute of the user (the bio- part), converts that reading into some numeric value or values (the -metric part), and compares that information to the biometric data stored in the authentication system for that user. Biometrics relies on the uniqueness of the biological attributes of different people and is the most expensive form of authentication but the strongest and most specific single form of authentication. Users tend to dislike the use of biometric systems because they invade one's personal space. Users are not fond of pressing their hand down on a palm reader platen where 3,000 other users just pressed their hands (especially when the user just before him had glazed donuts for breakfast!). Retina scanners require a close look into the pupil of the user, which can provoke a sense of violation of personal space and discomfort as the retina scanner draws close to the user's open, exposed, and vulnerable eye and so on.

Table 2-1 presents the more common forms of the "something you are" authentication mechanisms.

TABLE 2-1 Biometric authentication techniques

Technique	Definition
Fingerprint	Plots the points where the ridges of the fingerprint come to an end and where the ridges fork into multiple ridges, called bifurcations.
Finger scan	Similar to fingerprint but uses less data. Faster and cheaper.
Palmprint	Maps the palm's areas of contact with the platen and the creases in the palm. Some also use infrared to identify vascular structure within the hand.
Hand geometry	Maps the shape of the hand from a top view looking down at the hand.
Hand topology	Maps the shape of the hand from a side view, as if looking at a mountain range on the horizon.

Technique	Definition
Iris scan	Maps the color patterns around the pupil of the eye. Can be accomplished from some distance. Not as invasive as the retina scan.
Retina scan	Maps the pattern of blood vessels in the back of the eye. Requires close proximity to the user's eye.
Voiceprint	Maps the tones and lyrical quality of the user's speech patterns.
Signature dynamics	Behavioral attribute. Maps the speed and direction of motion as the user signs his name. Not dependent on the visual appearance of the signature.
Keystroke dynamics	Behavioral attribute. Maps the timing of keystrokes as the user enters her password on a keyboard. Not dependent on the accuracy of the characters.

ENROLLMENT

Before the user of a biometric authentication system can log on, he must first have a user account on the system. Then, an enrollment process for the biometric system must be completed for the user, which links the user's biometric data to the associated user account. This typically involves multiple scans of the target biological attribute (fingerprint, palm scan, and so on), often 10 or more, the calculation of the metrics, the numeric representation of the biological attribute, and an analysis of the convergence of the data collected from the scans. A sufficient number of points must agree a sufficient number of times for the biometric data to be acceptable as an authenticator mechanism for the user. If the user is inconsistent in the placement with regard to the scanner, additional scanning is likely be required until a sufficient level of consistency can be achieved.

After an acceptable level of consistency is achieved, the biometric data is obfuscated for security purposes and then stored within the authentication system and linked to the appropriate user account.

The time it takes to enroll users is often considered a cost associated with the use of the particular biometric system.

ERRORS IN THE BIOMETRIC SYSTEMS

Biometric authentication systems are not perfect. From time to time, errors occur in the authentication process. When a legitimate user fails to authenticate to her user account, this is called a *Type I error - False rejection rate*; the user is falsely rejected authentication and is denied access. When a legitimate user is successfully authenticated as the incorrect user, when someone without a user account is successfully authenticated as a legitimate user, or when one user is incorrectly authenticated as a different user, this is called a *Type II error - False acceptance rate*; the user is falsely authenticated and is then granted inappropriate access.

Although neither type of error is a good thing, the Type II error - False acceptance error is by far the more threatening and risky type of error because it provides inappropriate access to the incorrectly authenticated user. This constitutes a security breach. The Type I error - False rejection error simply denies a legitimate user access. Although this might be frustrating for the legitimate user and degrades his productivity, it does not expose the valuable assets of the organization to the unauthorized.

The accuracy of biometric authentication systems is commonly indicated by the statistical rate or frequency of Type I and Type II errors the system produces. As the sensitivity of the biometric authentication system is increased from a very low sensitivity to a very high sensitivity, the rate of false rejection will go from low to high. As the sensitivity of the biometric authentication system is increased from a very low sensitivity to a very high sensitivity, the rate of false acceptance will go from high to low. The accuracy of the biometric authentication system is based on this plotted profile for the biometric device and is called the *crossover error rate* (*CER*). The CER is defined by the intersection of these two lines, the *false rejection rate* (*FRR*) and the *false acceptance rate* (*FAR*), plotted versus the device's sensitivity.

The graph showing an example of the CER is shown in Figure 2-1.

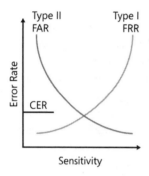

FIGURE 2-1 Crossover error rate

EXAM TIP

Remember that the lower the CER for a biometric authentication system, the greater the accuracy of the system. However, be aware that every control must be cost justified. The budget might not support the use of the best.

Another form of failure of the system stems from periodic changes that can occur to physical attributes of the users. Imagine a cut or burn on a finger used for biometric authentication. The fingerprint no longer has the same metrics, and the legitimate user authentication fails. Consider the user with a cold and sore throat, when the voiceprint is used for authentication. Pregnancy, physical strain, and drug therapy can alter the size, paths, and quantity of blood vessels in the back of the eye, causing the retina scan to fail. Consider the loss of the digit or an eye. In these cases, the legitimate user's authentication will fail, and re-enrollment is required to authenticate these users successfully again.

FINDING A MATCHING RECORD

Biometric systems can perform their authentication using one of two methods. In the first type, the user first identifies his claimed identity by inputting a claim of identity, such as a user name or employee ID number, some nonsecret information that links the user to his account. The user then allows the system to perform its scan. This is called the *verification method*; the user first claims a specific identity, and then the scanned data is compared to the data stored on the back-end authentication system for the claimed user identity in a *one-to-one* fashion. Only one record will ever be reviewed for a match for this specific logon attempt, shown in Figure 2-2. This one-to-one method, the verification method, is typically faster and more secure but carries with it the increased cost of requiring a user input device, a keyboard, or keypad at every location authentication must occur to enable the user to input his claim of identity.

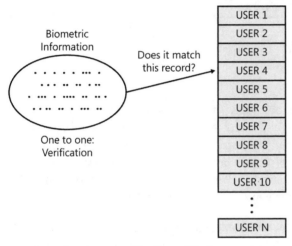

FIGURE 2-2 One-to-one verification method

The one-to-one verification method carries with it the risk of Type I errors - False rejection but greatly minimizes the risk of Type II errors - False acceptance because it would only ever test and potentially match the one record from the user's claim of identity. Remember that false acceptance, minimized in this case, is the more dangerous form of error on biometric systems, making false rejection the more secure form of biometric system.

In the second commonly used method, the user does not provide any claim of identity but simply allows the system to perform its scan. The user cannot claim any specific identity. This is called the *identification method*; the system must figure out which record in the back-end authentication system matches the scanned data, if any. After the scan of the user's biological attribute is complete, the scanned data is compared to all the biometric data stored in every user record on the back-end authentication system in a *one-to-many* fashion, as shown in Figure 2-3. Every biometric record will be reviewed for a match, and if a match is found, the system now identifies the user (based on the matching user account) and authenticates her.

This identification method is typically slower and less secure but is also less expensive by not requiring any user input device from the user to claim an identity.

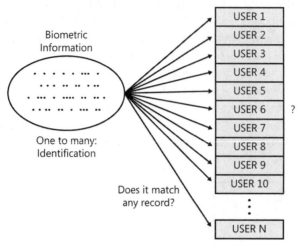

FIGURE 2-3 One-to-many identification method

The one-to-many identification method carries with it the risk of a Type I error - False rejection and the risk of a Type II error - False acceptance because it checks every record for a match without relying on the user's claim of a single identity. This makes the identification method less secure than the verification method on biometric authentication systems. Remember that the Type II errors (FAR) are substantially more risky than the Type I errors (FRR), and the identification method does not help minimize the chance of the Type II errors.

DRAWBACKS OF BIOMETRIC AUTHENTICATION (SOMETHING YOU ARE)

One drawback of the use of biometric authentication systems is the high cost of the biometric scanning systems required at every location authentication must occur. This hardware cost can put a serious dent in the allocated budget for the security program. An indirect cost of these systems is the time it takes to enroll and re-enroll users and the time it takes during the authentication process, especially when the users must overcome the errors (hopefully, only Type I errors). These systems tend to be slow.

Another drawback is the lack of acceptance by the users. The scanning process invades the user's personal and private space, and many users find this uncomfortable. This resistance to accept might lead to increased Type I errors because users squirm or are too quick to extract themselves from the invading devices. There could be privacy issues with the use of biometric devices, such as when a failed authentication from a retina scan leads to an inference by the system administrator that a female user might be sick or pregnant—an invasion of the user's privacy.

Yet another drawback to the use of biometric authentication systems is that if the store of biometric information is ever really compromised, the users' personally identifying information cannot ever be changed. If a password (something you know) is exposed, changing it is easy. If you lose your token device (something you have), disable that one and issue a new one. However, if your fingerprint (something you are) is captured by the bad guys, that same fingerprint will be your fingerprint, uniquely identifying you, for the rest of your life, and it is now in the hands of the bad guys. Although the manufacturers of these systems understand this, and go to lengths to obfuscate these uniquely identifying details, have they gone far enough? What will the bad guys figure out with these in the next 10 or 20 years? Will they be able to crack these obfuscation techniques and recover usable biometric data? Who can say? The device vendors assure you there is little or no risk in this area. They need to sell systems. Can you believe them? Some questions and risk remain in this area for some time to come.

> **NOTE   A FOURTH AUTHENTICATION TYPE?**
>
> Some references describe another type of authentication, to include something you know, something you have, something you are, and the fourth, someplace you are. The examples of "someplace you are" as a method of uniquely identifying authorized users don't seem to hold up to scrutiny. One example is a user in the middle of the desert. How do you know whether the user is in the right place in the middle of the desert? You give him a GPS device that you can track (isn't that something you have?). How do you know there aren't unknown and unauthorized people in the middle of the desert? You restrict the area and allow only those intended users in. (Isn't that authorization coupled with some form of prior authentication to identify who to let into the restricted area?)
>
> Another example is people in a grocery store being authenticated by their proximity to the grocery store and, therefore, being authorized to use the shopping carts, with the shopping carts having proximity locks (restricting to a location) on the wheels. In this case, the people aren't being identified and authenticated by their proximity to the store. The carts are, and the proximity locks on the wheels are something you have (in this case, the carts).
>
> Someplace you are might be used to adjust the level of strength of the authentication process. For example, if a user is inside the facility (someplace you are), a user name and password is acceptable, but when the user is away from the facility, stronger authentication, such as multi-factor authentication, might be required. Other than this, someplace you are seems to fall short as a mechanism for uniquely identifying and authenticating authorized users. Stick to the three authentication mechanisms—something you know, something you have, and something you are.

Multi-factor authentication

Attackers can crack passwords, and users accidentally expose their passwords. Users lose their token devices, smart cards, and memory cards, and at least in the spy movies, the bad guys painfully remove the required body parts of the authorized users to defeat biometric authentication systems. When used alone, each of the three authentication mechanisms is relatively easy to defeat, but when used in combination, the authentication system is notably strengthened. This is referred to as *two-factor authentication* or, more generically, *multi-factor authentication*.

Requiring the use of a password along with the use of the smart card greatly improves the strength of the authentication system by strengthening both mechanisms. If the user's password is exposed, the attacker must also acquire the smart card before she can compromise the system. If a user loses his smart card, a would-be attacker cannot use it without first cracking the user's password.

Two-factor (or multi-factor) authentication requires at least two authentication mechanisms from at least two types of authentication (something you know, something you have, or something you are), such as a token device and a password or a biometric scan and a PIN. A PIN and a password are not considered two-factor (or multi-factor) authentication because they both come from the same type of authentication mechanisms—something you know.

EXAM TIP

Be sure that multi-factor authentication mechanisms come from two of the three groups: something you know, something you have, and something you are.

Mutual authentication

Another approach to strengthening the authentication system is with *mutual authentication*, by which the subject authenticates himself to the authentication system, and the system authenticates itself to the user. This has become more important because of the increased use of remote access such as dial-in computing, virtual private networks (VPNs), and wireless networking.

When a user must come into the building and connect to that network by using a physical cable, physical security controls are in place to ensure that only authorized users can accomplish this. A stranger sitting at a long-time coworker's computer is obvious and will likely be detected and responded to quickly. Further, when an authorized user comes into the building and connects to the network there by using a physical cable, that authorized user is quite certain that she has connected to the correct and legitimate corporate network. It is unlikely that a rogue network is attached to the Ethernet jack in the wall of your office.

However, in these cases of remote access (dial-in, VPN, and wireless), the user cannot be seen by the authorized users and does not need to pass through any type of physical security. Therefore, the authentication process for the remote user should be stronger. Further, because the user is dialing up from some remote location, how does he know that he dialed the correct number and is connected to the correct network? If the connection is a VPN over the Internet, how does the user really know that she has connected to the correct and legitimate corporate network? Many attacks can hijack connections to bogus Internet locations without the user being aware of the deception. When connecting over wireless networking, even if you are physically located within the building, the wireless network interface card (NIC) attempts to associate with the access point by using the correct service set identifier (SSID) that is providing the strongest signal to the client location. How can the user be certain that a rogue access point isn't using the corporate SSID? It only takes about $15 in hardware for an attacker to set up a rogue access point and use the corporate SSID. In all three examples, the user cannot be certain of the network he has attached to unless the user requires the network to authenticate itself. In these three examples, and perhaps others, mutual authentication should be implemented.

THE ZERO KNOWLEDGE PROOF

Imagine this: It is finally Saturday night, the night you've been waiting forever since you found out the password to get into the greatest party this town has seen in decades. You grab your date and head out into the cold, dark, and rainy night. The directions you've been given lead you into an even darker alleyway that ends at a lone door that seems to have been made in the middle ages. The door is tall and broad and is mounted and reinforced with heavy, black metal hardware. You can see a cloud from your breath as you pound on the heavy wooden door. In a moment, just below eye level in the center of the door, a small opening appears. You realize you are holding your breath as you see a scruffy, unshaven chin and mouth move to the opening from behind the door. A deep and coarse voice barks at you, "What's the password?"

You hesitate as you recall that when you were quietly and secretly slipped the password, it came with a warning that you understood. Without additional explanation, you knew you had to take this warning seriously. The warning was, "Do not tell anyone the password."

You definitely want to get into the party, but if you break the rule, violate the warning, and tell the chin with the voice what the password is, you might be revealing the password to someone who should not know the password. What if you're at the wrong door? What if someone is lurking deep in the shadows of the alleyway and overhears? You can't tell him the password. You just can't say it to him. You realize that you're holding your breath, now, as you stand there in the cold and the dark and the rain, puzzled, torn, and filled with both anxiety and desire. You realize that your date, standing close and next to you, is holding her breath, too.

This is the dilemma that prompts us for the zero-knowledge proof. You must prove to the authentication service that you know the password without telling the service what the password is, just in case you are connected to the wrong (spoofed) authentication service or someone is listening to the communication. You cannot openly reveal the password to any-one, but you must successfully authenticate by using the password. So how do you do that?

 The open-standard *Challenge Handshake Authentication Protocol* (CHAP) does just that. It relies on a randomly generated string of characters called challenge text and on a *hashing algorithm*. Hashing algorithms, also called *message digests*, produce a unique fingerprint for a given message. Hashing algorithms are covered in detail in Chapter 3, but a brief introduction is needed here.

Data is stored on computers as long strings of binary bits. By treating the binary bits of a message as numbers instead of as the characters of the message, the hashing algorithm per-forms mathematical calculations and transposition manipulations on the numbers to produce an answer. The product of the math and manipulation performed on those numbers represents a unique fingerprint of the message. Running the same hashing algorithm on exactly the same message always produces exactly the same answer. However, if any character or even a single bit is altered in the message, the hashing algorithm produces a distinctly different answer. In addition to producing this unique fingerprint of a message, hashing algorithms perform a one-way function; you can take a message and generate a hash value, but you cannot take a hash value and re-create the original message. Now, back to CHAP.

A user wants to authenticate by means of a password, as shown in Figure 2-4, but she does not want to reveal the password openly.

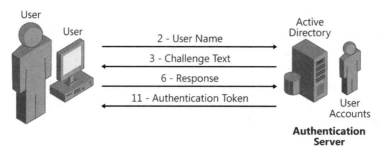

FIGURE 2-4 The zero-knowledge proof and the Challenge Handshake Authentication Protocol (CHAP)

The following procedure generically describes the CHAP process. There are many more details and components for those with a higher level of interest and understanding, but this procedure generally describes the key points of CHAP as might be test-worthy on the CISSP certification exam.

1. The user enters his user name and password in a logon screen and clicks the Login button.

2. The logon process on the user's workstation sends the user name (and not the password) over the network to the authentication server.

3. The authentication server verifies that the user name exists in the user database and then generates a unique string of challenge text and sends it over the network to the user.

4. The logon process on the user's workstation receives the challenge text. The logon process on the user's workstation produces a hash value of the password the user entered. The logon process on the user's workstation appends the hash value of the password to the challenge text it received from the authentication server.

    CHALLENGE_TEXT + HASH (PASSWORD)

5. The logon process on the user's workstation runs a hashing algorithm over the challenge text plus the hash value of the password to produce a hash value.

    HASH (CHALLENGE_TEXT + HASH (PASSWORD))

6. The logon process on the user's workstation sends the resulting hash value over the network to the authentication server.

7. The authentication server holds the user database where the user's account resides.

8. The authentication server looks up the user account and extracts the stored hash value of the user's password on record.

   HASH (PASSWORD)

9. The authentication server appends the retrieved hash value of the user's password to the challenge text it generated and then sent to the user.

   CHALLENGE_TEXT + HASH (PASSWORD)

10. The authentication server runs a hashing algorithm over the challenge text plus the retrieved hash value of the password to produce a hash value.

    HASH (CHALLENGE_TEXT + HASH (PASSWORD))

11. The authentication server compares its calculated hash value with the hash value it just received from the user:

    - If the two hash values are identical, the user must have known the correct password, correct down to each binary bit. The user is successfully authenticated. The authentication server (typically) produces and provides the user an authentication token as proof of the user's successful authentication.

    - If the two hash values are different, the authentication fails. Either the user didn't know the correct password or simply mistyped it. The user is denied access to all resources except the authentication service (to retry the logon process).

Most computer-based authentication systems rely on some form of the zero-knowledge proof to authenticate the users. CHAP is the default authentication protocol for virtually all enterprise-level network operating systems (those that use directory services).

Single sign on

The concept of *single sign on* (SSO) is to have the user log on once and, based on that single sign on, allow the user to access every resource, enterprise-wide, that the user has been granted permission to access. This extends to the networked information system that includes resource servers from different vendors, servers running different operating systems, and potentially even different authentication systems.

Having to log on only once and then gain access to all resources when privilege has been granted is a wonderful thing for the user and tends to simplify the life of the administrators. However, with single sign on technologies in place, an attacker now only needs to (illegitimately) log on once as an authorized user to gain access to all resources privilege has been granted to—to the authorized user, not the unauthorized and illegitimate attacker! SSO is certainly a double-edged sword.

In the early days of networking, in the 1980s and even into the early 1990s, it was common for each network server that provided resources to the network users to hold its own discrete user database. Therefore, if an environment had five servers, each user had five discrete user accounts, an account on each server, each with, potentially, a different user name and a different password. Although five servers, five user accounts per person, and five passwords to remember might sound somewhat functional, imagine an environment with 20 servers or 100 servers, and you begin to understand the need for SSO technology.

Back then, a commonly employed SSO solution to even a few servers, a few user names, and a few passwords was to write yourself a *batch file* (login.bat, for example) that contained the command-line logon instructions to log on to each account you owned. As soon as you started your workstation, you could run the batch file *script* to log on to each account on the network servers. In those days, a sample script might look something like this:

```
Login [<Server1>] [<Username1>] [<Password1>]  [</options>]
Login [<Server2>] [<Username2>] [<Password2>]  [</options>]
Login [<Server3>] [<Username3>] [<Password3>]  [</options>]
```

Back then, this was a slick solution, and you were bright for figuring out how to do it. However, today, as security concerns have matured, this solution would violate multiple policies and would introduce multiple unacceptable vulnerabilities by storing and transmitting user names and passwords in plaintext. There must be a better way. There is.

Kerberos

Recognizing the need for SSO in the 1980s, engineers at the Massachusetts Institute of Technology (MIT) developed an SSO network authentication service for information systems called *Kerberos*. The original development project was named *Project Athena*. Kerberos (also Cerberus) is named after the three-headed dog from Greek mythology that guarded the gates of Hades, the underworld. In the case of SSO, the three heads of the dog represent the client, the resource server, and the Kerberos server. The Kerberos server is a third party, trusted by the users of the network. The users and the resources within this Kerberos environment are referred to as *principals*.

Kerberos is an open standard and was initially classified as military technology because of its use of the Data Encryption Standard (DES). It was restricted from export by the US government until 2000, when the United States loosened its export restrictions on encryption technologies. The most recent version of Kerberos, version 5, was published in 2005 and is embedded in most network operating systems and *directory services* from vendors, including Microsoft, Linux, Unix, Apple, Oracle, and IBM, to name a few. If the operating system needs Kerberos but does not yet have it installed, the system is said to need to be *Kerberized* (have Kerberos installed).

The Kerberos system provides mutual authentication and uses *symmetric key cryptography* and *tickets* to convey authentication details to the principals securely. The *Key Distribution Center (KDC)* is the trusted Kerberos server that also supports the AS and the *Ticket Granting service (TGS)*, shown in Figure 2-5. Symmetric key cryptography is covered in Chapter 3.

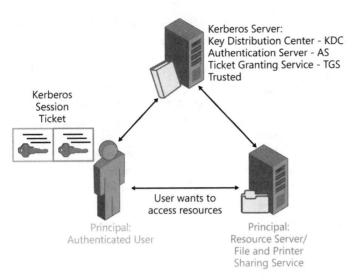

Kerberos Server:
Key Distribution Center - KDC
Authentication Server - AS
Ticket Granting Service - TGS
Trusted

Kerberos
Session
Ticket

User wants to
access resources

Principal:
Authenticated User

Principal:
Resource Server/
File and Printer
Sharing Service

FIGURE 2-5 The Kerberos KDC and principals

The KDC is a single point of failure for the information system and, therefore, should be implemented to support *high availability* (*HA*), usually providing multiple KDCs in each location. Further, the KDC is a juicy target for the bad guys. The KDC should be installed on a *bastion host system*, a hardened system performing, largely, a single dedicated function, in this case, the Kerberos (KDC, AS, and TGS) function. For starters, hardening a system includes regular updating of the operating system, regularly updated antimalware protection, restricted network access, file integrity verification, minimized user accounts, minimized software installed, minimized services running, and all processes running under the least privilege possible. The bastion host server is covered in more detail in Chapter 7.

The presence of one or more open-standard Kerberos KDCs, and its collection of trusting and trusted principals, forms a Kerberos *realm*. The Kerberos realm is implemented on Microsoft networks as the Active Directory directory server *domain*. The realm (domain) has a boundary that is called its *namespace*. All objects belonging to the same realm have the same namespace, such as server1.contoso.com and user27.contoso.com. This namespace boundary is a logical boundary. On Windows 2000 networks and later, these Kerberos services (KDC, AS, and TGS) form the core of the Active Directory *domain controller* (*DC*). Each DC is actually a Kerberos KDC.

The operating system that implements the realm (or domain) includes technical controls that enforce the boundary defined by the namespace. Principals within the realm are trusted by and trusting of the other principals within the realm. The namespace boundary and the technical controls that enforce the boundary form a *security domain*; the collection of objects (such as users and computers) with a common namespace are trusted by and trusting of all other objects within that same realm and with that same namespace. To gain access to a resource, trust for the identity of the principal, plus permissions granted to those principals are required. Kerberos includes the element of trust within the realm.

> **NOTE TRUST VERSUS PRIVILEGE**
>
> **All objects within a realm are trusted by and trusting of all other objects within that same realm, but trust is not privilege. Without trust between objects, permissions cannot be granted and access cannot occur, so there can be no privilege. Therefore, trust must first exist, either through common membership within the same realm or through an external trust with a different realm. After trust has been established, access still cannot occur until permissions are granted. Prior to granting permissions across the trust, even with the trust in place, the default permission of No Access is in place, so an access request would be denied. Both trust and permissions are required to allow access in the Kerberos environment. Kerberos is a very complex protocol, with much more complexity than can be described here. The CISSP exam requires a certain level of understanding, and the following description targets that level of understanding. As described about CHAP earlier in this chapter, there are many unmentioned details and complexities, but if you can grasp the concepts described here, you should do just fine on the certification exam. Many very technical and detailed resources are available online for Kerberos if you need more information.**

Kerberos relies on an initial authentication of the principal (the user) using its AS and is commonly based on CHAP in network operating systems. After the initial CHAP-based authentication is successful, the TGS generates a Kerberos ticket granting ticket (TGT) that the TGS on the KDC provides to the now authenticated user. The TGT is the user's *access token* for this logon session, is (typically) good for 10 hours, and is protected using symmetric key cryptography. This TGT proves that the user has successfully authenticated to the trusted KDC and that the KDC believes this user is who she claims to be. Because all principals in the realm trust the KDC, all users in the realm trust what the KDC says and, more specifically, what the KDC's tickets say.

The user is now successfully logged on and is holding his TGT. When he attempts to access any network resource (another Kerberos principal within the Kerberos realm, for example), he sends a copy of his TGT back to the KDC along with the details of his request for access to a trusted network resource. The KDC validates the TGT and generates a new and different ticket called a *session ticket*. The KDC sends the session ticket back to the user at this point.

The session ticket has two halves. One is encrypted so that only the user can decrypt it. The other half is encrypted so that only the resource server can decrypt it. The encrypted halves contain authenticator details to validate and substantiate the legitimacy of requests within the trusted realm, and each half of the ticket contains a copy of a symmetric session key as the mutual authenticator. The KDC generates a new pair of symmetric session keys for each request for access from principals. The session ticket (typically) has a lifetime of only five minutes. This limited lifetime, along with the use of sequence numbers, is designed to defeat the replay attack, described earlier in this chapter. Five minutes is not long enough for the bad guys to crack the symmetric key encryption, alter the ticket, re-encrypt the ticket, and send the ticket to the resource server to exploit the resources.

The user, who now holds the session ticket, decrypts his half of the session ticket and extracts his symmetric session key. The user writes (again) the details of his request for resource access in his half of the ticket and then encrypts it with the newly acquired symmetric session key. The user now sends the session ticket to the resource server. This is the user's request to authenticate to the resource server, and it includes the details of the requested access, such as the desired path and filename, and whether the request is to create, read, modify, or delete the desired file.

The resource server can only decrypt its half of the session ticket at this point and, in doing so, decrypts the authenticator details of the request for access as documented by the KDC, along with the resource server's copy of the symmetric session key that the same KDC provided. At this point, the resource server knows what the KDC understands about the request for access and, using the symmetric session key provided within the session ticket, can decrypt and read the user's request.

The resource server verifies that everything the KDC said about the request for access is exactly what the user says about it. The resource server validates the time stamps on the two ticket halves, to be sure the ticket hasn't expired, along with several other validation checks. Because the symmetric session key the KDC provided to the resource server was the correct key to decrypt successfully the portion written and encrypted by the user (who used his copy of the symmetric session key the KDC provided), the resource server trusts that the ticket was legitimately supplied by the trusted KDC. At this point, because the authenticator data and the validation checks are accurate, the resource server trusts that the KDC successfully authenticated the principal, the user who made this request for access. The user has now successfully authenticated to the resource server, and the details of the request for access are known.

There is one more step to complete the mutual authentication processes of Kerberos. Using the symmetric session key provided by the KDC within the session ticket, the resource server encrypts a portion of the user's authenticator data from the now decrypted user half of the session ticket and sends the encrypted message to the user. When the user can successfully decrypt the message from the resource server, using the symmetric session key provided to him by the KDC on the original session ticket, he can verify that the message from the resource server contains the authenticator details he wrote. He knows that the resource server is the one, trusted resource server in the Kerberos realm that he was looking for. Mutual authentication is successful.

With the session ticket now validated by the resource server and the associated trust for the user's identity, Kerberos has finished its work. The resource server knows who the user is and knows what resource(s) the user is requesting access to. This is the end of the Kerberos functions. The resource server now moves to the authorization phase, but Kerberos has nothing to do with that. Kerberos only authenticates the two ends to each other in a trusted manner.

If any part of tickets used in this process does not decrypt correctly, the endpoint that discovers the failure discards the ticket. If the ticket lifetime, based on the time stamp from the KDC, has expired, the ticket is discarded. If any of the authenticator details do not match correctly on any of the tickets, the ticket is discarded. There are several additional TGT and session ticket validation steps, and if any fail, the Kerberos authentication process fails.

Because Kerberos relies on this relatively short ticket lifetime, clock synchronization of the KDCs and all principal systems is critical. If an environment is suffering from unexpected Access Denied errors, one of the first places to check is the clocks on the KDCs and the principal systems involved. The *Network Time Protocol (NTP)*, using port 123, is often used to resolve this time synchronization issue. Kerberos uses port 88 by default. The NTP port numbers are covered in Chapter 7.

WEAKNESSES WITH KERBEROS

The Kerberos TGT is issued based on the initial (typically) password-based authentication of the user. As described earlier in this chapter, passwords are the weakest form of authentication. If an attacker can get access to a user's password by social engineering or password cracking, Kerberos will never know, will trust the unauthorized user as the legitimate user, and will issue that attacker a legitimate TGT, professing trust for the user's true identity. Further, based on that trust, all the other principals within the realm will trust the unauthorized user as the legitimate user.

Kerberos uses only symmetric key cryptography. Symmetric key cryptography only provides one cryptographic service strongly, confidentiality (keeping the secrets secret). It provides a weak form of authentication and a weak form of integrity validation. Again, symmetric key cryptography is covered in detail in Chapter 3.

> *NOTE* **KERBEROS PROVIDES AUTHENTICATION SERVICES, NOT AUTHORIZATION SERVICES**
>
> Kerberos is designed strictly to provide mutual authentication between trusted principals within a Kerberos trusted environment. As soon as the user (principal) authenticates the resource server by using Kerberos and the resource server (principal) authenticates the user using Kerberos, Kerberos is finished with this transaction. Authorization is performed by other services on the resource server, such as the network-based server service, the file system, and perhaps even a security structure built within an application, but authorization services are never provided by Kerberos.

Directory services

At about the same time Kerberos was being developed at MIT to solve the single sign on problem, another visionary entity, called the *International Telecommunications Union - Telecom division (ITU-T)*, formerly the *International Telegraph and Telephone Consultative Committee (CCITT)*, was recognizing that computer networks were growing. Imagine a large computer network: an information system with about a billion user accounts, about a billion or so computer accounts, all the administrative tasks that a network like that would require, the security aspects of that network, the geographic diversity that a network of that size might encompass, and the networking issues related to that geographic diversity that would arise. The ITU-T, also working with the *International Organization for Standardization* (*ISO*), envisioned the issues that a large information system would create and began designing a model that would address those issues. This model was first published in 1988 and is known as *X.500 Directory Services*. The ISO released its relatively equivalent model as ISO/IEC 9594.

Implementation of the X.500 model within enterprise-level network operating systems first occurred with the *Banyon VINES* operating system, followed by *Novell Directory Services* (*NDS*) (renamed *eDirectory*), and eventually followed by *Active Directory* in the release of Windows 2000.

The directory in X.500 directory services is large and complex but is nonetheless just a database. The structure of databases (in general) is called the *schema* of the database. Schema elements include rules restricting the type of data allowed in a field, such as requiring all alpha characters or all number characters in a specific field in the database, and limiting the number of characters to some maximum in a field in the database. Schema also includes the defined relationships between different sets of data within a database.

Different implementations of the X.500 database model might vary slightly, causing their schemas to differ as well. Something called the *metadirectory* is commonly included in the directory services to facilitate the interoperability issues between implementations of the X.500 databases with their different schemas. The metadirectory is essentially an *open database connectivity* (*ODBC*) *driver*, a piece of software that recognizes the differences in the two schemas and adjusts the format or structure of the data flowing between databases to accommodate the differences required by the different schemas. ODBC drivers are covered in more detail in Chapter 9. The metadirectory allows one X.500 database with its unique and specific schema to communicate successfully and flow data with a different X.500 database with its unique and specific schema.

X.500 defines a trusted directory server that holds the database of trusted network entities, users, and computers primarily and supports and performs all the related and required directory services. These services include:

- Ensuring that the database is scalable to support a billion or so user objects, about a billion or so computer objects, and other objects (such as trust objects) along with all the descriptive and controlling attributes of each object.

- Because of these large numbers of computers and users, all these physical people and computers cannot exist in a single room or building or even a single city, so this directory must scale to essentially a global networking environment. The database must be globally distributable.

- The different geographically dispersed copies of the database must be regularly, securely, and reliably synchronized so they all hold the same information (called *knowledge consistency* or *convergence*). Directory server to directory server synchronization processes (also called replication) are included in the directory services.

- Communications channels for queries and changes to the database must occur. X.500 incorporates the *Lightweight Directory Access Protocol* (*LDAP*) for client to directory server communications.

- A security structure (access controls) must protect the directory services, their communications, and the objects and information they hold.

- Administrators, the more trusted type of user, are authorized to create, modify, and remove objects, so authoritative controls for these differing levels of privilege, in contrast to standard users with no authority to make changes to directory services, must be in place within directory services.

- Kerberos was designed to interoperate with the X.500 model and has become the de facto standard as the authentication system used in directory services–based network operating systems to establish trust between and authenticate directory objects (principals) to each other.

To support federated identity management and single sign on, in addition to the use of the metadirectory for communicating with other X.500 directory databases, other tools are often required to synchronize user passwords between different types of user databases. Many systems that support their own form of user database also provide these *password synchronization* scripts, processes, or applications so that a user can log on once, and those cached credentials are usable and correct when the user attempts to access content on these typically non-X.500 user databases.

> **NOTE X.509 CERTIFICATE SERVICES**
>
> The ITU-T also developed the model for the design, implementation, and ongoing administration of the PKI used to manage digital certificates and the use of asymmetric key cryptography to provide strong security services within the X.500 Directory Services environment. The set of security services provided includes Confidentiality, Integrity, Authentication, Nonrepudiation, and Secure Key Distribution. These topics are covered in detail in Chapter 3.

Secure European System for Applications in a Multivendor Environment (SESAME)

Secure European System for Applications in a Multivendor Environment (*SESAME*) is very similar to Kerberos, with a few changes. Instead of using symmetric key cryptography on the ticket getting ticket (TGT), SESAME uses asymmetric key cryptography and symmetric key cryptography. In addition, SESAME calls its equivalent to the TGT a *privileged attribute certificate* (*PAC*) (a certificate versus a ticket) and then relies on symmetric key cryptography for its other services. Asymmetric key cryptography and symmetric key cryptography are covered in detail in Chapter 3. The system that generates the PAC that uses the asymmetric keys in SESAME is called a *privileged attribute server* (*PAS*), not a Ticket Granting service (TGS). The SESAME services are shown in Figure 2-6.

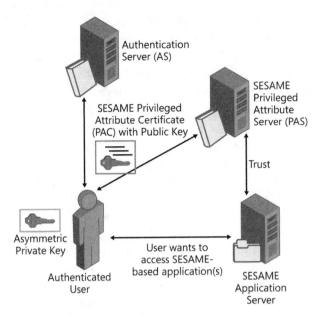

FIGURE 2-6 The SESAME authentication system

SESAME is used primarily within applications and not on the operating system level. It depends on the initial user authentication, just as Kerberos does, so SESAME has the same vulnerability to attacks on the user's password as Kerberos does. If an attacker can successfully authenticate as another user during the initial authentication process (typically password and CHAP-based), the SESAME system will provide all privileges to the attacker, by way of the PAC, that have been granted to the legitimate user.

Web-based authentication

As our infrastructure, platforms, applications, and data migrate more and more into the cloud environment, more of the applications are being accessed through web interfaces. This is placing the user interface for authentication processes more often on web servers, and that interface communicates with back-end authentication services such as X.500 directory ser-vices. The good news is that by using *Secure Sockets Layer* (*SSL*), and its newer SSL version 3.1, called *Transport Layer Security* (*TLS*), secure, web-based, and mutual authentication can be accomplished.

SSL and TLS begin by using an X.509 digital certificate on the web server to authenticate strongly on the web server to the supplicant (the unauthenticated client). After this initial server authentication is verified, and the client now knows and trusts the web server's identity, a secure, encrypted channel is constructed between the supplicant system and the web server. Then, within the encrypted channel, and with the use of the *Extensible Authentication Protocol* (*EAP*), the user authentication can be negotiated and then completed using back-end authentication services. SSL, TLS, and EAP are covered in more detail in Chapter 7.

Web servers or, more specifically, the HTTP protocol the web server uses, is a stateless proto-col, which means that the web server doesn't keep track of each user session and the specific state of each session on an ongoing basis. An HTTP-GET request arrives at the web server from a client. The web server pushes down the requested collection of files to the client and then has no idea what that client might be doing after that. End of the session.

As the first web-based applications were being implemented, when the application run-ning on the web server had to know a little more about the client's session—such as whether the user is authenticated, what the user name is, whether the user completed form 1 before allowing him access to form 2, and so on—some technique was required for the application running on the web server over the HTTP protocol to understand something about the state of the client session. *Cookies* to the rescue! The web application running on the web server would document the state of the client session in a cookie file that would be pushed down to the client computer. When the client submitted each request to the web application, the application would first retrieve and read the session state data written the client's cookie and then keep track of it and operate in a stateful manner. The cookie would be updated and pushed to the client computer by the application as the application completed each request from the client. Because cookies can also carry information about user authentication, they initially provided a form of web-based, SSO capability, but it was not the most secure way to accomplish this.

A newer technology that supports web-based authentication and single sign on is an authentication-related extension to *Extensible Markup Language (XML)* called *Security Assertion Markup Language (SAML)*. Similarly to how Kerberos works in the network operating system, SAML uses three primary roles, the principal (the user), the service provider (the web app or service the user wants access to), and a trusted identity provider such as the KDC. The service provider and the identity provider are back-end services.

The user requests access to the services that the service provider provides on the web server. The service provider must make an access control decision: Who is this user, and is this user authorized to access this service or data? The service provider then queries the identity provider for the user's authentication. If the user has not already been authenticated, the identity provider prompts the user for authentication information. If the user has already been authenticated, the identity provider, using SAML, forwards a security (identity) asser-tion conveying the user's identity and successful authentication status to the service provider so the service provider can trust the user's identity. Now the service provider can make an appropriate access control decision based on trusted user authentication and the permissions granted to that now-known user.

Cookies, XML, and SAML are covered in Chapter 9.

Authorization

After authentication has completed, and the resource server knows and trusts who the user is, the resource server must now control the access the user has, based on a predefined set of privileges granted to that user account. Some form of access control must be designed into the system to accomplish this.

> **NOTE NOT JUST FOR INFORMATION SYSTEMS**
>
> In many of the examples provided, the resources being protected are held on an information system resource server, like a file and printer-sharing server. However, recognize that the identification, authentication, authorization, and auditing processes apply to the access control of the physical environment as well as to the networking environment and information systems that provide soft resources.

A user's *privilege* is commonly defined by her collection of *rights* and *permissions*. In general, rights are assigned to users to allow the administration of system services, such as the right to change the system clock, the right to add or remove computer accounts to the directory, the right to manage the audit and security logs, or the right to back up and restore files. Permissions are typically assigned to resources such as read, write, execute, and delete permissions on files and directories. Collectively, rights and permissions define a user's level of privilege to access resources and objects.

The collection of rights and permissions for users should always be granted, strictly following the principle of least privilege. Grant only and ever the most restrictive collection of rights and permissions that enable a user to perform his work, based on his need to know and access resources, and not any more than that—the barest minimum of privilege.

Other than the built-in default system accounts and (typically) one administrator account, most systems default to *No Access* on every resource for every user, and access can only be accomplished by users if and when specific *allow* permissions are applied. In addition to allow permissions for access, many systems also provide an all-powerful and overruling *deny* permission to manage the instances when a user might unexpectedly gain inappropriate access. For example, if the members of the marketing group should never have access to the documents in the research and development (R&D) department, assign an explicit deny permission in addition to the default No Access permissions implicitly assigned. This prevents a member of the marketing department inadvertently being granted an allow permission to the documents in the R&D department through some other group membership. The explicit deny permission dominates any combination of allow permissions.

Different environments, such as commercial enterprises versus government environments, have different needs for access controls. Some require the strongest possible forms of access control, and others can tolerate some level of risk or weakness that usually affords some cost benefits. Remember that all controls, including access controls, must be cost justified. Remember also that access controls come from three families of control. They are:

- Physical
- Technical
- Administrative

 If an access control that is implemented within the environment has a particular weakness, you can often implement an additional *compensating control* of a different type to establish an acceptable level of protection. This is an example of the need for *defense in depth*. For example, if sensitive documents are well protected when they exist in a digital form, as on the information systems (computers and the network), but those controls cannot protect the same documents if they are printed, an additional administrative control, such as a *nondisclosure agreement* (NDA), can be implemented as a compensating control to protect the printed version.

The authorization life cycle

 As resources are developed in an information system, a notion of who specifically should be able to access the resource must also be developed along with a notion of who specifically should not be able to access the resource. The process of defining and implementing controls that limit who should and should not have access to any specific information asset is called *provisioning*. Provisioning must occur just prior to when a resource is first made available to users and for every new user as she is added to the system.

The provisioning process must be fully documented in the policy documents of the organization, and all those involved with the provisioning process must fully understand and adhere to the required provisioning procedures. The data custodian, the administrator who implements the rights and permissions, should not perform those tasks unless the provisioning request has been fully documented and fully approved by the appropriate individuals. Typically, those approving individuals include the direct supervisor (manager) for the user, the data owner, and, sometimes, a member of the HR department. A member of the security team should also be a required approver to identify potential conflicts of interest, violations of policy, or the excessive aggregation of privilege—too much authority that could lead to fraud.

 Periodically, a review of the assigned privileges should be performed to verify that the principle of least privilege is being applied in every instance. This *privilege review* might be a random spot-check or a comprehensive review of all assigned privileges. Users with access to the greatest value of resources should be reviewed more often than those with minimal access. This is typically considered an auditing function. The ongoing and routine monitoring of the environment will also identify areas in which users might have an excess of privilege. The periodic auditing and routine monitoring of privileges might also be required by applicable laws and regulations.

Any time a user no longer requires access to a resource or no longer needs to perform administrative tasks, the unneeded rights and permissions should be removed for that user. *Privilege revocation* processes should occur regularly to maintain adherence to the principle of least privilege.

Over time, it is common for users to transfer to different positions or departments or be promoted in an organization. As a user changes positions for any reason, his resource access requirements often need change. This requires granting access to new resources, an increase of privilege. However, all too often while the addition of privilege is accomplished to allow access to new resources, the revocation of privileges needed for the previous position that are no longer needed is overlooked. This results in an excess of privilege through authorization creep, or authorization aggregation, which violates the principle of least privilege. Provisioning procedures must include requirements to document the former access and verification of the revocation of those unneeded privileges for the user. The aforementioned auditing procedures help identify instances of authorization creep and should trigger the appropriate adjustments in the user's privileges.

Mandatory access control

One of the strongest technical authorization (access control) mechanisms is the mandatory access control (MAC) model. The MAC model is implemented primarily when the value of the resources is very high, so high, in fact, that this model is rarely used in the commercial world but finds its home mostly within the government and military information systems. When the protection of the information assets equates to, for example, the safety of human lives and the global economic balance or the secret that Elvis Presley still lives and is actually an alien from planet Zennon, the higher costs associated with the MAC model of access control are justified.

The MAC model is structured on a logical lattice and relies on documented definitions of the sensitivity levels of data elements (objects) called *classifications*. Each classification level is assigned a *label*, and the appropriate label is assigned by the system to any objects that meet that definition of sensitivity. Further, this assignment of the labels on objects cannot be overridden. That label becomes bound to the object and becomes the object's classification. Similarly, users (subjects) of the system are assigned a *clearance* label based on the level of trust that management has for the subject and the subject's need to know. Changing the clearance label on a subject is slow and difficult by design.

MAC systems often use four or five levels of sensitivity. In the government world, a common set of labels is:

- **TOP SECRET** Breach would lead to exceptionally grave damage to national security.
- **SECRET** Breach would lead to serious damage to national security.
- **CONFIDENTIAL** Breach would cause damage or be prejudicial to national security.

- **SENSITIVE BUT UNCLASSIFIED or RESTRICTED** Breach would cause undesirable effects to national security.
- **UNCLASSIFIED** Although a label but technically not a classification, includes all other information assets. Users without a clearance might be able to access these information assets.

The descriptions provided for these government labels are how the US government defines these classifications. They are provided as a reference only. Remember that the exam is an international exam and very likely will not focus on US-centric laws or definitions.

In the commercial world, management can choose any labeling scheme it prefers, such as:

- CRITICAL
- RESTRICTED
- INTERNAL
- PUBLIC

At a basic level on MAC systems, when the subject's clearance matches the object's classification, information can flow. If the subject has a clearance of SECRET, and the object has a classification of SECRET, the subject can access the object. Figure 2-7 shows an example of the MAC model.

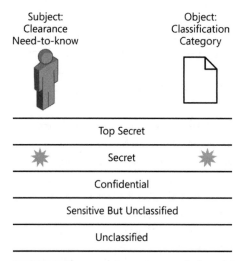

FIGURE 2-7 The mandatory access control model

 At the next level of complexity, also shown in Figure 2-7, not only must the subject's clearance equal the object's classification but a second set of parameters is set for the subject and the object to control access. A second label is applied to the subject, called the subject's *need to know*, and a second label is applied to the object called the object's *category*. This second level of control enables the system to further limit the subject's access to objects. For example, if a subject works on Project XYZ, his need-to-know label can be assigned as XYZ. The objects related to Project XYZ will receive a category label of XYZ. At this second level of complexity within the MAC system, the subject's clearance label and his need-to-know label must match the object's classification label and category label for the access to be granted and for the information to flow.

In operation, the MAC system, not a user, makes the determination of the sensitivity of any data element, and after a label is assigned to an object, that label is difficult to change. This inertia, or the resistance to change designed into the MAC system, is an extension of the *tranquility principle*, the intent to maintain strict stability within the system. Any change can only occur through a lengthy review period that carefully considers any increase in vulnerability, exposure, conflict of interest, and so on that might occur from the proposed change. This long delay and resistance to change is one of the areas of increased cost of the MAC system and one of the main reasons the MAC model is usually unacceptable in a commercial environment, where fast adjustments are required to maximize revenue and profits continuously.

Following is a word-association list to help you memorize the attributes of the MAC model. Every time the mandatory access control model is referenced, this collection of terms should come to mind:

- Strong
- Expensive
- Slow
- Government
- Lattice

- Labels
- Clearance
- Classification
- Need to know
- Category

Because the controls for the MAC model are implemented within the information system (the server), the protection of the information assets is functional only when the information asset remains on the system. Typically, an administrative control, like an NDA, a confidentiality agreement, an acceptable use policy, a data protection policy, and strict laws that carry massive penalties, helps protect the asset if a user were to print a copy of a sensitive document and take it away from the system. Nevertheless, you are relying on the user to be trustworthy aware of the administrative control, and willing to abide by it for it to be effective.

MAC is implemented in several operating systems, including:

- **SELinux** Secure Edition Linux (National Security Agency (NSA))
- **SCOMP** Secure Communications Processor (Honeywell)
- **Blacker** (Unisys)
- **AppArmor** SUSE, Ubuntu (Novell, Canonical Ltd.)
- **FreeBSD** TrustedBSD project
- **Purple Penelope** A MAC hybrid (UK Defense Research Agency (DRA))

Interestingly, elements of MAC are being implemented in the latest version of Windows Server 2012, a classically discretionary access control (DAC)–based operating system, forming a MAC/DAC hybrid operating system. Although complex to implement and manage, and definitely not for beginners, Windows Server 2012 includes mandatory integrity controls, automatic system-assigned clearance labels for users, automatic system-assigned classification labels for files, and access restrictions based on these labels. Expect to see these MAC elements develop further over time and perhaps eventually become a standard component of the security architecture of these commercially used implementations of information systems.

Systems that use the MAC model can be implemented using different combinations of controls but primarily fall into four modes that enforce the rules of the MAC model but vary based on the number of technical filters, or controls implemented on the system. Fewer technical controls means that administrative controls, physical controls, or both are likely being used in conjunction with the technical MAC-based controls to establish the level of security required by policy. The first mode relies solely on physical controls, simplifying the security structure required on the information system. In effect, no security structure is required on the system in the first mode. The other modes add one technical control to the preceding mode, making the security structure more complex, but provide a more granular level of control for the information assets and greater versatility in the use of the system. As previously described, administrative controls are added to these MAC systems to protect any content that is taken away from the system, such as a printed copy or a copy of the file burned to a CD-ROM or copied to a USB flash drive. The four MAC modes are:

- **Dedicated Security Mode**   All users who can gain physical access to this system can access all data. All data on this system has the same classification label. For example, a user with a SECRET clearance can access all content on the SECRET classified system. This system has no technical controls.

  - The clearance of the subject matches the classification of all data on the system.

  - The need to know of the subject matches the category of all data on the system.

- **System High-Security Mode**   All users who can gain physical access to this system can access some of the data, based on their need to know. All data on this system has the same classification label but might have different category labels. For example, a user with a SECRET clearance can access some of the content on the SECRET classified system as long as her need to know matches the category of the data. This system has one technical control—a control to deny access if the need to know does not match the category.

  - The clearance of the subject matches the classification of all data on the system.

  - The need to know of the subject matches the category for *some* of the data on the system.

- **Compartmented Security Mode**   All users who can gain physical access to this system can access some of the data, based on their need to know and access permissions assigned by management. The data on this system has classification labels that match or are lower than the user's clearance. The data on this system might have different category labels. For example, a user with a SECRET clearance can access some of the data on the system that is holding SECRET, CONFIDENTIAL, SENSITIVE BUT UNCLASSIFIED, and UNCLASSIFIED content as long as his need to know matches the category of the data, and management has not assigned restricting permissions on the data. This system has two technical controls—a control to deny access if the need to know does not match the category and a control to deny access if deny permissions are assigned on the data.

- The clearance of the subject matches *the highest level* of classification of data on the system.

- The need to know of the subject matches the category for *some* of the data on the system.

- Management approves access to specific content and *assigns permissions* to restrict access to some content.

- **Multi-Level Security Mode**   All users who can gain physical access to this system can access some of the data, based on their clearance, need to know, and access permissions assigned by management. The data on this system has classification labels that might be different from the user's clearance, higher or lower. The data on this system might have different category labels. For example, a user with a SECRET clearance can access some of the content on the system that is holding TOP SECRET, SECRET, CONFIDENTIAL, SENSITIVE BUT UNCLASSIFIED, and UNCLASSIFIED content as long as her clearance equals or exceeds the classification of the content, her need to know matches the category of the content, and management has not assigned restricting permissions on the content. This system has three technical controls—a control to deny access if the need to know does not match the category, a control to deny access if deny permissions are assigned on the data, and a control to deny access if the classification of the data is higher than the clearance of the user.

- The clearance of the subject matches or dominates *some* classification of data on the system.

- The need to know of the subject matches the category for *some* of the data on the system.

- Management approves access to specific content and *assigns permissions* to restrict access to some content.

Discretionary access control

Discretionary access control (DAC) is a commonly used technical access control model on commercial information systems and on many government systems that do not store, process, or transmit classified data. Most computers in use today have the DAC model implemented in the operating system. DAC establishes the premise that the creator of the data is the owner of that data, and the owner of the data has full control of his data, including the ability to assign (grant) permissions on the data to other users at the owner's discretion (thus the name). Administrative controls, such as policy and, more specifically, the data classification program, typically define how access permissions should be granted and controlled for each data element (file, database record, and so on), but DAC leaves it up to the owner to implement the permissions in a manner that meets the policy specification. This makes DAC easier to implement and easier to adjust but makes it weaker than MAC. Individual users can forget the rules of the policies, willfully violate the policies "because it is easier," or ignore the policies because of social compatibility objectives (such as when BoBo is sweet on LuLu and decides to grant LuLu full control of his files in violation of policy). These inconsistencies weaken the security posture of the information system and of the enterprise at large.

DAC is a technical, identity-based access control typically requiring a user authentication process to establish trust for the identity of the user before any access to data or resources can even be considered. Each user logs on to a unique user account, one account per user. DAC provides for the assignment of permissions on objects such as files, directories, network shares, and other resources. Classically, DAC defaults to No Access for all objects and then supports the assignment of allow permissions to provide access to the data. A kernel-mode component of the operating system called the *security reference monitor* compares the trusted identity of the user, based on a prior authentication process, to the *access control list (ACL)* bound to the object and then provides access based on the permissions on that ACL granted to the identified user account.

DAC binds an access control list (ACL) to each object at the creation of that object. This ACL is a list of all users who have permissions on the object and defines those specific permissions for each user, such as read, write, execute, and delete. Figure 2-8 shows an example of an ACL as implemented in Windows.

FIGURE 2-8 An access control list (ACL)

In most enterprise-level information systems, the information assets of the enterprise are stored on servers, and those servers are administered by a central network operations team such as administrators who act as the system custodians and, often, as the data custodians as well. In this case, the administrators assume the role of the owner of each object on the server(s) and then manage the permissions in this centralized administrative model. In this example of a DAC implementation, the permissions typically are applied much more consistently, ideally by strictly following policy, and provide a stronger security posture for the information system.

The use of DAC introduces a vulnerability or two. It enables the escalation of privilege and the transfer of privilege on objects. If a user creates an object such as a data object, that user is the owner of the object and has full control of the object. If the owner grants a user the read permission only, the intent is that the user should be allowed only to read the data, never escalate his level of privilege, and never be able to grant others privilege on the data object. The DAC system supports this intent, but only on this one copy of the data object.

When the user accesses the file and reads the file based on her read-only permissions, unfortunately, the DAC system allows her to perform a Save As function to create and save a second copy of this read-only file. Because the user created the copy of the file, the user is the owner of this second copy, with full control permissions. This is escalation of privilege, and it violates the intended privilege level granted to the user. The user can now modify this copy, an unintended level of privilege. Further, as the owner of the second copy of the file, the user can grant others permissions on the file. This is transferring privilege, again in violation of the intended privilege level of the file. The technical controls built into the DAC-based system fail to protect the content in these cases, so administrative controls are required to support the intended security objectives. Policy documents must be developed, and users who are trusted and agree to abide by the company's policies must be taught these rules. Management must then monitor and enforce these policies and address any violations effectively.

In DAC, the user's identity is known, and permissions are granted to the user. As the user launches programs, the user's access token is bound to each process the application spawns. As that application attempts to access resources, the user's access token that was bound to the process is compared to the ACL that lists the users and their respective privilege (access levels) on the target object. In this manner, the process seemingly becomes the subject, the active entity desirous of access to the object. However, the process is inanimate and is performing tasks on behalf of the user whose access token is bound to the process. The subject virtually always links back to a user object, a human person, or a service account.

Because of the way the user's access token is bound to the process acting as the user's delegate, when an attacker can exploit an active process through vulnerabilities introduced in the software application by poor coding, he gains access to the user's access token. Having access to the user's access token means that the attacker's malware is now being executed at the privilege level of the user whose process code was compromised. The attacker's malicious code can also access everything the user can access. This is why processes should always be executed at the least level of privilege possible that still allows the process to complete its work.

DAC is implemented in many operating systems, including:

- Windows
- MAC OSX
- Linux
- UNIX

An extension of the ACL in DAC is the *access control matrix*. Each object (such as a file) in a DAC-based information system has an ACL bound to it that describes the users who have permissions on the object and what each user's permission level is on that object. The access control matrix is the collection of all ACLs for all the objects in the information system. It lists every subject (user) in the enterprise on the left vertical axis and every object (file) in the enterprise on the top horizontal axis. It then fills the matrix at the intersection of each subject and object with the permission level the subject has been granted on the object. Figure 2-9 shows an example of an access control matrix.

	Objects				
Subjects	Object 1	Object 2	Object 3	Object 4	Object N
User 1	R	RW	No Access	No Access	Full Control
User 2	RW	No Access	RW	Full Control	R
User 3	No Access	No Access	RW	Full Control	RW
User 4	R	No Access	RW	R	R
User N	No Access	RW	Full Control	RW	RW

Capability

ACL

FIGURE 2-9 The access control matrix

The row in the matrix lists a user and every permission that user has been granted on every object in the information system. The row is defined as the user's *capability*. Capability is bound the user. The column in the matrix lists an object and every permission that object has available for every user in the information system. The column is defined as the object's ACL. As previously stated, the ACL is bound to the object.

Role-based access control

Role-based access control (RBAC) is a technical control model. It is much like a simplified implementation of DAC. However, instead of each user logging on to a unique user account, one account per user, which could be hundreds or thousands or even tens of thousands of user accounts like DAC, RBAC defines only a few user accounts, maybe three or four, such as SysAdmin, DBAdmin, and User, for example. These accounts are based on a job role in the organization or application. Permissions are granted to each role (account) as appropriate, and then multiple users who can perform the same types of functions log on to the same role (account) and access resources based on the permissions granted to the role. The reduction of user accounts from tens of thousands down to three or four greatly reduces the complexity of the security system and the administrative effort required and simplifies the ACL for each object.

EXAM TIP

Discretionary access control implies that the owner of an object controls the permissions assignment at his discretion. Nondiscretionary access control implies that the system, and not the owner of an object, controls the permissions assignment. MAC and RBAC are both forms of nondiscretionary access controls.

In the classic RBAC model, discrete user identities are not captured. Individual users do not log on to their individual user accounts. Many users log on to the same role-based account by using the name of the role as the user name and the shared password for that role account. The access control system, and the logging (or auditing) system, cannot identify which individual logged on to the DBAdmin role and performed some task. Dozens of people might be logged on to the User role at any given time, and there is no way to identify the actions of any one person from the actions of another person. The classic implementation of RBAC can be used whenever the need to track the individual is not required.

In actual use, RBAC is often implemented within larger applications such as database applications. RBAC can also be used when an enterprise has a high rate of turnover, and the administrative effort required to create, provision permissions, and remove accounts continually is prohibitive.

However, the classic model of RBAC is commonly violated when RBAC is implemented at the operating-system level. In most cases, it is unacceptable to lose track of individual identities on information systems. Most policies, laws, and regulations require an audit trail, so discrete user identities are required. To satisfy this need to track identities in the logs and take advantage of the simplified security architecture and administrative benefits of RBAC, the roles of RBAC are often implemented as *security groups* at the operating-systems level within DAC-based systems that support discrete user identities.

A few security groups are defined that map to common functional needs, such as the job roles of Accounting, R&D, and Production. For example, suppose all members of the Accounting group need access to 80 percent or 90 percent of the same resources. Those common permission requirements are granted to the Accounting security group, simplifying the security structure, like RBAC does. Then, the appropriate (DAC-based) user accounts from the Accounting department are added to the security group and inherit the permissions granted to the group. In this manner, user identities are available for logging and auditing purposes as well as individual and granular permissions, and because of the role-based security groups, the ACLs and the administrative effort are reduced. Explicitly assigned permissions can still be granted to the individual user accounts as needed to accommodate the user's needs for the 10 percent or 20 percent of the permissions not already granted through the group membership.

When implemented in this manner, security groups differ from the classic model of RBAC in a second way. In a classic RBAC system, a user can only log on to one role at a time to acquire the collection of privileges granted to that one RBAC user account and role. However, when roles are implemented in the form of security groups, technically a violation of the academic RBAC model, a user can be a member of multiple security groups at one time. He can then acquire all the privileges granted to the individual user as well as the collection of all privileges granted to the multiple security groups the user is a member of.

EXAM TIP

Explicit permissions are assigned directly to a user account. Implicit permissions are permissions that are assigned to a security group, and the user inherits those permissions through group membership.

Rule-based access control

Rule-based access control is a technical control model. In the classic model, as in role-based access control, the discrete user identity is not required. In the classic model for rule-based access control, the rules apply to all users. An example of a rule-based access control is a firewall rule that rejects inbound Simple Network Management Protocol (SNMP) packets. (SNMP is used to interrogate and reconfigure network systems, and you generally don't want those types of communications from the Internet. SNMP is covered in more detail in Chapter 7.) It doesn't matter who the sender is, SNMP is not allowed to enter the corporate network from the Internet.

Another example of a rule-based access control is a disk space quota on users' home folders or their mailbox. Regardless of who the user is, if her mailbox has more than 500 GB of content, the user account associated with the mailbox is not allowed to send email.

In addition, like role-based access control, the academic model for rule-based access control is commonly violated in implementation. Most implementations of rule-based access control are aware of discrete user identities. Therefore, a rule is established for all users without regard to identity, but then exceptions to the rule might be granted on an individual basis. For example, a rule might be set to allow all users access to the Internet from 7 A.M. to 6 P.M. only.

Then, as an exception to the rule, the identity of the user can be used to adjust the firewall rule base in proxy firewalls—one user, BoBo, is only allowed to browse the Internet from 2 P.M. until 5 P.M. Another rule for all users might be a 250 MB limit on email mailboxes. If the boss wants an extra 500 GB for his mailbox, the implementation of rule-based quota access controls on mail servers can typically take into account the discrete user identity and allow one user a different mailbox quota.

Decentralized access control

With decentralized access control, individual users manage the access control to their information assets, and there is no central administration for the information system. Users are to apply access controls in compliance with the corporate policy. The workgroup type of network and ad hoc networks are implementations of decentralized access–controlled information systems. This form of access control is faster than centralized access control but often inconsistent and incomplete in the implementation of permissions. (Centralized access control is covered in the next section, "Centralized access control.")

Administration of decentralized access–controlled environments typically occurs faster because of the low level of formality and procedure. When a change is warranted, the individual user simply makes the change to his local system on the spot. But these environments are incomplete and less consistent because if a user is away from the office or her computer when the need for a change is identified, that user cannot make the change at that time and might not ever make the change, leading to inconsistencies and holes in the security of the information system. Users might also forget the rule defined in policy and even willfully violate policy because it is easier or because of social compatibility objectives, similar to user-managed DAC.

Centralized access control

Centralized access control is managed by a central person or team in compliance with the corporate policy. The centralized access control structure is typically slower to respond to a needed change than the decentralized model, largely due to the well-developed structure and procedure for making changes to the security of the environment. Typically, a person or team is dedicated to network administration and therefore more likely to follow policies and procedures more closely. This form of access control is better at full compliance with the corporate policy, resulting in improved consistency and completeness for each adjustment required.

Hybrid access control

In all actuality, the real world primarily operates in a hybrid access control implementation in which different administrative teams autonomously manage their location or division (centralized) and then communicate and coordinate as peers with other administrative teams within the organization (decentralized). Further, within the locations or divisions, although the central administrative team manages the information systems (centralized), most users are allowed to manage many of their own information assets, perhaps even storing them locally on their laptop or workstation computer (decentralized).

Centralized access control technologies

A family of technologies helps support centralized access control for remote users that need to access the corporate network environment. These technologies are designed to provide remote access and implement the AAA services, authentication, authorization and accounting (back in those days). They include:

- **RADIUS**   Remote Authentication Dial-In User Service
- **TACACS**   Terminal Access Controller Access Control System
- **Diameter**   The next generation of RADIUS
  (Diameter is twice as good as RADIUS: *d = 2r*)

RADIUS

RADIUS was developed by Livingston Enterprises, Inc. in 1991 to satisfy the needs of AAA. It was released and has been adopted as IETF RFC 2865 and 2866 open standards. The demand for AAA services came from the proliferation of modems and dial-up bulletin boards. (The Internet was still embryonic compared to today.) Today, these technologies manage not only the dial-in user; remote access has evolved to include access by VPN and wireless connection, and these technologies have grown to manage the AAA services on these connection types as well.

In the early days, a common approach for the bulletin board was to charge a monthly membership fee for various levels of access—like a gold membership, a silver membership, and a bronze membership—and then charge a small fee for each minute you were on the bulletin board, for each kB uploaded, for each kB downloaded, or some combination thereof.

A RADIUS server would be positioned between the network access server (NAS) and the resources the dial-in users wanted access to. The NAS server would have one or as many as 256 modems attached by serial (Comm) cables. Each modem would be connected to a tele-phone line.

As a call would come in, the NAS server would answer the call and forward the authen-tication details to the RADIUS server. The RADIUS server would have a user database to authenticate against or could back-end into other user databases, such as a directory service database (domain controller), for authentication services. The RADIUS server would manage the user authentication processes (authentication). If all went well and the user was a member subscriber and able to log on, RADIUS would identify and then manage the access level of the user (authorization)—the gold level, silver level, or bronze level of access, for example. Meanwhile, the RADIUS server would be keeping track of the ongoing billable amount for the user, based on the user's activities on the bulletin board (accounting). Today, the accounting component isn't quite what is needed; auditing of the users' activities is needed, so the third A in AAA now commonly and more accurately refers to auditing or accountability. Figure 2-10 shows a typical implementation of RADIUS.

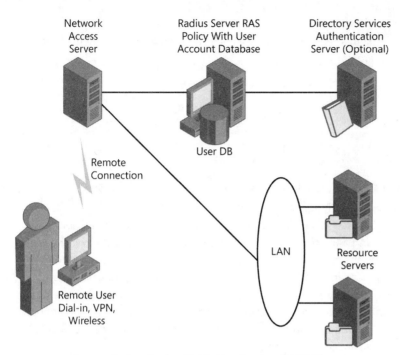

FIGURE 2-10 Remote Authentication Dial-In User Services (RADIUS)

Newer implementations of RADIUS include the ability to define various policies that can control many aspects of the remote access session. These policies can be linked to individual users and to security groups. After a user successfully authenticates, the user and the collection of groups the user is a member of is determined. Then the policies linked to each one (user and groups) are aggregated to define the access control rules to be applied to this remote access session. Policy filters can include day of week, time of day, source phone number or IP address, destination phone number or IP address, encryption requirements, and many more. This feature provides strong security and control for remote access for dial-in, VPN, and wireless connections.

TACACS

Terminal Access Controller Access Control System (TACACS) operated as an AAA service mostly on UNIX systems and was replaced by RADIUS and by XTACACS (eXtended TACACS), a proprietary implementation from Cisco Systems. A later implementation is TACACS+, which is open standard. XTACACS and TACACS+ separate the three AAA services onto three systems.

DIAMETER

Diameter is the latest implementation of an AAA service. It has made improvements over RADIUS in the following areas:

- Authentication
- Security
- Proxying
- Message Transport
- Session control
- New support for several higher-layer protocols

More important, Diameter is designed to provide AAA services for wireless and cellular networks. A requirement of true 4G cellular networks is to provide connection reliability as if you were connected using a physical wire. To accomplish this, it is likely that whichever cellular carrier is providing the strongest signal to your phone is the carrier required to carry your connection, even if that carrier isn't the one you subscribe to from your cellular service. Diameter supports switching your connection not just from cell to cell but also from cellular provider network to a different (competing) cellular provider network and providing enough detail to ensure proper accounting. Figure 2-11 shows how Diameter is intended to allow a user to roam between cellular carrier networks.

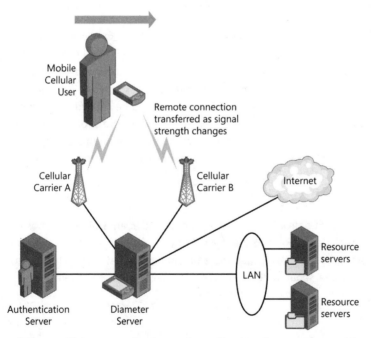

FIGURE 2-11 Diameter transfers from cell to cell and carrier to carrier to achieve the strongest possible signal for the user

As Diameter is implemented within the cellular network structure, that third A in AAA returns to imply accounting once again.

> **NOTE 4G CELLULAR? NO, IT DOES NOT EXIST YET.**
>
> True 4G cellular is quite a ways away. Current implementations often claim to be 4G but are actually 4G LTE - Long Term Evolution, an improvement over 3G but nowhere near the true 4G specification from the ITU-T.

Other types of access controls

Following are several other technologies that help support access control for local and remote users who need to access information assets and networking resources.

THE CONSTRAINED INTERFACE

The constrained interface limits users' access to the underlying software and data resources. Many automatic teller machines (ATMs) are computers running Windows XP, but they are configured to launch into a single, full-screen application that only allows the few functions appropriate for the self-service bank customers. Kiosks are also often full-blown computers with full-featured operating systems but disallow all functions except those few that are appropriate for their users. Menuing systems, like those often used on Telnet servers, are a form of the constrained interface, as are database views that limit a user to viewing the 50 records she has permission to read from the database of 2,000 records.

THE HARDWARE GUARD

The hardware guard is implemented as two network interface cards (NIC) installed in a single computer system, with one NIC attached to a network segment with data and processes of one sensitivity level and the other NIC attached to a network segment with data and processes of a different sensitivity level. The system is configured to allow only one NIC at a time to be active and never to route packets from one NIC to the other NIC.

THE SOFTWARE GUARD

The software guard is a software front-end application that filters access based on some form, limited by the user's identity and privilege level.

TEMPORAL ACCESS CONTROLS

Any access control that controls based on some time, date, or condition is a temporal access control. If the user can access the Internet on Mondays and Tuesdays from noon to 5 P.M., this is a temporal access control. Another form of temporal access control is a user account made active for seven days at the beginning of each quarter and then automatically disabled for the remainder of the quarter. Alternatively, if a user is working on a project for widgets this month, he can access the widget database for only this month.

Another, less obvious, form of a temporal access control is implemented when a user is accessing database A but may not access database B. However, anytime the user is not accessing database A, she can access database B. The hardware guard described earlier in this section is an example of this type of temporal access control.

 Quick check

1. Which authorization model is the strongest and most commonly used on government information systems?

2. Which authorization model allows the owner of the file to grant permissions on the file freely?

Quick check answers

1. The mandatory access control (MAC) model

2. The discretionary access control (DAC) model

Auditing

Auditing is primarily a detective control but also acts as a deterrent when users are aware of the auditing activities. Auditing is the capture, protected storage, and review of events that occur within the corporate environment. Auditing should be the trigger for response when anomalies are detected. Anomalies that are identified should be added to a watch list. Most systems perform some level of event logging by default and, typically, store those event logs on the local system. Some systems with limited or no storage for the logs only support the generation of the logs and then have to send the logged data over the network to a log repository for storage and later review. The syslog protocol was designed to provide that networking service.

Historically, logged data was only ever looked at for troubleshooting purposes when the system was malfunctioning. The logging system has now become a new facet of many corporate networks. In recent years, various industry, financial, and privacy laws and regulations have been implemented with rigid compliance requirements that have forced companies to build and maintain a whole new networked system to satisfy logging, monitoring, and auditing requirements.

The requirements for logging and the details of the logging systems should be defined within the policy documents of the organization and must include related requirements from any applicable laws and regulations. The requirements and the procedures for the real-time monitoring and periodic review of the logged events must also be fully documented. Criteria must be defined that establish anomalous events that require additional investigation as well as the point at which the event is escalated to incident status, requiring a response.

Logged events should, at a minimum, capture the following details, and these details may be extended if the enterprise is subject to legal or regulatory compliance requirements:

- Date
- Time
- Source system (IP address)
- User ID
- Event category
- Event details
- Success/Failure status

Laws and regulations that define a standard for the logging system generally include requirements similar to the following:

- All systems within the scope of compliance, and those systems that monitor or administer systems within the scope of compliance, must produce event logs that contain a defined level of detail as previously described.
- All logs within scope must be recorded locally (for local auditing and troubleshooting) and must be transmitted in real time to a network-based log repository.
- The transmission of logged data must use guaranteed delivery protocols.
- The transmission and storage must be protected against unauthorized access, unauthorized monitoring, and tampering (encryption).
- At the time of reception, the log repository system must produce integrity validation information to be used to verify the integrity of the log data at some point in the future.
- Access to logged data must be restricted to those with a business need to know.
- All logged data must be reviewed on at least a daily basis for anomalies. Real-time monitoring is preferred.
- All access (read, modify, delete) to the logging path and the logged data must be logged.
- Log reviewers may not have the authority to modify the logs (read-only access).
- For correlation purposes, all systems being logged must be configured to use a (typically hierarchical) time synchronization mechanism (such as the network time protocol (NTP)) and use industry standard time sources.
- Time synchronization must be periodically verified on all systems within scope.
- Time clocks on systems within scope must be protected from unauthorized modification.
- Modification to the time clocks on systems within scope must be logged.
- The logged data must be retained for some defined period in a manner that supports the immediate access, review, and integrity verification for any logged data (for review and auditing purposes).

Figure 2-12 shows the basics of such a logging system.

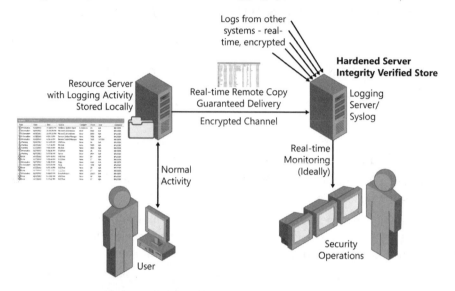

FIGURE 2-12 A typical logging system

Targeted and specialized logging is often referred to as auditing. In Windows, auditing is enabled through the local computer policy or through the Group Policy Object (GPO) when the computer is joined to a directory service domain. Figure 2-13 shows the GPO configuration for generating audit logs on a system when the computer becomes a member of the directory service domain.

EXAM TIP

Strong policies, laws, and regulations typically require the use of internal auditing to identify gaps in compliance and external auditing by a hired, unbiased, third-party auditor to perform the formal compliance report. This form of internal plus external auditing has become a common standard of due care. An enterprise is, in theory, negligent if not performing both internal and external auditing.

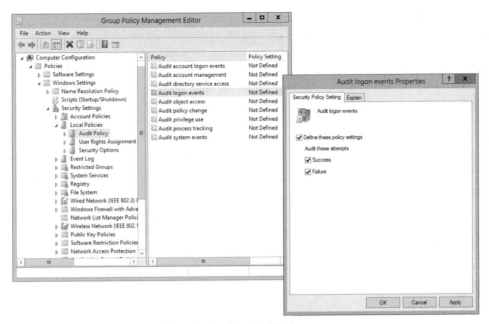

FIGURE 2-13 Configuring targeted logging (auditing) in Windows

The protections required of the logging system are to defend against an unauthorized user or an attacker deleting or modifying the logged events related to an attack. The unauthorized alteration or deletion of log data is commonly called *scrubbing the logs*.

Real-time monitoring systems are commonly called *security information and event management (SIEM) systems*. SIEM systems can also be referred to as SIM and SEM systems. These systems have been developed to help companies satisfy legal and regulatory requirements and minimize losses by quickly identifying misconfigurations, breaches, and attacks within the information systems. SIEM systems often include secure and guaranteed transmission, a hardened and secure log repository like the logging systems described earlier, but also take it a step further. Most SIEM systems implement various levels of artificial intelligence to parse the logs programmatically from virtually every type and vendor of systems found within the corporate network, correlate events from every system, and recognize anomalies ranging from the basic and obvious to those that are very sophisticated and stealthy.

The SIEM system is often very time-consuming and expensive to acquire, implement, maintain, and monitor over time. The monitoring of the SIEM systems typically requires specialized training and should be accompanied by a solid background in network technologies, network architecture, penetration testing, and IT security.

After the retention period has expired for logged data, if the company has no business need for the log data, the *secure disposal* of the expired data should be performed. Simply deleting the data from the log repository server is not sufficiently secure. Secure disposal of digital data (commonly stored on magnetic media such as hard disk drives) is to overwrite the files with random binary bits, save the overwritten file, and then delete the overwritten file. Otherwise, numerous recovery techniques could recover the deleted content. Another technique is to destroy the media fully by drilling holes through the disk drives, shredding the disk drives or backup tapes, or disposing of the storage media in an incinerator. The legal department is often eager for the secure disposal of expired and valueless data.

EXAM TIP

A security assessment, vulnerability scanning, and penetration testing can be considered auditing functions because these will identity the state of security for the environment, They can detect changes in that security posture as compared with a baseline and a previous assessment, scan, or test. These are covered in more detail in Chapter 10, "Operations security."

Intrusion detection systems and intrusion prevention systems

Intrusion detection systems (IDS) and intrusion prevention systems (IPS) are two of the security systems that might be required to satisfy legal and regulatory requirements but even if not mandated by laws and regulations are often a standard part of an enterprise-level network infrastructure. The output from these systems should be sent to the logging system and to the SIEM or other system for real-time monitoring if possible. IDS and IPS systems are nearly identical, with one exception:

- The IDS monitors, detects anomalies, and alerts.
- The IPS monitors, detects anomalies, alerts, and implements a defensive response.

The types of response an IPS can implement might be to detect an attack from a specific source IP address and then dynamically assemble a rule to deny traffic from that source IP address (or a range of source IP addresses). Another response mechanism is to send the legitimate client reset packets or de-authentication packets, causing the client's session with an attacker to fail repeatedly. Another IPS response is to *quarantine* the malicious or suspicious executable process and disallow its execution, now or in the future. When the IPS implements the quarantine process, it typically encrypts the executable so it cannot be executed and moves the encrypted executable to a secured directory. Only the IPS process has the decryption key, and only the IPS process may retrieve the file from the secured directory. An authorized user, by way of the IPS application, could have the IPS application restore the quarantined executable (decrypt and return the file to its original location) if he trusts the executable and requires its continued operation.

There is a middle ground on these two systems as well, although not all that common. A system called an *IDS response system* uses the classic IDS, but the alert from the IDS is sent to a different, network-based security system that can parse (read) the alert and dynamically implement a defensive response. The IDS does not implement any response other than its alert. A second security system is required to implement the response.

> **NOTE IDS AND IPS**
>
> To keep the remainder of this section clutter free, when the term IDS is used, recognize that the IPS does everything the IDS does plus implement the defensive response.

IDS and IPS are well known for their difficulty to configure and tune and their tendency to trigger a high number of false positive alerts. Attackers can use the IPS against the enterprise; this is described later in this section.

There are *network-based IDS* (*NIDS*) and *host-based IDS* (*HIDS*). The IDS and IPS systems can be used to monitor the network to detect known network attacks, anomalous network traffic, and protocol configurations. This type of system is called a network-based IDS (NIDS or NIPS). The NIDS monitors a segment on the network and inspects each packet on the segment. It does not understand anything other than the packet, including its payload and its header. For example, the NIPS would identify an attack such as the SYN flood from a specific IP address and would dynamically implement a rule to deny all traffic from that source IP address (the attacker's system) past this point on the segment.

The IDS and IPS systems can also be used on network endpoints to monitor the processes and execution code for known malicious and suspicious activities. These systems are called *host-based IDS* (HIDS or HIPS). A *host-based IPS* analyzes activity only within a single system and not anything on the network. The host-based systems are typically capable of quarantining the suspicious or known bad process, so these systems are typically HIPS. For example, the HIPS systems would quarantine a text editor that opened a network listener. Text editors have no need to listen to the network. This is an indication of a Trojan and malicious application that should be quarantined.

These IDS and IPS systems use different detection mechanisms. *Signature-based or knowledge-based detection* is a commonly used detection mechanism. Signature-based detection systems compare the packet or code to the stored signature of a previously detected attack. This detection mechanism tends to produce the fewest false positive alerts but cannot detect new attacks. The attack signatures are stored in a signature database that requires frequent updating.

Another form of signature-based analysis is the verification of the system's configuration. Core operating system files are integrity verified regularly (to detect tampering), using hashing algorithms and other metrics. System logs, configuration parameters, and configuration files are monitored for changes from day to day, compared either to a previous state with a known good configuration or to a gold-standard system with the approved standard configuration and only the approved, installed applications.

 Another detection mechanism is *behavior-based* or *anomaly-based*. This detection mechanism monitors normal behavior to learn and establish a normal baseline. Then thresholds, also called *clipping levels*, are defined to establish the acceptable amount of deviation from the baseline. The thresholds statistically establish a boundary of tolerance on the deviation from the normal level of traffic (or activity). A network behavior-based IDS would, for example, monitor the volume of FTP traffic over time and establish a baseline normal level. The sensor uses a sliding average over time to adjust the statistical boundaries of tolerance for deviation automatically, based on the most recently learned state of normal. If the level of FTP traffic jumps suddenly, breaching the upper threshold, the IDS would send an alert. Often, when a clipping level is breached, the event is analyzed and, if warranted, added to a watch list, like a new signature, to identify the occurrence of similar events in the future.

 Host-based IPS systems can use a third type of detection called *static heuristics*. The host-based IPS scans executables during system idle time and analyzes the actions the executable is to perform. Based on the perceived behavior, if the executable were to be launched, the HIPS, using static heuristics, could conclude that the activities could be harmful and would quarantine the executable.

Therefore, a network IDS could have a signature database to detect known attacks (knowledge) and could monitor the trends in traffic, looking for aberrant behavior (misuse of protocols, changes in traffic patterns, and so on) to detect new attacks (behavior).

The host-based IPS could have a signature database filled with the signatures of known good executables and known bad executables and then identify unknown executables (knowledge). The unknown executables are sometimes automatically submitted to the vendor for analysis and a decision on being known good or known bad along with its signature (knowledge) or might be scanned using static heuristics to detect potential aberrant behavior (behavior). The host-based IPS will scan log files to identify suspicious activities (behavior) and can monitor a process in action to detect suspicious activities (dynamic behavior).

The implementation of the IDS system requires some understanding and planning. The major components are:

- **Network IDS sensor**   Hardware network appliance or software on network systems
- **Host IPS sensor**   Software application on a network system such as on a computer
- **Administrative console**   Typically, a software application installed on an administrator workstation
- **Vendor**   For regular signature updates, application updates, and firmware updates, typically delivered over the Internet

Figure 2-14 shows an example of an IDS system's architecture.

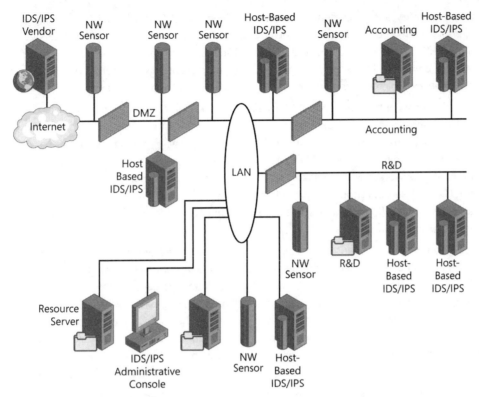

FIGURE 2-14 An example of IDS and IPS architecture

The administrative console is used to monitor the sensors; configure them, like for identifying friendly traffic in response to a false positive alert; to fetch all system updates from the vendor; and to deploy updates to sensors.

The administrative console should be the only system capable of communicating directly to the IDS sensors. Communications from any other source directed at the sensors are likely attacks on the sensors, a common tactic by attackers. Attackers target the sensors to defeat your vision and knowledge of the impending attack. The longer the attacker can keep you in the dark about the attack, the greater the losses you will suffer. The sensors should drop all packets directed to them other than packets from the administrative console and should alert on this activity.

Another mechanism used to defeat the sensors is to flood the segment or system and make the sensor analyze so much activity that some activities must be ignored and passed by without being analyzed. Yet another is the use of encryption to hide malicious activities from sensors. Because the sensors cannot decrypt the packets, the sensors cannot analyze the packets.

The use, quantity, and placement of network IDSs and host IDSs is optional. Generally, you need sensors where you need vision on the critical network segments (NIDS) and critical network hosts (HIPS). Where do you need this vision? The answer is "approximately everywhere." Quantity will be dictated largely by budget, and use and placement of sensors should be defined by policy, which is sometimes driven by applicable laws and regulations.

Network sensors outside the external firewall will tell you what the Internet is throwing at you. Network sensors inside the external firewall on the perimeter network will tell you how effective your external firewall is and what is getting through the external firewall. Network sensors behind the perimeter network on the corporate network will tell you how effective your perimeter network is and provide a clearer picture of user communications across the Internet. Network sensors should be placed at network choke points to monitor the busiest links and the most traffic and should be placed on segments where critical (high-value) data and processes must commute.

The NIC on the network sensors must operate in a mode to receive and process all packets, even packets not addressed to the sensor. This is called *promiscuous mode*. The vast majority of NICs operate in *nonpromiscuous mode* by default and are capable only of receiving and processing packets addressed to them (unicast), broadcasting packets that are addressed to everyone, and multicasting packets that the client system has opted in for. More detail on unicast, broadcast, and multicast packets is presented in Chapter 7, "Telecommunication and network security." Placing the network sensors in promiscuous mode enables the sensor to analyze every packet it sees on the network segment, providing the required level of vision.

Placing the network sensors in promiscuous mode is not yet sufficient to monitor network traffic. Because nearly all network segments are established using network switches (that replaced the older hubs), the network sensors being attached to the segment through the switch keeps the sensor isolated from the network traffic because of the layer-2 MAC address filtering function of the switch. The sensors must be attached to the switch by using a *span port*, also called a *mirror port* or *diagnostic port*. These ports are persistently switched into the backplane of the switch, so the sensor sees all network traffic that commutes through the switch. Another tool you can use to attach the network sensor to a segment is a *hardware tap*. The hardware tap operates like a hub and is commonly used between two or more switches to connect the sensor to the backplanes of the multiple switches. More detail on the layer-2 MAC address filtering function of switches is presented in Chapter 4.

The honeypot, the honeynet, and the padded cell

These are for the more sophisticated and mature networking environments and not for the beginner. The honeypot is a system built with no real valuable assets, but with existing and known vulnerabilities, and deployed on a (usually somewhat remote) network segment. It is hoped that the easily found vulnerabilities will attract the attackers there to the remote honeypot and away from real systems that have real and valuable assets. The honeypot system and the segment are often well equipped with monitoring technologies to identify early on when an attack has begun and to record the actions, code, methodologies, targets, exploits, and so on that the attacker(s) uses. The honeypot is implemented to isolate the attackers, to learn from them for better defenses, and possibly to gather evidence to prosecute them.

Honeypots are almost always implemented on *virtual machines* to minimize hardware costs and for ease of resetting to a known state after an attack has occurred (reverting to a previous snapshot).

The honeypot, a single, vulnerable system out on a remote segment all by itself, might be a little too obvious to seasoned attackers, so the honeypot is often deployed in multiples to present a more realistic target to the attackers. A collection of honeypots on a remote segment and filled with stealthy monitoring technologies is commonly called a honeynet or a padded cell. The longer the attacker is busy hammering away on these systems with no assets, the more the security team can learn about the malicious intent, code, and methodologies of the attackers; the more evidence can be gathered for a more certain prosecution; and the less time the attackers spend hammering away on the real systems.

In some states, counties, or local environments, the evidence gathered from the use of honeypots, honeynets, and padded cells might not even be admissible in court for the prosecution of the attacker(s). In their good light, these systems form an *enticement* to the would-be attackers. An enticement is typically defined as the presentation of a vulnerability to elicit criminal action to identify and, possibly, prosecute those who might be willing to commit a crime. In most cases, evidence gathered from enticement is admissible in court for the purposes of prosecution.

In their not-so-good light, these systems form an *entrapment* to the would-be attackers. An entrapment is typically defined as the presentation of a vulnerability and the spread of the information about the vulnerability to elicit criminal action to identify and, possibly, prosecute those who might be willing to commit a crime. In most cases, evidence gathered from entrapment is not admissible in court for the purposes of prosecution.

In a legal sense, there is a thin line between enticement and entrapment. Be sure to check with your local legal department for these types of issues before implementing the honeypots, honeynets, or padded cells.

 Quick check

1. What term describes the unauthorized modification or deletion of logged data?
2. What type of sensor monitors a single network system and responds with a defensive control when it detects a malicious process in action?

Quick check answers

1. Scrubbing the logs
2. Host-based intrusion prevention sensor using dynamic behavior detection

---

Exercises

In the following exercises, you apply what you've learned in this chapter. The answers for these exercises are located in the "Answers" section at the end of this chapter.

Exercise 2-1

Locate the logs on your computer that show successful and failed authentication. On a Windows system, they can be found by right-clicking My Computer and selecting Manage. Then, in the computer Management dialog box, expand the Event Viewer in the left column. Expand Windows Logs and select Security. On a Ubuntu Linux system (and many other Linux distributions), the authentication logs can be found in /var/log/auth.log.

Locate any failed logon attempts.

Document how you would configure the maximum size of a log file and what the system will do when that maximum size is reached.

Exercise 2-2

Identify five access controls relative your local computer and its use. Determine their primary group (technical, physical, administrative) and sub group(s) (deter, delay, prevent, detect, assess, correct, recover, direct, compensate). When multiples exist, list the groups in order of their intended effect.

Chapter summary

- Subjects (active) use computers and programs to access (information flow) objects (passive repository of data). A trusted path must be established between the subject and the object.

- Access controls are technical controls, administrative controls, or physical controls. Controls are driven by threats and are implemented to deter, delay, prevent, detect, assess, respond (correct, recover), compensate, or direct.

- Controls of various types should be implemented in layers. Remember: Defense in depth.

- AAA = authentication (something you know, something you have, and something you are), authorization, and accounting. (The third A is also auditing or accountability.)

- Attacks on authentication include the brute force, the dictionary, the hybrid, the rainbow, the replay, and social engineering attacks.

- Multi-factor authentication and mutual authentication can be added to strengthen a single factor authentication system.

- Single sign on techniques include the use of scripts, Kerberos, X.500 Directory services, and SESAME.

- When you think mandatory access control (MAC), think government, strong, expensive, lattice, and labels.

- When you think discretionary access control (DAC), think commercial, weak, inexpensive, and the owner has full control.

- When you think role-based access control (RBAC), think simplified DAC, few roles, and used in high employee turnover environments.

- When you think rule-based access control, think firewalls, and quotas, and they apply to everyone.

- The remote access systems RADIUS, TACACS, and Diameter provide AAA services.

- Auditing, as a control, is the process of capturing, securely storing, and reviewing logs and events from critical systems, and should trigger a response when needed.

- Intrusion detection systems (IDS) monitor, detect, and alert.

- Intrusion prevention systems (IPS) monitor, detect, alert, and respond.

- Network based IDS/IPS systems analyze packets on a segment, require promiscuous mode on the network interface card, connect to the switch through with a span, mirror or diagnostic port, or connect between switches with a hardware tap.

- Host-based IDS/IPS systems analyze processes on one system.

- IDS/IPS systems may detect threats by using a knowledge base (known threat signatures), or may be behavior-based, monitoring for anomalous and threatening process actions.

Chapter review

Test your knowledge of the information in this chapter by answering these questions. The answers to these questions, and the explanations of why each answer choice is correct or incorrect, are located in the "Answers" section at the end of this chapter.

1. Which type of control describes the attacker seeing the guard dogs and deciding not to attack?

    A. Physical deterrent

    B. Subject preventive

    C. Technical detective

    D. Physical corrective

2. Authentication in the AAA services includes which of the following functions?

    A. One-time password

    B. Identification

    C. Integrity verification

    D. A transponder

3. Which of the following is convincing the authentication service you know the password without revealing the password?

    A. A Type I error

    B. SESAME

    C. A privilege attribute certificate (PAC)

    D. The zero-knowledge proof

4. A network intrusion prevention system (IPS) sensor must be connected to the segment using which of the following?

    A. TACACS

    B. A hybrid card

    C. A supplicant

    D. A span port

5. Which of the following controls depends on the attacker being unaware of the asset or vulnerability?

   A. Provisioning

   B. Subject deterrent

   C. Security through obscurity

   D. Separation of duties

6. If there is a concern that the use of separation of duties is becoming ineffective due to the length of time coworkers have worked together, which of the following should be implemented to help manage fraud?

   A. Dual control

   B. The principle of least privilege

   C. Dynamic separation of duties

   D. Job rotation

7. Which of the following uses only symmetric keys and tickets to perform authentication services?

   A. Biometrics

   B. Kerberos

   C. SESAME

   D. The extensible authentication protocol (EAP)

8. Which of the following access control models requires unique user identities?

   A. Discretionary access control (DAC)

   B. Mandatory access control (MAC)

   C. Role-based access control (RBAC)

   D. Rule-based access control

Answers

This section contains the exercises and the "Chapter review" section in this chapter.

Exercise 2-1

In Windows, the maximum size of a log is defined by right-clicking the log and selecting Properties. Then adjust the size in the Maximum Log Size field. Control what the system should do when the log size has been reached just below that by selecting Overwrite Events As Needed (called circular logging; overwrites and loses events), Archive The Log (saves the events in the full log as a separate file and will not lose events), or Do Not Overwrite Events (log must be cleared manually; log stops accepting new events and could lose event when full). See Figure 2-15.

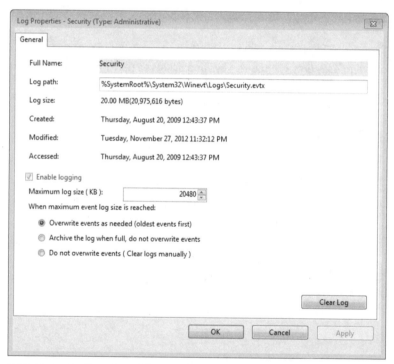

FIGURE 2-15 Configuration of the security event logs (Windows)

In Ubuntu Linux, the default approach to managing the log file is by date and not by size specifically. The period for rotating the file is configured through the /etc/logrotate.conf file. Logrotate is called from the cron.daily directory, and the specific parameters are pulled from the aforementioned logrotate.conf file. By default, the log files are set to rotate weekly, and the system is configured to archive the last four logs. An alternate to the use of the logrotate daemon is the use of the sysklogd daemon. Figure 2-16 shows a sample of the auth.log file.

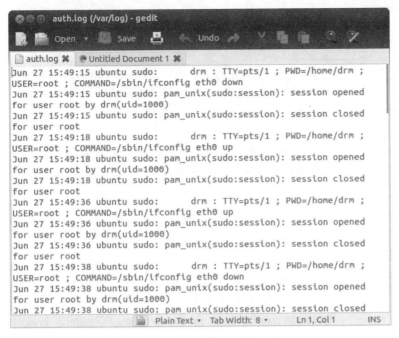

FIGURE 2-16 The authentication event log, Ubuntu Linux

Exercise 2-2

Following are examples of access controls likely to be in place:

- **Acceptable use policy** Administrative preventive (based on trust of the user), Administrative deterrent (penalties for violation described as a warning)
- **Logon password** Technical preventive, technical delay, technical deterrent
- **File permissions** Technical preventive
- **File system auditing** Technical detective, technical deterrent
- **Share permissions** Technical preventive

Chapter review

1. **Correct answer:** A

   A. **Correct:** The guard dog is physical, and the attacker's awareness of the dog convincing him not to attack is a deterrent.

   B. **Incorrect:** Subject is not an access control type.

   C. **Incorrect:** The dog is physical, not technical. If the attacker had entered and been held down by the dog, that would be preventive.

   D. **Incorrect:** The dog is physical, but corrective is the initial response to an attack. In this case, the attacker chose not to attack.

2. **Correct answer:** B

   A. **Incorrect:** The one-time password is a form of the "something you know" authentication mechanism but isn't a function.

   B. **Correct:** The subject first claims an identity, and then the back-end authentication service verifies that claim. Identification is the first stage of authentication.

   C. **Incorrect:** Integrity validation confirms data has not been altered since it was known good.

   D. **Incorrect:** A transponder communicates with proximity memory cards for contactless authentication but is not a function of authentication.

3. **Correct answer:** D

   A. **Incorrect:** A Type I error is a term used in biometrics to describe a false rejection.

   B. **Incorrect:** SESAME is a single sign on (SSO) authentication scheme used in applications.

   C. **Incorrect:** A privilege attribute certificate (PAC) is the access token provided to the authenticated user in a SESAME environment.

   D. **Correct:** The zero-knowledge proof is used to prove to the authentication service that you know the password without ever revealing the password.

4. **Correct answer:** D

   A. **Incorrect:** TACACS is an AAA server used primarily on UNIX systems. It was largely replaced by XTACACS (now TACACS+) and RADIUS servers.

   B. **Incorrect:** A hybrid card is a smart card with both contact-oriented and contactless communications mechanisms that also has two CPU circuits for increased security by means of physical segregation.

   C. **Incorrect:** A supplicant is another term for a system prior to authentication.

   D. **Correct:** A span port receives all packets that flow through the switch.

5. **Correct answer:** C

   A. **Incorrect:** Provisioning is the process of managing user accounts and their permissions.

   B. **Incorrect:** Subject deterrent is not a control type.

   C. **Correct:** Security through obscurity relies on the attacker being unaware that an asset or vulnerability exists.

   D. **Incorrect:** Separation of duties limits a user's access so he does not have enough authority to commit fraud singlehandedly.

6. **Correct answer:** D

   A. **Incorrect:** Dual control requires two (or more) authorized users to perform a critical process.

   B. **Incorrect:** The principle of least privilege should be applied 100 percent of the time, not just under special circumstances.

   C. **Incorrect:** Dynamic separation of duties is a subset of separation of duties; an authorized user can perform operation A or operation B but may never perform operations A and B for the same transaction.

   D. **Correct:** Job rotation cycles a new worker into a process. If workers had entered into collusion to commit fraud, this new worker would likely recognize the anomalies, have no relationship with the other workers (yet), and therefore be likely to report the anomalies.

7. **Correct answer:** B

   A. **Incorrect:** Biometrics use numeric representations of biological attributes to accomplish authentication.

   B. **Correct:** Kerberos is a single sign on (SSO) authentication scheme used in network operating systems. It uses only symmetric keys and authentication data on tickets.

   C. **Incorrect:** SESAME is a single sign on (SSO) authentication scheme used in applications. It uses symmetric and asymmetric keys and authentication data on certificates.

   D. **Incorrect:** The extensible authentication protocol is an application programming interface that enables different and new authentication mechanisms to be used on standard authentication systems.

8. **Correct answer:** A

   A. **Correct:** The academic DAC model requires discrete user identities.

   B. **Incorrect:** The academic MAC model is based on a user's clearance, not specifically on her unique identity. In implementation, MAC systems do support discrete user identities.

   C. **Incorrect:** The academic RBAC model allows multiple users to log on to a single role-based account and does not require unique identities. In implementation, RBAC systems do support discrete user identities.

   D. **Incorrect:** The academic rule-based access control model applies the rule set to all users regardless of unique identities. In implementation, academic rule-based access control model systems do support the use of discrete user identities.

CHAPTER 3

Cryptography

For thousands of years, humans have needed to keep secrets, whether the secret had to do with the strategy for the attack on a walled city, conspiracies to overthrow some unpopular political system, or the protection of credit card numbers that are transmitted during online purchases. So for these thousands of years, we have continued to design and use cryptosystems to help keep these valuable secrets secret.

Exam objectives in this chapter:

5.1 Understand the application and use of cryptography

    5.1.1 Data at rest (e.g., Hard Drive)

    5.1.2 Data in transit (e.g., On the wire)

5.2 Understand the cryptographic life cycle (e.g., cryptographic limitations, algorithm/protocol governance)

5.3 Understand encryption concepts

    5.3.1 Foundational concepts

    5.3.2 Symmetric cryptography

    5.3.3 Asymmetric cryptography

    5.3.4 Hybrid cryptography

    5.3.5 Message digests

    5.3.6 Hashing

5.4 Understand key management processes

    5.4.1 Creation/distribution

    5.4.2 Storage/destruction

    5.4.3 Recovery

    5.4.4 Key escrow

5.5 Understand digital signatures

5.6 Understand non-repudiation

What is cryptography?

Cryptography is defined as hiding the meaning of a message and the revelation of that meaning at some later time or other place. As security needs became more complex and cryptographic algorithms evolved into sophisticated cryptosystems, cryptography grew to provide more than just confidentiality services. Contemporary cryptosystems provide five major services:

- **Confidentiality**   Encryption provides confidentiality: *keeping the secrets secret*. Confidentiality can provide a form of access control or authorization. If a message is encrypted and the decryption key is only provided to those who are authorized to read the message, then those without the decryption cannot access the information within the message.

- **Authentication**   Cryptography can provide a *claim of identity* by a sender and a *verification of that claim* by a recipient to authenticate the sender. Symmetric key cryptography provides a weak form of authentication, and asymmetric key cryptography can provide a strong form of authentication.

- **Nonrepudiation**   If the identity of a sender can be strongly verified (proven) through strong authentication techniques, then not only does the recipient know the sender's identity, but *the sender cannot deny being the sender*. As stated previously, asymmetric key cryptography can provide this authentication mechanism, identifying the sender strongly enough to provide nonrepudiation. Symmetric key cryptography cannot provide nonrepudiation because it provides a weak form of authentication, as described in the "Symmetric key algorithms and cryptosystems" section later in this chapter.

- **Integrity** When the integrity of information is known to be good, the information is believed to be *complete, consistent*, and *accurate*. Information considered to have high integrity is information that is considered not to have been altered or tampered with and that can be trusted to some extent. As a security objective, integrity has two components: *integrity protection* and *integrity verification*.

  Cryptography (confidentiality) can protect the integrity of a message by encrypting the message. If an unauthorized person cannot access and read or understand the meaning of a message, that person cannot intelligently modify the meaning of the message, so the integrity of the message has been protected.

  Cryptography provides integrity verification by calculating a message digest (also called a hash value) of the message at the time of its creation, when the integrity of the message is known to be good. This message digest acts as a fingerprint of the message. Then, at the time of use, a new message digest is calculated. If these two digest values are identical, this proves that the message has not been altered since the time of the creation of the message. The integrity of the message has been verified.

- **Secure key distribution** Symmetric key cryptography requires both the sender of a message and the recipient of the message to have a copy of the key used to encrypt the message. Somehow, the sender must provide this copy of the encryption key to the recipient, and this must be accomplished in a secure manner. Contemporary cryptosystems can provide this secure key distribution service.

Sometimes the objective is to protect sensitive (valuable) content from others while you store it for use at a later time (*data at rest*). Examples might include the protection of the secret sauce recipe for your top-selling product or protection of your collection of passwords in your password vault. Whole disk encryption and smaller encrypted volumes might be used to provide protection for data at rest. An example of a whole disk encryption tool is BitLocker Drive Encryption, a Microsoft product. An example of an encryption tool for whole disk and for smaller encrypted volumes is the open source TrueCrypt application.

Other times, you must communicate your valuable information over hazardous network connections or other communications channels, such as by broadcasting radio signals into the air, and you are concerned that someone might steal the information. This is *data in transit*. A virtual private network (VPN), such as the Microsoft Point-to-Point Tunneling Protocol (PPTP) or the open standard Internet Protocol Security (IPsec), provides protection for data in transit from local area network (LAN) to LAN. Secure Sockets Layer (SSL) provides protection for data in transit over the Internet between anonymous clients and servers.

Cryptography can help solve both of these types of problems. The developers of applications, operating systems, and networking services and protocols cryptographically enable their software by including cryptographic code and linking to cryptographic application programming interfaces (APIs) that might be available.

There is another area of protection of data. As the user is actively accessing and using the information, sensitive data can be presented on video displays or in printed reports. This is an example of *data in use*. Data in this state cannot be protected by cryptography because it must be in a human-readable form. It must be protected by physical security measures and the user's awareness and defenses against social engineering, described in the "Cryptanalysis" section later in this chapter.

In this chapter, you explore the history of cryptography and the evolution of cryptosystems over time. You review symmetric key algorithms, asymmetric key algorithms, and hashing algorithms, and then you study the combination of these technologies in contemporary, hybrid cryptosystems that can provide all the required protective services. Cryptographic functions are added to the discussion as necessary to provide a balance between the need for strong security and the price paid in processing time to perform the various cryptographic functions.

The basics of cryptography

Cryptology is the study of all things crypto. This includes *cryptography*, the process of hiding the meaning of a message and revealing it at a later time, as well as cryptanalysis, cryptographic algorithms, cryptosystems, and key management, for example.

Although contemporary cryptosystems use many components and processes, strictly speaking, cryptography requires three components to operate:

- **A *cipher* (also called an *algorithm*)**   A data manipulation process
- **A *key* (also called a *cryptovariable*)**   Kept secret and used to impose a unique randomness on the message
- **A plaintext message**   In need of protection

Encryption converts the plaintext message into *ciphertext*. The plaintext message is processed by the cipher, and the processing is altered by the encryption key. Ciphertext is (generally) not readable by humans; therefore, it provides secure storage and transmission over otherwise untrusted communications channels. The message is recovered (made readable by humans again) by *decrypting* the ciphertext into the readable message, this time by using the decryption key, as shown in Figure 3-1.

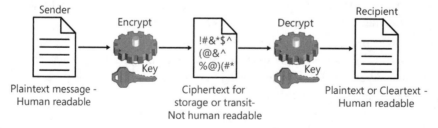

FIGURE 3-1 The encryption and decryption processes

The cryptographic algorithm (cipher) is the series of manipulations (logical or mathematical steps) performed on data to encrypt and decrypt the content. You can consider the cryptographic algorithm (cipher) to be like the engine in a car. Consider the cryptosystem to be the car that is built around that engine to provide the complete collection of functions that might be desired to satisfy the security objectives. The cryptosystem will include a cryptographic algorithm and might include many other components, such as symmetric algorithms, asymmetric algorithms, hashing algorithms, one or more key pairs, and other randomizer-type variables, such as an initialization vector, a salt, a seed, or a nonce.

The car (cryptosystem) needs a well-built engine (cipher), but the engine alone does not provide all the services needed, so additional components are added to the strong engine to increase the capability of the car and improve its utility and performance.

The goal is to build or implement a cryptosystem that provides as many of the five desirable cryptographic functions (confidentiality, authentication, nonrepudiation, integrity, and secure key distribution) as needed and to do it in a way that *adequately protects* the data without spending more time and money than is required to process the data through the cryptosystem.

Tying this all together, as described in Chapter 1, "Information security governance and risk management," all valuable information assets were identified, and the value of each information asset was determined during the risk assessment. Then, following policy, a specific level of protection was required for each data classification level based on the asset's value. The cryptosystem must be designed to provide the cryptographic portions of that protection at the level of protection required by the policy of the organization. Therefore, policy defines what the term *adequate protection* means. Providing stronger protection costs more in technology (cryptographic hardware and software) and in time to perform the process through the cryptosystem. Implementation of the right level of protection, balanced against the additional costs that go along with stronger protection, should be used to implement the correct cryptosystem.

Generally, as functions are added to a cryptosystem to improve its strength, the performance of the system degrades and the cost of using the system increases. All security measures, including cryptography, must be cost justified. Implement strong enough cryptography to satisfy the security needs for the data being protected but without spending more on the cryptography than can be justified.

Cryptanalysis

Cryptanalysis, a subset of cryptology, is the science or process of cracking a cryptosystem. Cryptanalysis is performed by the good guys and by the bad guys. The bad guys want to steal confidential messages to gain unauthorized access to valuable information or, better yet, to crack or reveal decryption keys so they can steal many confidential messages.

The good guys try to crack cryptosystems and reveal messages and keys to identify and validate the strength of the cryptosystem. They measure the amount of time and resources necessary to reveal messages or keys. The time and resources required to crack a cryptosystem is defined as the *work factor* of the cryptosystem. The larger the work factor, the stronger the cryptosystem.

One type of attack to crack a cryptosystem is the *brute force attack*, in which every possible key is tested to see whether it accurately decrypts the message. This is an exhaustive attack and typically takes a very long time, but it is guaranteed to be successful eventually.

A smaller subset of the brute force attack is the *dictionary attack*, by which the attacker uses a list of words from a dictionary to test as the password. Because many users choose passwords or keys that are easy to remember, such as commonly used words found in a dictionary, this attack is often successful in a relatively short period. These words are tested as the password until a match is identified or the words on the list are exhausted.

A combination of the brute force attack and the dictionary attack is the *hybrid attack*. In this attack, words from the dictionary are tested as the password or key. If a word fails, a collection of additions and substitutions is made to the word to produce variations, such as:

- Mustang
- Mu5tang
- mu$tang
- Must/\ng
- &&Mu$tang!!

These variations are then tested as the password until a match is identified or until the word list and the set of variations are exhausted.

A relatively new attack on passwords is the *rainbow attack*. Many applications and operating systems that include a key store or user database avoid storing plaintext keys and passwords by calculating and storing the message digest of the password. Message digests, also known as hash values, are covered in the "Hashing algorithm/message digest" section later in the chapter. Message digests are like fingerprints of the message (key or password in this case) and cannot be directly reversed to reveal the original input value (the plaintext password). These message digests are also present wherever cached keys or user credentials might be stored on a computer system.

To perform the rainbow attack, attackers must first perform a brute force attack that includes every combination of characters for a specific length of password, and they record the message digest of each combination. This table of every possible password and its message digest is called a *rainbow table*. If an attacker can compromise a computer system and capture any of the message digests that are stored on the computer, he simply finds the matching message digest that are stored on the computer in the rainbow tables to reveal the plaintext key or password used to produce the message digest.

However, another attack vector is *pattern detection*, in which the ciphertext is analyzed for patterns that might reveal the nature of the cryptographic keys. Some algorithms and cryptosystems show more patterns in their ciphertext, making these weaker but often faster than others. Additional manipulations can be combined with these systems to abstract the nature of the keys further, diffusing these patterns and making the cryptosystems stronger. However, these additional strengthening manipulations take time and processing power, resulting in a higher cost. Generally speaking, if a cryptosystem shows patterns in the ciphertext, that cryptosystem should only be used to protect small amounts of data, giving the bad guys only a small sample of ciphertext to analyze—small enough not to expose patterns and should not be used on very valuable data.

Basic substitution ciphers, described in the "Historical review of cryptography" section later in this chapter, lend themselves to pattern-based frequency analysis attacks. Transposition ciphers (also called permutation ciphers) contain the entire plaintext message in the cipher-text, and it is a simple process, often a game, to rearrange these letters or words in the correct order (into recognizable words or sentence patterns) and reveal the message. An attack on the patterns in ciphertext is typically much faster than the brute force attack but is not certain to be successful.

Not classically part of cryptanalysis, but a very successful technique for revealing keys and messages, is *social engineering*, in which the bad guy tricks a user into providing unauthorized access and revealing keys and messages. Social engineering is very often the fastest of the attacks on cryptography, but again, it does not represent the strength of the cipher or cryptosystems. Social engineering attacks identify the weaknesses in the human element in the information environment. These weaknesses can be reduced by providing security awareness training to all users, reinforcing the need to choose strong keys and passwords, and introducing users to the techniques of social engineers who intend to steal the users' secrets, identity, and access.

> **NOTE** **FREQUENCY ANALYSIS ATTACK**
>
> Take any 10 pages of US English copy from any source—a newspaper, an encyclopedia, your favorite trashy novel—and count the number of times each character is used. The proportional usage of letters is very consistent, no matter what the source of the sample is, as shown in Figure 3-2. When a simple substitution cipher is used, attackers do exactly the same thing with the ciphertext—count the frequency of each character. They align that frequency of use with the frequency of use in a plaintext sample. This shows which plaintext characters to substitute for which ciphertext characters—typically with at least 80 percent accuracy. After that, simply eyeballing the results can tell them where corrections of the substitution need to be made to reveal the entire plaintext message.

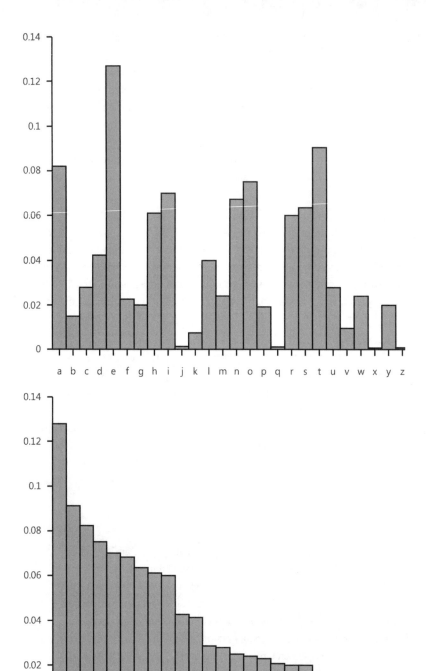

FIGURE 3-2 Frequency analysis of the use of US English letters

The strength of a cryptosystem—its work factor

In Chapter 1, in the discussion of the risk assessment and data classification processes, it was noted that the value of a particular data element (information asset) changes over time. For example, if a company has secretly developed a new product and is preparing to announce this new product next Monday, the value of this data would be very high today. However, Monday afternoon, after the announcement that grabs all the headlines has been made, the value of the information would be very low because it is now in the public domain.

If a competing company that has done no new product development were to learn of this information today, that competitor could make the announcement this Friday that it has developed the new product, to appear, untruthfully, to be the industry leader, superior to the legitimate company. Then, on Monday, when the legitimate company that had done the research and product development makes its announcement, that company appears to be nothing but a me-too follower in the industry and not the leader that it really is.

This example demonstrates more of a step function of how the value of data can change over time—in this case, very suddenly. Other data assets, such as your driver's license number, experience a more gradual change in value over time. Today, these numbers have value to you because they could be used to commit identity theft against you, but in a hundred years, this information will have very little relevance or value to anyone.

As the white-hat cryptanalysts work their magic and identify the work factor for a given cryptosystem, *they want the work factor of the cryptosystem to be substantially longer than the data the cryptosystem is protecting holds its value.* If your data will hold its value for 10 years, you should protect that data with a cryptosystem whose work factor is in the centuries (hundreds of years) or even greater—thousands of years or even millions or billions of years.

 Why such an exaggerated time for the work factor? Because of a persistent nibbling away at the work factor called *Moore's Law.* Contemporary cryptosystems operate on computers. In 1965, Intel cofounder Gordon E. Moore predicted that the number of transistors packed into CPU chips (indirectly, the chip's processing power) should double every one to two years. His prediction has held true for more than 50 years of CPU chip development (1958–2008), as suggested by the graph shown in Figure 3-3. This means that if processing power used on our cryptosystems doubles every two years, the work factor of a particular cryptosystem will be cut in half every two years. This is why exceptionally long work factor values are needed for cryptosystems and why there is a constant evolution toward greater complexity with each new implementation of cryptosystems.

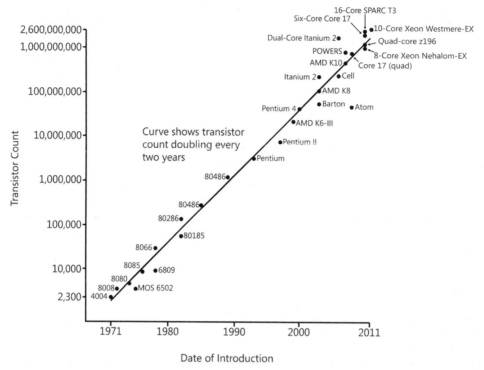

FIGURE 3-3 Moore's Law showing the number of transistors in a CPU chip doubling approximately every two years

> **NOTE** **MOORE'S LAW—LOOKING FORWARD**
>
> After the year 2015 or 2020, the increases in CPU power are predicted to slow to doubling only every three years.

Historical review of cryptography

Cryptography has been around for thousands of years. For almost all that time, there were only *symmetric key ciphers*, in which the key used to encrypt the message was exactly the same key used to decrypt the message. It was only when computers became commonplace (in the 1970s) that the computational horsepower was available to crunch numbers large enough to allow the invention of asymmetric key ciphers. *Asymmetric key ciphers* use two keys, a public key and a private key, that are mathematically related, and the content that one key encrypts can be decrypted only by the other key. The focus of this chapter will be the analysis of these symmetric and asymmetric key ciphers and cryptosystems.

Hieroglyphics: 3000 BC

Ancient Egyptians recorded events and concepts by using a defined set of characters or symbols to represent elements of the message being recorded. Hieroglyphics were readable only by those who were educated to read them. The intended recipient of the message had to be able to read hieroglyphics. This makes hieroglyphics a symmetric key *substitution cipher* because symbols were substituted to represent the meaning of the message, and the nature of the symmetric key was the education of the writer and the reader of the symbols.

The Atbash cipher: 500 BC

Atbash reverses the order of the characters in the ciphertext alphabet so that the plaintext letter A aligns with the ciphertext letter Z, the plaintext letter B aligns with the ciphertext letter Y, and so on. The characters in the plaintext message are substituted by using the characters on the ciphertext line, as shown in Figure 3-4.

A	B	C	D	E	F	G	H	I	J	K	L	M	N	O	P	Q	R	S	T	U	V	W	X	Y	Z
Z	Y	X	W	V	U	T	S	R	Q	P	O	N	M	L	K	J	I	H	G	F	E	D	C	B	A

FIGURE 3-4 The Atbash cipher

The plaintext message "CRYPTO IS COOL" is converted to the ciphertext message "XIBKGL RH XLLO." The intended recipient of the message had to know the message was encoded using Atbash. The recipient simply performs the same character substitution. Atbash is a symmetric key, substitution, mono-alphabetic cipher, and the nature of the key is that both sender and recipient know the messages are encrypted using Atbash. It is a *monoalphabetic* cipher because it uses a simple one-line substitution function. (A *polyalphabetic* cipher, such as the Vigenere cipher, discussed later in this section, uses multiple lines of characters for its substitution function.)

Atbash is a very weak cipher because there is no variability in the substitution characters. The letter A is always substituted with the letter Z, the letter B with the letter Y, and so on. With practice, this cipher could easily become human readable.

The Scytale cipher: 400 BC

The Scytale cipher was implemented by wrapping a parchment, papyrus, or leather strap around a log of a specific diameter. Then the message was written across the log, one character per wrap of the leather strap around the log. When the leather strap was removed from the log, the letters appeared, one above the other on the strap, out of order. The strap would be given to a runner or horseman who carried it across the battlefield to the recipient. The intended recipient of the message had to know the diameter of the log used during the encoding process. The recipient would know to wrap the leather strap around the correct size of log. This would cause the letters to align and be once again human readable, as shown in Figure 3-5.

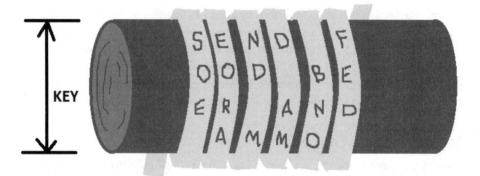

FIGURE 3-5 The Scytale cipher

  The Scytale cipher is a symmetric key *transposition* cipher because the characters within the original plaintext are rearranged, or transposed, making them unreadable. The nature of the symmetric key is the diameter of the log used to encode the message.

The Caesar or Shift cipher: 100 BC

The Caesar or Shift cipher simply shifts the character set of the plaintext message by a specified number of letters and then uses the new character set as the substituted ciphertext characters. For example, if you choose a key value of 5, then you would substitute each character of the plaintext message with the character five places to the right in the alphabet, as shown in Figure 3-6.

A	B	C	D	E	F	G	H	I	J	K	L	M	N	O	P	Q	R	S	T	U	V	W	X	Y	Z
F	G	H	I	J	K	L	M	N	O	P	Q	R	S	T	U	V	W	X	Y	Z	A	B	C	D	E

FIGURE 3-6 The Shift cipher using 5 as the key value

The plaintext message, "CRYPTO IS COOL" in this case, is converted to the ciphertext message, "HWDUYT NX HTTQ." The intended recipient of the message has to know how many characters to shift for the message. The recipient simply reverses the direction of the shift to reveal the plaintext message. The Shift cipher added variability to the cryptosystem, allowing a different key from message to message.

Notice how the letters wrap around on the ciphertext line, beginning again at the letter A after the letter Z. This is referred to as *Modulo 26 addition*, which says, "After you reach the 26th character (which in the English alphabet is the letter Z), start at the beginning and get the next character from the beginning, the first character."

This is a symmetric key, mono-alphabetic, substitution cipher, and the nature of the key is the number of places to shift for the substituted ciphertext character. It is often said that the Caesar cipher always uses a shift (key) of 3, whereas the Shift cipher can shift by up to 25 characters. ROT-13 (rotate/shift by 13 places) is an example of the Shift cipher still in use today (mostly on UNIX and Usenet systems). In the English alphabet, with its 26 characters, if you rotate (shift) 13 places (encryption) and then rotate again 13 places (decryption), you end up where you started, with the cleartext message. The Caesar cipher can be referred to as a ROT-3 (rotate by 3 places) cipher.

A weakness in this type of cipher is that if any one plaintext letter/ciphertext letter mapping is known, the entire substitution mapping is now known. Another weakness of this type of cipher is that encrypting the message twice does not increase the strength of the ciphertext. Instead of decrypting with two shifts of 3, an attacker can successfully decrypt with a single shift of 6. This makes the shift cipher a member of the *group cipher* family of ciphers. Algorithms whose ciphertext is strengthened with multiple encryption processes (such as DES, described later in this chapter, in the section "Symmetric key algorithms and cryptosystems") are not group ciphers, and the ciphertext is strengthened by encrypting it multiple times.

An extension of this cipher is an *arbitrary substitution cipher*, in which the one plaintext letter/ciphertext letter mapping is randomized. The substitution letters on the ciphertext line have been randomly transposed. The symmetric key just became much more complex, but so did the ciphertext. With an arbitrary substitution cipher, if one plaintext letter/ciphertext letter mapping is known, only that one character mapping is known.

Cryptanalysis: AD 800

The first known recorded instance of cryptosystems cracking occurred in the ninth century by Al-Kindi, an Arabian mathematician in a manuscript entitled *A Manuscript on Deciphering Cryptographic Messages*. The document described the use of frequency analysis to attack contemporary symmetric key, mono-alphabetic substitution ciphers.

The Vigenere cipher: AD 1586

The Vigenere cipher used multiple lines of substitution characters to defeat frequency analysis attacks on ciphertext, making this the first recorded polyalphabetic cipher. In the Vigenere cipher, a string of characters would be chosen as the key, and those characters would be aligned with the characters of the plaintext message—for example, you could use the plaintext message "CRYPTO IS COOL" and a key of "BOBOVILLE." The characters of the key would be repeated as necessary to cover the plaintext message characters, as shown in Figure 3-7.

Plaintext	C	R	Y	P	T	O		I	S		C	O	O	L
Key	B	O	B	O	V	I		L	L		E	B	O	B

FIGURE 3-7 Plaintext and key material for use with the Vigenere cipher

These characters would then be used in the Vigenere table, as shown in Figure 3-8, aligning the first plaintext character on the top horizontal line and the first key character on the leftmost vertical line.

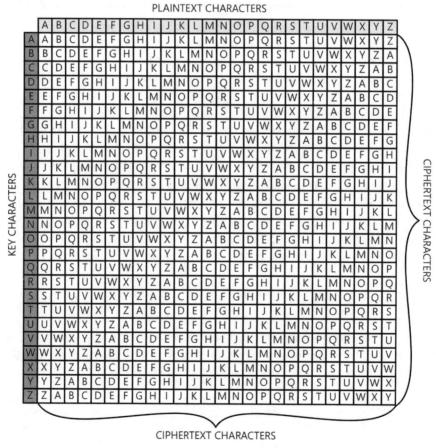

FIGURE 3-8 The Vigenere cipher table

In Figure 3-8, every row and every column contains the entire alphabet, but the characters in each adjacent row or column are shifted by one character and apply the modulo 26 function. The 26 x 26 matrix is completed with the cell at the intersection of row Z (plaintext characters) and column Z (key characters) being filled with the letter Y. The first combination of plaintext C and key material B intersects at the substituted ciphertext character D; the next plaintext character R and the second character of the key material O intersect at the substituted ciphertext character F, and so on, to produce the ciphertext message shown in Figure 3-9.

Plaintext	C	R	Y	P	T	O		I	S		C	O	O	L
Key	B	O	B	O	V	I		L	L		E	B	O	B

Ciphertext	D	F	Z	D	O	W		T	D		G	P	C	M

FIGURE 3-9 Plaintext, key material, and ciphertext using the Vigenere cipher

As always, the intended recipient of the message has to know the symmetric key characters the sender used during the encryption of the message. The recipient locates the first character of the key in the leftmost vertical column and follows the horizontal line from that first character of the key to the right until she hits the ciphertext character. Following that line up to the top horizontal line reveals the plaintext character.

The Vigenere cipher added a notable increase in randomness to the ciphertext because it used multiple lines of substitution ciphertext characters, making this a relatively strong symmetric key, substitution, poly-alphabetic cipher.

The Vigenere cipher also introduces a critical concept that carries forward into today's cryptosystems. Suppose the key used was only a single character long. It would have to be repeated to cover all the characters of the plaintext message. This dramatically reduces the randomness of the ciphertext that the Vigenere cipher would otherwise provide. Further, suppose the key used was ABCD. This easily recognizable pattern or sequence would also dramatically reduce the potential randomness of the ciphertext. The Vigenere cipher introduced the concept that a stronger key would contain many characters, and those key characters would be highly randomized, a concept that remains intact on contemporary cryptosystems.

The Jefferson disk: AD 1795

The Jefferson disk included a set of 36 leather disks. The alphabet was stamped on the edge of each disk but in a randomized order on each disk. There was a hole in the center of each disk so it could be placed on a central axis or spindle. Each disk was uniquely numbered from 1 to 36 and was placed on the spindle in a specified order, which was the key for the message to be encoded or decoded.

The sender would then rotate the disks until the desired message was spelled out along a row of the letters on the edge of the wheels. The sender could then choose any other row of characters to be the ciphertext message to send to the recipient.

The recipient would rebuild his Jefferson disks in the correct order, rotate the wheels so one row of characters was the ciphertext message received from the sender, and then simply look for a row of characters that was a readable message elsewhere on the set of disks.

This system was the basis of the cryptography later used by the US Army from about 1922 until about 1945. The later evolution of this device the US Army used was called the M-94.

The Vernam cipher/the one-time pad: AD 1917

Named after Gilbert Vernam, who worked for AT&T Bell Labs, the Vernam cipher took the concepts of the Vigenere cipher to the full extent. Gilbert Vernam deduced that to strengthen the ciphertext against cracking, the number of characters in the key should be equal to the number of characters in the plaintext message to be protected, and those key characters should be highly randomized with no observable patterns. Each key should only be used once and then never reused, and, of course, the key must be kept secret. The Vernam cipher, which implements these characteristics, is also called the one-time pad. It is a symmetric key, poly-alphabetic, substitution cipher.

> **NOTE** **GILBERT SANDFORD VERNAM**
>
> Gilbert Vernam also invented the symmetric keystream cipher, a family of ciphers that will be reviewed in the "Symmetric keystream ciphers" section later in this chapter.

The Enigma machine: AD 1942

The Enigma machine was an electromechanical cryptographic machine based on a Hebern rotor-based system. Enigma used mechanical rotors to alter the pathway of electricity and light up ciphertext characters on the display. It was invented in Germany in the 1920s for commercial purposes. However, when World War II broke out, Nazi Germany relied on it heavily for its secure communications. Interestingly, just prior to the outbreak of World War II in 1939, a team of Polish cryptographers cracked the Enigma ciphers and secretly provided their findings to the French and British governments. This allowed the Allied forces to decipher many German communications and shorten the duration of the war in Europe.

The Enigma machine is a symmetric key, poly-alphabetic, substitution cipher system. Two models of the Enigma were built, one using a three-rotor system, and another using a four-rotor system (shown in Figure 3-10). Code names used by the Allied forces for the Enigma machine during the war were Triton and Shark.

The Japanese Red and Purple machines and the US Sigba machine are variations of the rotor-based Enigma machine.

FIGURE 3-10 The Enigma machine

Hashing algorithms: AD 1953

Hashing algorithms are an integral component of virtually all cryptography systems today. Although technically not cryptographic ciphers (no key, no way to reveal the original message from the hashed value), they are commonly used to provide integrity verification of data and authentication of one or more endpoints in a data transmission. The first hashing algorithm was invented by Hans Peter Luhn while he worked at IBM. The term *hashing* came from the chopping and mixing of the input data to produce the hashed output value. However, at that time, this functionality was viewed more as a mathematical curiosity than as something useful. This same Mr. Luhn invented the Luhn calculation used by virtually every credit card company to encode a validation check into the credit card number.

It was Robert Morris (the father of the man who released the infamous Morris worm [1988]) who, while working at the National Security Agency (NSA), recognized the importance of hashing algorithms in cryptography and converted the mathematical peculiarity into contemporary crypto-technology.

The Data Encryption Algorithm (DEA) and the Data Encryption Standard (DES): AD 1976

In the early 1970s, the US government recognized a need for establishing a standard for protecting sensitive but unclassified content as part of the *Federal Information Processing Standard (FIPS)*. After surveying the marketplace for ciphers, the government in 1976 selected the Lucifer algorithm submitted by IBM. Lucifer is a symmetric key block cipher, encrypting 128-bit blocks at a time and using a 128-bit key. As in virtually all contemporary symmetric key block ciphers, Lucifer uses multiple rounds of substitution and transposition to introduce confusion and diffusion into the ciphertext. This cipher was considered stronger than what was needed, so the National Institute of Standards and Technology (NIST) watered it down to a 64-bit block size and 64-bit key size to produce the Data Encryption Algorithm (DEA), used as the core of the Data Encryption Standard (DES) in FIPS. The DEA key is actually made up of 56 bits of key material and 8 bits of parity to produce the 64-bit key. DEA is a symmetric key block cipher. It performs 16 rounds of substitution and transposition to produce its ciphertext. DES is discussed in more detail in the "Symmetric key algorithms and cryptosystems" section later in this chapter.

Diffie-Hellman (or Diffie-Hellman-Merkle): AD 1976

After approximately 5,000 years of nothing but symmetric key cryptography and the weaknesses therein (described in the "Symmetric key algorithms and cryptosystems" section later in this chapter), computers became available to perform complex mathematics on unbelievably large numbers, and the very first asymmetric key algorithm was invented by Whitfield Diffie and Martin Hellman (1976). The Diffie-Hellman algorithm was invented to solve one of the major weaknesses in symmetric key cryptosystems: secure key distribution. In 2002, Martin Hellman recognized Ralph Merkle's contribution to the asymmetric algorithm mathematics and proposed adding his name to this revolutionary and evolutionary advancement in cryptography. The Diffie-Hellman algorithm is discussed in more detail in the "Asymmetric key algorithms and cryptosystems" section later in this chapter.

> **NOTE** **CRYPTOGRAPHIC SERVICES**
>
> Although the Diffie-Hellman asymmetric key algorithm provides only one cryptographic service, secure key distribution, asymmetric key algorithms can potentially provide all five desirable cryptographic services in a strong manner. The five services are confidentiality, authentication, nonrepudiation, integrity, and secure key distribution.

RC4: AD 1987

Ron Rivest of Rivest, (Adi) Shamir, and (Len) Adleman (collectively known as RSA) produced a family of ciphers referred to as Rivest ciphers (hence the acronym RC, though some say that stands for "Ron's Code"). RC4 (1987) is a symmetric *keystream cipher* that operates on binary bits, not characters. Stream ciphers, invented by Gilbert Vernam in 1917, encrypt a single binary bit at a time but introduce a high level of randomness in the resulting ciphertext. Although RC4 is a proprietary algorithm, it was leaked to the public domain in 1994. RC4 is by far the most prevalently used symmetric keystream cipher, finding its place in the original version of PPTP, in Wired Equivalent Privacy (WEP), and in Netscape's SSL, web-based, secure channel. Symmetric keystream ciphers are discussed in more detail in the "Secure channels for LAN-based applications" section later in this chapter.

Triple DES (3DES): AD 1999

In 1997, a specialized computing system called Deep Crack with 1,856 crypto-cracking processor chips was able to crack DES in 96 days (that is a work factor of approximately three months). Shortly thereafter, another cryptanalysis team was able to crack it in about six weeks, then in a little over two days, and then in less than a day.

In 1999, DES was reaffirmed as the minimum standard, but the use of triple DES (3DES) was recommended. 3DES is three passes through DES by using two or three keys.

Today, relatively typical systems can routinely crack DES keys in about 4.5 days, with some weak keys revealed in less than a day.

Triple DES is discussed in more detail in the "Symmetric key algorithms and cryptosystems" section later in this chapter.

The Rijndael algorithm and the Advanced Encryption Standard (AES): AD 2002

With the observable weaknesses in DES and its relatively short keyspace, the US government needed a new standard. After surveying the marketplace once again, the government selected the Rijndael (pronounced rain-doll) algorithm by Belgian cryptographers Vincent Rijmen and Joan Daemen. The algorithm was incorporated into the Advanced Encryption Standard (AES) and in 2002 replaced DES and 3DES as the US FIPS standard for protecting sensitive but unclassified content. It is also approved by the NSA for protecting top secret data. AES is a symmetric key block cipher using a 128-bit block. AES can use key sizes of 128, 192, or 256 bits and performs 10, 12, or 14 rounds (respectively) of substitution and transposition.

Some say that AES is uncrackable. AES is discussed in more detail in the "Symmetric key algorithms and cryptosystems" section later in this chapter.

Other points of interest

Following are some additional ciphers and significant events in the history of cryptology.

- **Running key cipher**   Both the sender and recipient have a shelf of books, exactly the same books in exactly the same order. This is the symmetric key. Ciphertext is created by locating the first word of the secret message in one of the books, identifying its location by writing the book number, page number, line number, and word number. Then the sender locates the second word in the secret message in another of the books and documents its location by using the four numbers described. The ciphertext is a page full of numbers. This is a symmetric key, substitution cipher, and the nature of the key is the common bookshelf of books. Its ciphertext might look like this (book, page, line, word):

  4, 112, 17, 18, 11, 253, 6, 9, 9, 23, 31, 12

  This cipher was also used to distribute symmetric keys securely for character substitution ciphers, with the ciphertext of this message identifying a line from a book to use as the symmetric key for the encryption and decryption of another message.

- **Concealment cipher**   The concealment cipher is a symmetric key, transposition cipher in which the words or characters of the plaintext message are embedded in a page of words or characters at a regular interval. For example, the key could be that every fourth letter is a plaintext letter in the message. The other letters simply diffuse the meaning of the message, making it unreadable for those without the key. The key is the frequency of plaintext elements in the sheet of ciphertext. So the plaintext message "CRYPTO IS COOL" might look like this in ciphertext when the concealment cipher is used and the key is 4:

  JBECPSLRUNXYAWUPNVSTIHGOEAZIKMWSTHJCJSROYPLOVBWLPDU

- **AD 1815 to 1864: George Boole**   A British mathematician largely regarded as the founder of the field of computer science and digital computer logic, George Boole studied the binary number system and developed a series of logical functions called *Boolean logic* and truth tables commonly used in integrated circuits, computers and, more relevantly, in cryptography. The binary Exclusive Or (XOR) function is the basis of a large proportion of contemporary symmetric key algorithms and cryptosystems.

- **AD 1883 - *Kerckhoffs's principle***   Auguste Kerckhoffs worked as a cryptographer for the French military and identified six design principles for cryptosystems. The most critical of these states the following (translated and paraphrased):

  "The strength of a cryptosystem should not be in the secrecy of the algorithm but in the secrecy of the key."

  This allows the algorithm to be published, studied, and scrutinized by the brightest minds on the planet in hopes of verifying the strength of the cryptosystem or to reveal its weaknesses. If the cryptosystem is strong, as long as the secret keys are maintained securely, unauthorized persons are unable to reveal the protected messages or reveal the nature of the keys.

- **AD 1915 to 1990 - Horst Feistel**   This German-born physicist, mathematician, and cryptographer moved to the United States in 1934 and developed the Feistel Network while working at IBM. The *Feistel Network* has been the foundation of many symmetric key block ciphers, including DES, 3DES, RC5, RC6, IDEA, Blowfish, Twofish, Lucifer, CAST, GOST, MARS, and Skipjack. A key feature of the Feistel Network is that the algorithm is most often identical when performing the encryption and decryption functions. This allows developers to use the same code for the two processes with only minor adjustments (key scheduling). The Feistel Network includes an iterated cipher and introduced a popular and often used *round function*.

> ✔ **Quick check**
>
> 1. What type of algorithm is the Vernam cipher?
> 2. Mixing and moving the characters of a plaintext message around to produce ciphertext describes what type of cipher?
>
> **Quick check answers**
>
> 1. A symmetric key, poly-alphabetic, substitution cipher
> 2. A transposition cipher

Cryptographic keys

Cryptography relies on keys. In symmetric key cryptography, the key that is used to encrypt the content is the same key that is used to decrypt the content. The sender and the recipient must each have a copy of the key to perform the encryption and decryption process, so these two copies must be identical.

In asymmetric key cryptography, often referred to as *public key cryptography*, a pair of related keys is used. One key is a private key, created and stored securely and never shared. The mathematically related key in the key pair is the public key. These keys are related such that what one key encrypts, only the other key can decrypt. If you encrypt using the private key, only the public key can decrypt the content. If you encrypt using the public key, only the private key can successfully decrypt the content.

Key management becomes a core component of any cryptosystem. Key management includes the creation, distribution, storage, archiving (escrow), recovery, and disposal of the key material. Moreover, this must all happen securely so that attackers can never access your keys.

Key creation

In contemporary cryptosystems, cryptographic keys are generated on a computer system by a specialized kernel mode process called a *cryptographic service provider* (*CSP*). Different CSPs produce different types of keys, as requested by the crypto-enabled application. The keys are strings of binary bits.

Key length

Symmetric keys are typically 64 bits to 512 bits long. Asymmetric keys are typically 768 bits to 4,096 bits (4 kilobits) long, with the current recommendation at 3,072 bits (3 kilobits) long. The key length used is typically defined by the developer of the crypto-enabled application and the algorithm or cryptosystem chosen.

Generally speaking, the longer the length of the key, the stronger the cryptosystem. Specifying a key length is very much like the childhood game of "I am thinking of a number between 0 and 9. Guess which number I am thinking of." As the range of the possible chosen numbers increases, it becomes more difficult for the bad guys to guess which secret number you have chosen. Your key is a number chosen from this range of possible numbers, otherwise called the *keyspace*. Key lengths are defined by the number of binary bits. The range of possible numbers to choose your key from is directly related to the number of binary bits in the key, following the function 2 to the power of N, where N is the number of bits in the key. So a 64-bit key has a keyspace of 2 to the power of 64, or 18,446,744,073,709,551,616 possible choices of the symmetric key used. Your chosen key is a number somewhere between 0 and 18,446,744,073,709,551,615. The bad guy has to guess which number you chose. Then she can decrypt your messages. This is considered to be such a weak key length that it is not recommended. Table 3-1 shows the keyspace for some standard key lengths.

TABLE 3-1 Keyspace calculation

Bits	Keyspace - approximate	Cryptosystem
2^{64}	18 with 18 zeros behind it	SYMMETRIC
2^{128}	34 with 37 zeros behind it	SYMMETRIC
2^{256}	11 with 76 zeros behind it	SYMMETRIC
2^{512}	13 with 153 zeros behind it	SYMMETRIC / ASYMMETRIC
$2^{1,024}$	18 with 307 zeros behind it	ASYMMETRIC
$2^{2,048}$	32 with 615 zeros behind it	ASYMMETRIC
$2^{3,072}$	58 with 923 zeros behind it	ASYMMETRIC
$2^{4,096}$	10 with 1,232 zeros behind it	ASYMMETRIC
$2^{15,360}$	66 with 4,622 zeros behind it	ASYMMETRIC
$2^{32,768}$	14 with 9,863 zeros behind it	ASYMMETRIC

In May 2011, in SP800-57 (Part 1, Rev. 3), NIST recommended a minimum symmetric key length of 64 bits for 3DES using three keys (also called 3DES or TDES) and up to 256 bits for AES, using a single key. They recommend that asymmetric public keys should be a minimum of 2 kilobits (2,048 bits) long, up to as many as 15,360 bits. These minimums are currently expected to remain viable until the year 2030.

Key distribution

For the several thousand years of symmetric key cryptography, key distribution was a problem. If you had to get a sensitive message to a recipient in a different location, and the space between you was potentially hazardous, where an attacker might try to steal your data, you should encrypt your sensitive data. Right? But because you only had symmetric key cryptography, you had to get the recipient a copy of the symmetric key first. How would you get a copy of a symmetric key to that recipient securely? If you could get the key to your target securely, why not just tell the recipient the message by using that secure communications channel? Most often, the answer was that there was no secure way to get the key to the recipient unless you knew in advance that you would need this secure communication channel; thus, you would share a symmetric key prior to needing it, when you were in close proximity to one another. In other words, you needed a prior association with the recipient and had to anticipate the future need for secure communications.

If you had not anticipated this need, you had to have some alternative communications channel that might not be monitored by the bad guys. This is referred to as an *out-of-band* communications channel. Today, you might pick up the phone and tell the recipient that the password is BOBOVILLE. Or you might copy the key to a thumb drive and carry it (sneaker-net it) to the recipient instead of sending the key across the potentially hazardous network.

Symmetric key cryptography creates the problem of needing some secure mechanism to get a copy of the symmetric key to a recipient.

Today, Diffie-Hellman and the family of asymmetric algorithms, with their public keys and private keys, not only do not have this problem but finally solve this five-thousand-year-old problem by providing secure key distribution services. The way this works is described in detail in the "Asymmetric key algorithms and cryptosystems" section later in this chapter.

Secure key storage

Contemporary information systems exist on computers; therefore, contemporary cryptosystems exist on computers too. Typically, it is the responsibility of the operating system to provide a secure storage mechanism and location for cryptographic keys. Most operating systems establish and protect various key stores to achieve this. Because the keys are usually generated on the system by the operating system, it becomes natural for the operating system to store the keys securely, as needed.

Quantities of keys

As the number of participants (users) in a cryptosystem increases, you should consider the number of keys to be created, distributed, and stored for the life of the cryptosystem. Even very basic symmetric key cryptosystems require many keys, and every copy of every symmetric key must be protected for the life of the cryptosystem. The number of keys required can be determined by using the following formula, where N = the number of users in the cryptosystem:

$(N \times (N - 1))/2$

Table 3-2 shows the number of unique symmetric keys required as the number of users in a cryptosystem increases.

TABLE 3-2 Symmetric key requirements

Users	Number of keys
5	10
10	45
100	4,950
1,000	499,500

As you can see, the number of keys rises dramatically as the number of users in the symmetric key cryptosystem increases, and 1,000 users is not at all uncommon in today's IT infrastructure. Nevertheless, this isn't the worst part. Two copies (so double these numbers) of each of these keys must be protected for the life of the cryptosystem. Otherwise, there is a breach of security, and secrets will be lost.

Asymmetric key cryptography provides a distinct improvement in this area. In a basic asymmetric key cryptography, only two keys are required per user, providing the following formula, where N = the number of users in the cryptosystem:

$2N$

Table 3-3 shows the number of unique asymmetric keys required as the number of users in the cryptosystem increases.

TABLE 3-3 Asymmetric key requirements

Users	Number of keys
5	10
10	20
100	200
1,000	2,000

This shows a dramatic improvement in reducing the number of keys required in the cryptosystem, and the good news continues. Only the private key in the public/private key pair must be kept private. The public key can be shared with anyone without any risk at all. So only half of the asymmetric keys must be protected for the life of the cryptosystem.

Key escrow (archival) and recovery

One of the common responsibilities of IT personnel is to ensure the recoverability of all the organization's valuable information assets. So if a user has encrypted content and somehow loses his copy of the decryption key, it is IT's responsibility to be able to recover (decrypt) that content, making it usable and recovering its value. One technique used to accomplish this is to escrow all decryption keys. You can imagine that this repository of all the decryption keys for an organization would be a juicy target for the bad guys, so you recognize the need for the utmost security to protect these escrowed decryption keys. If someone could get into this repository and gain access to the archived keys, he might be able to decrypt all protected content within the organization and steal the identity of every user participating in the cryptosystem.

 Many companies use specialized *hardware security modules* (*HSMs*) to store and retrieve these escrowed keys securely. These HSM systems typically detect and prevent tampering by destroying the key material if tampering is detected (kind of like in *Mission: Impossible*).

 Recovery of these archived keys is usually considered to be too much authority for a single individual, so these HSM systems are typically designed to support dual control, or an *M-of-N function* requiring several people to come together and agree on the recovery of even a single key. Typically, the system provides several recovery keys, which might be like USB thumb drives. The HSM manufacturer might provide, for example, eight recovery keys. Then, based on company policy and the HSM system's configuration, it might require five of the eight recovery agents with their recovery keys to come together and agree on the recovery of any escrowed keys.

> **NOTE** **CRYPTO CONTENT JOURNALING**
>
> Content journaling is another approach to solving the problem of recovering encrypted content. With content journaling, the cryptosystem is configured to send a copy of all encrypted content to a highly secured, service-type user account, often called a recovery agent account. The cryptosystem is set up to allow this recovery agent user to decrypt all content. Recognize the technology requirements and the storage capacity issues that might arise from this type of solution in addition to the massive sensitivity (value) of this repository and the need for serious protection and auditing. No user should ever log on to this account unless authorized for the strict purposes of data recovery of specified content.

Key lifetime or the cryptoperiod

Keys should be changed regularly, just as most systems require you to change your password every 60 or 90 days. Company policy should define how frequently these passwords and the other keys used in the organization must be revoked and replaced with new keys. This is called *key rotation*, and the useful lifetime of a key pair is called the key's *cryptoperiod*. Keys used on a user's digital certificates often are good for 1 or 2 years. Keys on the certification authority servers are often good for 5, 10, or even 20 years. However, some keys, such as those used on a high-security VPN channel, might be changed as frequently as every few milliseconds (thousandths of a second), and other cryptoperiods range between these extremes.

It takes administrative effort, time, and system processing to rotate keys, so this must be balanced—as always, cost justified—against the need for increased security. Policy should dictate the cryptoperiod for the various types of keys used within a cryptosystem. Following are a few of the issues that would indicate the need for a short cryptoperiod:

- Weak algorithm(s) being used and the implementation details
- A high value assigned to the data that is being protected with the keys
- A lower level of trust for the entity (or entities) using the keys
- Use of keys or ciphertext in very hostile environments
- A high frequency of access to the keys
- A large quantity of data to be protected with keys (a larger sample of ciphertext)

The following lists some terms you should become familiar with; these provide an indication of the cryptoperiod of a key:

session key = short-term key = temporal key

secret key = persistent key = static key = long-term key

Session keys, also called short-term or temporal keys, have a relatively short cryptoperiod, typically the duration of a session. This can be as short as a few milliseconds to as long as a day or so.

Secret keys, also called persistent, long-term, or static keys, have a comparatively longer cryptoperiod. This can be as short as a day or a few days to as long as a few years or even decades.

In 2011, NIST recommended a cryptoperiod of less than or equal to two years for most cryptographic keys used to protect sensitive but unclassified content.

When the cryptoperiod expires, or when the administrator of the cryptosystem has just cause, the keys a user uses in a cryptosystem can be revoked and destroyed. These expired or revoked keys should not be used again for additional cryptographic functions other than to recover existing encrypted content if necessary.

Initialization vectors

A common issue to be concerned about with any cryptosystem is to what extent the nature of the encryption key presents itself in the resulting ciphertext. This is one of the most common attack vectors. If all things are working correctly, the only thing the bad guys have access to is the ciphertext as it flows between trusted entities over relatively untrusted network segments. If the ciphertext shows patterns, it might lead to insights into the nature of the encryption key, which leads to cracking the key.

One technique used to abstract the nature of the encryption key further in the resulting ciphertext is the addition of one or more *initialization vectors* (*IVs*) in the algorithm or in the implementation of the cryptosystem. This IV is a *nonsecret variable* that affects the processing of the plaintext data during encryption. Generally, the longer the IV value is, the greater the randomization and the stronger the resulting ciphertext. The goal is to make the ciphertext more randomized, diffusing potential patterns and hiding any insights or clues into the nature of the encryption key used to produce the ciphertext.

The IV must be shared with the recipient and can be sent in plaintext. If the bad guys see the IV and the ciphertext only, they gain less insight into the nature of the encryption key than without the use of an IV.

Other terms that you might see that refer to values that operate like an IV are *salt*, *seed*, or *nonce*.

Hashing algorithm/message digest

Hashing algorithms, also called message digests, are primarily used for the verification of the integrity of information at the time of use of the information. The hashing algorithm is applied to the message to produce a hash value. The hash value acts as a *fingerprint* of the message and is initially calculated at the time of creation of a message or at other times when the information in the message is known to be complete and accurate. Then at a later time or place, when the information in the message is about to be used, the calculation is performed again and compared to the original hash value. If the two values are identical, it is concluded that the message says exactly what it did at the time it was known to be good.

Hashing is also used in cryptosystems to provide authentication services, providing some level of trust that the sender is who he claims to be.

Hashing algorithms can accept any size of message as input and produce a fixed-size hash value (also called a *message digest*) output. Messages on computers are stored as a contiguous string of binary bits. In a simplified description, the hashing algorithm breaks that long contiguous string of binary bits into smaller chunks of binary bits. The algorithm then treats those chunks of binary bits as numbers and runs mathematical and logical functions on those numbers to produce a fixed-length hash value output as the answer.

A hashing algorithm will produce the same answer (hash value) on the same message every time as long as none of the binary bits that make up the message have been changed.

If any binary bits in the original message, even one, are changed between the original hash value calculation and the time-of-use calculation, the chunk of binary bits that contains the changed bit or bits results in a different number, and the mathematics performed on those different numbers will produce a different answer, a different fingerprint. This difference in the before (creation) and after (altered) fingerprints identifies that a change has occurred in the data. This is used commonly in cryptosystems to identify a violation of the integrity of the original data, called integrity verification.

The greater the number of bits in the hash value output from a hashing algorithm, the more specific the fingerprint of the message. More bits in the hash value, therefore, make the hashed message more difficult to alter yet provide the same hash value to make the altered message believable and trusted (called spoofing a message). Table 3-4 shows several commonly used hashing algorithms and their hash value output bit lengths.

TABLE 3-4 Hashing algorithms and their output lengths

Algorithm	Output bits	Notes
PARITY	1	The crudest of all hashing functions. Invented in ancient Greece.
CYCLIC REDUNDANCY CHECK (CRC)	32	Appended as a trailer to Ethernet packets to detect corruption, not tampering. 1961, 1975.
MESSAGE DIGEST v2 (MD2)	128	By Ron Rivest. Optimized for 8-bit computers. Rare but still used in some public-key infrastructures (PKIs). 1989.
MD4	128	Ron Rivest. Used in NTLM authentication. 1990.
MD5	128	Ron Rivest. Flaws found. 1991.
MD6	512	Ron Rivest. Flaws found. 2008.
SECURE HASHING ALGORITHM v1 (SHA1)	160	Developed by NIST. FIPS PUB 180-1 Standard 1995–2002.
SECURE HASHING ALGORITHM v2 (SHA2)	256-512	Developed by NIST. FIPS PUB 180-2 Standard 2002.
SHA3	Arbitrary	NIST has chosen a base algorithm called Keccak for the upcoming SHA3 standard. SHA3 will use a mathematical sponge construction by which input data is absorbed into the algorithm. Examples currently show output sizes ranging from 244 bits to 512 bits, but the algorithm's functionality allows an expansion of this range.
HAVAL	128-256	128-bit, 160-bit, 192-bit, 224-bit, and 256-bit output options. 1992.
RIPEMD	128-320	128-bit, 256-bit, and 320-bit output options. 1996.
TIGER	192	128-bit, 160-bit, and 192-bit output options. 1995.
WHIRLPOOL	512	ISO Standard. Vincent Rijmen (co-inventor of Rijndael used in AES). 2000.

The output from the hashing algorithm, called the hash value or message digest, is typically written in hexadecimal characters. For example, the SHA1 (160-bit) hash output for the input P@ssword is:

9e7c97801cb4cce87b6c02f98291a6420e6400ad

SHA-256 hash output for the input P@ssword is:

28efb68dcba507ecd182bead31e4e2d159b0f9185861d1ebfe60a12dfb310300

The same input should *always* produce the same hash output when the same hashing algorithm is used. Several websites will calculate the hash value for your input. Feel free to try some of them. You should get the same output values when using P@ssword as the input.

Hashing algorithms perform a one-way function. They can take any size of input, 10 bytes or 10 terabytes, and produce a fixed-length output. In the case of SHA1, this would be a 160-bit output hash value. Although this is an accurate fingerprint of the original 10-terabyte message, you certainly cannot convert the 160-bit hash value back into the original 10 terabytes of data.

Hashing algorithms do not use any kind of key as encryption and decryption algorithms do. Although hashing algorithms are commonly referred to as cryptographic hashing algorithms, because of the lack of a key and their one-way functionality (being unable to reveal the meaning of the original message from the hash value), hashing algorithms are, strictly speaking, *not* cryptographic functions.

Hashing algorithms, like all other algorithms, must be designed well to be usable. The more bits there are in the hash value output, the more specific the fingerprint of the message is and the stronger the hashing algorithm is. The algorithms must provide good strength versus their performance (time required to process). They must have a high avalanche effect; in other words, it should only take a little change at the top of the mountain (the message) to cause a huge change at the bottom of the mountain (the hash value output). The hash value for the message "IOU 10 beers." should be very different from the hash value of the message "IUO 11 beers." Equally important is for the hashing algorithm to be resistant to *collisions*. A collision is when two different messages produce the same hash value output—like two people with the same fingerprint—and this is a bad thing. The lower the frequency of collisions for an algorithm, the stronger the algorithm.

Attacks on hashing algorithms

The bad guys want to alter your data to gain some sort of benefit, usually to steal money. They want to alter the inventory count so they can take your inventory without detection. They want to inject malicious code into a downloadable application or device driver to compromise your computer. They want the contract to read that you must pay them $10,000 instead of $1,000.

The good guys don't want that alteration and loss to happen. So the good guys run hash values of the known good content so that later, at the time of use, the user of the data can verify that the data has not been altered from its known good state.

The bad guys must now defeat the integrity verification process and trick you into believing that the altered version of the data is the known good data, so they alter the data, the file, the program, whatever, in a way that provides them the illegitimate benefit, and then run the hash on the altered version. This produces a hash value that is different from the original, so they make another slight change to the altered version and run the hash again. Again, the result is different. Another change and hash. Different. They repeat this process until their altered data produces a hash value that exactly matches the original hash value you created at the time you knew the data to be good. This attack is called the *birthday attack*. Its goal is to make the hash value of the attacker's altered document collide with, or match a specific value (like someone else having the same birthday as you). The value she wants to match is the hash value of the original, known-to-be-good, trusted document to create a collision.

Now the user downloads the data or the application, verifies that the hash value is correct, trusts the integrity of the content, and moves forward, completely unaware that he has been successfully compromised by the bad guys.

The longer the hash value output of an algorithm, the larger the scope of possible hash values there will be and, therefore, the more difficult it is to match the original hash value exactly. If your hash value output was only 4 bits, the bad guy only has to hit one specific number in 16, a relatively easy thing to do. If the hash value has 256 bits, the bad guy has the very difficult challenge of matching one specific number in approximately 116,000,000,000,00 0,000,000,000,000,000,000,000,000,000,000,000,000,000,000,000,000,000,000,000 values.

Strong cryptography

So what does it take to make a good algorithm and cryptosystem? Following are some of the primary components of a strong algorithm and cryptosystem.

- The algorithm and system must not have any mathematical or logical weaknesses that might provide a back door for the attacker.

- The keys used should be of sufficient length and highly randomized, and key management issues should be addressed and securely managed.

- The next thing to consider is the notion that when an IT environment is implemented securely, the only thing the bad guys ever get to see is ciphertext, so you must hide the nature of the encryption key in the resulting ciphertext. To say it another way, the ciphertext should not be linearly related to the encryption key.

  To accomplish this, you add functions to abstract and randomize the ciphertext. These functions include substitution (confusion) and transposition (diffusion) functions, possibly the use of symmetric and asymmetric cryptographic algorithms, the use of a strong initialization vector, the use of different types of algorithms together within a cryptosystem, and the addition of hashing algorithms to provide integrity-verification and authentication capabilities. Such a system is called a hybrid cryptosystem.

The addition of these randomizing functions, which will degrade performance, should be balanced with the need for stronger security. This balance must be defined by the policies of the organization that specify the level of protection required for specific classifications (values) of data. Provide an appropriate level of security and not more. Otherwise, you are paying too much for security.

This last bullet point is debatable. Many believe that the world, including potential attackers should also know the details of the algorithm. Kerckhoffs's principle says to publish your algorithms and let them be tested under fire by the brightest mathematicians and cryptographers on the planet. If no one can find flaws or weaknesses, and you can verify a sufficiently long work factor, then you have a pretty good level of trust that the algorithm or system is strong. The strength of your cryptosystem should come from the secrecy of the keys, not the secrecy of the algorithm.

Very often, this is not done with algorithms and cryptosystems for government use, but it is common in the public sector.

> *NOTE* **STRONG CIPHERTEXT**
>
> Strong ciphertext should not provide any insight into the nature of the encryption key that was used to create the ciphertext. Furthermore, no patterns within the ciphertext should provide any insight into the nature of the encryption key. Strong ciphertext should not compress well because compression algorithms identify patterns and then substitute smaller markers for the multiples of the pattern to reduce the file size. If the ciphertext is highly randomized, there should be no multiples of patterns.

EXAM TIP

Different types of ciphers and cryptosystems provide different cryptographic services (can you list the five desirable cryptographic services?) at varying levels of strength. Understand which services and levels of strength of those services each cipher and cryptosystem can provide.

Symmetric key algorithms and cryptosystems

As stated previously, a cryptographic cipher is a manipulation process that transforms organized, readable information into unreadable content and can be used later to recover the meaning of the information by making it readable again. Algorithms introduce confusion or diffusion, often by performing substitution, transposition, or mathematical functions on the data.

Cryptographic algorithms fall into two major categories:

- Symmetric key algorithms
- Asymmetric key algorithms

This section and the following sections cover these algorithms in depth, starting here with symmetric key algorithms.

The term *symmetric* implies that the key used to encrypt the content is the same as the key used to decrypt the content. This means that the sender and the recipient must each have a copy of the symmetric key.

Symmetric key cryptography is *fast* compared to asymmetric key cryptography. Depending on the specific ciphers used and the other features of the cryptosystem, symmetric key cryptography is estimated to be somewhere between 100 times faster and, in many cases, more than 1,000 times faster than asymmetric key cryptography. So virtually all bulk encryption, when the volume of content is undefined or known to be more than a few kilobytes (KB), uses symmetric key cryptography.

Today, information systems rely on cryptography to provide five critical cryptographic services:

- Confidentiality
- Authentication
- Nonrepudiation
- Integrity
- Secure key distribution

Symmetric key ciphers provide only one of the five desirable cryptographic services strongly, confidentiality. Encryption and decryption processes that use symmetric keys perform very well and can produce *strong ciphertext for strong confidentiality.*

Symmetric keys can be used to provide weak authentication. If you receive a message that is successfully decrypted by using a symmetric key you share only with BoBo, then it is very likely that BoBo sent you the message because no one else but you and BoBo should have a copy of the key that encrypts the message. Therefore, you have a level of trust that the message came from BoBo. This is authentication. However, because there are two keys (you have one and BoBo has one) that could have been used to encrypt the message so that your copy of the symmetric key successfully decrypts the message, it can never be proven which key was used to produce the ciphertext. This makes symmetric key cryptography a *weak source of authentication.*

Because the authentication services provided by symmetric key cryptography are weak, BoBo could deny sending the message, and there is no way ever to prove he is lying. So symmetric key cryptography *does not provide nonrepudiation.* To provide nonrepudiation, the cryptosystem would need to prove with certainty that BoBo was the source of the encrypted message. With this provability, BoBo could not deny being the source.

If you add a hashing function to a symmetric key cryptosystem, it can be used to prove that a message has not been altered since the time it was sent. This is integrity validation. However, because you cannot be certain who sent you the message (weak authentication), you cannot trust the message any more strongly than you trust the authentication. Symmetric key cryptography provides *weak integrity validation*.

Finally, symmetric key cryptography not only does not solve the problem of needing some secure mechanism to distribute symmetric keys over nonsecure channels, it creates the problem. *It does not provide secure key distribution services; it causes the problem.*

The following list of services shows what symmetric key cryptography can provide and at what level of strength:

- **Confidentiality** Strong
- **Authentication** Weak
- **Nonrepudiation** No
- **Integrity** Weak
- **Secure key distribution** No, the use of symmetric keys causes the problem

Users of a cryptosystem typically only consciously recognize two services they need. These are commonly referred to as *signing* and *sealing*.

 In a symmetric key cryptosystem, *signing* a message provides weak authentication and weak integrity validation services (with the addition of a hashing algorithm). Nothing else. Recognize the need to distribute the symmetric key securely to the recipient.

 In a symmetric key cryptosystem, *sealing* a message provides strong confidentiality services. Nothing else. Recognize the need to distribute the symmetric key securely for decryption to the recipient.

A message can be signed, sealed, or both at the discretion of the user, based on policy, or as imposed by the cryptosystem.

In addition, recall the issues regarding the number of keys required in a symmetric key cryptosystem, described earlier in this chapter: $(N \times (N - 1))/2$.

Symmetric key algorithms operate by performing substitution, transposition, or both functions on the data. Substitution replaces a plaintext character with a ciphertext character and introduces confusion in the ciphertext. Substitution ciphers are sensitive to the frequency analysis attack. Transposition mixes and relocates plaintext characters in the ciphertext, introducing diffusion in the ciphertext, as in the popular game that gives you jumbles of the letters of words for you to figure out what the secret message is. Transposition ciphers leave all the data from the original, sensitive plaintext message in the resulting ciphertext message. When used alone, both substitution and transposition ciphers present vulnerabilities, but when they are used together, as is common in contemporary symmetric key cryptosystems, those vulnerabilities are greatly reduced.

Present-day information systems store and process data on computers, and therefore, the symmetric key cryptographic systems operate on the binary bits that represent the data we use and understand.

Symmetric key algorithms come in two types: block ciphers and stream ciphers.

Symmetric keystream ciphers

Invented by Gilbert Vernam in approximately 1917 at AT&T Bell Labs, stream ciphers encrypt and decrypt a single bit at a time and operate like a one-time pad. The algorithms typically use a symmetric key and an IV as inputs, a *pseudo-random number generator (PRNG)*, and the symmetric keystream algorithm itself to produce a *keystream* of binary bits. This keystream output should be made up of long periods of nonrepeating sequences and provide bits in a statistically unbiased manner (over a sampling, an equal number of 1s and 0s). Further, although the keystream is a byproduct of the key, the keystream should not show any linear relationship to the key. The initialization vector and the PRNG help avoid this issue.

The binary XOR function is then used on the keystream with the bits of the plaintext to produce the ciphertext. This is shown in Figure 3-11.

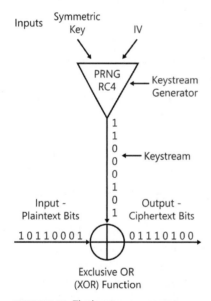

FIGURE 3-11 The keystream generator

George Boole, the nineteenth-century British mathematician, was mentioned earlier in this chapter. This is where his magic comes into play—inside the Exclusive Or (XOR) function. Boole developed a series of binary logic functions called Boolean logic, and their resulting *truth tables*: functions such as AND, OR, NAND, NOR, and XOR, to name a few. These functions are the basis of digital circuitry and are heavily used today. The XOR logic function lends itself beautifully to cryptography. With this *XOR function*, if two binary bits (A and B) are provided as input, the result (R) will be true (a binary 1) if one bit or exclusively the other bit is a 1. Otherwise, the result is false (a binary 0), as shown in Figures 3-12 and 3-13.

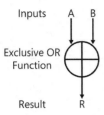

FIGURE 3-12 The Exclusive OR (XOR) function

EXCLUSIVE OR (XOR)			
Input A	B		Result R
0	0	=	0
0	1	=	1
1	0	=	1
1	1	=	0

FIGURE 3-13 The XOR truth table

When this function is used on binary plaintext data as input A and binary key material as input B, it performs a reversible, symmetric key substitution process to produce ciphertext (R). The XOR function is a core component of the stream cipher and is the basis of the S-box function used in block ciphers, described in the "Symmetric key block ciphers" section later in this chapter. Figure 3-14 demonstrates the XOR encryption process and decryption process.

```
   Plaintext   1 1 0 1 0 0 1 0
Symmetric Key  1 0 0 1 1 1 0 0
      XOR
  Ciphertext   0 1 0 0 1 1 1 0

  Ciphertext   0 1 0 0 1 1 1 0
Symmetric Key  1 0 0 1 1 1 0 0
      XOR
   Plaintext   1 1 0 1 0 0 1 0
```

FIGURE 3-14 Encryption and decryption using the XOR function

Notice that the ciphertext binary string is different from the plaintext binary string. The plaintext bits have been substituted by the ciphertext bits. This ciphertext can now be securely stored or transmitted over untrusted channels because it does not reveal the original information. The recipient, who must also know the same symmetric key, can decrypt the ciphertext into the original plaintext message. Notice that the two keys are identical (symmetric). The bad guy, who might see the ciphertext message, does not know the symmetric key, and therefore, cannot convert the ciphertext back into the original, readable message. Confidentiality of the message has been provided.

Work through your own sample of plaintext and key material by using the XOR function (encryption) to produce ciphertext and then recover the plaintext from the ciphertext (decryption). You might be a cryptographer now!

Symmetric keystream ciphers produce stronger ciphertext than block ciphers because of the reduction in potential patterns within the resulting ciphertext, but they are generally considered about 1,000 times slower than block ciphers.

Because they encrypt a single bit at a time, and because of their relative slowness when compared with block ciphers, stream ciphers are better used to encrypt small amounts of data, often single bits or single bytes (8 bits) at a time. When block ciphers are used to encrypt small amounts of data, specifically smaller than their block size, they must generate padding bits to fill the block. This padding often presents patterns and further weakens the strength of the block cipher.

Most symmetric keystream ciphers rely on a function well-performed on an integrated circuit chip (hardware) called a *Linear Feedback Shift Register* (*LFSR*). Most stream ciphers *tend not to code well* in applications without that hardware, and the code without the use of the LFSR chip does not process efficiently on CPUs. Therefore, it is said that *symmetric keystream ciphers are best implemented in hardware*. This should be compared to the implementation of symmetric key block ciphers, described in the next section.

Following is a list of symmetric keystream ciphers to become familiar with:

- RC4
- A5/1, A5/2
- Rabbit
- FISH
- SNOW
- SOBER, SOBER-128
- ISAAC
- MUGI
- Scream

In approximately 2004, the European Union established a project called *eSTREAM* to evaluate new stream ciphers, hoping to accelerate their development and adoption as international standards for cryptography.

RC4

Designed in 1987 by Ron Rivest, RC4 is the most prevalently used symmetric keystream cipher. RC4 can use key sizes ranging from 40 bits to 256 bits. Although it is proprietarily owned by RSA, RC4 was leaked into the public domain through Cypherpunks in 1994 and then out into the wild from there. Because the term *RC4* was trademarked by RSA, it might also be referred to as ARCFOUR and ARC4 to avoid trademark issues with RSA. It is used in the original implementation of PPTP, Secure Shell (SSH), Remote Desktop Protocol, (RDP), WEP, Wi-Fi Protected Access (WPA), SSL, and Transport Layer Security (TLS). It is believed that RC4 became so popular due to its speed and its simplicity of implementation. RC4 does not require the use of hardware LFSRs, unlike most stream ciphers.

Symmetric key block ciphers

Block ciphers encrypt and decrypt a block of data at a time, making these ciphers the fastest of all. However, these blocks of ciphertext tend to be the most revealing of patterns and therefore require additional consideration in their use. It would be unacceptable to choose a block cipher because of its excellent performance (speed) but allow the decryption key to be revealed in its ciphertext. The next section looks at multiple modes of operation for block ciphers that progressively improve the randomization in the ciphertext, further abstracting the nature of the encryption key.

Virtually all contemporary symmetric key block ciphers use both substitution and transposition functions. The substitution box, or S-box, performs an XOR function on a binary bit of plaintext and a binary bit of key material, a block of it at a time. An S-box function and a transposition function together is called *one round* of cryptographic processing, as shown in Figure 3-15. Different algorithms perform different numbers of rounds to produce their ciphertext. For example, DES performs 16 rounds of substitution and transposition. The International Data Encryption Algorithm (IDEA) performs eight rounds of substitution and transposition.

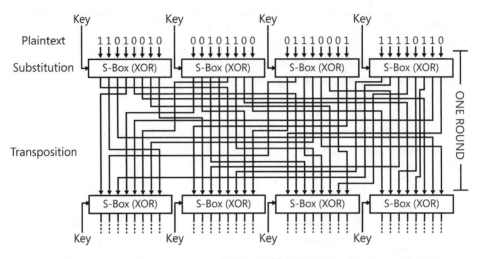

FIGURE 3-15 One round equaling one substitution (S-box) function and one transposition function

In general, symmetric key block ciphers code well in applications, and that code processes efficiently on CPUs, so it is said that *symmetric key block ciphers are best implemented in software.* This is compared to the implementation of symmetric keystream ciphers described earlier in this chapter.

Following is a list of symmetric key block ciphers to become familiar with:

- DES, 2DES, 3DES
- AES
- IDEA
- RC5, RC6
- Blowfish, Twofish
- CAST
- MARS
- SAFER

 EXAM TIP

Several of these are examined in detail in this chapter. Learn them. Be aware of the others, not so much to know details about what they are, but as to know what they are not. They might be used as distractors on the exam. Just know that they are symmetric key block ciphers.

Data Encryption Algorithm (DEA) and Data Encryption Standard (DES)

DES was established as the US recommendation for protecting sensitive but unclassified content in 1976. DES is based on the Lucifer algorithm that was developed by Horst Feistel at IBM. Lucifer uses a 128-bit block and a 128-bit key, but it was redesigned as DEA to use a 64-bit block with a 56-bit key plus 8 parity bits to form 64 bits of key material. DES uses 16 rounds of substitution and transposition. In the late 1990s, DES was cracked and is now considered insecure.

Double DES (2DES)

In the late 1990s, when DES was cracked, researchers looked for a quick replacement, and 2DES was considered. However, after analysis, it was concluded that 2DES suffered from a vulnerability that allowed a known plaintext, meet-in-the-middle attack, which showed that 2DES was negligibly more secure than DES. For this reason, 2DES was and is considered insecure. An attacker who knew the plaintext and resulting ciphertext that was encrypted using double DES could brute-force the encryption process on the plaintext. The attacker would then brute-force the decryption process on the ciphertext. By comparing the brute force–encrypted messages with the brute force–decrypted messages and locating the two matching messages, the attacker would know the two keys used in the 2DES process.

Triple DES (TDES or 3DES)

In 1999, 3DES was added as the recommended implementation of the DES algorithm by the US government for protecting sensitive but unclassified content. 3DES passes plaintext through DES three times, using two or three keys. This increased the work factor back into a reasonable but still largely unsatisfactory level. The search began for the next generation of encryption algorithms.

3DES can operate in several modes, using two or three keys and performing the processes in different directions. The four modes of 3DES are:

- EEE-3 - Encrypt with key 1, then encrypt using key 2, then encrypt using key 3
- EEE-2 - Encrypt with key 1, then encrypt using key 2, then encrypt using key 1
- EDE-3 - Encrypt with key 1, then decrypt using key 2, then encrypt using key 3
- EDE-2 - Encrypt with key 1, then decrypt using key 2, then encrypt using key 1

These modes are shown in Figure 3-16.

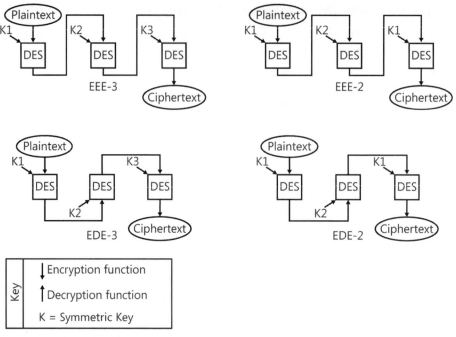

FIGURE 3-16 The modes of 3DES

The use of two keys is a tad more efficient than having to generate and securely distribute three keys, but it is also considered a tad less secure. 3DES is now considered insecure and, in 2002, was replaced with AES as the US recommendation for protecting sensitive but unclassified content.

Advanced Encryption Standard (AES)

AES is an iterative symmetric key block cipher based on the Rijndael algorithm, developed by Belgian cryptographers Vincent Rijmen and Joan Daemen. It uses a block size of 128 bits and can use key sizes of 128 bits, 192 bits, or 256 bits. It performs 10, 12, or 14 rounds of substitution and transposition, based on the key size used. It performs four basic crypto functions to accomplish confusion and diffusion:

- **AddRoundKey**   An XOR substitution function
- **ShiftRows**   A transposition function
- **SubBytes**   A byte-level substitution (S-box) function
- **MixColumns**   A mathematical function

On May 26, 2002, AES became the US recommendation for protecting sensitive but unclassified content, and it remains so currently. It is FIPS 197–compliant and is expected to perform in this role until approximately the year 2020.

The NSA has approved AES to protect Secret and Top Secret classified content.

It is said that if you could crack DES in one second, AES would take 149 trillion years to crack. The universe is only approximately 13.7 billion years old, so that work factor should be satisfactory for most purposes.

International Data Encryption Algorithm (IDEA)

IDEA was first described in 1991 and was intended to be the replacement for DEA/DES. It was developed under contract in Zurich by James Massey for a Dutch networking and telecom corporation. IDEA has been patented in numerous countries by MediaCrypt AG. IDEA is used in Pretty Good Privacy (PGP) and OpenPGP. It uses a 64-bit block size, a 128-bit key, and performs eight rounds of substitution and transposition.

A newer version of IDEA, called IDEA NXT, was released in 2005.

Rivest Cipher 5 (RC5) and RC6

Rivest Cipher v5 (RC5) was released in 1994. It can use block sizes of 32 bits, 64 bits, or 128 bits and key sizes ranging from 0 bits to 2,040 bits. Although the original implementation recommended 12 rounds, the algorithm supports 1 to 255 rounds. RC5 introduced data-dependent rotations and relatively simple implementation. RC5 is a proprietary algorithm and must be licensed from RSA for use. In response to a challenge by RSA, Distributed.net has cracked RC5 keys of 56 bits and 64 bits and is currently cracking the 72-bit keyspace by using a brute-force attack. At its current pace, the brute-force attack is expected to take 90 years to complete.

Rivest Cipher v6 (RC6) was proposed as a submission to replace DES and 3DES when AES won the competition for adoption as the NIST recommendation. RC6 was released in 1998. It uses a block size of 128 bits; key sizes of 128 bits, 192 bits, or 256 bits; and 20 rounds. RC6 uses data-dependent rotations, like RC5, and relatively simple implementation. Because of its submission as a candidate for a US standard, RSA was willing to provide free licensing for the use of RC6. However, although RSA has declared nothing certain, because RC6 was not adopted as the NIST standard, the company has kept its rights open to require licensing and royalty payments for its use.

Blowfish and Twofish

Designed in 1993 by Bruce Schneier, Blowfish has stood the test of time and remains popular in use in virtually every facet of computing and networking. There are currently no known successful attacks on Blowfish. The algorithm was released into the public domain and can be used freely. Blowfish uses a 64-bit block size and can use key sizes ranging from 1 bit to 448 bits. It performs 16 rounds of substitution and transposition.

A closely related algorithm by Schneier is Twofish, considered by many to be the second generation of Blowfish. Twofish was released in 1998 and has not (yet) been cracked. It uses a 128-bit block size and can use key sizes ranging from 128 bits to 256 bits. It performs 16 rounds of substitution and transposition. Twofish has also been released into the public domain and can be used freely.

Modes of symmetric key block ciphers

Remember that in the best situation, the bad guys only ever get to see ciphertext. They try to figure out the encryption key by analyzing the ciphertext and looking for patterns or other clues to the nature of the key. If the bad guys can figure out the key, they can steal all messages. Ciphertext that does not show these patterns and clues to the key is the result of a strong cryptosystem. Some cryptosystems are better at this than others are.

Generally speaking, the stronger the cryptosystem, the higher the price you will pay in performance and perhaps even for crypto-hardware (cost versus security). So when might you need to pay the higher price to get stronger security? Following are some examples:

- When you are protecting very sensitive (valuable) content
- When you are communicating in or through very hostile environments
- When you are producing large amounts of encrypted content
- When performance (cost) is less important than security (when cost is not an issue)

When you need to pay a higher price for stronger security from your cryptosystem, you have a range of choices. As described earlier, symmetric key block ciphers are quite fast (less expensive)—about 1,000 times faster than stream ciphers. However, the ciphertext from block ciphers tends to show patterns that might reveal the nature of the key used to produce the ciphertext. This, of course, is a bad thing. Cryptographic components can be added to the core block cipher within the cryptosystem to improve the strength of the ciphertext. These additional cryptographic components improve the strength by further separating the encryption key from the resulting ciphertext, further abstracting the encryption key from the resulting ciphertext, and further randomizing the ciphertext. There are five standard modes that symmetric key block ciphers can use that provide a range of performance versus strength to choose from. Each mode offers different combinations of cryptographic components or different orders of processing into the cryptosystem to randomize the ciphertext. The five modes of block ciphers are:

- Electronic Code Book (ECB)
- Cipher block chaining (CBC)
- Output Feedback mode (OFB)
- Cipher Feedback mode (CFB)
- Counter mode (CTR)

These five modes can be applied to any symmetric key block cipher, including DES, 3DES, IDEA, and AES. You will need to know these five modes and be generally familiar with how they operate.

Electronic Code Book (ECB)

Electronic Code Book (ECB) is the fastest and weakest mode of symmetric key block ciphers. It simply performs its encryption on each block of plaintext, as shown in Figure 3-17.

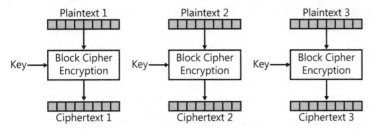

FIGURE 3-17 Electronic Code Book (ECB) mode encryption

There is no effort or attempt to randomize the ciphertext other than what happens within whatever block cipher was used. In theory, identical blocks of plaintext could produce identical blocks of ciphertext. This would be a very obvious pattern for the bad guys to see and guide them toward revealing the encryption key. Even without identical blocks of plaintext, patterns might be readily observed in ECB ciphertext.

ECB is typically used to protect small amounts of data, such as on personal identification numbers (PINs) on electronic payment terminals and ATMs, to keep the sample of ciphertext small. Smaller samples make it harder to recognize patterns that would present themselves readily in larger samples.

Cipher block chaining (CBC)

A little slower and a little stronger than ECB is cipher block chaining (CBC). This mode is fast enough and strong enough for many applications and has been the most popular mode of block ciphers. CBC was invented by the cryptography team at IBM in 1976 and adds one step to ECB. It applies an XOR with an IV to the first block of the plaintext (PT1). (This requires the IV to be the same size as the plaintext block.) Then it passes that through whatever symmetric key block cipher is being used to produce ciphertext block 1 (CT1). Then, CBC XORs a copy of CT1 with the next block of plaintext, PT2, *chaining the ciphertext* into the next block of plaintext. This block is passed through the block cipher to produce ciphertext block 2, CT2. A copy of CT2 is XORed with PT3, and so on, as shown in Figure 3-18.

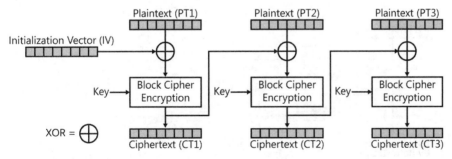

FIGURE 3-18 Cipher Block Chaining (CBC) mode encryption

This extra XOR step helps randomize the resulting ciphertext, reducing the likelihood of patterns that might lead to revealing the key. Notice that if any bit in the plaintext is altered, accidentally or intentionally, that change will propagate to and affect every block of ciphertext from that point forward to the end of the message.

CBC is slower than ECB because of the extra XOR processing and because the second block of plaintext cannot be processed until the first block of plaintext has been encrypted. (And the third block cannot be processed until the second block has been processed.) CBC must be processed sequentially rather than in parallel like ECB.

Output Feedback mode (OFB)

Output Feedback mode (OFB) is often called a stream cipher mode of a block cipher. OFB makes the block cipher behave like a stream cipher because it takes an IV as the first block of input where plaintext data would normally be entered, and it encrypts the IV by using the symmetric key. This behavior is similar to the stream cipher. The key and IV are inputs into the block cipher, as they are in a keystream generator. The output from this process is XORed with the first block of plaintext, PT1, to produce the first block of ciphertext, CT1, again as with a stream cipher. Next, the *output from the block cipher* (this is the original IV that has been encrypted—not the encrypted plaintext) is used as the IV input for the next block. This output feedback continues across all blocks until the entire message has been encrypted. The OFB process is presented in Figure 3-19.

OFB requires sequential processing, like CBC. OFB does not propagate errors in the plaintext through remaining blocks of ciphertext, whereas CBC does.

Further, the IV can be processed (encrypted) without the plaintext, so if there is any delay in accessing the plaintext—for example, due to reading it from a slow hard disk drive or waiting for the user to finish typing it in—much of the preprocessing can be accomplished and ready when the plaintext arrives. This output can also be fed to the next block for preprocessing. Then the relatively fast XOR process is the only thing left to complete to produce the ciphertext. This can improve the performance of OFB mode.

OFB is often used to protect satellite communications.

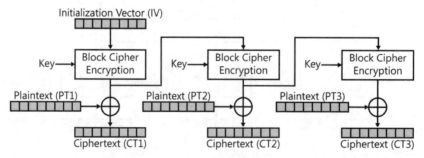

FIGURE 3-19 Output Feedback (OFB) mode encryption

Cipher Feedback mode (CFB)

Cipher Feedback mode (CFB) is another stream cipher mode of a block cipher. It operates like a cross between OFB and CBC. CFB encrypts an IV as the first block of input into the block cipher where plaintext data would normally be by using the symmetric key. The output from the block cipher is then XORed with the plaintext block 1 (PT1) to produce ciphertext block 1 (CT1). Then CFB takes a copy of CT1 to the next block cipher process and encrypts it by using the symmetric key, *feeding the ciphertext* into the block cipher. This CT1 block is passed through the block cipher, and the output is XORed with the second block of plaintext, PT2, to produce ciphertext block 2, CT2. A copy of CT2 is encrypted and then XORed with PT3, and so on, as shown in Figure 3-20. This ciphertext feedback continues across all blocks until the entire message has been encrypted.

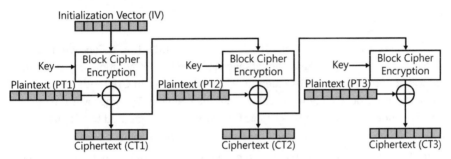

FIGURE 3-20 Cipher Feedback (CFB) mode encryption

CFB must be processed sequentially; note that if an error occurs during the encryption of the data in any block, that error will be propagated in each subsequent block through the rest of the message, just as in CBC mode. In contrast, when using OFB, errors in any one block of encryption will not propagate beyond that one block because the encrypted data is not chained.

As in OFB, the IV in CFB can be preprocessed (encrypted) without the plaintext. In CFB, however, the XOR function must be completed before the ciphertext output can be fed to the next block for processing.

CFB is often used to encrypt the mouse clicks and keystrokes upstream, and the video content downstream, within terminal services and RDP communications.

Counter mode (CTR)

Counter mode (CTR) is the newest mode of the group. CTR is both fast and strong. It adds another component to the process: a counter. This counter value is combined with an IV (also called a *nonce*) to produce the input in the symmetric key block cipher. This value is then encrypted through the block cipher by using the symmetric key. The encrypted output from the block cipher is then XORed with the first block of plaintext (PT1) to produce the first block of ciphertext, CT1. For the next block, the same IV is combined with the next value from the counter and is encrypted using the symmetric key. This output is XORed with PT2 to produce CT2, and so on. Counter mode is presented in Figure 3-21.

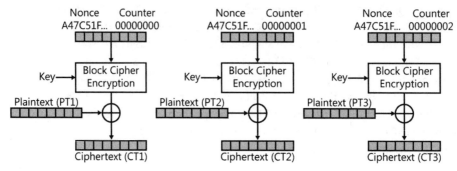

FIGURE 3-21 Counter (CTR) mode encryption

Notice that nothing is chained from one block to the next. This is how CTR mode gets its speed. Multiple blocks can be processed simultaneously, as in ECB. In addition, any errors in the plaintext will not propagate to subsequent blocks of ciphertext. In CTR mode, the nonce and counter can be preprocessed (encrypted) without the plaintext. This improves the performance of CTR mode. The extra cryptographic functions (when compared to ECB) used to abstract the key and produce stronger ciphertext make CTR quite strong.

The counter function can be as simple as a true counter, progressing from 0 to 1, 2, 3, and so on. However, many believe this is too simplistic. Remember that the IV (nonce) is a nonsecret value, so the bad guy might see it being sent from sender to recipient. And if the counter value is easily guessed and predictable, following a pattern, this value might also be easily obtained by the bad guys. It is these two values that are actually encrypted using the block cipher. Therefore, the bad guys could actually know the plaintext (the IV and the counter value) that goes into the block cipher. This is referred to as the *known plaintext attack* and provides the bad guys with more information than many are comfortable with. They feel that this is too much information and therefore choose a much more complex counter function with substantially less predictability.

CTR is used in the strongest implementation of 802.11i, W-Fi Protected Access v2 (WPA2), and is used in IPsec VPNs.

> **NOTE   KNOWN PLAINTEXT ATTACK?**
>
> There will be more on the types of attacks on cryptography in the "Attacks on cryptography" section later in this chapter.

Signing and sealing using symmetric key algorithms

Although IT professionals know that there are five desirable cryptographic services, from a user's perspective, signing and sealing are the two recognized services needed within information systems. They are often the check boxes available in an application.

- Signing messages provides authentication and integrity validation services.
- Sealing provides confidentiality services.

Symmetric key cryptosystems can provide these services, but in a limited sense. As you recall from earlier in this chapter, the following list of services shows what symmetric key cryptography can provide and at what level of strength:

- **Confidentiality**   Strong
- **Authentication**   Weak
- **Nonrepudiation**   No
- **Integrity**   Weak
- **Secure key distribution**   No, the use of symmetric keys causes the problem

If you receive a message that decrypts correctly when you use a key you share only with the user BoBo, you have a pretty good idea that the message really came from BoBo. Nevertheless, remember that because there are at least two copies of the symmetric key, it is not possible to prove a single and undeniable source. There is a potential that the other key was used to produce the message, and it is never certain or provable which copy of the key was actually used to produce the ciphertext. This limitation provides only a weak level of authentication and does not provide nonrepudiation. This weaker form of authentication based on symmetric keys is often called *data origin* or *system authentication*.

If a hashing function is added to the symmetric key cryptosystem, it can be used to prove that a message has not been tampered with since it was sent, but if you cannot prove who sent the message, the integrity (level of trust) for the message cannot be any greater than the level of trust for the authentication. However, it is an indication of some level of trust for the integrity of a message, and that is better than no indication of integrity.

Signing by using symmetric key algorithms

When symmetric keys are used to provide authentication and integrity validation of messages, it is referred to as *message authentication code (MAC)*. When this term is used, it is understood that the authentication and integrity validation is weak but better than nothing. Several techniques can provide MACs:

- Hashed message authentication code (HMAC)
- Cipher block chaining message authentication code (CBC-MAC)
- Cipher-based message authentication code (CMAC)

MAC VERSUS DIGITAL SIGNATURE

Although the use of a MAC on a message might be called "signing the message," MAC uses symmetric keys and provides only weak authentication and weak integrity validation. It should not be confused with signing a message by using a digital signature (covered in the "Cryptography in use" section later in this chapter). Digital signatures use asymmetric keys and (typically) public key infrastructure (PKI) digital certificates along with a hashing algorithm. Digital signatures provide strong authentication, strong nonrepudiation, and strong integrity validation.

MAC and digital signatures are competing technologies; MAC is regarded as the poor man's version (faster and cheaper but weaker) of a digital signature.

MAC types of authentication are used in the open standard Challenge Handshake Authentication Protocol (CHAP) and Microsoft proprietary implementation of CHAP, MS-CHAP, currently in version 2. These are forms of a zero-knowledge proof, in which a user can prove his identify (in a weak sense) without revealing the symmetric key (the user's password) to the authentication service. CHAP is used in Kerberos protocol, a symmetric key authentication system. CHAP, Kerberos protocol, and the zero-knowledge proof are covered in Chapter 2, "Access control."

HASHED MESSAGE AUTHENTICATION CODE (HMAC)

Hashed message authentication code (*HMAC*) is performed by adding a symmetric key to a message and then running the message and key through a hashing algorithm. This produces a MAC value, called the sender's MAC or MACs in Figure 3-22, which is the sender's hash value. (Actually, it is more than a hash value because it contains properties of the symmetric key as well as properties of the message.) Next, the plaintext message (without the symmetric key) and the MAC value are sent to the recipient. The recipient would have to have acquired a copy of the symmetric key through some other secure mechanism, as always.

To verify the HMAC, the recipient adds her copy of the symmetric key to the message and runs the message and key through the same hashing algorithm. This produces a MAC value, called the recipient's MAC or MACr in Figure 3-22, which is the recipient's MAC, the hash value that includes the recipient's copy of the symmetric key. If the message has not been modified, and if the sender and recipient have the correct and same copies of the symmetric key, MACs should equal MACr, as shown in Figure 3-22. In this case, the authenticity of the sender and the integrity of the message can be trusted to some level but cannot be proven.

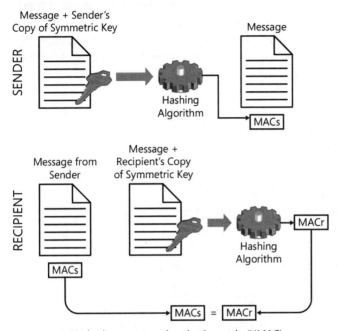

FIGURE 3-22 Hashed message authentication code (HMAC)

If the two MAC values are not equal, either the message *has* been modified, or the sender and recipient *do not* have the correct and same copies of the symmetric key. The message cannot be trusted, and most applications will discard the message.

Notice that no encryption was involved, and no confidentiality was provided. That is not the objective of signing a message. If you need confidentiality, you need to seal the message, not sign it. HMAC only provides weak authentication and weak integrity validation.

CIPHER BLOCK CHAINING MESSAGE AUTHENTICATION CODE (CBC-MAC)

Cipher block chaining message authentication code (CBC-MAC) operates quite differently. Remember the CBC discussion in an earlier section of this chapter—understand the statement that errors or alterations in the plaintext propagate through all ciphertext blocks, following the error to the end of the message. This is the basis for CBC-MAC.

The sender runs the message through a block cipher in CBC mode, using her copy of the symmetric key. Each block of ciphertext is XORed with the next block of plaintext. This is what carries any alterations forward through the message. The very last block of the sender's CBC ciphertext, S in Figure 3-23, is the culmination of every bit contained in the message and is a product of the sender's symmetric encryption key.

The plaintext message and the very last block of CBC ciphertext are sent to the recipient. The recipient verifies the signature by running the plaintext message through the same block cipher in CBC mode and using the recipient's copy of the symmetric key. The very last block of the recipient's CBC ciphertext, R in Figure 3-23, is then compared to the block of CBC ciphertext from the sender, S. If R and S are equal, then the message can be trusted, to some level, as not modified. It can be trusted on some level that the message was most likely sent by the claimed sender because only the sender and recipient share the correct and same copies of the symmetric keys. In this case, the authenticity of the sender and the integrity of the message can be trusted to some level but cannot be proven.

CBC-MAC is shown in Figure 3-23.

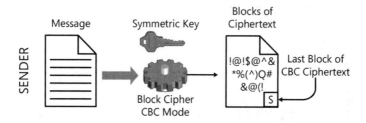

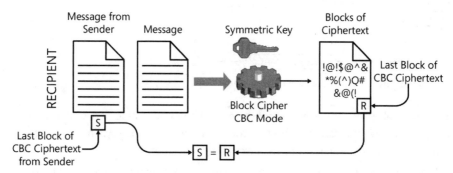

FIGURE 3-23 Cipher block chaining message authentication code (CBC-MAC)

If the two CBC-MAC values are not equal, either the message *has* been modified, or the sender and recipient *do not* have the correct and same copies of the symmetric key. The message cannot be trusted, and most applications will discard the message.

Notice that encryption *was* involved, but no confidentiality was provided. The message was sent to the recipient in plaintext. Confidentiality is not the objective of signing a message. If you need confidentiality, you need to seal the message, not sign it. You could sign and seal a message, but that is two different functions and two different security objectives. CBC-MAC provides only weak authentication and weak integrity validation.

CBC-MAC had been approved in FIPS Publication 113, using DES as the block cipher, and is included in the International Organization for Standardization/International Electromechanical

Commission ISO/IEC 9797-1 (1999) but is now considered insecure for variable-length messages. CBC-MAC is used in the strongest implementation of 802.11i WPA2.

CIPHER-BASED MESSAGE AUTHENTICATION CODE (CMAC)

Cipher-based MAC (CMAC) is an improved variant of CBC-MAC that was developed to correct the vulnerabilities in CBC-MAC on variable-length messages. CMAC is documented in the NIST Special Publication series 800-38B, May 2005, which is the US recommendation for performing authentication with symmetric key block ciphers.

Sealing by using symmetric key algorithms

Symmetric keys are commonly used to provide confidentiality. They can provide strong confidentiality and strong encryption. When cryptography is used to provide confidentiality, it is often called sealing the message, like putting the message in an envelope and sealing (encrypting) it in a way that only the intended recipient can open (decrypt) the envelope.

Weaknesses in symmetric key algorithms

Most of these issues have been mentioned already, but the topic is so broad that a summary is warranted.

Basic substitution ciphers (confusion) are easily cracked by using frequency analysis. Transposition ciphers (diffusion) contain all the characters in the original plaintext message and simply need to be correctly repositioned. Used alone, each of these is pretty easy to crack, but when the two are used together, they can produce strong ciphertext.

If two different keys produce the same ciphertext from the same message, this is called *key clustering*. Key clustering is an undesirable characteristic of some cryptosystems because it means that two (or possibly more) different keys could also decrypt the secure content. This increases the chances for attackers to guess the key and statistically reduces the time it will take to crack any one of the keys that will decrypt the protected message and reveal the meaning of the message. A strong cryptosystem has a low frequency of key clustering occurrences.

Symmetric key cryptography only provides strong confidentiality services, and provides weak authentication and weak integrity verification services. The use of symmetric keys cannot provide non-repudiation, and they cause the problem of needing some mechanism to securely distribute the symmetric keys to the participants of the cryptosystem.

The next two weaknesses of symmetric key cryptosystems fall into the category of key management. First, somehow the sender must securely communicate the symmetric key to the recipient (secure key distribution), but if there were a way to accomplish this within the symmetric key cryptosystem, why not just tell the recipient the message securely? This problem historically was solved by establishing and sharing a symmetric key before it was needed usually when the sender and recipient were in close proximity in a nonhostile environment.

Finally, recall that the number of keys required within a symmetric key cryptosystem grows very rapidly as the number of users grows ($N \times (N - 1))/2$ and that typically two copies of each key must be protected for the lifetime of the cryptosystem.

EXAM TIP

Be sure you understand the strengths, weaknesses, and solutions available within symmetric key cryptosystems.

 Quick check

1. Why are symmetric key block ciphers weaker than symmetric keystream ciphers?

2. What new mode of block ciphers is both fast and strong?

Quick check answers

1. Block ciphers tend to show patterns in the ciphertext that might reveal clues to the nature of the encryption key.

2. Counter mode

Asymmetric key algorithms and cryptosystems

For nearly 5,000 years, only symmetric key cryptography existed, with all the weaknesses and problems that symmetric key cryptography introduced. The most critical of those issues was that of secure key distribution. How do you get a copy of the symmetric key to the recipient securely? In the 1940s, John Mauchly and John Eckert developed one of the first computers, the Electrical Numerical Integrator And Computer (ENIAC, 1947). In the 1950s and 1960s, computers and the computational power they bring became more available, allowing researchers and scientists to write programs to crunch larger and larger numbers. Then, in the early 1970s, with computers more available than at any time in history, the paths of two mathematician/cryptographers, Whitfield Diffie and Martin Hellman, intersected. They had both independently been working on a solution to this 5,000-year-old problem of secure key distribution. When they compared their research and began collaborating, they realized that together they had the solution.

The very first asymmetric key algorithm was introduced in 1976 to solve the problem of secure symmetric key distribution. It became known as the Diffie-Hellman algorithm (DH), a key agreement protocol. In 2002, Whitfield Diffie suggested adding the name of their co-inventor, Ralph Merkle, to the name of the algorithm, so you might sometimes see the name of the algorithm as Diffie-Hellman-Merkle.

This asymmetric algorithm not only provided the solution to secure symmetric key distribution, it cracked open a new era in cryptography. When other new asymmetric algorithms are used, all five of the desirable cryptographic services can be provided in a strong manner. Once again, they are:

- Confidentiality
- Authentication

- Nonrepudiation
- Integrity
- Secure key distribution

Asymmetric key cryptography uses two different but mathematically related keys. This key pair includes a *public key* and a *private key*. What one key encrypts, only the other key can decrypt.

- If you encrypt content by using your private key, the private key cannot decrypt the content. Only the public key can decrypt this ciphertext.

- If you encrypt content by using your public key, the public key cannot decrypt the content. Only the private key can decrypt this ciphertext.

The public key can be shared with anyone: a good guy, a bad guy, and even an unknown guy. Another person can do you no harm by having your public key.

The private key should never be shared or exposed to anyone. If the private key is exposed to someone else, this key pair should immediately be replaced and never used again. All content protected by the exposed key pair should be protected by using the replacement key pair.

With a public key, you can:

- Encrypt content (providing confidentiality, sealing) to the owner of the mathematically related private key.

- Verify (decrypt) the digital signature of the sender (signer) of a message.

With a private key, you can:

- Produce a digital signature by encrypting a hash value of a message.

- Decrypt content that has been encrypted with the mathematically related public key.

EXAM TIP

The relationship between the private key and the public key is a critical concept to understand in asymmetric key algorithms and cryptosystems. The functions that each provides are also critical knowledge for the exam.

Although symmetric algorithms are largely based on substitution (confusion) and transposition (diffusion) of binary bits, asymmetric algorithms are based primarily on mathematic formulas. The keys (numbers) used in asymmetric key cryptography are notably longer than those used in symmetric key cryptography. A short key in asymmetric key cryptography is 768 bits long (DH Group 1), providing a keyspace range of zero to approximately the number 15 with 230 zeros behind it. Today, this key size is considered too short to use. In 2003, the IETF published RFC 3526, which identifies key lengths up to 8,192 bits (8 kilobits, known as DH Group 18), providing a keyspace range of zero to approximately the number 1 with 2,466 zeros behind it. These keys are so large and unique (random) that it is statistically impossible for someone to guess your private key. The recommendation today is to use a key longer than 1 kilobit, and typically 2 kilobits or 3 kilobits in length is preferred, with the NIST recommendation in 2011 to use a 2-kilobit key minimum.

Key management in an asymmetric key cryptosystem is much easier than in a symmetric key cryptosystem. Only two keys are required per user (2N, where N is the number of users) in the asymmetric key cryptosystem. Further, only the private key requires protection, cutting in half this very low number of 2N keys. Because you can readily share the public key with anyone, there is no problem of secure key distribution, and the asymmetric key cryptosystem solves this problem for the symmetric key cryptosystems. Secure key distribution will be described in full detail in the "Cryptography in use" section later in this chapter.

The primary detriment with asymmetric key cryptosystems is the performance. Crunching numbers that fill a page takes some processing power and time. With this in mind, cryptographers have assembled hybrid cryptosystems that take advantage of the best features of the various cryptographic functions.

The great security benefits provided by the asymmetric key cryptosystem has led to its use with digital certificates and the PKI system that has become a standard for security in contemporary information systems. Another hybrid cryptosystem of note is Pretty Good Privacy (PGP). These two commonly used technologies are explored in more detail in the "Cryptography in use" section later in this chapter.

Signing by using asymmetric key algorithms in a hybrid cryptosystem

 When asymmetric keys are used to provide authentication and integrity validation, it is called a *digital signature*. Because of the strength of the authentication provided by the asymmetric key pair, the digital signature also provides nonrepudiation. This digital signature uses a hashing function and an asymmetric key pair. It also typically uses *digital certificates*, provided by a PKI and *certification authorities* (CAs), the systems that produce the digital certificates. The digital certificate adds the element of trust to the cryptographic functionality of the asymmetric key pair. The digital certificate binds the user's identity and the user's asymmetric public key to the X.509 digital certificate and is then signed by the CA that created the certificate. PKI is described in the "Cryptography in use" section later in this chapter, but for now, it is enough for you to know that after a recipient verifies a digital certificate, the recipient knows and believes that the public key embedded in the certificate belongs to the user whose name is documented on the certificate.

The digital signature provides the following three cryptographic services:

- **Authentication**   Strong
- **Nonrepudiation**   Strong
- **Integrity validation**   Strong

If a sender digitally signs a message, he proves these three things to the recipient. The digital signature does not provide confidentiality services. If you need confidentiality, you need to seal the message, not sign it.

Here is how the digital signature (signing), using asymmetric keys and a hashing function, works. Suppose that BoBo (the sender) wants to send LuLu (the recipient) a digitally signed message to prove to LuLu that he sent the message, that he cannot deny sending the message, and that the message has not been altered since BoBo created the message.

1. BoBo, the sender, has an asymmetric key pair. The public key is embedded in a digital certificate from a trusted CA. BoBo holds the mathematically related private key securely and never shares the private key with anyone.

2. BoBo creates a message.

3. BoBo runs a hashing algorithm on the entire message, producing a hash value as the output of the hashing algorithm. The hash value acts as a fingerprint of the message. If any one or more binary bits that make up the message are changed, the hash value will change. Because BoBo, the creator of the message, is running the hashing algorithm on the message at the time of creation, the message is known good at this time.

4. BoBo uses his private key to encrypt the hash value of the message. This is the digital signature for the message. BoBo is the only person on the planet who can access this private key, therefore BoBo is the only person on the planet who can produce this signature for the message.

5. BoBo sends the plaintext message and the digital signature (the encrypted known good hash value) to LuLu, the recipient (see Figure 3-24).

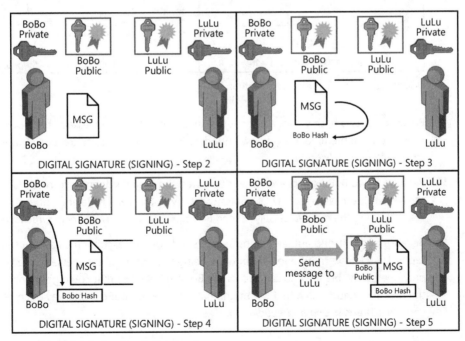

FIGURE 3-24 Producing the digital signature

6. Upon receiving the digitally signed message, LuLu acquires BoBo's digital certificate.

7. LuLu verifies BoBo's digital certificate and concludes, with certainty, that the public key embedded in the BoBo digital certificate belongs to BoBo.

8. LuLu uses BoBo's public key from the BoBo digital certificate to decrypt the digital signature and reveal the hash value that BoBo created at the time when the message was known good.

9. LuLu runs the same hashing algorithm on the entire message and produces a second hash value, the LuLu at-time-of-use hash value.

10. LuLu compares the BoBo known good hash value to the LuLu at-time-of-use hash value (see Figure 3-25).

    If the two hash values are identical, LuLu can conclude that three cryptographic services have been provided strongly.

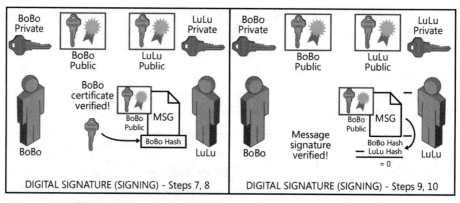

FIGURE 3-25 Verifying the digital signature

11. Because the two hash values are identical, LuLu knows that the message has not been modified from the time it was known good by BoBo, at the time of creation. This is *strong integrity validation*.

12. Because it was BoBo's public key that decrypted the digital signature correctly (so that the hash value was correct), LuLu knows that only BoBo could have encrypted the hash value by using the mathematically related BoBo private key. This is *strong authentication*.

13. Because of the strong authentication services provided by asymmetric key cryptography, LuLu knows that BoBo cannot deny being the sender of the message. He is the only one on the planet who can access the BoBo private key that could have encrypted the digital signature such that the mathematically related BoBo public key decrypts it correctly. This is *strong nonrepudiation*.

Sealing by using asymmetric key algorithms in a hybrid cryptosystem

Sealing messages means providing confidentiality for messages. Although asymmetric key cryptography can provide strong confidentiality, remember that it is approximately 1,000 times slower than symmetric key cryptography, and symmetric key cryptography can provide strong confidentiality. The messages sent between users in an information system could be large—perhaps tens of megabytes, hundreds of megabytes, or even several gigabytes. You wouldn't want to encrypt that bulk with asymmetric keys that are 1,000 times slower when the much faster symmetric keys can provide good, strong ciphertext. The symmetric keys, however, are quite small, ranging from 64 bits to 512 bits in length. These small symmetric keys could easily be encrypted with the slow asymmetric keys to provide the secure key distribution that is required of symmetric key cryptosystems.

With this in mind, it becomes obvious why hybrid cryptosystems use *symmetric session keys* and asymmetric keys together to provide confidentiality (sealing) of messages. Here is how providing confidentiality of messages, with the use of asymmetric and symmetric keys, works:

1. LuLu, the recipient, has an asymmetric key pair. The public key is embedded in a digital certificate from a trusted CA. LuLu holds the mathematically related private key securely and never shares the private key with anyone.

2. BoBo, the sender, creates a message.

3. BoBo acquires LuLu's (the recipient's) digital certificate.

4. BoBo verifies LuLu's digital certificate and concludes, with certainty, that the public key embedded in the LuLu digital certificate belongs to LuLu.

5. BoBo uses a cryptographic service provider (CSP) on his local computer to create a pair of symmetric session keys. Remember that symmetric key cryptography uses small keys (typically only 64 bits to 512 bits) and is approximately 1,000 times faster than asymmetric key cryptography.

6. BoBo uses one of the symmetric session keys to encrypt the message intended for LuLu.

7. BoBo uses LuLu's public key from the LuLu digital certificate to encrypt the second copy of the symmetric session key. Remember that this copy of the symmetric session key can be used to decrypt the sealed message.

8. BoBo sends the encrypted message and the encrypted symmetric session key to LuLu (see Figure 3-26).

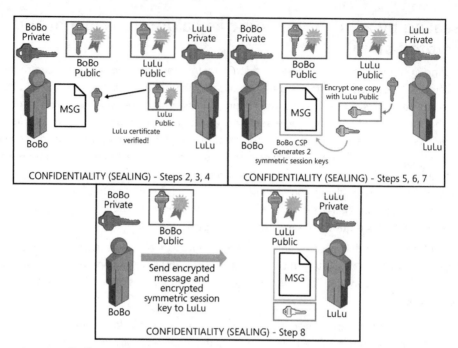

FIGURE 3-26 Sealing a message

9. LuLu receives the encrypted message that has been encrypted with the symmetric session key and the symmetric session key that has been encrypted with her public key.

10. Only LuLu has the private key that can correctly decrypt the symmetric session key. LuLu uses her private key to decrypt the symmetric session key.

11. LuLu uses the symmetric session key to decrypt the encrypted message, revealing the meaning of the message. The message was securely delivered to LuLu, and only LuLu could decrypt the message successfully. Secure key distribution (the symmetric session key) was also accomplished to facilitate the secure delivery of the message (see Figure 3-27).

FIGURE 3-27 Unsealing a message

Sealing messages provides the cryptographic service of confidentiality and secure key distribution. Notice that the symmetric session key is used for one message only and is then destroyed after its one-time use, "session" implying short-term or temporary. Notice also that the public and private key pairs are long-term keys (also called static, persistent, or secret keys). These keys are typically good for one or two years before expiring.

Sending to multiple recipients when sealing

If the sender wants to send a message securely to multiple recipients, all the sender has to do is perform the following steps. See Figure 3-28.

1. Acquire and validate the digital certificate for each intended recipient.

2. Duplicate the symmetric session key, one copy for each intended recipient plus the one copy the sender needs to encrypt the message.

3. Extract the public key from the verified digital certificate for each intended recipient.

4. Encrypt a copy of the symmetric session key, one key at a time, using the public key of each intended recipient so that there is one encrypted symmetric session key for each intended recipient that has been encrypted using that recipient's public key.

5. Distribute a copy of the encrypted message to each intended recipient along with a copy of the symmetric session key that has been encrypted with that recipient's public key.

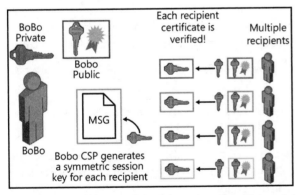

FIGURE 3-28 Sending a confidential message to multiple recipients

The intended recipient decrypts the copy of the symmetric session key by using her private key and then uses the decrypted symmetric session key to decrypt the securely distributed message.

Signing and sealing messages

So how would signing and sealing a message work? This would require all five desirable cryptographic services. Here is how the digital signature (signing) and sending of secure messages (sealing) works, using asymmetric keys, symmetric keys, and a hashing function: BoBo (the sender) wants to send LuLu (the recipient) a secure and digitally signed message. This keeps the message secret, for only BoBo and LuLu, and proves to LuLu that Bobo sent the message, that he cannot deny sending the message, and that the message has not been altered since BoBo created the message. The following steps detail the procedure (see Figures 3-29 and 3-30). Feel free to review the individual pieces as shown in Figures 3-24, 3-25, 3-26, and 3-27.

1. BoBo, the sender, has an asymmetric key pair. The public key is embedded in a digital certificate from a trusted CA. BoBo holds the mathematically related private key securely and never shares the private key with anyone.

2. LuLu, the recipient, has an asymmetric key pair. The public key is embedded in a digital certificate from a trusted CA. LuLu holds the mathematically related private key securely and never shares the private key with anyone.

3. BoBo creates a message.

4. BoBo runs a hashing algorithm on the entire message, producing a known good hash value as the output of the hashing algorithm.

5. BoBo uses his private key to encrypt the hash value of the message. This is the digital signature for the message.

6. BoBo acquires and validates a copy of the LuLu digital certificate, and concludes, with certainty, that the public key embedded in the LuLu digital certificate belongs to LuLu.

7. BoBo uses a cryptographic service provider (CSP) on his local computer to create a pair of symmetric session keys.

8. BoBo uses one of the symmetric session keys to encrypt the message intended securely for LuLu.

9. BoBo uses LuLu's public key from the LuLu digital certificate to encrypt the second copy of the symmetric session key. Remember that this copy of the symmetric session key can be used to decrypt the sealed message.

10. BoBo sends the encrypted message, the encrypted hash value of the message (the digital signature), and the encrypted symmetric session key to LuLu.

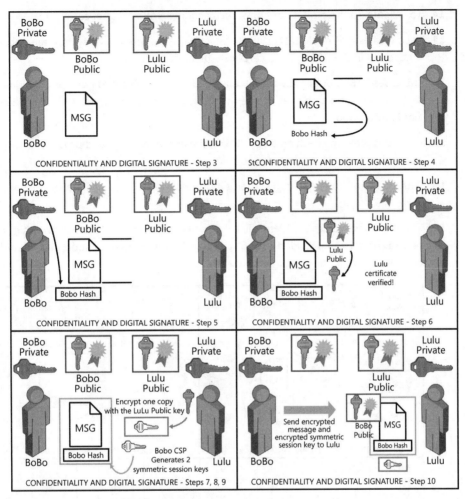

FIGURE 3-29 Signing and Sealing a message

11. LuLu receives the encrypted message, the encrypted hash value of the message (the digital signature), and the encrypted symmetric session key that has been encrypted with her public key.

12. LuLu uses her private key to decrypt the symmetric session key.

13. LuLu uses the symmetric session key to decrypt the encrypted message, revealing the meaning of the message. The message was securely delivered to LuLu, and only LuLu could decrypt the message successfully. Secure key distribution (the symmetric session key) was also accomplished to facilitate the secure delivery of the message.

14. To validate BoBo's digital signature, LuLu acquires BoBo's digital certificate.

15. LuLu verifies BoBo's digital certificate and concludes, with certainty, that the public key embedded in the BoBo digital certificate belongs to BoBo.

16. LuLu uses BoBo's public key from the BoBo digital certificate to decrypt the digital signature and reveal the hash value that BoBo created at the time when the message was known good.

17. LuLu runs the same hashing algorithm on the entire message and produces a second hash value, the LuLu at-time-of-use hash value.

18. LuLu compares the BoBo known good hash value to the LuLu at-time-of-use hash value.

19. If the two hash values are identical, LuLu can conclude that three cryptographic services have been provided strongly: authentication, nonrepudiation, and integrity validation.

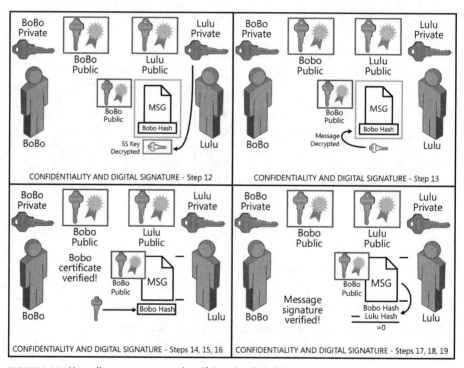

FIGURE 3-30 Unsealing a message and verifying the digital signature

Wow! If you were able to follow that, you might have become a cryptographer! (Did that happen again?!)

The signing and sealing of messages requires all five desirable cryptographic services and requires both BoBo, the sender, and LuLu, the recipient, to have an asymmetric key pair and (typically) digital certificates. Content can be signed and sealed and then sent to one or more recipients (protection for data in transit), or it can be signed and sealed to self, so that the creator can protect and verify the integrity of his own secret content in secure storage (protection for data at rest).

Asymmetric key algorithms

Asymmetric key algorithms have only been in existence since the mid-1970s, when computers became available to the masses, and they are based on relatively heavy mathematics with large, perhaps unbelievably huge, numbers.

Following is a list of the most commonly used asymmetric algorithms:

- Diffie-Hellman-Merkle (or just Diffie-Hellman [DH])
- RSA (Rivest, Shamir, Adleman)
- Elliptic Curve Cryptography (ECC)
- ElGamal
- Digital Signature Standard (DSS)
- LUC (Reference only)
- XTR (Reference only)

By culling data from RSA, NIST, IETF, and other sources, Table 3-5 shows how the key length used in different algorithms align with approximately equivalent strength.

TABLE 3-5 Comparison of approximately equivalent key strength vs. key length (values are estimates and shown in bits)

Symmetric	ECC	XTR	LUC	RSA
80	163	342	512	1,024
112	233	683	1,024	2,048
128	283	1,024	1,536	3,072
192	409	2,560	3,840	7,680
256	571	5,120	7,680	15,360

Invented in 1976 and based on large numbers and mathematics, asymmetric key cryptosystems are the latest and greatest addition to cryptography. They rely on a pair of mathematically related numbers (keys); one is a private key and the other is a public key. What one key encrypts only the other key can decrypt. You can share your public key with anyone. You can never share your private key with anyone. Because you have only the public key of another, you have no insight into the nature of the other's private key.

Most asymmetric key algorithms use variations of mathematics from the following list:

- Calculating discrete logarithms in a finite field
- Factoring large numbers into their prime values
- Calculating discrete logarithms in a finite field, limiting that finite field to pairs of numbers plotted on an elliptic curve or other mathematical or numeric sequences

Although some asymmetric key cryptosystems provide only a few services, when used with symmetric key algorithms and hashing algorithms (a hybrid cryptosystem), most can provide all five desirable cryptographic services in a strong manner. They form the basis of the PKI that adds the element of trust to the functionality of the asymmetric key pair. The PKI binds a user's public key to her identity by using an X.509 digital certificate and ensures trust through a hierarchical trust model.

The key lengths in asymmetric key cryptosystems are typically at least twice as long as symmetric keys and are often more than 10 times the length of symmetric keys. This causes them to be notably slower than symmetric key cryptosystems. The quantity of keys generated ($2n$) and protected (n) are substantially lower than those of symmetric key cryptosystems ($n \times (n-1))/2$, especially as the number of users participating in the cryptosystem grows.

Diffie-Hellman-Merkle (or just Diffie-Hellman)

Diffie-Hellman was introduced in 1976. It was designed to solve that 5,000-year-old problem with symmetric key cryptography—the necessity to distribute copies of symmetric keys securely without some prior relationship or arrangements. Following are several key concepts to understand about the Diffie-Hellman (DH) algorithm.

- DH was the first asymmetric algorithm ever.
- DH provides *only one* of the five desirable cryptographic services: secure key distribution.
- DH is commonly referred to as a *key agreement protocol*.
- DH is based on mathematics described as *calculating discrete logarithms in a finite field*.
- DH does not perform any kind of authentication of the endpoints.

When using Diffie-Hellman, the two participants use public keys and private keys to generate the same symmetric session key simultaneously in essence, providing secure key distribution. This can be accomplished across any communications channel, even when an attacker might be eavesdropping, because they only need to send public keys. Although the bad guy will see these public key values (remember that keys are nothing more than numbers), without knowing the private keys of the two participants, the bad guy cannot produce the same symmetric session key.

Here is how Diffie-Hellman works:

1. BoBo and LuLu have no prior relationship and have never communicated previously. Today however, their paths cross, and they need to exchange confidential information securely over an unsecured communications channel.

2. BoBo and LuLu agree on a public key value. Anyone monitoring their communications channel can see this number.

3. BoBo calculates a mathematically related private key based on the agreed-upon public key value.

4. At the same time, LuLu calculates a mathematically related and different private key based on the agreed-upon public key value.

5. BoBo performs math by using his private key value and the agreed-upon public key value (Pub1). This produces BoBo's public key 2 value (BoBo Pub2).

6. LuLu performs math by using her (different) private key value and the agreed-upon public key value (Pub1). This produces LuLu's public key 2 value (LuLu Pub2).

7. BoBo sends BoBo's public key 2 value (BoBo Pub2) to LuLu. Anyone monitoring their communications channel can see this number.

8. LuLu sends LuLu's public key 2 value (LuLu Pub2) to BoBo. Anyone monitoring their communications channel can see this number.

9. BoBo performs math by using his private key value and LuLu's public key 2 value (LuLu Pub2). This produces BoBo's copy of the symmetric session key.

10. LuLu performs math by using her (different) private key value and BoBo's public key 2 value (BoBo Pub2). This produces LuLu's copy of the symmetric session key, the same symmetric session key that BoBo just produced (see Figure 3-31).

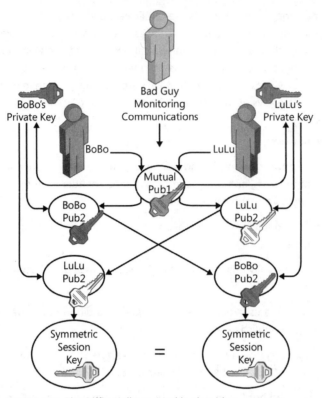

FIGURE 3-31 The Diffie-Hellman-Merkle algorithm

BoBo and LuLu now have copies of the same symmetric session key and can use these keys to encrypt and decrypt content to one another. The freshly and independently calculated symmetric session keys never commuted through the unsecured communications channel, so they remain secure.

An attacker could see three public keys commute through the unsecured communications channel—Pub1, BoBo Pub2, and LuLu Pub2—but without knowing either of the two private key values BoBo and LuLu used, she cannot calculate the same symmetric session key value (in a reasonably useful period).

The Diffie-Hellman algorithm can be used to calculate different lengths of symmetric session keys. The different length keys produced by DH are categorized by DH group ID numbers and are defined in IETF RFCs 2409, 3526, and 4492.

DH is most commonly used when digital certificates (PKI) are not present in the information environment. DH is a competing technology with other asymmetric, secure key distribution algorithms.

As stated before, Diffie-Hellman does not perform any kind of authentication of the endpoints, the two entities who want to establish symmetric keys. This vulnerability lends itself to identity spoofing (someone claiming to be someone he is not) and the man-in-the-middle attack, when an imposter convinces two legitimate endpoints that she is the other endpoint. When identity spoofing and man-in-the-middle attacks are successful, the bad guy can affect the confidentiality, integrity, and availability of the valuable information assets of an organization.

This indicates that before you perform a Diffie-Hellman key exchange with another endpoint, you should strongly authenticate the other endpoint by using some other means of authentication.

RSA

While at the Massachusetts Institute of Technology (MIT), Ron Rivest, Adi Shamir, and Leonard Adleman, the founders of RSA, developed the RSA asymmetric key algorithm. The RSA company is now a division of EMC Corporation. The algorithm was introduced in 1978 and has become one of the most widely used asymmetric key algorithms. It is the preferred algorithm for PKI digital certificates used for signing and sealing content in mature and well-developed information systems.

- The RSA algorithm can be used to provide all five desirable cryptographic services.
- RSA is based on the difficulty of *factoring giant numbers into prime integers*.
- RSA keys typically range between 1 kilobit (1,024 bits) and 4 kilobits (4,096 bits) and are commonly used on PKI X.509 digital certificates.
- The RSA algorithm is commonly called a *trapdoor function* because the ease with which you can multiply many numbers to reach an answer, producing the public key, is like going up a ladder through a trapdoor into an attic compared with the difficulty of finding the closed trapdoor in the floor to come down the ladder from the attic (unless you know the secret).

The algorithm was patented in 1983 but was released into the public domain in September 2000. There have been cracks of up to a 786-bit key (they have been factored), but the use of these relatively short key lengths has been deprecated.

Elliptic Curve Cryptography (ECC)

Introduced in 1985 simultaneously by two mathematicians, Neal Koblitz and Victor Miller, this asymmetric key algorithm is based on pairs of numbers plotted on an elliptic curve and calculates discrete logarithm functions. ECC has the beneficial characteristic of using a relatively short key length and providing similar cryptographic strength to much longer keys used in other asymmetric key algorithms. According to the IETF in its RFC 4492 published in May 2006, a 163-bit key used in ECC has similar cryptographic strength to a 1,024-bit key used in the RSA algorithm. A 233-bit key used in ECC has similar strength to a 2,048-bit key used in RSA, and so on. The shorter keys used in ECC are much more efficient with CPU usage and therefore with power consumption. The ECC algorithm naturally finds a home in battery-operated or handheld devices, in which battery life can be extended without giving up cryptographic strength. This includes mobile phones, PDAs, and smart cards.

Because of this reduction in key length and the resulting reduction in computational effort required, ECC can be used to provide confidentiality for bulk content without the use of symmetric key cryptography for its performance benefits.

- ECC can provide all five desirable cryptographic services.
- ECC is based on pairs of numbers plotted on an elliptic curve.
- Keys typically range between 163 bits and 571 bits.
- ECC is desirable for its high speed, low processing power, low energy consumption, and low memory consumption.
- ECC is the preferred asymmetric algorithm for handheld and battery-operated devices.

NIST recommends that an ECC key should be at least twice the length of a symmetric key to provide equivalent strength. In FIPS-186-2, the US National Security Agency has approved the use of ECC-256 with SHA256 for protecting classified SECRET content and the use of ECC-384 with SHA384 for protecting classified TOP SECRET content.

ElGamal

ElGamal was published in 1984 by Taher ElGamal. ElGamal uses two schemes, one to provide encryption and another to provide a digital signature. It is used in the commercially available PGP asymmetric cryptosystem and in the free GNU Privacy Guard. The ElGamal Signature Scheme was used as the basis of the NIST Digital Signature Algorithm (DSA) used in the NIST-recommended DSS.

- ElGamal is an extension of the Diffie-Hellman algorithm and is based on mathematics described as calculating discrete logarithms in a finite field.
- ElGamal (the two schemes) can provide all five desirable cryptographic services.

ElGamal has a tendency to inflate the size of a message as it converts plaintext into ciphertext, often at a 2:1 ratio.

Digital Signature Standard (DSS)

In August 1991, NIST introduced the DSS based on the underlying DSA. It was adopted in 1993 as the Federal Information Processing Standard (FIPS) 186, which as of 2009 is on its third revision, FIPS 186-3. DSA is a variant of the ElGamal Signature Scheme. The DSA algorithm was patented in 1991 by two entities, Claus Schnorr (disputed) and David Kravitz of the NSA.

Recall that a digital signature relies on asymmetric key cryptography and a hashing algorithm. Because NIST recommends the use of its SHA family of hashing algorithms, it is easy to understand why SHA is a component of DSA and DSS. Remember that today SHA1 is not recommended, and the SHA2 family has become the NIST recommendation.

Several asymmetric key algorithms have been approved for use within DSA and DSS, including ElGamal, ECC, and RSA.

- DSA and DSS can be used to provide only digital signatures, only three of the five desirable cryptographic services.

- DSA can use different approved asymmetric algorithms but requires the NIST-approved SHA family of hashing algorithms.

EXAM TIP

The DSS can provide three desirable cryptographic services. They are strong authentication, strong nonrepudiation, and strong integrity validation.

LUC

LUC is a relatively fast asymmetric key algorithm. The name is from the mathematics on which the algorithm is based, called *Lucas sequences* (a family of mathematical functions that produce related integers, such as the Fibonacci series [1, 1, 2, 3, 5, 8, 13, 21 . . .]). LUC adds to this the calculation of discrete logarithms (such as those used in Diffie-Hellman). LUC can use relatively short keys (about half the size of an RSA key) and produce relatively strong ciphertext (compared to RSA). ECC is faster and similarly strong, so LUC gets little attention.

XTR

XTR gets its name from Efficient and Compact Subgroup Trace Representation (ECSTR). If pronounced, "ECSTR" sounds like "XTR." XTR uses mathematics very similar to LUC, but through the addition of another specialized function, it can reduce the key length to about one-third the length of an RSA key while maintaining strength similar to RSA. ECC is faster and similarly strong so, like LUC, XTR gets little attention.

Knapsack

First introduced by Ralph Merkle and Martin Hellman, this algorithm is based on the much older knapsack problem. The problem poses a set of items, each with a specified weight and value, and a fixed-size knapsack to be filled with the best combination of the items based on the value versus the weight of the items. This problem is implemented mathematically to use a public key and a private key for contemporary cryptosystems. Unfortunately, several vulnerabilities have been identified in this family of algorithms, so it has fallen out of favor in recent years.

 Quick check

1. Which asymmetric key cryptosystem is based on pairs of numbers on a plotted curve?

2. What services does the Digital Signature Standard provide?

Quick check answers

1. Elliptic Curve Cryptosystem

2. Authentication, nonrepudiation, and integrity validation

Cryptography in use

By now, you should have a solid view of how cryptography works, but where and how does cryptography fit into a contemporary information system? Remember that the primary objectives of a cryptosystem are to provide the following security services, ideally in a cost-justified manner, balancing the need for security (required protection for the valuable information assets) with the cost of implementation.

- Confidentiality
- Authentication
- Nonrepudiation
- Integrity
- Secure key distribution

This balance links to the risk assessment and information classification covered in Chapter 1 and the resulting policies that dictate what satisfactory protection is for each data element based on that classification. These policies define the strength of the security controls to be implemented to protect these assets while they are in storage (data at rest) and when they must be sent to some other recipient or location for use (data in transit).

A significant component of the cost of implementation is the price paid for slow performance of cryptographic services. Generally speaking, the strength of a cryptosystem is inversely proportional to its performance. In most cases, as strength gets better, performance gets worse, and you pay a higher price for the stronger security. Pay the minimum sufficient amount for the appropriate level of security as required by the data's classification and the company's policy.

You need to protect content while it is at rest and while it is in transit. Choose and implement the technologies that provide the needed service or services at the appropriate level of strength. This section addresses the various commonly used technologies to satisfy these issues in contemporary information systems.

They include:

- Link encryption
- End-to-end encryption
- Public-key infrastructure (PKI) with X.509 digital certificates
- Pretty Good Privacy (PGP)
- Secure communications channels for local area network–based (LAN-based) applications in the form of a virtual private network (VPN)
- Secure communications channels for web-based applications
- Steganography

Link encryption

Link encryption is a class of (typically) symmetric key encryption technologies used to protect data in transit. It is commonly implemented when the source and destination systems exist within two relatively trusted IT environments but these two locations must connect over a communications mechanism that cannot be properly secured otherwise (see Figure 3-32).

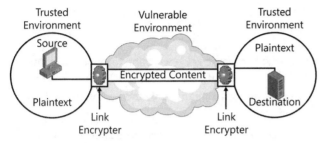

FIGURE 3-32 Link encryption

Link encryption devices are almost always configured with symmetric keys (which are faster for bulk encryption). You can think of link encryption as similar to a garden hose. What goes in one end is encrypted, making it unreadable, and it can only be decrypted (become readable) where it comes out at the other end. Nothing is readable in the middle. Because all content going into the link-encrypted channel becomes unreadable, there can be no intermediate infrastructure devices, or hops, that need to be able to read forwarding or routing information, and no error detection or correction can be performed, except at the endpoints of the encrypted channel or beyond the endpoints, on the trusted network.

If there are infrastructure systems that must read header or trailer information from the encrypted frame, those systems must decrypt the entire frame, read the required information, and then re-encrypt the frame. The infrastructure devices would need the symmetric key, and the content becomes exposed at the infrastructure device. This is usually not good, so if the connection between trusted networks does have to read frame data for forwarding, routing, or error detection, or for any other reason, link encryption is probably not the best solution and should be avoided. End-to-end encryption (described in the following section) should be considered for when infrastructure systems need to be able to read framing data in transit.

Examples of communication systems that might use link encryption include point-to-point T1 and T3 lines (described in more detail in Chapter 7, "Telecommunications and network security") and telephone lines—for example, to secure sensitive fax transmissions. Another use for link encryption is to secure satellite communications channels. A link encryption device is placed inline between an Earth-based IT network and the uplink satellite dish. All communications are encrypted before transmission to the satellite. The satellite retransmits the encrypted content back down to Earth, where hundreds or thousands of antennas within the satellite's footprint receive the signal. Only the link encryption device at the intended and authorized Earth-based destination IT network has the correct symmetric key to decrypt the encrypted satellite retransmission. The plaintext content is then forwarded to the destination node on the intended, trusted network.

Notice that the information is in plaintext from the source to the uplink link encryption device and from the downlink link encryption device to the destination and is therefore potentially vulnerable. This exposure of plaintext data should be considered to ensure compliance with the policy of the organization.

End-to-end encryption

End-to-end encryption is a class of (typically) symmetric key encryption technologies that encrypts content at the source and decrypts it only at the destination, so that the protected data is never in plaintext while in transit. This helps ensure that only the authorized and intended recipient can access the protected content.

For this end-to-end encrypted content to make it over a standard routed network, forwarding information (a Layer 2 header), routing information (a Layer 3 header), and error detection information (used by routers and the recipient at Layer 2 but appended as a frame trailer) must remain in plaintext. Therefore, end-to-end encryption typically begins encrypting at the Layer 4 (Transport layer—also called the end-to-end layer) header of the standard Ethernet frame and stops at the end of the payload, just before the cyclic redundancy check (CRC) trailer used for error detection at each *hop* (router). This encryption structure is shown in Figure 3-33.

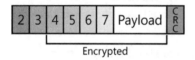

Encrypted

FIGURE 3-33 End-to-end encryption

End-to-end encryption is commonly used today in secure channel technologies such as IPsec, VPN, and SSL used over the Internet.

EXAM TIP

Understand the differences between, and uses for, link encryption and end-to-end encryption.

Public key infrastructure

The *public key infrastructure (PKI)* is a specific implementation of a hybrid cryptosystem. A PKI combines the functionality of symmetric, asymmetric, and hashing algorithms with the trust that can be provided by X.509 digital certificates in a hierarchical trust structure. The X.509 digital certificates and the PKI were developed by the ITU-T to provide strong security services within an X.500 directory service environment. A PKI can provide all five desirable cryptographic services in a strong manner. When strong security matters, PKI is the recommended solution. However, it is an expensive solution, and it requires a large amount of administrative effort to establish and maintain. PKI is strong enough to have become the basis of assignment of formal legal liability in court.

Digital certificates from PKI systems are commonly used to provide user authentication of smart cards and system authentication on corporate networks and the Internet. They are used to provide SSL/TLS channels for many networking applications and protocols such as secure email, secure file transfers, and HTTPS to support secure e-commerce. They are used in dialup, wireless, and VPN authentication schemes such as the Microsoft Lightweight Extensible Authentication Protocol (LEAP) and Protected Extensible Authentication Protocol (PEAP).

The formation of a viable PKI begins with policies and procedures that define the structure and requirements of the PKI. Then technology (PKI-related hardware and software) must be implemented and specific roles and assignments of responsibility must be made. Users must be trained on the secure and approved use of the PKI and related technologies.

The PKI is implemented on computers or other specialized computing devices called certification authorities (CAs). These are the systems that create the digital certificates, binding a user identity to a public key. That public key is mathematically related to the private key accessible *only* to the aforementioned user, the user named on the digital certificate. The CA then digitally signs the digital certificate to provide strong proof that the CA created the certificate and that the certificate has not been altered or tampered with since it was created. The digital signature provides authentication so strong that it provides nonrepudiation and strong integrity validation at time of use.

The systems within a PKI trust the CA, and if the CA creates and issues a digital certificate that states that a user is BoBo, for example, all systems in the PKI trust that the user really is BoBo. As stated previously, in many cases, this declaration by the CA becomes a legally binding statement.

When the user submits the certificate as proof of identity to a system and the system validates the certificate, the system trusts the information written on the certificate and trusts that the public key embedded in the certificate belongs to the user named on the certificate. Now that user's public key can be used to accomplish secure and trusted cryptographic functions and communications, such as signing and sealing content, as needed in an IT environment.

The certification authority (CA)

The certification authority, and the hierarchy of CAs, is the structure of trust within a company. CAs are implemented to satisfy three roles within the PKI hierarchy:

- The root CA
- Policy CAs, subordinate CAs
- Issuing CAs, subordinate CAs

The *root CA* is the pinnacle of trust for an organization (or for the PKI). There is typically only one root CA within an organization. This system is so important to the PKI that to avoid the possibility of compromise, in most implementations, the root CA never connects to any network, operating as a stand-alone system for its entire useful lifetime. The root CA is only rarely needed for service, so the system is usually powered off and is stored in a secured location. The root CA is used to generate subordinate CA certificates that authorize policy and issuing CA systems. These subordinate CA certificates must be sneaker-netted to the subordinate systems by using removable media, such as a floppy disk, writable optical media, or a USB thumb drive. This removable media must be verified to be free from malware before use. The root CA is certified by issuing itself a self-signed certificate.

A *subordinate CA* is any CA other than the root CA. Subordinate CAs can be policy CAs or issuing CAs. They are certified by a CA from a higher tier in the PKI hierarchy.

Policy CAs define a branch of the PKI hierarchy intended to comply with a business partner's PKI requirements. When the business partner—whether it is a supplier or a customer—is considered important enough and relies on PKI, companies will often commit the resources and add a branch to their internal PKI specifically to facilitate trusted business transactions with the partner. All CAs within the branch defined by the policy CA will be strictly managed following the policies and procedures declared on a certificate practices statement (CPS). The statement should match or exceed the PKI-related requirements of the intended partner. The CPS is usually published so that the intended partner can review the certificate practices promised by the company to ensure compliance with the partner's requirements and needs. The policy CA then is used to create one or more subordinate CA certificates for (typically) the issuing CAs within that branch governed by the stated policies. The policy CAs are kept online.

Issuing CAs are the systems that generate the X.509 digital certificates that are issued to the end entities. End entities include users, computers, and, more often these days, infrastructure systems such as routers, switches, and firewall appliances. These end entities are often called the subscriber or the subject of the certificate. This type of CA is accessed most often as users request and are issued certificates and when any certificate or certificates that were issued by the CA need to be revoked. The issuing CAs are kept online.

These CA systems should be hardened and dedicated-purpose systems, performing only the collection of CA functions. They must be protected from compromise. If attackers can compromise a CA, they would be able to generate digital certificates that certify a level of trust by the company that owns the PKI for themselves. They could claim any identity and have it certified by the company on the digital certificate. This places the company in a position of liability, and all users in the PKI and any trusting PKI would automatically trust the attackers' claimed but illegitimate identity, blindly facilitating their unauthorized and likely malicious activities.

It is generally considered that a PKI hierarchy should be at least two tiers deep, and most are three or four tiers deep. Multiple CAs are recommended at each tier and in each branch to provide redundancy, capacity, and perhaps geographic diversity to provide a local CA for faster and more reliable access.

An example of a relatively mature three-tier PKI hierarchy is shown in Figure 3-34.

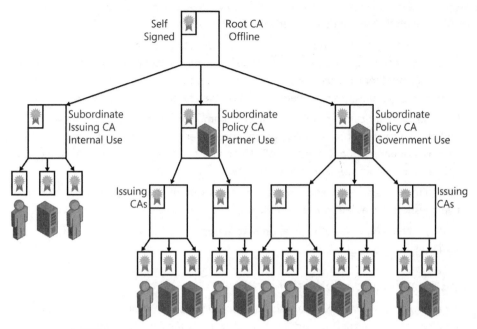

FIGURE 3-34 A PKI hierarchy

The registration authority (RA)

With all this formalized trust happening within a PKI, the issue of authenticating the user who is requesting a digital certificate surfaces as a critical issue. The PKI accommodates this with the use of a registration authority (RA). It is the job of the RA to authenticate end entities satisfactorily and attest to the CA that the required proof has been received and validated. The levels of required proof vary based on company policy and the class of certificate being requested. A higher value class of certificate is intended to protect higher value information assets, and the authentication requirements for those are more stringent. Certificate classes range from 1 to 5. For example, VeriSign uses the following descriptions for its certificates:

- Class 1 for individuals, intended for email
- Class 2 for organizations, for which proof of identity is required
- Class 3 for servers and software signing, for which independent verification and checking of identity and authority is done by the issuing certificate authority
- Class 4 for online business transactions between companies
- Class 5 for private organizations or governmental security

Companies might choose to use these class descriptions, use their own classes, or reference no classes on their certificates. The following list shows some examples of different levels of user authentication that might be required within a PKI system:

- A basic level is successful user authentication in directory services so that the authentication server trusts the identity claim of the user. The authentication server is accepted as the RA. Another example is a supervisor's declaration of the user's identity by using an official communication mechanism. In this case, the supervisor acts as the RA.

- In-person authentication requires the user to complete and sign an application form and present to an authorized RA (a person) one federal government official photo ID, such as a Department of Defense (DoD) ID or a passport, or two nonfederal issued IDs such as a driver's license and birth certificate.

- Add to the in-person authentication an interview with the (human) RA in which cognitive questions are asked from an on-file profile of the user to verify identity further.

- Add to that a biometric authentication mechanism.

- Add to that a DNA verification.

Trusting a certification authority or PKI

Subjects participating within a PKI establish trust for the PKI by importing the digital certificate from the root CA into their *Trusted Root Certification Authorities Store*. Importing a root CA certificate from a different organization's PKI provides cross-certification to establish trust for the other organization. Importing a digital certificate from a nonroot CA from a different organization's PKI establishes subordinated trust for that CA and its subordinates from the other organization.

By acquiring and storing the certificate from a CA, a system now has access to the public key for the CA and can validate the CA's digital signature attached to every certificate the CA issues. This strongly proves to the system that a certificate was issued by a trusted CA and that the certificate has not been tampered with since it was created and issued by the trusted CA. The system can now trust the information presented on the digital certificate and can trust that the public key embedded on the digital certificate belongs to the subject named on the certificate. This facilitates the signing and sealing processes required by the PKI-enabled information system.

Typically, the provider of the operating system (such as Microsoft) automatically adds the collection of globally recognized trustworthy public CAs to the Trusted Root Certification Authorities Store to provide PKI functionality right out of the box for an operating system. If you decide you don't want to trust a CA or PKI, simply remove that CA's certificate from the Trusted Root Certification Authorities Store.

The X.509 digital certificate

The *X.509 digital certificate*, currently in version 3, is an *International Telecommunication Union Telecommunication Standardization Sector (ITU-T)* standard format for certificates and certificate revocation and validation. It was introduced in July 1988 as an additional component to provide strong security services for the X.500 Directory Services standard. In 1999, the IETF adopted the X.509 standard in RFC 2459 and has updated that with the current RFC 5280 (issued in 2008), often called PKIX (PKI X.509).

The X.509 standard defines the following fields for the digital certificate:

- Certificate
- Version
- Serial Number
- Validity
    - Not Before
    - Not After
- Algorithm ID
- Issuer
- Subject
- Subject Public Key Info
    - Public Key Algorithm
    - Subject Public Key
- Issuer Unique Identifier (optional)
- Subject Unique Identifier (optional)
- Extensions (optional)
- Certificate Signature Algorithm
- Certificate Signature

The following describes a typical commercial scenario:

1. The subject presents a claim of identity and a certificate request to the RA.

2. The RA validates the subject's identity by following the authentication standards in place for the organization and, based on the type of certificate being requested, typically defined in the policies of the organization.

3. After the RA has successfully completed the verification process, the RA requests the issuance of the certificate by the CA on behalf of the subject.

4. If the certificate has been authorized by management for the subject, the CA requests the public key from the subject.

5. On the subject's local computer, this triggers a call to the cryptographic service provider (CSP) that generates keys, matching the key requirements specified by the CA for the requested certificate. The CSP generates a public key/private key pair and securely stores the private key in the local computer's key store.

6. The subject's system then sends the public key to the CA.

7. The CA binds the details of the subject, the details of the certificate, and the public key into the digital certificate.

8. The CA digitally signs the digital certificate by generating a hash value of the certificate, including the subject's public key, and encrypting the hash value by using the CA's private key.

9. The certificate is then issued to the subject and is generally forwarded to the certificate repository for the PKI-enabled application where the digital certificate is to be used.

Figure 3-35 details this process.

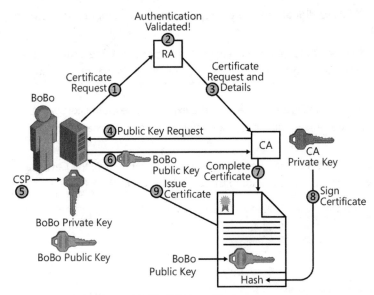

FIGURE 3-35 Acquiring an X.509 digital certificate

 In government use, it is common for a CSP on the CA to generate the private key and public key pair. The private key is then encrypted on the *common access card* (*CAC*) smart card, and the public key is bound to the digital certificate. The digital certificate might also be copied to the CAC card, but it isn't typically necessary to encrypt the digital certificate with the public key.

Digital certificates usually specify an intended purpose. The following is a list of the commonly used intended purposes:

- Client authentication
- Server authentication
- Smart-card logon
- Secure email
- Code signing
- IPsec/IKE intermediate
- KDC authentication
- Certificate request agent
- Private key archival
- Key recovery agent
- Online Certificate Status Protocol (OCSP) signing
- Microsoft Trust List signing (Microsoft systems)

An example of how an X.509 v3 digital certificate is represented on a computer is shown in Figures 3-36, 3-37, and 3-38.

If there is a certificate practices statement from a higher-level policy CA, the Issuer Statement button, which is unavailable in Figure 3-36, will be active and link to that policy statement.

The Copy To File button shown in Figure 3-37 allows the export of the digital certificate for manual distribution on removable media or through email or some other networking file copy function.

If the certificate shown in Figure 3-38 had been issued by a subordinate CA, the Certification Path tab would show the chain from the issuing CA to the root CA of the PKI.

FIGURE 3-36 A sample X.509 digital certificate showing the General tab

FIGURE 3-37 A sample X.509 digital certificate showing the Details tab

FIGURE 3-38 A sample X.509 digital certificate showing the Certification Path tab

When a certificate is presented to initiate a secure cryptographic function, the server should validate the certificate before trusting the certificate. This is a process written into the PKI-enabled application. The higher the value of the information assets that the certificate is intended to protect, the more strictly the certificate should be verified and the more likely the program should be to reject the requested protected function if the certificate fails to validate completely and successfully. Certificate validation checks should include the following:

- Verifying that the certificate was issued by a CA hierarchy that is trusted
- Verifying the digital signature of the certificate to prove the source CA of the certificate and the integrity of the certificate
- Verifying that the details of the certificate match the nature of the request, such as that the name of the subject on the certificate matches the name of the requester, or the name of the web server, and that the requested function matches the certificate's intended purpose
- Verifying that the certificate hasn't expired, as shown in the Valid From and Valid To dates
- Verifying that the algorithms and key lengths satisfy the company's policy and security requirements for the type of transaction requested
- Verifying that the certificate revocation list (CRL) is accessible and that the certificate has not been revoked (discussed shortly)

Sometimes, to prevent a program from appearing to fail, a developer might allow the user to bypass a failed certificate validation, allowing the nonsecure process to execute and exposing the system and data to potential compromise. This defeats the whole purpose of implementing a PKI. Strong security should dictate that all certificates receive full validation checks, and any certificate validation failure fails the related process.

The certificate repository

When application developers enable PKI in their applications, the application server typically becomes the certificate repository for that application. Client-side applications natively connect to the application server for routine operations, making that server the most efficient distribution point for storing and accessing digital certificates for the participants using the application.

For example, if the certificates are used for user authentication within directory services, the directory service server becomes the certificate repository. If the certificates are used for signing and sealing email messages, the email server is designed as the certificate repository.

Certificate revocation

To limit the exposure and liability of an organization, it often becomes necessary to revoke certificates that have been issued, and the organization no longer wants those certificates to be honored if presented for use. An issued certificate must be revoked at the CA that issued the certificate. When an administrator revokes a certificate, the serial number for the certificate is added to a *certificate revocation list* (*CRL*). This CRL must be published so that systems that are presented with a certificate can verify whether that certificate has been revoked. The issued certificates include where the CRL is published. These locations are called *CRL distribution points* (*CDPs*). A CDP location is often:

- A publicly accessible website.
- A location within directory services, accessible by a Lightweight Directory Access Protocol (LDAP) query.
- On a network share, accessible over the corporate network.
- On an FTP server for download, often accessed by partners participating with the organization's PKI.

According to RFC 5280, there are currently 10 reasons to revoke a certificate. (Although the list contains 11 items, 7 isn't used.) They are:

0. Unspecified
1. Key Compromise
2. CA Compromise
3. Affiliation Changed
4. Superseded
5. Cessation Of Operation
6. Certificate Hold
7. (not used)
8. Remove From CRL
9. Privilege Withdrawn
10. Compromise

The only one of these that is reversible is the Certificate Hold, which is typically used when a subject will not be participating in the PKI for some period of time, such as when going on sabbatical or an extended leave of absence.

Another technique to publish and access the CRL is by using the newer OCSP. This provides greater accessibility and faster response to revocation status queries.

EXAM TIP

The use of X.509 digital certificates can provide all five desirable cryptographic services in a strong manner.

Pretty Good Privacy (PGP)

Pretty Good Privacy (*PGP*), currently in its tenth version, is a commercially available hybrid cryptosystem that includes the use of asymmetric algorithms, symmetric algorithms, and hashing algorithms. PGP is a competing technology with PKI and provides most of the same services and functions. It was created by Phil Zimmermann in 1991 and was published as an open standard called *OpenPGP* in the IETF RFC 2440 in 1998. The RFC was updated in 2007 in RFC 5581. PGP does not use X.509 digital certificates natively, but it has been updated to participate with and, to some level, integrate with the PKI system.

PGP provides services that include:

- Signing and sealing email messages and attachments (protection for data in transit).
- Whole-disk encryption (protection for data at rest).
- Scalable encrypted volumes (encrypted store to self) (protection for data at rest).
- PGP NetShare (encrypted store to authorized others) (protection for data at rest).
- Protection of instant messaging (IM) (protection for data in transit).
- Secure deletion (overwriting remnants).

The most significant difference between PKI and PGP is that PKI uses a hierarchical trust model, whereas PGP uses a less structured, *web of trust* model. This model has several vulnerabilities, including the need to verify authentication codes manually on the certificate form (not X.509) used by PGP to establish trust for the certificate. Another weakness is the issue of associative trust, by which user BoBo trusts user LuLu, and user LuLu trusts user Willis. If the trust is not managed strictly in PGP, user BoBo will have a level of trust for Willis without ever knowing Willis, trying to trust Willis, or even being aware of his trust for Willis.

The public key of the other PGP user is stored on a *key ring* versus a key store as in PKI.

> **NOTE** **A COLORFUL PAST**
>
> Zimmermann named PGP after a fictional business named Ralph's Pretty Good Grocery, a store in a radio program. The original algorithm was called BassOmatic, from a Saturday Night Live skit. BassOmatic is a 128+ bit symmetric key algorithm. The original version was distributed free and was provided by Zimmermann to hide antinuclear activist content on Bulletin Board Systems (BBS) and the Usenet.
>
> In 1993, due to violations of US export regulations, Phil Zimmermann became the formal target of a criminal investigation for "munitions export without a license." Anything larger than 40 bits was considered to be weaponry and was restricted for export. In an act of defiance, Zimmermann published the entire source code in a book and continued to distribute the code because books are protected under the First Amendment and are therefore exportable. The code was designed to be scanned and then run through optical character recognition (OCR) software, resulting in the easy distribution of the source code. The federal investigation was eventually dropped after several years without any charges filed against anyone, ever.
>
> PGP 2 bumped into patent violations with respect to the CAST, DSA, and ElGamal algorithms. PGP v3 and v4 bumped into patent violations with the RSA algorithm. These patent violation disputes were eventually resolved.

After going through several owners, PGP was purchased in 2010 by Symantec Corporation and is part of their Enterprise Security Group.

Secure channels for LAN-based applications

It is often necessary to protect content during transit between two endpoints over a corporate network or between different geographic network locations. In this scenario, the endpoints are often somewhat trusted, but the connection between these previously known and somewhat trusted endpoints is potentially hazardous and untrusted, such as a connection over the Internet between headquarters and a branch office. The technology commonly deployed to solve this problem is called the *virtual private network* (*VPN*).

The VPN works by isolating the network frames from the surrounding networking environment, often referred to as *encapsulation*. VPN protocols are also often referred to as *tunneling protocols*. In most cases, the protection provides encryption and some form of authentication and integrity validation.

Following are several commonly used VPN technologies:

- Secure Shell (SSH)
- Point-to-Point Tunneling Protocol (PPTP)
- Internet Protocol Security (IPsec)
- Layer Two Tunneling Protocol (L2TP)
- Secure Socket Tunneling Protocol (SSTP)

Secure shell (SSH)

In the earliest days of networking, to avoid needing to be physically close to computers to perform maintenance and configuration changes, administrators used a protocol called *Telnet* to perform remote administration. However, Telnet performed its authentication in cleartext, and all information commuted on the wire in cleartext. In 1995, SSH was introduced as an encrypted channel to perform this authentication and remote administration securely.

Telnet uses TCP port 23, and SSH uses TCP port 22. SSH is an Open Systems Interconnection (OSI) Model Layer 7 protocol. Servers must run the SSH daemon (server service), and the administrative workstation must run the SSH client.

SSH uses asymmetric keys to authenticate users, and its implementation does not verify ownership of key pairs or identities bound to key pairs. It originally used IDEA for bulk encryption of the data and a 32-bit CRC for integrity verification. The most recent version, SSH-2, uses DSA, RSA, ECDSA, or X.509 digital certificates for authentication. It can use Diffie-Hellman for secure key exchange and Message Authentication Code (MAC) for authentication and integrity validation. Many implementations support the use of passwords (symmetric keys) for endpoint or user authentication.

Although not originally designed or intended to be used as a VPN, its inherent functionality allows for this. It is not considered to be the strongest encryption, but SSH has nonetheless become popular for use in securing FTP traffic in the *SSH File Transfer Protocol* (*SFTP*).

Point-to-Point Tunneling Protocol (PPTP)

Point-to-Point Tunneling Protocol (*PPTP*) was designed to secure Point-to-Point Protocol (PPP) connections. Published in IETF RFC 2637 in 1999, PPTP uses TCP port 1723. The PPTP protocol doesn't specify any encryption technology but refers to the use of generic routing encryption (GRE). Microsoft implemented PPTP by using Microsoft Point-to-Point Encapsulation (MPPE), which uses RC4. Although it is widely used on Microsoft systems, versions are available for Linux and Macintosh operating systems.

With the relatively recent addition of the Extensible Authentication Protocol (EAP), Microsoft has included support for its Protected EAP (PEAP) for secure authentication. PPTP is considered relatively weak, and several vulnerabilities have been identified.

Internet Protocol Security (IPsec)

It is clear that TCP/IP has become the standard for Transport layer and Network layer protocols, and although the rest of the world has pretty much migrated on to IPv6, the United States is still largely operating on IPv4. IPsec was created to provide security capabilities for IPv4 network traffic, regardless of its higher layer source. IPsec has become the de facto VPN because of its strength and tremendous versatility. It is defined in the IETF RFC numbers 2401, 2402, 2406, 2408, and 2409 and uses UDP port 500.

> **NOTE   SECURITY BUILT INTO IPV6**
>
> Internet Protocol version 6 (IPv6) has security features built into it and therefore does not require a different protocol, as IPv4 needs IPsec, for security.

In its default state, IPsec uses symmetric key cryptography and therefore can provide strong encryption and weak authentication and integrity validation. IPsec can be strengthened to provide the cryptographic services strongly through the addition of digital certificate–based authentication.

IPsec can provide host-to-host, host-to-subnet, or subnet-to-subnet VPN connectivity. These implementations are shown in Figure 3-39.

The use of different IP subnets causes the routing system on the LAN or LANs to forward the plaintext packets through the IPsec VPN gateway systems, where they are encrypted in the host-to-subnet and subnet-to-subnet designs.

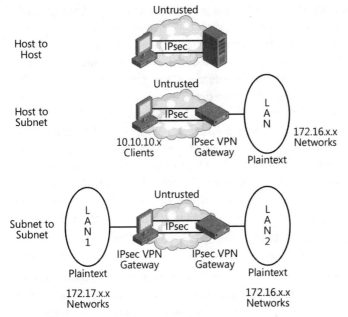

FIGURE 3-39 IPsec in host-to-host, host-to-subnet, and subnet-to-subnet implementations

INTERNET KEY EXCHANGE (IKE)

The IPsec VPN is highly customizable. Different types and levels of protection can be configured differently based on many issues, such as:

- Authentication type: Kerberos protocol, digital certificates, or a pre-shared key (such as a password)
- Direction: inbound/outbound/mirrored
- Protocol
- Port numbers
- IP addresses
- Data authentication and integrity verification (AH Mode)
- Data encryption (ESP mode; the default behavior is to provide AH + ESP for data)
- Encryption algorithm
- Key distribution technique
- Encryption key rotation frequency (typically every 100,000 KB or every 60 minutes, whichever comes first)
- Hashing algorithm
- Transport mode vs. Tunnel mode
- Perfect Forward Secrecy—On/Off

The list of options goes on and on.

These details are figured out and documented by a protocol called *Internet Key Exchange* (*IKE*), currently in version 2. In the first phase of IKE, a protocol called *Internet Security Association and Key Management Protocol* (*ISAKMP,* pronounced *isa-camp*) establishes a secure channel, and then it establishes the framework for the negotiation of the details of the IPsec VPN. However, ISAKMP itself does not negotiate the details. IKE negotiates all the numerous details of the IPsec VPN and records the agreed-upon details in two lists called *security associations* (*SA*). There is one SA with details for the inbound connection and one SA with details for the outbound connection. These two SAs are stored on each endpoint in a database. One endpoint's inbound SA is the other endpoint's outbound SA and vice versa. There might be as many as four SAs per IPsec VPN, one SA pair for the AH protocol and one SA pair for the ESP protocol. The AH and ESP protocols are covered shortly within this section. To improve performance and keep track of potentially hundreds of active VPN connections, these SAs are indexed, and the index is assigned a numeric value called the Security Parameter Index (SPI).

In the second phase of IKE, the *Oakley* Key Determination Protocol allows the two endpoints to agree on how to exchange symmetric keys securely for encryption and decryption.

After all the details are understood, it is almost time to start sending data packets through IPsec. But first, IKE must generate and distribute the symmetric encryption keys to be used for data authentication and encryption. This typically is accomplished by using Diffie-Hellman. However, IPsec supports a protocol called the *Secure Key Exchange Mechanism* (*SKEMe*), which allows various key distribution techniques to be implemented such as the use of static and manually input symmetric keys or the use of public key/private key secure key distribution. As soon as the SAs are complete and the symmetric keys are distributed, IKE is done, and data packets can finally flow, protected by the security mechanisms just negotiated.

AUTHENTICATION HEADER (AH)

Authentication header (*AH*) is a security component of IPsec that performs symmetric key authentication and integrity validation but not encryption (confidentiality). The negotiated and agreed-upon details of AH are documented within a pair of SAs at each endpoint. AH runs a hashed message authentication code (HMAC) algorithm from the beginning of the Layer 3 header to the end of the payload to produce an integrity check value (ICV) for the IP packet, as shown in Figure 3-40.

AH Transport Mode Packet Structure

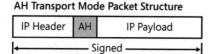

FIGURE 3-40 Authentication header (AH) in IPsec

The recipient validates this ICV to provide authentication and integrity validation.

Notice that the ICV is calculated over the Layer 3 header. This means that if the Layer 3 header data is changed, the ICV validation will fail, and the packet will be discarded by the recipient. This is why IPsec and Network Address Translation (NAT) have potential conflicts that must be avoided. NAT is covered more in Chapter 7.

AH is defined as Protocol ID 51.

ENCAPSULATING SECURITY PAYLOAD (ESP)

Encapsulating Security Payload (*ESP*) provides symmetric key authentication, integrity validation, and encryption (confidentiality). The negotiated and agreed-upon details of ESP are documented within a pair of SAs at each endpoint. The encryption begins at the end of the Layer 3 header and before the Layer 4 header, and then a Message Authentication Code (MAC) value is calculated across a portion of the Layer 3 header and the entire encrypted payload of the packet, as shown in Figure 3-41.

ESP Transport Mode Packet Structure

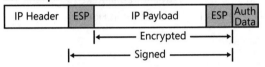

FIGURE 3-41 Encapsulating Security Payload (ESP) in IPsec

The recipient validates the ESP MAC value to provide authentication and integrity validation. ESP also provides a sequence number for anti-replay protection. Because ESP does not encrypt Layer 3 or include the source and destination IP addresses in its MAC calculation, ESP alone does not have any trouble passing through a NAT server. This is referred to as IPsec NAT-T (NAT Traversal).

ESP is defined as Protocol ID 50.

TRANSPORT MODE

The *Transport mode* of IPsec implements encryption at the beginning of the Layer 4 header, the Transport layer. This encryption continues until the end of the payload and before the 32-bit CRC trailer, as shown in Figure 3-42.

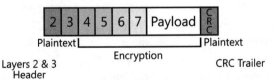

FIGURE 3-42 The Transport mode of IPsec

This allows the forwarding information (destination MAC address information) in the Layer 2 header, the routing information (destination IP address), and the 32-bit CRC trailer to remain in plaintext so that the network infrastructure systems can successfully transmit the packet to its destination.

The plaintext presentation of actual source and destination IP addresses reveals network architecture and might be considered too much information to provide to the unauthorized (attackers). If the security requirements of the organization dictate that this information must also be protected, Transport mode should not be used, but IPsec has an alternative that will satisfy these concerns.

TUNNEL MODE

To protect the actual source and destination IP addresses with encryption, run IPsec in *Tunnel mode*. This encrypts the entire packet from the beginning of the Layer 3 header to the end of the payload. Then it adds a new, plaintext Layer 3 header that contains the destination IP address of the IPsec VPN gateway system on the remote side of the IPsec VPN. Finally, at Layer 2, it adds a plaintext Layer 2 header and the CRC trailer to complete the frame. This leaves Layer 2 information, Layer 3 information, and the CRC trailer in plaintext, just enough information to pass the frame through a routed network. This is shown in Figure 3-43.

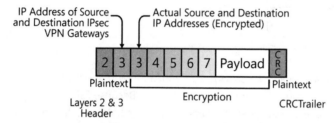

FIGURE 3-43 Tunnel Mode of IPsec

Tunnel mode protects the true source and destination IP addresses, hiding all indications of the internal corporate network architecture and indications of interesting targets (endpoints) for any potential attackers who might just be watching the encrypted packets commute on the public networks.

Layer Two Tunneling Protocol (L2TP)

Published in 1999 as the IETF RFC 2661, *Layer Two Tunneling Protocol* (*L2TP*) was developed jointly by Cisco and Microsoft, merging Layer 2 Forwarding (L2F) Protocol and PPTP. L2TP was designed to tunnel many types of protocols from many applications using Point-to-Point Protocol (PPP) connections over IP (or other) networks to connect to an L2TP network server (gateway). Interestingly, L2TP does not provide any encryption. If confidentiality services are required, some additional encryption technology must be implemented. In common practice, IPsec is used to provide this encryption service. This is referred to as an *L2TP/IPsec tunnel*. When L2TP is used with IPsec, X.509 digital certificates for server authentication can be used. By using these certificates, L2TP/IPsec provides strong authentication of the endpoints in addition to strong integrity verification. The Encapsulating Security Payload of IPsec provides encryption for confidentiality. This implementation is shown in Figure 3-44.

FIGURE 3-44 L2TP over IPsec

Although L2TP can work on an IP network, it can also be used on wide area network (WAN) Layer 2 networks such as X.25, frame relay, and Asynchronous Transfer Mode (ATM). L2TP uses UDP port 1701, but when it is used with IPsec implemented at the same gateway node, IPsec encrypts the L2TP frame and exposes only IPsec's UDP port 500.

EXAM TIP

The initiating protocols, authentication mechanisms, key exchange mechanisms, security protocols, and modes of IPsec should be understood for the exam.

Secure Socket Tunneling Protocol (SSTP)

Secure Socket Tunneling Protocol (*SSTP*) was introduced as an encrypting VPN technology in approximately 2008. SSTP is a client to the VPN server (gateway) encrypted channel designed to transport PPP or L2TP protocols securely over IP networks. SSTP requires a digital certificate on the server side. Client authentication is optional but can include no authentication, CHAP, and certificate-based authentication mechanisms when the EAP is used. SSTP establishes an SSL tunnel (described in the next section) and ports all encrypted traffic over TCP port 443, the same port used by HTTPS. This facilitates its use through corporate firewalls, in which HTTPS must already (typically) be allowed.

SSTP does not support subnet-to-subnet VPN connectivity.

Secure channels for web-based applications

There certainly is a need to protect information in transit over the Internet between client computers and web-based servers. In this arena, and in contrast to VPN technologies, there is a greater expectation that the endpoints of a web-based session are less trusted and are more likely to have no prior relationship. The security goals remain the same to provide confidentiality and some form of authentication and integrity validation. If authentication can be implemented strongly, you can get nonrepudiation, and because you will typically need to send bulk data, you will probably need to distribute symmetric session keys securely.

The following technologies are or have been commonly used to provide secure communications for web-based traffic:

- Secure Sockets Layer (SSL) and Transport Layer Security (TLS)
- Hypertext Transfer Protocol over Secure Sockets Layer/Transport Layer Security (HTTPS)
- Secure Hypertext Transfer Protocol (S-HTTP)
- Secure File Transfer Protocol (SFTP) and FTP over SSL (FTPS)
- Secure Electronic Transaction (SET)
- Secure Multipurpose Internet Message Extensions (S/MIME)

Secure Sockets Layer (SSL) and Transport Layer Security (TLS)

Secure Sockets Layer (SSL) is the predecessor to Transport Layer Security (TLS). SSL/TLS has become the de facto standard for protecting web-based content in transit. SSL was developed by Netscape and is defined in the IETF RFC 5246 (the latest update). Due to security flaws, the first stable version of SSL was version 3, published in 1996. TLS version 1 was released in 1999, and although it is very similar, it is an upgrade to SSL version 3, improving security and fixing flaws. TLS is currently in version 1.2, with its most recent update released in March 2011, IETF RFC 6126. SSL version 3.1 is approximately equivalent to TLS version 1.2. This release upgrades TLS to the use of AES with counter mode and SHA-256, and disallows the negotiation down to the weaker SSL version 1 and version 2. Almost all current browsers support TLS version 1, and Internet Explorer 8 and later supports TLS version 1.2.

SSL/TLS typically requires an X.509 digital certificate for server authentication (now often called an SSL certificate). This provides strong authentication of the server to the client, so the client can trust that it has connected to the correct remote system. (Figure 3-45, in the next section, shows the use of SSL/TLS to protect HTTP traffic [HTTPS]).

Hypertext Transfer Protocol over SSL/TLS (HTTPS)

Hypertext Transfer Protocol over Secure Sockets Layer/Transport Layer Security (HTTPS) might also be called Hypertext Transfer Protocol Secure. HTTPS was designed to provide strong authentication, nonrepudiation, confidentiality, and integrity validation services for HTTP-based traffic. HTTPS was invented by Netscape in 1994 and was accepted by Microsoft, being implemented in the two most popular browsers in their time. Although not a perfect cryptographic protocol, HTTPS has risen to the top of the list to provide strong cryptography for HTTP traffic and web-based applications. HTTPS is defined in IETF RFC 2660 and typically uses port 443 for its HTTPS traffic.

HTTPS requires a digital certificate for server authentication (often referred to as an SSL certificate) on the HTTPS web server. The establishment of the SSL/TLS tunnel is described in the following steps (see also Figure 3-45):

1. The client initiates a session with the web server. This is often done using the HTTP-Get command sent to the server's port 80.

2. The server is configured to run HTTPS and notifies the client of the protocol change. Cryptographic algorithms are negotiated, and the server sends its X.509 server certificate to the client.

3. The client validates the server's X.509 digital certificate (confirming a trusted CA, that the digital signature validates, that the details on the certificate are accurate and match the session, that the certificate is not expired or revoked, and so on). After the certificate is validated, the client trusts the certificate and that the embedded public key belongs to the server whose name appears on the certificate (strong server authentication and nonrepudiation).

4. The client system activates the correct cryptographic service provider (CSP) on the client system to generate a pair of symmetric session keys that satisfy the cryptographic algorithm or algorithms negotiated earlier.

5. The client uses the server's public key from the digital certificate to encrypt one of the newly created symmetric session keys.

6. The client sends the encrypted symmetric session key to the server (secure key distribution).

7. The server uses its private key to decrypt the symmetric session key from the client.

8. The client and server now switch to the HTTPS protocol. The client switches to destination port 443 for its outbound traffic to the server. The client and server now encrypt everything outbound in the session and decrypt everything inbound in the session (strong confidentiality). Most implementations include the use of some form of message authentication code (MAC) (integrity validation).

   Depending on the nature of the services provided on the web server, client authentication might be required by the server. This authentication can be negotiated and performed within the secure SSL/TLS channel. In a Microsoft implementation, this is called Protected Extensible Authentication Protocol (PEAP). In a Cisco implementation, this is called Lightweight Extensible Authentication Protocol (LEAP).

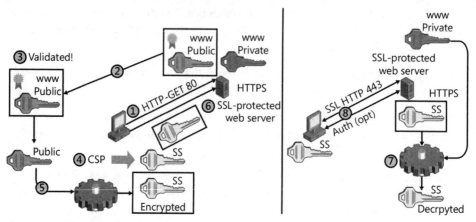

FIGURE 3-45 Hypertext Transfer Protocol over Secure Sockets Layer/Transport Layer Security (HTTPS)

On a publicly accessible web server running HTTPS, the digital certificate is typically acquired from an external public certification authority (CA) such as VeriSign, Entrust, Equifax, GeoTrust, or Thawte. To support internal users, for example for user authentication within a directory services environment, the certificate can be generated by an internal, private, but trusted CA.

Secure Hypertext Transfer Protocol (S-HTTP)

Secure Hypertext Transfer Protocol (S-HTTP) and HTTP over SSL (HTTPS) are competing technologies used to secure web-based traffic. They were both introduced in the mid-1990s and can use similar encryption, authentication, and hashing algorithms. Both support the use of digital certificates. However, S-HTTP performs a message-based encryption, whereas HTTPS encrypts the entire channel, providing session-based encryption.

S-HTTP is defined in IETF RFC 2660 and can use the same port 80 for its traffic. S-HTTP hasn't been accepted nearly as well as HTTPS and has largely fallen by the wayside. S-HTTP was designed to be very flexible, allowing many options for application developers to design S-HTTP into their applications. This has been likened to giving the developers enough rope to hang themselves. Due to the lack of strict specification, application developers, who very often are not cryptographers, can implement the cryptographic protocols improperly, allowing the potential for massive vulnerabilities.

Secure File Transfer Protocol (SFTP) and FTP over SSL (FTPS)

The File Transfer Protocol was one of the early networking protocols designed to transfer bulk content by using guaranteed delivery TCP. FTP includes user authentication but performs that authentication in plaintext. This is a bad thing. Plaintext authentication is never preferred because many users use their directory services logon account user names and passwords for the FTP server so that they don't have to remember so many credentials. This exposes their corporate logon credentials. SFTP and FTPS were invented to help resolve this problem.

SFTP uses an SSH connection and then runs the FTP protocol through the secure shell. The latest version of SSH is version 2. The FTP client software must support the SFTP protocol. SFTP typically runs on SSH port 22. An early and fallback technology uses the UNIX/Linux secure copy (*scp*) utility.

FTPS establishes an SSL secure channel and then runs the FTP session through SSL. Both FTPS and SFTP seem to be getting business, and current implementations of both are common. IANA assigned ports 989 (data) and 990 (control) for FTPS, but vendors often use custom port numbers. Remember that SSL requires the use of a digital certificate from a trusted CA.

Secure Electronic Transaction (SET)

As the Internet became more popular and e-commerce became the name of the game, the payment card industry (PCI)—that is, the banks that issue credit cards—recognized the need to protect credit card information when it is used for Internet transactions. Their first attempt to protect this information was called *Secure Electronic Transaction (SET)*.

When a client browsed to an e-commerce website and wanted to make a credit card purchase, SET, using X.509 digital certificates, would validate identities and encrypt the credit card information. That encrypted credit card data was sent through the vendor (the e-commerce website) to the vendor's bank, called the merchant bank. The credit card data would be decrypted at the merchant bank, where the issuer and the client's information would be revealed. This kept the credit card data encrypted and secure in transit from the client computer, across the Internet, to the vendor's bank, a trusted endpoint. The vendor never has access to the plaintext credit card numbers, so the credit card data can never be exposed by the vendor. The vendor's bank would then contact the issuing bank for approval of the charge. If the issuing bank approved the charge (its promise to pay), the vendor's bank would notify the e-commerce website to accept the order. The settlement of payments would typically occur within three days of the approval, and the vendor's bank account would receive funds from the issuing bank. The issuing bank would then bill the client on the pre-established monthly billing cycle (see Figure 3-46).

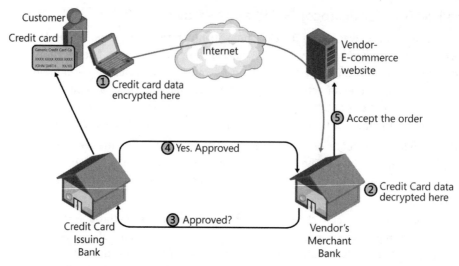

FIGURE 3-46 Secure electronic transaction (SET)

This sounds wonderful until the vendors learned that the banks wanted to charge them a transaction fee of a small percentage of the transaction plus another small percentage for the use of SET. Vendors refused to pay this second fee to help protect the banks, and SET never had a chance of survival.

The banks then decided that if the vendors would not pay the SET fees, the vendors must provide adequate security for the credit card data and implemented the Payment Card Industry Data Security Standard (PCI-DSS). This obligates all vendors who accept credit cards to meet and verify information system security standards designed to protect the credit card data.

Secure Multipurpose Internet Message Extensions (S/MIME)

Earlier in this chapter, you saw how email messages can be secured by using digital certificates for signing and sealing. What about the email attachments? Multipurpose Internet Message Extensions (MIME) is the Layer 6 protocol that enables the Simple Mail Transfer Protocol (SMTP), the protocol that is used to send email and include file attachments with the email messages. By default, MIME does not provide any security protections. Secure MIME (S/MIME), developed by RSA, uses X.509 digital certificates, and the S/MIME feature has been built into virtually every email system to encrypt and digitally sign the attachments of protected email messages.

Steganography

In a category within cryptography, somewhat of its own, is steganography. The term *steganography* is from Greek, meaning "covered writing." It was recognized that data can be relatively easily hidden within certain types of files. Digital audio, video, and still photographs provide this opportunity. On a typical digital camera today, photographs contain 10 megapixels or more. That is approximately 10,000,000 color dots that collectively make the image. Each pixel has six attributes:

- Red
- Green
- Blue
- Hue
- Saturation
- Luminance

Each of these attributes is described by at least eight binary bits, providing 256 shades of red, from no red (00000000) to maximum red (11111111), 256 shades of green, and so on. (Many cameras today provide 32-bit color, which equates to about four billion shades of red and green and blue and so on.) The human eye cannot detect the subtle change from one level of red to the next 1/256 level of red, so binary data can be written as the least signifi-cant bit of each attribute (six bits per pixel) and across the entire picture of 10,000,000 pixels. This simple algorithm would allow you to hide approximately 7.5 megabytes ((6 bits per pixel × 10,000,000 pixels)/8 bits per byte = 7.5 MB) of data in a single photograph without visibly altering the photograph. Furthermore, consider that many of the original least-significant bits will already be the bits required by the hidden data, causing even less visual perturbation to the photo.

Although the steganography algorithms are more complex, the concepts remain the same. Hide your data invisibly within these color dots (pixels), or audio clips, or video clips. Only you and your counterpart know there is data to be found and how to find it. This awareness of the hidden data is the nature of the symmetric key in steganography. For greater protection, you could encrypt the data before encoding it into an image file. In this case, steganography becomes a protected, covert storage channel.

Steganography provides a different service than most encryption technologies—secrecy in-stead of confidentiality. If a sender is concerned that an attacker could intercept and compro-mise a sensitive message during transmission to a remote recipient, the sender can apply an encryption process (cryptography) to the message and then transmit the ciphertext securely. Although an attacker might see the ciphertext transmission, he can't read or understand the encrypted message, but he is fully aware that a sensitive message has just been transmitted. Cryptoprocesses provide confidentiality services—C for crypto and C for confidentiality.

However, if the sender chose to use steganography instead of cryptography, the sensitive message could be encoded in an image file (or any of the other file types that support good steganography); an attacker would see an uninteresting image file and would be unaware that a hidden message exists or was communicated. This is secrecy of information flow, not confidentiality. Stego provides secrecy services—S for stego and S for secrecy.

To take this process a step further, the sender could first encrypt the sensitive message to provide confidentiality (just in case the message is discovered) and then use steganography to provide secrecy, embedding the ciphertext message in an appropriate carrier file. Combining these two technologies provides secrecy and confidentiality. Cool.

Watermarks

Steganography can be used for another purpose as well. To identify proprietary image, audio, and video digital content, steganography can be used to hide an invisible digital watermark. Then active processes can search web content for these watermarks that are acting as a hidden fingerprint identifying the true owner of the content. These active processes are referred to as spiders, crawlers, robots, and sometimes just bots. If a spider locates one of its watermarks, the spider reports back to the owner, who would verify whether proper licensing fees have been paid for the use of the content.

Watermarks might also be visible to act as directive control labeling the content for a certain type of use or protective control, as an advertisement to steer sales to the legitimate owner, or to act as a deterrent for illegitimate use.

Attacks on cryptography

The following are classes of attacks on cryptography. They describe how much information and access the attacker has while actively attacking the cryptosystem. The attacker's goal is to crack (reveal) the encryption keys, decryption keys, or both.

Ciphertext-only attack

When all is designed and implemented in its best forms, a cryptosystem shows only one thing to the unauthorized bad guys: ciphertext. The bad guys have no information about the plaintext data or the nature of the keys the cryptosystem uses. This is the good guy's strongest position and the bad guy's weakest position. Considering that the bad guy wants to steal your messages and crack your keys, put the bad guy in this position whenever you can.

Known plaintext attack

If the bad guy knows what plaintext was entered to produce the resulting ciphertext, he gains insight into the nature of the encryption keys used to create the ciphertext. It is this type of insight that reduces the work factor of the cryptosystem, weakening the security in the environment.

When an attacker knows the plaintext and sees the resulting ciphertext, the attack on the keys becomes more direct. The attacker's position just got a little stronger, and your position just got a little weaker. If a bad guy had captured some ciphertext and could learn something about the plaintext content that was part of the message, she could more easily crack the encryption key.

Chosen plaintext attack

If the bad guy could choose some plaintext to be encrypted using the victim's key, he could choose patterns of plaintext that might more likely lead to patterns within the resulting ciphertext. Suppose that a coworker tends to take long breaks and often fails to lock her workstation. An attacker could use the unlocked system to generate plaintext messages at will and then use the victim's encryption key to produce ciphertext. Another example is the use of someone's public key to encrypt any content desired and then inspect the resulting ciphertext, hoping to gain insight into the private key of the victim.

Symmetric key cryptosystems present a vulnerability in this area. If an attacker chooses a plaintext message that is the same size as the key length and is all zeros and then encrypts the message with the victim's system, the resulting ciphertext will be the victim's symmetric key, as demonstrated in Figure 3-47.

```
Chosen Plaintext  0 0 0 0 0 0 0 0 0 0 0 0 0 0 0 0
           Key    1 1 0 0 0 1 1 1 0 1 0 1 1 0 1 1

   Ciphertext     1 1 0 0 0 1 1 1 0 1 0 1 1 0 1 1
```

FIGURE 3-47 Chosen plaintext attack on symmetric keys

The chosen plaintext attack is useless on asymmetric key ciphertext messages because these are encrypted by using the potential victim's public key that is already available to the attacker. The attack does not in any way expose the potential victim's private key.

Chosen ciphertext attack

This attack moves in the opposite direction. In the chosen ciphertext attack, the attacker creates ciphertext, usually some patterns of characters. Then he runs the ciphertext through the victim's system to reveal the decrypted plaintext. This direction produces a stronger link to the nature of the decryption key of the victim. Cryptosystems are designed to produce strong ciphertext by hiding (randomizing) any nature of the key within the resulting ciphertext. The concern was never to hide the nature of the key in the decrypted plaintext.

This attack puts the good guy in her weakest position and the attacker in his strongest position.

Adaptive attacks

The adaptive attack is a variation or an extension of either the chosen plaintext or the chosen ciphertext attack. By gaining some initial insight to the nature of the key, an attacker might adjust the attack vector and attack again, gaining some additional insight and adjusting her attack vector to improve her position once again. These can also be called iterative chosen plaintext and iterative chosen ciphertext attacks.

Exercises

In the following exercises, you apply what you've learned in this chapter. The answers for these exercises are located in the "Answers" section at the end of this chapter.

Exercise 3-1

Download a cryptography utility from a trusted source. An example might be TrueCrypt from *http://www.truecrypt.org*. Install the application and establish an encrypted volume. Notice the cryptographic functions required to build and mount the encrypted volume, including the encryption algorithm, password creation, and key creation.

Identify the cryptographic ciphers and the hashing algorithms implemented by the application and the type of cipher.

Exercise 3-2

Locate the Trusted Root Certification Authorities list on your computer. In Internet Explorer, this can be found by choosing Tools | Internet Options | Content | Certificates | Trusted Root Certification Authorities. Open and examine several root certificates. On the public CA's website, locate and review the certificate practices statement (CPS) for one or more of the public root CAs.

Identify the algorithms used for the following attributes in three of the digital certificates stored in the Trusted Root Certification Authorities store on your computer:

- Signature cryptographic algorithm
- Signature hashing algorithm
- Public key algorithm
- Public key length
- Thumbprint (hashing) algorithm

Chapter summary

- Cryptanalysis is the science of cracking cryptosystems. It might be done for good cause, to prove the strength of a cryptosystem, or for bad cause, to steal secret messages and keys.
- Hashing algorithms produce a fingerprint of a message and can be used to provide integrity validation and authentication.
- Contemporary symmetric key cryptography is fast and includes two types of algorithms: block ciphers and stream ciphers.

- Block ciphers and stream ciphers might use initialization vectors (IVs) to randomize and strengthen the resulting ciphertext. The IV is a nonsecret value and might also be called a salt, a seed, or a nonce.

- Block ciphers tend to show patterns and might require the use of randomizing modes. The five prevalent modes of symmetric key block ciphers are: Electronic Code Book (ECB); cipher block chaining (CBC); Output Feedback mode (OFB); Cipher Feedback mode (CFB); and Counter mode (CTR).

- Symmetric key cryptography causes the need to distribute symmetric keys securely but can provide three cryptographic services: confidentiality (strong), authentication (weak); and Integrity validation (weak).

- Hybrid cryptosystems use combinations of symmetric key algorithms, asymmetric key algorithms, and hashing algorithms and can provide all five cryptographic services in a strong manner. They include confidentiality, authentication, nonrepudiation, integrity validation, and secure key distribution.

- The first asymmetric algorithm, the Diffie-Hellman-Merkle algorithm, was introduced in 1976. It is based on calculating discrete logarithms in a finite field. It was designed to solve only one of the five cryptographic services: secure key distribution.

- A public-key infrastructure (PKI) is based on a hierarchical trust model of certification authorities (CAs). It uses X.509 digital certificates to bind a public key to a user's identity.

Chapter review

Test your knowledge of the information in this chapter by answering these questions. The answers to these questions, and the explanations of why each answer choice is correct or incorrect, are located in the "Answers" section at the end of this chapter.

1. Which feature or mode of IPsec protects the actual source and destination IP addresses?

    A. Transport mode

    B. Tunnel mode

    C. Internet Key Exchange (IKE)

    D. Security Parameter Index (SPI)

2. What network location needs to be checked to verify whether the issuer of an X.509 digital certificate has withdrawn its claim of trust for the subject of the certificate?

    A. The certificate revocation list (CRL)

    B. Directory services registry

    C. The email server for the organization

    D. The CRL distribution point (CDP)

3. Which of the following is not a characteristic of the one-time pad?

   A. The key must be as long as the message.

   B. The key is never reused.

   C. The key is bound to a certificate.

   D. The key should be highly randomized.

4. Which of the following describes an attacker attempting to create a collision by using a hashing algorithm?

   A. The brute force attack

   B. The rainbow attack

   C. The birthday attack

   D. The ciphertext-only attack

5. Which of the following accurately describes the requirements to produce a signed and sealed message?

   A. Sender's public key, sender's private key, and a hashing algorithm

   B. Sender's private key, recipient's public key, and a hashing algorithm

   C. Sender's private key, recipient's private key, and a hashing algorithm

   D. Sender's private key, recipient's public key, and recipient's private key

6. Which of the following accurately describes the attack used to reveal the sender's symmetric key easily?

   A. Ciphertext only

   B. Known plaintext

   C. Chosen plaintext

   D. Chosen ciphertext

7. Which of the following is the fastest and strongest mode of symmetric key block ciphers?

   A. Counter mode

   B. Output Feedback mode

   C. Cipher Feedback mode

   D. Cipher block chaining

8. Which function is used in the S-box in contemporary symmetric key cryptosystems?

   A. Transposition

   B. Hashing

   C. Pseudo-random number generation

   D. Exclusive Or

Answers

This section contains the answers to the exercises and the "Chapter review" section in this chapter.

Exercise 3-1

Following is the list of cryptographic ciphers implemented by the TrueCrypt v7.1 application:

- AES
- Serpent
- Twofish
- Combination of these

Following is the list of hashing algorithms implemented by the TrueCrypt v7.1 application:

- RIPEMD-160
- SHA512
- Whirlpool

NOTE: A different version of the TrueCrypt application might implement different algorithms.

Exercise 3-2

Following are examples of three certificates that might be found in the Trusted Root Certification Authorities store on a computer system.

- Entrust.net Certification Authority (2048):
    - Signature cryptographic algorithm: RSA
    - Signature hashing algorithm: SHA1
    - Public key algorithm: RSA
    - Public key length: 2048 bits
    - Thumbprint (hashing) algorithm: SHA1
- Equifax Secure Certificate Authority:
    - Signature cryptographic algorithm: RSA
    - Signature hashing algorithm: SHA1
    - Public key algorithm: RSA
    - Public key length: 1024 bits
    - Thumbprint (hashing) algorithm: SHA1
- Microsoft Root Certification Authority 2011:
    - Signature cryptographic algorithm: RSA
    - Signature hashing algorithm: SHA256

- Public key algorithm: RSA
- Public key length: 4096 bits
- Thumbprint (hashing) algorithm: SHA1

Chapter review

1. **Correct answer: B**

   A. **Incorrect:** Transport mode presents the actual source and destination IP addresses in plaintext.

   B. **Correct:** Tunnel mode encrypts the actual source and destination IP addresses and is added to the beginning of the packet with a new Layer 3 header.

   C. **Incorrect:** IKE is used to negotiate the terms of the IPsec VPN securely.

   D. **Incorrect:** The SPI is used to look up the processing details quickly for each IPsec packet.

2. **Correct answer: D**

   A. **Incorrect:** The CRL is the list of revoked certificates. It is not a network location.

   B. **Incorrect:** The directory services registry is used to record details for directory services. It does not contain a list of revoked certificates.

   C. **Incorrect:** An email server might be used as a certificate repository but not a CRL distribution point.

   D. **Correct:** The CDP is a network location where the CRL is published.

3. **Correct answer: C**

   A. **Incorrect:** The one-time pad requires a key that is as long as the message.

   B. **Incorrect:** A key is never reused in a one-time pad.

   C. **Correct:** The public key in a PKI is bound to a digital certificate. This has nothing to do with a one-time pad.

   D. **Incorrect:** The one-time pad avoids patterns in the ciphertext by using highly randomized key values.

4. **Correct answer: C**

   A. **Incorrect:** The brute-force attack is an exhaustive attack on cryptographic keys.

   B. **Incorrect:** The rainbow attack uses rainbow tables to reverse-lookup passwords from a password store that hashes the passwords.

   C. **Correct:** The birthday attack is an attempt to produce the same hash value for a modified message.

   D. **Incorrect:** In the ciphertext-only attack, the attacker only sees ciphertext. This makes the attacker's job more difficult.

5. **Correct answer: B**

   A. **Incorrect:** The digital signature requires the sender's private key and a hashing algorithm. The sealing of a message requires the recipient's public key.

   B. **Correct:** The digital signature requires the sender's private key and a hashing algorithm. The sealing of a message requires the recipient's public key.

   C. **Incorrect:** The digital signature requires the sender's private key and a hashing algorithm. The sealing of a message requires the recipient's public key.

   D. **Incorrect:** The digital signature requires the sender's private key and a hashing algorithm. The sealing of a message requires the recipient's public key. The recipient's private key is only needed to decrypt the message, not to produce the message.

6. **Correct answer: C**

   A. **Incorrect:** The ciphertext-only attack is the most difficult of all attacks.

   B. **Incorrect:** The known plaintext attack allows the attacker to compare the plaintext to the resulting ciphertext and is used to perform the meet-in-the-middle attack, like that used on 2DES.

   C. **Correct:** By choosing a block of all zeroes as the chosen plaintext, the results should show the symmetric key used to encrypt the messages.

   D. **Incorrect:** The chosen ciphertext attack is used to reveal the recipient's asymmetric private key.

7. **Correct answer: A**

   A. **Correct:** Counter mode (CTR) is the fastest and strongest mode of symmetric key block ciphers.

   B. **Incorrect:** Output Feedback (OFB) is faster than CFB but slower than CTR, ECB, and CBC modes of symmetric key block ciphers.

   C. **Incorrect:** Cipher Feedback (CFB) is slower than CTR, ECB, CBC, and OFB modes of symmetric key block ciphers.

   D. **Incorrect:** Cipher block chaining (CBC) is faster than OFB and CFB but slower than CTR and ECB modes of symmetric key block ciphers.

8. **Correct answer: D**

   A. **Incorrect:** Transposition mixes the order of the characters of the message.

   B. **Incorrect:** Hashing produces a fingerprint of a message.

   C. **Incorrect:** The PRNG is used in most stream ciphers to help produce a keystream.

   D. **Correct:** The Exclusive Or (XOR) function is used inside the S-boxes in symmetric key block ciphers. The S is for substitution.

CHAPTER 4

Physical (environmental) security

Physical security is an access control that establishes boundaries to impede intruders. It is a required component of comprehensive and prudent security. If an attacker can approach and handle the valuable information assets of an organization, security, overall, has failed.

Exam objectives in this chapter:

10.1 Understand site and facility design considerations

10.2 Support the implementation and operation of perimeter security (e.g., physical access control and monitoring, audit trails/access logs)

10.3 Support the implementation and operation of internal security (e.g., escort requirements/visitor control, keys and locks)

10.4 Support the implementation and operation of facilities security (e.g., technology convergence)

    10.4.1 Communications and server rooms

    10.4.2 Restricted and work area security

    10.4.3 Data center security

    10.4.4 Utilities and Heating, Ventilation and Air Conditioning (HVAC) considerations

    10.4.5 Water issues (e.g., leakage, flooding)

    10.4.6 Fire prevention, detection and suppression

10.5 Support the protection and securing of equipment

10.6 Understand personnel privacy and safety (e.g., duress, travel, monitoring)

Physical security in a layered defense model

Physical security is applied to an environment as a layer in a layered defense model. This layered methodology ensures that the organization is not relying solely on one specific area of security; that can leave other areas vulnerable to compromise. A layered physical defense also ensures that if the organization is the target of an attack, whether logical or physical, the attacker must get through multiple levels of security to reach any critical information. If a single security mechanism fails or is breached, the other measures would continue to protect the asset. The first layer of a layered defense model should reside on the perimeter and apply additional layers as you move inward toward the valuable assets.

Organizations must remember that hacking, a technical attack, is not the only way information is stolen and information assets are compromised. Physical security encompasses a different set of threats, vulnerabilities, and risks than the types of security controls previously discussed. Physical security considerations include the design and layout of the organization's facility, environmental components, availability and response of emergency services, physical intrusion detection and protection, electrical power, and fire protection. The specific threats that are applicable to physical security include physical destruction, intruders, environmental issues, theft, and vandalism. Physical security is also largely concerned with the safety of personnel and visitors, whose safety are always the top priority for the security professional.

When the security of information assets is considered, physical security is often overlooked. However, even if an organization has the most expansive and capable technology-oriented countermeasures in place, they are futile without the integration of proper physical security components. Physical environments that house corporate structures are built with an emphasis on functionality and aesthetics, often with very little attention to providing protection for files and databases—the information assets they hold.

Within an organization's security program, the physical security portion should be composed of both safety and security mechanisms. Safety considerations directly relate to the protection of human life and the organization's assets against fire, natural disasters, threats by willful human actions, and destructive accidents.

Security needs to protect the assets of the organization while minimizing the impact of countermeasures on the productivity of the employees by providing a secure and available work environment. Good security mechanisms and practices enable employees to focus on their jobs and areas of responsibilities while reducing the risk of breach or incident.

Planning the design of a secure facility

Many threats must be considered when planning to build or expand a facility for an organization. These considerations include location, environment design to improve physical security, construction design, and the countermeasures that should be installed to secure the facility.

Such countermeasures include preventing or deterring an attack from happening, delaying the attacker's progress, detecting the attack as early as possible, and assessing the situation to determine the severity of the attack and introduce a response to the situation that is properly targeted and scaled.

Developing a physical security program consists of spending the time needed to identify vulnerabilities inherent in the assets and business functions, the threats to those assets and functions, and the countermeasures that should be incorporated to establish and maintain a safe and secure environment.

First line of defense

Keeping in mind the layered defense model, the perimeter defenses of an organization are the key to minimizing the ability of an intruder to damage, steal, or otherwise compromise the information assets or, worse yet, to cause harm to the employees of the organization. Human safety is always the first objective. Minimizing risks and losses for the organization is a close second in the list of objectives.

EXAM TIP

Physical security is often considered the first line of defense.

Threats to physical security

The physical threats that an organization typically tackles can be grouped into natural threats, threats to the supply system, and human-made threats. Each of these threat groups has specific vulnerabilities, and countermeasures can be applied to help ensure not only continual operations but safety of life.

Natural threats are threats to the organization's information assets and its people from incidents such as fire, flood, hurricanes, tornados, and earthquakes. Defining what the organization should do when confronted with a natural disaster is important to the continuity of business operations.

Supply system threats include service disruptions in power, communications, heating, ventilation, air conditioning (HVAC), and water. The security design needs to consider what processes the organization should perform to ensure minimal impact from disruptions of the supply system to the security and productivity of the enterprise.

The last group of physical threats is *human-made threats*. These threats include intentional or accidental damage, fraud, vandalism, and theft of data or physical assets from the organization. Human-made threats also include politically motivated incidents such as strikes, riots, and even terrorist acts that could disrupt productivity, generally by affecting the availability of assets.

A well-known security consultant, Donn B. Parker, author of *Fighting Computer Crime: A New Framework for Protecting Information* (Wiley, 1998), has identified seven sources of potential loss or damage to physical assets. They are:

- Temperature
- Gases
- Liquids
- Organisms
- Projectiles
- Movement
- Energy anomalies

Liability of physical design

Organizations and security professionals are often not aware of the civil liability and the potential lawsuits that stem from businesses not practicing due diligence and due care pertaining to physical security. It is important for security professionals to assess an organization's security from the position of a possible criminal and to detect (due diligence) and remedy (due care) points of vulnerability that could be exploited by a potential attacker.

Some examples for which organizations could be sued because of improper physical security considerations are:

- A woman reports a broken lock to her apartment landlord, and after many months of no response, the woman's apartment is robbed with her there.
- A convenience store provides an exterior ATM machine. However, the maintenance of the surrounding bushes is lax and provides a hiding spot for criminals to attack individuals as they withdraw money.

An organization is legally obligated to understand the vulnerabilities and risks inherent in its environment. Developing that understanding is performing due diligence. Due diligence continues with the ongoing monitoring and maintenance of appropriate countermeasures that are in place. An organization is also legally obligated to address those vulnerabilities and risks in some manner to mitigate them. This is performing due care. Not performing due diligence and due care is often construed as negligence in court. If an organization is found to be negligent in any regard relevant to the target of a lawsuit, the court will almost always find the organization liable for damages. Negligence very nearly equals liability in court. Organizations must avoid the appearance of negligence and, therefore, must perform due diligence and due care to mitigate or avoid risks and unnecessary losses due to negligence and liability.

Designing a physical security program

The organization's leadership establishes the organization's security policy to define the security posture of the organization, which is also influenced by the laws and regulations that might be applicable to it. The objectives of the physical security program depend on the level of protection required by the information assets of the organization and the organization's tolerance for risk.

The individuals involved in creating the physical security program must be able to identify the threats to the work environment. To identify these threats, the team must define who or what could compromise the organization's information assets (the threat agent), what attacks could occur (the exploit), and the likelihood that the threat will affect the asset (the level of risk). The team must comprehend the impact on the business that these threats pose (the exposure factor). Then, finally, the physical security program should detail the type of countermeasures required to mitigate those threats.

The process of designing a solid physical security program contains several steps to ensure that all potential threats are recognized and appropriate countermeasures identified. These steps typically are:

1. Select a team to build the security program. This team should consist of a team lead, one or more security professionals, representatives of the major facets of the organization—usually employees—and can include outside consultants to fill capability gaps.

2. Perform a risk analysis to identify the vulnerabilities and threats and calculate the likelihood and business impact of each threat.

3. Work together with leadership to determine an acceptable risk level, at least partially based on the organization's compliance requirements or applicable laws.

4. Consider any existing countermeasures in place and derive the business requirements and performance baselines that accommodate the acceptable risk level.

5. Determine what new countermeasures could complement existing ones or supplement existing security based on the layered security methodology. Remember that each proposed countermeasure must be cost justified, as described in Chapter 1, "Information security governance and risk management."

6. Acquire management approval and implement countermeasures.

7. Continuously monitor and evaluate countermeasures to ensure effectiveness.

The key to a successful physical security program is not only in the methodical approach of risk management, but in the evaluation of the newly implemented countermeasures. This evaluation ensures that the organization is fulfilling its responsibilities pertaining to due diligence. Remember, the primary goal of a physical security program is life safety.

When developing the organization's physical security program, the emphasis is on introducing countermeasures that relate to goals of the perimeter and deeper layers of security:

- Deter
- Delay
- Detect
- Assess
- Respond

Building the layered defense, as discussed earlier, is pertinent to ensuring the safety of people and security of the assets of the organization. Figure 4-1 shows an example of this layering.

Deter, Delay, Detect, Assess, Respond

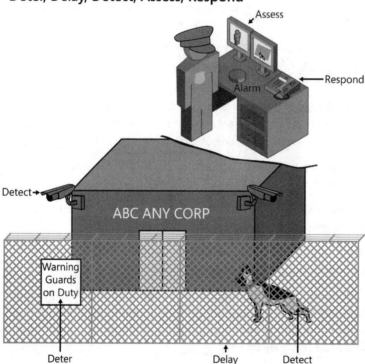

FIGURE 4-1 Physical security countermeasures

Remember that within the physical security program, the focus is not only on human-made threats but also on natural threats and threats to the supply system of the organization. It is essential for each of these categories to be included in the layered defense strategy the organization implements during the establishment, monitoring, enforcement, and maintenance of physical security.

Deterring an intruder from performing some unlawful activities is the first step to providing a secure environment. An organization wants to show a presence of security in its environment. The idea is that when the organization displays a defensive posture, potential intruders are persuaded to find an easier target for their malicious acts. When the security mechanisms are visible, potential attackers understand the penalty they might suffer by initiating an attack. Some deterrent countermeasures are:

- Fences and barbed wire
- Security warning signs
- Visible security guards and dogs
- Visible CCTV cameras

If an intruder is unfazed by the deterrent security mechanisms, the next obstacle that she will face is the collection of delay tactics the organization employs. These security mechanisms might stall intruders long enough to change their mind about committing the attack or delay them long enough for the organzation to detect the attack so that the incident can be assessed and responded to before significant losses are incurred. Some of the countermeasures that offer the delay capability are:

- Fences and barbed wire
- Locks on doors to stall entry
- Wide-open distance between the perimeter fence and first cover
- Access controls that require authentication

If the perpetrator continues her quest to infiltrate the organization's confines and the delay tactics are fulfilling their role within the security process, the detection methods are the next focus of attention. These mechanisms assist the organization in monitoring the internal and external boundaries and alert the required individuals of the presence of an intruder. Some of the countermeasures that offer the ion detection capability are:

- CCTV cameras and security guards
- Door and window sensors and alarms
- Motion detectors and alarms

The successful detection of an intruder warrants an assessment of the severity of the event. Some systems provide automatic assessment and response, such as a sprinkler system triggered from a smoke detector. Nevertheless, the human element provides the best assessment, allowing for a calibrated response. The human first responder must quickly assess the severity of the incident, the potential losses, and the risk to the safety of personnel. Some examples of potential assessment processes and capabilities are:

- Adjusting the CCTV camera to survey the target area.
- Sending security guards to inspect the location of the alarm.
- Determining whether in-house staff can manage the situation or will require emergency services (police, fire, medical, or other outside professionals).
- Engaging communication and command structure— for example, security guards contact management with information and for instructions and approval to take action.

Different situations warrant different levels of response. The appropriate response should be based on an accurate assessment of the security-related event. As mentioned in the assess phase, the response might be different based on the severity of the security breach or incident. These responses rely on an appropriate and knowledgeable assessment of the situation. The response might be initiated automatically or manually by a person who is witnessing or monitoring the environment. In case of an intruder, some examples of appropriate responses might include the following:

- A security guard monitors the intruder on the CCTV while the intruder figures out where the appropriate exit door is.
- A security guard confronts intruder and escorts the intruder to visitor reception.
- A security guard confronts the intruder with gun drawn and orders the intruder to stop what she is doing and put her hands in the air.
- A security guard immediately contacts police for emergency response.

 Quick check

1. What are the desired goals when implementing perimeter security?
2. Signage that notifies passersby of the danger and presence of an electrified fence is an example of which of these five goals?

Quick check answers

1. Deter, delay, detect, assess, and respond
2. Deter

Crime prevention through environmental design

Crime Prevention through Environmental Design (CPTED) is a methodology that details how to design a physical environment properly to reduce crime by directly affecting human behavior. This methodology specifies how combining proper facility construction with the surrounding environmental elements by addressing landscaping, entrances, facility layouts, lighting, road and parking lot placement, and traffic patterns can prevent crime.

Whether you are designing a facility from the ground up or performing a build-out, using the CPTED methodology can reduce the potential of malicious activity. CPTED is intended to deter the attacker, to convince the potential attacker that the risk of being caught is too great, weaken the attacker's confidence, and ultimately prevent the crime from being committed. CPTED elements include open or glass-encased (highly visible) stairwells; designing break areas in view of potential crime areas such as the parking lot; landscaping that does not allow an intruder to hide; and natural physical boundaries, such as a cliff or body of water, to prohibit access. Natural obstructions that limit the capability of an intruder to enter a building by using anything other than the common and intended entrance should also be considered when an organization is deciding the location of a facility. Having a natural barrier such as a lake, hill, or cliff makes it difficult for an attacker to enter the facility and blends the building into its environment so that it doesn't draw unneeded attention. Using nature as a protection mechanism to deter intruders from targeting the organization can prevent an incident from happening.

CPTED introduces psychological, or subconscious, apparent boundaries to keep people in desired walkway channels and out of areas they should not enter, with landscaping (plants) or bollards that produce the illusion of a fence. For the good guy, CPTED should provide an increased confidence in the apparent safety of the area.

Everyone knows that a big part of building a successful business is about location, location, location. Costs are often the motivation behind the choice of location for a new facility; however, you might also need to consider access to public transportation, highways, freeways, and airports. These factors assist in getting customers to the facility, make it easier to attract skilled workers, and simplify inbound deliveries and outbound shipping.

A primary challenge for any business is finding workers who have the requisite knowledge and capabilities to perform the tasks that keep an organization producing its products or services. If the local area cannot provide the required employee pool, the aforementioned factors need to be considered if the organization needs to rely on a workforce that isn't local.

An additional consideration concerning the location of a new facility is the crime rate of the surrounding area. If the organization is driven to a specific high-crime area because of cost, the savings are likely to be at least partially offset by the increased costs of additional security.

Understand the potential of natural disasters such as earthquakes, floods, tornados, or hurricanes. Even though locating the facility in a tornado alley or an area prone to floods might provide tremendous benefits, it might not be a good idea to locate there because the cost of rebuilding, loss of information assets, and lost business while the facility is shut down due to damages from natural events can be extreme.

Regardless of whether a natural or human-made incident occurs, the proximity of emergency services must be evaluated. The time it takes for services to respond to an emergency might be long enough for the theft to be accomplished, the fire to consume the building, or, worse yet, lives to be lost. The results of any incident can be minimized by the efficiency of response from the necessary emergency services. If community-sponsored emergency services are too far away, consider the need to include these skills and capabilities within the organization's emergency response team.

Another consideration should be the amount of pass-by traffic at the location of the facility that provides visibility and access to it. For retail businesses, high visibility is usually a good thing, bringing in the impulse shopper. For other businesses, such as a weapons research and a development (R&D) company, high visibility is a bad thing because it can attract the interest of thieves or just curious people.

When stakeholders consider the location of a facility, they must address joint tenants and shared spaces. Having to share space within a building with another business could present a challenge to the organization's reputation, operations, and security. You cannot pick your neighbor, so if the tenant sharing the building has less desire or need for security, a resolute intruder could gain access to your facility through this shared tenant's space.

As was mentioned earlier, visibility of actions around the facility can be addressed by controlling traffic patterns, automobile or pedestrian, that create a natural surveillance mechanism. To improve physical security, most organizations provide limited entry points to facilitate ingress access controls and monitoring. Install highly visible pathways to the front door to force individuals to use those limited points of entry. Entry doors are often automatically locked outside of business hours and can require a swipe card or proximity card (user authentication) for access.

Fire code typically dictates the number and location of doors that provide exit capabilities, but it is important to ensure that those egresses accommodate exit-only functionality. Emergency exit doors are usually locked, preventing access from the outside, but use the spring-loaded crash bar on the inside for opening during an emergency. Use of the crash bar should trigger an alarm to notify security personnel of its use.

Using the layered defense methodology and taking into account these CPTED considerations can assist in deterring and preventing crimes by not making the facility a target in the first place. If an intruder still intends to target the building, the natural barriers, visibility traffic patterns, access control, and highly visible area make it more difficult for the intruder to succeed.

Physical controls

After the site's location has been established with the previously discussed considerations taken into account, the next step in building a facility concerns the physical controls to ensure a secure environment. The results from the risk analysis will assist the organization in determining the type of material to use in the construction, which is based on the needs of the business, the applicable fire and construction codes, and the identified threats to the facility.

BUILDING MATERIALS

Depending on the building's purpose, consider the various construction factors, such as the weight on the supporting structures and the fire resistance of materials. Although the local building codes dictate the standard requirements, based on the zone in which the facility is being built and the intended use of the building, certain construction materials should be used.

If the building will be used as a data center that processes and stores classified government information, it would be wise to use concrete with reinforced steel construction methods. These materials enable a prolonged penetration time if the building is subjected to a bomb; if the concrete is damaged, it will take longer to cut or break through the reinforced steel bars. This type of construction would also be beneficial to the organization if it is in an area prone to hurricanes because the concrete could withstand the wind speeds and airborne projectiles. These construction materials are more expensive than the others that will be discussed, but they provide additional strength in the event of a natural catastrophe or any attempted forced entry.

If the function of the building does not warrant the cost of concrete and reinforced steel—for instance, if it will be used as a retail outlet or clothing manufacturing facility—other materials can be used. However, although these materials have some cost benefits when compared to concrete, they have some security deficiencies as well.

A light timber construction method comprises lumber that is used primarily in building residences. These materials are more combustible. Fire could consume a building of this type in approximately 30 minutes, so its *burn rating* is 30 minutes. Light frame construction materials provide only adequate strength for loads imposed by other materials and the building's contents. From a security perspective, the use of light frame materials provides minimal resistance against a forced entry or fire.

Heavy timber construction uses some lumber but requires the thickness of that lumber to be a minimum of 4 inches. This type of construction is used primarily in office buildings and some larger facilities. The heavy timber materials provide more protection in the event of a fire, with the building typically being consumed in approximately one hour, which would be its burn rating. As mentioned earlier, heavy timber materials provide more strength and capacity to support a heavier load on the structure. From a security perspective, heavy timber materials provide more resistance than light timber in the event of a forced entry or fire.

SECURITY ZONES

The internal space should be divided into *security zones* that provide differing levels of security. These zones could be assigned based on the sensitivity of the assets, the related risk to the contents, and the personnel who need access to that security zone. Every zone should have access controls that control which individuals can go from one security zone to the next, as shown in Figure 4-2.

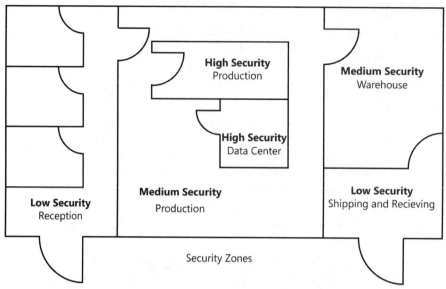

FIGURE 4-2 Security zones

DATA CENTER LOCATION

A very important function that an organization might need to build a new facility for is that of a data center. Keeping in mind that the choice of building materials depends on the intended function of the facility, because of its relatively high value, a data center will most likely need to be constructed of concrete and reinforced steel. Not only will this construction method provide additional strength for the loads to be placed on the supporting structures, it provides security and protection in the event of incidents, including human-made and natural disasters.

What makes a data center construction so unique is that an organization puts all its figurative eggs in that basket. The amount of hardware, software, data, and human capital is in a single location. The amount of loss that an organization would suffer from a security incident affecting a data center could be enormous.

Ideally, the data center should be located in the center of the facility, with offices surrounding it to make it difficult for external threats to enter or damage the data center. No external windows should look into the data center, and access should be strictly controlled and audited, allowing only authorized individuals access during the times that are required for them to perform their job tasks.

A data center should not be located on the top floor of a multistory building. Roofs often leak, and fire burns and consumes floors in an upward direction. It should not be located on the first floor or below ground for similar (catastrophic) reasons. The basement and first floor are the first areas to be destroyed in case of flood. The first floor also typically provides the easiest access for intruders. In addition, avoid building plumbing above the data center.

Target hardening

The target-hardening method is another approach to designing physical security for an environment. CPTED uses environmental factors such as trees, bushes, and placement of sidewalks to facilitate particular security results. Target hardening uses multiple layers of barriers to secure the facility. The physical barriers implemented—obstacles such as fences, locks, and controlled doors—make it very difficult for an attacker to gain access to a facility.

Full wall versus partition

Full walls and partitions separate areas within a larger space into individual or team work areas and can be used as boundaries to provide controlled access to security zones. A *full wall* extends from the floor to the ceiling structure. A *partition* is a wall that extends only from the floor to the drop-down or acoustic ceiling and attaches to the framing members above but does not reach the underside of the ceiling material.

In less-secure areas, where the primary function of the internal structure is simply to separate working groups, the use of a partition is appropriate. For a more secure zone, such as a confidential area, it is advisable to use a full wall structure. The partition wall is not recommended in higher-security areas because it allows an intruder to bypass access control mechanisms by climbing over the partition, through the drop-down ceiling, and into the more secure zone.

Window design

Windows should be placed where they provide egress per applicable fire codes, and framing should be of a necessary strength and include any glazing materials or protective coverings as required. Table 4-1 describes the various types of windows and their accompanying structural capabilities.

TABLE 4-1 Window types

Window type	Description
Standard	Cheapest option, lowest level of security. Often used in residential construction.
Tempered	More expensive; during fabrication, the glass is heated and then cooled quickly to increase integrity and strength.
Acrylic	Uses plastic instead of glass; stronger than standard glass. Because of the chemicals used, could be fire code hazard and produce toxins when burning.
Wired	Uses two sheets of glass or acrylic with a wire mesh in between. Increases strength and prevents shattering.
Laminated	Uses a sheet of plastic between two sheets of glass. Increases strength of glass on impact.
Film	Can use tinted films for increased privacy; transparent plastic film for increased strength; can also be metalized and grounded to minimize electromagnetic emanation.

When placing windows at the ground floor level, the organization should consider a size or type of window to prohibit access because these could likely be an intruder's first point of entry.

Doors

Commonly overlooked weaknesses within door construction are the frame, the hinges, and the material the door is made of. The frame and the hardware that supports the functionality of the door, such as the hinges and bolts, need to provide the same level of strength as the door itself.

The type of door construction should depend on the identified threats, balanced with management's definition of acceptable risk, as determined by the risk analysis. When hardening a target, think about security beginning at the perimeter and continuing in toward the asset. Consider the layered defense method when selecting types of doors for the facility, placing the stronger doors on the exterior of the building and in any high-security areas. Place the weaker doors in areas within the facility that do not house sensitive information or critical assets.

Choose the type of door based on the location of the door and the potential forced-entry threats or natural threats. Hollow-core doors are lightweight and cost less. This type of door provides very little strength and can easily be kicked down to gain access. Hollow-core doors are typically used internally to provide more of a separation of space than a high level of security.

Solid-core doors are much heavier and are more expensive than hollow-core doors. They provide greater strength and can be built by using various fire-rated materials that provide increased levels of protection from fire, *resistance to forced entry*, and natural threats.

Bulletproof doors should also be considered as an option. They are constructed by layering bullet-resistant and bulletproof material with an exterior layer of wood or steel veneers. This external layer will provide some aesthetic quality to a very strong door.

No matter what type of door you consider, keep in mind that the hardware and doorframe must be of equal protective quality as the door itself. Exterior doors and doors used as access to high-security areas should use long and well-anchored screws or bolts to attach hinges and strike plates, and the hinges should have pins that cannot be accessed or removed by a would-be intruder.

Locks

Locking systems, using keys or other devices, are among the most common form of access control mechanisms. A *conventional lock* uses a mechanical key to open the lock. The inclusion of a dead bolt provides more strength because the bolt is projected from the door into the door frame, increasing protection from unauthorized entry. Conventional locks maintain physical security but introduce a key-management challenge. Locks should be changed and new keys distributed every time an employee with a key quits or when a key is lost.

Pick-resistant locks are conventional locks whose complex and difficult-to-reproduce keys are an additional security mechanism that makes it nearly impossible to pick the lock. The use of pick-resistant locks also has the same key-management issues to consider, and the cost of the locks and keys are notably greater than those conventional locks use.

Cipher locks are keyless locks that use mechanical keypads to control access to an area or facility. The lock requires a specific combination to be pressed on the keypad. Cipher locks cost more than traditional locks; however, their additional security capabilities increase the protection of the areas they secure. The combination to unlock a cipher lock can be easily changed; specific combination sequences can be locked out; and in an emergency situation, personnel can enter a predefined code that opens the door and initiates an alarm if configured. Although cipher locks are similar to electronic locks, cipher locks typically do not connect to a centralized database for increased versatility and access verification. All authentications for access are based on the code entered.

 Electronic locks provide a centralized control and auditing capability that is lacking with a cipher lock. This auditing capability makes it easier to manage and administer the access capabilities of each entrance. Users can be issued individual combinations, and electronic locks can enable access to specific individuals based on the hours that they work. If someone tries to access an area through an electronically locked door outside of business hours, she will not be able to enter the area.

Key management

As mentioned earlier, an additional challenge is created when conventional locks are used for physical security. It is not that these locks do not provide a certain level of physical strength; the problem lies with the management of keys and key distribution within the organization. Keys can easily be lost, stolen, or duplicated, which makes key management a priority. To facilitate a proper key-management process, an accounting of all keys and spares must be made, and audits of these keys should be conducted frequently.

Another option for key management is to use a master key system. A select few members of administrative personnel can access all doors, with each lock also having its own unique key. If an organization chooses the master key system, auditing these master keys must be conducted often and randomly to ensure that all issued keys are accounted for.

It is good practice to make sure that perimeter doors are keyed to a separate keying system than internal doors. Minimize the number of perimeter doors using the same keying system, too, and provide only the minimum number of keys necessary to satisfy the business needs of the organization. The primary motivation for having differing keying systems is that in the event of a key-related breach, the extent of unauthorized access will be minimized, and fewer locks and keys will need to be replaced.

Fences

When an organization is applying the layered defense model, a fence can be an effective physical barrier not only by physically impeding an intruder but by providing a psychological deterrent. When a potential attacker sees a tall and strong fence surrounding the site, she might be more likely to move on to a less challenging target unless she is intent on targeting the facility.

When the security team is considering the type of fencing to use, several factors should be considered. The gauge of the metal, the mesh size, and the height of the fence should correlate with the types of physical threats determined during the physical risk analysis.

The gauge of fence wiring is the thickness of the wires used in the fence mesh. A lower-number gauge is a thicker wire. The mesh sizing is the clear distance between the wires. It is more difficult to climb or cut a fence with small mesh sizes, and the heavier gauged wiring is harder to cut. However, tighter mesh and larger wire increases the cost of the fence.

The following list details the common applications of fencing based on the mesh and gauge and defines the various levels of security.

- Extremely high security: 3/8-inch mesh, 11 gauge
- Very high security: 1-inch mesh, 9 gauge
- High security: 1-inch mesh, 11 gauge
- Greater security: 2-inch mesh, 6 gauge
- Normal industrial security: 2-inch mesh, 9 gauge

Fences come in varying heights, and each height provides a different level of security:

- Fences 3 to 4 feet (approximately 1 meter) high deter the casual trespasser.
- Fences 6 to 7 feet (approximately 2 meters) high are usually considered too high to climb easily.
- Fences 8 feet or higher (2.5 + meters) deter even the more resolute intruder.

In some instances, barbed wire can top the fence. If the intent is to keep people out of the facility, the barbed wire should be tilted out. If the intent is to keep people inside the barrier, the barbed wire should be tilted in.

Critical areas that can be accessed from the outside should have fences at least 8 feet high to provide the proper level of protection. The fencing must be well maintained to mitigate risk and liability, should not sag, and should be tightly and securely connected to the posts. Posts should be mounted securely, buried several feet in the ground, and fixed with a poured concrete base.

Earlier in this section, you learned that the strength of a door's frame and hardware should be equivilent to the strength of the door. Strong and secure gates must be used when securing the perimeter of a facility with high-quality fencing. Underwriters Laboratories (UL) developed and maintains four classifications of gates; it tests, inspects, and classifies devices and certifies tested devices that comply with national building codes. Gates have four distinct classifications as defined by UL:

- Class I: Residential usage
- Class II: General public, commercial usage
- Class III: Limited public access, industrial usage
- Class IV: Restricted access

Perimeter Intrusion Detection and Assessment System (PIDAS) is a fencing system consisting of mesh wire and passive cable vibration sensors. PIDAS systems detect and alert if an intruder is attempting to cut or climb the monitored section of the fence. It is very sensitive and can unfortunately cause many false alarms.

Bollards are posts or barriers that typically allow foot traffic to pass between them but that form the appearance of a boundary. Some are small and provide the visual image of a boundary. Others are heavy concrete barriers designed to stop a vehicle from being driven through the passageway. Bollards are often placed along walkways, between the facility and a parking lot, or between the facility and a road that runs close to an exterior wall.

EXAM TIP

Be familiar with the security aspects of the different heights of fences.

Emanations protection

Many electrical devices and conducting media emanate electrical signals that bring up several issues to consider, including attenuation, interference, and emanations detection. As signals (electron flow) pass through devices and transmission media such as cables, an electromagnetic field is generated around the media. The propagation of this electromagnetic field into the air is an electromagnetic *emanation*, as shown in Figure 4-3.

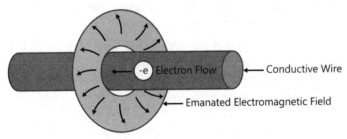

FIGURE 4-3 An emanation field around a cable

As nearby wires intersect this radiated field, the emanated field introduces an electron flow in the nearby wire, taking energy from the original signal and causing the signal in the transmission cable to degrade. Signal degradation over distance is called *attenuation*.

This same radiated energy around the transmission media can be detected by unintended, unauthorized users and reconstructed into the information being transmitted over the transmission media. This emanations detection is information theft.

The electron flow induced in the nearby cable, which might be transmitting signals of its own, becomes interference or crosstalk in the nearby cable and degrades the signal in it.

The propagated field around the signal-carrying cable degrades rapidly in the air, so simply moving the nearby cable a few inches away from the signal-carrying cable will reduce or eliminate the interference and crosstalk. Shielding reduces the size and strength of the propagated field, making shielding an effective method for reducing or eliminating the interference and crosstalk. Space to move cables apart isn't always available, but increased shielding makes the cabling system more expensive.

Any electron flow or signal on the signal transmission media that is not specifically part of the intended signal is commonly called noise, or electromagnetic interference (EMI). EMI is a broad category of induced, unwanted electron flow in transmission media; there are two primary types of this interference.

Transient noise is generally considered spurious and inconsistent in nature. Sources of transient noise include lightning, squirrel-cage induction motors (a type of electric motor), and static discharge. In addition to the signal degradation transient noise introduces in intended signals and power lines, it can damage devices attached to the affected wires.

Radio frequency interference (RFI) is the second subset of EMI, but as its name implies, this induced, unwanted signal has a consistency or regularity because it has a frequency. This type of interference often comes from wireless networks, AC power lines, cell phones, radar, and radio transmissions such as those from AM or FM radio stations.

WIRELESS COMMUNICATIONS

Wireless communications, such as Wi-Fi networks, transmit all their data through the use of emanations. Wireless networks, by design, propagate their signal into the air, using the air as their transmission medium and, therefore, make wireless communications the most susceptible to the technological and security issues regarding emanations.

To protect the data traversing the wireless network against unauthorized detection (in this case, through the use of a wireless sniffer), organizations should always use encryption for data transmission, and strong authentication mechanisms should be implemented to ensure that only authorized users can attach to, and communicate using, the wireless network.

CABLES

Twisted-pair cabling is a type of wiring in which two conductors are twisted together to reduce electromagnetic emanations from within and interference (crosstalk, EMI, and RFI) from external sources. It is often used in data networks for short and medium-length connections because of its relatively low cost compared to optical fiber and coaxial cable. The more frequent the twists in the pairs of wires, the more effective the shielding (emanations protection) the twisted pair provides. Ethernet cables, commonly used on corporate and home networks, use four twisted pairs of wires (eight wires total).

Unshielded twisted-pair (UTP) cabling is commonly used for standard Ethernet networks and provides significant cost benefits for an organization. The twists in the pairs of wires provide minimal protection against outbound emanations and inbound EMI.

Shielded twisted-pair (STP) cabling is a little more expensive than UTP but provides shielding around the groups of twisted-pair wires. This shielding enhancement to UTP provides a little more protection from emanations and EMI.

Coaxial cable, or coax, is an electrical cable with an inner, signal-carrying conductor surrounded by a flexible, tubular insulating layer, which itself is surrounded by a tubular, conductive shield layer that is electrically grounded. The solid and grounded shield around the central signal-carrying conductor minimizes the production of the electromagnetic field around the cable, reducing attenuation, interference, and emanations detection capabilities. This allows coaxial cable runs to be longer and useful in slightly more electromagnetically hazardous environments.

A fiber optic cable is a very effective countermeasure against emanations. Fiber optic cables use photons, not electrons, to carry their signals. Photons do not produce the propagated electromagnetic field, eliminating the performance and security concerns of emanations. A fiber optic cable is a cable containing one or more optical fibers that conduct light pulses. The optical conductors are typically individually coated with plastic layers and then contained in a protective tube suitable for the environment in which the cable will be deployed. Optical fiber cables are difficult to install and are very expensive to implement.

TEMPEST

In the 1960s and 1970s, the United States government conducted research to understand and mitigate electromagnetic emanations and interference in signaling circuits. The project was code-named *Tempest*. The term has grown synonymous with *emanations security* (*EMSEC*), and many attempts have been made to retrofit emanations security words to cast TEMPEST as an acronym. Technologies and methodologies that provide emanations security and reduce interference are often referred to as *Tempest technologies and methodologies*.

FARADAY CAGE

A Faraday cage, a Tempest technology, is a box, room, or entire building that is designed with an external metal sheathing around it. This skin is often made up of a conductive wire mesh that fully surrounds the cage on all sides, including the top and bottom of the area. This metal covering is grounded and helps prevent emanations from exiting or entering the protected area.

WHITE NOISE

Another Tempest technology is the use of white noise, the propagation of nonsense radio-frequency energy into an area being protected from emanations detection. The white noise effectively drowns out (jams) the small signal emanations that could otherwise be detected by unauthorized users and used to steal data.

Security guards: Advantages and disadvantages

Some organizations employ security guards to assist in ensuring a proper physical security posture. This presence also provides a visual force that can typically deter an attacker from targeting the organization. Security guards are considered the most effective single physical security control. They provide a level of flexibility, intelligent assessment, and appropriate response to an incident that is unparalleled by other physical controls.

Security guards provide expedient, process-based, and sometimes dynamic responses than other security mechanisms available for physical protection. Regardless of whether an organization employs a security force or contracts these tasks from a third party, security guards are considered the best physical security countermeasure, but an expensive one.

Security guards can be required to monitor a specific entrance or perform foot patrols to inspect defined areas visually. They should have clear and decisive tasks to perform and be trained to perform those tasks consistently.

Some of the advantages of providing this level of security are the following:

- They can make judgments (assessment) and adjust to rapidly changing conditions. Some responses, though procedural, might require thought and reasoning to expedite an appropriate resolution to an offense.

- Their visual presence can be a deterrent and assist in strengthening the target profile of an organization.

- They provide increased presence and monitoring and improved security and safety response in more sensitive areas of the facility such as the server room or data center and other restricted areas.

- They can provide assistance with routine employee monitoring to improve safety and deter potential malicious insider activities.

- If a security incident occurs, a security guard can provide procedure-based responses based on policy, which can also assist in controlling and containing the situation.

- As an added benefit for an organization that employs a security guard force, the guards can provide customer and visitor reception, verify identity and authorization, and escort visitors to ensure that appropriate physical and access controls are met.

Some of the disadvantages of the use of security guards are as follows:

- Security guards are typically required around the clock to ensure a consistent level of protection. This is expensive and often difficult to manage administratively (24 x 7 availability of guards).

- When an organization employs a security guard directly, thorough pre-employment screening should be performed. This is time-consuming and expensive and is no guarantee of the intent or professionalism of the guard. Background checks should be repeated periodically for the security guards.

- Security guards are one of the more expensive control types, though they provide multiple benefits as previously described and include many complementary services.

Several of the disadvantages can be mitigated by using third-party companies to provide this service. The best security program an organization can have is a combination of technical, administrative, and physical security mechanisms, one that does not depend on just one component of security. Thus, security guard deployment should be accompanied by other physical security mechanisms.

Guard dogs

Guard dogs are very useful in detecting intruders and other unwanted conditions such as drugs, drug paraphernalia, or other such items. Typically, guard dogs go through intensive training to detect a wide range of contraband, to respond to a wide range of commands, and to perform many tasks. Dogs can be trained to hold an intruder at bay until security personnel arrive or to chase an intruder and attack. Some dogs are trained to smell smoke so they can alert others to a fire.

Dogs cannot always know the difference between an authorized and an unauthorized person because they do not have the judgment capabilities of a human. Dogs can provide a good supplementary security mechanism.

Guard dogs can be expensive and require a great deal of maintenance.

EXAM TIP

Guards and guard dogs are effective security measures but are more costly than many other countermeasures.

Piggybacking or tailgating

One of the ways in which intruders, whether authorized or not, attempt to access a facility or area is to use a method called piggybacking. Piggybacking, also called tailgating, occurs at unmonitored but authenticated entry points, such as a door that unlocks only after an appropriate ID card is swiped. After an authorized user successfully authenticates and the door unlocks to provide access, a second person, the intruder, simply follows the authenticated user through the unlocked door without providing the required authentication credentials.

One of the best methods to ensure that a facility will not be compromised by this simple social engineering method is to provide security awareness training that identifies the breach to the users. Train authorized users to interrupt the piggybacking process and either notify security of the breach or require the tailgater to provide appropriate authentication, as long as the authorized user is not placing themselves in any additional risk of harm.

Another countermeasure for piggybacking is to have a security force monitor the activities of individuals attempting to gain access.

Physical access controls

Entryway barriers can be implemented in an environment to enhance the physical security of an organization. These barriers, some of which have been mentioned previously, can include turnstiles and mantraps.

Turnstiles and revolving doors can be introduced to control the flow of traffic entering a building. These devices, in combination with other control mechanisms, can ensure that only approved individuals can enter the facility. Adding an automatic lock or proximity card reader ensures that the turnstile allows only authorized individuals to enter and can prevent anyone from exiting if he has somehow gained unauthorized access.

Mantraps can be implemented to control the potential for piggybacking. A mantrap comprises two doors using access control technology with an area in between. When someone gains access through the first door, she will be momentarily trapped between the two doors because the first door must close before the second door will open, either automatically or with the use of a proximity card, much like an air lock on a spacecraft.

In selecting which type of barrier to implement in the environment, the security program team must consider fire code requirements. The ability to allow a quick exit in the event of a fire is of the utmost importance because safety is a priority. Revolving doors and turnstiles can be set for freewheeling egress when interfaced with building fire systems. Additional exit-only doors can be used to limit the number of entry doors but provide code-satisfying exit doors in sufficient quantity.

Fail safe and fail secure

In the event of an emergency, such as a fire, the organization's security structure must comply with the safety and fire codes and any other local requirements. Access controls, specifically doorways, can fall into two specific reactionary stances when an emergency occurs. Each one of these capabilities provides some advantages and disadvantages to the people and the information assets that they are protecting. The two categories of these devices are:

- **Fail-safe**   In the event of an emergency or a power failure, the access control device opens the lock to allow quick and efficient exit for the internal associates. Most fire code and local building regulations require all exits to fail into this safe mode.

- **Fail-secure**   In the event of an emergency or a power failure, the access control will lock down the facility to ensure that no one can enter or exit the building. In military compounds, the entry and exit gates, not doorways, often impose a fail-secure status in case of emergency. Fail-secure on doors is often not allowed due to the safety risks but could be accomplished by locking doors and exits inbound (fail secure), and allowing all outbound traffic (fail safe).

Signage

Signage that provides instructions for guidance and safety is a directive control, and signage that issues warnings to potential intruders is a deterrent type of control. It is a defensive measure that can assist in deterring an attacker, warning of security controls such as electrified fencing, guard dogs, and alarms. These warning signs indicate to the intruder that targeting this facility carries an increased risk of being caught or injured.

EXAM TIP

Many local safety codes are changing exit signage to use green-lighted signs, replacing the original standard of red-lighted signs. It has been recognized that green light is more visible than the original red signs used in fire situations. Although green exit signs are likely the way of the future, stick to answering "red exit signs" on the exam.

Lighting

Lighting should be used to deter intruders and provide safety for personnel. A well-lit area typically is not a good place for a crime to occur because the criminal will favor a poorly lit target over a more visible one to avoid being detected, recognized, or identified. Proper lighting reduces an organization's risks and potential liability. When considering an organization's lighting requirements, ensure that there are no areas of inadequate lighting.

Light is measured in terms of foot candles. One foot candle is the amount of light required from a point source to illuminate 1 square foot of flat surface uniformly from 1 foot away. General guidelines indicate that critical areas should be illuminated at a level of 2 foot candles from 8 feet high. There are different approaches to creating lighting that benefits the physical security posture of an organization. The use of continuous lighting assists in deterring an attack from happening. As mentioned, a well-lit area will deter an attacker from performing malicious intent. Always ensure that there is continuous lighting in critical areas such as entrances, parking lots, and garages.

Using motion-triggered lighting can deter an intruder from attempting to target a facility, especially attacks in those areas that do not require a continuous light, such as side entry doors. Motion-triggered lights might make attackers flee because they believe that they have been caught.

The use of random lighting will also deter an attacker. If lights are on a timing device, they will turn on in a random fashion, and the attacker might believe an uninhabited area is populated, ultimately scaring him off the premises.

CCTV cameras

Depending on the requirements of the organization, a proactive security stance typically involves providing surveillance to ensure that unacceptable events are detected and responded to expeditiously. An organization can use various surveillance technologies to monitor and detect activity by using visual detection or devices that use sophisticated means of detecting abnormal behavior or unwanted conditions.

The primary motivations for implementing a closed-circuit TV (CCTV) system are:

- To detect motion, or the presence of an intruder, before she can accomplish her malicious task
- After the intrusion has been detected, to recognize what is being done and by whom, to ensure that this intruder is actually doing something malicious, and that the organization can determine any specific actions to take (assess, respond)
- To identify the intruder or any details of the intruder to prove that this individual was in fact the intruder, to be able to press charges, or to provide appropriate grounds for dismissal (detect, collect evidence)

Prior to purchasing a CCTV system, an organization should consider several factors that will determine the investment in these surveillance systems:

- **The purpose** Typically, CCTVs are used to detect, recognize, and identify intruders, to assess developing events, and to record events for later review and evidence collection.

- **The environment** Different camera types are used, depending on whether they are located inside or outside of the facility.

- **The view** Depending on the area to be monitored, some specific capabilities will also be required. These include fixed or adjustable (motorized) positioning, fixed or variable aperture (lighting considerations), and fixed or adjustable focal length.

- **Available light** Will night vision be required?

- **Monitoring and recording stations** The CCTV system typically requires human review, assessment, and response actions. The video data is commonly recorded for later review and perhaps prosecution purposes. This recorded content must be protected similarly to logged data to avoid its unauthorized access, alteration, or deletion.

- **Enhancing security** CCTV systems can integrate with other physical controls to enhance the physical security posture.

The items in this list need to be considered prior to investing in a CCTV system because many types of cameras, lenses, and monitors make up the diverse CCTV products that are available. Each of these capabilities and environmental variables affects the output of the video, which will affect the organization's ability to detect, identify, and prosecute an intruder. Cameras have become inexpensive, even including infrared-based night vision. A camera with infrared night vision is shown in Figure 4-4.

FIGURE 4-4 A monitoring camera with infrared night vision

Depending on the size of the implementation, a CCTV system comprises cameras, transmitters (for wireless cameras), receivers (for wireless cameras), multiplexers, monitors, and recorders. The cameras might be wired, requiring cable runs from the monitoring station to each camera, or wireless cameras that might be subject to unauthorized monitoring, interference or intentional jamming. Cameras all require a power supply of some sort. The signal and power cables should be tamperproof so that an attacker cannot interfere with the camera's performance. Wireless cameras should include encryption of the wireless signal to defend against unauthorized monitoring.

In a small implementation, a CCTV system comprises cameras that capture the data and transmit it to a receiver. The receiver then connects to a monitor that presents the images and all data to be recorded. In a larger, more complex CCTV implementation, multiple cameras provide surveillance to cover more areas. These cameras connect to a multiplexer, which interleaves multiple video signals to a single monitor. Again, all data should be recorded.

FIELD OF VIEW AND FOCAL LENGTHS

To ensure that the camera is capturing the appropriate amount of detail, consider the focal length of the lens. The focal length of a camera relates to the field of view that can be achieved.

Fixed focal-length lenses are available in various fields of views: wide, medium, and narrow. A wide-angle lens has a short focal length, and a telephoto lens has a long focal length. As the name implies, a fixed focal-length lens is stationary, and the guard cannot manipulate it by using a remote control, nor will the lens provide the ability to focus on the object automatically.

To have remote control capabilities to move the camera's focus and change the field of view to different angles and distances, with zoom capabilities, a camera with a motorized and remotely controlled zoom lens should be implemented. For more flexible monitoring capabilities, selecting a camera with a zoom lens is recommended because it allows the focal length to change from wide-angle to telephoto while maintaining the focus of the image. This makes the camera more expensive and subject to needing repairs and maintenance more often.

DEPTH OF FIELD AND IRISES

The depth of field refers to the portion of the environment that is in focus when shown on the monitor. The depth of field varies, depending on the size of the lens opening (the aperture), the distance of the subject, and the focal length of the lens. The depth of field increases as the size of the lens opening decreases, the subject distance increases, or the focal length of the lens decreases.

CCTV lenses have irises, which control the amount of light that enters the lens through the aperture. The two types of available irises are:

- **Fixed or manual iris lenses** A ring around the lens is either a fixed size or must be manually turned and controlled, providing a fixed level of exposure. Fixed or manual iris lenses should be used in areas that have a relatively constant level of lighting.

- **Auto iris lenses** The lens will automatically adjust itself based on the light available in the viewed area. Auto iris lenses should be used in outdoor settings or where the light changes. This makes the camera more expensive and subject to needing repairs and maintenance more often.

CAMERA MOUNTING

Depending on the requirements of the area the camera will survey, how the camera is mounted to the wall will determine the appropriate type of camera for that environment. Two types of mounting capabilities are available:

- **Fixed mounting**   Provides a stationary mount; the camera will not move or respond to commands sent to it. To change the view of the camera, it must be physically moved.

- **PTZ capabilities**   Provide pan, tilt, and zoom (PTZ) capabilities and can be manipulated by remote commands sent from the controller in response to an incident. These cameras can also be programmed to swing slowly from side to side automatically. This makes the camera more expensive and subject to needing repairs and maintenance more often.

MONITORING STATION

To realize the capabilities of a CCTV system fully, consider a monitoring station with operators. There is no point in investing the money and time required to implement a sophisticated CCTV system if no one watches the monitor.

A primary vulnerability of a CCTV system is that the cameras are often located in potentially hazardous areas. This requires the protection of the signal cable and power feed to the cameras so that they are protected from tampering.

The use of enunciators can make it easier for the security force to recognize an event efficiently without having to stare at a monitor. An enunciator listens to activity and can perform some sort of action, such as turning on a light, sounding an alarm, or moving a PTZ camera into position and starting to record.

Securing portable devices

Organizations need a mobile workforce that can work from home or other remote locations, connecting to the company's network from laptop computers through a secure channel, a virtual private network (VPN). It is common for remote users to store sensitive customer or company information on the remote computer for easy retrieval and use. Maintaining sensitive information on a portable device is a dramatic increase in risk because laptop and cell phone thefts continue to rise around the world; attackers are targeting these mobile devices specifically to obtain information for fraud, identity theft, or corporate espionage, for the value of the data, and not just for the value of the hardware anymore.

Cable locks

One of the simplest security mechanisms for preventing an attacker from stealing a laptop is a cable lock. This device connects to the frame of the laptop and is long enough to wrap around a solid, fixed object. Then it uses a lock to secure the laptop. It is true that a determined attacker can still cut the lock or break the table leg the laptop is connected to, but it makes it more difficult for a thief simply to walk by and take the portable device.

Password policy

If a laptop or smart phone is stolen, and for general security precautions that will be discussed throughout this book, a couple of protection mechanisms should be employed.

The use of strong authentication in any environment, but especially on portable devices, should be implemented. A strong password consists of a minimum of 8 to 15 characters, including uppercase letters, lowercase letters, special characters, and numbers. Passwords should not contain a word found in the dictionary, and they should expire periodically, such as every 90 days. After a password has been used, it should not be used again for a minimum of three cycles of expiration (270 days). Users should not use the same password on different authentication systems, and an account lockout should be implemented in the case of multiple failed logons.

Disk encryption

The use of disk encryption is especially important on portable devices such as laptop computers, removable media, and even cell phones. With the spread of small and removable devices such as USB thumb drives and other easily accessible media, encryption should not simply be an option anymore but a requirement when transferring sensitive or confidential information from one location or machine to another. Most portable devices can be purchased to include an encryption mechanism to make it easier to deploy and maintain.

Asset tracking

Security applications can be installed on the laptop computer and cell phones that can locate the device in the event the laptop is lost or stolen. This tracking software can be installed so that the laptop can "phone home" on its next connection to the Internet if it has been stolen.

When this software has been configured on the laptop, the software reports to a centralized station hosted by the software vendor. If the owner reports the laptop to be lost or stolen, the phone-home software vendor will work with Internet service providers and law enforcement to track down and return the stolen laptop.

Lost or stolen smart phones can be located by use of GPS or cellular triangulation but there may be higher costs associated with the effort compared to wiping the device securely and replacing it.

Wiping the disk

As a last resort, to protect sensitive data that was stored on the stolen laptop or smart phone, it is possible to wipe the device remotely. On laptops and cell phones, this can be performed by installing software on the portable device and configuring it to overwrite the contents of the drive(s) when a certain number of failed password attempts have occurred. If a laptop or cell phone is stolen, the thief might try to guess or brute-force the password to gain access. Many failed attempts at logging on to the system will automatically wipe the local drive.

If the organization does not want to wipe a system automatically after a certain number of failed logon attempts, administrators at a centralized monitoring station can initiate the overwrite remotely. The laptop or cell phone can be sent a signal simply to wipe the device's contents to ensure minimal data loss of the organization's sensitive information.

Suggested target-hardening procedures

The following list describes additional security procedures and mechanisms that should be employed with the aforementioned suggestions to provide a layered defense in protecting the data stored on the asset:

- The organization must inventory all laptops and phones issued to workers.
- Harden the operating system. This includes applying all updates promptly and removing unneeded user accounts and software. All unused services should be disabled. Install and update antimalware software. Enable and configure a personal firewall using strict controls on inbound access. Impose a strong password policy and require data encryption or whole-disk encryption.
- Use the BIOS's password protection.
- Register all laptops and cell phones with the vendor and file a report when one is stolen. If a stolen laptop is sent in for repairs, the vendor will flag it.
- Do not check a laptop or phone as luggage when flying.
- Never leave a laptop or phone unattended and carry it in a nondescript carrying case.
- Engrave the laptop or phone with a symbol or number for proper identification.
- Back up the data from the laptop and phone regularly to a secure and stationary machine.
- When storing a laptop or phone in a car, be sure to place it in the trunk (prior to arrival at the destination).

Intrusion detection

Physical Intrusion detection systems (IDSs) identify and alert the organization to an unauthorized access or general changes in the physical environment. Using magnetic contacts or vibration detection sensors, these systems can monitor building entrances, emergency exit doors, easily accessible windows, stationary devices, open spaces, or any cover that is protecting or hiding equipment. If there is a change in the environment such as movement, the IDS device sounds an alarm either in the local area or in both the local area to scare off the intruder and at a police or guard station.

Acoustic sensors

An acoustical IDS typically uses microphones located on or near glass windows. These microphones detect the sound made during a forced entry. Due to the sensitivity of these microphones, these devices often trigger on loud noises, such as thunder or the sound of a garbage truck dropping a dumpster, issuing false alarms.

Photoelectric sensors

A photoelectric system IDS uses a photoelectric cell to emit a beam of light that is captured by the system's receiver. If this beam of light is interrupted for any reason, an alarm sounds. This beam of light can be visible or invisible and can be cross-sectional so that one area can have several beams extending across it. This is achieved by using hidden mirrors to bounce the light beam from one place to another until the receiver captures the light.

It is important to know that because photoelectric sensors require the use of beams of light, these sensors should be deployed only in environments that have controlled exposure to sunlight.

Proximity detectors

IDSs are often deployed using proximity detectors. A passive infrared proximity detector monitors an area and identifies localized temperature changes in the sensing field such as body heat given off from an intruder. An infrared proximity detector is shown in Figure 4-5.

FIGURE 4-5 Infrared proximity sensor to detect motion

Other forms of proximity detectors emit a measurable electromagnetic (RF or microwave) or acoustic (ultrasound) field and sound an alarm if this field is penetrated. These types of IDSs use the Doppler effect, which detects motion by sensing the signal reflected from the environment. When there is no motion in the sensing field, the reflected frequency matches the transmitted frequency. If something in the field moves toward the receiver, the frequency of the reflected signal is higher. If something in the field moves away from the receiver, the frequency of the reflected signal is lower. If the reflected frequency changes, the IDS activates an alarm.

Pressure mats

Pressure mats are designed to detect a person standing or walking over them. Using a built-in transducer that converts a change in pressure (weight on the mat) into an electric signal, pressure mats can sound an alarm or send a signal to a receiving station, alerting the station to the presence of an intruder. Pressure mats can be used internally to detect an intrusion around or in secure areas. If used within a facility, the mat should be mounted on a flat and even surface and then covered with a conventional floor covering. These mats can also be used outside because they are weatherproof and can be buried by dirt and grass to hide them from a potential attacker.

Contact switches

Magnetic contact switches work by detecting a break in the closed circuit established by the magnets. Magnetic contact switches are often installed on windows and doors so that if the contact is separated because the window or door is opened, an alarm will sound or be sent to the monitoring station.

Heating, ventilation, and air conditioning systems

Another, often overlooked, aspect of physical security is the heating, ventilation, and air conditioning (HVAC) systems in a facility. These systems, like many other infrastructure components, are also vulnerable to attacks by a determined adversary. Almost all electronic infrastructure assets, as well as an organization's personnel, must operate in a climate-controlled environment. Humans are comfortable within a temperature range from about 68°F to about 86°F. As the ambient temperature approaches the edges of this range, productivity drops dramatically, and workers typically stop working when temperatures go outside this range.

Temperature and humidity considerations

Because of the enormous amount of heat created by components within a data center or in confined areas that contain many computing devices, challenges must be considered when dealing with these types of environments. Usually, a data center needs to have its own HVAC system to ensure that its specialized temperature considerations are dealt with.

Improper levels of heat and humidity can cause damage to critical information assets because high humidity can cause condensation, and low humidity can cause damage by static discharge. Static electricity discharge can short out devices and can cause the loss of availability.

As a rule, humidity in these environments should be kept between 40 percent and 60 percent, and the temperature should be between 70°F and 74°F (21°C and 23°C). Table 4-2 describes the maximum temperature that a component can be exposed to before there is damage or loss.

TABLE 4-2 Temperature considerations

Component	Damaging temperature
Computer systems and peripheral devices	175°F or 80°C
Hard disk drives	100° F or 38°C
Paper products	350° F or 177°C

The ventilation systems in facilities should produce *positive air pressure*. This forces a small amount of air out of the facility through small cracks and crevices throughout the building. If a negative air pressure were allowed to exist, dirty outside air, filled with dust, smoke, and other contaminants, would be pulled in through these small openings, decreasing the facility's cleanliness and potentially damaging systems over time.

External air intakes of the ventilation system should be protected. These could be used by an attacker to introduce toxins or other contaminants into the entire facility.

Failure recovery

Hard disk drives will fail. There will be power outages. Operating systems will be corrupted. Data will be corrupted or accidentally deleted. Expect it to happen. When information systems shut down, they must be brought back online as quickly as possible within previously identified recovery timeframes. Whether the operations department keeps an inventory of spare parts or the company hires an outside organization to perform the repairs, failures of any type should be planned for, and satisfactory recovery solutions should be put in place.

Service-level agreements

Companies often use service-level agreements (SLAs) with servicing organizations that define a maximum repair time for the specified systems and components the agreement covers. In this manner, companies can transfer some of the responsibility for critical information system recovery to these specialized service organizations. The greater the demand for performance and availability, the more expensive the SLA contract will be. Stiff penalties are often imposed if the service provider does not meet the terms of the SLA.

Secondary power supplies

Depending on the criticality and required availability of the information assets within an organization, various types of secondary power should be incorporated. These secondary power sources are mostly for temporary power in the event that a disaster, fault, or failure affects the available power coming into a facility. Organizations that require high availability (HA) for their IT systems often must identify and implement this supplemental AC power for the data center. A simple and common thing like a power failure can destroy a commonly guaranteed uptime of 5 nines (99.999% uptime = less than 6 minutes of downtime in a year).

Solutions range from immediate sustained power, in the form of a connection to a separate power grid, to a short-term supply provided by a relatively inexpensive uninterruptible power supply (UPS) attached to the asset.

Large organizations that require full-time availability of their data, such as government facilities, hospitals, or large data processing centers, could suffer catastrophic losses if power were lost. These facilities often require an alternate power source, such as connectivity to a completely separate second power grid or power substation, or a properly sized power generator. Although these configurations are expensive, the potential losses from power outages could be drastically greater.

UPSs provide battery backup AC power and typically provide surge suppression (short-term overvoltage protection). UPSs use battery packs that range in size and capacity to provide power to supported systems for some estimated length of time, typically in the minutes. They are often used as a temporary measure, keeping critical systems powered until the primary power source returns or until another supplemental power supply system is initiated.

Smart UPSs connect to computer systems by using a serial or USB cable. As batteries begin to deplete during an AC power failure, the UPS signals the operating system on the attached computer and triggers a clean shutdown, so the computer doesn't suddenly lose power and shut down unexpectedly.

Two commonly used UPSs are the online UPS and the standby UPS:

- **Standby UPS**   During normal use, the standby UPS connects supported systems (the load) to the primary AC power through surge suppression filters. Parallel to that, the standby UPS charges a bank of batteries. When the AC power fails, the UPS detects the failure and switches to providing power to the load from the batteries. The switchover time from AC power to the battery might cause problems in some systems. The DC voltage from the batteries is sent through an inverter that changes the DC output from the batteries to AC to feed the load. The standby UPS is common and relatively inexpensive.

- **Online UPS**   During normal use, the online UPS connects supported systems (the load) to the primary AC power through surge suppression filters, the battery, and the inverter circuit. When the AC power fails, the battery is already attached to the load, eliminating the switchover time delay, making it a more reliable alternate power source for the attached systems. Running the power through the battery and inverter all the time causes these components to fail more rapidly. A parallel AC path, with only the surge suppression filters, is switched in to keep systems powered in case the battery or inverter fails.

Another solution to provide supplemental AC power is the use of a generator. Some generators can detect a power failure and automatically start up and engage the AC power circuits of the facility to provide power. Generators typically run on gasoline or diesel and are limited to the amount of fuel available. The generator will require a quantity of fuel sufficient to power the generator for the planned duration of the power outage. The fuel supply must be maintained properly and arrangements should be made for a resupply when needed.

No matter what type of alternate power source is implemented, each of the backup mechanisms needs to be tested periodically to ensure that it will be available in the event of a true power failure.

Electricity considerations

Electricity provides the needed power to run many parts of the digital world, including the systems that keep information assets available. When the power supply experiences no interference or voltage fluctuations, it is considered clean power. Unfortunately, the power company does not always provide clean power nor do standard power lines. Most of these considerations can be resolved with a UPS or line conditioner.

If there is interference or voltage fluctuations in the flow of power, an organization could implement line conditioners, which can ensure a clean and smooth distribution of power throughout the facility. The primary power runs through a line conditioner that can absorb extra power in the event of a surge or spike and can store some energy to add current to the line if there is a sag, or drop in power. Line conditioners attempt to keep the electrical flow at a steady level so that no damage is done to the attached devices. Line conditioners are intended to provide supplemental AC power for brief periods. A secondary connection to a separate power grid and generators often feeds through line conditioners when they are installed.

As mentioned previously, *static* will discharge to balance a positive and negative electrical imbalance. It can cause damage to computers, ranging from system reboots to chip or disk damage. Static electricity is produced in low-humidity environments and can be harmful to internal components of the devices that provide the various services to an organization's computing environment.

- A *spike* is a sudden and short jolt of energy (nanoseconds to milliseconds) that can cause damage to devices instantly or over time. Some common causes of spikes on the AC power lines are nearby lightning strikes, tripped circuit breakers, and unplugging live systems without performing a clean shutdown, among others.

- Unlike a spike, a *surge* is a prolonged rise in energy (milliseconds to seconds). It can also damage components immediately or cause effects that are not apparent for some time. Some typical sources of a surge are lightning strikes, a power plant going online or offline, a shift in the commercial utility power grid, or electrical equipment within a business starting and stopping.

- An *inrush* is the initial draw of current to start a load. It happens when an electrical device is turned on. During the inrush, the newly activated device could take in so much power that it causes a momentary dip in the power distributed to the devices around it.

- A *fault* is a momentary power outage, which can also damage components. This brief or enduring loss of power is often caused by a fluctuation originating at the power company or by lightning strikes.

- A *blackout* is when the voltage drops to zero and requires intervention from a backup power source to provide business continuity. Blackouts are generally not issues with the power plant itself but with the AC power distribution system, such as lightning, the failure of distribution system components such as transformers, or accidents that result in damage to a power line or transformer.

- A *brownout* is a reduction of voltage; this typically occurs when power companies are experiencing high demand. Using a device known as a constant-voltage transformer to normalize this fluctuation of power helps ensure an appropriate level of required voltage.

- A *sag* is a momentary drop of electrical current, which can last from a second to minutes. Sags can cause data loss and damage to assets if those assets are constantly subjected to the fluctuations of current. Low voltage situations cause electron flow (the amperage) to increase. This will cause a temperature rise in the wires and circuits affected by the low voltage. The excessive heat can degrade or destroy components, and in extreme cases, can cause a fire.

Two types of possible disturbances to the flow of electrical power as it travels across a power line can be problematic to information assets' ability to obtain clean power. These interferences make it difficult to keep these devices properly running and can hinder network communications if not addressed. Any unwanted electrical activity on a wire or system, in this case the AC power system, is known as electromagnetic interference (EMI) or noise. If that EMI has a regularity or pattern to it, it is classified as a subset of EMI called radio frequency interference (RFI). If the EMI does not have a pattern or regularity, it is called spurious or transient noise.

The power company that supplies the electricity to the organization's facility can be the source of some of these electrical conditions. However, some of these issues can be the result of poor electrical planning and implementation by the organization itself, such as the excessive or inappropriate use of extension cords or power strips to provide power to more devices in a localized area. This bulk-of-power demand on a typical wall outlet can cause additional line noise, sags, and inrush of currents and can result in spikes of power that can damage the components connected to the power strip or extension cord and could cause harm to the electrical system itself.

When dealing with electric power issues, the following measures can be implemented to assist in the protection of an organization's information assets:

- Ensure that every device is plugged into a surge suppressor and/or a UPS.

- Gracefully shut down devices as instructed in each device's manual.

- Use power-line monitors and regulators.

- Protect electrical panels, master circuit breakers, and transformer cables.
- Consider using shielded cables for long-distance data runs.
- Do not run data or power lines directly over fluorescent lights or near other high-voltage components.
- Do not daisy-chain outlet strips and extension cords or otherwise overload AC circuits.

Water detectors

Water can cause extensive damage to components and technology, including information assets, walls, furniture, and the foundation of the facility itself. It is important for an organization to be able to detect the presence of harmful water.

Detectors should be placed under raised floors and above drop ceilings to detect water coming from the floor above. The location of the detectors should be documented and their location marked for easy access.

Water detectors should be actively monitored from a centralized location and provide alarms to staff members who are responsible for correcting the situation.

Periodic walkthroughs and inspections

To ensure the highest quality of physical security, security controls must be monitored, inspected, tested, and audited to ensure that the controls in place are providing the expected levels of protection. This type of activity shows that the organization is maintaining security prudently, so that if any accidents were to happen, the company can prove it has attempted to perform due diligence and due care, specifically avoiding being negligent.

A security professional should periodically perform a walkthrough inspection of the facility and document any breaches of the policies of the organization. If unsafe or insecure elements in the physical environment are observed that are not currently managed by policy, new policy components should be added, awareness training should be performed, and these elements should be eliminated from the environment.

In addition to the safety of personnel, another aspect of routine monitoring should include an awareness by management and security personnel of potential stress, duress, and frustration of personnel. Workers are more likely to make mistakes or commit willful malicious acts when most fatigued, stressed, or frustrated in the working environment. Events such as promotions, bonuses, and reorganization can be stressful and aggravating times for employees (especially for those who didn't get the promotions or bonuses they expected) and might indicate the need for elevated diligence in the care and monitoring of the affected personnel.

The list of duties of a security guard often includes the details of the walkthrough inspections he is required to perform while on shift. This is especially important during the night and early morning because that is when most break-ins to businesses occur.

The security guard should perform standard walkthroughs within the facility to ensure that no unauthorized personnel are on the premises, and she should inspect windows and doors to make certain they are secure and have not been tampered with. During this inspection, the security guard should turn on lights in individual rooms and open closet doors or any other areas of the building that could provide a hiding place to an intruder. Any violations of policy or conditions that might present safety concerns should be documented and reported for timely remediation. Failure to do so could be considered negligence. These types of conditions often result in the development of new policies and the requisite employee training.

Security guards should also walk the perimeter of the building, looking for any trespassers or loiterers and confirming that all windows and doors are securely locked from the outside. They should inspect window casings, doorframes, and all surveillance hardware to ensure that they have not been tampered with.

The security guard should also sporadically walk through the facility in between these defined intervals, performing many of the same tasks, especially inspecting the integrity of the doors, windows, and surveillance hardware. These occasional walkthroughs ensure that if the facility is being surveyed by a possible intruder, the timing of the security guard's activities cannot be determined, making it more difficult for the planned intrusion to progress.

During these walkthroughs, or at any point during the day, a security guard must document what has happened. Whether an attempted access has occurred or everything checks out, these conditions need to be logged and reviewed daily by the physical security force when shifts change. It is very useful and necessary also to have a security professional or the facility's manager review them. Once again, timely remediation should take place for all issues found.

Auditing and logging

When using logging for facility and secure area access, the following information should be logged and reviewed if an incident happens. It should also be part of the physical security policy to review these audit logs daily:

- The date and time of the access
- The entry point of the access
- The ID used for the access
- Any unsuccessful access attempts
- Any other anomalies regarding the access or activities within heightened security areas

Audit and access logs are ineffective unless someone reviews them. Within the physical security policy, a security professional should be responsible for reviewing the access to the facility and secure areas. To defend against oversight and collusion, someone other than the security professional overseeing access should occasionally review these logs. These types of auditing mechanisms are both detective and deterrent. They should be securely retained in case an investigation is required. Secure retention might also be required for compliance requirements.

Fire prevention, detection, and suppression

Generally speaking, damages from fire attack the availability of an asset. Understanding how to protect an organization's information assets, facilities, and people from a fire must begin at understanding the components and conditions that instigate a fire. These originating elements are addressed within this section along with the detection devices that assist in alerting the appropriate individuals of the presence of smoke and fire.

Fires are classified based on the fuel that is combusting. An appropriate suppressant must be used on these different classifications of fire. Failure to use the appropriate suppressant could easily cause increased damages and increase the potential harm to people.

Four legs of a fire

Fires present a security threat unique to an organization from any of the other threats previously discussed. Fires can damage information assets and their data and can put human life in jeopardy. A fire is initiated from an ignition source such as an electrical fault, a faulty heating device, or intentional arson.

A fire needs four elements to ignite and continue to burn. These elements are:

- Fuel
- Oxygen
- High temperature
- Chemical reaction

Consider each of these elements to understand the best way to extinguish a fire. Sufficiently reduce or remove any one or more of these elements of a fire to suppress it. Table 4-3 shows common combustible elements, their suppression methods, and what these suppression methods do to the fire. The suppression methods are detailed in the "Fire suppression agents" section later in this lesson.

TABLE 4-3 Combustion elements and an example of their suppression methods

Combustion element	Suppression methods	Suppression results
Fuel—cooking oil	Soda acid	Removes fuel
Oxygen	Carbon dioxide	Removes oxygen
Temperature	Water	Reduces temperature
Chemical reaction	Gas, Halon (Halon substitute)	Interferes with the chemical reaction between elements

Fire detection

The first step in alleviating the damage and safety concerns as they pertain to fire and the damage it can cause is to detect the fire as early as possible. Fire detection systems should sound an alarm near the detected fire and are often configured to call the local fire station and/or trigger a fire suppressant system, like sprinklers. Detectors should be placed approximately everywhere, including where people are and where people are not. Fire detectors should also be placed above suspended ceilings, under raised floors, and inside air ducts.

It is important for an alarm to sound as early as possible so that damage to information assets can be minimized, fire suppression activities can be invoked as quickly as possible, and enough time can be given to direct people to evacuate the area as soon as possible.

Different detection methods differ by the stage of the fire that is identified to sound the alarm. Two types of commonly used detectors are activated by smoke, one type of detector identifies thermal changes, and another type recognizes the infrared light produced by the flame from a fire.

Fire detectors

Types of detection mechanisms are ionization, photoelectric, thermal, and infrared:

- **Ionization detector** The ionization detector contains a small radioactive source that ionizes nearby clean air. (An ion is an atom or molecule with an imbalance between the negatively charged electrons and the positively charged protons. An ion has a positive or negative charge.) The detector then senses these ions, indicating a normal condition. When smoke is present in the air, the smoke neutralizes the ions, eliminating the charge, and the detector senses a lack of ions in the air, triggering the alarm.

- **Photoelectric detector** The photoelectric detector contains a light-emitting diode (LED) that emits a light (photons) through a tube that passes air from the room. At a right angle to this light and air tube is another tube that has a photoelectric sensor at the far end of it. When the air is clean, the light shines straight out the far end of the tube. When smoke is in the air, the smoke particles reflect the photons at all angles, including at a right angle, down the tube where the photoelectric sensor is mounted.

When the photoelectric sensor sees any light from the LED, indicating the presence of smoke, it triggers the alarm.

- **Thermal detectors** Thermal detection mechanisms can be configured to sound an alarm under two conditions: at a predefined, elevated temperature (fixed temperature) or when the temperature increases rapidly over a short period (rate of rise). Fixed-temperature detectors are not very sensitive and can cause false alarms, which can be an expensive situation for an organization. Rate-of-rise detectors can provide a quicker reaction to temperature increases because they are more sensitive to the surrounding environment.

- **Infrared detectors** Infrared detectors use a photon detector that sees light in the infrared range. Flames give off infrared light, so if the infrared detector sees the pattern of light that matches a flame, it triggers the alarm.

Most computer systems are made of components that are not combustible but that can melt or suffer damage if overheated. If a fire is ignited in a data center, it will probably be an electrical fire caused by overheating of wire insulation or the ignition of surrounding elements by those overheated components. Smoke usually occurs before ignition of a fire, so smoke-activated detectors are a good early warning device. They work well to sound an alarm prior to the activation of the suppression system in response to the fire.

EXAM TIP

Know the four types of fire/smoke detectors and how they work.

Five classes of fires

There are five classes of fires, based on the elements that ignite and provide the characteristics of the fire. Each of these is important to understand not only for the CISSP exam but to ensure that an organization is applying the correct suppression methods to make certain that the fire is extinguished as quickly as possible.

- Class A fires are the most common and involve common combustibles such as wood and paper. As you often see on the news, firefighters commonly use water for these types of fires.

- Class B fires involve flammable liquids such as alcohol, oil, tar, gasoline, and other petroleum products. Water is typically unacceptable as a suppressant because it will cause the fuel to splash and flow to other areas, spreading the fire. A gas, dry chemical, or wet foam suppressant is commonly used on class B liquid fires.

- Class C fires are electrical fires. Gas suppressants are the most effective at putting out the class C fire. The suppressant used on electrical fires should not be electrically conductive. As quickly as possible, the electrical energy source should be shut off.

- Class D fires involve burning metals. These fires often burn at very high temperatures. Thus, it is dangerous to use water as a suppressant on metal fires. The water on this high temperature fire would cause a steam explosion that is likely to be more devastating than the metal fire itself. Dry powder suppressants are the recommended approach to extinguishing class D fires.

- Class K fires are kitchen fires involving overheated cooking oil or grease. This classification was added because of the high frequency of this specific type of fire, but some references do not include this Class K fire classification. Baking soda or a wet foam to smother the class K fire is recommended.

These fire classes and their associated suppressants are detailed in Table 4-4.

TABLE 4-4 Classes of fires

Fire class	Type of fire	Fuel (examples)	Suppressants
A	Common combustibles	Wood, paper, and fabrics	Water, soda acid
B	Flammable liquids	Petroleum products and combustible gas	Gas: CO2, FM-200
C	Electrical	Electrical equipment and wires	Gas: CO2, FM-200, or non-conductive wet chemicals (foam)
D	Combustible metals	Magnesium, sodium, potassium (burn at very high temperatures)	Dry chemicals
K	Kitchen fires	Grease, oil	Wet chemicals (foam)

EXAM TIP

Know the five classes of fire, the combustible material for each, and the appropriate suppressant for each class.

Sprinkler systems

As discussed previously, water reduces the temperature of a fire to extinguish the flames. One of the mechanisms that provides the distribution of water to perform these actions is a sprinkler system.

When a fire suppression system using sprinklers is employed, all the mechanisms need to work in conjunction to alert the personnel to the presence of a fire and provide ample time for a safe and expedient evacuation from the facility. The most commonly used types of water sprinkler systems are wet pipe, dry pipe, pre-action, and deluge.

Wet pipe sprinkler systems

In a sprinkler system that employs wet pipe mechanisms, the water is pressurized and consistently present within the pipes up to the sprinkler heads themselves; the pipes are wet inside. When a fire is detected, the sprinkler heads open, and the water is released from the pipes. This is the most commonly used sprinkler system and the least expensive to install. However, this system typically causes a large amount of water damage when triggered. Another concern with the wet pipe sprinkler system is its use in thermally uncontrolled areas such as warehouses. If these pipes freeze, the water inside expands and can burst the pipe, causing water damage.

Dry pipe sprinkler systems

To avoid the damages that can occur from frozen pipes in thermally uncontrolled areas, a dry pipe sprinkler system is often used. The water is shut off from the dry pipes by a valve within a temperature-controlled area. The dry pipe areas are filled with pressurized air to keep water from seeping into the dry pipes over time. When the fire alarm is triggered, the valve is opened, filling the dry pipes with water and forcing water out of the sprinkler heads to extinguish the fire. These are a little slower to respond after an alarm because the water must travel the length of the pipes before reaching the hazard area, but they are a requirement if there is a risk of the pipes freezing. This system is more expensive to install than the wet pipe system.

Pre-action sprinkler systems

A pre-action system begins with a dry pipe system but adds a second trigger to activate before the water is released. The pipes are kept dry, but the heads are plugged with a plastic bulb or billet that melts at a specific temperature. A benefit of this release mechanism is that only the sprinkler heads that are affected by the heat from the fire will release the water, minimizing unnecessary water damage. When the fire alarm is triggered, the valve is opened, and the water is released through the pipes to the sprinkler heads. The water will not be distributed until the plug at the sprinkler head melts. The billets come in different colors. Each color represents the maximum temperature the area can reach before the billet melts. The colors are orange (135°F/57°C), red (155°F/68°C), yellow (175°F/79°C), green (200°F/93°C), and blue (286°F/141°C). Local fire code typically dictates the required melting point for these billets.

Deluge sprinkler systems

A deluge system is used where the threat of fire presents a very high level of risk, such as at a munitions factory, a fireworks factory, or a paper mill, where the nearby materials are highly flammable, and a fire is likely to become very dangerous quickly. The deluge system uses the same mechanism as a dry pipe system except that the pipes are a very large diameter, the water supply is larger, the sprinkler heads are open, and the water is charged with greater pressure to flood the protected area very quickly. The fire alarm opens the deluge valve and drenches the area. The deluge system causes a great deal of water damage, but compared to an uncontrolled fire in this very hazardous environment, the losses are considered acceptable.

 Quick check

1. What type of fire detector uses a radioactive isotope?
2. What suppressant should be used on a class C fire?

Quick check answers

1. Ionizing smoke detector
2. Gas

Fire suppression agents

An organization can provide fire-extinguishing methods in many ways. As discussed previously, these include water; dry chemicals; wet, nonconductive foam; and gas. Although water is considered the most common and usable suppressant, the type of agent depends on the class of fire expected within the specific areas of the facility. Each of these agents attempts to extinguish the flames by reducing one or more of the four legs of a fire.

Gases

Several types of gases can extinguish a fire. Each of these gases removes the oxygen component that fuels the fire. Each also carries a varying degree of risk because these gases can be harmful to the environment and to people. The two types of gas that can be used as suppression agents to extinguish a fire are FM-200 (the most common Halon alternative) and CO_2. These systems are often installed in the raised flooring in data centers because many of these gas suppressants are lighter than air and will rise.

HALON GASES AND THEIR ALTERNATIVES

Halon is a very effective fire suppression agent that provides a chemical reaction when it interacts with the fire, which consumes the energy and lowers the temperature of the flames. Halon is hazardous to the ozone and is currently being phased out. Due to revelations about the ozone-depleting properties of Halon gas, the Montreal Accord was established and enacted by the Montreal Protocol in 1989, which banned the production and consumption of Halon systems in developed countries by January 1, 1994. The Montreal Accord did allow existing Halon systems to remain but stated that no new systems shall be implemented. There is an effort to recycle existing Halon gas to enable organizations to move to a Halon alternative. There are exceptions to the use of Halon within the Montreal Accord; they include the use of Halon on airplanes and submarines where the threat of fire is exceptionally dangerous.

Because of the time that has passed between the Montreal Accord and the writing of this book, most Halon systems are being replaced simply because of their age. Some of the alternatives that can be used within Halon systems are:

- FM-200
- NAF-S-III
- CEA-410
- FE-13
- Inergen
- Argon
- Argonite

FM-200 is commonly implemented as a fire suppression agent within data processing and telecommunication facilities and in the protection of many flammable liquids and gases. FM-200 was the first non–ozone depleting replacement for Halon that was widely used within existing Halon-based fire systems. FM-200 requires a slightly higher concentration to suppress fires and will not leave any residue on electrical equipment or hardcopy materials after the gas has been released. FE-13 is the newest of the gas suppression agents and is considered a safe alternative to Halon that allows this gas to be breathed in concentrations up to 30 percent, whereas other Halon replacements are generally safe only up to 10 percent to 15 percent concentration.

CO2

Although CO2 is a very good fire suppression agent, certain risks are associated with its use. The primary risk is that CO2 is toxic to humans. Because it is odorless and colorless, humans are often unaware of the overdose they might be exposed to. CO2 suppression agents are recommended only in unstaffed areas. If it must be used in areas where humans will be subjected to it, the personnel should be trained. Gas masks are ineffective in protecting humans from CO2 gas, and oxygen tanks should be supplied to ensure safety. Remember that a gas mask might be able to filter toxic gases out of the air, but if the gas suppressant has replaced all the oxygen in the air, the gas mask will not add oxygen into the mask. A supplemental air supply, such as the drop-down air masks on all commercial airplanes, might be an alternative if you use gas suppressants in closed spaces such as a data center.

COUNTDOWN TIMERS

The use of CO2, Halon, and Halon substitutes within gas-based fire suppression systems often includes the use of a countdown timer, which can provide both a visible and an audible warning to alert all persons in the surrounding area before the gas is released. The time that elapses provides for personnel to evacuate the area calmly and quickly. Another benefit of using countdown timers is that if there is a false alarm, the system can be manually disabled to stop the costly release of the gas.

Dry chemicals

Dry or powder-based suppression agents separate the various elements of a fire—the oxygen, temperature, and fuel. These powders prevent a chemical reaction from occurring between these elements and halt the production of fire-sustaining free-radicals, thus extinguishing the fire. The following list describes some types of dry-chemical suppression agents and is provided as a reference only. These details will not be test worthy:

- Mono-ammonium phosphate suppression agent is also known as tri-class, multipurpose, or ABC. This type of agent can be used on class A, B, and C fires.

- Sodium bicarbonate suppression agent is also known as regular or ordinary. This type of agent is used on class B and C fires.

- Potassium bicarbonate is known as Purple-K because of its violet color. This type of agent is used on class B and C fires.

- Potassium bicarbonate & Urea Complex is known as Monnex/Powerex. This type of agent is used on class B and C fires.

- Potassium chloride is also known as Super-K and is not a popular suppression agent. This type of agent is used on class B and C fires.

EXAM TIP

Know the different fire suppressants and the types of fires they are designed to suppress.

Fire extinguishers

Fire extinguishers are designed to suppress one or more of the different types of fires the extinguisher can handle. Most newer extinguishers can suppress class A, B, C and K types of fires by using a nonconductive foam. Each fire extinguisher also has a numeric rating that serves as a guide for the size of the fire the extinguisher can appropriately manage. The higher the number, the more firefighting power the extinguisher has.

Fire extinguisher ratings

The number and placement of fire extinguishers that an organization should deploy are dictated by the National Fire Protection Association (NFPA), Document 10 - Standard for Portable Fire Extinguishers, 2010, Annex E, Distribution. The number and placement of these extinguishers are based on the classes of fires because the contents of the extinguisher will be truly safe and effective only if they are used on the appropriate fire type. The following are the general requirements as laid out by the NFPA:

- Fire extinguishers shall be provided for the protection of both the building structure, if combustible, and the occupancy hazards contained therein.

- Required building protection shall be provided by fire extinguishers suitable for class A fires.

- Occupancy hazard protection shall be provided by fire extinguishers suitable for such class A, B, C, or D fire potentials as might be present.
- On each floor level, the area protected and the travel distances shall be based on fire extinguishers installed according to the following specifications:
  - The travel distance from the class A hazard (common combustibles) area to an extinguisher is 75 feet or less.
  - The travel distance from the class B hazard (liquid combustibles) area to an extinguisher is 50 feet or less.
  - The travel distance from the class C hazard (electrical fires) area to an extinguisher is to match the placement pattern for existing class A or class B extinguishers. (If there are no class B extinguishers, place class C extinguishers within 75 feet. If class B extinguishers are used, place class C extinguishers within 50 feet.)
  - The travel distance from the class D hazard (metal combustibles) area to an extinguisher is 75 feet or less.
- Rooms or areas shall be classified generally as light (low) hazard, ordinary (moderate) hazard, or extra (high) hazard. Limited areas of greater or less hazard shall be protected as required.

Fire extinguisher suppressants

Several types of suppressants might be contained within a fire extinguisher to put out fires, based on the class of the fire. These suppressants are water, dry chemicals, wet chemicals, and gas. An organization should consult applicable local fire codes before implementing a fire suppression system.

All fire suppression agents work by attacking one or more of the four legs of the fire:

- Reduce the temperature.
- Reduce the oxygen supply.
- Reduce the fuel supply.
- Interfere with the chemical reaction.

Water suppresses fire by reducing the temperature below the kindling point, or ignition point. Water is the most commonly used of all suppressive agents and is recommended for extinguishing common combustible fires. In the event of an electrical fire, shut off the electrical power to the affected area to reduce the risk of electrocution. To facilitate this action in data centers, an emergency power off (EPO) button is often installed but protected with a switch cover to prevent accidental triggering.

Soda acid is used to pressurize the water contained within the fire extinguisher. This is an older method, by which a glass bottle filled with sodium bicarbonate is placed inside the extinguisher filled with water. Activating the extinguisher breaks the bottle, releasing the acid to react with the water and pressurizing the container, forcing the water out of the extinguisher.

Soda acid creates a layer of foam that will float on the surface of a liquid fire, removing the oxygen from the fuel and extinguishing the fire.

Dry powder suppressants work by lowering the temperature of the fire and removing the oxygen to assist further in extinguishing the flames. The dry powder often used is sodium chloride, which primarily puts out fires that are ignited and fueled by flammable metals. Metals burn at very high temperatures. Putting water on surfaces at these high temperatures could result in a steam explosion, potentially increasing damage.

Wet chemical suppression agents primarily comprise potassium acetate mixed with water to lower the temperature and remove the oxygen, smothering the flames. Because most of these wet foam suppressants are electrically nonconductive, these suppressants are typically useful in extinguishing type A, B, C, and K fires, as shown in Figure 4-6.

FIGURE 4-6 A wet chemical fire extinguisher

Nonflammable, suppressant gases should be used on class C electrical fires to penetrate the electronic systems, cabinets, and circuits easily. If possible, quickly shut off the electrical supply to the electrical fire to reduce the energy at the ignition and combustion sources.

Fire extinguisher status/inspection

As with other security mechanisms, ensuring that fire extinguishers are available and in working condition is of the utmost importance. All fire extinguishers are labeled with the class of fire they apply to and display warning stickers, instruction for use, and, especially, expiration dates. The facilities department often keeps track of these items, but it is imperative for the security professional to understand and oversee the logging and status of these items. If the extinguisher fails any of the tests, it must be replaced.

The NFPA standard number 10 specifies the inspection and testing procedures for fire extinguishers in a typical workplace. Monthly visual inspection is required and includes looking for damage, correct pressure, the functional condition of the hose and nozzle, broken seals, and proper documentation of the monthly inspections affixed to the extinguisher.

NFPA 10 also requires annual inspections that include the monthly inspection and some basic testing to verify that the extinguisher is not blocked by furniture or equipment, to verify the pressure gauge and check the weight, and to check the metal cylinder and hose for damage. The annual inspections require conducting a pull test on the pin and replacing the seal. Personnel conducting the annual inspection should replace and update the inspection tag.

Fire plan and drill

As with fire extinguisher placement and inspection, a well-laid-out fire plan cannot be fully realized unless it is tested to ensure that the policies are followed. Keeping in mind that safety is of the utmost importance, people need to know what they are supposed to do in the event of a fire. Roles and responsibilities should be assigned to individuals to ensure that the smooth evacuation and safety of people is attended to appropriately.

Roles and responsibilities

Within the security policy that defines what actions are to be taken when an emergency occurs, several key roles should be defined and assigned.

- The *safety warden* is responsible for making certain that all of the organization's personnel safely evacuate the facility.

- Crowd control personnel should ensure that traffic flows smoothly out of the facility toward the defined meeting locations.

- The *meeting point leader* ensures that all personnel are accounted for at the emergency meeting point. This is very important if the facility houses children.

- A notification agent should be assigned to contact the appropriate emergency services as well as internal first aid teams, key management personnel, incident response teams, disaster recovery teams, public relations department, news media, and so on as is appropriate and necessary.

- Facilities support, for HVAC emergency shutoff and electrical shut off, and often works with emergency services to provide information, access, and other forms of support.

With safety the primary concern, personnel with mobility challenges must be taken into account. Individuals who require extra time to evacuate include people in wheelchairs or with permanent crutches or those who have physical impairments that hinder the speed of egress. An organization should consider where to locate these individuals and the quickest routes they should take to ensure a speedy evacuation.

Evacuation routes

Evacuation routes should be defined and posted in highly visible areas within the facility. All personnel need to know what routes should be taken to provide a quick evacuation in the event of a fire. Again, the evacuation routes should be clearly marked and provide the location of the meeting point so that all personnel and visitors can be accounted for.

Training and awareness

An important part of ensuring a safe evacuation is to set expectations for what people are supposed to do when an emergency occurs. Training enables the organization to set expectations for the personnel who are to perform the various roles and what they are supposed to do to ensure life safety.

Training must be mandatory for all new employees and should be provided at least annually for all personnel to make certain that everyone knows what to do or what to expect if a fire requires evacuation from the facility. This training should be updated, and drills should be performed to ensure its accuracy and relevance to the environment. Lessons learned and improvements should be incorporated into updated procedures and training.

Exercises

In the following exercises, you apply what you've learned in this chapter. The answers for these exercises are located in the "Answers" section at the end of this chapter.

You are planning a new facility to house administrative offices, a production facility, and a warehouse with shipping and receiving capabilities. The facility will produce plastic toys for children. An estimated 1,200 employees will work at the facility. The facility will be staffed with two security guards, on duty 24 hours a day. Entry into the administrative and production areas must be controlled with detailed and accurate auditing. Local fire code requires at least one egress point (exit) for every 200 people in the building.

Exercise 4-1

Describe the emergency exit planning.

Exercise 4-2

Describe the type of entry access controls that should be implemented to satisfy the stated requirements.

Exercise 4-3

Because the temperature in the warehouse is uncontrolled, describe the type of sprinkler system that should be implemented and why that particular type is required.

Exercise 4-4

Describe the techniques you can use to prevent crime in and around the facility.

Exercise 4-5

Plan the appropriate and cost-effective fire suppressants for fire extinguishers in the following areas of the facility; explain your choices.

- Administrative area
- Production area
- Break room
- Warehouse/shipping/receiving area
- Data center

Chapter summary

- The primary responsibility of the security professional is to ensure human safety.
- Facilities can be hardened against the threats by addressing the following issues: location, construction, CPTED, entry and exit access controls, data center placement, emanations protection, lighting and surveillance cameras, and fences. Countermeasures should deter, delay, detect, assess, and respond to threats to the physical environment.
- Crime Prevention through Environmental Design (CPTED) addresses the use of environmental elements to improve security.
- Redundant power lines, generators, UPSs, and line conditioners are some of the possible countermeasures to improve the continuity of business in the event of power outages and other power problems.
- There are four legs of a fire, five classes of fire, and specific suppression agents for each class. Life safety policies include assigning a safety warden and meeting point leader, documenting and testing fire policies, training all employees in fire safety protocols, and posting evacuation routes in highly visible areas.
- Suppression designs include wet pipe, dry pipe, pre-action, and deluge, gas, Halon (banned by the Montreal Accord), FM-200 gas, carbon dioxide (CO_2), dry powder, and nonconductive wet foam.
- The common fire detection mechanisms are ionization, photoelectric, temperature, and infrared detectors.

Chapter review

Test your knowledge of the information in this chapter by answering these questions. The answers to these questions, and the explanations of why each answer choice is correct or incorrect, are located in the "Answers" section at the end of this chapter.

1. What are the five categories that a physical security program should detail when considering the threats and countermeasures to apply?

   A. Deter, detect, react, sustain, and maintain

   B. Deter, delay, respond, sustain, and maintain

   C. Deter, delay, detect, assess, and respond

   D. Detect, delay, assess, respond, and confirm

2. What is a Faraday cage?

   A. An enclosure that provides a complex access control implementation, including mantraps

   B. An enclosure that prevents all emanations from exiting or entering the area enclosed by the cage

   C. A wired room enclosed by a cage that does not allow entry to any unauthorized individuals and has only one way in

   D. The copper shielding around twisted-pair wiring that provides additional emanations protection and strength

3. What are the two types of uninterruptible power supplies?

   A. Internal and external

   B. Online and offline

   C. Internal and offline

   D. Online and standby

4. What are the four legs of a fire?

   A. Fuel, oxygen, contaminants, and chemicals

   B. Fuel, chemical reaction, water, and temperature

   C. Oxygen, fuel, Halon, and temperature

   D. Fuel, oxygen, temperature, and chemical reaction

5. What are the five classes of a fire?

   A. A, B, C, D, K

   B. A, B, C, D, E

   C. A, B, C, D, F

   D. L, M, N, O

6. What are the four primary results that a suppressant agent should accomplish individually or in conjunction with another agent?

   A. Reduce the temperature, reduce the smoke, reduce the free radicals, interfere with chemical reactions

   B. Deluge the environment, capture the smoke, control the flame, open doors in fail-safe mode

   C. Reduce the temperature, reduce the oxygen supply, reduce the fuel supply, interfere with the chemical reaction

   D. Simply put out the fire

7. What is the function of security zones?

   A. Security zones separate differing levels of security within a facility.

   B. Security zones are areas where piggybacking is not allowed.

   C. Security zones require armed guards standing at the door.

   D. Security zones is the term used for full walls that separate individuals into their appropriate departments.

8. Where should a data center be located within a facility?

   A. A data center should be in its own facility and should not be combined with any other function of an organization.

   B. A data center should be located in the basement of a facility, underground for added protection.

   C. A data center should be located on the top floor of the building to ensure that intruders cannot access it from the ground.

   D. A data center should be located in the center of the facility.

9. What is the difference between a full wall and a partition?

   A. A full wall extends from the floor to the ceiling, whereas a partition is only 38 inches high.

   B. A full wall is a 4-inch thick wall that requires concrete, whereas a partition can be made of wood.

   C. A full wall extends from the floor to the roof structure, whereas a partition extends from the floor to the acoustic ceiling.

   D. A full wall is an external wall, whereas a partition is an internal wall.

10. What is the function of key management in physical security?

   A. Key management is the process of accounting for all keys and spares, auditing the inventory of keys, and having a master key system.

   B. Key management is the use of cryptographic keys and how to distribute the certificates to users.

   C. Key management requires every lock to have a unique key, each assigned to only one person within the organization.

   D. Key management is a function of the safety warden.

11. What are the recommended heights of fences to deter intruders?

   A. There are no recommended heights.

   B. A height of 3 feet to 4 feet deters casual trespassers; 6 feet to 7 feet is considered too high to climb; and 8 feet deters more resolute intruders.

   C. A height of 4 feet to 6 feet deters casual trespassers; 8 feet to 10 feet is considered too high to climb; and 12 feet deters more resolute intruders.

   D. It really doesn't matter; fences are an inappropriate means to deter an intruder.

12. What is the most effective way to deter an attacker from stealing a laptop?

   A. Installing applications that provide GPS functionality

   B. Making it against policy to take laptops from the facility

   C. Cable locks

   D. Keeping the laptop in a backpack and not a laptop bag

13. What are the two types of smoke-detecting mechanisms?

   A. Photoelectric and rate of rise

   B. Ionization and fixed temperatures

   C. Class A and class B

   D. Ionization and photoelectric

Answers

This section contains the answers to the exercises and the "Chapter review" section in this chapter.

Exercise 4-1

There will be at least seven fire exits (because the number of employees might occasionally exceed 1,200) that include four front, main-entry doors. All entry doors will fail-safe (be unlocked) in case of emergency alarm. The other doors will be marked as fire exits only and will remain locked from the outside, with no handles or knobs on the exterior of the doors. These emergency exit doors will use an alarmed crash-bar handle on the interior to unlock the doors and sound an alarm when they are opened. These doors will be monitored by cameras with the display presented at the security guard station. Policies and procedures will be defined, will incorporate all required local and other laws and regulations, and will be part of the security awareness training for all employees. Exit routes will guide workers away from hazardous areas and will be clearly identified in all areas of the facility. Exit paths, both internal and external, shall be kept clear of obstructions at all times. Employee staging areas will be defined outside and away from the facility and will be used during the fire drills. Semi-annual fire drills will be performed. One individual will be assigned the responsibility to maintain the emergency exit plan and perform regular inspections to ensure compliance with company policy.

Exercise 4-2

Employee entry is allowed through four controlled main-entry doors near the security guard station. These doors remain locked and allow access only by use of an ID card reader. All employees are issued an ID card (a memory card or smart card) to provide entry to the facility. The security guard monitors incoming pedestrian traffic to ensure that no piggybacking occurs. Company policy states that each person entering must identify himself by using the ID card, and piggybacking is prohibited.

Employee entry through the shipping/receiving/warehouse into the administrative and production facility is discouraged but is allowed through the one ID card reader–controlled door. Company policy states that no entry into the administrative and production facility is permitted through the shipping/receiving/warehouse area except by using an authorized ID card. Cameras monitor this door; the display is presented at the security guard station.

Exercise 4-3

The warehouse should use a pre-action sprinkler system, which includes a dry pipe to avoid freezing and damage to the pipes and resulting water damage, and includes a plastic billet that must melt before the sprinkler head will open. This is to reduce water damage, primarily to the packaging of the products, when the sprinkler system is activated.

Exercise 4-4

Choose a location for the facility in a lower-crime area. Employ the techniques described by Crime Prevention through Environmental Design (CPTED). Avoid creating places where an attacker can hide. Keep shrubs cut lower than 3 feet high. Use natural elements, bollards, or landscaping to establish defined and controlled pedestrian areas and walkways. Use glass-enclosed stairwells. Place the smoking area in full view of the parking lot. Provide continuous lighting between the facility and the parking lot and throughout the parking lot.

Exercise 4-5

- **Administrative area** Use a wet chemical, nonconductive suppressant. This area will include common flammables, including paper, furniture, and fabrics (carpeting, curtains) but might also include electronic computer systems. You need a general-purpose suppressant that can be used on electric fires also.
- **Production area** Use gas suppressants because this area will house electrical machinery and might include liquid flammables.
- **Break room** Use water because this area should only house common combustibles and should not have cooking oils as a household kitchen might.
- **Warehouse/shipping/receiving area** Use water because this area should only house common combustibles. Place gas extinguishers on propane-driven forklifts used in this area.
- **Data center** Use gas suppressants not only because this area houses valuable electronic systems but to eliminate potential damage from other suppressant types.

Chapter review

1. **Correct answer: C**

   A. **Incorrect:** React, sustain, and maintain are incorrect categories. The five objectives of the countermeasures used in physical security are deter, delay, detect, assess, and respond.

   B. **Incorrect:** Respond, sustain, and maintain are incorrect categories. The five objectives of the countermeasures used in physical security are deter, delay, detect, assess, and respond.

   C. **Correct:** When developing a physical security program, countermeasures should be implemented to:
   - Deter: Convince the attacker not to attack.
   - Delay: Slow down the penetration of the intruder. Enhances deter and detect.
   - Detect: Identify the intrusion as soon as possible.
   - Assess: Identify the severity of the threat, the potential for harm to personnel, and the scale of the potential losses.
   - Respond: Policies and procedures should dictate how to respond to the various threats, based on the assessment.

D. Incorrect: Detect, delay, assess, respond, and confirm are incorrect categories. The five objectives of the countermeasures used in physical security are deter, delay, detect, assess, and respond.

2. **Correct answer: B**

   A. Incorrect: A Faraday cage can provide significant access control, as does any secure location, but is intended to prevent emanations from entering and exiting the area so that there cannot be any interference or listening on the communications being sent or received. A Faraday cage is not required to include mantraps.

   B. Correct: A Faraday cage is an area, mobile room, or entire building that is designed with an external conductive sheathing that reduces or prevents emanations from exiting or entering the area.

   C. Incorrect: A Faraday cage is not specifically required to control physical access or limit the number of entry points.

   D. Incorrect: This describes the shielding used on shielded, twisted-pair Ethernet cabling.

3. **Correct answer: D**

   A. Incorrect: The two types of uninterruptable power supplies are standby and online, not internal and external.

   B. Incorrect: The two types of uninterruptable power supplies are standby and online, not online and offline.

   C. Incorrect: The two types of uninterruptable power supplies are standby and online, not internal and offline.

   D. Correct: During normal use, the standby UPS connects supported systems (the load) to the primary AC power through surge suppression filters. Parallel to that, it charges a bank of batteries. When the AC power fails, the UPS detects the failure and switches to providing power from the batteries. The switchover time from AC power to the battery might cause problems in some systems. The DC voltage from the batteries is sent through an inverter that changes their output to AC to feed the load. The standby UPS is common and relatively inexpensive. During normal use, the online UPS connects supported systems (the load) to the primary AC power through surge suppression filters, the battery, and the inverter circuit. When the AC power fails, the battery is already attached to the load, eliminating the switchover time delay, making it a more reliable alternate power source for the attached systems. However, running the power through the battery and inverter all the time causes these components to fail more rapidly. A parallel AC path, with only the surge suppression filters, is switched in to keep systems powered in case the battery or inverter fails.

4. **Correct answer: D**

   A. **Incorrect:** Contaminants, and chemicals are not components of the four legs of a fire.

   B. **Incorrect:** Water is not a component of the four legs of a fire.

   C. **Incorrect:** Halon is not a component of the four legs of a fire.

   D. **Correct:** Combustion requires fuel, oxygen, temperature, and a chemical reaction if it is to ignite and continue to burn.

5. **Correct answer: A**

   A. **Correct:** The five classes of fires are based on the initiator and what fuels the fire. The five classes are class A, common combustibles such as wood, paper, and laminates; class B, liquids such as petroleum products and flammable gas; class C, electrical, which includes electrical equipment and wires; class D, combustible metals such as magnesium, sodium, and potassium; and class K, kitchen fires, including grease and oils.

   B. **Incorrect:** E is not one of the five classes of fire. The five classes of fires are A, B, C, D, and K.

   C. **Incorrect:** F is not one of the five classes of fire.

   D. **Incorrect:** L, M, N, and O are not the five classes of fire.

6. **Correct answer: C**

   A. **Incorrect:** Reducing the smoke and free radicals are good things to accomplish, but they are not mechanisms of fire suppression.

   B. **Incorrect:** Although deluging the environment, capturing the smoke, controlling the flame, and opening doors in fail-safe mode might be helpful in a fire event, they are not mechanisms of fire suppression.

   C. **Correct:** The primary activities that suppression agents should perform are to reduce the temperature, reduce or remove the oxygen supply, reduce or remove the fuel supply, and interfere with the chemical reaction.

   D. **Incorrect:** "Simply put out the fire" does not address how to put out the fire.

7. **Correct answer: A**

   A. **Correct:** A security zone includes access controls and is a division of areas to provide differing levels of security.

   B. **Incorrect:** Piggybacking should be disallowed at every managed entryway.

   C. **Incorrect:** Although guards can be used to control the access to security zones and within security zones, they are not a specific requirement or function of security zones.

   D. **Incorrect:** Security zones should be constructed with appropriately designed walls, but security zones do not only describe the design of the walls.

8. **Correct answer: D**

   A. **Incorrect:** Other security zones and structures around the data center provide additional protection to it.

   B. **Incorrect:** Basements are the first area of a building to flood.

   C. **Incorrect:** Fire rises in buildings, and roofs leak.

   D. **Correct:** Ideally, the data center should be located in the center of a facility with offices surrounding it. This makes it difficult for an attacker to gain access or damage the data center with an external attack. Avoid plumbing above the data center.

9. **Correct answer: C**

   A. **Incorrect:** Partitions are not limited in their height to 38 inches.

   B. **Incorrect:** The material used for walls and partitions is not mandated.

   C. **Correct:** A full wall extends from the floor to the roof structure, typically the underside of the roofing material. A partition wall extends from the floor to the framing members that support the acoustic ceiling.

   D. **Incorrect:** Both the full wall and the partition are internal walls.

10. **Correct answer: A**

    A. **Correct:** To facilitate a proper key management process, an accounting of all keys and spares must be made, and audits of these keys should be conducted frequently. An additional mitigation is to ensure that keys to restricted areas with access-controlled doors are not issued to staff. In case of emergency, keys must be available if the access control system fails; this circumstance will become more procedural and can be dealt with in a number of ways.

    B. **Incorrect:** Cryptographic keys are technical components and perform encryption and decryption functions.

    C. **Incorrect:** Management and operations personnel will often need keys to multiple doors.

    D. **Incorrect:** The safety warden ensures that all people have successfully evacuated the building in a fire drill or alarm.

11. **Correct answer: B**

    A. **Incorrect:** 3 feet to 4 feet deters casual trespassers; 6 feet to 7 feet is considered too high to climb; and 8 feet deters more resolute intruders.

    B. **Correct:** Fences are one of the first lines of defense in a layered defense strategy. 3 feet to 4 feet deters casual trespassers; 6 feet to 7 feet is considered too high to climb; and 8 feet deters more resolute intruders.

    C. **Incorrect:** 3 feet to 4 feet deters casual trespassers; 6 feet to 7 feet is considered too high to climb; and 8 feet deters more resolute intruders.

    D. **Incorrect:** Fences are one of the first lines of defense in a layered defense strategy.

12. **Correct answer: C**

   A. **Incorrect:** Although GPS functionality is an option to track a stolen laptop, it is not the simplest way to prevent the laptop from being stolen.

   B. **Incorrect:** Organizations provide laptops to enable mobile computing.

   C. **Correct:** One of the simplest security mechanisms to deter an attacker from stealing a laptop is a cable lock. This device connects to the frame of the laptop; is long enough to wrap around a solid, fixed object; and uses a lock to secure the laptop.

   D. **Incorrect:** Although it is true that keeping a laptop in a nondescript bag can help conceal the existence of the laptop, this advantage disappears when you have to take it out to use it.

13. **Correct answer: D**

   A. **Incorrect:** A photoelectric sensor is one of the mechanisms used within a smoke detector, but the rate of rise is used in a thermal detector rather than in a smoke detector.

   B. **Incorrect:** Ionization is one of the mechanisms used within a smoke detector, but fixed temperatures are used in a thermal detector.

   C. **Incorrect:** Class A and class B are types of fires, not mechanisms to detect smoke.

   D. **Correct:** An ionization smoke detector contains a small radioactive source that creates a small electric charge. A photoelectric smoke detector contains a light-emitting diode (LED) and a photoelectric sensor that generates a small charge while receiving light.

CHAPTER 5

Security architecture and design

The vast majority of information assets today exist on computer systems. This chapter takes the position that "subjects use computers and programs to access objects." It then explores the question, "How can you develop a sense of trust that the source of a breach of the confidentiality, integrity, or availability of the valuable information assets will not be the computer?" If the computer itself has unknown vulnerabilities that allow a breach, or has a covert device that specifically siphons off data to the bad guys, there is little point in spending the money to implement security for the protection of those assets. Somehow, there must be a way to develop some level of trust at which you can feel confident that the computer itself will not be the source of the breach. Only with this level of trust does it make sense to implement other forms of protection for information assets.

With this in mind, this chapter begins with an overview of the computer, often referred to as the bare metal system, and the operating system architecture, largely to identify opportunities within those architectures for security. How do these components lend themselves to providing—or better yet, improving—the security of the system?

Exam objectives in this chapter:

6.1 Understand the fundamental concepts of security models (e.g., Confidentiality, Integrity, and Multi-level Models)

6.2 Understand the components of information systems security evaluation models

6.2.1 Product evaluation models (e.g., common criteria)

6.2.2 Industry and international security implementation guidelines (e.g., PCI-DSS, ISO)

6.3 Understand security capabilities of information systems (e.g., memory protection, virtualization, trusted platform module)

6.4 Understand the vulnerabilities of security architectures

6.4.1 System (e.g., covert channels, state attacks, emanations)

6.4.2 Technology and process integration (e.g., single point of failure, service oriented architecture)

6.5 Understand software and system vulnerabilities and threats

    6.5.1   Web-based (e.g., XML, SAML, OWASP)

    6.5.2   Client-based (e.g., applets)

    6.5.3   Server-based (e.g., data flow control)

    6.5.4   Database security (e.g., inference, aggregation, data mining, warehousing)

    6.5.5   Distributed systems (e.g., cloud computing, grid computing, peer to peer)

6.6 Understand countermeasure principles (e.g., defense in depth)

Identifying architectural boundaries

As you review this architecture, focus on where natural boundaries exist. These boundaries provide isolation, a potential security opportunity. The boundaries come in many forms, and as described in many places in this book, more layers can provide a greater depth of security. Therefore, every one of these boundaries could be implemented to improve the security of the system. Watch for terms such as the following that identify boundaries within the architecture:

- Segmentation
- Perimeter
- Layering
- Isolation
- Encapsulation
- Black box
- Data hiding
- Abstraction
- Wrapper
- Time division
- Namespace
- Virtual/logical addressing

The goal is to find ways to separate high-value, highly trusted processes and data from lower-value, less-trusted processes and data. For example, if you have a computer with two or more processors, to improve security you could run only top-secret processes and data on one processor and all other processes on the second processor. This is an example of physical segmentation that could be implemented on a multiprocessor system. There is a potential for increased security in this example. As with almost all aspects of information system security, no single security control will satisfy all security concerns, so, as usual, you need to consider the use of multiple layers of security—defense in depth.

When you understand these natural and potential boundaries, implementing them correctly as security control components is the next objective. To implement comprehensive security sufficiently so that it supports a level of trust of the security of a system, the designers of computer hardware and operating systems must consider academic proofs of security theory and refer to a collection of standards or specifications that are required to map out all the details and requirements of implementation. These policies, procedures, guidelines, baselines, and standards can be used to build a framework that defines how a computer should be designed, built, delivered, installed, maintained, and eventually decommissioned so that it supports a specified level of trust that it will not be the source of a breach of security. That was a long and perhaps complex sentence, but it is the crux of this domain. You might want to read it again to be sure you understand what the goal is.

Recognize that building a computer to that heightened specification and then testing it to verify that the security features exist (functionality) and operate correctly under every specified condition (assurance) will certainly increase the cost of the system. Moreover, as stated in Chapter 1, "Information security governance and risk management," every security countermeasure must be cost justified—the losses avoided should be greater than the cost of the security control.

The "Frameworks for security" section later in this chapter includes a collection of academic models that mathematically prove the effectiveness of specific security functions. They are abstract, but parts of these models are mixed together and implemented by operating system and application developers to satisfy security at a specified level. That section also includes an introduction to enterprise frameworks and their security subset components. This chapter includes the testing and evaluation models defined by governments that the hardware and operating system vendors must abide by if they want to sell their wares to governments, who buy a lot of systems and will pay the notably higher price for certified systems.

The section finishes with a brief overview of legal and regulatory compliance standards imposed on commercial markets to ensure adequate security of systems for which the industry or government feels that security breaches might negatively affect the public. These include the Payment Card Industry-Data Security Standard (PCI-DSS), the Sarbanes-Oxley Act, the Healthcare Insurance Portability and Accountability Act (HIPAA), and similar standards.

Computer hardware and operating systems

Because most of the valuable information assets that need to be protected exist on computer systems, the computer hardware and the basic software must support the protection of those information assets. This chapter focuses on the computer hardware, the low-level software that initially boots the computer system, and the computer's operating system that supports higher-level drivers and provides the platform for applications and human interaction. Software development security is covered in Chapter 9, "Software development security."

Figure 5-1 presents an overview of this relationship.

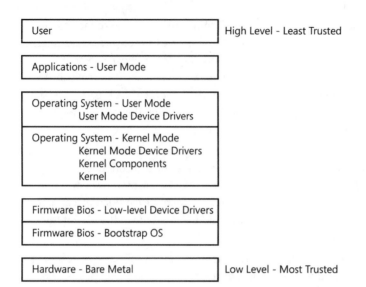

User	High Level - Least Trusted

Applications - User Mode

Operating System - User Mode   User Mode Device Drivers

Operating System - Kernel Mode
         Kernel Mode Device Drivers
         Kernel Components
         Kernel

Firmware Bios - Low-level Device Drivers
Firmware Bios - Bootstrap OS

Hardware - Bare Metal	Low Level - Most Trusted

FIGURE 5-1 Architecture of a computer system, operating system, and applications

The lower an item is in this structure, the more trusted it is, or must be, as you move toward access of valuable information assets at the higher levels near the subject (user) and applications. Computer systems are built with hardware and specialized software, called *firmware*, that is stored in the computer in a specialized memory component called the *basic input/output system* (*BIOS*). This combination of hardware and firmware provides the basic functionality of the system.

As a user powers up the computer, the *bootstrap operating system* is read from this BIOS memory and starts the system. From here, the bootstrap operating system loads low-level device drivers that provide basic functionality of the various hardware components, such as the video card to provide a basic display for the user, and the disk controller to enable initial access to the hard disk drives. Device drivers are software that allows the computer to communicate with and control hardware devices.

After the BIOS has loaded itself into memory, the bootstrap operating system locates a bootable device, typically a hard disk drive. This is where the higher-level operating system, such as Windows or Linux, is stored. The bootstrap operating system loads the higher-level operating system, providing the platform for applications and human interaction. After the kernel of the operating system is initialized, taking control of the system from the bootstrap operating system, higher-level, kernel-mode device drivers are loaded into memory to provide all the high-power, high-performance, fancy bells and whistles the hardware devices can provide. The kernel is the core of the operating system and is the most trusted software component in the computer system. The kernel is in control of the entire system. If the kernel doesn't bless (approve) a request for access, the access is denied.

The computer system is now ready for applications and human interaction.

Computer hardware

A computer system is built using *integrated circuit* (*IC*) chips mounted on a printed circuit (PC) board called a *motherboard*, which is installed in a case with a power supply for power and protection. The case typically includes storage locations for hard disk drives and optical CD/DVD drives. The case has interfaces or connectors to attach *peripheral devices* such as a video display, a keyboard, a mouse, external storage drives, a microphone, a camera, speakers, and a printer. A typical motherboard is shown in Figure 5-2.

FIGURE 5-2 A computer motherboard

The two large, square objects in the lower-right corner of the figure are heat sinks that draw heat off the two Xeon CPU assemblies below them. Just above the heat sinks, mounted vertically, is the random access memory (RAM). The actual memory IC chips are mounted on small PC boards and are often referred to as memory sticks. The power supply is the square block in the upper-left corner. Hard-disk drive storage is in the lower-left corner.

The central processing unit (CPU)

The core of the computer system is the *central processing unit* (*CPU*). This is an integrated circuit, often an assembly that performs the main part of the processing, manipulating data elements as defined by instruction code (software). The CPU typically includes a specialized component called the *arithmetic logic unit* (*ALU*), which performs the mathematic and

Boolean logic functions. (Remember George Boole [1800s] from Chapter 3, "Cryptography"?) It also includes small and fast memory locations, called *registers*, and a specialized traffic-cop type of function called the *control unit*.

The registers are physically and electrically close to the CPU circuit for speed and are used as temporary storage locations, like a scratchpad for the CPU. Access times are in the range of 1 nanosecond or sub-nanosecond, related to the clock speed for the CPU. A *nanosecond* is 1/1,000,000,000 second. The size of the register memory is in increments of the architecture of the processor. For example, a 16-bit processor has multiple registers, each 16 bits wide.

The control unit stages instructions and their related data elements in the registers, moving them closer and closer to the CPU for processing, keeping the CPU fed with work as efficiently as possible. The control unit performs a *fetch* function when it is moving data or instructions, and when the data and instructions are in the CPU and ready for processing, the control unit orders an *execute* function.

If the instruction requires math or logic (always in binary on a computer), the CPU doles the work out to the ALU and then can continue working on other tasks.

The premier producer of CPU chips is Intel. It introduced its first 16-bit CPU chip, the Intel 8086 chip, in 1978. The 8086 is a one-core processor operating at 4.77 megahertz (MHz, or millions of cycles per second) and has 29,000 transistors. The CPU chips have steadily become faster—today's 64-bit Sandy Bridge Core i7 eight-core processors operate at nearly 4 gigahertz (GHz, or billions of cycles per second) and have 2.27 billion transistors.

CISC AND RISC CPU CHIPS

The CPU chip contains a collection of instructions that it inherently understands and can perform, called the *instruction set* for that CPU. Application program code ultimately must call instructions from this instruction set for the CPU to run its programs and process its data. There are two primary types of instruction sets: *Complex Instruction Set Code* (*CISC*) and *Reduced Instruction Set Code* (*RISC*).

CISC includes a larger collection of instructions for the application developer to call from. Having many instructions enables the developer to write very straightforward code, more directly achieving the desired programmatic tasks. However, this larger instruction set consumes more of the valuable memory on the CPU chip. As an example, imagine a CISC instruction set that includes the following instructions:

- Turn right 90 degrees
- Turn left 90 degrees
- Turn right 180 degrees
- Move forward
- Move backward

RISC has fewer instructions, reducing the burden on the memory on the CPU chip, but now the application developer has fewer choices of instructions to accomplish the same programmatic tasks. For example, imagine a RISC instruction set that includes the following instructions:

- Turn right 90 degrees
- Move forward

To be able to turn left, it now requires three turn-right instructions. To move backward, it requires two turn-right instructions, a move-forward instruction, and two more turn-right instructions.

CPU chips that use the CISC instruction set include the Intel x86 family, the IBM System/360, and the Motorola 68000 series. CPU chips that use the RISC instruction set include the DEC Alpha, AMD 29k series, the Sun SPARC, the MIPS family of CPUs, and the Motorola 88000 series.

UNI-PROCESSING SYSTEMS AND MULTIPROCESSING SYSTEMS

Early CPU chips had only one core or processing channel. Because of the high cost of these new devices at the time, most systems had only a single CPU. A computer system with one CPU chip that has only one core is called a *uni-processing system*. A uni-processing system can process only one instruction, also called a *thread*, at a time. The system uses *time-division multiplexing* to provide different processes access to the CPU in small time slices. The system performs this *multiplexing* so quickly that it gives the illusion of running multiple applications simultaneously.

When additional CPU chips are installed in a system, it is called a *multiprocessing system (MPS)*. It can process multiple threads simultaneously, one thread per core. In the early days, this required a motherboard designed to accept multiple single-core CPU chips. Today, many CPUs are built with multiple cores to accomplish this in a single device such as the aforementioned Intel i7 processor.

SCALAR, SUPERSCALAR, AND PIPELINED PROCESSORS

Some CPU chips include the capacity to accelerate the execution of instructions by using various techniques. A basic uni-processor CPU chip that can only execute a single instruction at a time is the most common and performs what is called *scalar* processing. A faster but much less common CPU is called *superscalar*; though having a single core, it can execute more than one instruction at a time. The application code must also be written to support this faster functionality. Other types of CPU chips can support an acceleration technique called *pipelining*, by which the output from one instruction is the data for the very next instruction, allowing an overlap of the two instructions and eliminating a fetch of the data because it is already in the CPU register. Again, to support this faster pipelining functionality, the application code must be written to take advantage of this hardware (CPU) capability.

Memory

 The next component is *cache memory*. It typically has a 1-nanosecond to 2-nanosecond access time and is a little farther away from the CPU chip electrically and physically. Level 1 cache memory is often on the same substrate as the CPU chip or is mounted on the same assembly as the CPU chip. Level 2 cache memory is typically mounted on the motherboard near the CPU assembly. The typical volume of Level 1 cache memory on a CPU is less than 10 megabytes (MB, 1 MB is approximately 1,000,000 bytes), but some motherboards support up to 1 gigabyte (GB, 1 GB is approximately 1,000,000,000 bytes) of Level 2 cache memory.

 A bit farther away electrically and physically is *random access memory* (*RAM*), the volume of memory most users are aware of. The volume of RAM is usually provided as a main part of the system specification and today ranges from 1 GB to about 8 GB of RAM for a typical workstation. The access time for RAM is approximately 10 nanoseconds. RAM is where the bootstrap operating system, firmware, operating system, drivers, and applications reside during the operation of the computer system. RAM currently costs about $13 USD for 1 GB and $20 USD for 4 GB. The register memory, the cache memory, and RAM are all *volatile memory*; if the power to the systems is shut off, whatever was stored in these memory locations is lost.

 RAM is based on a technology called *dynamic random access memory* (*DRAM*), which is volatile (requires a constant supply of DC voltage to retain what is stored within) and requires a power refresh about 1000 times per second. This power refresh consumes additional DC power; therefore, DRAM is not commonly used in battery-operated, handheld, portable types of devices. The cache memory is based on a technology called *static random access memory* (*SRAM*), which is also volatile. However, SRAM does not require the power refresh cycles. This reduces the power consumption. SRAM is the type of RAM used on most battery-operated, handheld, portable types of devices such as smart phones and pad-type devices. Notice that the farther away from the CPU memory is, the slower it is and the larger the volume typically is. As memory gets faster, it also gets more expensive. As you read further, you will see that these trends persist as the computer and its accompanying hierarchical storage system are described.

 Another memory component in a computer system is *read-only memory* (*ROM*). This is the memory location where the firmware BIOS (bootstrap operating system and low-level device drivers) is stored. This ROM is *nonvolatile*; it retains its content in memory even with the power removed. In earlier days, this ROM data was stored on erasable/programmable ROM (EPROM), which used a high-intensity ultraviolet light shining through a glass window over the memory chip to erase the contents, making it rewritable with a new program. Today, this memory is usually flash memory, such as that used on a USB thumb drive. Flash memory is slower than or equal to RAM in terms of access times.

This flash memory is electrically erasable, read-only under normal operations, and nonvolatile; it carries the Electrically Erasable, Programmable, Read-only Memory (EEPROM) label. These ROM components come from a family (superset) of programmable logic devices (PLD).

Finally, the farthest, slowest, cheapest, and largest volume of memory typically used on a computer system is *virtual memory*. When a system doesn't have enough RAM, rather than tell the user he cannot run any more applications or load any more data, the system spools some content currently in RAM out to the hard disk drive on the system to make room in RAM for additional application code or data. The typical hard disk drive access time is about 10 milliseconds (10/1,000 seconds). Notice that the hard disk is approximately 1 million times slower than RAM. This becomes painful for the computer system but keeps the user supplied with the needed RAM. It's similar to your car going 1 million times slower when you go to the nearby convenience store. Hard disk drives today are available in the range of 1 terabyte (TB, approximately 1,000,000,000,000 bytes) and 3 TB and cost about $60 USD for 1 TB and about $160 USD for 4 TB. The process of using virtual memory is managed by an operating system kernel component called the virtual memory manager, which will be described in the section titled "The memory manager" later in this chapter.

To summarize the relationship of the various types of memory within a computer system, the closer the memory is to the CPU, typically, the faster it is; the more expensive it is; and, therefore, the smaller the amount provided or available to the system. The order of the memory types is as follows, from nearest the CPU to the farthest away:

- **Nearest to CPU**   Fastest, most expensive, smaller amount
  - **Registers**   Read/write, volatile
  - **Cache (Level 1)**   SRAM, Read/write, volatile
  - **Cache (Level 2)**   SRAM, Read/write, volatile
  - **RAM**   DRAM, Read/write, volatile
  - **EPROM/EEPROM**   Read-only, nonvolatile
  - **Virtual memory**   Read/write, nonvolatile
- **Farthest from CPU**   Slowest, cheapest, largest amount

The address bus and the data bus

An important part of the operations in a computer system is moving data from one location, such as a hard disk drive, to another location, such as RAM. This is accomplished using the address bus and data bus. A *bus* is a series of conductors (wires), typically run in parallel beside one another and connecting various components inside the computer system. These wires are usually printed on or within the motherboard. The more wires there are (the greater the *bus width*), the faster the system can operate. Many systems today use a 64-wire bus. This allows for addressing or flowing data at 64 bits per clock cycle.

The address bus identifies the location on one of the memory devices at which data bits are to be accessed, read from, or written to. When the location is defined by its address, the data bus latches onto that location, and the data bits can flow as voltage on the wires, one bit per wire per clock cycle.

Peripherals

What happens inside the computer system is important, but the only reason that computer exists is to empower and enable its user. Somehow, the user must be able to interact with this computer. This is accomplished through *human interface devices* (*HIDs*). Items such as the keyboard and mouse for input and the display and printer for output are examples of these peripheral devices. They connect to the computer system through *ports*, or interfaces. Some ports are designed specifically for one device, such as a video port, but others are more generic and capable of connecting to a large number of devices, such as a *universal serial bus* (*USB*) port.

These interfaces then typically connect to controller devices and the address or data buses inside the computer. When hardware devices need work done by the CPU, the device driver for the hardware issues an interrupt request (IRQ) to signal its need for attention. Peripheral devices operate on speeds compatible with humans—meaning eons-slow compared to the subnanosecond CPU.

Figure 5-3 shows an overview of the major components of a computer system and the general flow of information within the system.

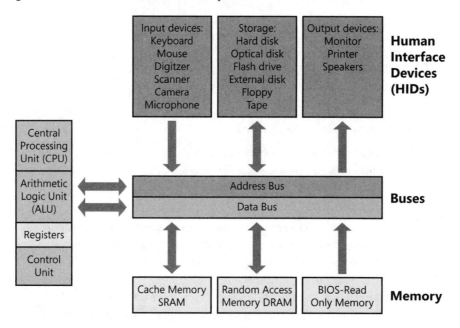

FIGURE 5-3 Overview of the major components of a computer system.

Security opportunities within the computer hardware

One opportunity to improve security by using computer hardware is the addition of secondary authentication mechanisms such as a smart card reader or a biometric device—for example, a fingerprint scanner, but in the basic computer system, there are a few opportunities as well.

As mentioned earlier in this chapter, the opportunity for *physical segmentation* appears when multiple CPUs are installed in a system and when multiple RAM sticks are installed. Isolation can be implemented if the system supports the control of processes and data so that one memory stick and one CPU handles only top secret data and processes, and all other data and processes are handled by the other memory sticks and CPUs.

Yet another security opportunity presents itself in the computer hardware. A relatively new and still largely optional security device for computers is called the *trusted platform module* (*TPM*) chip, a cryptographic processing device that includes secure storage of asymmetric keys. The chip is mounted on a computer motherboard during the manufacturing process and cannot be removed. It is typically used to provide *whole disk encryption* for the hard disk drive or drives installed in the system. If the disk drives are removed from the system that uses the TPM chip, all content on the removed disks remains encrypted and protected because the decryption keys are stored inside the TPM chip. This feature defends against a common attack vector if the computer is lost or stolen. To bypass common access controls such as rights and permissions, an attacker removes the disk drives from the original system and mounts the disk drives on a system on which the attacker has full authority and privilege. Without the TPM chip and the whole-disk encryption, the attacker now has access to all content on the disk drives. With the TPM chip and whole-disk encryption, the attacker can see only ciphertext on the stolen and remounted disk. She still has the physical asset, but she cannot access the more valuable data, and no breach of data occurs.

Many TPM chips include a feature called *remote attestation*. At the time of the computer's installation, when the system configuration is complete and is considered to be in a known-good and trusted configuration, a hash value is calculated over the system's firmware, configuration details, and perhaps some core components of the operating system's kernel, and this hash value is securely stored within the TPM chip. Then at each startup, a new hash value is calculated over the same components and compared to the original. If the two hash values match, the startup is considered good and trusted, and the process is allowed to continue. If the two hash values do not match, it indicates that an unauthorized configuration or software change has occurred, and startup is halted. The TPM chip in the computer system will not allow the system to start in this altered and untrusted state.

There has been a successful attack on the TPM chip, called the *cold boot attack*, in which the decryption key for the disk drive was captured during startup. The key could then be used later to decrypt the disk drives. The cold boot attack is a type of side-channel attack in which an attacker with physical access to a computer can retrieve encryption keys from a running operating system after using a cold reboot to restart the machine. The attack relies on the data remanence characteristics of DRAM and SRAM to retrieve memory contents that remain readable in the seconds after power has been removed.

The operating system

The operating system is a collection of software programs that is typically stored on a hard disk drive and is loaded into RAM at startup. The computer hardware and the operating system provide the platform for the applications needed by the user.

The core of the operating system is called the *kernel*; it is the most powerful and trusted component of the operating system and is responsible for the overall computing environment of the system. Being in charge of so many specialized functions required in a computer is more work than one piece of software can perform, so the kernel has many specialized support components to help administer the system. These processes that support the kernel are referred to as kernel components or *executive services*. Kernel components include:

- Memory manager
- Security kernel
- Process manager
- Device drivers
- File system drivers
- Other components

The kernel, kernel components, and most device drivers operate with heightened trust and privilege in a state of operation called *kernel mode*, commonly called system mode, supervisory mode, trusted mode, or privileged mode. When any of these kernel components needs the CPU to do work, the system switches into the kernel mode execution state, also called the kernel mode execution domain. In this mode, the procedures have full authority over the system, so this mode must remain highly protected to retain its required high level of trust. As the kernel components of the operating system load into RAM, the memory space where the kernel resides is protected, and nonkernel processes are denied access.

When users launch their software, this software operates with the lowest level of trust and privilege in a state of operation called *user mode*, commonly called problem mode or less-trusted mode. When these processes need the CPU to do work, the execution domain switches into user mode, in which all requests are sent to the kernel for approval before any work can be performed. Figure 5-1 showed this kernel mode/user mode relationship and their relative levels of trust and privilege supported by the system architecture.

Figure 5-4 presents an overview of user mode and kernel mode and several of the kernel components.

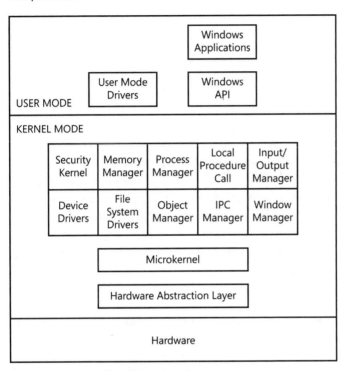

FIGURE 5-4 User mode and kernel mode

Communications occur between these layers by using application programming interfaces (APIs), software pathways across the boundaries. APIs should be implemented as security control points, not as holes in the boundaries that simply allow information to flow.

Another view of this model is called the *ring architecture*. In this model, the kernel and all kernel mode components exist in Ring 0 surrounded by a security boundary. Outside that is Ring 1 and its boundary with Ring 2, Ring 2 and its boundary with Ring 3, and, finally, Ring 3. Ring 3 is where all user mode functions, the least trusted functions, occur. As stated previously, for the user to do any work, a request must be sent to the kernel. In this model, that request must use an API to pass to Ring 2, another API to pass to Ring 1, and then a third API to pass to Ring 0, where the kernel resides. Information flowing from the kernel out to the user must also commute through APIs and the boundaries.

This ring architecture is designed to protect the kernel from misbehaving software and willful attack. Figure 5-5 shows the ring architecture.

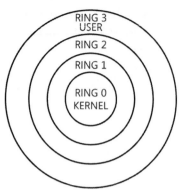

FIGURE 5-5 The operating system ring architecture

> **NOTE   RISKY DEVICE DRIVERS**
> Most hardware device drivers operate in kernel mode, right next to the kernel, and are often developed by third-party vendors. It is not uncommon for users and administrators to download and install device drivers on a system. Recognize the risks associated with installing this software unless it comes from a trusted source and has verified its integrity. If a device driver contains a trojan, the malware can run in kernel mode and operate with a high level of privilege, including the ability to cover its tracks.

Multiprogramming

Multiprogramming is a feature the operating system provides. In the early days of mainframe computing, when a program needed to access a peripheral device, the program would simply wait until the peripheral device could supply the data or perform whatever the function call was. This kept other programs from running. Peripheral devices are still slow today, but they were substantially slower back then. This was terribly inefficient.

So multiprogramming was introduced. This enabled a program to run until it needed to access a peripheral device. Then the system would record the state of the program and give the next program its turn until it needed some slow device. The system would then record the state of the second program and give the next program its turn. This procedure would continue to cycle through all loaded programs until all programs completed in this batch-style operation.

Multiprogramming was the prelude to multitasking.

Multitasking

Multitasking is a feature the operating system provides. In the early days of personal computing, a computer running DOS could only run a single application at a time. If you were running a word processor and needed some numbers from a spreadsheet file, you had to save your document, exit the word processing application, launch your spreadsheet application, open your file, and retrieve the desired numbers. Then you would have to exit the spreadsheet application and launch the word processing application again. Early operating systems such as DOS did not support multitasking.

Windows 3, the Macintosh operating system, and IBM's OS2 Warp then provided the opportunity to seemingly run multiple applications simultaneously by multitasking, sharing the CPU with multiple programs through time-division multiplexing. These early implementations

supported *cooperative multitasking*. The multitasking operating system would give control of the CPU to a program. The developer coded the program with a series of instructions that needed CPU time and would code into his program when the program would return control of the CPU to the operating system, cooperatively sharing the CPU with other programs. The program was in control of when its turn in the CPU ended.

However, if a program failed during its turn in the processor, the program would never reach its CPU release statement. The program was stuck, and the CPU was locked on the stuck program. The computer had to be restarted to clear the stuck program, and any unsaved data from any of the applications was lost.

Then, in the early 1990s, the Windows NT 3.1 and Windows 95 operating systems changed this behavior. The kernel of the operating system assumed control of whose turn it would be in the CPU. The kernel would issue time slices to programs and interrupt the program to share

the CPU with other programs preemptively. This is called *preemptive multitasking*. Now, if a program failed and locked up, the kernel of the operating system could still switch the CPU to other programs, keeping them alive. Only the failed program would need to be restarted, not the whole system.

Multithreading

As the operating system implemented the concept of multitasking, the concept of the thread also grew. The thread is a small instruction the CPU performs on data elements. The ability of

a process to spawn more than one thread is *multithreading*. Threads are coded in human-readable programming languages but then are compiled or interpreted into *machine language* so the CPU can execute them. The CPU only understands machine language, which is not readable by humans.

In the early days of computing, like in DOS, an operating system would only support running a single application. That application could spawn a single process. That one process could spawn a single thread. Today, users can start multiple applications simultaneously, each application can spawn one or more processes, and those processes can spawn one or more threads, as shown in Figure 5-6.

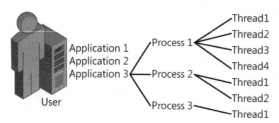

FIGURE 5-6 Applications, processes, and threads

Processes

As a user launches an application, that application spawns one or more processes. A *process* is a collection of instructions or threads that tell the CPU how to manipulate (process) the related data elements. The developer who wrote the program knows how much space, in memory, the set of instructions will consume and how much space, in memory, the data that the instructions must work on will consume. Therefore, as the process is launched, a request is made by the program and on behalf of the user to the memory manager kernel component for a specified amount of RAM to support the process.

The memory manager, a kernel component of the operating system, allocates the amount of RAM requested. This memory space is referred to as a *buffer*. The memory manager then notifies another kernel component, the *security kernel*, of the allocated memory. It is the job of the security kernel to protect the allocated memory space for the process. If an unauthorized process attempts to access the memory location, the security kernel terminates the offending process.

> **NOTE   BEFORE PROTECTED MEMORY**
> In early implementations of operating systems, all processes were stored and operated within one common and shared memory space, and there was no protection. This meant that any process on a system could access any other process's instructions and data on the same system. Then, in the early 1990s, protected memory became the norm for operating systems.

In addition to being allocated a protected memory space, the new process is issued a process identifier (PID) and is listed on the *process table* indicating the *process state*. The control unit in the CPU monitors this table to identify which processes need to be fetched and staged closer to the CPU for processing.

Process states can be:

- **Blocked**   A process is in a blocked state when it is waiting for its data elements and cannot be executed yet.
- **Ready**   A process is in a ready state when it has all its required data elements, and its collection of instructions is ready to be executed. These are the processes the control unit is most interested in.
- **Running**   A process is in a running state when it is being executed in the CPU.

After the memory is allocated and protected, the process begins loading its instructions (threads) into the buffer from the bottom of the memory space toward the top. At the top of the set of instructions in the buffer, a pointer is added to identify what process or instruction is to be carried out after this process completes the execution of its instructions.

Instructions work on data, so next, the data elements are retrieved and placed in the buffer memory space. Data elements load into the buffer from the top toward the bottom. The data elements can also come from various places, from a database or files on the hard drive, or they might be the output from some other process. Data can also come from user input in a form as the user types in information and moves to the next field in the form. The retrieval of data can take some time, so the process remains in the blocked state until all required data elements are available in the buffer. Processes tend to spend most of their lives in the blocked state.

Eventually, all required data elements become available in the buffer memory. The process changes its state from Blocked to Ready, signaling the control unit that it needs to be staged, using time-division multiplexing, toward the CPU for processing. This process is shown in Figure 5-7.

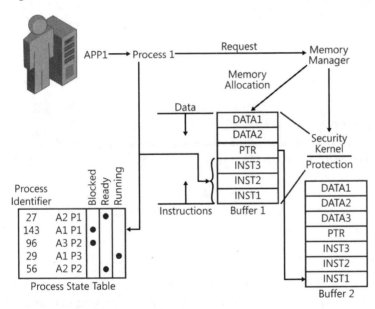

FIGURE 5-7 The process and buffer memory

After the process has its turn in the CPU and its instructions run on the data elements to produce the desired output, the process should clean itself up. To avoid the possibility of leaving sensitive information lying around in unprotected memory, the process should overwrite the entire buffer with bits, either all 1s or all 0s or a pattern of random bits, but by no means any sort of data. After fully purging all viable data contents of the buffer, the process should return the buffer memory space to the memory manager, freeing up the memory so another process can use it. This purging of data in the buffer and returning the buffer memory is called *garbage collection*. Data that remains after a process frees the storage space is referred to as *remnants*.

If a process doesn't return the memory to the memory manager as it should and continues to collect and keep memory after it has finished its work, this is called a *memory leak*. A process with a memory leak will continue to consume more and more RAM, depleting the system of available RAM, degrading performance, and eventually triggering an automated reboot or requiring a manual reboot. When attackers find a memory leak in an application, they might develop ways to trigger these processes remotely as a denial of service (DoS) attack. You can identify applications and processes with memory leaks by monitoring them with the Windows Task Manager on the Processes tab, as shown in Figure 5-8.

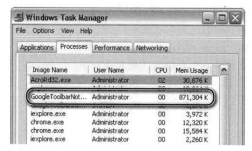

FIGURE 5-8 A memory leak

> **NOTE SELECTING COLUMNS IN TASK MANAGER**
> If necessary, in the Windows Task Manager, on the View menu, choose Select Columns to enable the fields you want to display on the Processes tab.

If you must run an application that has a memory leak, you can simply restart the application to release the acquired memory back to the memory manager and then restart the application as necessary.

The buffer overflow attack

The buffer overflow attack is one of the most prevalent attacks on software. As described, the instructions and the pointer are loaded from the bottom of the buffer toward the top. Data elements load from the top down. The developer who wrote the code for the process knows how much memory needs to be allocated for the instructions, pointer, and data elements and asks for just that much memory. If the developer does not manage the size (in bytes) of the data elements coming into the buffer carefully, this presents the vulnerability called *buffer overflow*. If an attacker can find processes where the data input is not carefully qualified, he can inject malicious code instead of the expected data and overfill (overflow) the data portion of the buffer to overwrite the pointer. He redirects the pointer to execute his injected malicious code, which compromises the security of the system, as shown in Figure 5-9.

The malicious code executes with the privilege level of the legitimate user who originally launched the application or process. This gives the attacker access to everything the user has access to on this system and, potentially, across the network.

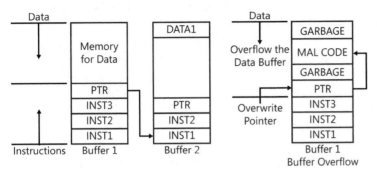

FIGURE 5-9 The buffer overflow attack

Interestingly, if developers improved their secure coding habits, the buffer overflow vulnerability could be eliminated with all new software. All user input and data input into buffers should be programmatically qualified and controlled to match specifically what the developer is expecting for the data elements, truncating or rejecting anything that doesn't match the expectations. Some of the newer programming languages include some protections along these lines; however, developers should accept the responsibility for their code and verify that correct and complete protective measures are in place before releasing their code.

The memory manager

The memory manager is an operating system kernel service responsible for all things related to memory. This includes providing memory to applications and processes, reclaiming memory as processes perform garbage collection, and coordinating with the security kernel to protect allocated memory. The memory manager also works with a subordinate kernel service called the *virtual memory manager.*

LOGICAL MEMORY ADDRESSING

The memory manager allocates memory to the operating system and to applications in logical address assignments of 2 GB each. The computer might only have 1 GB of RAM, but the operating system and each application thinks it has been assigned a full 2 GB for its private use. As additional applications are launched, they are assigned the next available 2-GB increment in this logical memory addressing. The logical address is assigned as a *base address* of 2 GB, for example, and the application can use up to, but not including, the 4-GB address. The memory manager actually allocates memory, typically in 4-KB pages, only as the applications and their processes use memory. Most applications use only a small fraction of the allocated 2-GB logical address space.

As a user launches an application, the memory manager adds the application to its *memory map* and assigns the application the 2-GB logical memory address space. The memory manager maps this logical address space to true physical memory addresses, keeping the true physical address hidden from the application. Remember that applications run in user mode and are the least trusted processes.

As the application spawns processes, those processes request memory, in the form of a buffer, from the memory manager. As that memory space is allocated, the application keeps track of where, within the application's 2 GB of logical address space, the process has been allocated by identifying its base address and then the *offset* within that logical address space where the specific process resides. Again, the memory manager maps this logical address (base plus offset—for example, a 4-GB base address plus a 64-KB offset) to the secret physical memory address where the content truly resides on the system. Although there are other benefits to the operating system for this logical addressing, it acts as a security control, protecting (hiding) the actual location in physical RAM where sensitive processes and data reside from the less-trusted applications and their processes. This memory map and its logical memory addressing is shown in Figure 5-10.

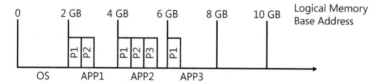

FIGURE 5-10 Logical memory addressing

VIRTUAL MEMORY

Applications and their processes need to be loaded into RAM to be executed. When a system has allocated all its RAM to applications and the demand for RAM continues, the memory manager puts a kernel mode subordinate service, the virtual memory manager (VMM), to work. Because of the relatively high price of RAM (as compared to the price of hard disk drive space), many systems have substantially less RAM (typically a few gigabytes) than hard disk drive space (typically a few hundred gigabytes to a few terabytes). To free up space in physical RAM, the VMM identifies which processes in RAM have not been accessed for the longest time and relocates this content, typically 4-KB pages at a time, to a temporary storage space

on the hard disk drive. This location on the hard disk drive is commonly called the *swap file* or the *page file*, and the process is called a *page out*. The VMM keeps track of what has been paged out and where in the swap file the paged-out content is.

When the user toggles back to an application that has been paged out to the swap file, the VMM recognizes this *page fault* event. The VMM often has to make new space in physical RAM for the paged-out content to be moved back into RAM, so once again, the VMM identifies which processes in RAM have not been accessed for the longest time and relocates this content to the swap file. Then the VMM *pages in* to RAM the content identified by the page fault.

The VMM coordinates with the memory manager to update the memory map when the VMM restores content into physical memory because it might not put the content back from where it was originally pulled.

The use of virtual memory is transparent to users, other than the delays of writing to and reading from the comparatively slow hard disk drive, which is roughly 1,000,000 times slower than physical RAM.

Kernel mode processes typically cannot be paged out to virtual memory for security and performance reasons.

SHARED CONTENT IN MEMORY

Although the security kernel must protect the process instructions and data (the buffers) in RAM, some content is intended to be shared among multiple processes. This includes dynamically linked libraries (DLLs) of content shared by many applications (such as the OK button used in virtually every application) and shared processes when a system is running a shared, multiuser application. This shared content typically is stored in the 2 GB allocated to the kernel mode processes for security purposes.

The mandatory access control (MAC) model and security modes

Access control systems are commonly implemented within operating systems. The mandatory access control (MAC) model is the strongest of the access control models in IT systems and the most expensive in implementation. It is so costly to implement that typically only governments, who can afford it and have the greater need for the strongest security, will pay the higher price.

The MAC model divides subjects and objects into layers of a *lattice*, each layer having a different *label*. Subjects get a *clearance* label based on a combination of need, risk, and trust level, and objects get a *classification* label based on the sensitivity (value) of the information asset. The higher a subject is on the lattice, the more privilege that subject has been granted. The higher an object is on the lattice, the more sensitive (valuable) the object is.

The labels are affixed to subjects, granting a specific level of privilege, and to objects, identifying the level of sensitivity of the object, by a rigid system policy and process. After these labels are assigned, they are purposely difficult and slow to change to prevent any rapid change that might introduce unexpected weaknesses and exposure in the system. This feature is what makes MAC the strongest access control model used in IT systems. Its tight and slow-to-change bond between subjects and objects and their labels prevents a subject from altering its label (level of privilege) and the unauthorized transfer of privilege. Other access control models, such as discretionary access control (DAC) and role-based access control (RBAC), aren't this strong and might allow the unauthorized transfer of privilege. This phenomenon is described in Chapter 2, "Access control."

In a simplistic MAC implementation, if the clearance of a subject matches the classification of an object, access is granted, and information can flow. The lattice structure the MAC model uses is shown in Figure 5-11.

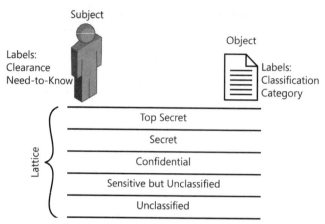

FIGURE 5-11 The lattice structure of the MAC model

EXAM TIP

For the MAC model, remember the following key descriptive terms (word association): MAC, strong, expensive, governments, lattice, labels, clearance, classification, need-to-know, and category.

Four common MAC model security modes provide greater versatility and granular control but at the price of greater complexity of the technical controlling mechanisms. When considering these MAC model security modes, consider the nature of the technical controls implemented within the operating system (stronger security means greater complexity and greater cost to implement) compared with the sensitivity levels (classification) of information the system could hold and the types of subjects (clearance levels) that could use the system.

These MAC security modes use controls to match clearance to classification and formal authorization to access the content from management as well as need to know and category. The need-to-know and category match describes topics in the content within the object. For example, a subject working on projects related to Korea doesn't need to know information about China.

These modes also consider that a subject could print a hard copy of the content, eliminating the technical controls in place in the MAC-based operating system or application. To maintain control over these copies, these four modes include the administrative control of a signed nondisclosure agreement (NDA) between the subject and the organization.

The four MAC model security modes and their primary access controls are:

- Dedicated
- System High
- Compartmented
- Multi-Level

As you progress through these security modes, recognize that they become progressively more granular with the need for controls but that the systems lend themselves to supporting a wider range of subjects.

DEDICATED SECURITY MODE

The Dedicated security mode suggests a system that will only ever hold one classification of data and that the only subjects authorized to use this system have a clearance that matches the classification of all data on the system. Management has authorized these users to access all content on the system, and the subjects' need to know matches all the content on the system. The following statements further define this mode.

- Clearance that matches ALL information on the system
- Formal authorization to access ALL information on the system
- Need-to-know that matches ALL information on the system
- All subjects can access all objects on the system

SYSTEM HIGH SECURITY MODE

The System High security mode suggests a system that will only ever hold one classification of data, and the only subjects authorized to use this system have a clearance that matches the classification of all data on the system. Management has authorized these users to access all content on the system, and the subjects' need to know matches some of the content on the system. The following statements further define this mode.

- Clearance that matches ALL information on the system
- Formal authorization to access ALL information on the system
- Need-to-know that matches SOME information on the system
- All subjects can access some objects, based on their need to know

COMPARTMENTED SECURITY MODE

The Compartmented security mode suggests a system that will hold multiple classifications of data, and the only subjects authorized to use this system have a clearance that matches the highest classification of all data on the system. Management has authorized these users to access some content on the system, and the subjects' need to know matches some of the content on the system. The following statements further define this mode.

- Clearance that matches the highest level of data classification on the system
- Formal authorization to access SOME information on the system
- Need-to-know that matches SOME of the information on the system
- All subjects can access some objects, based on their formal access approval and need to know

MULTI-LEVEL SECURITY MODE

The Multi-Level security mode suggests a system that will hold multiple classifications of data, and some content might have a classification higher than the subject's clearance. Users are granted access to some content based on their clearance matching or exceeding the classification of the objects. Management has authorized users to access some content on the system, and the subjects' need to know matches some of the content on the system. The following statements further define this mode.

- Clearance that matches SOME information on the system
- Formal authorization to access SOME information subjects will access on the system
- Need-to-know that matches SOME of the information on the system
- All subjects can access some objects, based on their clearance, formal access approval, and need to know

Table 5-1 summarizes these MAC-based security modes and the type of information the subject is allowed to access on the system. (ALL = all information on the system can be accessed by a subject. SOME = some information on the system can be accessed by a subject and requires a technical control to limit access.)

TABLE 5-1 Security modes of MAC systems

	Signed NDA	Clearance	Approval	Need to know
Dedicated	ALL	ALL	ALL	ALL
System High	ALL	ALL	ALL	SOME
Compartmented	ALL	ALL	SOME	SOME
Multi-Level	ALL	SOME	SOME	SOME

EXAM TIP

You should be able to identify these four security modes from their descriptions. Remember their order of strength: Dedicated, System-High, Compartmented, Multi-Level—DSCM. To remember this order, you can memorize the mnemonic "Durable Security Costs Money." Then remember that each successive model adds another security control. This can help you memorize these models.

Application architecture

To improve availability, performance, and security, many enterprise-level client and server applications are constructed in layers. On the client side, users launch client applications and browsers. This *front-end*, client-side function usually requires limited processing, primarily providing connectivity to presentation servers. The presentation servers accept inbound connections from clients and establish communications with *back-end application servers*. The back-end application server is where the real number crunching and processing occurs and is often where some valuable intellectual property, in the form of custom program code, exists. These back-end application servers connect to one or more *data repositories*. The data repository is typically where the most value lies within the application architecture. If the types of data repositories are different, an extra layer between the application and data repository layers, called *middleware*, might be required. It is the job of middleware to perform a form of *data normalization*, standardizing the formatting of the data coming in from those data sources to the applications. This architecture is shown in Figure 5-12.

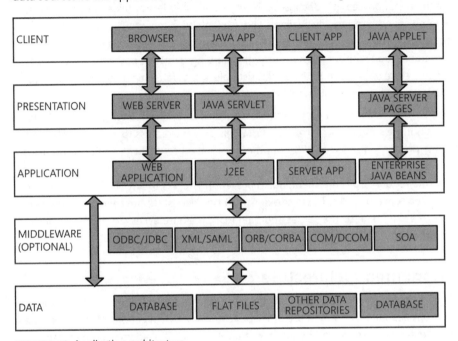

FIGURE 5-12 Application architecture

Notice that between each layer is a boundary that can be implemented as a security control layer. Information must flow through those boundaries in APIs and through direct network connections and protocols. Firewalls and other data filtering can be implemented at the boundary between each layer in this structure to introduce preventive and detective (logging) measures. VPNs might be implemented over all network connections to provide confidentiality and integrity controls. Corrective measures might include cluster servers at the presentation, application, data repository layers (described in Chapter 10, "Operations security"), and trusted recovery techniques (described in the "Trusted Computing System Evaluation Criteria (TCSEC)" section later in this chapter). Clustering of servers lends itself to minimizing or eliminating single points of failure in the application architecture providing high availability. (Remember C, I, and A?)

Web-based applications should be reviewed to ensure that clients are forced to follow the intended sequence of processing. Because web servers are stateless applications, by default, clients can request and jump to any available URL (called *URL jumping*). This might allow an attacker to cause a web app to perform its processes out of order, such as completing an e-commerce transaction without passing through (jumping over) the payment screen. This attack is called a *state attack* due to the stateful/stateless characteristic of applications. (Web applications are stateless, which allows this attack.)

A common protection used to prevent the state attack is server-side environment variables that keep track of the state of the current session. This prevents access to any URL unless it is the next in the proper sequence of URLs. Another tool is the use of client-side encrypted session cookies that store the satisfied steps in the process. The cookie is then read by the server at each new URL request from the client, again preventing access to any URL unless it is next in the proper sequence of URLs. These cookies must be encrypted; otherwise, an attacker could edit the cookie to lie to the server and gain inappropriate access to processes of the web-based application.

Service-oriented architecture

An emerging collection of technologies, called *service-oriented architecture* (*SOA*), operates mostly in the application layer, where the SOA applications offer collections of interoperable services and detect services offered by other SOA applications. Developers couple these application services, as desired, to pass and parse information contained in messages and produce the output they want. The information within these messages typically describes data or is data that has already been processed to some extent and is therefore more accurately described as data about data, referred to as *metadata*. Instead of using the traditional API, SOA makes its coupling through well-defined application protocols and functionality.

The goal of SOA is to assemble a collection of services offered by applications on potentially many platforms and federate all the information resources these applications have access to through these standardized messages. Earlier forms of SOA include distributed computing and modular programming. SOA is now extending into newer technologies such as cloud computing, software as a service (SaaS), and mashups. Cloud computing and SaaS are covered in the following sections. Mashups are a relatively new family of web applications that aggregate data and content from multiple SOA-based sources to produce a single web page for a user.

Distributed systems

Distributed systems were first implemented in the late 1970s and early 1980s. To improve processing power, several autonomous computer systems can be connected so that they share the workload to accomplish a common task. The connection between the distributed systems takes the form of a *distributed program* that communicates with other computers running the same distributed program over a computer network. These communications between computers are called messages. The computer systems can operate on different platforms, and each computer system operates on a portion of the overall solution. Computers can be added to the overall distributed system and can go offline from time to time. This lends itself to minimizing or eliminating single points of failure in the information system.

> **NOTE PARALLEL PROCESSING**
> The major difference between distributed systems and parallel processing is that of memory. Each distributed system has its own independent memory, whereas parallel processing systems share a common memory space.

Peer-to-peer networks

The computers in a *peer-to-peer (P2P) network* operate independently of a central infrastructure system in a decentralized administrative model. They operate in a client or server mode, or both, providing access to files and peripheral resources to other members of the P2P environment over a computer network.

The P2P environment can be constructed to operate as a distributed system with the addition of a distributed program; however, this begins to form a central infrastructure, moving the model further away from the classic P2P model. Napster and torrents are examples of P2P systems that become associated by means of a distributed program.

Virtualization

Virtualization enables the implementation of one or more guest operating systems on a single host hardware system and operating system. The host system runs an application, or *hypervisor*, to support one or more guest operating systems. The hypervisor exposes virtualized hardware resources to the guest operating system so that the guest system thinks it is installed on true physical hardware. This guest system is referred to as a *virtual machine (VM)*. The VM includes all the necessary virtual hardware that would be needed on a standard workstation or server, including virtual hard disk drives, virtual optical disk drives, virtual network interface cards (NICs), virtual USB ports, and so on.

There are numerous benefits to the use of VMs in computing:

- Most physical computer systems use only a fraction of the system resources. By running multiple VMs on a single hardware system, the use of this capital expense (computer hardware) is used much more efficiently.

- Decreased power consumption can be achieved in data centers by reducing electricity and cooling demands due to having fewer physical computer systems.

- The VM provides a security boundary, providing layers of isolation between the host operating system, the guest operating system, and the additional guest operating systems.

- The VM can run many operating systems on a single host operating system. This is useful for testing and development purposes.

- Many aspects of virtualized systems perform much faster in a virtual environment. For example, networking between two virtual machines on the same host hardware system can operate on CPU timing, not the timing of physical networking hardware such as network interface cards, routers, and switches.

- VMs provide centralized administration of virtual systems.

- VMs are easily duplicated or cloned. This lends itself to simplified administration for new system generation and disaster recovery. It also supports compliance with policy and standardization of system configuration.

- Many commercial hypervisors support clustering of the host hardware systems to provide dynamic resource allocation for efficient load balancing.

Specialized CPU chips and computer systems have been developed to support direct access by the kernel of the hypervisor for performance and security purposes.

Several vendors have developed and support hypervisor software, including VMware, Hyper-V from Microsoft, Oracle's VM VirtualBox, Sun's Java VM, and Parallels for Mac.

The ease of administration, scalability, and redundancy, and the much greater use of capital hardware of virtualization, are reasons that most cloud computing environments are based on virtualization. However, virtualization introduces one or more additional attack vectors that must be considered and included within the security assessment and program. In addition to all the standard system and network hardening and monitoring systems for the virtual machines, you must now monitor and protect the host operating system and its hypervisor. In a VM Escaping attack (accomplished through exploiting guest VMs), the attacker can gain control of multiple virtual machines simultaneously by compromising the host operating system or hypervisor.

Cloud computing

Cloud computing has become the buzz phrase of the decade. In a *cloud computing* environment, the computing services are provided in the cloud and are not required on the workstation. The cloud is a potentially massive collection of clustered, load-balanced, often virtualized servers tightly coupled with applications and data that client systems can access over a network such as the Internet. This keeps the hardware and software requirements on the many client systems to a minimum—for example, to a thin client—reducing these costs.

Because the applications and data reside in the cloud, a user can access this content from any location that has connectivity, and from any system, without much regard for the configuration (and security level) of the client system. This architecture has led to the concept of *bring your own device (BYOD)*, whereby users can supply a large array of personally owned computing hardware and still access all the applications and data, further reducing hardware costs to organizations. Ensuring the security level of these various BYOD devices is a difficult challenge for security operations and is just now evolving in contemporary IT systems.

Cloud computing architecture typically has three tiers, beginning at the core with *infrastructure as a service (IaaS)*, which provides servers (virtual and physical), storage, and networking services. On top of IaaS, cloud computing can provide the *platform as a service (PaaS)*, which provides operating system and back-end application server support, such as database servers and web servers. The top tier provides *software as a service (SaaS)*, which includes the applications end users access more directly. This usually includes the client desktop and user interface, email, and other front-end applications.

Because the cloud provides the applications, there is no need to deploy to, and update software on, each client. The applications are centrally maintained on the server side (in the cloud), simplifying these aspects and reducing costs to the end users.

The cloud generally includes data management and storage services as well, so built into the administration of the cloud is the collection of high-availability, high-capacity, redundancy, disaster recovery, and geographically dispersed data storage and protection services.

Some large companies can develop their own private cloud for internal use. However, generally speaking, when the cloud is referred to, it is identifying this collection of computing services on the Internet. Clients often subscribe to these services, paying monthly fees and potentially additional usage fees.

Some concerns exist regarding the placement of privately owned valuable intellectual property and information assets on a large number of shared systems that are administered by personnel outside the controls of the organization. This security aspect must be carefully considered and coordinated with company policy and external compliance requirements. Often, a company loses control over granular security and auditing when it subscribes to cloud computing services.

Grid computing

Extending past the singular administrative body managing a cloud computing environment, a more loosely coupled collection of cloud computing environments has evolved. These are administered by different entities and are referred to as *grid computing*. Scale up the cloud to include the use of resources from multiple clouds and you have grid computing. However, recognize that a common thread connects these clouds to define the grid. The computing power and data elements from the multiple clouds are pulled together to accomplish a specific task, a common goal. In addition, when the task is complete, this common thread is disconnected, reverting to discrete clouds once again, only to be combined in perhaps a different combination of clouds for the next large-scale common task. Specialized grid middleware defines and assembles these threads that connect to the cloud resources of the grid.

This highly scalable collection of distributed parallel computing resources essentially produces a virtual supercomputer. Highly demanding projects, such as those involving artificial intelligence processing, lend themselves to the use of grid computing.

The security concerns scale similarly as you scale from cloud to grid computing. Now instead of concerns with the security management of one external administrative body, the grid presents the challenges of the security management of multiple external administrative bodies.

However the architecture of the system is designed, security checks should include those for the threat of covert channel attacks, which is discussed in more detail in Chapter 9, and emanations attacks, which are discussed in more detail in Chapter 7, "Telecommunications and network security."

 Quick check

1. What is another name that describes an instruction in machine language?

2. What execution domain does the system move to when the memory manager is having some work done?

Quick check answers

1. A thread

2. The memory manager is a kernel mode component and triggers the system to shift into the kernel mode execution domain.

Frameworks for security

 The secure enterprise must have a defined framework, an administrative control to define and maintain the prudent governance of the organization. This framework must be initiated, driven, and supported by top-level management. The collection of policies, procedures, guidelines, baselines, and standards that document this organizational framework is collectively called the *policies* of the organization. These policies establish the *security posture* of the organization and define the framework of the *security program* for the enterprise. These documents should describe the prudent management of the specialized security concerns of the organization (because no two organizations have the same security concerns) and have integrated into this the collection of policies, all laws, and regulations the organization is subject to. These documents also provide the platform for senior management to establish ethical standards for the employees to abide by.

The security requirements the policies define must provide adequate security yet allow for the overall functionality of the business, with the underlying goal of maximizing corporate profits. This implies that all security countermeasures must be cost justified, as described in Chapter 1. So that this risk management can be performed and losses minimized, the policies of the organization must describe the performance of due diligence and due care with the implementation of safety and security controls following the *prudent person rule*. Legally, this shows that the organization is not negligent, which minimizes risk and liability and therefore losses.

The development of this comprehensive security program is generally considered a three-year project, from the time the organization reaches the point of maturity at which it recognizes and acts on the need to implement security until the organization has performed the risk assessment, implemented its controls prudently, provided the appropriate awareness training for all subjects, and is enforcing and refining the policies of the security program.

The security program should also include some form of monitoring and the use of metrics to evaluate the security status and performance of the enterprise continuously. This monitoring can come in the following forms and others, and laws and regulations might dictate monitoring processes:

- Internal auditing
- External auditing
- Vulnerability assessment and scanning
- Penetration testing
- Secure code review

There are many collections of enterprise frameworks, security frameworks, recommendations, and best practices. As you develop your policies, use these as the fundamental structure and checklist and modify or customize them as necessary to satisfy the specialized and unique security posture your organization requires.

International Organization for Standardization (ISO) 27000 series

The ISO 27000 series is a collection of internationally recommended information security standards, largely based on the *British Standard 7799* (*BS7799*). Organizations can become ISO 27000 certified if they can prove their compliance to an accredited testing entity.

- **27000** This document provides an overview of the 27000 series of *information security management systems* (*ISMS*).
- **27001** This document describes requirements for how to establish, implement, operate, monitor, review, maintain, and improve an ISMS. It replaced the original BS7799-2 standard and follows a *Plan-Do-Check-Act* (*PDCA*) model.

- **27002** This document was originally the BS7799 standard and then was republished as the ISO 17799 standard. It operates as a code of practice and lists hundreds of security controls and control mechanisms that might be useful within the ISMS. It also describes ways to develop security standards (policies) to establish a security program within an organization.

- **27003** This document focuses on implementation and describes ways to establish, implement, review, and improve the ISMS.

- **27004** This document describes metrics, the ways to measure the effectiveness of the ISMS.

- **27005** This document describes the standard for Information System Risk Management (ISRM).

- **27006** This document is titled "Information technology - Security techniques: Requirements for bodies providing audit and certification of information security management systems," and it defines the guidelines for accreditation of vendors who certify and register certified ISMSs.

Although there are many other documents in the ISO 27000 series, these provide the core of the ISO's ISMS standards.

EXAM TIP

Be aware of the ISO 27000 series of standards and guidelines for the exam.

The Zachman Framework for enterprise architecture

Created by John Zachman in 1987 for IBM, the Zachman Framework for enterprise architecture is a way to structure policy documents for information systems, within an organization, that focuses on the object a policy targets and the issue that the policy is targeting. It has been modified several times since its introduction and focuses on the who, what, where, when, why, and how of information systems

This model has been adapted to many specific frameworks. An independently designed but later integrated subset of the Zachman Framework is the *Sherwood Applied Business Security Architecture (SABSA)*. This architecture, published in 1996 by John Sherwood, describes an architecture that secures information systems in an organization by using the policy structure and concepts from the Zachman Framework. Notice the similarities to the Zachman Framework in the SABSA model.

EXAM TIP

Remember that the Zachman Framework describes the structure of policies for the entire enterprise, and SABSA is a subset of the Zachman Framework that focuses only on the security aspects of the information system in an organization.

The Committee of Sponsoring Organizations of the Treadway Commission (COSO)

COSO is a five-member group of accounting, financial, and auditing professional associations that develops enterprise-level frameworks and guidance for accounting on:

- Enterprise risk management
- Internal control
- Fraud deterrence

It was organized in 1985 to sponsor the National Commission on Fraudulent Financial Reporting; its name refers to its first chairman, James C. Treadway Jr. COSO regularly publishes "Thought Papers" on the three security topics previously described.

Control Objectives for Information and Related Technology (COBIT)

Control Objectives for Information and Related Technology (COBIT) is an IT governance framework and toolset of controls, developed by the Information Systems Audit and Control Association (ISACA). You can consider COBIT the IT security arm of COSO. COBIT is currently on version 5, released in 2012.

COBIT breaks this control into four aspects of the IT services. They are:

- Planning and organization
- Acquisition and implementation
- Delivery and support
- Monitoring

COBIT focuses on the requirements of the business, the IT processes, and the IT resources that satisfy those requirements.

ISACA also sponsors the Certified Information Systems Auditor (CISA), the Certified Information Systems Manager (CISM), the Certified in Risk and Information Systems Control (CRISC), and the Certified in the Governance of Enterprise IT (CGEIT) certifications.

EXAM TIP

Remember that the COSO framework describes the structure of policies for the governance of accounting data within the entire enterprise, and COBIT is a subset of the COSO framework that focuses only on the security aspects of the information system in an organization.

Information Technology Infrastructure Library (ITIL)

The Information Technology Infrastructure Library (ITIL) is a collection of best practices for *IT service management*. ITIL's approach is to help manage the services that IT provides from end to end rather than just managing the discrete infrastructure technologies. ITIL presents a service life cycle that includes:

- Service strategy
- Service design
- Service transition
- Service operation
- Continual service improvement

Generally Accepted Information Security Principles (GAISP)

Sponsored by the Information Systems Security Association (ISSA), a nonprofit international organization, the Generally Accepted Information Security Principles (GAISP) is currently on version 3. GAISP sprang from the earlier Generally Accepted System Security Principles (GASSP). Its recommendations are based on "experience, reason, custom, usage, and, to a significant extent, practical necessity." The principles the GAISP present are that:

- Computer security supports the mission of the organization.
- Computer security is an integral element of sound management.
- Computer security should be cost effective.
- Systems owners have security responsibilities outside their own organization.
- Computer security responsibilities and accountability should be made explicit.
- Computer security requires a comprehensive and integrated approach.
- Computer security should be periodically reassessed.
- Computer security is constrained by societal factors.

National Institute of Standards and Technology (NIST) Special Publication 800 (SP 800) series

The *Computer Security Resource Center (CSRC)* of NIST has published a series of recommended practices for computer security called the Special Publications 800 (SP 800) series. These publications are issue-specific and system-specific recommendations that include the following titles, to name a few examples:

- **SP 800-153** Guidelines for Securing Wireless Local Area Networks
- **SP 800-146** Cloud Computing Synopsis and Recommendations
- **SP 800-68** Guide to Securing Microsoft Windows XP Systems for IT Professionals

- **SP 800-53** Security and Privacy Controls for Federal Information Systems and Organizations
- **SP 800-37** Guide for Applying the Risk Management Framework to Federal Information Systems

Security models

As referred to in the concept mentioned earlier in this chapter, "Subjects use computers and applications to access objects," somehow on these computer systems, you must provide some control over how and when that access is allowed. On computer systems, control is implemented by means of software, so developers must identify some mechanisms or methodologies that can be implemented in software and control access in a manner that satisfies company policy. Developers identify different types of access control models as examples of how security of different strengths could be implemented.

These security models are academic models, with their rules often proven secure through abstract mathematical formulas and calculations. The models often have more than one facet—multiple rules—that can be proven mathematically. Developers must locate the proper type of control in these models (based on policy and a specific need for security within a program or operating system) and then implement the selected rules in the form of program code. There is a difference between the academic security rules from the models and the implementation of those rules in software.

You can think of these rules as like a recipe for a cake, written in a book and sitting on a shelf above the oven. The recipe is a model for how to produce a cake, but it is not a cake. Someone must implement the recipe (model) by baking a cake (implementation) based on the recipe (model). After implementation, you have the cake, the implementation of the model. While using a single recipe for cake—during implementation—you might decide you need to deviate somewhat from the academic recipe to implement the cake in a way that satisfies your immediate needs. For example, today you might need chocolate icing (the birthday girl's favorite!) instead of the vanilla icing that the recipe specifies. As long as the chocolate icing does not violate some policy (such as an allergy to chocolate or the prohibitively high cost of chocolate flavoring) and satisfies your specific needs, this deviation from the academic model (recipe) might be acceptable by management.

These models are implemented within program code in some larger, more complex applications, but they are usually implemented in computer operating systems and network operating systems to control how subjects use computers and applications securely to access objects.

Remember that the purpose of these models is based on these concepts:

- Subjects use computers and applications to access objects.
- You must protect the valuable information assets that these computer systems store, process, and provide access to.
- You must be able to develop some level of trust that the computer system will not be the source of compromise of the valuable information assets.

Only if you can do this can you hope to implement effective security within an organization.

The first three models address lower-level aspects of developing this sense of trust for the computer system. These three low-level models must be secure in implementation for the remaining higher-level models to be effective. If any one of these first three models fails in the implementation of a system, the higher-level models are useless because these lower-level aspects of the computer system will be massively vulnerable. The higher-level security structures can be circumvented easily if security is breached in the lower-level area. It is like believing that your house is secure because you locked the front door, but if you did not lock the back door, the expensive and strong lock you installed and configured on the front door might thus have been wasted time and money.

The three lower-level models are:

- The state machine model
- The information flow model
- The noninterference model

The higher-level models of primary interest are:

- The Bell-LaPadula model
- The Biba model
- The Clark-Wilson model
- The Brewer-Nash model

State machine model

The state machine model recognizes that a computer system in operation exists in one of several states at any point in time. There are steady states and transition (also called transformation) states. The system might be powered down, or it might have just been powered up. It might be loading its bootstrap operating system, initializing its low-level drivers, loading the higher-level operating system and drivers, launching an application, waiting for user input, taking input, or closing an application. A device or process running on the system might have failed, it might be providing output, or it might be shutting down.

The concept of the state machine model is that no matter what the state of the system is throughout its lifetime, the system will remain secure. If this is true, then no matter what happens on or to the computer, the computer system's state at any point in time will not be the source of a breach of security of the valuable information assets the system is storing, processing, or providing access to.

If you could implement a computer system for which this is true, you could build higher-level security structures on this system, and those higher-level security structures could provide effective security.

Information flow model

An extension of the state machine model, and based on it, the information flow model recognizes that within information systems, information needs to flow. Information will flow from the keyboard, along a data bus, and into RAM. It will flow from RAM along the data bus to a database record written onto a hard disk drive, and so on. However, this model states that the information will only flow in ways that do not violate the security policy of the system.

If you could implement a computer system for which this is true, you could build higher-level security structures on this system, and those higher-level security structures could provide effective security.

Noninterference model

The noninterference model continues to build on the state machine and information flow models. It identifies a security domain for a subject that consists of the subject itself and the collection of all objects the subject is authorized to access. The model states that whatever a subject is doing within his security domain, those actions cannot alter (interfere with) the security of objects within the security domain of other subjects.

An example might be 10 records in a database that BoBo has access to but that LuLu is not authorized to access. The database and the 10 records exist within BoBo's security domain. They do not exist within LuLu's security domain. The noninterference model states that if BoBo accesses the 10 records, this action does not trigger some unauthorized change that suddenly allows LuLu to access the 10 records.

If you could implement a computer system for which these three lower-level models are true, you could build higher-level security structures on this system, and those higher-level security structures could provide effective security.

If any of these three lower-level models is proven false, you cannot rely on the security of the system, regardless of the implementation of any higher-level security models.

Bell-LaPadula model

The Bell-LaPadula (BL) model is one of the higher-level security models and is strictly concerned with confidentiality—keeping secrets secret. Published in 1973, BL strictly applies to the mandatory access control (MAC) model. Apply everything you know about MAC here, including the terms mentioned earlier: strong, slow, expensive, government, lattice, labels, clearance, classification, need-to-know, category, and so on. BL is based on the three lower-level security models: the state machine model, the noninterference model, and the information flow model. They must all be true for BL to be useful and effective.

BL has a collection of rules that have been mathematically proven to maintain or improve confidentiality in the MAC environment. These rules are largely intuitive, and several of them must be understood for the exam.

Here are the rules you should know for the exam:

- **The simple property: No read up** This says that to maintain or improve confidentiality of information in the MAC environment, you should not let subjects read from objects with a classification higher than the subject's clearance. For example, a subject with a Secret clearance is not allowed to read Top Secret classified objects.

- **The * property (the star property): No write down** This says that to maintain or improve confidentiality of information in the MAC environment, you should not let subjects write to objects with a classification lower than the subject's clearance. For example, a subject with a Secret clearance is not allowed to write to classified objects with a Classified label. This is because the Secret subject might inadvertently divulge details that the Classified subjects are not authorized to know.

- **The strong * property (the strong star property): No read up. No read down. No write up. No write down** The subject is constrained to accessing objects within her clearance layer only.

Try to avoid adding to the rules with assumptions. The simple property—No read up—does not address prohibiting reading down. Other factors of implementation might address reading down, but the simple property from the model does not address this. Associate "simple" with "reading," and "*" (star) with "writing."

EXAM TIP

Use word association lists to remember these models. For Bell-LaPadula, remember confidentiality, * = writing, simple = reading, no read up, no write down, strong * = limited to one layer, MAC, strong, slow, expensive, government, lattice, labels, and so on.

Biba model

The Biba model is one of the higher-level security models and is strictly concerned about integrity, which is keeping the information accurate, complete, and highly trustable. Biba, published in 1975, is not at all concerned with the confidentiality of information. Biba strictly applies to the MAC model. Apply everything you know about MAC here, including the terms strong, slow, expensive, government, lattice, labels, clearance, classification, need-to-know, category, and so on. Biba is based on the three lower-level security models: the state machine model, the noninterference model, and the information flow model. They must all be true for Biba to be useful and effective.

Before the rules of Biba make much sense, an analysis of the *aggregation and inference attack*, and the defense against this attack, is required. Subjects in a MAC environment are authorized to know a certain collection of sensitive information, based on their clearance. For example, a subject who works at a military naval base might be authorized to know that the military ship at the nearby (and in plain view) dock is making ready to set sail. It is obvious, with all the busy workers painting, grinding, loading, and hustling around. However, the subject might not be authorized to know where the ship is destined. Later, when the ship leaves and the subject notices the large, empty space at the dock and the absence of all the people and activity, curiosity sets in. Curiosity is a naturally occurring phenomenon in humans. With no malicious intent, and perhaps even subconsciously, this hole in the subject's knowledge triggers a mental effort to reach a conclusion and fill that hole in his knowledge. This is the aggregation of authorized information assembled to infer a conclusion that is perhaps correct and that the subject is not authorized to know. If the subject happens to guess (infer) the whereabouts of the missing ship correctly, a breach of security has occurred because the subject is not authorized to know the destination of the ship. Malicious or not, willful or not, a breach of security has occurred.

The security structure of an organization must be designed to prevent breaches of security, so a security control is required here, one that defends against an aggregation and inference attack, even the accidental one. The security control commonly introduced in this case is to tell the unauthorized subjects plausible lies, fill the hole in their knowledge, and avoid triggering curiosity, which leads to the attack. If the subject knows where the ship is going, curiosity does not occur and, therefore, does not trigger the aggregation and inference attack that leads to the breach in security. The information the subject has been told is not accurate, but the subject doesn't know that. When the authorized tell the unauthorized plausible lies to defeat the aggregation and inference attack, it is called *polyinstantiation*—multiple (poly) instances (instantiation) of the truth.

Now that you are armed with the awareness of polyinstantiation (and all those plausible lies commonly told to subjects at the the lower layers of the MAC model), the rules of Biba become more intuitive and make more sense. The collection of rules from the Biba model has been mathematically proven to maintain or improve integrity in the MAC environment. You must understand several of these rules for the exam.

- **The * integrity axiom (the star integrity axiom): No write up**   This says that to maintain or improve integrity of information in the MAC environment, you should not let subjects write to objects with a classification higher than the subject's clearance. Because the subject has been told more lies (polyinstantiation, inaccuracies) than those at higher levels of clearance, the subject might, unknowingly and with the most honorable intent, degrade the integrity of the information at higher layers by injecting the lies that she had been told (and believes).

- **The simple integrity axiom: No read down**   This says that to maintain or improve integrity of information in the MAC environment, you should not let subjects read from objects with a classification lower than the subject's clearance because the objects at the lower layers contain willfully injected lies (polyinstantiation) as a security control against the aggregation and inference attack. If subjects read from lower layers, they are degrading the integrity of their information by reading and believing the lies.

- **The invocation property: No requests up**   This property addresses controlling aggregation and inference attacks at higher layers that might lead to inaccurate conclusions.

  Suppose, in the earlier story of the ship with the unknown destination, the ship was really heading to an area with military activity and carrying military supplies. However, the subject was told, because of his unauthorized status and lower clearance, and by means of polyinstantiation, that the ship was heading to Antarctica with exploration supplies. Now suppose that the subject posts a question to a higher layer: "How long will the ship be unavailable on its mission to Antarctica?" Subjects at the higher layer have just been fed misinformation in the request, degrading the integrity of their information.

Clark-Wilson model

The Clark-Wilson (CW) model was published in 1987 and is an integrity model. In the frame of "subjects use computers and applications to access objects," Clark-Wilson focuses on the subject, the application, and the object pieces and calls these three the *access triple*. CW is not based on MAC, DAC, or other access control models but targets the control of fraud. In most cases, fraud involves violating the integrity of information (commonly called cooking the books) to cover up the theft of valuable assets. CW relies on well-formed transactions, the separation of duties, and auditing to help mitigate the threat of fraud.

To maintain or improve the integrity of information, the rules of CW state that the system should:

- Prevent unauthorized users from making modifications to the data.
- Prevent authorized users from making improper modifications of the data.
- Maintain internal and external consistency. Internal consistency says that the application should manipulate the data accurately—20 plus 20 equals 40. External consistency says that the data should match physical reality—when someone claims to deposit two $100 bills using an ATM, someone else needs to open the envelope and see the two $100 bills.

CW dissects the application to identify where greater risk exists and how you might reduce those risks, as follows:

- **Users (Subjects)** The active entity that desires information flow; also the least trusted entity on the system.
- **Transformation procedures (TPs)** Components of applications (processes) that access or manipulate information. Through testing and verification, these TPs become trusted.
- **Constrained data items (CDIs)** Data elements that are stored within the system and can only be accessed by TPs, not by users. These are more isolated from the users and are more likely to contain information of high integrity.
- **Unconstrained data items (UDIs)** Data elements that are directly accessible by users. These are like data input fields and are more likely to handle information of low integrity (unverified).
- **Integrity verification procedures (IVPs)** Verification of internal consistency—that the TPs manipulate the data correctly, such as balancing the books at the end of the day—and verification of external consistency—that the stored data matches physical reality, such as performing a physical inventory count to compare against what is recorded in the inventory database.

The Clark-Wilson model groups these five items into three primary components, often referred to as the Clark-Wilson triple. These three components are:

- The users
- The program (transformation procedures and integrity verification procedures)
- The data (constrained and unconstrained data items)

Brewer-Nash model

Published in 1989, the Brewer-Nash (BN) model is a commercial model designed to defend against conflicts of interest. BN is also called the Chinese wall model. The Chinese wall is constructed by dynamically implementing access controls when unwanted conditions exist. Before a subject accesses any objects, he can access any object. However, as soon as he accesses an object, a collection of access controls is dynamically assembled to prevent him from accessing any other objects that might introduce a conflict of interest. This makes BN context oriented rather than content oriented, as are most other types of controls.

An example of the Brewer-Nash model in practice is the following. When a lawyer is representing a plaintiff in an upcoming lawsuit against a large and wealthy corporation, she identifies the top lawyers that would typically represent the defendant company to be sued. She then reaches out to those defendant lawyers and the top handful of expert defense witnesses and offers them some unrelated legal work for good pay. Any defendant lawyers and expert witnesses who accept the work will now not be allowed to represent or testify for the defendant in the upcoming lawsuit because it is a conflict of interest for the lawyer(s) and expert defense witnesses to work for both sides of any legal activities. This legal trick takes away the defendant corporation's best legal support, weakening its ability to defend itself. This use of a well-intended protective measure has unfortunately become a common implementation of the Brewer-Nash model.

Two other models to be aware of are:

- **Graham-Denning**   Focuses on securely creating and deleting user accounts and how to provision those accounts securely with permissions.
- **Take-Grant**   A testing model to validate the security of access control systems by taking, granting, and removing permissions on objects and creating new objects.

 Quick check

1. How long does it typically take an organization to complete the development of its security program?
2. Which model addresses the integrity of programs?

Quick check answers

1. Three years
2. The Clark-Wilson model

Certification and accreditation (C&A)

After frameworks that might support some level of trust in the security of computer systems have been created and identified, how would a buyer verify that a specific product actually meets the standards and specifications so that he could actually trust the system to some extent? *Certification and accreditation (C&A)* is the solution. C&A is nicely defined by NIST in its Special Publication (SP) 800-37 entitled, "Guide for Applying the Risk Management Framework to Federal Information Systems," as follows.

- Security certification is performed "to determine the extent to which the security controls in the information system are implemented correctly, operating as intended, and producing the desired outcome with respect to meeting the security requirements for the system."

- "Security accreditation is the official management decision given by a senior agency official to authorize operation of an information system and to explicitly accept the risk to agency operations, agency assets, or individuals based on the implementation of an agreed-upon set of security controls."

Computer systems are tested and evaluated for the functionality and assurance of the declared collection of security features. If the testing and evaluation meet a specified standard, the system is certified as meeting that standard.

Functionality is verification that the security control exists and that it works correctly at least once. *Assurance* is the verification that the security control operates correctly every time under a potentially wide range of specified conditions. A higher level of trust required in a system warrants more thorough testing and evaluation.

As the buyer purchases a collection of certified computer systems, and those systems are assembled into complete information systems, including infrastructure devices and applications, the buyer authorizes specialists to accredit the information system for the trusted and secure handling of valuable (perhaps classified) information assets.

All this testing and evaluation of security controls costs money. This means that the certified computers will be more expensive. Typically, only governments are willing to pay the higher prices for these systems and can justify the cost to acquire the (believed) higher level of trust security. For governments, the cost of a breach of security could include people's lives or a disruption of the economic balance of their own or foreign countries, so a higher price for stronger security is more often warranted.

To manage the C&A processes, governments have developed standards, defined criteria that map out how computer systems must be designed, manufactured, delivered, installed, maintained, and decommissioned in a manner that supports specified levels of trust that the computer system will not be the source of a breach of the security of the valuable information it stores, manipulates (processes), and provides access to. The three sets of criteria are:

- The Trusted Computing System Evaluation Criteria (TCSEC)
- The Information Technology Security Evaluation Criteria (ITSEC)
- The Common Criteria

Trusted Computing System Evaluation Criteria (TCSEC)

The TCSEC was defined in the Orange Book by the United States in August 1983 and describes security standards for a computer system that will store, process, and provide access to sensitive and classified information. The Orange Book was based on the proofs and rules introduced in the Bell-LaPadula security model that addresses only confidentiality. The Orange Book was the first of the now 30-plus books in the Rainbow series, a collection of IT security standards and guidelines published by the US Department of Defense Computer Security Center and the US National Computer Security Center, a branch of the National Security Agency. The Orange Book was retired in 2005 when it was replaced by the Common Criteria.

The TCSEC defines a concept called the *Trusted Computing Base* (*TCB*) that includes the computer hardware, firmware, and software components that collectively establish the security of the computer system. The TCB requires these security mechanisms to protect themselves automatically from tampering to maintain correct and trustworthy operation. The TCB establishes a conceptual perimeter around these components that identifies the trusted components and software, and those outside the perimeter are identified as untrusted. If any untrusted element can affect a trusted element, the TCB perimeter is probably destroyed, eliminating any ensured level of trust for the system.

Another concept included in the TCSEC is the *Security Reference Monitor* (*SRM*) (also called the Reference Monitor). This concept identifies the requirement for a security boundary between subject and object, isolating the two. For every request from a subject for access to an object, the SRM must qualify the level of privilege on the object that has been granted to the subject and reports that level of access to the security kernel. The system (security kernel) then allows access at that level or denies access altogether if no access privilege has been granted.

The SRM must satisfy these three rules:

- The SRM must be invoked for every access and cannot be circumvented.
- The SRM must be tamperproof.
- The SRM must be small enough to be verifiable in a comprehensive manner.

The Security Reference Monitor is depicted in Figure 5-13.

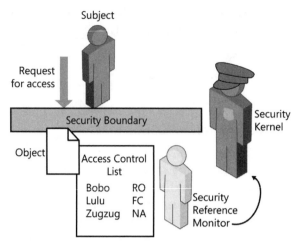

FIGURE 5-13 The Security Reference Monitor

 The TCSEC also identifies the need for a system to perform a *trusted recovery* attempt if some form of system crash or failure occurs such as a misbehaving process in kernel mode. An example of trusted recovery, in implementation, is the stop error that displays a blue screen. This is actually a security feature designed to satisfy the need for attempted trusted recovery. Upon a breach or failure, the system immediately stops processing to defeat any attempt to access content inappropriately. The system then copies the contents of RAM, where the offending process currently resides, to the page file on the hard disk drive to provide a record of the event for an investigation. (Remember that RAM is volatile, and its contents will be lost with a restart.) Finally, the system restarts in an attempt to clear the failed state from the system and, hopefully, resume to a secure state. The stop error that performs an automatic restart is an example of an *emergency system restart.* When the user restarts the system after detecting or suspecting some sort of instability, this manually initiated restart is called a *system cold start.*

 After one of these restarts, the system might default to *safe mode.* The operating system starts and loads only the minimum number of device drivers. Many times when a system stops, it is due to a violation or breach in kernel mode. Because the operating system itself is largely single source and trusted, commonly the third-party device drivers that load into kernel mode would misbehave and trigger the stop error event. You cannot replace the driver if the operating system has mounted the driver, so safe mode loads and mounts only a minimum of these drivers to enable the administrator to replace the offending device driver software.

EXAM TIP

Be aware of the Trusted Computing Base, the Security Reference Monitor, and the details of trusted recovery.

The TCSEC identifies seven levels of security, each building on many of the elements of the lower level, providing stronger security as you move up the scale, as shown in Table 5-2. Notice that the C class uses the DAC model, and the B class uses the MAC model. Verified protection includes a formal secure code review and verification methods (often mathematical proofs) when possible.

TABLE 5-2 Levels of the Orange Book/TCSEC

TCSEC rating	Access control model	Description
A1		Verified protection
B3	MAC	Security domains
B2	MAC	Structured protection
B1	MAC	Labeled security protection
C2	DAC	Controlled access protection
C1	DAC	Discretionary security protection
D		Minimal protection

If you want to connect an Orange Book–certified computer system to a network and keep it Orange Book certified, you can only connect to a Red Book network. The *Red Book* is called the *Trusted Network Interpretation* (*TNI*) of the TCSEC; it describes the security requirements of a trusted network to support Orange Book computer systems.

Although the Orange Book has largely been retired, older systems remain that were purchased and implemented through the Orange Book specifications. The Orange Book still gets some business because of the ongoing support for these older systems.

Information Technology Security Evaluation Criteria (ITSEC)

In 1991, a collection of European countries (the United Kingdom, the Netherlands, France, and Germany) published their version of the TCSEC called the ITSEC. The ITSEC broke the testing and evaluation of security controls into two sets: Functionality (the F rating) and Assurance (the E rating). The ITSEC was still based on Bell-LaPadula, which addresses only confidentiality, but it extended the rating scale to include integrity and availability to complete the AIC triad (availability, integrity, and confidentiality). The ITSEC rating scale is shown in Table 5-3.

TABLE 5-3 Levels of the ITSEC

ITSEC E rating	ITSEC F rating	TCSEC rating	Access control model	Description
	F10			High integrity and confidentiality requirements for data transmission
	F9			High confidentiality requirements for data transmission
	F8			High integrity requirements for data transmission
	F7			High availability functions
	F6			High integrity requirements for data and programs
E6	F5	A1		Verified protection
E5	F5	B3	MAC	Security domains
E4	F4	B2	MAC	Structured protection
E3	F3	B1	MAC	Labeled security protection
E2	F2	C2	DAC	Controlled access protection
E1	F1	C1	DAC	Discretionary security protection
E0		D		Minimal protection

Although largely replaced by the Common Criteria, the ITSEC is still used today.

Common Criteria

Introduced in 2005, the Common Criteria for Information Technology Security Evaluation (CC) was designed by a team from several countries to replace the TCSEC and ITSEC with standards based on real-world security needs rather than on what could be proven mathematically. It is currently in version 3.1 and has been adopted as the *ISO 15408* series.

The CC defines the following components in the evaluation and certification process:

- **Protection Profile**   This is the prospective buyer's statement of need for security in a computer system—a description of the required real-world security objectives.

- **Target of Evaluation (ToE)**   This is the vendor's product that potentially satisfies the buyer's Protection Profile requirements.

- **Security Target**   This is a report prepared by the vendor, describing how its product, the ToE, satisfies the security requirements described in the Protection Profile.

- **Testing and Evaluation**   If all looks good and the buyer and vendor want to move forward, the vendor submits the Protection Profile, the ToE, the Security Target, and a check to an accredited testing center to have the ToE evaluated and, hopefully, certified at the targeted Evaluation Assurance Level (EAL). The testing validates that the claimed security mechanisms exist and work correctly as required by the Protection Profile. Systems are tested for functionality and assurance of the security mechanisms.

- **Evaluation Assurance Level (EAL)/Evaluated Products List (EPL)** The EAL identifies the increasing levels of testing and evaluation of the ToE. It scales from EAL 1 to EAL 7. A higher EAL means that the security elements in the system have been more thoroughly tested and therefore can be trusted to a higher level. If the system passes the required testing and becomes EAL-certified, it is added to the EPL. When a product is listed on the EPL, buyers can simply order it from the list.

  - **EAL 7** Formally verified, designed, and tested
  - **EAL 6** Semi-formally verified, designed, and tested
  - **EAL 5** Semi-formally designed and tested
  - **EAL 4** Methodically designed, tested, and reviewed
  - **EAL 3** Methodically tested and checked
  - **EAL 2** Structurally tested
  - **EAL 1** Functionally tested

The International Organization for Standardization (ISO) adopted the CC as its standard ISO/IEC 15408. It broke the CC into three parts:

- **ISO/IEC 15408-1** Introduction and general model
- **ISO/IEC 15408-2** Security functional components
- **ISO/IEC 15408-3** Security assurance components

Legal and regulatory compliance

Aside from the government's needs for security in its information systems, legal and regulatory compliance requirements are standards placed on the commercial world by the government or by marketplace and industry leaders who dominate and therefore can regulate a vertical industry such as the payment card industry (PCI). These laws and regulations are imposed on businesses because the businesses are believed to be unwilling to manage their information systems securely and prudently. The government and regulating bodies are protecting the public from unscrupulous businesses by mandating appropriate security frameworks for IT systems and imposing financial penalties for violation of these compliance standards.

These laws and regulations can be considered frameworks for the security of information systems in businesses' specialized areas of business and should be incorporated in the policies of the businesses they target, combined with the unique security concerns that management recognizes and needs to address for its organization.

Examples include the standards described in the following sections.

Payment Card Industry-Data Security Standard (PCI-DSS)

Originally released in 2004, the PCI-DSS was imposed by the payment card industry to protect credit card, debit card, ATM card, and POS card numbers and the personally identifiable information (PII) associated with the cardholder of the account. It includes 12 areas of security for computers and networks that store, process, and provide access to this type of data. This is the only industry-imposed regulation. Participating brands include Visa, MasterCard, American Express, Discover, and JCB (Japan Credit Bureau).

The 12 major requirements defined by PCI-DSS are:

Build and maintain a secure network

1. Install and maintain a firewall configuration to protect cardholder data.

2. Do not use vendor-supplied defaults for system passwords and other security parameters.

Protect cardholder data

3. Protect stored cardholder data.

4. Encrypt transmission of cardholder data across open, public networks.

Maintain a vulnerability management program

5. Use and regularly update antivirus software or programs.

6. Develop and maintain secure systems and applications.

Implement strong access control measures

7. Restrict access to cardholder data by business need to know.

8. Assign a unique ID to each person with computer access.

9. Restrict physical access to cardholder data.

Regularly monitor and test networks

10. Track and monitor all access to network resources and cardholder data.

11. Regularly test security systems and processes.

Maintain an information security policy

12. Maintain a policy that addresses information security for employees and contractors.

Sarbanes-Oxley Act of 2002 (SOX)

This act imposes security controls on information systems of publicly held companies to ensure truthful and accurate reporting of their financial activities and standing. The law was enacted because of massive financial losses shareholders experienced of several publicly held companies due to the companies' fraudulent financial reporting to the Securities and Exchange Commission (SEC).

Gramm Leach Bliley Act of 1999 (GLBA)

This act imposes security controls on information systems of companies that provide financial services to protect the PII of their customers and the integrity of their information assets.

Healthcare Insurance Portability and Accountability Act of 1996 (HIPAA)

In an attempt to encourage the use of electronic data exchange (EDI) in the medical industry, which would improve health care, HIPAA imposes security and privacy controls on the information systems of medical institutions and businesses.

Exercises

In the following exercises, you apply what you've learned in this chapter. The answers for these exercises are located in the "Answers" section at the end of this chapter.

Exercise 5-1

Download and review several of the frameworks described in this chapter. These might include the GAISP, several of the SP 800 series documents, and the Common Criteria. Identify five NIST SP 800 documents that relate to your specific responsibilities.

Exercise 5-2

Download and install a virtualization hypervisor such as VirtualBox or VMware Workstation. Within the hypervisor, install one or more virtual machines and configure networking sufficient to browse the Internet.

Although the use of virtual machines (VM) can provide additional security because of the boundary between the VM and the host operating system, identify several of the remaining vulnerabilities that exist with the VM.

Chapter summary

- Management must develop some level of trust that the organization's computer system will not allow a breach of security of the information assets it stores, processes, or provides access to. Laws and regulations require commercial organizations to ensure the security of the sensitive information their information systems store, process, and provide access to.

- The computer system includes the bare metal hardware, the firmware, and the operating system. The computer architecture provides natural opportunities to implement security controls. The application architecture provides natural opportunities to implement security controls. Application architectures include:

  - The client layer
  - The presentation layer
  - The application layer
  - The middleware layer
  - The data layer

- Distributed systems architectures include:

  - Peer-to-peer networks
  - Virtualization
  - Cloud computing
  - Grid computing

- The policy documents of an organization establish its framework for implementing security, should include its unique security concerns, and must include all laws and regulations that apply to it.

- General frameworks developed as an aid to organizations include:

  - ISO 27000 series
  - Zachman Framework and Sherwood Applied Business Security Architecture (SABSA)
  - Committee of Sponsoring Organizations of the Treadway Commission (COSO) and Control Objectives for Information and Related Technology (COBIT)
  - Information Technology Infrastructure Library
  - Generally Accepted Information Security Principles (GAISP)
  - NIST Special Publication 800 series
  - The state machine model
  - The information flow model
  - The noninterference model

- The Bell-LaPadula model
- The Biba model
- The Clark-Wilson model
- The Brewer-Nash model
- Frameworks for the certification and accreditation of systems include:
  - Trusted Computing System Evaluation Criteria (TCSEC)
  - Information Technology Security Evaluation Criteria (ITSEC)
  - Common Criteria
- The validation of the security mechanisms in computer systems evaluate the functionality and assurance of the security mechanisms.

Chapter review

Test your knowledge of the information in this chapter by answering these questions. The answers to these questions, and the explanations of why each answer choice is correct or incorrect, are located in the "Answers" section at the end of this chapter.

1. Which security model is specifically designed to protect the integrity of information in a government computing environment?

   A. The Sherwood Applied Business Security Architecture (SABSA)

   B. The Bell-LaPadula model

   C. The Biba model

   D. The Zachman Framework

2. Which of the following would eliminate the vulnerability that allows the buffer overflow attack?

   A. Monitoring the process state table

   B. Preemptive multitasking

   C. Compiling code instead of interpreting code into machine language

   D. Qualifying the data required by processes

3. The ODBC driver resides at which layer in the application architecture?

   A. The client layer

   B. The presentation layer

   C. The middleware layer

   D. The application layer

4. Which of the following types of memory is not volatile?

   A. EPROM

   B. Level 1 cache memory

   C. RAM

   D. Level 2 cache memory

5. Which system evaluation process can provide an Evaluation Assurance Level (EAL)?

   A. Capability Maturity Model Integration (CMMI)

   B. Trusted Computing System Evaluation Criteria (TCSEC)

   C. Information Technology Security Evaluation Criteria (ITSEC)

   D. Common Criteria

6. Which system evaluation process offers seven granular levels of certification and ranges from A1 through D?

   A. Capability Maturity Model Integration (CMMI)

   B. Trusted Computing System Evaluation Criteria (TCSEC)

   C. Information Technology Security Evaluation Criteria (ITSEC)

   D. Common Criteria

7. Which of the following best describes the difference between certification and accreditation?

   A. Certification shows that the system(s) can perform the function, and accreditation shows that the system(s) can perform the function every time under the specified conditions.

   B. Certification shows that the system(s) meets a specified standard, and accreditation shows that the system(s) can perform the function every time under the specified conditions.

   C. Certification shows that the system(s) meets a specified standard, and accreditation is management's acceptance of the risks of operating the system(s).

   D. Certification shows that the system(s) can perform the function, and accreditation is management's acceptance of the risks of operating the system(s).

8. Which of the following best describes a large array of computing systems and resources to provide exceptional accessibility, availability, performance, and scalability?

   A. Infrastructure as a service (IaaS)

   B. Service-oriented architecture

   C. Cloud computing

   D. Platform as a service (PaaS)

Answers

This section contains the answers to the exercises and the "Chapter review" section in this chapter.

Exercise 5-1

Following is the list of current NIST SP 800 series documents. Topics include the management of IT systems, risk assessment, cryptography, networking architectures, password management, portable device management, and technical implementation recommendations, to name a few. The current list can be downloaded from the NIST SP 800 series website and is subject to change.

800-12	An Introduction to Computer Security: the NIST Handbook
800-13	Telecommunications Security Guidelines for Telecommunications Management Network
800-14	Generally Accepted Principles and Practices for Securing Information Technology Systems
800-15	MISPC Minimum Interoperability Specification for PKI Components
800-16	Information Security Training Requirements: a Role- and Performance-Based Model
800-16	Information Technology Security Training Requirements: a Role- and Performance-Based Model
800-17	Modes of Operation Validation System (MOVS): Requirements and Procedures
800-18	Guide for Developing Security Plans for Federal Information Systems
800-19	Mobile Agent Security
800-20	Modes of Operation Validation System for the Triple Data Encryption Algorithm (TMOVS): Requirements and Procedures
800-21	Guideline for Implementing Cryptography in the Federal Government
800-22	A Statistical Test Suite for Random and Pseudorandom Number Generators for Cryptographic Applications
800-23	Guidelines to Federal Organizations on Security Assurance and Acquisition/Use of Tested/Evaluated Products
800-24	PBX Vulnerability Analysis: Finding Holes in Your PBX Before Someone Else Does
800-25	Federal Agency Use of Public Key Technology for Digital Signatures and Authentication
800-27	Engineering Principles for Information Technology Security (A Baseline for Achieving Security), Revision A

800-90A	Recommendation for Random Number Generation Using Deterministic Random Bit Generators
800-90A	Recommendation for Random Number Generation Using Deterministic Random Bit Generators
800-90B	Recommendation for the Entropy Sources Used for Random Bit Generation
800-90C	Recommendation for Random Bit Generator (RBG) Constructions
800-92	Guide to Computer Security Log Management
800-94	Guide to Intrusion Detection and Prevention Systems (IDPS)
800-94	Guide to Intrusion Detection and Prevention Systems (IDPS)
800-95	Guide to Secure Web Services
800-96	PIV Card to Reader Interoperability Guidelines
800-97	Establishing Wireless Robust Security Networks: A Guide to IEEE 802.11i
800-98	Guidelines for Securing Radio Frequency Identification (RFID) Systems
800-100	Information Security Handbook: A Guide for Managers
800-101	Guidelines on Mobile Device Forensics
800-101	Guidelines on Cell Phone Forensics
800-102	Recommendation for Digital Signature Timeliness
800-103	An Ontology of Identity Credentials - Part 1: Background and Formulation
800-104	A Scheme for PIV Visual Card Topography
800-106	Randomized Hashing for Digital Signatures
800-107	Recommendation for Applications Using Approved Hash Algorithms
800-108	Recommendation for Key Derivation Using Pseudorandom Functions
800-111	Guide to Storage Encryption Technologies for End User Devices
800-113	Guide to SSL VPNs
800-114	User's Guide to Securing External Devices for Telework and Remote Access
800-115	Technical Guide to Information Security Testing and Assessment
800-116	A Recommendation for the Use of PIV Credentials in Physical Access Control Systems (PACS)
800-117	Guide to Adopting and Using the Security Content Automation Protocol (SCAP) Version 1.2
800-117	Guide to Adopting and Using the Security Content Automation Protocol (SCAP) Version 1.0
800-118	Guide to Enterprise Password Management
800-119	Guidelines for the Secure Deployment of IPv6
800-120	Recommendation for EAP Methods Used in Wireless Network Access Authentication

Exercise 5-2

The use of the VM for additional isolation from the host operating system increases the number of computer nodes in the IT system. This increases the potential attack targets and the number of systems to maintain and protect.

The hypervisor is additional software that runs on the host operating system, with some of it running with a high level of privilege. This increases the attack surface (exposure) of the host. This hypervisor software must be updated on the host system regularly to mitigate vulnerabilities and risk.

The operating system and applications running within the VM will contain vulnerabilities and must be maintained (updated, configuration management, change management, hardened, monitored, audited, and so on) regularly, just as with every other system in the IT environment.

The VM is often configured to allow network access to the host system. This could become an attack vector.

Chapter review

1. **Correct answer: C**

   A. **Incorrect:** SABSA addresses security within the Zachman Framework.

   B. **Incorrect:** The Bell-LaPadula model addresses confidentiality in a government computer environment (MAC).

   C. **Correct:** The Biba model addresses integrity in a government computer environment (MAC).

   D. **Incorrect:** The Zachman Framework is an enterprise-level model for information systems.

2. **Correct answer: D**

   A. **Incorrect:** The process state table is monitored by the control unit in a CPU, watching for processes in the ready state.

   B. **Incorrect:** Preemptive multitasking gives the kernel of the operating system control of the time slices a process is granted in the CPU.

   C. **Incorrect:** Both compiling and interpreting code produces machine language code. Compiling produces an executable file; interpreting is performed at run time and is used during development.

   D. **Correct:** The buffer overflow attack is possible because developers allow users (attackers) to input more data than the buffer has space for. This overflows the data buffer and overwrites the pointer and possibly instructions with whatever the attacker wants to inject. Developers should control the quantity and type of data being sent to the buffer.

3. **Correct answer: C**

   A. **Incorrect:** The client layer is the client computer and front-end application that users use to connect to presentation servers.

   B. **Incorrect:** The presentation layer is often a web server that receives inbound client connections. It does not process or hold any data.

   C. **Correct:** The ODBC driver normalizes and converts data into a standard format as required by the application. It resides in the middleware layer.

   D. **Incorrect:** The application layer is where the application servers reside. This is where data is processed and fed to the presentation layer, giving clients access to the results.

4. **Correct answer: A**

   A. **Correct:** The erasable/programmable read-only memory (EPROM) is an example of nonvolatile memory. It retains its data even when the power to the system is removed.

   B. **Incorrect:** Level 1 cache memory is volatile. It loses its data if the power to the system is removed.

   C. **Incorrect:** Random access memory (RAM) is volatile. It loses its data if the power to the system is removed.

   D. **Incorrect:** Level 2 cache memory is volatile. It loses its data if the power to the system is removed.

5. **Correct answer: D**

   A. **Incorrect:** CMMI provides a process improvement map to help enterprises grow and improve. Software development companies commonly use it.

   B. **Incorrect:** The TCSEC was based on the Bell-LaPadula confidentiality model and identifies four primary levels of protection, ranging from A to D; (A) formally verified protection, (B) mandatory access control protection, (C) discretionary access control protection, and (D) minimal protection.

   C. **Incorrect:** The ITSEC was an extension of the TCSEC and includes 10 levels of protection, with different designations for functionality (F rating) and assurance (E rating).

   D. **Correct:** The Common Criteria provide seven evaluated assurance levels, EAL 1 through EAL 7.

6. **Correct answer: B**

   A. **Incorrect:** CMMI provides a process improvement map to help enterprises grow and improve. Software development companies commonly use it.

   B. **Correct:** The TCSEC was based on the Bell-LaPadula confidentiality model and identifies four primary levels of protection, ranging from A to D; (A) formally verified protection, (B) mandatory access control protection, (C) discretionary access control protection, and (D) minimal protection. The granular designations are, from weakest to strongest protection, D, C1, C2, B1, B2, B3, A1.

   C. **Incorrect:** The ITSEC is an extension of the TCSEC and includes 10 levels of protection, with different designations for functionality (F rating) and assurance (E rating).

   D. **Incorrect:** The Common Criteria provide seven evaluated assurance levels, EAL 1 through EAL 7.

7. **Correct answer: C**

   A. **Incorrect:** Functionality shows that the system(s) can perform the function, and assurance shows that the system(s) can perform the function every time under the specified conditions.

   B. **Incorrect:** Certification shows that the system(s) meets a specified standard, and assurance shows that the system(s) can perform the function every time under the specified conditions.

   C. **Correct:** Certification shows that the system(s) meets a specified standard, and accreditation is management's acceptance of the risks of operating the system(s).

   D. **Incorrect:** Functionality shows that the system can perform the function, and accreditation is management's acceptance of the risks of operating the system(s).

8. **Correct answer: C**

   A. **Incorrect:** Infrastructure as a service (IaaS) is a subset of cloud computing that provides network and IT infrastructure services.

   B. **Incorrect:** Cloud computing services are commonly based on a service-oriented architecture (SOA), so SOA is a subset of cloud computing.

   C. **Correct:** Cloud computing is a large array of computing systems and resources that provides exceptional accessibility, availability, performance, and scalability.

   D. **Incorrect:** Platform as a service (PaaS) is a subset of cloud computing that provides specialized computing services and server-level application services.

CHAPTER 6

Legal, regulations, investigations, and compliance

Cybercrime is more rampant, complex, and aggressive than ever. Prosecutors have a difficult time of successfully convicting cyber criminals due to many factors, even when well-founded proof exists. This domain presents a global overview of the laws and regulations designed to protect information assets, intellectual property, and personally identifiable information and identifies the governing bodies that define those laws and regulations. Not all regulations are government borne; some are developed and imposed by coalitions of leaders in an industry. Collectively, the laws and regulations that apply to the enterprise must be included within its frameworks of governance (its policy documents), and the enterprise must achieve compliance with these mandates. Further, this domain describes incident response and investigations related to computer crime, including evidence handling and forensic analysis of digital data.

Exam objectives in this chapter:

Computer crimes

They do it for many reasons. In the early days, they did it for fun, for the challenge of it all, and for the bragging rights that came with a successful exploit. Later on, it began to evolve toward doing it to get even on a grudge of some kind or to make a political statement, referred to as *hacktivism*. Today, the stakes have risen substantially. Most computer crimes are professionals, well sponsored and supported by organized crime, corporations, or even governments. A recent survey estimated more than $400 billion USD in losses in 2012 due to global cybercrime (see *http://securityaffairs.co/wordpress/9319/cyber-crime/ponemon-statistics-2012-on-cost-of-cybercrime.html*).

Historically, attackers would distribute their malware to as many potential targets as possible and reap the benefits of those targets who had not yet properly addressed the vulnerabilities in their systems and software. These are called shotgun attacks, also known as spray and pray, grazing, browsing, or drive-by attacks, in which no specific target was identified, and no specific bounty was desired but, rather, were opportunistic. The attackers simply compromised as many targets as possible and took whatever low-hanging fruit was accessible.

These shotgun attacks are still quite common, but more often today, attacks are carefully planned and strategized by skilled, determined, and sponsored hacking professionals. Specific victims and specific targets are carefully chosen and then studied. Highly specialized penetration methods are developed, and highly specialized payloads are crafted to compromise the very specific vulnerabilities already known about the target. These are elements of the relatively new breed of attacks called the *advanced persistent threat* (*APT*). Although relatively few targets will be compromised by the costly process of this attack, the payoffs of the successful APT attack are quite often spectacular.

Is it a crime?

As described in Chapter 1, "Information security governance and risk management," the corporate policy framework of governance describes the prudent management of the enterprise and embodies required protections from breaches of security. This framework is largely driven by four primary components:

- Vulnerabilities inherent in the business and the industry
- Specific threats to the enterprise
- Laws and regulations applicable to the enterprise
- Senior management's vision, ethical posture, and chosen style of management

A breach of security will always be a breach of policy and will always warrant an investigation. However, a breach of security and policy might not always be a criminal act. There is a huge difference between the incident response and investigation for a breach of policy and the incident response and investigation for a criminal act against the enterprise. Early on in an investigation, a conclusion must be made about whether this incident could be a criminal act and warrant the notably higher standard of reporting and investigative methodology that will come with a notably higher price tag.

There are several forms of computer crimes, and the specific definition of a crime varies greatly from country to country, state to state, and, sometimes, even county to county. (Check with your local legal department for the definitive conclusions of whether an incident is an actual crime.) Types of cybercrime include:

- **Data theft**   Might be taken for its direct value or used for extortion
    - Financial account information.
    - *Personally identifiable information* (*PII*), used for *identity theft*. PII generally includes a name and a related Social Security number, financial account number, driver's license number, or passport number. Additional supporting information, such as address, phone number, birthdate, gender, age, height, color of hair, color of eyes, spouse, and so on, strengthens the value of the PII.
    - Intellectual property, trade secrets.
    - Government or military secrets.
- **Denial of service (DoS)**   Ping of death, smurf, fraggle, christmas tree, syn flood, and many other types of attacks. The DoS attack temporarily shuts down a website or other network service.
- **Data alteration**
    - Fraud, cooking the books to steal money or other valuable property.
    - Salami attack, a little, unnoticeable slice of data taken from many places that nobody notices, so it remains undetected and financially productive.

- **System takeover**
  - Command and control.
  - Botnet, army of zombies.
- **Child pornography** As of a 2012 study (7th edition) by the International Centre for Missing & Exploited Children, laws against child pornography exist in 143 of the 196 countries that were reviewed.
- **Social engineering** Phishing, scams, stalking.
- **Dumpster diving** Not exactly a crime, but losses are still incurred due to exposure of sensitive information, intellectual property.

The first quarter of 2012 showed a 300 percent increase in the number of attacks against financial institutions over the preceding quarter in 2011. Although the trend sharply points toward financial gain as the primary reason, the motivations for cybercrime historically include:

- Fun; the technical challenges
- Grudge
- Financial gain
  - Intellectual property, trade secret theft
  - Account information theft
  - Corporate espionage
  - Sale of a botnet
  - Sale of PII, account information
  - Sale of illegal information and images
- Political
  - Hacktivism, often DoS attacks or exposure of sensitive data targeting governmental operations as a protest of some political action or event
  - Terrorism
  - Defense, such as the Israel Defense Force (IDF) allegedly launching Stuxnet in June 2010 to sabotage the efforts of the Iranian government to develop weapons-grade uranium; in January 2013, the Chinese government allegedly hacking into the network at the *Wall Street Journal* to monitor its coverage of China

A computer becomes involved in a cybercrime primarily in three ways. They are when the computer is:

- **The *target* system** The system being breached
- **The attacker system** The system the attacker uses
- **A support system** A system used during the act to support the act; used to develop exploitation code, store stolen intellectual property (IP), and so on

The *victim* of a computer crime is the owner of the breached system.

The types of people committing these crimes has evolved over time toward the more skilled, focused, and professional attacker, but they include:

- Script kiddies (little or no skill; attacker downloads an application or script and points it at one or more [typically] random targets to see what he can get away with)
- Insiders and coworkers
- Business partners
- Corporations
- Governments
- Organized crime
- Hackers
- Terrorists
- Hacktivists
- Skilled professionals committing APT attacks
- Proof-of-concept trials by (irresponsible?) researchers (such as the Morris worm)

A recent study reports the sources of cybercrime attacks as a percentage of reported computer-related crimes, shown in Table 6-1. (See *http://securityaffairs.co/wordpress/4468 /cyber-crime/ddos-detailed-analysis-of-the-phenomenon.html*.)

TABLE 6-1 Sources of cybercrime attacks by country: 2012

Source of the attacks	%
China	31
United States	19
Russia	13
India	10
Germany	7
France	5
Korea	5
Ukraine	4
United Kingdom	3
Brazil	3

Prosecutors are having a rough go of it in their attempts to prosecute computer crimes, for many reasons:

- Many computer crimes are not reported. Reporting the crime will likely formalize losses due to legal actions from damages. Businesses do not want their reputation damaged nor law enforcement to confiscate their assets as evidence. Most states in the United States have enacted laws requiring computer crimes to be reported.

- Laws might not yet exist or do not accurately describe the new nature of the evolving computer crimes.

- Countries around the world view computer crimes differently and, therefore, enact their laws to protect information assets differently. The laws that do exist vary greatly from country to country and even from state to state within the United States.

- Evidence is intangible and difficult to collect and analyze and then difficult to present in an understandable manner to judges and juries.

- Jurisdictional issues, extradition issues, and a lack of cooperation complicate apprehending the attacker, who can be thousands of miles away and in a different country, with different laws and legal interpretation, from the location of the target and victim of the attack. Everything is very close together on the Internet, and there are no international borders on the Internet.

- Lack of enough skilled investigative, forensic, and legal professionals to address the mountainous number of computer crime cases.

Another factor is affecting the ability of law enforcement to prosecute cybercriminals successfully. In the countries that use the common law system, such as in the United States and the United Kingdom, verdicts are based on *precedents*. If the case being tried before the court is similar (enough) to a case tried previously, the verdict in the current case must be the same as the verdict in the case that set the precedent. Because many of the computer crime laws are new and being tried for the first time, prosecutors are very hesitant to take the cases to court unless they are virtually certain of a conviction for fear of establishing the wrong precedent. Specifics of different legal systems are described in the following section.

EXAM TIP

An understanding of the reasons computer crime is difficult to prosecute successfully will likely be a target on the exam.

A global perspective of laws regarding computer crime

Legal systems around the world have evolved over the millennia and vary greatly. Following is a brief overview of the major types of legal systems and where they are currently in use.

The codified law system

The codified law system, also called the civil law system, is based on rules defined in a written codex, a book of law. This form of legal system was first identified in approximately 2100 BC in Mesopotamia (modern Iraq) and continues in use today. Political leaders collect and document rules or statutes for society to abide by. The Byzantine emperor Justinian of the 6th century AD receives historical credit for aggregating the collection of imperial enactments, rules, and codes to date in three books (codices), and they were given the force of law. Justinian's rulings were assembled into a fourth codex, and the four books form the basis of the contemporary codified law system. France, Spain, China, and most of South American countries use the codified law system.

 EXAM TIP

Don't confuse the civil law system with civil law, one of three subsets within the common law system described next.

The common law system

The United Kingdom and the United States use the common law system. It is based on rulings by judges that establish a precedent for a particular dispute rather than on written statutes. This legal system is divided into three areas of law:

- Criminal law
- Administrative law or regulatory law
- Civil law

Criminal law

This system of law is designed to protect the public from people who might threaten, harm, or endanger their safety or welfare. The victim of a criminal act is society. These laws address crime, such as burglary, robbery, and murder, and require a more stringent burden of proof *beyond a reasonable doubt*. This equates to a greater than 99 percent certainty that the accused is guilty. The government is responsible for the enforcement of criminal law. The penalties for criminal acts include financial payment, imprisonment, and even the death penalty in extreme cases. The more-serious crimes are called *felonies* and often carry prison sentences of greater than 1 year. The less-serious crimes are called *misdemeanors* and typically carry prison sentences of less than 1 year.

Administrative law or regulatory law

This kind of law manages administrative agencies of the government such as the Federal Communications Commission (FCC), the Federal Trade Commission (FTC), the Food and Drug Administration (FDA), and the Occupational Safety and Health Administration (OSHA). Laws such as the Healthcare Insurance Portability and Accountability Act (HIPAA), Sarbanes-Oxley (SOX), and the Gramm-Leach-Bliley Act (GLBA) are examples of administrative laws. Penalties are usually financial but can include imprisonment in extreme cases.

Civil law

Civil law, also known as *tort law*, addresses disputes between individuals or organizations such as contract disputes, damages to the property of another, and personal injury. The intent of civil law is more to reimburse the injured party than to punish the guilty. Civil law requires less of a burden of proof, referred to as a balance of the probability or a *preponderance of the evidence*. This equates to a greater than 50 percent certainty that the accused is guilty. The penalties are almost always only financial reimbursement. The level of liability (the amount of the reimbursement) in these cases is often tied to the losses incurred and demonstrated but can be greatly amplified if there is any indication of negligence by the offending party. Both criminal laws and civil laws can be applied to some types of activities, such as a criminal murder case followed by a civil wrongful death case for the same event.

EXAM TIP

Within the common law system, understand the three types of laws, the differing burden of proof required by each, and the different penalties that may be imposed.

The customary law system

This legal system is based on traditions and customs handed down from generation to generation within particular communities "because it has always been done this way." Customary laws are often related to the perception of rights and a collection of locally and socially prescribed rules. These customary rules are often used in addition to the more formally defined governmental laws (forming a hybrid law system described in the next section). Customary laws are generally considered inferior to the more formal governmental laws for the area. Examples can be found in virtually every corner of the planet, including among the Native American Indian, in regions of China, and in regions of India.

The religious law system

Initially, these laws were declared by a deity and were then written (codified) by the humans the God or gods spoke with. Like customary laws, religious laws are generally considered inferior to the more formal governmental laws for the area. Religious laws often address social obligations and responsibilities and the moral and ethical expectations defined by the deity. Examples include Canon (Christian) law, Halakha (Jewish) law, Hindu law, and Sharia (Islamic) law.

Hybrid law systems

These occur when more than one legal system is present and has influence in a specific geographic or political area such as on a Native American Indian reservation in Oklahoma, where customary law and common law both apply. Much of the world is influenced by more than one legal system.

The difference between laws and regulations

In the United States, Congress, and only Congress, can enact a law. The U.S. Code is the official collection of codified laws, and the U.S. Statutes-at-Large is the official chronologic collection of all laws.

Federal executive departments and administrative agencies other than Congress write regulations to implement the authority of laws. The Code of Federal Regulations is the official collection of regulations. Regulations (as well as executive orders and proclamations) are subordinate to laws, but both laws and regulations are administered by governmental law enforcement.

Industry leaders also may produce industry regulations to guide and manage activities performed by members of that industry. Violations of these industry regulations are not administered by governmental law enforcement but (typically) by coalitions of the industry leaders. Penalties are strictly financial or banishment, in a sense, from participating in the industry.

Protecting intellectual property

Several types of legal controls are available for the protection of IP to reward the inventor or creator and provide incentive for the inventor or creator to share his new creation with the world. These protections are supported in the United States and in some other countries, but the foreign support, if it exists at all, is often marginal and subject to the often varying interpretation of the foreign courts. Work with the legal department of the organization to decide the proper type of protection to apply for and rely on.

Patents

The patent is designed to protect an invention such as a form of technology. The invention must be novel and not obvious, and it must provide some utility. In other words, it must do something specific and (usually) beneficial. The patentable invention must be something that can be produced, and each patent may only cover a single idea.

For all participating members of the World Trade Organization, the protection of the invention, if the patent application is approved, should be good for 20 years from the date of application, but there are still variations from country to country. The invention must be disclosed in the application. After the patent application is submitted and prior to approval, there is no protection, and the intellectual property is exposed to the public domain. If approved, the patent (in those countries that choose to participate fully) prohibits others from producing, selling, distributing, or using the patented object without specific permission from the holder of the patent.

If a patent application remains inactive for a period of three years, it is considered abandoned, and the information disclosed within the patent is now declared to be in the public domain.

Copyrights

 The copyright was designed to promote the creation and publication of original works of authorship and protect the *expression of an idea*, not the idea itself. (Patents are typically used to protect the specific ideas.) The expression must be recorded on some media, such as written on paper or recorded on some magnetic media.

The protections are intended to allow the creator to benefit by being credited for the work and control the duplication, use of, and distribution of the work. Many countries participate with international copyright agreements, but the level of strict participation and protection, again, varies greatly. The protections are typically good for the entire life of the creator plus 50 to 100 years after the death of the creator. Although simply declaring a work to be copyrighted qualifies the work for legal protection in most instances, stronger protections are often afforded by formally registering the copyrighted materials.

The copyright can be used to protect all forms of source code, the expression of the idea for the application. It is compiled into machine language prior to its release, making it unreadable by humans. This is a form of protection—in essence, encryption—which qualifies it as a protection mechanism.

Trademarks

The trademark is intended to protect a recognizable name, symbol, image, icon, shape, colors, or sound (or combination thereof) that is used to represent a brand, product, service, or company and to distinguish that brand, product, service, or company from its competitors. The intent is to identify the source or origin of the trademarked item. The unregistered trademark is typically designated with the TM superscript. The unregistered *service mark*, used to brand services, is typically designated with the SM superscript. The registered and approved trademark is typically designated with the ® symbol.

Trade secrets

The trade secret is intellectual property developed by an entity (a person, business, or organization) at some cost, which provides competitive value, is proprietary to that entity (not generally known to the public), and is important to the entity for its ongoing survival. It is commonly a unique procedural know-how and produces some special quality or characteristic in the end product. The creator or owner of the trade secret must implement due care by adequately protecting the secret for the life of the desired protections. This is typically accomplished through nondisclosure agreements (NDAs), confidentiality agreements, and intellectual property agreements. (Anything invented by a worker under the agreement sells any inventions, secrets, intellectual property to the organization for $1 and so on.) Further, controls such as numbering copies of sensitive documents, logging the distribution of documents, carefully controlling copies, and so on will help substantiate any claims of breaches.

Recognize that for the fullest protections, the patent, the copyright, and the trademark all require registration, which places the IP in the public domain. If the application is approved, and the legal protection is subsequently granted, very often the registering organization is faced with the task of identifying and then pursuing litigation against one or more companies that have profited from the use of the now-protected IP. Typically, when successful, the registering organization must prove some specific level of loss, and only that amount can be recovered. Breaches of patents, copyrights, and trademarks are typically settled in civil courts (like contract disputes) and are generally not considered criminal matters, but this varies in different jurisdictions.

The trade secret does not require registration and remains the only legal control for intellectual property of the four types of legal controls that allows the IP to remain undisclosed and confidential.

Protecting privacy

Privacy deals with the collection and subsequent protection of (specifically, the confidentiality of) information about individuals. It begins with the protection of personally identifiable information, described earlier in this chapter, and continues with issues regarding the monitoring of employees at work. Various entities have the need or desire to collect information about people, such as customers, employees, and patients.

With the advances in connectivity, applications, and storage technologies over the past decade, this new form of vulnerability, called *data aggregation*, is rapidly evolving. Borders, travel time, and storage limits don't exist anymore. As these various entities amass details about us all, there is little about the individual that remains really private. With fewer cash transactions, virtually everything a person purchases is known, and every place a person purchases is known. Cookies in the web browsers and endpoint protection software track every website that is visited and often record times and paths followed through those websites. On the *social media sites*, people expose too much information about themselves, their families, and many (most?) other aspects of their personal history and their personal lives. (Look at me! Look at me!) Medical information is made readily available, for very good cause, to other medical facilities and carries a person's entire medical history. A person's favorite food, drink, shoe size, and entertainment preferences are all very easily identified in this ever-growing mountain of readily available personal information.

These collections of information are often shared, sold, or stolen, which builds an even larger collection of potentially sensitive information. Some companies apply *artificial intelligence* to this data and sell research services for marketing purposes. (Oh, great. More spam and commercials.) Others research this data to uncover enough information about individuals to do them harm from theft, fraud, or sometimes even extortion.

The EU Data Protection Directive

Governments have begun to recognize this threat and are enacting privacy laws that specify requirements for the protection of personal information. The European Union seems to be leading the pack in this area, with a collection of well-developed laws called the Data Protection Directive EU/95/46/EC. This directive includes the following principles:

- **Notice**   Subjects should be given notice when their data is being collected.
- **Purpose**   Data should be used only for the purpose stated and not for any other purposes.
- **Consent**   Data should not be disclosed without the data subject's consent.
- **Security**   Collected data should be kept secure from any potential abuses.
- **Disclosure**   Data subjects should be informed about who is collecting their data.

- **Access** Subjects should be allowed to access their data and make corrections to any inaccurate data.
- **Accountability** Subjects should have an available method to hold the data collectors accountable for following these principles.

A new draft of this directive also includes requirements for the protection of data held about children 13 years and younger, portability rules, and the right to be forgotten (having the records wiped clean if requested). Further, in case of severe breaches of the EU data protection law, authorities may impose penalties of up to 2 percent of a company's worldwide revenue.

The EU has drafted and, in 2000, approved a framework to accommodate differences in non-EU countries privacy laws to standardize a definition of adequacy for the protection of personal data being processed, stored, or transmitted within the EU. This framework is commonly referred to as the *EU Safe Harbor*. The 28 EU member states agree to and are bound by the Safe Harbor definition of adequacy for protecting the personal data. This greatly streamlines the ability of international enterprises to flow information into, out of, and within the EU.

US privacy laws and regulations

Unfortunately, there is no overarching federal law on privacy. However, 46 states, the District of Columbia, and four US territories have enacted cybercrime laws requiring the protection of PII and the reporting of breaches of PII. Because these laws and regulations vary from state to state, you must identify the specifics of the applicable laws and regulations that must be included within your organization's security program by consulting the local legal department for specific legal interpretation.

Laws and regulations are not optional, and they are not divisible. An enterprise is either compliant with the entire law or regulation, or it is not compliant. Noncompliance requires immediate action by the security professional if for no other reason than to advise management of the noncompliance.

Several federal laws address specific societal groups of individuals, such as:

- **Healthcare Insurance Portability and Accountability Act (HIPAA)** Addresses the sharing and protection requirements for related medical information of patients
- **Gramm-Leach-Bliley Act (GLBA)** Addresses the information protection requirements of the customers of financial institutions
- **Sarbanes Oxley Act (SOX)** Addresses information protections required of publicly held companies to ensure accuracy of information when reporting to the Securities and Exchange Commission (SEC) and to their shareholders
- **Federal Information Security Management Act (FISMA)** Addresses requirements to protect government information, assets and operations against natural or human-made threats

Although specific laws and regulations are reviewed in the official courseware, they are presented as examples of the elements and types of controls that may be included within the security program to ensure compliance when the laws and regulations apply to the enterprise. The nature of the types of laws and regulations that protect information systems may be test-worthy, but the specific details of these laws and regulations are not test-worthy.

Industry regulations that protect privacy

So-called self-regulated industries may also impose information security regulations on participating enterprises within that industry. The most prominent example of such a regulation is the *Payment Card Industry Data Security Standard* (*PCI-DSS*) that applies to any enterprise that stores, processes, or transmits payment card data. PCI-DSS defines 12 primary protection requirements for the information systems within the scope of compliance:

- Build and maintain a secure network

    - Requirement 1: Install and maintain a firewall configuration to protect cardholder data.

    - Requirement 2: Do not use vendor-supplied defaults for system passwords and other security parameters.

- Protect cardholder data

    - Requirement 3: Protect stored cardholder data.

    - Requirement 4: Encrypt transmission of cardholder data across open, public networks.

- Maintain a vulnerability management program

    - Requirement 5: Use and regularly update antivirus software or programs.

    - Requirement 6: Develop and maintain secure systems and applications.

- Implement strong access control measures

    - Requirement 7: Restrict access to cardholder data by business need to know.

    - Requirement 8: Assign a unique ID to each person with computer access.

    - Requirement 9: Restrict physical access to cardholder data.

- Regularly monitor and test networks

    - Requirement 10: Track and monitor all access to network resources and cardholder data.

    - Requirement 11: Regularly test security systems and processes.

- Maintain an information security policy

    - Requirement 12: Maintain a policy that addresses information security for all personnel.

The PCI-DSS regulations are the by-product of a failed prior attempt to protect cardholder data during transactions. The payment card industry attempted to implement a protection technology called Secure Electronic Transaction (SET) in the late 1990s. The technology used digital certificates to establish a secure channel and encrypt the cardholder data at the client PC through the e-commerce website (the vendor) and to the vendor's bank, where the cardholder data was decrypted. The vendor's bank would then communicate with the client's bank to approve the transaction. After approval, the vendor's bank would notify the e-commerce website (the vendor) to accept the order. This meant that the vendor never had access to the cardholder data. The technology was excellent.

However, the banks wanted to charge the vendors an additional fee of 2 percent to as much as 8 percent to use SET on top of the fees already charged to the vendors for processing the payment card transaction. The vendors refused to pay the additional fees, and SET failed as a technology. The payment card industry still had to protect that cardholder data, so PCI-DSS was created. SET is presented in more detail in Chapter 3, "Cryptography."

Auditing for compliance

Most of the laws and regulations that target the protection of information and information systems require verification of compliance on an annual basis. This verification is accomplished by auditing the enterprise, its policies, practices, and systems against the compliance standard. In some cases, the audit might be accomplished using internal auditors, accompanied by an attestation of compliance signed by one or more of the responsible corporate officials.

In other cases, the audit must be performed by an unbiased and accredited third-party auditing firm. These external audits can take a great deal of time and effort and can cost hundreds of thousands of dollars to complete.

These reports of compliance are submitted to the appropriate regulatory body for review and analysis. The regulatory body, in most cases, has the authority to require additional testing and auditing, to impose financial penalties, or, in some cases, even initiate legal action against the noncompliant enterprise.

Employee privacy issues

Monitoring employees has become a required tightrope that almost all employers must walk. As a standard of due care, it is the employer's responsibility to maintain a safe working environment for the workers and visitors in the workplace. Further, if an employee uses any company asset and in any way causes some harm, injury, or loss to someone else, whether intentionally or accidentally, the enterprise is held accountable and liable for the losses incurred in many cases. This combination of factors essentially mandates that the employer must prudently monitor all employee activities within the limits of the law. This monitoring should include:

- Entry and exit from the facilities and grounds
- Surveillance cameras
- Web browsing

- Email
- Keystroke logging
- Network activities
- Telephone conversations
- Voicemail
- Drug screening for sensitive positions

Employee privacy laws vary from country to country and from state to state. Work with the local legal department to establish appropriate employee monitoring policies and practices. The monitoring practices should be included in the employee security awareness training. The employees should be made well aware that they should have *no expectation of privacy* while on or using company property or when representing the enterprise.

Often, to satisfy the legal requirements of employee monitoring, the employees must be made aware that they are being monitored, should sign a statement declaring their awareness and approval of being monitored, and be reminded of the ongoing monitoring (as with logon banners). The monitoring should be routine and not target specific employees.

Trans-border information flow

As stated previously, information and privacy protection laws vary from country to country. Several countries have enacted information and privacy protection laws controlling certain types of information that can be transmitted, such as personal, medical, or financial information. In addition, certain types of cryptography may be restricted from use. It becomes the responsibility of the security professional to understand these restrictions and to ensure that the flow of information between offices, branches, partners, and so on does not violate these sovereign laws.

Typically, these remote locations where information must be shared are connected by means of a *virtual private network* (*VPN*), an encrypted channel, over the Internet. The Internet uses a packet-switched, mesh topology also known as cloud topology. Data-carrying packets leave the source office network and enter the cloud. The packets are routed following many paths through the cloud and then exit the cloud at a point nearest the destination network. The default behavior of the Internet does not allow the endpoints to manage the flow or path of the packets.

Trans-border information-flow concerns require this flow to be managed. Several wide-area networking (WAN) protocols support the management of the flow of the data packets between endpoints across the cloud-based Internet. The protocols that support the *pinned path* requirements include:

- Frame relay
- Asynchronous Transfer Mode (ATM)
- Multi-Protocol Label Switching (MPLS)

The cost of a pinned path from the WAN carriers is often higher than the default packet switching approach, but that price must be weighed against the possibility of violating a country's privacy and information-flow laws and opening the enterprise to the legal actions that could result from the violation.

Litigation

One of the many threats to an enterprise is the threat of litigation. Lawsuits are brought against an organization in an attempt to gain reimbursement for damages (or perceived damages) the organization caused. This can result from a breach of contract, from some violation of civil rights (discrimination), or from some form of injury resulting in losses, to name a few. Additional compensation, beyond just reimbursement, is often awarded if the plaintiff can demonstrate that the organization was somehow negligent, and that negligence directly or indirectly led to the damages, injury, or loss. It is the security professional's job to help management minimize and avoid unnecessary losses, so it becomes a responsibility of the security professional to perform due diligence and due care, to manage the enterprise prudently, as a reasonable person would under similar circumstances, and to avoid being negligent.

As presented in Chapter 1, due diligence is the development of knowledge and awareness of the risks present in the workplace and the marketplace and the ongoing maintenance of the protective controls that manage those risks. Due care is the management of risk and the implementation of safety measures, countermeasures, and controls to protect people and organizations from harm (physically and financially), largely based on the vision developed from the performance of due diligence. As you can see, these are core components of risk assessment and risk management.

 An aspect of liability that must also be considered and managed is that of *downstream liabilities*. A downstream liability is an organization or person who suffered losses because of negligence by another organization or person (perceived to be upstream from the organization with the losses). In the information systems world, this most commonly occurs when an attacker compromises one or more systems within an organization and, using those systems as the attacker systems, attacks a second, downstream, organization.

Governance of third parties

There are often insufficient internal assets, skills, and human resources to accomplish everything cost effectively that an organization requires. Many tasks and services must be outsourced to third parties that can support the requirements of the organization in a cost-effective manner. The prudent management of the enterprise and, often, the laws and regulations that apply to it require these third parties to comply *completely* with all the policies of the enterprise as if these third parties were employees of the enterprise. This means that the requirement to govern all third-party service providers must be included within the policy documents, and everything within the policies must be equally applied to every third-party service provider.

Third parties would include all types of external entities that gain access, in any way, to any information assets within the scope of corporate policy or any applicable laws and regulations such as the following:

- Contractors
- Consultants
- Lawyers
- Outsourced services
- Cloud services (of all kinds)
- Service-level agreement providers
- Maintenance providers
- Vendors
- Customers

These third parties must be legally bound and governed essentially as if they were internal employees; they must comply with every policy requirement, any applicable laws and regulations, and every element of the security program of the enterprise. This would include:

- Data classification
- Data protection requirements, based on classification
- Security awareness training
- Monitoring
- Auditing, including perhaps vulnerability scanning and penetration testing
- Consistent enforcement
- Risk assessment and risk management
- Disaster recovery and business continuity planning
- Remediation

This means that as an agreement is being considered and negotiated with any third party, these elements must be discussed, documented, and agreed on. This will likely increase the costs of these services. Training must be provided to the third-party personnel, and monitoring mechanisms must be in place prior to access to any valuable information assets. Monitoring and auditing must occur at a level that matches that of the internal organization during the third-party providers' presence, and consistent enforcement and remediation must occur for any violations of policy or breaches.

EXAM TIP

The topic of governance of third parties that gain access to the valuable information assets of the enterprise is a new item on the CISSP exam objective list, called the Candidate Information Bulletin (CIB) available from ISC2. Be sure you are aware of the management objectives and requirements for these third parties.

Software licensing

An often-overlooked component of the prudent management of an organization is that of using only fully licensed software. It becomes too easy simply to install another copy of an application without ensuring that the organization has purchased a valid license for it. A well-managed enterprise should never allow the use of pirated or otherwise unlicensed software.

One person or department should be assigned responsibility for the management of software licenses for the department, facility, location, or enterprise; there should be periodic audits of the number of copies of an application or operating system and the number of licenses that have been purchased. These licenses must be properly maintained (securely stored), ideally in a single location, and be readily available to show as proof of valid licensing and registration of this software. Most *end-user license agreements* (*EULA*) state that if you use the application, you choose to allow the software vendor to audit your organization for appropriate licensing of the software. Examples of the types of software licenses include:

- **Site license** Often unlimited use of the software within a specified location
- **Per server** Licensing binds to a server and prevents more inbound client connections than the number of licenses registered on the server
- **Per seat** Licensing binds to a single computer, no matter how many people use the computer
- **Per user** License allows the user to install the software on any number of computers, but only for that one user's use

Shareware, cripple-ware, and *unlicensed software* should be strictly forbidden within the policies of the enterprise. Shareware and cripple-ware are often the vehicles to install malware and are rarely supported in a manner that protects the organization from conflicts and potential system outages. Proper software licensing can be managed through security awareness training; the use of a documented, approved software list; by periodic audits of systems; and by using configuration management tools that would identify the software installed on each system.

The creation, distribution, or use of pirated software should be reported to the Business Software Alliance (BSA), a trade group of software developer industry leaders established in 1988 designed to identify and stop the copyright infringement of pirated software.

✔ Quick check

1. What term describes the legal, regulatory, and policy requirements imposed on external entities that operate with the organization?
2. What are the primary components of mitigating litigation?

Quick check answers

1. Third-party governance
2. Due diligence, due care, prudent management, avoid being negligent

---

Investigating computer crime

Computer crime is recognized as a significant global problem. There is a (slowly) growing global effort to improve the ability of countries to identify and prosecute the perpetrators of international computer crime.

 The *Group of 8*, or *G8*, is a collection of the eight countries with the largest economies; it includes Canada, France, Germany, Italy, Japan, Russia, the United Kingdom, and the United States. (The European Union also has representation in the G8, with some limited powers.) In 1997, the G8 adopted the Ten Principles to combat high-tech crime, including the provision that no computer criminal is provided safe harbor anywhere in the world.

 The *Council of Europe Convention on Cybercrime*, also known as the Budapest Convention, was the first international treaty attempting to harmonize laws and coordinate accepted investigative techniques, evidence collection, analysis, and presentation in courts. It came into force in 2004 and currently has 45 signatory countries, including the United States.

 The *International Organization on Computer Evidence (IOCE)* was formed in 1995; its objective is to establish and publish international standards for defining best practices for the forensic examination of digital evidence. It currently has published several documents, which are available for download at *www.ioce.org*.

Interpol is the largest international police force; its origin dates back to 1914 and comprises 190 participating countries. Interpol works in 16 areas of international crime, with one team specializing in cybercrime. In addition to the pursuit of criminals operating in Internet-based scams and child pornography, it fights terrorist activities that recruit members and target infrastructure systems such as power plants, electrical grids, and the information systems of governments and government agencies.

When to notify law enforcement

As an anomalous event is escalated toward the status of incident, a close eye must be kept to evaluate whether this event or incident is in fact a computer crime. It is the security professional's job to monitor the computer event and advise management of its status as soon as an appropriate judgment can be made. Not all events, incidents, or breaches will be criminal acts. The definition of computer crime varies from country to country and from state to state, so have the local legal department identify the specific threshold that separates the event or incident from computer crime. Don't be too eager to declare the event a crime; this greatly increases the complexity and cost of the investigation.

However, if the event escalates to incident level and appears to qualify as a computer crime that professional assessment must be forwarded to management. For many reasons, it is common for management to be reluctant and even unwilling to accept that the event is a crime. At a high level, following are some of the reasons management might want to avoid reporting the incident if possible:

- The cost of the investigation increases due to the need for much stricter investigative methodologies or the need for external professionals to perform the investigation.

- Management loses control of the investigation, of the assets of the organization, and of the crime scene.

- Law enforcement must confiscate evidence, items that are valuable and necessary assets of the organization. The assets include workspace (the crime scene), computers, logs, and work hours as workers are interviewed; productivity will be reduced or stopped altogether as the investigation progresses.

- The news of the incident or crime will be made public, damaging the reputation of the organization. This damage results in lower revenue, reducing the short-term and long-term profits of the organization.

From the standpoint of the CISSP, the decision to notify law enforcement agencies about a computer crime must be management's decision. However, in the United States, 46 states have enacted laws that require organizations to report breaches of (generally) PII to the appropriate law enforcement. This effectively makes it a crime to withhold a report of the computer crime. It is the CISSP's duty to follow management's instructions and not exceed or violate those instructions. However, if management refuses to report the computer crime, a higher ethical canon—the first and highest ISC2 ethical cannon, to protect society—must dominate, and the member of society (who in this case is also a security professional or CISSP) must report the computer crime. The four primary ISC2 ethical canons are described in Chapter 1 and include, in the order of priority:

1. Protect society, the commonwealth, and the infrastructure.

2. Act honorably, honestly, justly, responsibly, and legally.

3. Provide diligent and competent service to principals.

4. Advance and protect the profession.

EXAM TIP

You can expect at least one question on the ISC2 Code of Ethics and its relative priorities.

If law enforcement is brought into an incident, it will typically perform or manage the forensics and analysis of the evidence. The results of the forensics and analysis will be used to substantiate the claims of the criminal act as well as the motive, opportunity, and the means that will link the accused with the criminal act(s). The motive describes why the accused might have felt compelled and perhaps justified in performing the criminal act(s). Opportunity describes how the accused had the chance to commit the criminal act(s). Means describes how the accused had the ability to commit the criminal act(s).

Incident response

Sooner or later, in every enterprise, something will go wrong, or it becomes the target of malicious activity. Therefore, every prudently managed enterprise should be prepared for these incidents and have a planned and rehearsed approach to minimizing losses from these types of incidents. Incident response (IR) is an integral component of every security program and must integrate with the disaster recovery and business continuity plans and activities. Its charter and structure must be included within the policy documents. After the release of the Morris Worm in 1988, the US government issued a contract to Carnegie Mellon University (CMU) to establish procedures and a central control center to help manage malware outbreaks. CMU formed the first *Computer Emergency Response Team and Coordination Center* and registered the CERT and *CERT/CC* trademarks. In the corporate world, these are also commonly known as:

- Computer Emergency Response Team (CERT) (Not used often due to potential trademark infringement issues)
- Computer Security Emergency Response Team (CSERT)
- Computer Incident Response Team (CIRT)
- Computer Security Incident Response Team (CSIRT)

CSIRT

A CSIRT must be identified and trained. The core members are typically IT security professionals with a solid understanding of the enterprise information system and a varying mix of network engineering skills, programming skills, and familiarity with hacking skills and techniques. The team must have fairly direct access to senior management for the immediate flow of information and approvals typically required during in incident response. The team also often needs to coordinate with other internal and external entities, including:

- **Legal department**   For guidance with any potential legal matters
- **Human resources department**   When any employees might be involved
- **Network operations team**   The hands and eyes on hardware systems
- **Various divisional and department managers**   Whose areas might be affected by the incident, breach, or response
- **Public relations department**   If the incident goes public for any reason
- **External consultants**   When internal skills and knowledge is exceeded
- **Law enforcement**   If the incident is a crime

The CSIRT plan

The goal of the incident response program is to defend the information systems from outages and losses and breaches of the confidentiality, integrity, or availability of valuable information assets. The incident response plan should include discrete plans for the various types of incidents that would affect the information systems negatively and might be customized for different locations within the enterprise wide information system. These incidents commonly include (but are not limited to):

- Virus/worm/malware infection
- Hacker attack/DoS/DDoS attack
- Unauthorized disclosure
- Unauthorized or unacceptable access
- Lost or stolen equipment

An example of a high-level procedural flowchart is presented in Figure 6-1.

Computer Security Incident Response Procedure Flowchart

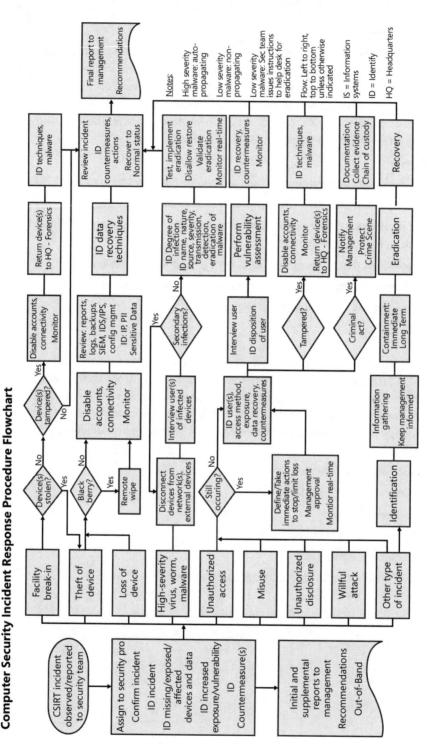

FIGURE 6-1 A computer security incident response plan flowchart

General procedures are often used because as an incident evolves, its scope, its impact, and the specific systems affected might change. Specific actions to be taken are often determined during the course of the incident response based on the specifics of the event. However, the incident should and usually does follow a particular flow of high-level stages, as follows:

- Monitor/detect/notify
- Triage
- Investigation
- Containment
- Analysis
- Tracking
- Recovery
- Reporting
- Prevention

> **NOTE   INCIDENT RESPONSE EXAMPLES**
>
> In the following sections on incident response, examples of a well-developed and well-funded incident response program are presented. The scenario(s) are by no means strict requirements but present a prudent approach to incident response, assuming the budget, human resources, skills, and other resources are available.

MONITOR

If you are not watching, you will never see the incident. Incident response begins with routine and ongoing monitoring of the enterprise. Although the occasional accidental discovery of a breach occurs, it is certainly not something the prudently managed security program should rely on. Monitoring is typically heavily focused on the information systems of the enterprise, especially those within the scope of legal and regulatory compliance and where the most critical and valuable information assets reside and are processed and transmitted. The monitoring should include system logs, such as those from:

- Firewalls
- Intrusion detection systems (IDS)/intrusion prevention systems (IPS)
- Network access systems (NAS) used for remote connectivity (VPN concentrators, RADIUS, TACACS+, and Diameter systems)
- Authentication servers
- File and print servers
- Application servers
- Internal DNS servers

- Publicly exposed servers (web servers, email servers, FTP servers, DNS servers)
- Data storage systems (such as storage area network [SAN] systems and database servers)
- Routers
- Intelligent switches
- Wireless access points
- Critical workstations

The routine and ongoing monitoring should also include output from host-based and network-based intrusion detection systems (IDS) and intrusion prevention systems (IPS) and the output from antivirus (AV) software on systems enterprise-wide. Many of these IDS, IPS, and AV systems can be configured to send their alerts and notifications to a centralized administrative console and collected, consolidated, and forwarded to the centralized monitoring systems from there.

In most cases, the amount of information pouring in from servers and other infrastructure systems in every corner of the network would overwhelm the human mind in just a few hours (if that long). When you consider that this gigantic flow of information runs at this pace during all business hours, and often 24 hours a day, you quickly realize that this is not a task for humans. This is a task for an automated monitoring system.

This automated monitoring system must have some special capabilities to perform this work. It must be able to collect and store these logs and events securely, read these logs in their various formats, and extract the pertinent information from each event (parse the logs) intelligently. This monitoring system must then correlate these numerous events from this wide array of differing systems and devices and develop some conclusion about the state of the security of the enterprise, probably through the use of artificial intelligence algorithm(s). This is no small order but what is needed to monitor the information systems of an enterprise diligently.

These highly specialized and sophisticated monitoring systems are called *security information and event management (SIEM) systems*. SIEM systems are tireless. They parse events from virtually any source device or system, they understand the nature of the system reporting, and they understand the significance of the event being reported. They correlate the events from each system and, using various and sophisticated artificial intelligence algorithms, develop a picture of the information systems within the enterprise.

> **NOTE SYNCHRONIZE THE CLOCKS**
>
> The clocks of the devices and systems being monitored must be synchronized to correlate events. The Network Time Protocol (NTP) is an automated time synchronization process designed to synchronize the clocks on information system devices. Most systems incorporate a way for this NTP time synchronization to operate correctly.

In addition to the automated aggregation and analysis of logs and events, the periodic manual auditing, spot checking, should be included in this process to verify that all the essential logs and alerts are making it to the monitoring systems.

DETECTION

The purpose of all this log aggregation, monitoring, and analysis is to be able to identify (detect) anomalous activities, system misconfigurations, outages, and willful malicious attacks on the information systems quickly. The quicker these can be identified, the more loss can be avoided, which maximizes the profits of the enterprise.

Some systems are designed to detect this type of activity automatically, such as IDS and SIEM systems. However, these automated systems are only as good as the algorithms and signatures built into them. They are prone to false positive alerts, which, if responded to blindly, would be very costly to the organization. In most cases, the systems should automatically monitor and analyze the millions of events and be designed to alert a human on the few, rare, suspected noteworthy events. Let the human judgment of a skilled security professional be the official trigger for the expenditure of the security budget and begin to commit that budget to investigations only when the security professional can rule out the event as a false positive.

 The incident response process begins with an *escalation process*. Automated systems identify anomalies and alert a tier 1 human for further investigation only on those rare few anomalies. The tier 1 security professional will spend some time (usually not more than 2 to 5 minutes) investigating the event in an attempt to rule it out as a false positive. If tier 1 cannot rule the event out as a false positive, she alerts tier 2. Tier 1 goes back to surveying the entire enterprise in case the anomaly appears elsewhere or repeatedly. An initial attack might be nothing more than a diversion to allow a much more harmful attack elsewhere on the network.

The tier 2 security professional, usually a more seasoned and skilled individual, will spend some time (usually not more than 2 to 10 minutes) investigating the event in an attempt to rule it out as a false positive. If tier 2 cannot rule the event out as a false positive, he alerts tier 3.

The tier 3 security professional, usually the senior security professional for the organization, will spend some time (usually not more than 2 to 10 minutes) investigating the event in an attempt to rule it out as a false positive. If tier 3 cannot rule the event out as a false positive, she alerts management with a summary report of the event and usually a recommendation to escalate the event to incident status.

Incidents might be accidental or the result of willful malicious acts. Incidents might be from a breach of policy, of a law or regulation, or of security. It might or might not be a criminal act. In any case, at this point, the security professional is required to report the incident to management. If management approves the upgraded status to incident, this is when the process really begins to get expensive.

If the breach is not introducing losses, and the level of confidence is high that the risk to the enterprise is minimal, the decision might be just to monitor rather than respond. Valuable lessons can be learned by studying and tracking the adversary in this never-ending game of cat and mouse.

NOTIFICATION

When events percolate up to an incident status and warrant additional investigation, involving senior management and often the legal department (among others), several questions require nearly immediate answers. They include:

- Is there a risk to safety? If so, determine whether evacuation is required and contact the appropriate emergency services (ambulance, police, fire). Remember that safety is always the top priority.

- Could this be a criminal act? If so, implement the incident response procedures and methodologies that support prosecution-level handling. Determine whether this is a violation of laws or regulations and whether law enforcement must be notified.

- Could this event trigger litigation other than, or in addition to, criminal prosecution? If so, implement the incident response procedures and methodologies that support prosecution-level handling of the investigation and evidence.

- Are in-house skills sufficient to handle (all investigative activities) this event? Determine what external skills are required and initiate communication with these entities. These external, highly skilled, professional services should already be identified and have a professional association with the enterprise. These consultants are often on a flat-fee, monthly retainer to ensure an acceptable response time. Increased costs are incurred when these consultants are used in an actual incident response event.

- Could an insider be assisting with the attack? If so, the response (typically) must occur covertly to avoid alerting the attacker of the detection.

These questions will be continually reappraised throughout the duration of the incident, and the answers might have an impact on the procedures, methodologies, and personnel used during the incident response.

Someone on the incident response team will begin notifying appropriate individuals based on a documented and prioritized call list. Although not everyone on the call list is notified for every incident, the call list would include services, names (when known), and periodically revalidated phone numbers. The details to be provided to each entity should be previewed and approved by senior management and, perhaps, even a member of the public relations department. These communications should use a communications channel that does not include any infrastructure the attacker might compromise. This is referred to as an *out-of-band communications* channel, and it is used to avoid letting the attacker know that he has been detected. The call list would include:

- Emergency services as appropriate
- The members of the incident response team
- Additional members of senior management as appropriate
- Managers of affected areas (divisions, departments, facilities, and so on) of the organization as appropriate
- External consultants as necessary
- Law enforcement

TRIAGE

Triage was originally a process developed in the battlefields during World War I to prioritize the allocation of medical resources and when resources are insufficient to respond to all that need attention. In its crudest form, triage determines which victims will most likely benefit the greatest from attention, based on the severity of the damages, as follows:

- Those victims who are likely to die, no matter what care might be given
- Those victims who are likely to live, no matter what care might be given
- Those victims who are likely to benefit if immediate care is given

Triage has been applied to incident response for information systems but includes an additional element in the analysis: the criticality (importance, value) of the victim—in this case, the criticality of the IT information, system, or device the incident has affected. As part of the initial impact assessment and report to management, the security professional in charge of the incident must continuously report to management the status of the incident as knowledge of the details evolve and make recommendations where to apply response efforts, with an understanding of:

- Whether the losses are still occurring
- The critical business processes and functions
- The IT systems that support those functions
- The value of the data being accessed
- Where the valuable information assets reside
- The affected systems
- The path the attack has taken into the network
- The scope of the systems being affected
- Whether the breach violates laws or regulations
- Potential suspects and potential witnesses

The security professional must determine which systems require the most immediate attention to identify the severity of the newfound breach of security. These questions must be continually reappraised throughout the duration of the incident.

INVESTIGATION

Some basic information will have been developed about the event as it escalated up through the security team, but much more detail and much less speculation will be required, and this information is needed in a hurry. The security team lead should be assigning specific investigative tasks to the members of the IR team to further understanding of the incident. The goal of this initial investigation is to understand how to minimize the losses and how to stop the expansion of the breach.

The logs of key systems should be reviewed, network sniffers might be deployed, and key people might need to be interviewed. Be sure the activities of the IR team do not expose more parts of the incident and response to the employees than is desired in case an insider is participating in the breach. In addition to internal investigations, many resources are available on the Internet that can provide much information about vulnerabilities, malicious software, the frequency of incidents around the globe, propagation mechanisms, containment and eradication techniques, and so on.

As details evolve, new priorities will arise, and new investigative tasks might be assigned. This information is developed to enable the security team lead to make recommendations to management for the next phase of the IR process—containment. Be sure the CSIRT team members and management use out-of-band communications channels to prevent the attacker from monitoring the network and cluing the attacker in on the status and nature of the response. Also recognize the need to protect the information gathered and shared during the investigation due to its sensitive nature.

CONTAINMENT

Based on the information gathered during the initial investigation, the security team lead reports the incident status to management and recommends actions to contain the incident and minimize losses. With management's approval to take action, the security team lead will (usually) reach out to the appropriate department (often the network operations team) with instructions on the specific actions to take.

Containment options might include applying patches or altering configurations on operating systems or applications, stopping various systems or services on the network, disconnecting areas of the network, and removing data from potentially compromised systems.

During the containment phase, the entire enterprise must be closely monitored to verify that the containment efforts are successful and that a secondary attack vector has not been initiated.

ANALYSIS

During this phase, monitoring of the entire enterprise continues, verifying that the containment efforts are successful. With a growing confidence that the containment efforts are successful, and that the losses are being stopped, the analysis phase identifies the vulnerabilities that led to the successful exploit, answering the question, "How did this happen?" Also during this phase, research is conducted to understand how to eradicate completely all traces of the malware or exploit from affected systems so that the steps to be taken to recover to a normal state are known.

TRACKING

With containment being verified in an ongoing basis, and an understanding of how to recover systems and data to a normal state, the tides begin to turn in favor of the enterprise. At this point, resources can often be redirected toward developing an understanding of who did this. This is when the IR team begins to track the attacker, with the possibility of gathering evidence for prosecution or other forms of legal action.

RECOVERY

Often parallel to tracking, resources are allocated toward eradicating all traces of the incident from affected systems and data to return the environment to a state of normal. A critical step is to ensure that all systems and data being brought back online are completely free of malware, and configurations are at least as secure as before the incident. With the vulnerability assessment that occurred during the analysis phase, there might be an improvement in the security posture of affected systems if those identified vulnerabilities can be mitigated or eliminated completely. The recovery phase is complete when all systems have been returned to their online status, the incident can be declared over, and the enterprise is operating as it would normally.

REPORTING

During the IR activities, reporting to management is ongoing and continuous as new information is learned about the incident and as new stages of the response are reached.

After the enterprise is operating normally, and the incident is over, an incident report is produced to perform the post mortem review of the incident and detail the incident timeline. This provides training for the IR team and management by reviewing the lessons learned during the incident, what went right, what went wrong, and what could be done to mitigate or prevent a similar incident from occurring in the future. Needed tools, training, support, and personnel can be identified to management to strengthen the security posture of the enterprise.

PREVENTION

Often after losses are suffered from an incident, management is more open to approving the acquisition of new controls to mitigate and avoid additional losses. The recommendations presented to management during the reporting phase might be approved and thus implemented. Recommendations might include:

- Modifying/updating the incident response plan
- Adding new skills (personnel) to the IR team
- Managing the out-of-band communications more carefully
- Managing the public relations (PR) aspects of public communications more carefully
- Improving security awareness training
- Acquiringadditional security hardware or software
- Modifying the policies to mitigate vulnerabilities
- Modifying (hardening) configurations on critical systems

These new controls become an integral component of the ongoing security program that establishes the security posture of the enterprise.

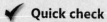
Evidence

Information is gathered at various stages during the incident to contain, eradicate, track the attacker, and recover from the incident effectively. This information will be used after the incident during the reporting phase and for ongoing prevention and improved incident response. However, if the incident was a criminal act, or if there might be other litigation as a result of the incident, this information and various physical assets might become evidence.

Evidence life cycle

Following are the stages that evidence passes through during the course of an investigation and perhaps prosecution. Consider the use of separation of duties throughout the evidence life cycle to ensure and substantiate the integrity of the evidence:

- **Preservation of the (crime) scene**   Prevent tampering or corruption of potential evidence.

- **Identification of the evidence**   What elements might be used to link a suspect to the act or crime or prove or disprove a claim or accusation?

- **Documentation**   Photograph everything, often using both still and video images. Describe details, using an audio recorder or written notes. This begins the *chain of custody.*

- **Collection**   Place evidence in protective control, usually in a sealed evidence bag to ensure that no alteration or corruption of the evidence can occur.

  - **Order of volatility**   As the time that a piece of evidence remains available decreases, the importance of collecting that evidence increases. This is especially true when gathering digital evidence on computers.

  - **Labeling**   Every piece of evidence must be accurately and fully labeled to maintain an appropriate chain of custody and document every time the evidence is accessed, by whom, and why the evidence was accessed. It should also provide some form of verification that the evidence has not been altered, tampered with, or corrupted since it was identified and collected as evidence.

- **Transportation**   After it has been identified, documented, collected, and labeled, the evidence must be transported to a secure storage location to ensure that it has not been altered, tampered with, or corrupted since it was identified and collected.

- **Secure storage**   Protect the evidence from being lost, altered, tampered with, or corrupted while it is stored.

- **Examination and analysis**   Forensic experts will likely analyze the evidence to validate and substantiate the relevance to the case.

- **Verification**   Proof must be offered to show that the evidence has not been altered, tampered with, or corrupted since it was identified and collected, usually performed just prior to presentation in court.

- **Presentation in court**   The evidence might be presented in court to validate and substantiate the relevance to the case, to link a suspect to the act or crime, or to prove or disprove a claim or accusation.

- **Return the evidence to the victim**   When the evidence is no longer needed after the trial, the evidence may be returned to the original owner. Consider the potential for appeal prior to giving up control of the evidence.

Admissibility of evidence

Both the prosecution and the defense teams will gather evidence. This evidence must be shared with the opposing party during the *discovery* phase of a case, prior to going to court. The defense will attack every piece of evidence with the hope of having it ruled inadmissible and thrown out. If the prosecution has no evidence, the case most likely will be dismissed. Every effort must be made to ensure that every piece of evidence remains admissible.

Several primary areas of dispute include:

- **Relevance**   The evidence must specifically relate to the claims and assertions of one team or the other (the prosecution or the defense). The evidence should link suspects to the criminal act(s) and prove or disprove elements of motive, opportunity, and means as well as identify specific actions, activities, and intent of the accused.

- **Unlawful search and seizure** Unless permission was given, law enforcement must attain a warrant to perform a search and seize evidence. The public (civilian) is not subject to this rule unless under the guidance of law enforcement making the civilian a police agent. Forced confessions, illegal recordings of conversations, and privacy violations disqualify evidence for court presentation.

- **Chain of custody** The evidence's handling must be fully documented and be in a secure state and disposition from the time it was identified and collected until presented in court. This documentation verifies that it has not been altered, tampered with, or corrupted during that time (proving the integrity of the evidence).

- **Enticement versus entrapment** Enticement is a means of collecting evidence when a vulnerability is exposed and then monitored. When an attacker exploits the vulnerability, the recorded events become evidence. Entrapment is a means of collecting evidence when a vulnerability is exposed, monitored, and then presented (such as blogging about the vulnerabilities on a hacker website). When an attacker exploits the vulnerability, the recorded events become evidence. In most cases, the evidence collected during *enticement is admissible* in court as evidence. However, in most cases, the evidence collected during *entrapment is not admissible* in court as evidence.

> *NOTE* **WARRANTS AND SUBPOENAS**
>
> A *warrant* is the required legal instrument to allow lawful search and seizure of objects as evidence. A *subpoena* is the required legal instrument to force a person (witness) to appear and testify as a form of evidence. When acquiring testimony from a witness, an interview is used to gather information, and an interrogation is used to gather evidence.

Types of evidence

Different types of evidence convey differing levels of credibility and certainty as proof of some claim. Of course, the more credible and certain the evidence is, the better it is for your side, prosecution or defense, on the issues being disputed in court.

The following terms describe types of evidence.

- **Real evidence** Physical evidence, something you can see and touch.

- **Best evidence** Not a copy of some other evidence but the original evidence. Copies or photographs instead of the original evidence increase the potential for alteration and therefore carries diminished credibility.

- **Direct evidence** Oral testimony given by a witness.

- **Documentary evidence** Printed records, reports, or manuals.

- **Demonstrative evidence** Maps, charts, models, and illustrations used to provide a visual aid to jurors.

The *hearsay rule* is evidence the court rules to be secondhand information provided by a witness or generated report such as the printed event logs from a server. Because of the possibility of bias or tampering, this type of evidence conveys diminished credibility, with two valuable exceptions:

- If the server or the disk drive that holds the logs is presented in court as the original, best evidence to support the more easily read secondary evidence, the printed report. The electronic bit is the original. The printed report is the copy.

- If the report is routinely generated during standard business operations, it is accepted as best evidence.

Forensic investigations

The forensic analysis of computer evidence is a specialized skill. In most cases, this work is performed by a professional who does only this for a living. An extensive knowledge of computer hardware, operating systems, applications, and programming languages is required before you can begin to think about how to extract the hidden details within these systems and applications and do so in a manner that keeps the evidence legally sound and usable. Highly specialized and complete hardware and software tool kits are available for those with the budget, such as EnCase and FTK, but there are also many less-expensive routes to accomplishing similar objectives, such as Helix, Backtrack, and others.

There are four primary types of forensic sciences related to information systems:

- Network
- Hardware
- Software
- Data

It is common for the forensic investigator to assemble and maintain a forensic field kit that contains hardware and software components to use on-site, in the field, for evidence extraction and collection purposes. This kit should be very transportable, something that can be grabbed easily on the way out the door, have everything the professional needs, and be sturdy enough to protect the contents yet travel well. (Consider acceptability as checked versus carry-on baggage on commercial airlines.) Some of the components to place in the forensic field kit might include:

- Evidence bags
- Antistatic bags
- Adhesive labels
- Chain-of-custody forms
- Pads, pens, and markers
- Crime scene (yellow) tape
- Camera(s) and batteries—still photos, digital, and video

- Flashlight and batteries
- Small tools—screwdrivers, pliers, tweezers, wire cutters
- Duct tape—required
- Cable ties
- Volatile memory extraction tools—hardware and software
- External (USB) drive(s)

Whatever tools are available, if the intent is to use the results for prosecution purposes, be sure the tools have been successfully validated in the courts.

Another piece of the equation for successful forensic analysis, especially for prosecution purposes, is a well-developed, documented, and practiced methodology for how the work is to be performed. Every action taken or not taken will be scrutinized by the opponent in court. The defense attorney will attempt to show total incompetence at every step in the process in an attempt to discredit or reject all condemning evidence. Have procedures documented. Follow those procedures carefully and completely. Document every action taken and document every step in the procedures not taken with some justification of why the step was omitted.

Management might conclude that the in-house tools, skills, or human resources are insufficient to perform the forensic analysis. This is solely management's decision but is probably heavily influenced by legal aspects. If the analysis is required as the result of a criminal act, and law enforcement is involved, the law enforcement officials will likely be responsible to perform this work.

EXAM TIP

Whoever will be responsible for performing the forensic analysis of the digital data, for the exam, you must have an understanding of the general concepts associated with the process and the requirement to use a strict procedure and methodology.

Forensic analysis

One of the first objectives of the forensic investigation is to verify and confirm that a crime has been committed, that the incident was not some honest mistake, the result of some misconfiguration or malfunctioning device or system, or some breach of corporate policy but a breach of the law. This will be a combination of the technical analysis of the digital data combined with the legal interpretation provided by the legal department or law officials.

The analysis will include content from many systems and must be correlated to produce a highly repeatable and complete picture and chain of events. The logs from the various systems involved in the incident will be reviewed to establish a timeline of activities. These would include infrastructure systems and ancillary systems as well as the target systems, including (but not limited to):

- Firewalls
- Routers

- Network access servers
- Authentication servers
- Domain name systems
- Web servers
- Email servers
- Application servers
- File and print servers
- Intrusion detection systems
- Intrusion prevention systems
- Endpoint protection systems
- Workstations

These logs will be analyzed to verify their integrity before conclusions can be made based on their data. A common practice by attackers is to disable logging of malicious events and to scrub the logs of the malicious events on the compromised systems. This is why most laws and regulations affecting information systems require the real-time, remote, and secure storage of all logs within the scope of compliance.

On the affected systems, the digital data typically should be collected in the order of volatility. Digital data is stored in many places on a system, as was described in Chapter 5, "Security architecture and design." The storage areas that are overwritten fastest and volatile memory locations should be collected first, followed with the more slowly updated (overwritten) storage areas and the nonvolatile storage locations.

Preparing clone disks

Many details can be revealed by analyzing the hard disks from a computer involved in a computer crime. Remember to follow the legally approved, defined methodology and document everything.

The analysis of hard disk drives should never be performed on the original disks but on identical, bit-level copies of the original disks called *clone disks*. The copy must be produced on a known clean disk with no remnants from any prior use. Even a brand new disk, just out of the manufacturer's packaging, might contain magnetic content and require wiping. The wiping process overwrites every bit on the clone disk to ensure that no intelligible data remains that could affect the analysis of data after the cloning process is complete.

There are several tools that can be used to accomplish the elimination of any *remnant* data on the disk drive, including HDDErase from UCSD and Darik's Boot and Nuke (DBAN), a Linux distribution disk. Use a disk-wiping tool on the clone disk that the local legal department has approved. Document the details of this action, including the make, model, and serial number of the clone disk, the time and date of the wiping, the wiping tool that was used, and who performed the wiping process.

Next, connect the original disk to the forensic system in a manner that ensures that it will not be written to. Several vendors produce hardware write blockers that have pins removed to accomplish this. After it is ensured that the original disk cannot be written to, run a hashing algorithm on the original disk to establish a known good fingerprint of the content on the disk. The current NIST recommendation is to use SHA256 (or greater); however, the use of MD5 or SHA1 might be acceptable. (As always, use the tools the local legal department advises.) Some automated tools run the hash function on every file, then on every directory, and then on each partition and then store this data securely on the forensic system. This information will be used later to validate the accuracy of the cloning process and confirm that this cloning process has not altered the original disk (evidence) in any way.

The next step is to attach the clone disk to the forensic system and make a *bit-level copy* of the entire original disk on the clone disk. A bit-level copy reproduces exactly the binary bits (ones and zeroes) of the original disk on the clone disk. Two tools that are available for this are an application called Adepto on a Linux distribution called Helix and the Linux command-line utility called dd. Be certain the order of the disks (source and destination) is correct before beginning the cloning process; with the requisite written methodology, experience, and practice, this should be easy.

After the cloning process is complete, run the hashing algorithm on the clone disk and again on the original disk. These two hash values should exactly match the first hash value calculated on the original disk earlier. This verifies that:

- The clone disk is an exact copy of the original disk.
- The original disk has not been altered in any way from the cloning process.

You might need multiple clone disks because some of the analysis will be destructive to some of the data; you might need to repeat the wiping, cloning, and hashing processes.

Analyzing the content on the clone disk

With this complete, the analysis of the disks can begin. Mount a clone disk as an extra disk in a write-protected mode on the forensic system. This keeps all the bits on the clone disk in the exact order as on the original disk. The first task is to recover deleted content from the free and slack space on the clone disk.

FREE SPACE AND SLACK SPACE

To use a hard disk in a computer to store data file, a partition must be created, and then that partition must be formatted. The formatting process builds a *file allocation table* for the partition. This file allocation table might also be called a master file table and is like a table of contents that keeps track of every file written to this partition. The file allocation table lists the name of the file and a handful of attributes for every file placed on this partition. This table also records where (the block) on the partition each file begins.

The formatting process divides the space on the disk first into concentric circles called *tracks*. Then it divides the tracks geometrically into *sectors*. This geometry that is formatted on a hard disk is shown in Figure 6-2.

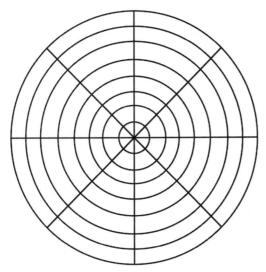

FIGURE 6-2 Tracks and sectors on a hard disk

Within the sectors, the formatting process further divides the space into (typically) 4-kilobyte (KB) *blocks*, also known as *clusters*. When a block is not allocated to any file, it is called *free space* and is available to be written to.

The binary bits that make up files are written in these blocks much like words are written on pages in a book. If a file named File 1 is 17 KB, the file allocation table locates free space on the disk to store the 17 KB of data. The file system writes data into the first 4-KB block and then links the end of that block to the beginning of the next 4-KB block for the file. The file system continues this writing to a 4-KB block and linking to the next block until the whole file is written. In this case, the file system consumes 4 blocks and then places the last 1 KB in a fifth block. The remaining 3 KB of the last block is called *slack space* and is not usable by any other file. This File 1 might grow into that space, but no other file may use that slack space.

> **NOTE SUBALLOCATION OF BLOCKS**
>
> Some older file systems could be configured to use this slack space for a second file (called suballocation of blocks), but this is not common today.

Figure 6-3 shows how files are written into blocks and shows free space and slack space.

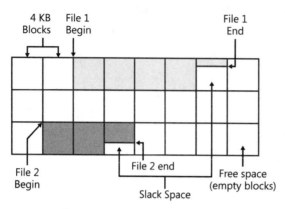

FIGURE 6-3 Free space and slack space

When a file is deleted from a hard disk, almost all file systems simply mark the space that the file occupied as free space by editing the file allocation table. The actual bits that make up the data in the file are not removed from the disk and remain intact on the disk until that space is needed for some other disk write. These data bits remaining from the deleted content are called remnants and are recoverable until they are overwritten. Remnants exist in many (most?) free blocks and in the slack space.

Some files can be a multiple of 4 KB plus 1 or 2 extra bytes, and some files might be just shy of some multiple of 4 KB. Statistically speaking, on average, 50 percent of the last block of each file is slack space. Because the (typical) block size is 4 KB, that says that for every file on a partition, there are 2 KB of remnants in slack space, and those remnants are recoverable forensic data with potential value as evidence. It is not uncommon for a disk to contain several hundred thousand files times an average of 2 KB slack space per file, equaling, potentially, hundreds of megabytes or even gigabytes of recoverable data from the remnants in the slack space:

(# of files on a partition) × 2 KB = potential volume of remnant data in slack space

 A tool called Foremost can recover remnants, available on the Helix distribution disk mentioned earlier. This process of recovering deleted content may be referred to as carving. The content that Foremost recovers must be captured to a different disk, called a *collection disk*, first because the clone disk should be mounted as read-only and, second, because you don't want to write on the disk you are recovering content from, which would potentially overwrite the content you are trying to recover. The collection disk should be at least as large as the disk being analyzed, and the collection disk should be wiped and documented prior to using it in the forensic investigation of the disk.

HIDDEN CONTENT

Another area of interest is to locate any hidden content. To cover their tracks, attackers will often hide their malware, tools, and captured data. They might use the simple hidden attribute on the file with the *attrib +H filename* command. (Remember RASH: read-only, archive, system, hidden?) Although this is easy for the bad guy to implement, it isn't very effective. Another simple but relatively easily detected technique to hide content is simply to rename the file extension. If the content to hide is an executable, tuck the file away in some rarely accessed directory and rename the extension from .exe to .inf, .cfg, or any other nonexecutable file extension. If the content to hide is an image file, rename the extension from .jpg to .inf,.. cfg, or any other nonimage file extension.

A good attacker will create hidden partitions or *stream* her covert files into other, innocuous files. Partitioning tools can create and identify hidden partitions. The cp utility from the NT 4.0 resource kit can stream any file of any size into a host file without changing the size of the host file. The hidden streamed file can be extracted and used when needed and then tucked back away for later use.

Another technique to hide data is through *steganography*, by which the data is embedded within an audio, video, or still photograph file. Steganography is covered in detail in Chapter 3.

Recover any hidden content that can be located to a separate collection disk for further inspection and analysis.

OTHER CONTENT FOR ANALYSIS

Begin with a review of all files on the disk. Due to the nature of the breach, there will probably be targets of particular interest. Be sure to identify any encrypted files and consider the cost benefit aspect of trying to crack the key (often based on or protected by a password). Look through the browser cookies, the favorites (bookmarks), and the temporary Internet files. Review the temporary operating system files and the swap file. Look into the shortcuts that are made conveniently available.

For any of the interesting files, examine the *modify/access/create (MAC) times* to help establish a timeline of activity. Create time is when the file was added to the file system, the access time is when the file was last read, and the modify time is when the file was last written to. Analyze any exploit code you find on the system. This analysis can identify the skill level of the attacker, the vulnerabilities the code relies on, and might even provide an indication of how and where communications occurred with the system.

Several additional areas can be explored better by booting into the operating system on the hard disk (if one exists) after all previously described analysis is complete. Consider reconfiguring the system to do this. Details such as the browsing history, email—sent, received, deleted, and unsent drafts—as well as network connections and mapped network drives can be pursued when the operating system is mounted. This will alter the data on the disk and might be hazardous to other networked systems. It should be done only when the system has no network connections and when you can afford to violate the integrity of this specific copy of the original disk.

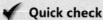

Quick check

1. What type of copy is required for forensic analysis?
2. What do you use to verify that the clone disk is identical to the original disk?

Quick check answers

1. A bit-level copy of the entire disk
2. Hashing algorithms

Exercises

In the following exercises, you apply what you've learned in this chapter. The answers for the exercises are located in the "Answers" section at the end of this chapter. There is no answer for Exercise 6-2.

Exercise 6-1

As a planning exercise for an upcoming forensic investigation of the remnants on a confiscated hard disk drive, you must identify the amount of free space on the hard drive of a system, one of the two places where remnants can be found on a hard disk. Further, you must calculate the estimated number of remnants to be collected from the slack space on the disk. Perform these functions on a hard disk drive in your computer and identify the free space and slack space.

Exercise 6-2

Download the Helix3 .iso file (Helix2009R1.iso) and the Darik's Boot and Nuke .iso file (dban-2.2.7_i586.iso). Both distributions are free. Burn these two ISOs to optical CD media.

The Helix3 .iso file can be found at:
https://www.e-fense.com/store/index.php?_a=viewProd&productId=11.

The Darik's Boot and Nuke .iso file can be found at:
http://www.dban.org/download.

> **WARNING!** **BE CAREFUL TO RUN THESE PROGRAMS ON UNIMPORTANT DISKS**
>
> Some of the utilities on the Helix3 disk could be destructive to data on your system. If you run any of the utilities, run them on a spare disk that contains copies of data that can be lost. Furthermore, do not run the DBAN wiping utilities on any disks that contain anything you want to keep. The point of using this utility is to destroy all data on the target disk completely.
>
> To return the system to its normal booting process, remove the bootable CD from the system and restart the system.

Boot a computer on the Helix3 disk and explore the tools and utilities. Launch the Adepto forensics tool. Observe the Restore/Clone tab where bit-level disk copies can be produced. What media types and drive interfaces does the Adepto utility support? This can be found on the Device Info tab in Adepto v2.0.

Boot a computer on the DBAN disk. Explore the various wiping algorithms, the disk selection options, and the wiping utility. Identify the disk wiping methods available on the DBAN utility and the number of overwrites (passes) each method uses.

Chapter summary

- The definition of a computer crime varies greatly from country to country and state to state but generally includes:
    - **Data theft**   Financial account info, personally identifiable information (PII), intellectual property, trade secrets
    - **Denial of service (DoS)**
    - **Data alteration**   Fraud
    - **System takeover**   Command and control, botnet, army of zombies
    - **Child pornography**
    - **Social engineering**   Phishing, scams
    - **Dumpster diving**   Not exactly a crime, but losses still incurred due to exposure of sensitive information, intellectual property
- A computer can become involved in a computer crime as the target, as the attack, and as a support system for the crime.
- Law systems around the world include codified law systems, common law systems, customary law systems, religious law systems, and hybrid legal systems. Legal instruments to protect intellectual property include patent, copyright, trademark, and trade secret.

- Formal agreements must be in place with any third-party service provider that has access to any information asset of the enterprise so that those third parties will be managed in a way that matches or exceeds the standards defined within the policies of the enterprise.

- Incident response typically envolves several stages, including monitoring, detecting, and notifying; triage; investigation; containment; analysis; tracking; recovery; reporting; and prevention.

- For evidence to be admissible, it must be properly collected with a properly documented chain of custody and be protected from alteration of any kind.

- Analyze a bit-level copy of magnetic media during the forensic analysis. Never analyze the original. Wipe and document all clone and collection media prior to using it during a forensic analysis.

Chapter review

Test your knowledge of the information in this chapter by answering these questions. The answers to these questions, and the explanations of why each answer choice is correct or incorrect, are located in the "Answers" section at the end of this chapter.

1. Which relatively new type of attack is sophisticated, targeted, slow, and stealthy?

    A. Dumpster diving

    B. A worm infection of email servers

    C. Advanced persistent threat (APT)

    D. A virus infection distributed in a file system utility download

2. Which of the following is used during forensic analysis to help establish a timeline of a computer crime?

    A. MAC times

    B. Chain of custody

    C. Codified laws

    D. Trans-border information flow

3. Which of the following is an example of self-regulation?

    A. Sarbanes-Oxley (SOX)

    B. Gramm-Leach-Bliley Act (GLBA)

    C. Payment Card Industry Data Security Standard (PCI-DSS)

    D. Third-party governance

4. A computer that is attacked and compromised and then used to attack deeper into a network, where valuable assets are stored, became involved in the computer crime in which manner?

   A. As an advanced persistent threat (APT)

   B. As a target

   C. As a support system used during a computer crime

   D. As a clone system

5. Which phase of incident response involves taking specific actions to reduce or stop the losses of an active breach of security?

   A. Triage

   B. Containment

   C. Prevention

   D. Recovery

6. Which of the following is the primary concern of the evidence life cycle when investigating a computer crime?

   A. Photograph the scene of the crime

   B. Present the evidence in court

   C. Collect digital evidence following the order of volatility (OOV)

   D. Document and protect the integrity of the evidence

7. Which of the following most accurately describes the priorities when forensically analyzing digital evidence?

   A. Analyze a bit-level clone of the disk.

   B. Review the log files on the clone disk.

   C. Perform a steganographic analysis on the clone disk.

   D. Identify malicious code on the clone disk.

8. Which of the following best describes the requirements to avoid printed data from being hearsay evidence in court?

   A. Present supporting data to show that enticement, not entrapment, was used to obtain the printed data.

   B. Present the printed data and the digital media or show that the printed data is generated on a regular basis for business purposes.

   C. Present supporting data to show that the appropriate chain of custody was completed.

   D. Prove that the printed data was obtained following proper search and seizure requirements.

Answers

This section contains the answers to the exercises and the "Chapter review" section in this chapter.

Exercise 6-1

On a Windows system, launch a DOS prompt.

Start > Run > CMD > Enter

At the command prompt, change to the root of the target disk.

C: > Enter

Enter the command to identify the free space on the disk and the number of files on the disk.

dir /s

The /s switch lists all files in all subdirectories. This command might run for a few minutes, depending on the size of the disk and the number of directories and files on the disk. A sample of the results is shown in Figure 6-4.

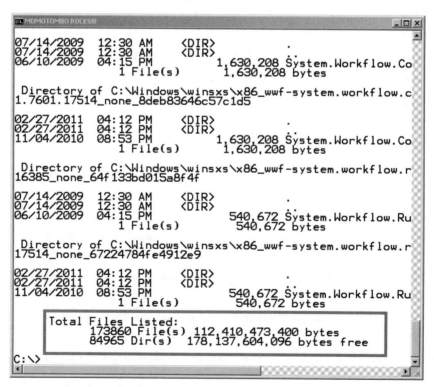

FIGURE 6-4 Sample results of executing the dir /s command

In the example shown, there is 178 GB of free space that could contain remnants. The example also shows that there are 173,860 files on the partition (the C volume). Using the statistical estimate that 50 percent of the last 4 KB block used by each file is slack space that could contain remnants, the calculation follows:

*173,860 files × (50% * 4 KB block) =*
173,860 files × 2 KB =
173,860 files x 2048 B = approximately 350 MB of slack space

178 GB of free space

350 MB of slack space

Exercise 6-2

Adepto (v2.1) from the Helix3 disk supports the following media types and drive interfaces:

- IDE drive interface
- USB drive interface
- Firewire drive interface
- RAID arrays
- CD/DVD drives
- Memory sticks
- Smart media flash memory drives

Darik's Boot and Nuke provides the following disk wiping options:

- Quick Erase 1 pass
- RCMP TSSIT OPS-II 8 passes
- DoD Short 3 passes
- DoD 5220.22-M 7 passes
- Gutmann Wipe 35 passes
- PRNG stream 4 or 8 passes

Chapter review

1. **Correct answer: C**

   A. **Incorrect:** Dumpster diving isn't sophisticated.

   B. **Incorrect:** A worm is a shotgun or grazing, opportunistic type of attack.

   C. **Correct:** The APT uses many tools and techniques over a long period to compromise a specific target covertly.

   D. **Incorrect:** A virus is a shotgun or grazing, opportunistic type of attack.

2. **Correct answer: A**

   A. **Correct:** The modify, access, create times recorded by most file systems are often used by forensic investigators to establish a timeline that supports the claim of a criminal act.

   B. **Incorrect:** The chain of custody tracks evidence from the time it is identified until it is presented in court to verify that it has not been altered in any way.

   C. **Incorrect:** Codified laws are written rules of conduct for various societies around the planet.

   D. **Incorrect:** Trans-border information flow is a concern because the information being sent across international borders might not be legal within that country.

3. **Correct answer: C**

   A. **Incorrect:** Sarbanes-Oxley is a law that requires publicly held companies to report their financial data accurately. This requires adequate protection of their information systems to ensure integrity of their data.

   B. **Incorrect:** GLBA is a law that requires financial institutions to protect the personally identifiable information of their customers adequately.

   C. **Correct:** PCI-DSS is an industry regulation developed and enforced by the payment card industry, an example of an industry regulating itself.

   D. **Incorrect:** Third-party governance requires any third party (nonemployee) that has access to any information assets of the enterprise to meet or exceed the requirements defined by the policies of the enterprise. This is commonly defined and enforced through contractual agreements.

4. **Correct answer: B**

   A. **Incorrect:** APT is a type of attack, not a computer system.

   B. **Correct:** The computer first was attacked. This makes it the target of that first attack and compromise.

C. **Incorrect:** The computer was first a target and then was used as the attack system, but nothing indicated it was used in any other way, such as a support system.

D. **Incorrect:** The term is incorrect and is based on a clone disk used to receive an exact, bit-level copy of an original disk. The clone disk is then used to analyze the data forensically.

5. **Correct answer: B**

A. **Incorrect:** Triage identifies priorities related to the breach to act on first, but does not yet take any action.

B. **Correct:** Containment is action taken to mitigate or stop the losses occurring from an active breach.

C. **Incorrect:** Prevention includes taking action to mitigate and stop losses, but not for an active breach.

D. **Incorrect:** Recovery includes actions to return the environment to a normal state after the losses have been mitigated or stopped.

6. **Correct answer: D**

A. **Incorrect:** Photographing the scene is an important step in the investigation process, but documenting and protecting the integrity of the evidence is critical for all forms of evidence.

B. **Incorrect:** Evidence can be denied in court if the integrity of the evidence cannot be substantiated.

C. **Incorrect:** Collecting evidence properly, like the OOV, is an important step in the investigation process, but documenting and protecting the integrity of the evidence is critical for all forms of evidence.

D. **Correct:** Documenting and protecting the integrity of the evidence is critical for all forms of evidence. Otherwise, the evidence can easily be deemed inadmissible and therefore of no value at all.

7. **Correct answer: A**

A. **Correct:** The analysis of digital data should only ever be performed on a bit-level copy of the original disk.

B. **Incorrect:** Log files should be reviewed but are often reviewed (read-only) on the functioning original system and, if on a clone disk, must be based on the bit-level copy to substantiate the integrity of the logs.

C. **Incorrect:** A steganographic review should be performed on a clone disk but must be based on the bit-level copy to substantiate the integrity of the findings.

D. **Incorrect:** Any malicious code identified should be reviewed on a clone disk but must be based on the bit-level copy to substantiate the integrity of the findings.

8. **Correct answer: B**

   A. **Incorrect:** Enticement and entrapment are evidence admissibility issues but are not directly related to hearsay evidence.

   B. **Correct:** The printed copy of digital data is hearsay unless the printed copy is generated on a regular basis, such as a weekly report that shows some evidence, or if the digital media can also be presented to validate the integrity of the actual original data, along with the printed copy as a more readable form produced directly from the original digital data.

   C. **Incorrect:** Appropriate chain of custody is an evidence admissibility issue but is not directly related to hearsay evidence.

   D. **Incorrect:** Appropriate search and seizure procedures are evidence admissibility issues but are not directly related to hearsay evidence.

CHAPTER 7

Telecommunications and network security

The vast majority of the valuable information assets of an organization either establish the networking infrastructure or are accessed over the networking infrastructure. Because the world has evolved to a state in which most information is stored and accessed electronically, a deep understanding of the architectures, systems, protocols, and processes that make up the networking infrastructure is required if you hope to secure these assets.

Although much of this chapter addresses the technical aspects, you should also recognize the need to secure physical access to the systems that make up the networking infrastructure, including the servers in the data center and elsewhere. The infrastructure systems consist of many elements, such as:

- Application and data storage servers.

- Directory services support systems.

- Routers, firewalls, and switches.

- Network access systems such as virtual private network (VPN) concentrators, Remote Authentication Dial-In User Service (RADIUS), Terminal Access Controller Access Control System (TACACS), and diameter systems.

- Wireless access points.

- Endpoint client systems such as stationary workstations, portable laptops, and mobile handheld devices such as smart phones for remote access and administration.

Exam objectives in this chapter:

Real world

Understanding network attacks

When I was a network engineering student studying for my first network engineering certification nearly a thousand years ago (so it seems), I was appalled at the notion that I had to learn this academic model related to networking, this OSI Model. What a waste of my time, when I had many juicier targets to study. I wanted to configure those ARCnet interfaces in the proper order, chase down a supply of 50-ohm BNC terminators (you never know when you're going to need one of these bad boys), install that Novell 2 server (from a tall stack of floppy disks), and build my own Ethernet cables. That was the cool stuff. Please, don't make me waste my valuable time studying this intangible, academic OSI Model.

However, over time, I came to realize how rational this model was and how I understood much more about how networks operate by understanding the model. I knew more about protocols and functions than I was ever told because I understood where and how these functions occurred and interoperated with other functions within the model. In retrospect, my instructors did me a favor by forcing this academic model down my throat.

Begin your networking studies with the classic OSI Model. Understand that first, but then recognize that this model is growing old, and many newer technologies don't fit into the model very well. That is OK. You know your network engineering foundation is strong when you can identify technologies that break the classic rules of the OSI Model.

The Open Systems Interconnection (OSI) Model

In the early days of network engineering, to be able to use an application over a network connection, the application itself would include the networking components. To run Lotus 1-2-3 on a network, the application would provide the network driver stack, which would need to be installed. If you wanted to use a second application on a network, it could not use the Lotus drivers; its own network driver stack had to be installed. Quite often, these sets of network drivers from different vendors would not play well together, and one or both would fail when installed on the same computer. A consistent implementation of the networking functions wasn't required for multiple applications to share a connection to the network.

Then came the OSI Model from the International Organization for Standardization (ISO). (The acronym is based on the Greek word *isos*, meaning "equal" so that it would be the same in every language.) The ISO was established in 1946 and is based in Geneva, Switzerland. It is an international, nongovernmental organization that defines and publishes standards intended for voluntary adoption by governments and industries. It has published more than 18,500 international standards to date.

The OSI Model organizes and divides the processes required for an application on a computer to access a network connection, transmit the data across the network, and return the data to a usable state for the application on a remote computer system. The model breaks up these processes into seven layers, with each layer only needing to perform its specific collection of tasks and to communicate with the layer directly above and the layer directly below. This segregates the work into specialized sections so the application developers can focus on developing their applications and remain isolated from the actual details of the networking processes; it enables the network hardware and software developers to remain isolated from the application that is using their network. The model provides one networking stack all applications can use and seven layers in the stack to allow for specialization of the required data processing outbound on the sending system, across the network, and then inbound on the receiving system.

The OSI Model is an academic reference model. It greatly improves the interoperability of networking components (hardware and software) and makes understanding the flow of data from application, down through the network stack, and across a network much easier. However, the model is growing outdated. Many newer technologies and protocols simply do not fit into the model as originally conceived. Although the model is worthy of study, don't become too rigid in the assignment of a device, process, or protocol to a specific layer because implementation of these devices, processes, and protocols in the real world is often different than this academic model specifies. Many ambiguities are to be found and debated; each position is potentially reasonable and accurate.

The seven layers of the OSI Model

The OSI Model breaks up the processes required to prepare, transmit, and reconstruct data from an application on one system to an application on a remote system. The seven layers of the OSI Model are numbered from one to seven, beginning at the bottom of the stack, and are shown in Table 7-1.

TABLE 7-1 The seven layers of the OSI Model

Layer	Name
7	Application
6	Presentation
5	Session
4	Transport
3	Network
2	Data link
1	Physical

EXAM TIP

For the exam, you need to know the order of the layers in the OSI Model and the various functions, devices, and protocols that operate at those layers.

Specific and discrete tasks are to be performed at each layer. A layer communicates with adjacent layers through application programming interfaces (APIs) that control how and when that communication occurs. A layer does its work, packages its results into a predefined structure, and then hands it up (or down, depending on whether inbound or outbound processing is involved) at the right time. Adjacent layers don't need to know or care what is happening at any other layer. A layer just needs to know when and how to receive information to do its own work and then to hand the information to the appropriate adjacent layer.

Many people use a mnemonic based on the acronym of the layers (from Layer 1 to Layer 7, PDNTSPA) to memorize the seven layers in order. The most common (and the most boring) mnemonic is shown in Table 7-2 as Mnemonic 1, read top to bottom. A slightly less boring (but not much less) mnemonic is shown as Mnemonic 2, read bottom to top. Feel free to make up your own, perhaps one a bit more colorful and memorable.

> **MORE INFO** THE OSI MODEL BY ISO
>
> For more information about the Open Systems Interconnection (OSI) Model, see the International Standard ISO/IEC 7498 (1984) at *http://www.ecma-international.org/activities/ Communications/TG11/s020269e.pdf*.

TABLE 7-2 Tools to memorize the seven layers of the OSI Model

OSI model		Mnemonic 1	Mnemonic 2
7	Application	All	Away
6	Presentation	People	Pizza
5	Session	Seem	Sausage
4	Transport	To	Throw
3	Network	Need	Not
2	Data link	Data	Do
1	Physical	Processing	Please

The sections following describe the seven layers of the OSI Model in detail, from Layer 7, the Application layer, to Layer 1, the Physical layer, where data is transmitted onto the network media. This order follows a process in which a user who runs applications *above* Layer 7 of the OSI Model attempts to transmit data from an application on the local computer (the source system) to a remote computer (the destination system). Recognize that on the remote computer, the system receiving the transmission, the process will be in the reverse order, beginning with Layer 1, the Physical layer, where the network interface card on the remote computer is receiving the inbound bits, and proceeding upward through the stack toward Layer 7, as shown in Figure 7-1.

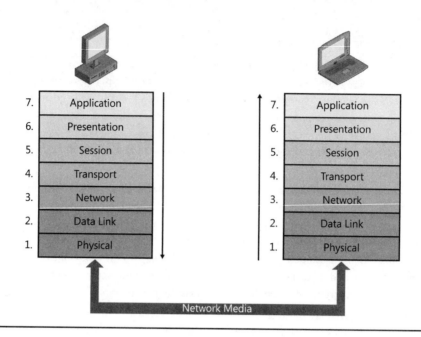

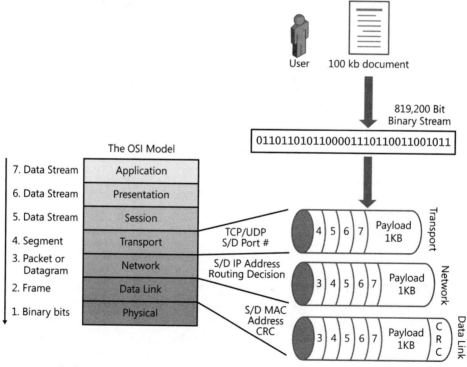

FIGURE 7-1 The flow of data through the OSI Model

As the seven layers are described in the following sections, many protocols and devices are introduced. Many of these are described in detail later in this chapter.

Layer 7: The Application layer

Layer 7 is the Application layer, which is considered the most intelligent layer and the most abstract from physical hardware. The primary function of this layer is to provide access to the network for the applications and processes the user and the operating systems use. This layer provides flow control and error recovery. It performs this work for an outbound network transmission and then communicates with Layer 6, the Presentation layer, to continue the processing. For inbound network transmissions, the Application layer receives information from the Presentation layer to complete the transmission.

The *gateway function* can operate at all layers of the OSI Model, so it can operate at the most intelligent layer; it's therefore often said to be a Layer 7 function. The gateway function converts one protocol to a similar but different protocol, like a Layer 7 Simple Mail Transfer Protocol (SMTP) gateway that converts to the earlier standard X.400 message transport protocol, or a Layer 4 and Layer 3 gateway between TCP/IP and Internetwork Packet Exchange/Sequenced Package Exchange (IPX/SPX) that was used in Novell days. Many hardware vendors sell devices that perform a gateway function and call the devices gateways. Recognize that the device isn't the gateway. The gateway is the function occurring within the device that is converting between two similar but different protocols.

Some protocols that operate at Layer 7 are:

- **HTTP**   Hypertext Transfer Protocol
- **FTP**   File Transfer Protocol
- **SMTP**   Simple Mail Transfer Protocol
- **DNS**   Domain Name System
- **DHCP**   Dynamic Host Configuration Protocol
- **SIP**   Session Initiation Protocol (used in VoIP)
- **NTP**   Network Time Protocol (used to synchronize system clocks on a network)
- **SSH**   Secure Shell (encrypted network channel)
- **Telnet**   Used to perform remote administration
- **LPD**   Line Printer Daemon (UNIX / Linux Print server services)

> **NOTE   DAEMON? WHAT IS A DAEMON?**
> The term "daemon" refers to a server service offered on computers that run UNIX-based and Linux-based operating systems. It is the Gaelic spelling of the word "demon," implying possession of mysterious and unseen powers, such as those offered by a remote server.

Imagine the user is working on a Microsoft Word document that is 100 KB in size, as shown in Figure 7-1, and that user wants to save her work. The user selects File | Save As and then pokes her way to a storage device, either connected to the local computer or perhaps on a network file server. The Application layer provides Word the option to save the file on some network location. If the user decides to save the file on her local hard disk drive, the network won't be needed. If the user decides to save the file to the remote file server, the process will work down through the OSI Model to pass the file to the network location.

> **NOTE** **TCP/IP AND STANDARD ETHERNET**
>
> Most corporate and home networks today use TCP/IP and standard Ethernet, so this analogy will be based on those standards.

When a user wants to save a file on a remote server or print to a print server, she identifies the remote system by its friendly name, either its hostname or its NetBIOS name. These names are often intuitive to humans and are designed to help us identify the system we want. However, the networking functions, the way in which data moves from the local system to a remote system, don't operate using names. That friendly, intuitive name must be resolved to the system's IP address so the networking functions can operate properly. Some form of name resolution must be present and correctly configured on every node on the network to facilitate this need. Most networks rely on DNS to provide this name-to-IP-address resolution. Other name resolution services can be provided by using a *hosts* file, an *lmhosts* file (LAN Manager hosts file), Windows Internet Name Services (WINS), or the older NetBIOS name resolution broadcast. Using one of these methods, a source system must identify the IP address of the destination system for any IP network transmission to occur.

At Layer 7, the data being prepared for transfer over the network exists in a continuous binary *data stream*.

Layer 6: The Presentation layer

Layer 6 is the Presentation layer; it converts file formats, as necessary, from whatever the application uses to a *standard format* that is compatible with the intended protocols and network. Layer 6 performs encryption and compression and can change the character set (for example, between ACSII and EBCDIC coded files) when required. The function that identifies whether the destination is local or remote, and then selects the correct network, is called the *redirector* and operates here at Layer 6.

For an outbound network transmission, the Presentation layer receives information from Layer 7 above and performs this work. It then communicates with Layer 5, the Session layer, to continue the processing. For inbound network transmissions, the Presentation layer receives information up from the Session layer for processing and then passes the processed information up to the Application layer.

Some protocols that operate at Layer 6 are:

- **XML** Extensible Markup Language
- **MIME** Multipurpose Internet Message Extensions

At Layer 6, the data being prepared for transfer over the network exists in a continuous data stream.

Layer 5: The Session layer

Layer 5 of the OSI Model is the Session layer. It negotiates and establishes session-related services with the application processes between the local system and the remote destination endpoint of the network transmission. It is responsible for naming resources and negotiates dialog control and the use of half-duplex or full-duplex over the network connection. For the sake of completeness and comparison, simplex, which isn't typically used on data networks, is also described here.

- **Simplex**   One-way communication, only and ever, from a transmitter to one or more receivers. Simplex is like an FM radio station broadcasting its signal to FM radios, but the FM radios can never communicate back upstream to the FM broadcasting system.

- **Half-duplex**   Both ends can send and receive, but the ends must take turns acting as transmitter while the other is receiving. Half-duplex operates like walkie-talkies. If both ends attempt to transmit at the same time, neither ever hears the other.

- **Full-duplex**   Both ends can send and receive at the same time. Full-duplex provides the best throughput.

If a network application requires multiple sessions, Layer 5 coordinates these different data streams to reassemble and synchronize them properly at the destination and performs session-based authentication and session restart for stalled sessions.

Layer 5 implements an efficient form of error detection and correction by inserting *checkpoints* into the data stream before transmission. If a section of the data stream is corrupted during transmission for any reason, only the section between the nearest checkpoints needs to be retransmitted.

For an outbound network transmission, the Session layer receives information from Layer 6 above and performs this work. The Session layer then communicates with Layer 4, the Transport layer below, to continue the processing. For inbound network transmissions, the Session layer receives information up from the Transport layer for processing and then passes the processed information up to the Presentation layer.

Some protocols that operate at Layer 5 are:

- **RPC**   Remote procedure calls
- **NetBIOS**   Network Basic Input/Output System
- **Named Pipes**
- **SQL**   Structured Query Language
- **NFS**   Network File System (file server on UNIX/Linux server)
- **PPTP**   Point-to-Point Tunneling Protocol
- **SSL**   Secure Sockets Layer (operates at Layers 4 and 5)
- **TLS**   Transport Layer Security (operates at Layers 4 and 5)

At Layer 5, the data being prepared for transfer over the network still exists in a continuous data stream.

Layer 4: The Transport layer

Layer 4 of the OSI Model is the Transport layer, also called the end-to-end layer or host-to-host layer. By the time the processes get to the Transport layer, the outbound network has been identified, and the payload size for each frame is known. The Transport layer breaks up the contiguous data stream into segments that fit into the payload. A standard Ethernet network uses a frame with about a 1 KB payload, so the data stream of 100 KB (in the earlier example and Figure 7-1) will be broken into approximately 100 segments (eventually frames) for transmission over the network. Each 1 KB payload is prepended with the Layer 7, 6, 5, and 4 header information, in that order, as shown in Figure 7-2. Layer 7, 6, and 5 header information tells the destination system what steps to perform to reassemble the payload into a copy of the original file as the payload is processed up the layers of the OSI Model. Layer 4 header information identifies the source and destination port numbers, a segment number (so that the segments can be reassembled in the correct order by the recipient at the destination), and information telling the destination system which transport protocol to use.

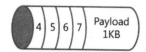

FIGURE 7-2 The Layer 4 segment—header and payload

For an outbound network transmission, the Transport layer receives information from the Session layer above and performs this work. The Transport layer then communicates with Layer 3, the Network layer, to continue the processing. For inbound network transmissions, the Transport layer receives information up from the Network layer for processing and then passes the processed information up to the Session layer.

Some protocols that operate at Layer 4 are:

- **TCP** Transmission Control Protocol
- **UDP** User Datagram Protocol
- **NetBEUI** NetBIOS Extended User Interface
- **SSL** Secure Sockets Layer (operates at Layers 4 and 5)
- **TLS** Transport Layer Security (operates at Layers 4 and 5)
- **SPX** Sequenced Packet Exchange (old Novell)
- **ATP** AppleTalk Transaction Protocol
- **WTLS** Wireless Transport Layer Security

 At Layer 4, the data and header information being prepared for transfer over the network exist in a *segment*.

TCP AND UDP

These days, almost every network uses the TCP/IP protocol suite for the transport and network protocols. The developer of the network-aware application designs the decision to use Transmission Control Protocol (TCP) or User Datagram Protocol (UDP) into the application as the Layer 4 transport protocol, based on the nature of the data and the application that uses the data. *TCP* is an expensive (slower), connection-oriented, guaranteed delivery transport protocol and guarantees no duplicate or missing segments. *UDP* is a less expensive (faster), connectionless, best-effort (not guaranteed delivery) transport protocol. TCP is like using an expensive letter or package delivery service, with the delivery being confirmed (signed for) with an acknowledgement of receipt from the recipient. UDP is like using the post office, costing much less, with only attempted and unconfirmed delivery to the identified destination. With UDP, the sender never really knows whether it was delivered to the right destination or even whether the intended recipient ever received the letter. The Layer 4 header on the segment identifies which transport protocol the network is to use for this delivery.

Many types of data become useless unless every single bit and byte of the file is received correctly. This includes most data files and program-related files. For this type of data, to ensure that every bit and byte is received correctly, the developer who writes the application that creates, edits, or transfers the file over a network decides that the sender will pay the higher price of using TCP to guarantee delivery and ensure that the transferred content remains usable. The higher price of using TCP comes in the overhead related to establishing and tearing down a TCP session by using the three-way-handshake, the flow control, the positive acknowledgements for each segment the destination receives, and the automatic retransmission of any packets the destination does not acknowledge. All this extra handshaking and acknowledging takes time and bandwidth on the network, so time and network bandwidth consumption are parts of the increased price when using TCP for the transport protocol. The TCP header is shown in Figure 7-3.

BYTE	\multicolumn{8}{c}{0}	\multicolumn{8}{c}{1}	\multicolumn{8}{c}{2}	\multicolumn{8}{c}{3}
BIT	0 1 2 3 4 5 6 7	8 9 10 11 12 13 14 15	16 17 18 19 20 21 22 23	24 25 26 27 28 29 30 31
0	\multicolumn{2}{c}{SOURCE PORT}	\multicolumn{2}{c}{DESTINATION PORT}		
4	\multicolumn{4}{c}{SEQUENCE NUMBER}			
8	\multicolumn{4}{c}{ACKNOWLEDGEMENT NUMBER (IF ACK SET)}			
12	DATA OFFSET / RES 0 0 0 / N S C W R E C E U R G A C K P S H R S T S Y N F I N		WINDOW SIZE	
16	CHECKSUM		URGENT POINTER (IF URG SET)	
20 ...	\multicolumn{4}{c}{OPTIONS (IF DATA OFFSET > 5) ...}			
BYTE				

FIGURE 7-3 The TCP header

There are six basic types of TCP segments, indicated by flag bits set to 1:

- **URG (Urgent)**   Identifies that some of the data payload contains urgent data and instructs that portion, identified by an Urgent Pointer value, to be processed immediately. This flag is rarely used, but when it is used, it is typically used in combination with the PSH flag.

- **ACK (Acknowledge)**   Confirms receipt and agreement.

- **PSH (Push)**   Instructs the recipient system to process this data up the stack now, without waiting for the receive buffer to fill.

- **RST (Reset)**   A one-frame session teardown used to terminate a TCP session quickly.

- **SYN (Synchronize)**   Synchronizes the source system's send buffer to match the size of the destination system's receive buffer and vice versa; initiates a TCP session during the TCP three-way handshake.

- **FIN (Final)**   Signals the end of the TCP session.

Three relatively new flags (as of 2001) identify network congestion and adjust the TCP flow controls to accommodate that congestion:

- **NS (Nonce Sum)**   Manages data flow and acknowledgements

- **CWR (Congestion Windows Reduced)**   Responds to an ECE flag identifying network congestion and enables congestion control mechanisms within the TCP session

- **ECE (Explicit Congestion Notification (ECN) Echo)**   Signals that the recipient is capable of using ECN (SYN = 1) or that a Congestion Experienced segment has been received (SYN = 0)

The transport protocol UDP, however, does not establish a session and does not handshake or acknowledge segments. It simply sends the segment out onto the network and hopes it gets to the destination. UDP is therefore faster, uses less network bandwidth, and is a cheaper transport protocol than TCP. If the segment makes it to the destination, that is great! That's the way the system is supposed to work. However, if the segment does not show up at the destination, oh well. The destination will just have to continue on without the information in that segment, or some higher-layer process will have to ask for a retransmission of the missing data, but UDP does not have any error detection or correction built into it.

UDP can be used when the data being transferred is not critical, and a few missing segments will be acceptable, as in time-sensitive audio or video transmissions. If a user is listening to a song over a network connection, and a segment containing the next few notes goes missing, the media player application just skips over the spot with the missing data. There isn't time to wait for a retransmission of the missing data. No need to retransmit that data. UDP is also used for multicast transmissions when one source server is streaming data to potentially thousands of destination multicast client computers. Establishing that many TCP sessions and managing acknowledgements and retransmissions would be quite demanding of the source server and network—if it were even possible. If the nature of a particular multicast transmission requires all data to be received without exception, the multicast application (not UDP) would have to have a mechanism built in at a higher layer to request retransmission of any missing pieces. The UDP header is shown in Figure 7-4.

BYTE	0								1								2								3							
BIT	0	1	2	3	4	5	6	7	8	9	10	11	12	13	14	15	16	17	18	19	20	21	22	23	24	25	26	27	28	29	30	31
0	SOURCE PORT																DESTINATION PORT															
4	LENGTH (UDP HEADER + DATA)																CHECKSUM															
BYTE																																

FIGURE 7-4 The UDP header

THE TCP THREE-WAY-HANDSHAKE

When TCP is selected within the network-aware application, at Layer 4 the client system establishes a TCP session with the server system through a three-way-handshake, using three frames, called SYN, SYN/ACK, and ACK (see Figure 7-5).

1. The client system sends the server system a synchronize (SYN) frame to initiate the negotiation of the TCP session. Included in the SYN frame is the size of the client system's Receive buffer, indicating to the server to synchronize the size of its Send buffer to optimize transmissions from server to client. This frame also defines a client sequence number (A). When the server responds, it increments this value by 1 (A + 1). This frame is called the *SYN* frame.

2. The server system responds with an acknowledgement (ACK) that it understands the client and server systems are entering a TCP session and that it has set its Send buffer to match the size of the client system's Receive buffer. This optimizes transmissions from server to client. In the same frame, the server system also sends a synchronize (SYN) flag and the size of its Receive buffer, telling the client system to synchronize the size of its Send buffer accordingly to optimize transmissions from client to server. This frame also defines a server sequence number (B). When the client responds, it increments this value by 1 (B + 1). This frame is called the *SYN/ACK* frame.

3. The client system responds with an acknowledgement (ACK) that it understands the client and server systems are entering a TCP session and that it has set its Send buffer to match the size of the server system's Receive buffer, optimizing transmissions from client to server. This frame is called the *ACK* frame.

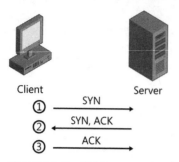

FIGURE 7-5 The TCP three-way-handshake

To terminate the TCP session, each side sends a frame to signal that it is the final (FIN) data to be sent. Each side then sends an acknowledgement (ACK) to confirm the termination of the TCP session. A brief waiting period follows before actual termination, in case any delayed packets are to be delivered that might have been sent before the FIN frame was sent. This is commonly accomplished in a three-way handshake called FIN, FIN/ACK, ACK.

PORTS AND SOCKETS

The Transport layer also identifies *port numbers* that represent different server services running on a system. A server service can also be called a listener or a daemon and is a process running on a network system that listens for inbound client requests for its service. Port numbers can range between port 0 and port 65,535 (64k). Services may use TCP ports, UDP ports, or both, based on the specifics of the function being requested; they often use both. Often, the port number used for a server service is fixed and doesn't change. Many listener (also called server service or daemon) port numbers are defined and reserved for network services by the Internet Assigned Numbers Authority (IANA). IANA defines the ports numbered between 0 and 1023 as the *well-known ports*.

In Table 7-3 are a few examples of some commonly used port numbers and the related server service. Protocols are described in detail later in this chapter.

TABLE 7-3 Commonly used protocols and their port numbers

Network service or protocol		TCP / UDP		Port #
FTP	File Transfer Protocol - Data	TCP		20
FTP	File Transfer Protocol - Control/Command	TCP		21
(Most implementations of FTP channel the FTP data (Port 20) through Port 21)				
SSH	Secure Shell	TCP	UDP	22
	Telnet	TCP		23
SMTP	Simple Mail Transfer Protocol	TCP	UDP	25
DNS	Domain Name System	TCP		53
DHCP	Dynamic Host Configuration Protocol Server		UDP	67
DHCP	Dynamic Host Configuration Protocol Client		UDP	68
TFTP	Trivial File Transfer Protocol	TCP		69
HTTP	Hypertext Transfer Protocol	TCP	UDP	80
	Kerberos Authentication	TCP	UDP	88
POP3	Post Office Protocol v3	TCP		110
NTP	Network Time Protocol		UDP	123
RPC	Remote Procedure Call	TCP		135
	NetBios Name Resolution		UDP	137
	NetBios Datagram Service		UDP	138
	NetBios Session Service	TCP		139
SNMP	Simple Network Management Protocol		UDP	161
SNMP	Simple Network Management Protocol Trap	TCP	UDP	162
LDAP	Lightweight Directory Access Protocol	TCP	UDP	389
HTTPS	Hypertext Transfer Protocol over SSL	TCP		443
SSTP	Secure Socket Tunneling Protocol	TCP		443

Network service or protocol		TCP / UDP		Port #
SMB	Server Message Blocks	TCP		445
IPsec	Internet Protocol Security		UDP	500
	Syslog - Remote logging service		UDP	514
LPD	Line Printer Daemon	TCP		515
L2TP	Layer 2 Tunneling Protocol		UDP	1701
PPTP	Point-to-Point Tunneling Protocol	TCP		1723
RDP	Microsoft's Remote Desktop Protocol	TCP		3389

 Therefore, when a client system wants to use a service on a remote system, it sends its request to the IP address of the server system and the port number of the requested service. The IP address combined with the port number builds a *socket*, which is typically written as IP:Port, so if the IP address of the web server is 192.168.101.50, and the requested service is HTTP (TCP port 80), the destination socket would be written like 192.168.101.50:80.

 Often, a system might run several server services and have several listener ports. Because the client might need multiple sessions with a server, the client tells the server service which client-side port to use when it responds back the client. This way, the client knows which process and request a response from the server is associated with. The client-side port number is usually chosen from a range of higher port numbers. The IANA allocates the range of 49,152 through 65,535 for client-side usage and calls this range the *ephemeral port numbers,* ephemeral meaning "temporary." However, different network operating systems often allocate client-side port numbers from different ranges.

> ✔ **Quick check**
>
> 1. What TCP flags are set to perform the three-way handshake?
> 2. What ports are used in HTTP, DNS, FTP, and SNMP?
>
> **Quick check answers**
>
> 1. SYN, SYN/ACK, and ACK
> 2. Port 80, port 53, port 20, and port 21 (usually just 21) and ports 161 and 162.

Layer 3: The Network layer

Layer 3 of the OSI Model is the Network layer. This is where IP operates. The Network layer deals with addressing hosts and performing routing functions that include the source system making a routing decision (that is, whether the destination is on the local subnet or on a remote subnet), routing at the routers, and possibly fragmentation (at the routers) and reassembly (at the destination system). The router and the packet filter firewall operate at Layer 3 because they make their networking decisions based on Layer 3 information.

For an outbound network transmission, the Network layer receives information from the Transport layer above and performs this work. The Network layer then communicates with Layer 2, The Data Link layer below it, to continue the processing. For inbound network transmissions, the Network layer receives information up from the Data Link layer for processing and then passes the processed information up to the Transport layer.

The router operates at Layer 3. Some of the protocols that operate at Layer 3 are:

- **IPv4** Internet Protocol version 4
- **IPv6** Internet Protocol version 6
- **ICMP** Internet Control Message Protocol
- **IGMP** Internet Group Management Protocol (multicasting)
- **IPsec** Internet Protocol Security (Virtual Private Network (VPN))
- **NAT** Network Address Translation
- **MPLS** Multiprotocol Label Switching (operates between Layers 2 and 3)
- **IPX** Internetwork Packet Exchange (old Novell)

At Layer 3, the data and header information being prepared for transfer over the network exist in a *packet* or *datagram*, as shown in Figure 7-6.

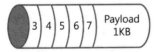

FIGURE 7-6 The Layer 3 packet or datagram, header and payload

Each host (also called *node*) on an IP network must have a minimum of two pieces of IP information configured to be functional on that network, an *IP address* and a *subnet mask*. If the system is on a routed network (and almost all of them are), a third piece of information is required for connection to different IP subnets. This third piece is the IP address of a router connected to the local subnet and other subnets; this router is called the *default gateway*. Although quite a few additional pieces of information might be configured in the IP properties of a system, one more piece of information becomes very helpful, if not absolutely required, and that is the IP address of the DNS server, the system that performs name-to-IP address resolution. The DNS server information is also required on computers that participate in directory services environments. This IP configuration information is shown in Figure 7-7.

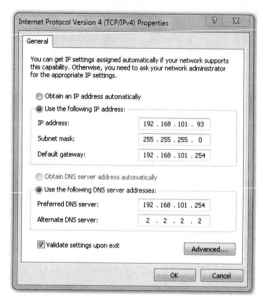

FIGURE 7-7 IPv4 properties configuration

INTERNET PROTOCOL VERSION 4

IPv4 is a 32-bit logical addressing scheme that assigns a unique address to each host on a network. These 32 bits are broken up into four sets of eight bits called octets, which are typically converted from binary to decimal and are separated by dots. The IPv4 address must be accompanied by a 32-bit subnet mask value to identify which part of the IP address represents the network (subnet) address and which part of the IP address represents an unambiguous host on that subnet.

Because every host requires a unique IPv4 address on the Internet, and with the explosive growth of the Internet, available 32-bit IPv4 addresses were running out. As a temporary solution for the problem, Network Address Translation (NAT) was introduced. It allows a boundary device, such as a firewall at the edge of a corporate network, to share a small number of public IPv4 addresses with many nodes on the private network, reducing the number of public IPv4 addresses a company needs.

Most networks in the United States still operate on IPv4 addressing, but the world is migrating to IPv6.

In IPv4, each packet is prepended with the Layer 3 header information to identify source and destination IP addresses, a time-to-live (TTL) value, fragmentation information, and type of service. The IPv4 header is shown in Figure 7-8.

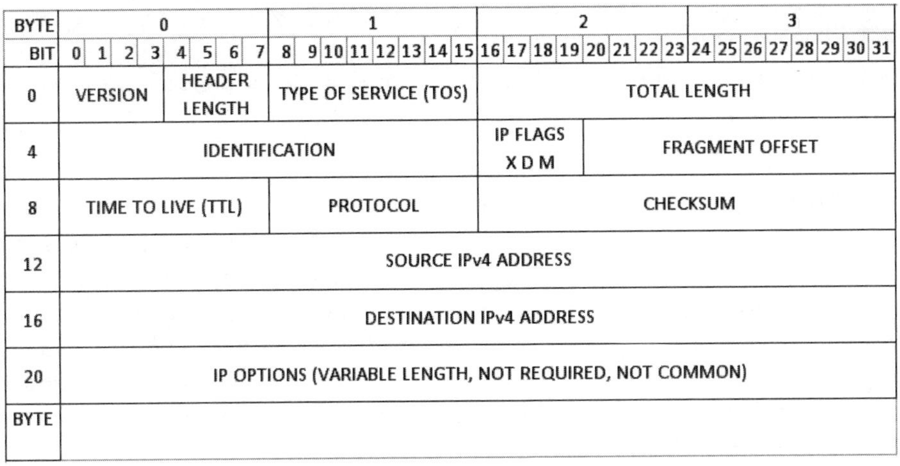

BYTE	0								1								2								3							
BIT	0	1	2	3	4	5	6	7	8	9	10	11	12	13	14	15	16	17	18	19	20	21	22	23	24	25	26	27	28	29	30	31
0	VERSION				HEADER LENGTH				TYPE OF SERVICE (TOS)								TOTAL LENGTH															
4	IDENTIFICATION																IP FLAGS X D M			FRAGMENT OFFSET												
8	TIME TO LIVE (TTL)								PROTOCOL								CHECKSUM															
12	SOURCE IPv4 ADDRESS																															
16	DESTINATION IPv4 ADDRESS																															
20	IP OPTIONS (VARIABLE LENGTH, NOT REQUIRED, NOT COMMON)																															
BYTE																																

FIGURE 7-8 The IPv4 header

NOTE **IPV4**

IPv4 is covered in more detail later in this chapter in the section "Protocols, protocols, and more protocols."

INTERNET PROTOCOL VERSION 6

To solve the problem of running out of IPv4 addresses, the Internet Engineering Task Force (IETF) introduced Internet Protocol version 6 (IPv6). IPv6 is 128 bits long, allowing for a tremendous number of unique IP addresses, approximately 34 with 37 zeros. With that many bits available, many new features can be identified in the IPv6 address, features that tend to violate the OSI Model because they exist outside Layer 3 where IPv6 theoretically operates.

The IPv6 header is shown in Figure 7-9.

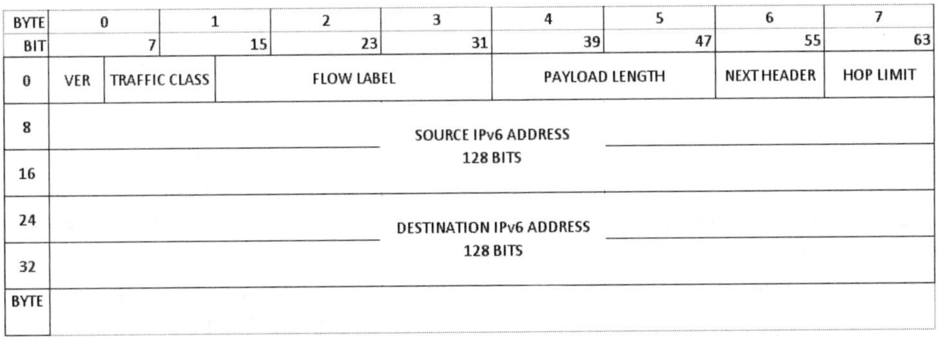

BYTE	0		1		2		3		4		5		6		7	
BIT		7		15		23		31		39		47		55		63
0	VER	TRAFFIC CLASS		FLOW LABEL				PAYLOAD LENGTH				NEXT HEADER		HOP LIMIT		
8	SOURCE IPv6 ADDRESS 128 BITS															
16																
24	DESTINATION IPv6 ADDRESS 128 BITS															
32																
BYTE																

FIGURE 7-9 The IPv6 header

NOTE IPV6

IPv6 is covered in more detail in the "Protocols, protocols, and more protocols" section later in this chapter.

NAME RESOLUTION TO GET THE DESTINATION IP ADDRESS

DNS operates at Layer 7 of the OSI Model. DNS is a database of mappings of *fully qualified domain names* (FQDNs) to IP addresses; it performs name resolution to the IP addresses of remote systems. A FQDN has a minimum of three names separated by dots, like www.contoso.com or fileserver1.somecorp.com. The first part (leftmost) of the FQDN is the hostname of the system. The middle part is the domain name (often the company name), and the last part (rightmost) is the top-level domain (TLD) that identifies the nature of the entity, such as .com for commercial, .edu for educational, or .mil for military.

Remember that when the user above Layer 7 identified the network file server she wanted to save her file to, she identified the file server by its name. That user-friendly, often intuitive computer name had to be resolved into the nonintuitive IP address of the destination server. This name resolution process is most commonly accomplished using DNS. Here at Layer 3, the destination IP address, which was most likely retrieved from a DNS server, determines whether the destination system is attached to the source system's local subnet or to a remote subnet so that the source system can figure out where to send the packet on its first hop. In the DNS system, the client system asking for the name resolution services is called the *resolver*.

THE ROUTING DECISION

The source system compares its own IP address to the IP address of the destination system to determine whether the destination system is on the same IP subnet as the local system. This is called the routing decision. (Is the destination system on the local subnet or on a remote subnet?) If the source and destination systems are on the same subnet, the source system can send the packet directly to the destination system. If the two systems are on different subnets, the source system must send the packet to a router (usually the default gateway) that is attached to the local subnet. That router presumably knows how to forward the packet to the destination system's IP subnet.

ROUTING

In processing data down through the network stack, the information is referred to as a segment at Layer 4. In networking architecture, the *segment* is the physical connection between collections of hosts on a network, usually connected by a switch, and is bounded by a router. (The router is an endpoint on the segment.) *IP subnets* are the logical network addressing imposed on those physical segments. One physical segment can have multiple logical IP subnets configured on it. Routers are devices that have multiple network interfaces that connect to multiple segments and provide the network paths between segments and subnets. They are configured with appropriate IP addresses for each network interface and with information about network paths to remote IP subnets through other routers. Routers make their routing decisions based on the IP addresses on their local network interfaces and on their routing tables that tell them how to send packets to remote networks. In Figure 7-10, Router A has local interfaces on 192.168.100.0 /24, 192.168.101.0 /24, 192.168.102.0 /24, and 192.168.103.0 /24. Router A will send packets out its 192.168.103.1 network interface to Router B at 192.168.103.2 to get packets to the 192.168.104.0 /24, 192.168.105.0 /24, and 192.168.106.0 /24 networks.

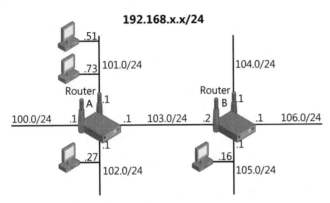

FIGURE 7-10 A routed network

The /24 notation (called slash notation or, more formally, Classless Inter-Domain Routing [CIDR]) represents the subnet mask by indicating how many of the 32 binary bits in the IPv4 subnet mask are 1s. The 1s in a subnet mask always begin at the left side, the most significant bit or high-order bit, and proceed to the right without any 0s mixed in, so a /24 will look like 11111111.11111111.11111111.00000000 in binary and translates to 255.255.255.0 in decimal.

Another process that functions at Layer 3 is fragmentation and reassembly. As a packet is commuting through routers on a network toward its destination, it might have to travel across one or more segments that require a smaller packet size, so the router that connects the larger packet segment to the smaller packet segment must break the larger packet into smaller fragments so they can fit onto the next segment. Each fragment is identified by a fragment number and offset to tell the destination system how to reassemble the fragments into the full-sized packet. Fragmentation occurs at the routers when necessary, and reassembly occurs at the destination system. For deep packet inspection, some security systems perform virtual fragment reassembly (VFR). They reassemble the fragments in memory so they can be interrogated for malicious or otherwise unwanted content.

Layer 2: The Data Link layer

Layer 2 of the OSI Model is the Data Link layer. In February 1980, the Institute for Electrical and Electronics Engineers (IEEE) established the 802 specifications that identified and defined several areas of networking technology at Layers 1 and 2 of the OSI Model. In addition, they divided the Data Link layer into two sublayers, the uppermost sublayer, called logical link control (LLC), and the lower sublayer, called media access control (MAC). Layer 2 provides the logical connection between the Network layer and the Physical layer. The LLC sublayer is primarily concerned with multiplexing between different networking protocols, such as between IP and IPX, and is rarely used in contemporary Ethernet networks. The MAC sublayer deals with physical (hardware) addressing using MAC addresses and merging frames onto the transmission media.

 Each network interface is built with a globally unique *media access control (MAC) address* that provides a local link to the network. The MAC address is 48 bits long and is commonly shown in pairs of hexadecimal characters separated by colons, as in 00:03:01:9a:bc:36. The first six characters represent the network interface card (NIC) manufacturer, and the last six characters form a unique identifier for that particular card. The MAC address is typically hard coded into the physical network interface device.

 A *frame* is the collection of binary bits that actually commute across the network. For Layer 2 to complete a frame so it can be transmitted onto the media at Layer 1, Layer 2 must place the source and destination MAC addresses in the Layer 2 header. Recall that at Layer 3, the destination IP address was known, and a determination was made whether the destination system was connected to the local subnet or to a remote subnet, in a process called the routing decision.

Layer 2 populates the source MAC address field with the MAC address of the NIC in the local (source) system that will be used to transmit the frame onto the network media. If the routing decision identified the destination system as connected to the local subnet, the source system uses the MAC address of the destination system in the destination MAC address field. As an example, in Figure 7-10, shown earlier, if the source system is using IP address 192.168.101.51, and the destination system is using IP address 192.168.101.73, the source and destination are on the same subnet, and the source system can forward the frame directly to the MAC address of the destination system.

If the routing decision at Layer 3 identified the destination system as connected to a remote subnet, the source system cannot send frames directly to the destination system but must send the frame to a router (usually the default gateway) that will know how to send the frame to the destination system. In this case, the source system must populate the Layer 2 header destination MAC address field with the MAC address of the router that will be the next hop for the frame on its way to the destination IP address. As an example, in Figure 7-10, if the source system is using the IP address 192.168.101.51 and the destination system is using the IP address 192.168.102.27, the source and destination are on different subnets connected by Router A, and the source system cannot forward the frame directly to the MAC address of the destination system. The source system must forward the frame to Router A at 192.168.101.1 and would need to use the MAC address for that 192.168.101.1 network interface as the destination MAC address in the Layer 2 header. Router A would then need to transmit the frame out from its 192.168.102.1 network interface to the destination system at 192.168.102.27. Router A would replace the source and destination MAC addresses in the inbound frame with the MAC addresses of those NICs addressed as 192.168.102.1 and 192.168.102.27 on the outbound frame.

Layer 2 uses *Address Resolution Protocol* (*ARP*) to acquire the appropriate next-hop MAC address of the host (sometimes the router) on the local subnet. The source system transmits an ARP broadcast frame onto the local segment and provides the IP address (Layer 3 data) of the next hop system, either the actual destination system (if the destination system is connected to the same subnet) or the IP address of the router that is connected to the same subnet as the source system (if the destination IP address resides on a remote subnet). Because the ARP request uses a broadcast, all nodes on the local segment process it. The one system that uses the IP address identified in the ARP request (the destination system if local or the default gateway if the destination system is remote) submits an ARP response that includes its IP address and its MAC address. The source system collects these addresses and stores them in its ARP cache (a location in memory) for future use. The source system also places the received, next-hop MAC address in the Layer 2 header of the frame as the destination MAC address.

When the correct source and destination MAC addresses are in place and the Layer 2 header is complete, the Data Link layer runs a 32-bit hash on the nearly complete frame and appends the hash value onto the frame as a trailer. The hash value is used by the next hop system to verify that the frame is intact and has not been damaged in transit. This error

detection function is called the *cyclic redundancy check* (CRC). The CRC value is appended to the frame as a trailer in a field called the frame check sequence (FCS).

Now that the Layer 2 header is complete and the CRC has been appended, the frame is complete and ready for transmission onto the network media. The MAC sublayer then feeds the binary bits down to Layer 1, which places the bits on the networking media. The MAC layer must time this transmission to avoid transmitting at the same time that another system on the local segment is transmitting. When two or more systems transmit onto the same segment at the same time, the frames collide, corrupting the transmissions.

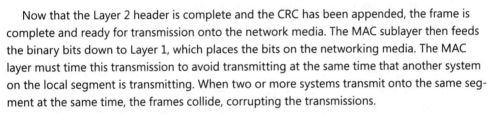

NOTE **MEDIA ACCESS METHODS**

Media access methods are covered in more detail in the "Transmission media and technologies" section later in this chapter.

For inbound network transmissions, the Data Link layer receives binary bits up from the Physical layer for processing. Upon receiving an inbound frame, the receiving system verifies that the destination MAC address is either its MAC address or a broadcast MAC address (indicating that the destination MAC address is all MAC addresses). A broadcast MAC address looks like ff:ff:ff:ff:ff:ff. (Forty-eight binary 1s converted to hexadecimal is 12 Fs). If the MAC address does not match the system's MAC address and is not a broadcast MAC address, the receiving system simply discards the frame because it is not the intended recipient. If the MAC address matches the system's MAC address or is a broadcast MAC address, the system is the intended recipient, and the inbound frame must be processed.

The receiving system then runs a CRC value on the frame (minus the trailer) for *error detection*. It compares its calculated CRC value on the received frame to the CRC that was calculated and appended to the frame before transmission at the source system. If the two CRC values are identical, the frame is intact and will be handed up to Layer 3 for further processing. If the two CRC values do not match, the receiving system discards the frame because the frame must have been damaged or otherwise altered in transit. The altered and discarded frame might or might not be retransmitted by the source, depending on error correction processes at higher layers such as those within TCP.

The NIC driver (software), bridges, switches, and wireless access points (bridging functionality) operate at Layer 2. Some of the protocols that operate at Layer 2 are:

- **ARP**   Address Resolution Protocol
- **VLAN**   Virtual local area network
- **L2F**   Layer 2 Forwarding
- **L2TP**   Layer 2 Tunneling Protocol
- **PPP**   Point-to-Point Protocol
- **SLIP**   Serial Line Internet Protocol
- **X.25**   For packet-switched wide area networks
- **Frame Relay**   For packet-switched wide area networks
- **ATM**   Asynchronous Transfer Mode ; for packet-switched wide area networks

> ***NOTE* ARP AT LAYER 2**
>
> Many people feel that ARP is not a Layer 2 protocol but a Layer 3 protocol because it broadcasts a Layer 3 IP address trying to resolve a Layer 2 MAC address. Inspection of the ARP frame in a protocol analyzer shows Layer 2 header information that includes the source MAC address and the destination MAC address that is the broadcast address (ff:ff:ff:ff:ff:ff), but the ARP frame doesn't have any Layer 3 header information. The source and destination IP addresses are provided in the payload of the ARP broadcast frame. This indicates that this protocol operates at Layer 2 and not Layer 3.

At Layer 2, the data, header, and CRC trailer information being prepared for transfer over the network exist in a frame, as shown in Figure 7-11.

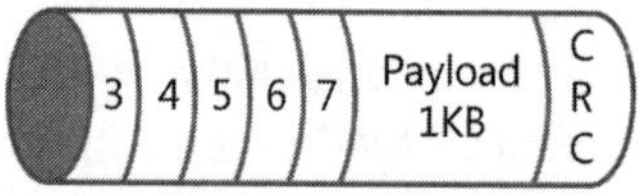

FIGURE 7-11 The Layer 2 frame—header and payload

Each frame is prepended with the Layer 2 header information to identify source and destination MAC addresses and the type of Ethernet framing, called the Ether type, that was used to construct the frame. The Layer 2 header is shown in Figure 7-12.

BYTE	0								1								2								3							
BIT	0	1	2	3	4	5	6	7	8	9	10	11	12	13	14	15	16	17	18	19	20	21	22	23	24	25	26	27	28	29	30	31
0	DESTINATION MAC ADDRESS - 48 BITS / 6 BYTES																															
4																	SOURCE MAC ADDRESS - 48 BITS / 6 BYTES															
8	SOURCE MAC ADDRESS - 48 BITS / 6 BYTES																															
12	ETHER TYPE - 16 BITS																															
BYTE																																

FIGURE 7-12 Layer 2 header

A frame might need to pass through several routers on its way from the actual source system to the actual destination system. Each time the frame is transmitted on the network media to the next system in this path, it is called a *hop*. The hop is accomplished from the source MAC address in the Layer 2 header to the destination MAC address in the Layer 2 header. In Figure 7-10, shown earlier, if the system using IP address 192.168.101.51 was sending frames to the system using IP address 192.168.105.16, the frame would need to travel through three hops. Each hop would use different source and destination MAC addresses in the Layer 2 header but would maintain the same Layer 3 data for source IP (192.168.101.51) and destination IP (192.168.105.16) addresses. Table 7-4 describes the three hops required for the frame to commute from the source computer at 192.168.101.51 to the destination computer at 192.168.105.16.

TABLE 7-4 Frames hopping the network

Hop #	Source system	Hop source	Hop destination	Hop destination system
1	Source computer	192.168.101.51	192.168.101.1	Router A
2	Router A	192.168.103.1	192.168.103.2	Router B
3	Router B	192.168.105.1	192.168.105.16	Destination computer

Each hop's source system will insert new source and destination MAC addresses and keep the source and destination IP addresses unchanged. Because the MAC addresses (Layer 2 header information) are different at each hop, a new CRC value is required at each hop, so the destination system for the hop can verify that the frame has been received intact, without corruption or damage in transit. Therefore, each hop's source system will calculate a new CRC value and insert it in the trailer of the frame. The frame is now ready for transmission onto the appropriate segment and subnet for its next hop.

THE INSTITUTE FOR ELECTRICAL AND ELECTRONICS ENGINEERS (IEEE) 802 SPECIFICATIONS

Because software interfaces with electronic hardware at Layers 1 and 2 of the OSI Model, the IEEE developed standards for different local area network (LAN) and metropolitan area network (MAN) systems to define the modulation and encoding (signaling patterns, voltages, and frequencies) and other specifications at these layers. The organization met in February 1980 and divided into working groups to focus and specialize in the different networking technologies. The IEEE 802 specifications are summarized in Table 7-5.

TABLE 7-5 The IEEE 802 specifications

802 Specification	Description	Notes
IEEE 802.1	Bridging (networking) and network management	
IEEE 802.2	LLC	Inactive
IEEE 802.3	Ethernet	
IEEE 802.4	Token bus	Disbanded
IEEE 802.5	Defines the MAC layer for a token ring	Inactive
IEEE 802.6	MANs	Disbanded
IEEE 802.7	Broadband LAN using coaxial cable	Disbanded
IEEE 802.8	Fiber Optic Technical Advisory Group	Disbanded
IEEE 802.9	Integrated services LAN	Disbanded
IEEE 802.10	Interoperable LAN security	Disbanded
IEEE 802.11	Wireless LAN (WLAN) & Mesh (Wi-Fi certification)	
IEEE 802.12	100BaseVG	Disbanded
IEEE 802.13	unused	
IEEE 802.14	Cable modems	Disbanded
IEEE 802.15	Wireless personal area networks (PAN)	
IEEE 802.15.1	Bluetooth certification	
IEEE 802.15.2	IEEE 802.15 and IEEE 802.11 coexistence	
IEEE 802.15.3	HighrRate wireless PAN	
IEEE 802.15.4	Low-rate wireless PAN (e.g., ZigBee)	
IEEE 802.15.5	Mesh networking for WPAN	
IEEE 802.16	Broadband wireless access (WiMAX certification)	
IEEE 802.16.1	Local Multipoint Distribution Service	
IEEE 802.17	Resilient packet ring	
IEEE 802.18	Radio regulatory TAG	
IEEE 802.19	Coexistence TAG	
IEEE 802.20	Mobile broadband wireless access	
IEEE 802.21	Media independent handoff	
IEEE 802.22	Wireless regional area network	
IEEE 802.23	Emergency services working group	New (March 2010)
IEEE 802.24	Smart Grid Technical Advisory Group (TAG)	New (November 2012)
IEEE 802.25	Omni-Range Area Network	Not yet ratified

Layer 1: The Physical layer

Layer 1 of the OSI Model is the Physical layer, which provides no intelligence or information to the frame. No negotiations or filtering or forwarding decisions occur at Layer 1. The Physical layer defines the physical, electrical, and optical characteristics of networking interfaces and transmission media along with *modulation* and *encoding* specifications. This includes specifications for connectors, pins, cables, voltages, radio frequency characteristics, and optical characteristics. Wired network interfaces modulate electrons and voltages on conductive cables to encode the *binary bits* from the Layer 2 frame. Wireless network interfaces modulate electromagnetic radio frequency (RF) waves in the air to encode the binary bits from the Layer 2 frame. Fiber optic network interfaces modulate photons on fiber optic cables to encode the binary bits from the Layer 2 frame.

The Physical layer adds a 64-bit preamble for synchronization purposes, but other than timing, these 64 bits provide no information. The preamble is a pattern of alternating 1s and 0s, ending in two consecutive 1s.

For an outbound network transmission, the Physical layer receives frame information in the form of binary bits from the Data Link layer above. The Physical layer then transmits the binary bits that make up a frame onto the network media, performing the appropriate modulation and encoding for that media. The bits are transmitted from the first byte of the preamble through the headers for Layers 2, 3, 4, 5, 6, and 7, the payload, and, finally, to the last byte of the CRC trailer. Bytes are transmitted from the least significant bit (the rightmost bit) to the most significant bit (the leftmost bit).

For inbound network transmissions, the Physical layer receives encoded signals from the media and converts them into binary bits to form a frame for Layer 2.

Some of the physical devices and components that operate at Layer 1 are:

- NIC (network interface card)
- Cabling Media
- Hub
- Repeater
- HBAs (host bus adapters—network interfaces for storage systems)
- MAU or MSAU (multistation access unit—old token ring hubs)
- Wireless access points (radios and antenna)

At Layer 1, the data and header information being transferred over the network exists as binary bits properly encoded on the network media.

The TCP/IP model

In the 1970s, the United States Defense Advanced Research Projects Agency (DARPA), an agency of the Department of Defense (DoD), was developing the first wide area network, called the Advanced Research Projects Agency Network, or ARPANET. ARPANET was the predecessor to the Internet. During that development work, DARPA produced a model to describe the functions of the TCP/IP protocol suite operating on the ARPANET.

In contrast to the OSI Model, the TCP/IP model primarily intended to detail the functions of the protocols relevant to the TCP/IP protocol suite. The researchers recognized that functions occurred below the layer where IP functions occurred, so they made that collection of functions one layer and called it Layer 1, The Link layer. This aligns with Layers 1 and 2 of the OSI Model.

DARPA called the next layer, where IP and all the network protocols operate, Layer 2, the Internetwork (or Internet) layer. This aligns with Layer 3 of the OSI Model, the Network layer.

DARPA called the next layer, where TCP and all the transport protocols operate, Layer 3, the Transport layer. This aligns with Layer 4 of the OSI Model, the Transport layer.

Finally, they recognized functions that occurred above the Transport layer, so they made that collection of functions one layer and called it Layer 4, the Application layer. This aligns with Layers 5, 6, and 7 of the OSI Model, the Session, Presentation, and Application layers.

Table 7-6 shows the alignment of the layers of the OSI Model to the layers of the TCP/IP model.

TABLE 7-6 The TCP/IP model compared to the OSI Model

The OSI Model		The TCP/IP model	
7	Application		
6	Presentation	4	Application
5	Session		
4	Transport	3	Transport
3	Network	2	Internet
2	Data Link	1	Link
1	Physical		

DARPA wasn't too concerned about the details of Layers 1 and 4 for its TCP/IP model, so the descriptions of these layers are notably more general than those in the OSI Model.

Transmission media and technologies

Valuable information assets are stored in data and file repositories throughout corporate networks. The data exists in databases and discrete data files on servers of different kinds, such as file servers, database servers, email servers, and even client systems. In many cases, for that information to be useful, users must access it over a network that uses shared media. To secure these valuable information assets properly when they commute over a network, it's important to understand the different types of networks and media that might be involved.

This section explores the types of media that carry these assets; it examines how the data is encoded on the different carrier technologies and the different topologies.

Finally, this section examines the different methods systems use to transmit data onto shared media while trying to avoid colliding with data being transmitted by another system on the shared media. This is called the network's media access method.

Media types

Cable is commonly used to conduct a signal from a source system to one or more destination systems and is therefore referred to as the media. A signal is encoded with data, usually in the form of bits. Most cable is made of one or more metal wires designed to conduct electrons, in either a digital or an analog fashion, down the length of the cable. Other cables, such as fiber optic cables, conduct photons (usually within a light spectrum not visible to humans) from source to destination to convey the encoded signal. Yet another commonly used medium is the air. Wireless networking, which has become so popular in the past few years, uses radio frequency waves that are encoded with data and transmitted through the air to destination systems.

Different types of media are used for networking because of their signal-carrying characteristics. The goal is to transmit a signal on the media and have it arrive at the desired destination intact and readable while minimizing the opportunity for bad guys to eavesdrop on it. This, of course, is always balanced with the cost of the media. Longer-running and more secure media is typically more expensive than most companies are willing to afford, so cheaper cabling is often used, with shorter runs, with greater potential for data leakage through emanations.

Emanations

 As an electron is conducted down the length of a wire (such as from a data-carrying signal), it propagates an electromagnetic field into the air around the cable. This propagation of energy takes energy away from the actual signal within the cable. This propagated field is called an *emanation* and can be detected without anyone ever touching or splicing into the cable itself. Bad guys can detect and record the emanations to steal data they are not authorized to access.

If another cable intersects this field, electron flow is induced within the second cable. This further reduces the quality of the emitting signal in the first conductor and introduces crosstalk into the second cable, degrading its signal as well.

 For these reasons, it is desirable to reduce emanations from signal-carrying cable media. *Shielding* contains and reduces the strength of the emanations around the cables and around the room or building where the emanations exist.

 Another technique used to defeat emanations detection is to transmit *radio frequency white noise* into the area where emanations from sensitive communications are occurring. This white noise is a stronger signal than the emanations, making it difficult—hopefully impossible—for an attacker to isolate the emanations from the sensitive signaling, but it does nothing to maintain or improve the quality of the data-carrying signal.

In the 1960s and early 1970s, the United States National Security Agency (NSA) ran a project codenamed *Tempest* to develop technologies to reduce these unintentional, intelligence-bearing emissions. This research and technology now falls into a classification called *emanations security (EMSEC)*.

> **NOTE TEMPEST**
>
> Tempest was the code name for the project and does not represent an acronym. Several back-ronyms have been suggested, though, including Tiny Electro-Magnetic Particles Emitting Secret Things.

Signal degradation

As electron-based signals transmit over distance, they degrade due to several types of phenomena. The natural resistance in the cable itself, the signal lost to emanations, and externally induced interference, collectively called attenuation, degrade the signal. As the length of the cable run increases, the attenuation increases. At some distance, the receivers at the destination systems can no longer understand the inbound signal due to it. This distance from the source of the signal to where the signal can no longer be understood defines the maximum cable runs for the types of cable and the types of signal being transmitted. Figure 7-13 shows an example of a transmitted signal and an attenuated signal.

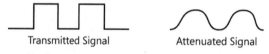

Transmitted Signal   Attenuated Signal

FIGURE 7-13 Signal attenuation

Another form of signal degradation falls into the arena of *electromagnetic interference (EMI)*. EMI is unintentional electric signal induced into the intentional, data-carrying signal. EMI includes spurious noise, such as from static discharge, lightning, or irregular transient noise from other electrical devices, that distorts and degrades the quality of the data-carrying signal. Another subset of EMI is *radio frequency interference (RFI)*. RFI is a more consistent and regular interference that induces unwanted signal into the data-carrying signal. Sources of RFI include the high-voltage ballasts used in fluorescent lighting, cell phone communications, radio communications such as those found around airports, and microwave ovens.

The *repeater* is a device designed to counter the effects of attenuation and other signal degradation. It is placed at the end of a cable run, where it receives an attenuated and degraded signal and regenerates it in a more pristine form, making it look much more like the original transmitted signal, so the signal can commute across another cable run and still be understood by the receiving systems at the far end.

Cables

Cables carry digital or analog signals for computer networks. Cables with electron-conducting wires include coax, shielded twisted pair (STP), and unshielded twisted pair (UTP) cables. Most common Ethernet networks use UTP cables.

COAX

Cables used in early computer networks were coaxial (coax) cables, which contain one center wire to carry the data signal and a ground shielding that surrounds the center conductor, as shown in Figure 7-14.

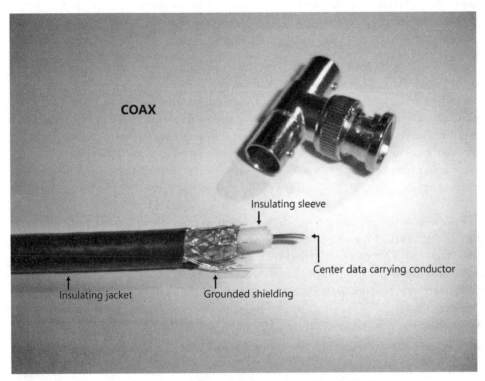

FIGURE 7-14 Coax cable shown with a BNC T connector used on 10Base2/Thinnet

The shielding is connected to electrical ground. It helps to keep the energy—that is, the signal—contained within the coax cable and isolated from other sources outside of the coax cable. This provides cleaner signals over the length of the cable and allows longer cable runs to reach greater distances for the network.

Early computer networks used 10BASE5 coax (RG-8/U, Thicknet) for long, backbone runs, and 10BASE2 coax (RG-58A/U, Thinnet) for shorter branch networks. The 10BASE5 coax provided a 10-megabits-per-second (Mbps) transmission speed, could run 500 meters, and handled like a frozen garden hose. The 10BASE2 cables were connected to the 10BASE5 backbone using a tap, often a vampire tap, that included a transceiver to boost the signal going onto the backbone and step down the signal going onto the 10BASE2 cable. The 10BASE2 cables were thinner and easier to work with. They provided a 10-Mbps transmission speed and could run 185 meters. The 10BASE2 cables would attach to computers using British Naval Connectors (BNC) (also called the Bayonet Neill-Concelman connector, named after its inventors) that twisted onto the network interface card installed in a computer.

> *NOTE* **BASEBAND VERSUS BROADBAND**
>
> The term *BASE* in 10BASE5 signifies that this system uses a baseband signaling scheme, by which one signal, or data stream, is all that can be transmitted over a wire. This is in contrast to the broadband signaling schemes, by which multiple discrete signals can be simultaneously transmitted over a single cable. Broadband systems used different frequencies (frequency division multiplexing) or different wavelengths (wavelength division multiplexing) to isolate the different data streams on the single cable. A pair of transmitters and receivers are tuned to the same frequency or wavelength at sender and receiver for each discrete signal.

These cable systems required 50-ohm terminators at each end of the cable to absorb signals as they reached the end of the cable. Without the terminator in place, the signal would hit the end of the cable and reflect back into the cable, destroying all signals on it. If any connector came loose, the entire network would be unusable until the loose connection was found and reconnected properly, making the cable itself a single point of failure in this network system.

Coax is more expensive and harder to work with than twisted-pair networking cables, but it provides the better emanations protection and longer data runs. Coax is rarely used for computer networks today.

TWISTED-PAIR CABLES—UTP AND STP

Most corporate networks today run Standard Ethernet. Standard Ethernet networks typically use *unshielded twisted pair* (UTP) cabling that consists of eight wires, with pairs of wires twisted around one another, producing four pairs. UTP was also called 10BASE-T; it can run up to 100 meters and can provide 10-Mbps, 100-Mbps, or 1-gigabit-per-second (Gbps) transmission speeds. The more twists of the paired wires per foot, the greater the transmission speed but, typically, the more expensive the cable becomes. One of the two wires in a pair carries the data signal; the other is connected to electrical ground to provide a level of shielding and signal protection. Although not a solid ground shield, this ground wire wrapped around the data signal wire tends to disrupt the electromagnetic field the electron flow is trying to produce, reducing the emanations and crosstalk and keeping the data signal stronger.

To reduce the emanations leakage and improve the signal integrity of UTP, *shielded twisted-pair* (STP) cable adds a conductive foil or metalized Mylar wrapping around the pairs of wires. This conductive shielding is then grounded at each end of the cable. STP was used on token ring and CDDI networks, covered in more detail in the "PAN, LAN, MAN, WAN, and more" section later in this chapter but is rarely used on corporate networks these days because of its high cost and difficulty to work with. However, academically speaking, STP is an improvement over UTP cable. A UTP cable and the RJ-45 connector commonly used on Ethernet networks are shown in Figure 7-15.

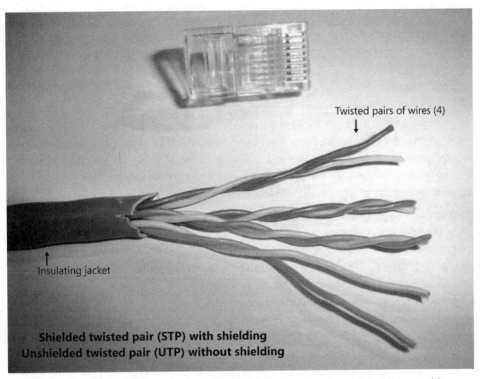

Twisted pairs of wires (4)

Insulating jacket

Shielded twisted pair (STP) with shielding
Unshielded twisted pair (UTP) without shielding

FIGURE 7-15 Unshielded twisted-pair cable shown with RJ-45 connector used on Ethernet cables

Network cabling is typically jacketed with polyvinyl chloride (PVC) plastic. It is cheap and easy to use on cables and effectively protects the wires inside. However, PVC burns at a relatively low temperature, and when it burns, it emits toxic smoke. This presents a particular problem when the cable is used within the plenum area, the air space below the true ceiling and a drop-down (pretty) ceiling. Air conditioning units commonly draw air in from this air space, chill it, and then blow it out through the air conditioning ducts to numerous areas within a building. If a fire breaks out in this plenum air space and ignites the PVC jacketing of the networking cables, the air conditioning system often distributes this toxic smoke to numerous areas, potentially risking the safety of humans in those areas.

In November 1980, the MGM Grand Hotel in Las Vegas, Nevada, caught fire. Eighty-five people were killed; seventy-five of them died from toxic smoke inhalation, and the majority of people were nowhere near the fire itself. The toxic fumes the burning PVC-jacketed cables produced were pumped throughout the hotel by the air conditioning system. This led the National Fire Protection Agency (NFPA) and the National Electric Code (NEC) to develop strict standards requiring the use of cables with plenum-rated jacketing that does not emit toxic fumes at low burning temperatures when the cables are run within the plenum areas in buildings. Plenum-rated cabling is jacketed with fluorinated ethylene polymer (FEP) that has increased fire resistance (it will only burn at high temperatures) and emits much less toxic smoke when it does burn. Cable that is jacketed with plenum-grade material is approximately twice the price of standard PVC-jacketed cable, making it impractical as the only cable type to use.

FIBER OPTIC CABLES

Fiber optic cables are made of glass fibers or clear plastic fibers and conduct photons, not electrons, that carry its data signals. Photons do not emanate electromagnetic fields as electrons do, so fiber optic cables are often used when emanations security is critical. In addition, fiber optic cables have significantly less attenuation than metal wires, so fiber optic cable runs can be significantly longer than wired cables, running several kilometers to tens of kilometers for fiber cables instead of a few hundred meters for metal cables.

Fiber optic cables are notably more expensive and usually require specialized devices and procedures to cut and terminate the cables. Single-mode fibers accept only a narrow angle of light (photons traveling in parallel), making them difficult to terminate properly, but they can run higher data rates over longer distances. Multimode fibers accept a wider angle of light (photons traveling in the same general direction, reflecting off the inner walls of the fiber), making them easier to work with, but they cannot carry signals as far as single-mode fibers due to multimode distortion. Fiber optic network interface cards convert the light signals from the cable into electric signals for the computer or other network device.

Fiber optic cables are used when high data rates or greater distances are required, such as between a LAN and a storage area network (SAN) and between the core connections of large corporate networks. They are often rated with a bandwidth-distance (MHz x km) rating because, as the required data rate increases, the usable distance decreases proportionally. For example, a low-end fiber optic cable could operate at 10 MHz x km, or the same cable could operate at 20 MHz x 0.5 km. Current typical networking transmission rates range from about 10 Gbps to about 40 Gbps, but high-end, single-channel systems (usually used in specialized backbone links) can exceed 110 Gbps over 160 km (approximately 100 miles).

Fiber can also carry different wavelengths of light without disturbing each other. In other words, multiple data signals transmitted at different ranges of the light spectrum (different colors of light) can run on one fiber optic cable, providing very high data transmission rates. This is called a fiber optic broadband digital network. Bell Labs in France has produced a 7000-km fiber optic link that can carry 155 100-Gbps channels by using this wavelength division multiplexing.

WIRELESS NETWORKING

In the past few years, wireless networking has become common in virtually every environment. Wireless networks often use a central *wireless access point* (AP) that mediates the wireless cell. (The wireless cell is the wireless AP, the wireless clients associated with the AP, and the area of coverage for the wireless signal.) Wireless networking clients associate with the AP and can then access the wired network attached to it, often providing access to the Internet. In this case, the air is the medium, and the AP and the wireless network interface cards (wireless NICs) transmit *radio frequency* (RF) waves in specified frequency ranges into the air and receive the waves from the air. Data bits are encoded into the RF waves.

Different countries allocate the frequency spectrum differently. In the United States, the frequency spectrum is regulated by the Federal Communications Commission (FCC), which provides frequency ranges for wireless networking at 2.4 gigahertz (GHz) and 5 GHz. Unfortunately, many other devices are allowed to operate in these ranges, especially in the 2.4-GHz range. These other devices introduce *interference* in the network's data signals, corrupting some or all of the useful data-carrying signal.

Wireless networks are inherently vulnerable because the transmission method is entirely emanations. It is easy to eavesdrop on communications being transmitted into the air. This is why security on wireless networks has become so important.

> **NOTE WIRELESS NETWORKING**
>
> Wireless networking is covered in more detail in the "Wireless networking" section later in this chapter.

To summarize a key point, emanations security is a target on the exam. EMSEC can be improved by choosing the appropriate media. The level of protection provided by the media types described are as follows (ranked from best EMSEC protection to worst protection):

1. **Fiber optics**   The signal is carried by photons, not electrons. This eliminates the security concerns of electromagnetic emanations.

2. **Coax**   The grounded shielding that encases the center data signal wire provides an improvement in EMSEC over the UTP and STP cable types.

3. **STP**   The grounded wire that is twisted around the data signal wire plus the additional grounded shielding provides some improvement in EMSEC over the UTP cable.

4. **UTP**   The grounded wire that is twisted around the data signal wire provides minimal EMSEC.

5. **Wireless**   Wireless communications are nothing but emanations. Strong authentication and encryption are recommended.

Encoding data into signals

The whole point of transmitting a signal over some media is for the signal to carry data or information from one system to one or more other systems, such as for saving a file on a remote file server or sharing a picture with a family member through email. Computers store data in a binary format, using only 1s and 0s called *bits*, so for the signal to carry these bits, the computer must encode them into a carrier signal that is appropriate for the network's media. By modulating the carrier signal, the system encodes bits into the signal that is transmitted over the media.

Some systems, such as wireless networks, encode binary bits into an analog carrier signal that looks like a sine wave. Other systems encode binary bits into a digital signal by varying DC voltage to encode 1s and 0s. Figure 7-16 shows an example of an analog carrier signal and a digital signal.

Analog   Digital

FIGURE 7-16 Analog and digital signaling

Analog encoding

Amplitude modulation (AM) is a form of analog signaling. Amplitude is the magnitude of change in the signal strength (positive and negative) of an oscillating wave shown on the vertical scale. To encode binary data in an AM encoding system, a carrier wave is defined with a standard amplitude. Then the amplitude of the wave is varied higher (stronger signal, more power) to represent a binary 1 and lower (weaker signal, less power) to represent a binary 0, as shown in Figure 7-17.

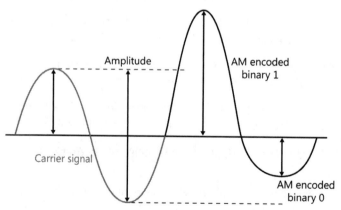

FIGURE 7-17 Amplitude modulation (AM) used to encode binary data

Frequency modulation (FM) is another form of analog signaling. Frequency is the number of occurrences of repeated cycles per unit of time, in this case, cycles of an analog RF wave. The number of analog waves transmitted in 1 second is the wave's frequency, expressed in hertz (Hz), meaning cycles (waves) per second. To encode binary data in an FM encoding system, a carrier wave is defined with a standard frequency. The frequency of the wave is varied higher (a shorter wave on the horizontal scale) to represent a binary 1 and lower (a longer wave on the horizontal scale) to represent a binary 0, as shown in Figure 7-18.

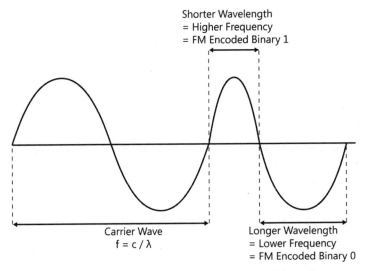

FIGURE 7-18 Frequency modulation (FM) used to encode binary data

Electromagnetic waves travel at approximately the speed of light (186,000 miles per second or 300,000,000 meters per second, 3 x 108 mps). If you were to put the number of waves transmitted in 1 second (its frequency) on a line 186,000 miles long (the distance light travels in 1 second), you could measure how long each wave is. This measurement shows the wavelength of a specific frequency, so the wavelength (λ, pronounced "lambda") is equal to the speed of light (c) divided by the frequency (f) of a wave, stated mathematically as $\lambda = c / f$.

It is also accurate to say that frequency (f) is equal to the speed of light (c) divided by the wavelength (λ) of the wave, otherwise stated as $f = c / \lambda$.

Phase-shift keying (PSK) is a third common method for encoding digital data into analog waves. A binary 1 is represented when the wave is modulated to reverse (shift) its phase between waves, and a binary 0 is represented when a phase shift does not occur between waves, as shown in Figure 7-19.

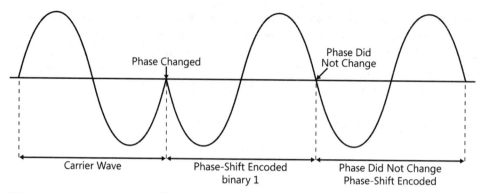

Phase Changed
Phase Did Not Change

Carrier Wave | Phase-Shift Encoded binary 1 | Phase Did Not Change Phase-Shift Encoded

FIGURE 7-19 Phase-shift keying (PSK) modulation used to encode binary data

To achieve higher data rates by encoding more data (binary bits) in each analog wave, combinations of amplitude modulation, frequency modulation, and phase-shift keying are employed on portions of each wave. The modulation and encoding scheme used to achieve the 54 Mbps in common wireless networks uses a combination of amplitude modulation and phase-shift keying called *quadrature amplitude modulation* (QAM), which encodes multiple binary bits in each quarter wave. By using two different amplitudes on the high side (positive voltage) and two different amplitudes on the low side (negative voltage) and allowing the phase to shift four times each analog wave, 16 bits can be encoded in each analog wave, as shown in Figure 7-20.

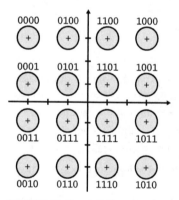

FIGURE 7-20 Constellation map for quadrature amplitude modulation (QAM) used to encode binary data

Digital encoding

Digital encoded signals can be unipolar or bipolar. Unipolar signaling uses the presence of a voltage as a 1 bit and the absence of voltage as a 0 bit. Bipolar signaling uses alternating positive and negative voltages as the 1 bits and the absence of voltage (0 volts) as 0 bits. Bipolar encoding is a bit more expensive to create but provides a more definitive data signal for transmission over greater distances, such as over a T1 wide area network (WAN) link. Examples of unipolar and bipolar signaling are shown in Figure 7-21.

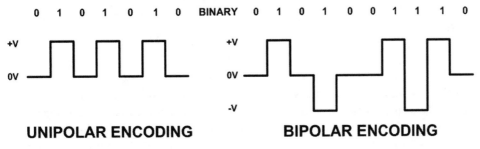

UNIPOLAR ENCODING   BIPOLAR ENCODING

FIGURE 7-21 Unipolar and bipolar digital signaling

Standard Ethernet encodes bits by using Manchester Coding (data bit XOR clock bit = Manchester Coded bit). A bipolar signaling scheme signals a 1 bit as alternating +2.5 volts of direct current (DCV) and –2.5 DCV and a 0 bit as 0 DCV.

SYNCHRONOUS AND ASYNCHRONOUS SIGNALING

Sending and receiving systems must establish a synchronized rhythm to identify when a unit of incoming data begins. Two schemes for this synchronization have emerged, called synchronous and asynchronous signaling. *Synchronous transmissions* are synchronized by using an *external clocking signal* (external to the data stream, such as on a separate wire) so that both systems understand the proper timing. This requires more than one wire or channel between the sender and the receiver. Synchronous systems provide greater throughput on the data channel but are typically more expensive than asynchronous systems.

Asynchronous transmissions do not use a clocking signal but include a *start bit* and a *stop bit* within the data stream to identify the beginning and end of each byte being transmitted. Asynchronous transmissions are typically performed when there is only one wire (or channel) for communications between the sender and the receiver. Asynchronous transmission systems are cheaper but carry more overhead because the data stream is peppered with control bits that are not useful data other than for timing purposes.

EXAM TIP

Synchronous signaling requires an external clocking signal, and asynchronous signaling does not require a clocking signal.

Networking topologies

As networks are assembled, the cabling that connects the networking infrastructure to the hosts (also called *nodes*) on the network forms a certain pattern based on the networking technology used. This pattern of the cabling is called the network's physical topology.

The shapes produced by the physical topologies of networks include:

- Bus
- Ring
- Star
- Mesh
- Tree

The cabling on early mainframe systems ran from the mainframe computer outward to many thin clients (also called dumb terminals because they had no processing power [intelligence] of their own). This pattern of cable runs produced a physical star topology, from a central point (the mainframe) outward in, theoretically, every direction, like the rays from a star. Early Ethernet networks used 10BASE5 and 10BASE2 coax cabling with a long cable run and nodes attached where needed. This was called a linear bus (or just bus) topology. Often, a 10BASE2 run would be tapped off a 10BASE5 backbone cable, producing a tree-shaped physical topology with the 10BASE5 cable run as the trunk of the tree and the 10BASE2 cable runs as multiple branches on the tree.

ARCnet networks were token-passing networks that attached nodes to a 93-ohm coax cable, also producing a bus topology. Token ring networks, including Fiber Distributed Data Interface (FDDI) and Copper Distributed Data Interface (CDDI) networks, ran a closed circle of cabling, producing a ring topology. IBM introduced a MAU central connection device for its token ring networks. Cables were run from the MAU to hosts located in any direction. These devices produced a physical star topology, but the token passing still ran in a ring order from the MAU out to the first node, back to the MAU, and out to the second node, and so on until the token returned from the last node in the MAU and then was passed back to the first node. Therefore, although this MAU device produced a physical star topology with the cables, it also produced a logical ring topology, following the path of the token.

Older Ethernet networks running over UTP cables attach nodes to a central hub, and today's popular Ethernet networks, also running over UTP cables, attach nodes to a central switch. These networks produce a physical star topology. If you connect several star networks by using a bus-type backbone, you have created a tree topology.

One cabling topology that might be used between routers is called a mesh topology. It makes connections between multiple systems within the network, providing redundant connection paths, usually for improved fault tolerance. A true mesh or full mesh connects every node (router) to every other node. This pattern is usually cost prohibitive and is rarely implemented. However, a partial mesh is quite often implemented, especially for critical data paths, when one router might have several paths to each router within the network system.

When different topologies are connected, a hybrid topology is created. This is probably the most common topology of all—a combination of networks and network types connected together.

Circuit-switched versus packet-switched networks

Networks can be either *circuit switched* or *packet switched*. An example of a circuit-switched network is the Public Switched Telephone Network (PSTN—which might also be called the plain old telephone system: POTS), in which the network consists of a mesh of wires connected to switches. A circuit-switched network might contain many paths between a sender (using the telephone example, the person dialing) and recipient (the dialed number). When a connection is requested, the circuit-switched network connects switches to create a point-to-point connection between the sender and the recipient for the duration of the call. An example of a circuit-switched network is shown in Figure 7-22.

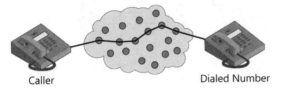

Caller   Dialed Number

FIGURE 7-22 A circuit-switched network

The wires and switches that make the connection are dedicated to the connection for the duration of the call (session) and are not shared during that time. When the call is disconnected, the wires and switches are released and made available for the next connection request. A second call between the same two points can be made using whatever wires and switches are available at that time to make the connection, sometimes using some of the same wires and switches and sometimes using completely different wires and switches.

Because the set of wires is dedicated for the exclusive use of the call (or session), the information flows from source to destination in series, and the information cannot arrive at the destination out of order. In addition, if there is a slow point in the connection, all information must pass through the same slow point, so all information will be delayed by the same length of time. This is called a fixed-delay, meaning that all information commuting across this circuit-switched connection is experiencing the same delay.

Circuit switching is very reliable. All data input flows along the same path to the output, so this type of network is best used for a fixed data rate of traffic, such as voice traffic, not for types of traffic that might be transmitted in bursts. When analog modems were the norm for connecting two computers, the telephone system was used as a circuit-switched network for computer data. Circuit-switched networks are largely being replaced with packet-switched networks because of the higher cost for effectively renting wires between a source and a destination.

Packet switching is the newer technology of the two. It breaks large amounts of digital data into smaller packets and then sends the packets into a cloud of routers. There are many potential paths between source and destination, as in circuit-switched networks, but on a packet-switched network, the packets are not required to follow each other and can be routed in any way possible to get them from the source to the destination. This type of behavior is called packet switching because the individual pieces of information are forwarded through the network based on the networking protocol (usually IP) that operates at Layer 3 of the OSI Model. At Layer 3, the information is referred to as a packet. An example of a packet-switched network is shown in Figure 7-23.

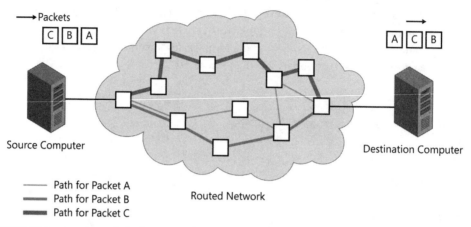

FIGURE 7-23 A packet-switched network

Because the packets can all travel the packet-switched network following different routes, some packets will be delayed more than others and might arrive out of order or even be lost in transit. All the packets must be placed in the correct order at the destination to reconstruct the original data stream, and missing packets might need to be retransmitted. Packet-switched networks can generally handle more traffic than circuit-switched networks, are less expensive, and are great for handling traffic in bursts, such as the data that computers send and receive over networks. Routed networks, such as the typical corporate network and the Internet, are examples of packet-switched networks.

Multiplexing

Within a session on a circuit-switched network, and on other point-to-point connections, the channel can be shared by dividing the circuit using different mechanisms such as time, frequency, or wavelength. This is referred to as *multiplexing*. *Time-division multiplexing* (*TDM*) provides time slices to different network endpoints. For example, Figure 7-24 shows three clients—named 1, 2, and 3—sharing a connection to another location, where they have sessions with systems A, B, and C, respectively. Multiplexers allocate the time slices to clients so that all clients have access to the shared connection. TDM is often used on baseband connections but can also be employed within individual data streams on broadband connections.

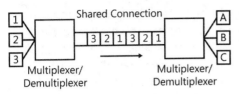

FIGURE 7-24 Time-division multiplexing (TDM)

Broadband systems that carry multiple data streams simultaneously on one connection can use *frequency-division multiplexing* (*FDM*), in which multiple signals are transmitted at different frequencies. Electromagnetic radio frequency signals at different frequencies can be transmitted on coaxial broadband connections. On fiber optic broadband connections, different colors of light (different wavelengths) can carry different data streams on the same cable. This is called *wavelength-division multiplexing* (*WDM*). Figure 7-25 shows an example of wavelength-division multiplexing.

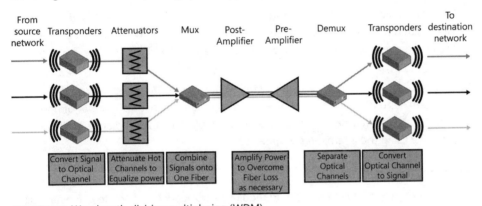

FIGURE 7-25 Wavelength-division multiplexing (WDM)

Whose network is it, anyhow?

Considering the various computer networks we connect to these days, some definition is necessary to describe the larger picture of the network, loosely indicating a trust level for the different network classifications. Networks are classified as one of the following:

- **Intranet** The most trusted of networks, this network is typically the privately owned network your computer is connected to. It is usually bounded by security devices (firewalls) at the boundary of the network where the intranet meets the Internet or an extranet. An intranet is managed by a central administrative person or team and can be subdivided into security zones, such as the perimeter network (also known as demilitarized zone, DMZ, and screen subnet) that hosts the publicly exposed services such as public web servers, email servers, name resolution servers, and other highly controlled segments where internal, sensitive data might be stored and accessed.

- **Extranet** From the perspective of the intranet, an extranet is a network outside your intranet but one with a regular connection path to it, such as to a partner's network or a branch office network. The connection path is often a dedicated, point-to-point channel, such as a T1 WAN link, or an encrypted channel such as a VPN running over a public network such as the Internet. The extranet is usually less trusted than the intranet but more trusted than the Internet and often has its own administrative person or team for network management. (Your intranet might be someone else's extranet.)

- **Internet** The Internet (almost always capitalized) is a global, public system of inter-connected networks called autonomous systems (AS). The Internet Corporation for Assigned Names and Numbers (ICANN) manages the namespace and IP address space on the Internet. It provides web services such as HTTP, FTP, VoIP, and VPN connections between private networks, to name just a few. The Internet is also called the World Wide Web (WWW), and it uses public IP addresses and blocks private IP addresses. The Internet might also be called a global area network (GAN).

The Internet should be considered a hostile network, and all precautions should be taken or at least considered before making connections to Internet-based hosts. Many bad guys lurk on the Internet, just waiting for the uninitiated to happen by, like bandits on a wooded trail in the olden days.

When asked, "How many nodes are connected to the Internet?" a good answer is "Too many." Although it is difficult to count and verify, many estimate that the number of nodes directly attached to the Internet exceeded 1 billion in 2009, with approximately 2 billion people regularly using the Internet (as of June 2010).

Packet transmission modes

To satisfy the many types of communication requirements needed to operate a network, different types of packet transmission modes are required. Sometimes a packet is intended for all to receive; other times, the packet is intended for a single, unambiguous destination host. The four types of packet transmission modes are:

- **Broadcast** *Broadcast mode* is one-to-all transmissions; it transmits packets to all hosts within a range of IP addresses. Broadcasts use all 1s for the destination MAC address at Layer 2 (binary) and might specify a broadcast IP address for the destination host address (all 1s in binary) at Layer 3.

- **Multicast** *Multicast mode* is one-to-many transmissions; it transmits packets to several hosts who have subscribed (opted in) to receive the multicast transmission from a single source server. Multicast transmissions use a special class of IP addresses in the Class D range of 224 to 239 in the first octet.

- **Anycast** *Anycast mode* is one-to-one-of-many transmissions; it transmits packets to the nearest node of several nodes that have the same anycast address. These anycast destination systems often provide the same type of service, and the goal is to provide the client with the nearest system that provides the desired anycast service. This transmission type is used primarily on IPv6 networks.

- **Unicast**   *Unicast mode* is one-to-one (also called host-to-host) transmissions. Because this transmission specifies a unique, unambiguous destination IP address, other systems will not receive or process these payloads (nonpromiscuous mode).

Media access methods

On most networks, the media are shared among multiple systems. These multiple systems contend for time on the media. When more than one system on a baseband segment (such as Ethernet) transmits a frame simultaneously, a *collision* occurs, destroying the intelligible information in both frames and requiring all collided frames to be retransmitted at a later time. This, of course, consumes network bandwidth without good benefit and degrades the performance of the network overall. Media access methods are designed to eliminate or reduce the number of collisions on a network.

Earlier networks tried to eliminate collisions and ran on *contentionless* or *deterministic* media access methods, where which system was allowed to transmit was predetermined, and all others were specifically not allowed to transmit. These methods include:

- **Polling**   In this method, which originated in the mainframe era, the mainframe server would poll each client to see whether the client system (dumb terminals in those days) needed to transmit anything. If a client system was not being polled at the moment, it was not allowed to transmit. Early 802.11 wireless network specifications include an optional polling mechanism to manage very busy wireless networks, but it is rarely made available to end users and even less often used due to its poor performance.

- **Token-passing bus**   With this method, one system on the network (usually the one that had been online the longest) would place one token on the linear bus media that would be passed from system to system in a predefined order. Only the system holding the token could transmit. All systems without the token were not allowed to transmit. ARCnet networks are a token-passing bus technology.

- **Token-passing ring**   In this method, one system on the network (usually the one that had been online the longest) would place one token on the circular media that would be passed from the nearest upstream neighbor on the ring to the nearest downstream neighbor on the ring in this predefined order. Only the system holding the token could transmit. All systems without the token were not allowed to transmit.

The contentionless and deterministic systems didn't perform as well as *contention-oriented* or *nondeterministic* media access systems and are used very little on contemporary networks. These better-performing, contention-oriented and nondeterministic media access methods try to reduce but do not eliminate collisions and include:

- **Carrier Sense Multiple Access/Collision Avoidance (CSMA/CA)**   A system that is ready to transmit listens (senses) the media to see whether another system is transmitting. If the media are clear (no one else is transmitting), the system transmits a small announcement frame and then listens to see whether it collided with another transmission from any other system on the shared media. If the announcement frame is successfully transmitted without colliding with another frame, the system has successfully reserved the media for the time it takes to transmit its frame, and no one else can transmit for the specified transmission time reserved in the announcement frame. The original AppleTalk protocol used on Macintosh networks used this type of CSMA/CA.

On early 802.11 wireless networks, the collision avoidance (CA) system also included reserved time for the destination system to transmit an acknowledgement frame to confirm successful receipt of the wireless transmission.

- **Carrier Sense Multiple Access/Collision Detection (CSMA/CD)**   Used on Ethernet networks, this media access method has proven to be the most popular and efficient. It does not include the overhead of the announcement frame on every transmission, as in CA technologies. Instead, it simply listens (senses) to the media to see whether another system is transmitting. If the media are clear, the system transmits its frame and then listens to see whether it collided with another transmission from any other system on the shared media. If another system begins transmitting during this transmission time, a collision occurs and is detected, and both systems must retransmit their frames later.

✔ **Quick check**

1.   On which media access method would collisions occur?

2.   Which type of network is best for bursty types of traffic and where data can arrive at the destination out of order?

Quick check answers

1.   Carrier Sense Multiple Access (CSMA) networks, including CA and CD

2.   Packet-switched networks

Network devices

It takes a lot of functions and systems to get a network going and keep it running efficiently. When it is done correctly, end users are virtually unaware of the network itself and just expect easy (and secure) access to their resources. Providing all the services required to keep the network running in this manner means that many infrastructure devices are required.

Devices within the OSI Model

Infrastructure devices are said to function at specific layers of the OSI Model based on the nature of the information they are designed to process.

Layer 1 devices

As described earlier in this chapter, Layer 1 of the OSI Model is the Physical layer. At the Physical layer, no intelligence is required, only physical connections between systems, with no filtering or forwarding decisions to be made. Layer 1 devices include:

- **Network Interface Card (NIC)** This device is imbedded in each network host and provides the physical connection between the host and the network media.

- **The media itself** The coax or Ethernet cabling for networks that use electrons and voltage on cables to carry its signals, fiber optic cables for optical networks, and the air for wireless communications.

- **Concentrator/hub** Connection blocks between hosts on a network. Originally, these were unpowered, but later they included amplifier (repeater) circuits to boost signal strength. Token ring systems introduced the multistation access unit (MAU or MSAU) as a concentrator that collapsed the physical ring into a physical star topology but kept the token passing in a ring-like manner, producing a logical ring topology.

- **Repeater** A signal-regenerating device placed inline on a network to boost the signal strength and defeat attenuation.

- **Wireless access point** The transmitting and receiving radios and the antenna of the wireless AP are physical components of the AP.

Layer 2 devices

Devices that operate at Layer 2 of the OSI Model, the Data Link layer, make filtering and forwarding decisions based on the MAC addresses found in the Layer 2 header information. These devices include the *bridge,* and the newer *switch* that has pretty much replaced hubs on corporate networks.

Bridges usually had relatively few interfaces due to their high cost, often having only two or four interfaces. They were used to break up crowded segments into smaller, less crowded segments. Bridges learn the MAC addresses that are connected to each interface by listening to the source MAC address in the Layer 2 header information of frames transmitted by the hosts on the segments. The bridge stores this MAC address information in a table for each interface. The bridge then uses these learned MAC address tables to make forwarding decisions by comparing the destination MAC address in the Layer 2 header information of a transmitted frame to the MAC addresses it has stored in its MAC address tables. Bridges forward frames to different interfaces only as necessary. This reduces the number of frames on each segment.

A frame transmitted on one segment attached to one interface on a bridge can never collide with a frame on a segment connected to a different interface on the bridge; therefore, the bridge creates a separate collision domain at each interface.

Broadcast frames use the broadcast MAC address of all binary 1s (which translates into all hexadecimal fs [ff:ff:ff:ff:ff:ff]) and are destined for all MAC addresses, so the bridge forwards all broadcasts to all interfaces.

As the price of bridges came down and people could afford to purchase bridges with many interfaces, these multiport bridges, called switches, became popular and replaced hubs on virtually every network. Switches greatly reduce the apparent traffic on any network. Switches have also evolved into more sophisticated devices, not only making forwarding decisions based on MAC addresses but often including configurable snooping functions to improve security, such as Dynamic Host Configuration Protocol (DHCP) snooping, Internet Group Management Protocol (IGMP) snooping, and configurable Virtual Local Area Network (VLAN) functions to provide logical isolation between hosts connected to the switch. Some switches are built with enough CPU and programming logic to perform basic routing functions and are often called Layer 3 switches.

 Another Layer 2 device is the *wireless access point* (*AP*). The AP acts as a moderator for the wireless infrastructure cell, which is the AP and all wireless nodes associated with the AP. The AP learns the MAC addresses of its wireless clients and then either relays wireless-to-wireless transmissions or bridges the wireless network to the wired network. The antenna, the transmitter, and the receiver of the AP are considered Layer 1 components, whereas the bridging function between the wireless nodes and the wired networks operates at Layer 2.

Layer 3 devices

 Devices that operate at Layer 3 of the OSI Model, the Network layer, make filtering and forwarding decisions based on the destination IP addresses found in the Layer 3 header information. These devices include the *router* and the *packet filter firewall*.

 As the interfaces on a router are configured with IP addresses, the router becomes aware of the networks that it directly connects to. Routers must be fed information about other networks that it does not directly connect to. This is called building the route table and can be done either statically, by manually entering the network addresses and the IP address of the correct gateway (router) that is the next hop on the path to the remote network, or dynamically, by implementing a *dynamic routing protocol*. Dynamic routing protocols are used on routers to tell other routers of the networks they know about, so that all routers know all the networks that can be reached and how to reach them. Dynamic routing protocols are covered in more detail in the "Routing protocols" section later in this chapter.

The packet filter firewall is a router with rules configured on an access control list (ACL) to filter (block, deny) unwanted traffic. Often, the packet filter firewall is configured with a default Deny All rule, and then only specified Allowed traffic rules are implemented to permit only limited, desirable network traffic. Packet filter firewalls are covered in more detail in the Firewalls section later in this chapter.

A frame transmitted on one segment attached to one interface on a router can never collide with a frame on a segment connected to a different interface on the router; therefore, the router creates a separate collision domain at each interface. In addition, because the router does not forward any broadcasts across interfaces, the router also acts as a boundary for broadcast domains.

Layer 7 devices

Although not exactly a device, the *gateway* function is said to operate at Layer 7 of the OSI Model. It is a translation from one protocol to a similar but different protocol for interconnection and interoperability purposes.

For example, to connect different email systems, an X.400 gateway might need to be installed. Because the SMTP and X.400 protocols operate at Layer 7 of the OSI Model, this is considered a Layer 7 function (or device that performs the function). To connect the older Novell IPX/SPX network to a TCP/IP network, the gateway function (translation of protocols from IPX to IP and SPX to TCP) must occur at Layers 3 and 4 of the OSI Model; this is usually described as a Layer 4 gateway.

Many vendors produce devices to perform specific and dedicated gateway functions, so many consider the gateway a device.

Mainframe computers

Some of the earliest networks (in the 1960s) were simply dumb terminals, also called thin clients, connected to mainframe computers. Some mainframe computers are still in use today. The mainframe computer is an expensive and powerful computer that performs the bulk, if not all, of the processing power for an organization. Often called big iron, most mainframes run on UNIX operating systems. Configuration changes and new devices are introduced during the startup process called the *Initial Program Load* (IPL). Restarting a mainframe computer is a significant event and is usually well planned and scheduled to avoid interrupting critical operations. The unscheduled IPL (restart) is cause for investigation because it might mean that unauthorized changes have been implemented.

Thin clients are systems used to access the mainframe. They are designed to be inexpensive and are basically a monitor, a keyboard, and a network interface card (NIC), with no processing capabilities of their own. The NIC on the thin client is configured with an erasable, programmable, read-only memory (EPROM) chip that contains a very basic startup program and a NIC driver, sufficient to connect to the network and communicate with the mainframe computer. The mainframe computer receives keystrokes from the thin client and returns display screens and information the client system requests. Thin client systems must be polled by the mainframe to authorize the client system's access to the network.

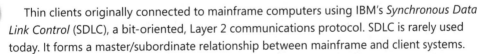

Thin clients originally connected to mainframe computers using IBM's *Synchronous Data Link Control* (SDLC), a bit-oriented, Layer 2 communications protocol. SDLC is rarely used today. It forms a master/subordinate relationship between mainframe and client systems.

The newer client-to-mainframe communications protocol, *High-Level Data Link Control* (HDLC), also a bit-oriented, Layer 2 communications protocol, was developed by the ISO and is still used today in Asynchronous Balanced Mode (ABM). The use of ABM in the HDLC network supports a peer-to-peer network in which any node can initiate transmissions.

The very recent use of virtual desktops and cloud computing, especially with bring your own device (BYOD)–type client systems, is approaching an architecture similar to the thin client systems and mainframe architecture of earlier days.

Client/endpoint systems

In most corporate settings, there are typically many more client systems than there are servers and infrastructure systems. There is more than one client system per human user in the computing environment. Many users have a desktop system in their office, a portable laptop computer, and a pad-type device as well. With mobile phones getting smarter and more powerful every day, these devices must also be included when considering endpoint security.

Physical security controls should be employed to protect the relatively stationary desktop systems. The portable laptops, pad devices, and mobile handheld devices present a more difficult security problem. This becomes especially difficult if users use their personally owned hardware to access or administer the network. A new realm of technology is being developed to address the BYOD endpoint connectivity and security concerns. Controls for endpoint systems, including BYOD, might include the following:

- Maintain hardened systems.
    - Install updates regularly of the operating system, device drivers, applications, and device firmware from trusted sources.
    - Keep antivirus and antispyware current with regular updates.
    - Enforce software policy and technical controls.
    - Perform configuration monitoring and enforce technical controls.
    - Maintain minimum services, user, and service accounts, using least privilege.
    - Maintain personal firewalls.
    - Use a host-based intrusion prevention system (IPS).
- Use strong authentication.
    - Require strong passwords.
    - Use multi-factor authentication.
    - Use mutual authentication.
- Use data classification, security control policies, and supporting technologies and enforcement.
- Use encryption.
    - Employ whole-disk encryption.
    - Use encrypted volumes.
- Perform automated routine data backup to centrally located servers.
- Enable remote wipe capabilities.

- Employ remote location tracking capabilities (such as LoJack, Phone Home, and Find My Device).

- Employ inventory control. Administrators should know what offsite devices the company owns, which devices are connecting to the network, and what type of data is stored on and accessed by those systems.

- Provide supplemental security awareness training for users of portable and mobile devices. The training should target the specific vulnerabilities and threats that could affect these devices and technologies and the elevated responsibilities these users face regarding increased protection and response to loss or theft. This training should be in addition to the standard user security awareness training and be required at least once a year for all portable and mobile users, more often as the value and risks increase and if policy breaches are identified (remedial security awareness training).

- Allow remote and BYOD access only through virtual desktops. In this case, the BYOD device operates more like a thin client that accesses a back-end server. The well-protected and secure back-end server is where the applications and data are stored and where all processing occurs. The BYOD device provides only data input and receives screen shots from the back-end systems. This can often be accomplished through web-based applications and through other virtual desktop client/server systems.

Remote access by client/endpoint systems

When client systems are used for remote access, as when a telecommuter works from home but accesses data and applications on the corporate network, another control technique to help secure the environment is the use of virtual applications and the virtual desktop. These operate like a platform as a service (PaaS), simulating a client desktop on the client machine through an instance of a virtual machine on the corporate servers, or as software as a service (SaaS), providing access to an application running on the corporate server but allowing the client to access it over a remote connection. This keeps the intellectual property, the data, and the applications on the corporate servers and provides screen shots of these to the telecommuting client.

A threat to even these technologies is the screen scraper. This malicious software captures these screen shots and forwards them to the attacker and can be used to steal data without ever gaining access to the back-end servers.

Bastion hosts/hardened systems

 A *bastion host*'s, or *hardened system*'s attack surface is drastically reduced. Although every system should be hardened to some extent, bastion host servers require a notably higher level of hardening.

One reason to create a bastion host is if the system is connected to the network in a hostile region, such as public-facing web resources placed in the perimeter network. A second reason to build a bastion host is if the system is to hold or connect with highly valuable assets. The level of hardening should align primarily with the sensitivity of the assets contained on the system or accessible through connectivity to the system and the level of hostility expected where the system is placed on the network.

Standard hardening of systems should include the following:

- Test and apply all operating system and application patches in a timely manner.
- Install and configure a host-based (personal) firewall.
- Install and regularly update antivirus protection.
- Install and regularly update antispyware protection.
- Disable unused services.
- Disable unneeded startup applications.
- Disable or delete unnecessary user accounts.
- Run any needed services and applications under the credentials of a lower-privileged user account—as low as possible but still supporting the required service.
- Implement all access privileges following the principle of least privilege.
- Define, document, and periodically verify the configuration settings.
- Periodically perform security inspections of the system to verify the effectiveness of the security controls.

These items should be properly installed, configured, and monitored on infrastructure servers, but they should be more aggressively configured for security and maintained on the bastion host systems. In addition, the bastion host should include some or all the following, depending on the level of hardening required:

- Build bastion host systems to perform limited, dedicated functions providing one or two services only.
- Install and regularly update a host-based intrusion detection/protection system.
- Regularly perform vulnerability scanning.
- Regularly perform configuration management scanning.
- Perform integrity verification of systems files and other critical files at time of use.
- Allow only a minimum number of users to access these systems.
- Allow only a minimum number of administrators to manage these systems.
- Uninstall all unneeded software.
- Delete any unneeded executables, scripts, and dynamically linked libraries (DLLs). This would include items such as Notepad.exe, Wordpad.exe, and Calc.exe.

- Follow the operating system vendor's instructions and harden elements of the operating system wherever possible (for example, by using the Specialized Security Limited Functionality (SSLF) settings suggested by Microsoft).

- Remove all administrative tools from the system. These administrative tools can be collected on a USB flash drive or on an administrative CD or DVD and mounted on the bastion host systems when needed for legitimate administrative purposes.

- Perform a security review of all custom code (software) installed on the system.

Every system in the perimeter network should be a bastion host system. Consider that any system exposed to the Internet in the perimeter network has already been compromised and put on those systems only what you are willing to give to the attackers. Every server on the corporate network that performs critical or sensitive processes or stores or manipulates sensitive data should be configured as some appropriate level of bastion host system.

Firewalls

Firewalls are security services or devices installed on a host or network. Network firewalls are usually installed as network choke points to enforce policy and can be configured to control network traffic by various methods. A host-based firewall (personal firewall) is installed on a network entry point to protect that one system from unwanted network traffic. Firewalls generally provide a default Deny All rule to block all traffic, and then narrowly defined and specific Allowed traffic rules are implemented to permit the desired network traffic. Firewalls are very often used at the perimeter of the trusted network where connections must be made to less-trusted extranets or to the Internet. They are also useful within the corporate network to segregate different security zones on the network.

Many firewalls can filter based on an imported list of Internet dark address space and known malicious websites and servers. Internet dark address space is the collection of unallocated public IP addresses that should not be used. Attackers often use these addresses to avoid being tracked. An alternate approach is to deny all websites except those listed on a company-approved list of safe and useful websites.

Virtually every firewall server is also a *network address translation* (*NAT*) server, used to share a limited number of public IP addresses with many internal, privately addressed hosts. NAT is covered in more detail in the "Network Address Translation" section later in this chapter.

Firewalls have evolved over time and can be classified into several generations, reflecting their filtering technologies. Contemporary firewalls often include several of these technologies in one system.

- **Generation 1 firewall**   Packet filter
- **Generation 2 firewall**   Proxy server
- **Generation 3 firewall**   Stateful inspection
- **Generation 4 firewall**   Dynamic packet filtering
- **Generation 5 firewall**   Kernel proxy

EXAM TIP

Understand the five generations of firewalls and their functionality. Contemporary firewalls often include generations 1 through 4 in a single firewall.

Generation 1 firewall: Packet filter

The first firewalls were routers with rules configured on their access control list (ACL) to deny unwanted traffic. They could filter traffic based on IP addresses (Layer 3 header information) and on port numbers (Layer 4 header information). Although they could be configured to filter on port numbers, they did not interact with Layer 4 in any other way and remained a Layer 3 device. When used internally, these firewalls often used deny rules that were configured to restrict traffic. When used at a network boundary between trusted and untrusted networks, they usually were configured with a default Deny All rule to block all traffic and then used narrowly defined and specific Allowed traffic rules to pass only the specific desired network traffic. These devices were generally relatively inexpensive, fast, and strong but unsophisticated, providing only wide-open IP addresses and ports and permanently closed IP addresses and ports.

Although not the most sophisticated firewalls, these packet-filtering devices still get their share of use on contemporary networks.

Generation 2 firewall: Proxy server

The *proxy server* is the second generation of firewall and is almost always used at the boundary between trusted and untrusted networks, rarely used on the internal network. The proxy server breaks the connection (proxying the connection) between the internal client and the external server and can be configured to require user authentication to apply access authorization rules. It can operate at Layer 5 (a circuit-level proxy) or at Layer 7 (an application layer proxy) of the OSI Model.

A circuit-level proxy breaks the connection between client and server and performs filtering based on IP addresses and port numbers. These firewalls are protocol and application independent. Because they don't perform content inspection like the application-layer proxy server, they are faster than those are. The SOCKS proxy is the most common circuit-level proxy server.

An application-layer proxy server breaks the connection between client and server, and proxy applications must be installed to support each protocol it is intended to proxy, such as SMTP, HTTP, or FTP. Because the application proxy understands the applications and protocols it is filtering, it can inspect the contents of the traffic against content rules to block unwanted content. This deep inspection is time-consuming, so the application proxy often includes a content cache for approved content after it has been inspected, to provide cached content more quickly, rather than retrieving and inspecting the same content multiple times.

A reverse proxy server acts as a front end to secure inbound access of internal resource servers such as a company's public-facing web and email servers.

Generation 3 firewall: Stateful inspection

The *stateful inspection firewall* is more intelligent than Generation 1 or 2 firewalls because it can keep almost all inbound ports closed by default. The stateful inspection firewall records all approved outbound requests and then can dynamically open ports to allow the stateful responses to those approved outbound requests. This allows more ports to be configured as closed by default, rejecting unsolicited inbound frames and dynamically allowing the stateful response frames that match approved requests on the state table.

To provide public-facing services, ports on the stateful inspection firewall can also be opened (always open) and forwarded to the appropriate internal server.

Generation 4 firewall: Dynamic packet filtering

The *dynamic packet filter* is a combination of the application-layer proxy firewall and the stateful inspection firewall, which allows ports to be closed by default but to open them dynamically as necessary to allow the stateful response frames to approved outbound requests, and it can perform content inspection to filter based on content-filtering rules.

Generation 5 firewall: Kernel proxy

The fifth-generation firewall, the *kernel proxy*, operates within the kernel of the firewall appliance, whereas all other generations of firewalls operate in user mode (less privileged). This makes the kernel proxy faster and stronger than earlier firewalls.

The kernel proxy interprets the inbound frame and dynamically constructs the appropriate session-dependent network stack to match the construction of the frame. This allows the kernel proxy to perform inspection at every header layer, including at the Application layer, where content inspection can be performed.

Firewalls in use

Firewalls are screening devices and shield systems from the abuses of the public Internet and other hostile network affronts. The devices behind and protected by the firewall are referred to generally as screened hosts that are connected to a screened subnet. Most firewalls are multihomed, meaning that they have more than one network interface card and connect to more than one segment. Figure 7-26 shows an example of the use of firewalls within a corporate network.

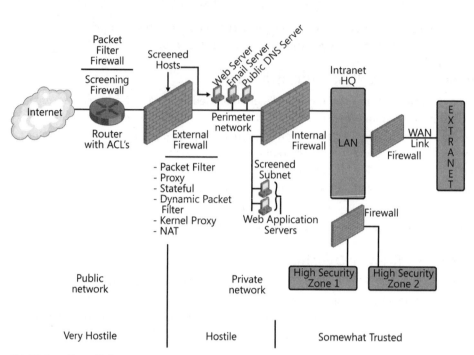

FIGURE 7-26 Firewalls in use

Ingress and egress filters

External firewalls that connect the corporate network to the Internet should typically have ingress and egress filter firewall rules in place.

The *ingress filter* is placed on the public interface of the external firewall and blocks any inbound frame using a private IP address as the source IP address. Because the Internet routers block all private IP addresses, this frame cannot be legitimate and is typically an attack on the internal host that uses the spoofed source IP address in the inbound frame.

> **NOTE PUBLIC AND PRIVATE IP ADDRESS SPACE**
>
> Details on private and public IP address space are covered in the "Internet Protocol Version 4" section later in this chapter.

The *egress filter* identifies an even more threatening, crafted frame. This firewall rule is placed on the internal interface of the external firewall and blocks any outbound frames that use a public IP address as the source IP address. Because all internal systems use private addresses, this frame cannot be legitimate and typically represents an internal host attacking a public system. It is generally assumed that the company's employees would not launch an attack on a public system using corporate computers, so the popular conclusion is that the actual sending system must be compromised and under the control of a malicious hacker and is acting as part of a distributed denial of service attack (DDoS). This system must be tracked down, taken offline, and investigated to understand the nature and severity of the compromise.

The next question that must be asked is, "If this one system is compromised without being detected, how many other corporate systems are compromised and being used for some unknown and, almost certainly, malicious purposes?" An investigation must be initiated to identify any other compromised and externally controlled systems.

Network address translation

For the past 30 to 40 years, the world has been connecting to remote computers by using Internet Protocol version 4 (IPv4) addresses. These addresses are based on 32 binary bits, which limits them to about 4 billion unique addresses, and many of those cannot be used. Of the addresses that can be used, some are allocated for use only on private networks (private address space), and some are allocated for use only on the Internet. The routers on the Internet are configured to drop any packets that are using private addresses.

In the mid-1990s, as the Internet grew in popularity, the number of available of public IPv4 addresses began to drop to critical numbers, and a more efficient use of these public IPv4 addresses became a requirement. *Network Address Translation* (*NAT*) was introduced to share public IPv4 addresses among many internal hosts that use private IPv4 addresses.

> **NOTE INTERNET PROTOCOL VERSION 6 (IPV6)**
> IPv4's replacement, IPv6, was introduced in 1998 and is slowly being phased in, eventually to eliminate the need for IPv4 addresses. IPv6 is based on 128-bit addresses and should provide sufficient quantities of addresses for the continued growth of the Internet and the need for public address space.

NAT is commonly implemented on the boundary device (usually the external firewall) between the private network and the public Internet. For full-featured NAT, *port address translation (PAT)* is also required, so the two systems are almost always required to be on the same system and are almost inseparable. One or more public IPv4 addresses are bound to the external, public interface of the NAT server, and one or more private IP address are bound to the internal, private interface of the NAT server. NAT replaces the outbound private IP addresses in the Layer 3 header of a packet with public IP addresses so the packet can commute across the Internet. NAT also replaces the public IP addresses in inbound packets with private IP addresses so that they work on the private network.

> **NOTE NAT HIDING**
> NAT also provides a thin layer of security because it hides the internal IP addresses from systems on the Internet. This is called *NAT hiding*.

NAT operates in three basic modes:

- **One-to-many (also called many-to-one)**   Used to share one public IPv4 address with many internal clients that use private IPv4 addresses. When internal clients, using private IPv4 addresses, attempt to access the Internet, the NAT server assigns the client a specific port number and maps that port number to the client's private IP address and source port address. The NAT server then removes the client's source IP address from the Layer 3 header and replaces it with the NAT server's public IP address. The NAT server also replaces the client's original source port address with the port number the NAT server assigned to the client. The NAT server records this NAT port number to client IP and port number mapping. When the public server responds to the outbound request from the NAT server, the public server uses the port address that the NAT server assigned to the internal client as the destination port number. When this packet arrives at the NAT server, the NAT server looks up the port number and modifies the header with the IPv4 address and source port number of the client's original packet, and then forwards the packet on to the internal network.

  In this manner, the NAT server can share one public IP address with many internal clients that use private IPv4 addresses. Note that this one-to-many process uses NAT and PAT together.

- **Port forwarding**   Used to share one public IPv4 address with multiple public-facing services that reside on the internal network, usually on the perimeter network. The NAT server is configured with the port numbers used and private IPv4 addresses of the servers that are providing public-facing services such as HTTP, SMTP, public DNS, and FTP. Typically using the same public IP address as the one-to-many NAT used to share access to the Internet, inbound requests arrive at the NAT server, and the destination port number identifies which internal server the NAT server must forward the inbound packet to. As inbound packets arrive at the NAT server from the Internet, the NAT server inspects the destination port number to determine which service the client is requesting and then replaces the public, destination IP address with the internal, private destination IP address of the server that provides the requested service. This way, several internal servers can share one public IPv4 address and provide multiple services to clients on the Internet.

- **One-to-one**   Used to dedicate one public IPv4 address to one internal, private IPv4 address when the internal service uses a range of port numbers. On occasion, application servers use dynamically allocated port numbers. When these applications must be made available to clients on the Internet, and the destination port number cannot be controlled, the NAT server must be configured with a dedicated IP address for this one server and with all inbound ports mapped to one internal server using its private IPv4 address. This one dedicated public IPv4 address cannot be shared with any other internal system or service.

Name resolution

Users refer to computers by their name and rarely know the IP address of the system. Names are intuitive and easy to remember for humans, unlike IP addresses. However, networks cannot forward frames and packets based on names. Networks require the IP addresses of destination systems to complete their forwarding and routing functions. The service required for networks is like the phone book for the telephone system.

Early networking systems relied on static, text-based listings of name-to-IP address mappings. In the UNIX and Linux worlds, they relied on a file named *hosts*. In the Microsoft NetBIOS world, they relied on the *lmhosts* file. However, as the number of nodes on the network grew, keeping a current hosts or lmhosts file became impractical. Server-based name resolution services became the standard for name resolution. Microsoft introduced the *Windows Internet Name Service* (*WINS*) server to map NetBIOS names to IP addresses. *NetBIOS names* are simple 15-character names such as FILESERVER1.

The sockets-based world developed *Domain Name System* (*DNS*) to map fully qualified domain names to IP addresses. A *fully qualified domain name* (*FQDN*) includes a *hostname* (such as www), a domain name (such as contoso), and a top-level domain (TLD) name (such as com) to build an unambiguous network destination such as *www.contoso.com*. FQDNs are the required naming structure for systems on the Internet. These name-to-IP-address mappings are stored in *resource records* in a database that is divided into *zones* based on the domain name and TLD for the FQDN. The Linux-based *Berkeley Internet Name Domain* (BIND) daemon (currently on version 9) was the first name server of this kind in public use and still holds a large share of DNS servers today.

In addition to helping humans use their friendly computer names on a network, DNS provides critical assistance in the use of X.500 directory services such as the Active Directory service. Most corporate networks rely on directory services to establish trust boundaries and maintain a database of trusted users, computers, and other directory objects. DNS provides mappings to directory services on the network and can identify directory service resources close to the users who need them.

Endpoint systems are configured with the IP address of a DNS server and automatically submit name queries to that configured DNS server whenever the network stack needs resolution of a name to an IP address. Clients query the DNS server on UDP port 53. If the target DNS server does not have the name-to-IP-address mapping information requested by a DNS client (called the resolver), the DNS system can relay a query to higher-level DNS servers, hoping for a successful resolution. DNS servers can be configured with an upstream DNS forwarder that might have access to additional mappings or, if the DNS server uses the *root hints* information, it can use the public, Internet-based DNS system, first querying the root server, then the TLD server, and, finally, the authoritative name server for the requested FQDN.

DNS servers that support directory services contain a map of the corporate network and computer resources. This information should not be made available to unknown or untrusted entities such as the bad guys on the Internet, so internal DNS systems that support directory services do not share information with Internet-based DNS systems. However, most companies also provide public, Internet-facing servers to provide access to their email system, websites, and other public services. These systems must be identified within the public DNS system so the public can find them. To solve these conflicting requirements, most companies run two DNS systems, one for internal, directory service support, and one for external, public resource support. This use of separate, noninteracting DNS systems is called *split DNS*.

Without correctly functioning public DNS systems, the use of the Internet as we know it would fail miserably. This came into focus shortly after the 9/11 terrorist attack, when the United States Department of Homeland Security performed a risk assessment on possible terrorist acts. This realization of the vulnerability and threat to the DNS systems, and therefore the Internet, prompted the development of a more secure DNS system and spawned *Domain Name System Security Extensions* (*DNSSEC*). DNSSEC requires all name resolutions to DNS clients from public DNS servers to be digitally signed by a trusted sender, using public key infrastructure (PKI) and ITU-T X.509 digital certificates. A pilot program was implemented in Sweden, and DNSSEC is now slowly being phased into the rest of the public DNS systems throughout the world.

Dynamic Host Configuration Protocol

All hosts on an IP network must have properly configured IP information to use the IP network. This configuration information can be manually (statically) configured on each system or automatically (dynamically) provided to the hosts as part of the startup process. In general, all infrastructure systems, such as routers, file servers, web servers, and VPN servers, should have statically assigned IP information. However, client systems are commonly configured dynamically because there are so many more clients than servers, and client systems are more likely to change their connection point on the network.

The infrastructure system that provides IP configuration information is called a *Dynamic Host Configuration Protocol* (*DHCP*) server. This system is configured with a pool of available IP addresses and a subnet mask, called a scope, along with additional IP configuration information such as a default gateway, the IP address of one or more DNS servers, and possibly other IP network–related information.

When a DHCP client starts up, it broadcasts a DHCP Discover frame from its port 68 to the DHCP server's port 67. This broadcast says, "This is my MAC address. Can someone please tell me what my IP address is?" A DHCP server listens for these DHCP Discover broadcasts and responds to the client with a DHCP Offer. The client system returns a DHCP Request to the server, and finally, the DHCP server transmits a DHCP Acknowledgement. With these four frames complete—*Discover, Offer, Request, Acknowledgement* (*DORA*)—the DHCP client binds the new IP information to its network interface and goes live on the IP network. The client is authorized to use this IP configuration for a specified lease period and must refresh the lease over time to accommodate potential changes to the configuration details.

The original protocol that provided IP addresses to clients was Reverse Address Resolution Protocol (RARP). This was followed by the Boot Protocol (BootP). Finally, in a third generation, DHCP can provide much more IP configuration information to clients than its predecessors.

An attacker can hijack a network by implementing a rogue DHCP server on a victim network, issuing IP configuration information to victim clients that route them to the attacker's network instead of to the legitimate network. To defend against this attack, newer switches offer a DHCP snooping capability, by which only the authorized DHCP server can communicate over the switch, and the switch rejects all other DHCP server traffic.

The virtual private network server

 Very often, communications over public and private networks carry sensitive information that should not be shared with unauthorized users. To secure these network transmissions, encrypted channels, called *virtual private networks* (VPNs) are commonly used. A VPN can be constructed between the sender and the recipient, but end users often don't have the technical savvy to initiate a VPN. Many times, the VPN is constructed between VPN servers in remote locations, and end users remain unaware of the security measures that protect their sensitive information. In the case of remote or telecommuting workers, a VPN server is positioned to receive inbound connections from client systems. These client systems are generally preconfigured with a VPN client, and users are provided with the additional instructions to initiate the VPN. VPN technologies are covered in more detail in the "Virtual private network protocols" section later in this chapter.

Protocols, protocols, and more protocols

A protocol is simply an agreement on how a process will work. Networking protocols describe how network devices or hosts communicate over a network. Because of the many types of communications that can be conducted over a network, there are many protocols to target the numerous specialized requirements placed on networks. Several protocols have been introduced already in this chapter.

Internet Protocol version 4

 Internet Protocol version 4 (IPv4) is a Layer 3 protocol that performs addressing and routing. Its basic functionality was described in an earlier section in this chapter on the OSI Model. The address space that is available for the 32 binary bits that make up an IPv4 address is commonly written in dotted decimal form for easier human interpretation, using four sets of eight bits, as in 192.168.200.15. Each section between the dots is referred to as an octet.

 The IP address is not complete or usable without its *subnet mask*, which identifies which part of the IP address represents the network address, called the subnet, and which part of the address represents the host address. The subnet mask is often shown in a format called *Classless Inter-Domain Routing* (CIDR) notation, also called slash notation. The number represents the number of binary 1s in the subnet mask, starting with the leftmost bit (also called the most significant bit or the high-order bit) and proceeding consecutively toward the rightmost bit (also called the least significant bit or the low-order bit). All bits to the right of these 1s in the subnet mask must be 0s. Some examples of subnet masks in CIDR notation and equivalent dotted decimal format are:

- /8 = 255.0.0.0
- /12 = 255.240.0.0
- /16 = 255.255.0.0
- /21 = 255.255.248.0
- /24 = 255.255.255.0

The subnet mask is used at Layer 3 to make the routing decision, answering the question, "Is the destination IP address on my local subnet, or is it on a remote network?" If it is local, the source can forward the frame directly to the destination. If it is remote, the source must forward the frame to a router, which, in turn, forwards the frame on toward the destination.

The IPv4 address space is divided into five classes, providing address ranges for large, medium, and small network structures (Classes A, B, and C); a range to provide multicast addresses (Class D); and a range for some potential use to be developed in the future (Class E), as described in Table 7-7.

TABLE 7-7 IPv4 address classifications

Class	First octet	Default or classful mask	Intended use	Number of networks	Number of hosts per network
A	1–126	/8	Larger organizations	126	16,777,214
B	128–191	/16	Midsized organizations	16,384	65,534
C	192–223	/24	Smaller organizations	2,097,152	254
D	224–239	N/A	Multicast/IGMP	N/A	N/A
E	240–255	N/A	Experimental	N/A	N/A

EXAM TIP

The IP address range of 127.0.0.0 /8 is the loopback network address. These addresses are reserved, and administrators cannot assign them to systems. The 127.0.0.1 address is typically used as the loopback address of the localhost, assigned by the IP stack.

Addresses from the A, B, and C classes can be used to address any IPv4 hosts. Class D addresses can be allocated for use only with the Internet Group Management Protocol (IGMP), or multicast transmissions. Addresses from Class E cannot be used on a standard IPv4 network.

When a network uses the default mask (based on the value in the first octet, as shown in Table 7-7), the network is said to be *classful*. Using any mask other than the default mask makes the network *classless*. Classful networks are commonly broken up into smaller networks by using a process called *subnetting,* in which the number of binary 1s used in the subnet mask is increased, making the subnet classless. Each additional binary 1 added to the subnet mask doubles the number of subnets available in the network but (approximately) cuts in half the number of hosts allowable on each subnet. Networks that use classless subnet masks are using Variable Length Subnet Masking (VLSM), and the routing functions that support VLSM use CIDR.

To isolate private network traffic from the more hazardous traffic on the Internet, and to make the use of public IPv4 addresses more efficient through NAT, ranges of IP address space are defined for use only on private networks. Private networks typically exist behind the external firewall for an enterprise and include the perimeter network(s) and the LAN. The routers on the Internet are configured to discard all packets that use addresses from the *private address space.* The following list shows the IPv4 address ranges that are designated for use only on private networks:

- 10.0.0.0 /8 = 10.0.0.0 through 10.255.255.255
- 172.16.0.0 /12 = 172.16.0.0 through 172.31.255.255
- 192.168.0.0 /16 = 192.168.0.0 through 192.168.255.255
- 169.254.0.0 /16 = 169.254.0.0 through 169.254.255.255 (APIPA Address)

All other Class A, B, or C address space is considered *public address space.*

Not all public address space has been issued for use. These unissued public addresses are called Internet dark address space. Some public IPv4 addresses have been issued for use but are not being used. Illegal hosts that use these unallocated addresses, usually to attack and send spam to systems, are called bogons. Some firewalls can be configured to retrieve the list of dark address space and bogon addresses automatically and block them.

Internet Protocol version 6

Internet Protocol version 6 (IPv6) is the replacement for IPv4 and might be referred to as IP Next Generation (IPng). IPv6 uses a 128-bit address space (versus the 32-bit addresses in IPv4), allowing for substantially more usable IP addresses and the configuration of many more network layer services. The IPv6 address is written by using eight groups of four hexadecimal characters separated by colons, something like this:

`fe80:0000:0000:0000:1d9a:78e9:4c48:0823`

Groups of zeros can be omitted by using a double colon, and leading zeros in a group can be omitted, so the preceding address would typically be written:

`fe80::1d9a:78e9:4c48:823`

IPv6 is being phased into most networks today. The most common approach to converting from IPv4 to IPv6 is to run both protocols simultaneously on each network interface, sometimes called running a dual (network) stack.

Following are several of the preallocated IPv6 prefixes and standard addresses:

- **2000:: /3**   Global Unicast Address; similar to public IPv4 addresses
- **fc00:: /7**   Unique Local Addresses; similar to private IPv4 addresses
- **fe80:: /10**   Link Local; not routable; similar to APIPA addresses in IPv4
- **ff00:: /8**   Multicast addresses
- **2001:0db8:0000:: /32**   Documentation/example address use; nonroutable
- **:: /128**   An unspecified address
- **::1 /128**   Loopback address
- **:: /0**   Default route

> **NOTE** **FEC0::**
>
> The IPv6 prefix fec0:: /10 had been identified for use as the Link Local address, now re-named Unique Local Address (ULA). The use of fec0:: was deprecated by the IETF in September, 2004, and its replacement, the new fc00:: /7 ULA, was adopted for use in October 2005.

Most IPv6 addresses are auto-allocated, and end users rarely need to interact with these addresses. With the many additional bits available in the IPv6 address, many additional services and features are available, such as Quality of Service (QoS) for time-sensitive transmissions and IPsec to provide built-in encryption and authentication.

The Windows operating system automatically issues fe80:: addresses to the local host and runs a dual IPv4 and IPv6 network stack.

Many of the protocols described in this chapter are compatible with IPv6, but after the removal of IPv4, many will no longer be needed because IPv6 has such enhanced capabilities compared to the older IPv4.

The TCP/IP Protocol suite

Some commonly used protocols that are part of the TCP/IP protocol suite include:

- **Transmission Control Protocol (TCP)**   Transport protocol that provides reliable, session-oriented, guaranteed delivery. High overhead.
- **User Datagram Protocol (UDP)**   Transport protocol that provides unreliable, best-effort delivery. No error detection or correction. Low overhead.
- **Internet Group Management Protocol (IGMP)**   Also known as *multicast*. A one-to-many transmission system in which a single source server streams data to many client systems that must opt in for the multicast transmission. Routers in between server and clients duplicate and distribute the streamed packets as necessary. Commonly used in audio, video, and gaming transmissions. IGMP is often disabled on corporate routers to reduce the workload on the routers.

- **Internet Control Message Protocol (ICMP)**   Enables hosts and infrastructure systems to send messages to one another autonomously to tune the network, such as the ICMP Source Quench and the ICMP Destination Unreachable messages. Many ICMP functions have been used in exploits and have had to be disallowed on many networks.

- **Address Resolution Protocol (ARP)**   Used to broadcast a destination IP address on the local subnet requesting the related MAC address of the destination host. This information is required to complete the Layer 2 header of the nearly ready frame. The retrieved IP-address-to-MAC-address mapping is stored in the requesting system's ARP cache for 10 minutes (on Windows-based systems).

Commonly used protocols

Other commonly used (and historic) protocols include:

- ***Bootstrap Protocol (BootP)***   Used on early diskless workstations on which a boot-strap operating system was embedded in an erasable, programmable, read-only memory (EPROM) basic input/output system (BIOS) chip. This BIOS chip would be installed on the network interface card (NIC). On powering up, the bootstrap operating system would mount the NIC, acquire an IP address, and then download an operating system from a Trivial File Transfer Protocol (TFTP) server into the system's RAM. The system would then complete starting up to an operational state on the downloaded operating system in RAM. On systems with a floppy disk drive, the BootP drivers could be installed from a floppy disk instead of the BIOS chip. BootP is the parent of DHCP.

- ***Telnet***   An older, text-oriented protocol used to administer systems remotely or provide a command shell on a remote system. Telnet uses a plaintext authentication scheme, so it was replaced by Secure Shell (SSH). The Telnet daemon is considered a vulnerability on a system, so running the Telnet daemon is typically disallowed on systems.

- ***Secure Shell (SSH)***   The replacement for Telnet. SSH is an old, text-oriented protocol used to administer systems remotely, provide a command shell on a remote system, or tunnel other protocols, such as SSH File Transfer Protocol (SFTP). SSH creates a secure channel that provides encryption and integrity protection. Although not originally considered so, SSH can be considered a VPN because of these features.

- ***File Transfer Protocol (FTP)***   An older protocol used to transfer files. FTP uses a plaintext authentication scheme, so it is typically run within an SSH (SFTP) or Secure Sockets Layer (SSL) secure (FTPS) channel.

- ***Trivial File Transfer Protocol (TFTP)***   An older protocol used to transfer files. Similar to FTP, but TFTP does not provide authentication. Used in early networks to support diskless workstations and BootP.

- ***Secure FTP (SFTP)***   FTP through a secure shell (SSH)

- **FTP over a Secure Sockets Layer (SSL) tunnel (FTPS)**   Uses X.509 digital certificates to establish a secure channel, then runs the nonsecure FTP through the SSL channel.

- **Simple Network Management Protocol (SNMP)**   Used to monitor and configure remote systems. An SNMP agent is installed on each monitored system and managed by an SNMP administrative console. The list of query-able items was stored in a management information base (MIB), and the individual items were delineated by a unique object identifier (OID). Authentication was based on a shared secret, one for reading data from a remote system, one for writing data to a remote system. This shared secret was called a *community string*. The default read community string was *public*. The default write community string was *private*. SNMP supported four basic functions: Get, to read a specific OID; Get Next, to read the next OID; Set, to write data to the target OID; and Trap, if an identified event happened, to record the event (trap it) and send the (trapped) information to the management console.

- **Domain Name System (DNS)**   A hierarchical name resolution system for fully qualified domain names mapped to its IP address. DNS clients, called resolvers, query the DNS server for these name-to-IP-address mappings.

- **Simple Mail Transfer Protocol (SMTP)**   Used to send email messages from client to server and server to server but not to download email messages to client systems. The SMTP protocol was based on a 7-bit-per-byte ASCII character set.

- **POP3**   Used by an email client to connect to an SMTP (email) server, authenticate, download inbound email messages, send outbound email messages, and then disconnect. By default, POP3 deletes messages from the SMTP server after the client downloads them.

- **IMAP4**   Used by an email client to connect to an SMTP (email) server, authenticate, download inbound email messages, and send outbound email messages. This session persists to allow the client to access additional resources that might be available on the SMTP server.

- **Multipurpose Internet Mail Extensions (MIME)**   Used on SMTP email messages and email attachments to encode 8-bits-per-byte characters into 7-bits-per-byte characters so that SMTP can handle them, and they can traverse the network and the Internet without being destroyed and then to reassemble the message and attachments into the 8-bits-per-byte characters on the recipient side.

- **Secure MIME (S/MIME)**   Used to encrypt email attachments, typically using public/private key pairs.

- **Hypertext Transfer Protocol (HTTP)**   Used as a means of requesting and presenting information from web server to web browser (also called a user agent). HTTP resources are referred to by their Uniform Resource Locators (URLs). Webpages (such as documents) are coded by using Hypertext Markup Language (HTML). Currently on version 1.1.

- **HTTP over SSL (HTTPS)**   HTTP content through an SSL secure channel, based on public/private key pairs.

- **Line Printer Daemon (LPD)**   Used to submit print jobs to a remote print server running on a Linux or UNIX system.

- **Network File System (NFS)**   Used to access shared files and directories on a remote file server on a Linux or UNIX system.

Routing protocols

Routers connect segments (physical) and subnets (logical addressing assigned to the physical segments) and are responsible for forwarding packets toward the destination network by using network (Layer 3) addressing. For this to work correctly, each router in the network must know about all the subnets in the network and how to get to those remote subnets. On smaller networks, this routing information can be manually configured on each router by an administrator. This is called *static routing*.

As a network grows, this administrative work quickly becomes too demanding to keep up with, so routing protocols were invented. Routers use routing protocols to share their routing information with other routers. This way, the routers dynamically configure each other with all the subnets in the network and the information on how to connect to those remote subnets.

Dynamic routing protocols fall primarily into two categories; *distance vector dynamic routing protocols* for small networks, and the more complex *link state routing protocols* for medium and large networks.

- **Routing Information Protocol (RIP)**   A distance vector dynamic routing protocol used on small networks. RIP was limited to 15 hops (called a metric), in which each router in a network path represented one hop (or one count on the metric). A packet was discarded when it reached its 16th hop, and the destination would be declared unreachable. The original RIP (v1) broadcast its entire route table on each interface every 30 seconds, making it a very chatty protocol. A router running RIP would accept all received RIP broadcasts, without authentication, and would update its route table with the new information. This led to an attack called *route poisoning*, by which an attacker would broadcast bogus networks and routes to disrupt or hijack the traffic on a network. Another weakness in RIPv1 was that it could only support classful IP addresses.

- **RIPv2**   Introduced in 1993 to address the need to support VLSM and CIDR (classless networks), authenticated RIP announcements, and multicast or unicast incremental updates to the route table instead of broadcasting the entire route table every 30 seconds, as RIPv1 did.

- **Interior Gateway Routing Protocol (IGRP)**   Cisco's proprietary implementation of RIPv1, a distance vector dynamic routing protocol.

- **Enhanced Interior Gateway Routing Protocol (EIGRP)** Cisco's proprietary implementation of RIP with enhancements to address performance of network paths. Still a distance vector dynamic routing protocol.

- **Open Shortest Path First (OSPF)** A link state dynamic routing protocol designed for use on medium to large networks. OSPF supports incremental, authenticated, and controllable routing updates, VLSM, and CIDR. OSPF detects network performance and adjusts its preferred path to accommodate the fastest path to a destination network. OSPF divides the network into collections of well-connected subnets (LAN speed 10 Mbps or better) called *autonomous systems (AS)* or areas, where route table synchronization occurs very rapidly. Route table updates between areas are controlled through specified *area border routers (ABRs)*.

- **Border Gateway Protocol (BGP)** A link state dynamic routing protocol designed for very large networks such as the Internet. BGP is in fact used on the routers on the Internet. Like OSPF, BGP uses autonomous systems and area border routers.

- **Multi-Protocol Label Switching (MPLS)** A relatively new, high-performance, protocol-independent telecommunications protocol. A cloud of MPLS routers is established. The edge MPLS router (called the label edge router [LER]) adds a label (also called a tag) to the front of each inbound packet with information that helps the next-hop MPLS router forward the packet without ever having to process the header or other contents of packet. The LER at the outbound point of the MPLS cloud removes the label and forwards the packet to the standard IP routing system.

 To prevent routing loops that could occur with distance vector dynamic routing protocols, *split-horizon* route advertisements are often used. Split-horizon prevents a router from advertising a route back on the interface where it learned the route. A more aggressive approach to split-horizon to avoid these routing loops is the use of a *poison reverse* advertisement, by which the router announces that a network cannot be reached on an interface where it learned of the network. *Holddown timers* are also often employed to prevent a router from receiving or announcing any new routes for some time (typically three minutes) after networks are added or removed, to allow the network to stabilize.

Virtual private network protocols

In the old days, companies connected to networks in remote sites (called extranets) by using dedicated network lines, usually T1s or T3s. Today, most companies use the Internet as their connection to networks in their remote locations. However, using these public connections, which are shared with good guys and bad guys alike, poses a security risk. To mitigate the risk of sensitive information leaking as it commutes over the Internet, companies are using encrypted channels on their connections over the Internet. These encrypted channels are called virtual private networks because even though the network is used as a public network, without the decryption key, the information is as secure as if it were being sent over a private network. The public network is, therefore, virtually private.

VPN protocols might also be called tunneling protocols because they encapsulate (or wrap) the original packet, providing a layer of isolation between the original packet and the network that the encapsulated packet is about to enter. Not all VPN technologies provide encryption for confidentiality and integrity protection, but most encapsulate the packet to make it compatible with the surrounding network, for example, to run a Layer 3 IP packet over a Layer 2 X.25 network.

Following are descriptions of some of the more popular VPN protocols.

- **Secure Shell (SSH)**   Not originally designed as a VPN but can be used as one. Provides encryption and authentication, usually based on public/private keys.

- **Layer 2 Forwarding (L2F)**   Cisco's proprietary tunneling protocol designed to tunnel point-to-point (PPP) dial-in traffic. L2F does not provide encryption.

- **Point to Point Tunneling Protocol (PPTP)**   Designed to tunnel PPP traffic over various networks, including IP, Internet Packet eXchange (IPX), and Network Basic Input/Output System Extended User Interface (NetBEUI). The original specification does not include authentication or encryption, but most implementations include both. Encryption is typically done using the RC4 symmetric key stream cipher.

- **Internet Protocol Security (IPsec)**   The de facto standard for a VPN. This protocol is extremely versatile and customizable, negotiating a *security association (SA)* for each direction of packet flow within the VPN. IPsec can use different forms of authentication, including passwords and digital certificates. IPsec, by default, includes an authentication header (AH) and Encapsulating Security Payload (ESP). AH provides weak authentication and integrity validation. ESP provides strong encryption and integrity validation. IPsec can operate in transport mode, in which encryption begins at the Layer 4 header and runs through the payload, allowing access to the forwarding and routing components of a packet. It can also operate in tunnel mode, in which the entire frame is encrypted, and a new Layer 2 and Layer 3 header and a new CRC trailer are added to the encrypted frame.

- **Layer 2 Tunneling Protocol (L2TP)**   An encapsulation protocol that commonly uses digital certificate-based authentication on the endpoints of the L2TP tunnel. L2TP does not require an IP network and can commute over Layer 2 networks such as X.25, asynchronous transfer mode (ATM), and Frame Relay. L2TP does not provide encryption. If confidentiality is required, an additional encryption protocol, such as IPsec, is required.

- **Secure Sockets Layer (SSL)**   The de facto secure channel for securing web-based protocols and transmissions (such as HTTP, SMTP, and VoIP). SSL was developed by Netscape and provides strong authentication, encryption, and integrity validation. SSL uses a digital certificate to authenticate the web-based server to the client and then performs secure symmetric session key distribution. SSL is finding its way onto the corporate LAN as a VPN in the newest VPN technology from Microsoft, Secure Socket Tunneling Protocol (SSTP).

- **Transport Layer Security (TLS)**   The latest version of SSL, TLS can require digital certificates on the client system and the server system for strong mutual authentication, strong confidentiality, and integrity validation. TLS also improves several other aspects of SSLv3.0.

- **Secure Socket Tunneling Protocol (SSTP)**   The LAN-based implementation of SSL on recent Windows-based systems. SSTP servers must use a digital certificate. Clients can be authenticated by using passwords or digital certificates (equating to TLS). SSTP uses TCP port 443, the same as HTTPS, to pass easily through firewalls and proxy servers.

Many administrators of corporate networks implement a filter to disallow *split tunneling*. Split tunneling occurs when a client connects to the corporate network over a VPN while also connected to another network (of most concern would be the Internet) using the same network interface. This could allow an attacker on the other network to gain access to the corporate network over the client's VPN connection.

Authentication protocols

Authentication is a process to verify the claimed identity of a user, client system, or server system. Historically, only users and client systems needed to authenticate to servers, and the server was typically not required to prove its identity to the clients. Today, with perils rampant on the Internet, and with many more remote connections, such as VPN, wireless, and some residual dial-up connections, servers are much more often required to authenticate themselves to clients.

- **Password Authentication Protocol (PAP)**   An older authentication protocol that transmits passwords over the network in plaintext, making it insecure. Its use is discouraged in almost all cases.

- **Challenge Handshake Authentication Protocol (CHAP)**   An authentication protocol that does not require the claimant to send a password over the network; this is called a zero-knowledge proof. A client requests to be authenticated by an authentication server. The server sends the client challenge text. This text typically contains a session identifier and a random string of ASCII characters. The client authentication process performs a one-way hash of the challenge text, the session ID, and the client's password. This hashed response is then sent from the client back to the authentication server, where it is then verified against the hash that the authentication server produced using the same process as the client. If the two hashes are identical, the client must have known the correct password and is successfully authenticated.

- **Microsoft CHAP version 2 (MS-CHAPv2)**   The Microsoft implementation of the open-standard CHAP protocol used on Windows logons.

- **Extensible Authentication Protocol (EAP)**   An application programming interface on the authentication service that allows additional authentication mechanisms to be used, now and in the future. EAP allows the use of digital certificates for user and system authentication.

PAN, LAN, MAN, WAN, and more

Networks come in all shapes and sizes to satisfy the needs of the users and the entities that build them. From very small peer-to-peer networks to networks that span the globe and beyond (satellites), different technologies are required to satisfy this broad range of needs; those technologies are updated and replaced over time as newer, faster, and more reliable technologies emerge.

Personal area networks

A *personal area network* (*PAN*) is usually defined as a network contained within about a 10-meter (33-foot) range from the user. The PAN is usually a wireless connection between peers because the size of the network usually doesn't warrant infrastructure systems such as dedicated servers. Devices are often mobile and battery powered, so the signal strength, and therefore transmission range, is usually limited. The PAN might include an uplink to a larger network or, perhaps, the Internet. Several commonly used PAN technologies include:

- **Infrared Data Association (IrDA)** Signaling uses infrared light and requires a point-to-point, unobstructed line of sight. Connectivity with closer peers (1–2 meters) is better than with farther peers. Data rates are typically low, 1 or 2 Mbps, but some technologies can reach 1 Gbps. Bright sunlight can overpower the signal and destroy or degrade the transmission capabilities. IrDA has been deployed in LAN environments where cabling is problematic and where 802.11 wireless communications might be impractical due to RF interference, but it is rare.

- **Bluetooth**   Probably the most popular PAN technology, Bluetooth was created by Ericsson and is used to connect many types of devices wirelessly. It is defined by the IEEE 802.15 specification and uses frequency-hopping spread spectrum (FHSS) radio frequency signaling in the 2.4-GHz frequency range. A Bluetooth PAN (called a *piconet*) can include up to eight active nodes, usually one master node and seven subordinate nodes, and up to 255 inactive (parked) subordinate nodes. Most Bluetooth PANs have a range from about 1 meter (Class 3), to 10 meters (Class 2), and up to 100 meters (Class 1). It currently supports data rates of about 2.1 Mbps maximum (version 2.1, coincidentally) but is targeting 24 Mbps in upcoming releases when used with additional 802.11 wireless technologies called Alternate MAC/PHY (AMP, using 802.11 MAC and Physical layers). Bluetooth is now managed by the Bluetooth special interest group (SIG).

- **Zigby**   Targeting the wireless control and monitoring market, Zigby focuses on connecting low-cost and low-power (battery operated) devices. It provides data rates up to 250 Kbps at a range of up to 75 meters. Zigby builds a mesh cluster of nodes and then forms a cluster of clusters to relay data. Zigby uses direct-sequence spread spectrum (DSSS), is a subset of the IEEE 802.15 Bluetooth specification, and uses the RF ranges of 868 MHz (Europe), 915 MHz (United States and Australia), and 2.4 GHz (worldwide).

Local area networks

A *local area network* (*LAN*) is typically defined as one or more owned (versus leased, as with telecommunications lines) and well-connected segments (10 Mbps or greater) in a limited geographical area. A typical LAN consists of the cabling media and a concentrator or switch that creates a segment and possibly includes routers that connect multiple segments. The LAN is usually bounded by firewalls, which are security devices at the connection points with remote networks and typically extends to a few hundred meters maximum. LAN technologies include:

- **Attached Resource Computer Network (ARCnet)**   A token-passing bus network technology invented in the late 1970s and popular in the early to mid-1980s. Network interface cards were configured with a unique 8-bit number on the segment, and the token would transmit from a node to the node with the next higher number. It supported data rates of 2.5 Mbps and ran on a 93-ohm coax physical star or linear bus requiring 93-ohm terminators at each end of the cable. The cable could run just over 600 meters maximum. The popularity of less expensive Ethernet over twisted-pair cabling and the better-performing token ring networks led to the demise of ARCnet in the mid-1980s. Token bus was defined by the IEEE 802.4 specification.

- **Token ring**   Introduced in the mid-1980s, token ring passes a 3-byte token frame around a cable ring to manage transmissions and avoid collisions. Most commonly implemented on twisted-pair cabling, token ring supported data rates of 4 Mbps (1985) and 16 Mbps (1989). One system on the ring (usually the first one powered up on the ring) acted as the *active monitor* (also called the token master) and would place one (4 Mbps) or more (16 Mbps) authorized tokens on the ring. Higher-end token ring implementations included Fiber Distributed Data Interface (FDDI) and Copper Distributed Data Interface (CDDI) networks that used redundant rings; eliminating the cable is the single point of failure. Of course, the fiber implementation also improved data rates and distance and increased the cost significantly. IBM introduced a token ring concentrator called a multistation access unit (MAU or MSAU) that collapsed the logical ring into a physical star topology. Token ring was defined by the IEEE 802.5 specification.

- **Ethernet**   Ethernet was introduced in the early 1980s by Xerox and was based on the ALOHAnet technology but was expensive at the time. It originally ran on 10BASE5 (Thicknet) linear bus, 50-ohm coax backbones and 10BASE2 (Thinnet) linear bus, 50-ohm coax branches. However, in the late 1980s, Ethernet began switching to the use of twisted-pair cabling (10BASE-T), four pairs of wires twisted around one another, which is relatively cheaper and easier to work with. This twisted-pair cabling attached to unpowered concentrators or powered hubs but now mostly connects to Layer 2 switches to improve performance and security and forms a star topology. Ethernet can also run over fiber optic cabling for greater data rates and transmission distances.

- Ethernet relies on a media access control method called Carrier Sense Multiple Access with Collision Detection (CSMA/CD), a contention-oriented, nondeterministic media access method. Ethernet has become the standard for LAN-based networks, but wireless is growing in popularity. Ethernet originally ran at 10 Mbps and used 48-bit source and destination addresses, but now it typically runs at 100 Mbps or 1 Gbps and uses IP addresses and 48-bit MAC addresses in half-duplex or full-duplex modes. Ethernet LANs are defined by the IEEE 802.3 specification.

- **Wireless**   Wireless networks are growing rapidly in popularity due to price reductions and the ease of installation. Wireless networks are inherently insecure because the signaling is entirely based on emanations that are easily intercepted by unauthorized users. Wireless LANs typically operate in the 2.4-Ghz or 5-GHz radio frequency ranges and offer standard data rates ranging from 1 Mbps to 54 Mbps. They use frequency-hopping spread spectrum (FHSS), direct-sequence spread spectrum (DSSS), and orthogonal frequency division multiplexing (OFDM) and quadrature amplitude modulation (QAM, a combination of amplitude modulation and phase-shift keying) encoding schemes at the higher data rates. Wireless LANs are defined by the IEEE 802.11 specification. Wireless technologies are described in the next section.

- **Virtual Local Area Network (VLAN)**   Not a true LAN in a classic sense, but the VLAN is a way to segregate or group clients logically. Prior to VLANs, physically reconnecting clients to the appropriate segments (hubs or switches) was required to accomplish this. VLANs are implemented in the switch by defining different VLANs and then assigning MAC addresses to the appropriate VLAN. With a little help from Layer 3, these VLANs can span across routers, logically placing nodes in the same collision and broadcast domains, even though they may be hundreds of miles apart and connected to different switches and routers.

Metropolitan area networks

Metropolitan area networks (*MANs*) typically range from a few hundred meters to tens of miles and are commonly owned or managed by a single entity. They are often used to connect multiple LANs and might be referred to as a campus area network (CAN). In addition to the MAN connecting multiple LANs, MAN technologies also include the huge market called the *last-mile* connectivity provided by Internet service providers (ISPs) between LANs such as your home network and the Internet. MAN technologies include:

- **Cable modem** Cable television companies have been installing infrastructure into the last-mile areas for years, perhaps decades, so that they can sell cable TV service to every home. As the demand for higher-speed connectivity to the Internet grew, these providers realized that they had big pieces of infrastructure in place and available bandwidth to provide this service. The cable modem typically receives RF broadband signals over coax from the cable company and translates that into digital Ethernet signaling used on the LAN. Many cable modems now include a router, a firewall, a NAT server, and a DHCP server and are assigned MAC and IP addresses to operate as a residential gateway between the home LAN and the Internet. Some cable modem systems are currently achieving data rates of over 160 Mbps, but data rates typically range between 2 to 8 Mbps. Original cable networks allowed connectivity between customers that shared the same cable trunk, so finally, in the early to mid-2000s, cable companies began using VLANs to separate or isolate the customers logically that shared the same cable trunk.

- **Digital Subscriber Line (DSL)** DSL is a high-speed Internet connectivity (last mile) technology that uses telephone lines and frequency division multiplexing (FDM). DSL data rates are typically about half those of cable modems, ranging between 1 and 3 Mbps. *Symmetric DSL (SDSL)* matches the uplink speeds to the downlink speeds, whereas *asymmetric DSL (ADSL)* optimizes the link to the way most home users actually consume bandwidth: a few characters in a URL and a few mouse clicks to uplink and then substantially more content being received on the downlink. Therefore, ADSL provides a small portion of the bandwidth—256 Kbps, for example—for the uplink traffic and the remainder of the bandwidth for all the stuff the typical home user is downloading from the Internet. High-rate DSL (HDSL) is symmetric and used on T1 lines, offering 1.544 Mbps over about 12,000 feet (approximately 2 miles). Very-high-data-rate DSL (VDSL) is asymmetric and provides between 13 Mbps and 52 Mbps downstream, with 1.5 Mbps to 2.3 Mbps upstream over about 4,500 feet (less than 1 mile).

- **Worldwide Interoperability for Microwave Access (WiMAX)** WiMAX is a wireless last-mile technology that provides data rates of about 40 Mbps, with 1 Gbps targeted in the near future, providing high data rates and good mobility. The technology competes with cable modems and DSL for stationary clients and might either compete with or be used to complement the upcoming 4G cellular network for mobile clients. It runs in a smattering of frequencies between 2 and 66 GHz and uses scalable OFDM and multiple input, multiple output (MIMO) transmitters, receivers, and antennas to achieve its greater distances and data rates. WiMAX is defined by the IEEE 802.16 specification.

- **Fiber Distributed Data Interface (FDDI)**   A fiber optic, double–token ring network that is often used as a backbone for MANs. Introduced around 1990 at 100 Mbps, a very high data rate for that time, and with a maximum distance of 124 miles and cable fault tolerance, this was the Cadillac of networks in its day. If fault tolerance wasn't the priority, the second ring could be used to carry data, increasing capacity to 200 Mbps.

- **Copper Distributed Data Interface (CDDI)**   The copper (twisted-pair, UTP) version of FDDI, with data rates at 100 Mbps and a maximum distance of 100 meters.

- **Synchronous Optical Network (SONET)**   SONET is an optical network that uses broadband digital fiber optics to carry large amounts of data and is used as both a MAN and a WAN technology. SONET is largely protocol independent and can carry Layer 2 communications (such as ATM communications) and Layer 3 communications (such as IP and Ethernet communications). Its channels are either Optical Carrier (OC) units at about 52 Mbps or Synchronous Transport Module, level 1 (STM-1) units at about 155 Mbps, equivalent to three OC units, commonly called an OC-3.

Wide area networks

 Wide area networks (*WANs*) span the globe and then some, ranging tens of miles to thousands of miles. They connect end users and LANs and MANs to faraway network resources. They are typically leased connections or are now more often the long-haul backbones that cross, connect, and form the Internet. Since the time when telephone service was common, there were WAN links. Early systems used analog couplers to telephone handsets. Then came the electronic modem to connect these computing devices, so the Public Switched Telephone Network (PSTN) became the first WAN technology. Other technologies grew from there. The FDDI and SONET MAN technologies can extend to WAN distances, and other WAN technologies include:

- **Serial Line Interface Protocol (SLIP)**   Designed to carry encapsulated IP frames over serial ports on computers through modems, SLIP was the dial-up protocol introduced on UNIX and Linux systems. However, SLIP had several deficiencies. It could not perform compression or encryption, and client systems could not be dynamically assigned an IP address, meaning that although a client might only connect for 10 minutes a month, the client had to be assigned a permanent IP address, consuming that static, preassigned address for (approximately) the life of the system.

- **Point-to-Point Protocol (PPP)**   PPP resolved the deficiencies that SLIP had by providing compression, encryption, and dynamic assignment of IP addresses. PPP has become the de facto standard for dial-up protocols, and much of the contemporary VPN and wireless connection technologies either rely on, or have evolved from, PPP.

- **Integrated Services Digital Network (ISDN)** Running on circuit-switched telephone wires, ISDN was presented as the new voice and data high-speed connection to the Internet for home users. ISDN offered data rates at 144 Kbps, of which 128 Kbps were usable, and 16 Kbps were an unusable control channel. This is made up from two B or Bearer channels at 64 Kbps each and one D or Data channel from a T1 line and is called a Basic Rate Interface or BRI. Unfortunately, to get these data rates, all the phone company's in-place wiring to households had to be replaced. While the wiring was being replaced, technology leapfrogged right past ISDN.

- **T1** The T1 is a digital, dedicated, point-to-point, circuit-switched connection providing 1.544 Mbps for voice and data that was developed by Bell Labs. The T1 can be broken into 24 user channels (called *DS0 channels*) at 64 Kbps each by using time-division multiplexing (TDM). In terms of ISDN, the T1 is called a Primary Rate Interface or PRI. A PRI contains 23 B channels at 64 Kbps and one D channel at 64 Kbps, totaling 1.536 Mbps, approximately consuming the T1.

- **E1** The European equivalent of a T1, the E1 provides 2 Mbps and 32 DS0 channels.

- **T3** The T1 architecture but with bandwidth up to 44.736 Mbps; 672 DS0 channels.

- **E3** The European equivalent of a T3, the E3 provides 34.368 Mbps and 512 DS0 channels.

- **X.25** An International Telecommunications Union Telecommunication Standardization Sector (ITU-T) standard for the first global, packet-switched WAN technology. It was developed in the 1980s and was used heavily into the 1990s on dumb terminal-to-mainframe connections. Data rates ranged from the common 56 Kbps up to the much less common 2 Mbps. Although X.25 is rarely used today, some older but secure and well-trusted financial applications still require X.25 communications. Asynchronous peripherals used a packet assembler/disassembler (PAD) to connect to the X.25 network.

- **Frame relay** A low-cost, packet-switching WAN technology that was largely based on X.25 technology but that has pretty well replaced X.25. At its low end, data rates ran at 56 Kbps, but that could be scaled up to a committed information rate (CIR) approaching 45 Mbps. A frame relay connection could also be configured as a permanent (or private) virtual circuit (PVC), where the connection path is predefined and not easily changed, or a switched virtual circuit (SVC), where the connection path is figured out on demand with each new connection. Another performance boost for frame relay came from doing error checking only at the endpoints and not on frames while in transit.

- **Asynchronous Transfer Mode (ATM)** The fastest WAN technology, commonly used for Internet backbone connections, typically over SONET fiber channels. ATM uses a mix of circuit-switching and packet-switching technologies. It uses a fixed 53-byte cell to simplify handling decisions; this improves performance by approximately 100 times versus variable-length packet switching (Ethernet). ATM provides 1.544 Mbps at its low end, up to 155 Mbps.

- **Satellite** A technology by which transmissions are relayed from a ground station to a geosynchronous satellite and then relayed back to earth-based ground stations within the satellite's coverage area on the earth's surface, which is called its footprint. Satellite communications are usually encrypted and typically use microwave-based transmissions.

EXAM TIP

WAN link T carriers (T1, T3) and E (E1, E3) carriers use time-division multiplexing (TDM) to share the media among multiple systems or customers.

Private Branch Exchange (PBX)

Not all information commuting over these various networks is data. With improved performance and priority-rating mechanisms such as QoS, digital networks carry time-sensitive payloads such as voice and video. One such system is the PBX.

The *PBX system* is a privately (business) owned telephone exchange that connects to a T1 or T3 dedicated line. Each B channel represents another phone extension on the system, or the unused channels could be aggregated to provide high-speed Internet connectivity.

PBXs have been the target of various attacks and are often overlooked during security audits and penetration testing. Most PBXs can be remotely configured by way of an analog modem connected to the device's administrative console. These connections are often forgotten and left unsecured by strong and changing passwords. Many attacks have occurred by an attacker dialing in to the administrative console and configuring remote, long-distance calling accounts. The attacker would sell long-distance service, but the PBX owner would pay the long-distance charges. The attacker could also interrupt or eavesdrop on phone calls on the PBX.

Voice over Internet Protocol

VoIP is another WAN technology. By using audio and video *codecs* (encoder/decoders) to encode speech into digital data, VoIP places voice (and possibly video) data into the payloads of IP packets for delivery to the recipient. If the recipient is also on a VoIP system, the packets will quite likely commute directly to the recipient wholly over the IP network. This can drastically reduce or eliminate long-distance charges, something that used to take their toll on the company budget. If the recipient is not on a VoIP phone, the packets will be delivered to a *VoIP media gateway* that connects VoIP to many telecommunications systems, such as PSTN, cellular, and PBX.

Session Initiation Protocol (*SIP*), by the IETF, is commonly used to create, modify, and terminate two-party (unicast) or multiple party (multicast) VoIP sessions. Interestingly, SIP is largely based on HTTP request and response mechanisms to establish the VoIP calls. A competing technology to SIP is the *H.323 protocol* from ITU-T for initiating audio and video sessions over a network.

VoIP is not without its share of technological and logistical problems. Audio and video data is time sensitive and must arrive promptly, or it has lost its usefulness. Because packet-switched networks, like most IP networks today, can introduce variable delays in the delivery of packets, VoIP is subject to latency (time lag) and jitter (interruptions in the voice stream). To overcome this, VoIP relies heavily on QoS features to require priority forwarding of the VoIP packets through the IP network. The *Real-Time Protocol* (*RTP*), another IETF protocol, assists with these time-sensitive communications, which helps improve QoS and session initiation.

With VoIP, because IP networks are based on logical IP addressing that can easily be relocated, versus a fixed address assigned to a phone number on an analog land line, emergency 911 calls are not routed correctly to the nearest emergency services center. Most emergency services identify addresses based on phone numbers, and they cannot identify the address of the caller when the caller is using a VoIP phone. Several solutions have been introduced, such as adding one PSTN line connected to the VoIP system that all 911 calls are routed to, or the use of the Enhanced 911 (E911) service, in which VoIP providers register VoIP phone numbers to addresses. As a result, most systems now can resolve this problem.

Because the network and the phone system are integrated in VoIP, if for any reason the network or the Internet connection goes down, the telephone system also is down. VoIP might also be called IP telephony.

Wireless networking

Wireless networks have become a fast-growing technology because of their low cost and ease of deployment. With no cabling infrastructure to deploy, the network installs very rapidly, and is just as easily moved, with no cabling to be pulled out or left behind. But beware! The low cost and ease of installation of wireless networks, coupled with their emanations-based transmission technology, make a legitimate wireless network inherently vulnerable to attack and breach and makes wireless technology a useful attack tool for the bad guys.

Wireless LAN is defined by the IEEE 802.11 family of specifications with quite a few subdivisions for individual wireless technologies. Table 7-8 presents a brief summary of the 802.11 family of specifications and principal technologies.

TABLE 7-8 802.11 Wireless technology summary

Spec	Frequency	Data rate	Maximum distance	Notes
802.11	2.4 GHz	2 Mbps	100 m	FHSS, DSSS, WEP
802.11b	2.4 GHz	11 Mbps	140 m	FHSS, DSSS
802.11g	2.4 GHz	54 Mbps	140 m	FHSS, DSSS, OFDM
802.11a	5 GHz	54 Mbps	120 m	FHSS, DSSS, OFDM

Spec	Frequency	Data rate	Maximum distance	Notes
802.11n	2.4 and / or 5 GHz	150 Mbps	250 m	Multiple input, multiple output (MIMO) up to 4 transmitters, receivers, and antennas for multiple simultaneous data streams over a single channel
802.11i				Security for 802.11 technologies; WPA and WPA2; replacement for WEP
802.11e				Quality of Service (QoS) for priority and time-sensitive data
802.11f				Inter-Access Point Protocol (IAPP): secure, fast roaming and load balancing; withdrawn in 2006
802.11h	5 GHz			Compatibility with European satellite and radar frequency allocation conflicts between 5 GHz and 6 GHz
802.11j	4.9 GHz			Compatibility with Japanese satellite and radar frequency allocation conflicts between 5 GHz and 6 GHz
802.11ac Draft	5 GHz	Approaching 3.5 Gbps	Potentially miles or tens of miles	Multiple input, multiple output (MIMO), up to 8 transmitters, receivers, and antennas for multiple, simultaneous data streams over a single channel

The FCC is responsible for frequency allocation in the United States and has allocated these two ranges (2.4 GHz and 5 GHz) for wireless network communications. Other countries have similar regulating bodies to allocate the use of the frequency spectrum in their countries but, on occasion, allocate the ranges differently. This is why 802.11h and 802.11j are needed.

Wireless networking basics

Wireless networking uses the air as the medium and radio frequency (RF) signaling to transmit data between wireless networked devices. The typical hardware wireless networks use is a wireless network interface card (NIC) in each wireless client system and a wireless access point (AP) that is usually connected to a wired infrastructure. A wireless access point acts as the mediator of a collection of associated wireless clients, called a cell, and typically has one transmitter/receiver installed for operation at the 802.11, 802.11b, and 802.11g frequencies of 2.4 GHZ, and/or a transmitter/receiver that operates at the 802.11a frequency of 5 GHz. Most APs include several switched ports for wired client connectivity. The AP needs to be configured to define many of the parameters that the wireless clients must match for network connectivity to occur. The required parameters to be configured on the AP include:

- The service set Identifier (SSID), which identifies the wireless network.
- The specific RF frequency range (channel number) on the transmitter/receiver.
- The security type (WEP, WPA, or WPA2).

- Security settings, including personal versus enterprise authentication, password, passphrase, and encryption algorithm.

- The IP configuration, including IP address and subnet mask.

Wireless APs also typically have several optional components that can be configured, including those that do the following:

- Change the administrative user name and password.

- Provide an uplink configuration—a bridged or routed connection to a wired infrastructure.

- Enable or disable transmitter/receiver (in a multi-transmitter/receiver [2.4 GHz/5 GHz] system).

- Change the time, time zone, or time source.

- Provide the domain name.

- Enable or disable remote administration (using the uplink/WAN port).

- Enable or disable the DNS relay function.

- Enable or disable the DHCP server, including scope and lease time.

- Enable or disable SSID broadcast—when SSID broadcast is on (which is the default), the AP broadcasts its SSID every 0.1 seconds; often disabled for security purposes.

- Enable or disable MAC address filtering.

- Enable or disable the firewall, including rules and URL filtering.

- Enable or disable the NAT server, including port forwarding.

- Enable or disable VPN pass-through.

- Enable or disable multicast.

- Set advanced wireless AP configuration, including data rates, power, RTS, CTS, and more.

Wireless clients must have a wireless NIC that matches the transmitters and receivers in the AP (2.4 GHz or 5 GHz) and must be configured with the SSID and security settings to match the AP. Client systems are typically set to match the radio channel defined by the AP automatically.

Because technology developed quickly and, with technology leading the standards, wireless hardware vendors were all rapidly designing and offering their own versions of devices with their own special, proprietary, and often incompatible, features. To help ensure vendor-to-vendor device compatibility, the wireless device vendors formed the Wireless Fidelity Alliance, or Wi-Fi Alliance. When a device is marked Wi-Fi, it means the device meets the specifications and is likely to be compatible with other vendors' Wi-Fi-certified products (but you might still give up some proprietary features if you don't standardize by using the gear from a single vendor for the entire wireless infrastructure).

EXAM TIP

The Wi-Fi Alliance is a consortium of wireless device manufacturers with the goal of improving the interoperability of wireless devices from different vendors.

Wireless networks operate in one of two modes:

- **Ad Hoc**   A peer-to-peer mode of operation by which wireless nodes communicate directly with one another. Ad hoc implies the absence of an AP. All wireless clients participating in the same ad hoc network share the administrative tasks for the network and must use the same SSID.

- **Infrastructure**   A wireless access point that acts as the mediator of a collection of associated wireless clients, called a cell. Wireless clients communicate with the AP, and the AP relays (bridges) clients' frames to other wireless destinations or to a wired infrastructure. All wireless clients participating in the same infrastructure mode network must use the same SSID. Figure 7-27 shows a typical configuration for a wireless access point.

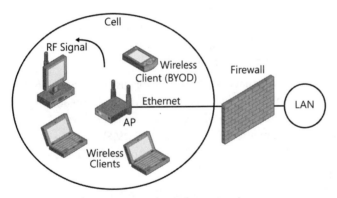

FIGURE 7-27 Infrastructure mode wireless network

FREQUENCY HOPPING SPREAD SPECTRUM

Wireless networks were originally defined to use *frequency-hopping spread spectrum* (*FHSS*) and direct-sequence spread spectrum (DSSS). FHSS was invented by Hedy Lamarr, the 1940s actress, and composer George Antheil among others. To avoid common narrow-band RF interference, the technology uses 75 narrow-band frequencies within a 78-MHz spectrum of frequencies (thus the term *spread spectrum*). FHSS transmits data in one narrow band frequency, typically for 100 microseconds, quickly hops to a different frequency to transmit data for the next 100 microseconds, and then hops again, and so on, much like playing different notes on a piano, as shown in Figure 7-28. The transmitters and receivers must agree on a hop pattern prior to data transmissions.

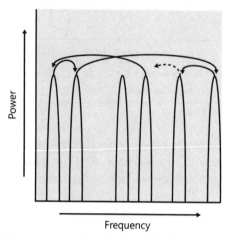

FIGURE 7-28 Frequency-hopping spread spectrum

DIRECT SEQUENCE SPREAD SPECTRUM

Direct sequence spread spectrum (*DSSS*) does not change its transmission frequency like FHSS, but it transmits its data over a wide, 22-MHz frequency range. This way, common narrowband interference might corrupt a portion of the range being used but typically will not interfere with the whole, wide range of the spread spectrum, allowing the transmitted data to be received correctly in frequency ranges without interference.

To achieve higher data rates, wireless networks now primarily use orthogonal frequency division multiplexing (OFDM), which is often incorrectly referred to as a spread spectrum technology. OFDM uses 48 discrete narrowband channels at close but different frequencies to transmit its data. This is like going from a serial cable (FHSS and DSSS) with one signal channel to a parallel cable (OFDM) with 48 signal channels. OFDM occupies a frequency range similar to FHSS and DSSS but carries much more data.

With DSSS and OFDM, the receivers must adjust to match the transmitter's transmission channel prior to data transmissions. Subdivisions (channels) within a frequency range allow multiple entities to use the same transmitter/receiver (802.11g at 2.4 GHz or 802.11a at 5 GHz) in close proximity and avoid or minimize interference.

In the United States, when the 2.4-GHz frequency range is used, DSSS and OFDM have 11 channels. However, because the spread spectrum uses such a wide band (22 MHz), to minimize overlap and interference when using single frequency transmissions, like those in 802.11, 802.11b, and 802.11g, only three channels should be used. Channels 1, 6, and 11 provide the smallest amount of overlap and interference, as shown in Figure 7-29. In the United States, using any channel other than 1, 6, or 11 in the 2.4-GHz range is generally a mistake. Japan allows 14 channels when using DSSS. Most of the rest of the world allows 13 DSSS channels.

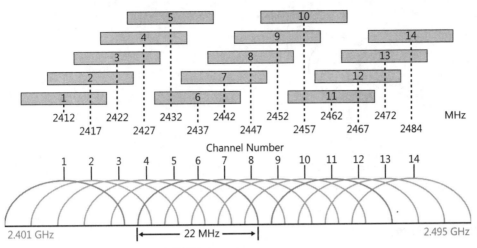

FIGURE 7-29 The 2.4-GHz DSSS and OFDM channel map

More than 20 channels are available in the 802.11a 5 GHz to 6 GHz frequency range in the United States, Europe, and Japan. Each of these channels is 20 MHz wide. These channels do not overlap, and all can be used. Eight channels are intended for internal LAN use.

> **NOTE   802.11N, 802.11AC, AND MIMO**
>
> When 802.11n, the new IEEE draft 802.11ac (due Feb. 2014), or MIMO is used, the channels might overlap. Powerful digital signal processors (DSPs) sort through the interference and multi-path signals to reassemble clear and readable transmissions. 802.11n, 802.11ac, and MIMO are covered in the "802.11n and 802.11ac: Multiple input, multiple output" section later in this chapter.

ROAMING

Wireless cells can be overlapped by using the same SSID on the APs but a different channel number. This allows the wireless client to move from one cell to another and remain attached to the same wireless network. The wireless client associates with the AP with the strongest signal, based on the client's present position. As the client moves to a point where another AP with the same SSID has a stronger signal, the client disassociates with the first AP and associates with the second AP, the one with the now stronger signal. This is called *roaming* and is shown in Figure 7-30. In the figure, each circle is the coverage area from an 802.11g access point, and the numbers inside the cells represent the channel numbers. All cells use the same SSID.

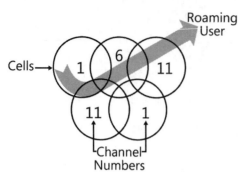

FIGURE 7-30 Roaming through a five-cell wireless network

Wireless security

Wireless networking is inherently vulnerable to eavesdropping, man-in-the-middle attacks, and attacks that acquire unauthorized access to the wired infrastructure. Security for wireless networks should be carefully considered and implemented to the fullest extent the network infrastructure supports to satisfy the network access requirements and to follow the principle of least privilege. Following are security controls available on wireless networks, approximately in the order they should be considered and, if possible, implemented.

- Change the administrative user name (if possible) and password.

- Change the SSID.

- Disable the SSID broadcast. (This is an option only if all clients can be preconfigured. It is not an option in a public hotspot, for example.)

- Implement MAC address filtering. (This is an option only if all clients can be preconfigured. It is not an option in a public hotspot, for example.)

- Implement enterprise authentication for the corporate environment, personal for the home environment. (Personal authentication might also be called pre-shared key [PSK] or shared-key authentication [SKA].)

- Implement WPA2 security (stronger; also called Robust Secure Network [RSN]) or WPA security (weaker but might be required for compatibility with older wireless hardware). WEP is not recommended due to multiple vulnerabilities.

- Implement Advanced Encryption Standard (AES) (stronger) or Temporal Key Integrity Protocol (TKIP) (weaker but might be required for compatibility with older wireless hardware) for confidentiality.

- Perform cell shaping to reduce signal strength where coverage is not desired. For example, place the AP in the center of the desired coverage area.

Although these security controls should be implemented, many are relatively easily over-come by a skilled and dedicated attacker. Implement them nonetheless. They send the signal to the attacker that this won't be an easy attack. They will cost the attacker time and effort, and he will risk exposure during the lengthy attack attempt. This signal acts as a deterrent and might convince him to focus his efforts on easier targets.

Beyond AP and wireless environment configuration, the following security controls should be considered and implemented if possible:

- Treat the wireless environment as hostile and keep it isolated from the wired, internal network by using a firewall.

- Require all clients to use strong authentication (as strong as the infrastructure will permit). Use enterprise authentication if possible. If using personal authentication, require compliance with a strong password policy.

- Require all clients to use wireless encryption (AES [preferred] or TKIP).

- In addition to the wireless encryption, require all clients to use a VPN into the corporate LAN for all data transmissions when connecting by the wireless network.

- Perform security awareness training for all corporate wireless users.

WEP, WPA, and WPA2

The original 802.11 specification included security for the wireless network called *Wired Equivalent Privacy* (*WEP*). WEP includes the following security controls:

- **Authentication**   Pre-shared key (PSK) or open (no authentication).

  Due to vulnerabilities in the authentication scheme that expose the authentication key, and the fact that the same key is used for data encryption, using open authentication (no authentication) became recommended along with required data encryption.

- **WEP key**   The same key is used for authentication and data encryption, and all users in the cell use the same WEP key.

  - Short: 40 bits long + 24-bit initialization vector (IV).

  - Long: 104 bits long + 24-bit initialization vector (IV).

- **Data encryption**   Based on RC4.

- **Data integrity**   Based on a 32-bit cyclic redundancy check (CRC) hash.

Unfortunately, WEP had numerous vulnerabilities, including its use of the authentication password as the data encryption key, that all users shared the same password (and encryption key), lack of an easy password/key rotation, and an initialization vector that was too short. It was quickly realized that WEP should not be used because it could be completely cracked and violated in a very short time.

To address the security problems with WEP, the IEEE developed the standards for *802.11i*, which introduced *Wi-Fi Protected Access version 2* (*WPA2*), also called the RSN. Because WEP was based on RC4, a symmetric key stream cipher, and WPA2 is based on the much more CPU-demanding Advanced Encryption Standard (AES), wireless hardware that was designed to meet the original 802.11 specification using RC4 would have to be replaced with devices having more powerful CPU chips to handle the demands of AES. Replacing a wireless infra-structure (especially one that might have just been installed) would take time and money.

To fix the problems with WEP immediately, and without forcing companies to replace wireless hardware (APs and NICs) immediately to run WPA2, *WPA* (version 1) was included in the 802.11i specification as a temporary measure. WPA fixes all the known vulnerabilities with WEP and, like WEP, WPA is based on the RC4 encryption algorithm, so original 802.11 hard-ware would be able to run WPA. WPA was designed to require only a firmware update on the original hardware to upgrade from WEP to WPA and fix the security issues.

WPA uses TKIP and Message Integrity Check (MIC or Michael). TKIP is based on RC4 and provides the following improvements over WEP:

- Enterprise or personal authentication (explained in more detail in this section)
- Separate data (per user) and broadcast (per cell) encryption keys
- Per-packet key rotation
- A sequence counter to prevent replay attacks
- An increase of the IV to 64 bits
- Integrity validation using MIC, a 64-bit hash

Although these improvements over WEP were very much needed, they were designed as temporary improvements to be replaced with WPA2. With the release of the updated 802.11 specification in 2009, now that people and companies have had the time to upgrade their wireless hardware to run WPA2, the use of WPA has been removed, and all wireless networks should be running only WPA2.

WPA2 replaces TKIP with AES in a special mode called Counter mode (CTR) with cipher block chaining (CBC) Message Authentication Code (MAC) protocol, collectively referred to as CCMP. In this implementation, AES uses a 128-bit key and block size.

Both WPA and WPA2 provide personal and enterprise authentication. Personal authen-tication is aimed at the home user and is based on a pre-shared key, such as a password, to authenticate the users of the cell to the AP.

Enterprise authentication targets the corporate network environment with the expectation of a full-featured networking infrastructure, including Remote Authentication Dial-In User Service (RADIUS) server (or similar), an X.509 digital certificate for server authentication on the RADIUS server, and an authentication system, such as directory services, that accepts EAP authentication mechanisms. Enterprise authentication in 802.11i includes 802.1x port-based authentication built into the AP that forwards EAP authentication traffic from a prospective wireless client to the wired network but disallows any other type of traffic until the client has been successfully authenticated and authorized. Figure 7-31 shows a typical 802.11i enter-prise authentication system.

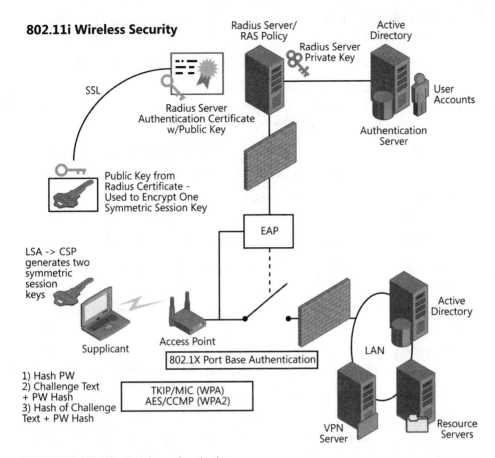

802.11i Wireless Security

SSL

Radius Server
Authentication Certificate
w/Public Key

Public Key from
Radius Certificate -
Used to Encrypt One
Symmetric Session Key

Radius Server/
RAS Policy

Radius Server
Private Key

Active
Directory

User
Accounts

Authentication
Server

EAP

LSA -> CSP
generates two
symmetric
session
keys

Supplicant

Access Point

802.1X Port Base Authentication

1) Hash PW
2) Challenge Text
+ PW Hash
3) Hash of Challenge
Text + PW Hash

TKIP/MIC (WPA)
AES/CCMP (WPA2)

LAN

Active
Directory

VPN
Server

Resource
Servers

FIGURE 7-31 802.11i enterprise authentication

The steps in the enterprise authentication process are as follows:

1. The wireless client (also called the supplicant) requests association to the access point. The user typically has entered her user name and password in a logon form on her local system.

2. The AP negotiates WPA enterprise or WPA2 enterprise authentication for the wireless association with the client. The AP is in the unauthorized state for this session at this point, forwarding only EAP authentication traffic to the wired network. Notice the open switch to the LAN but the connected path to the RADIUS server.

3. The AP notifies the RADIUS server of the authentication request.

4. The RADIUS server sends its server authentication certificate to the client.

5. The client verifies the server authentication certificate.

6. The client generates a pair of symmetric session keys to secure the authentication process.

7. The client encrypts one symmetric session key with the RADIUS server's public key from the digital certificate.

8. The client sends an encrypted copy of the symmetric session key to the RADIUS server.

9. The RADIUS server uses its private key to decrypt the symmetric session key. This is now a completed SSL-encrypted tunnel between the supplicant and the RADIUS server used to secure the authentication process.

10. The RADIUS server notifies the authentication server of the authentication request.

11. The authentication server creates challenge text and sends it to the RADIUS server.

12. The RADIUS server encrypts the challenge text using the symmetric session key and sends the encrypted challenge text to the client.

13. The client uses its symmetric session key to decrypt the challenge text.

14. The client calculates a hash value of the user's password and appends this hash value to the challenge text.

15. The client calculates a hash value of the challenge text and the appended hashed password.

16. By using the symmetric session key, the client encrypts the hash value of the challenge text with the appended hashed password and sends this to the RADIUS server.

17. The RADIUS server uses its symmetric session key to decrypt the challenge text with the appended hashed password and passes this to the authentication server.

18. The authentication server calculates a hash value of the user's password and appends this hash value to the challenge text it previously sent to the client.

19. The authentication server calculates a hash value of the challenge text and the appended hashed password of the user.

20. The authentication server compares its generated hash value of the challenge text and the appended hashed password of the user to the one received from the client. If the two hash values *are identical*, the user must have known the correct password and must be the correct user. In this case, the user is successfully authenticated. If the two hash values *are not identical*, the user did not know or did not correctly type the correct password. In this case, the user is *not* successfully authenticated.

21. If the user is successfully authenticated, the authentication server identifies the now authenticated user to the RADIUS server, including user name and group membership.

22. The RADIUS server identifies the correct RADIUS policy that applies to the user and identifies the rules in the policy governing the user's wireless connection.

23. The RADIUS server notifies the client and the AP of the successful authentication and provides the RADIUS policy for this user to the AP.

24. The AP changes the state of the 802.1x port from the unauthorized state to the authorized state, allowing access to the wired network for data. All wireless transmissions between client and AP are protected, using TKIP (WPA) or AES/CCMP (WPA2). If the user violates any parameters of the RADIUS policy, the AP changes the state of the 802.1x port to unauthorized and disconnects the user.

802.11n and 802.11ac: multiple input, multiple output

The newest technology on the scene is MIMO. *Multiple input/multiple output* (*MIMO*) provides greater data rates and greater transmission distance. MIMO uses two or more transmitters, two or more receivers, two or more antennas, a wider frequency spectrum (40 MHz versus 20 MHz or 22 MHz) (optional), and spatial division multiplexing to provide multiple data streams in either the 802.11g or the 802.11a frequency ranges. The 802.11n specification allows up to four transmitters, receivers, and antennas each, with which data rates can reach 600 Mbps and transmission distances can reach 250 meters. Greater distances are accomplished through antenna spatial diversity (physical distance between antennas) and RF beamforming techniques (phased array controls). The client NIC and the AP must both support MIMO for MIMO to be effective.

A new draft standard called 802.11ac increases the number of transmitters, receivers, and antennas up to as many as eight each, which is expected to bring wireless MIMO connections to the range of 1Gbps or more and potentially miles of transmission distance. Many vendors are already making 802.11ac-certified hardware, preceding the ratification of the new standard. Data rates are currently in the range of 3.5 Gb/s with coverage areas approaching 6 miles radius.

Worldwide Interoperability for Microwave Access

The *Worldwide Interoperability for Microwave Access* (*WiMAX*) specification targets fixed and mobile wireless clients; it is defined by the IEEE 802.16 specification. It currently operates at about 40 Mbps and targets 1 Gbps; it is growing in popularity as a last-mile Internet connection technology in remote locations. WiMAX is being incorporated in cellular telecommunication's 4G networking technologies. With its relatively high data rates, it is becoming popular as a triple-play technology, providing voice, data, and IP TV. Client-side WiMAX modems are called subscriber units (SUs) and can operate in ad hoc mode or infrastructure mode, like 802.11.

WiMAX doesn't have any allocated unlicensed frequency ranges, but it has presented licensing profiles at 2.3 GHz, 2.5 GHz, and 3.5 GHz, with the United States' implementation falling primarily at 2.5 GHz. Other frequency ranges can be added to the WiMAX spectrum.

Cellular networking

The cell phone has become the communications device, personal assistant, and entertainment device of virtually everyone in the industrialized world. The communications system behind the phones is moving toward the fourth generation (labeled International Mobile Telecommunications Advanced, or IMT-Advanced), which offers 100 Mbps and a connection (in theory) as reliable as a wired network. Cellular systems operate much like wireless networks that are set up for roaming, with a specific geographic coverage area for a cell in which users disassociate from one cell and associate with a new cell as its signal becomes stronger. However, cellular cells range in size from about a 12-km radius to about a 48-km radius versus 802.11's few-hundred-meters radius.

Cellular systems use different technologies to manage the many simultaneous sessions (calls and data accesses) within each cell. Early first-generation (1 G) analog systems used frequency-division multiple access (FDMA). The second generation of cellular services introduced Global System for Mobile Communications (GSM), code division multiple access (CDMA), and time division multiple access (TDMA). The third generation uses enhanced data rates for GSM evolution (EDGE), Universal Mobile Telecommunications Systems (UMTS), and Evolution-Data Optimized (or Data Only) (EV-DO). As we approach the fourth generation, the technologies include time-division duplexing (TDD), frequency-division duplexing (FDD), and 802.16's WiMAX. Table 7-9 shows a brief history of the advancement of cellular technologies.

TABLE 7-9 Cellular technology summary

	Years	Technology	Frequency	Data rate	Details
1G	1990–1994	Analog: FDMA	900 MHz	2.4 Kbps	Voice only
2G	1994–2001	Digital: GSM, CDMA, TDMA	1.8 GHz	14.4 Kbps	Voice, email, paging, caller ID
3G	2001–2005	Digital: UMTS, EV-DO, CDMA2000	2 GHz	2 Mbps	IP-based networking and web services

	Years	Technology	Frequency	Data rate	Details
4G LTE	2011	Digital: TDD, FDD, WiMAX	Many (41 so far) 700 MHz through 3.6 GHz	100 Mbps Peak	4G Long Term Evolution, intermediate step toward true 4G
4G	20??	Digital: OFDM, IMT-Advanced	40 GHz, 60 GHz	100 Mbps	Reliable, high-speed, IP-based networking and web services

Cell phones must be included in security reviews performed for organizations. The organization often issues them to employees, and they are often a vehicle for the unauthorized distribution of sensitive data, either by sending sensitive data by using the unmonitored cellular system or as a storage device, potentially containing multiple gigabytes of sensitive data. Most cell phones have built-in cameras that can be used to take still or video images. In highly sensitive areas (security zones) within an organization, cell phones should be disallowed, with policies, signage, pointed questions by guards, and possibly searches to verify that they do not penetrate the perimeter.

Attacking the network

The bad guys are out there and keeping busy. Existing network technology and software is loaded with vulnerabilities yet to be found. Every time networking technology and security professionals make an improvement in the security structure of an organization or network, the bad guys are there to find new ways to violate it. It seems it will forever be a costly game of cat and mouse.

Types of attacks

Some attackers simply peruse the Internet looking for easy prey, targets of opportunity—grazing, in a sense. These attacks are referred to as *browsing attacks*. Whoever presents himself with vulnerabilities becomes the next victim. The attackers who commit browsing attacks are usually motivated by the thrill of the challenge and the feeling of accomplishment after a successful exploit and are less often driven by greed or revenge.

Greed and revenge most often have a finer focus, like a spear tip pointed at a source of anger and frustration or the soon-to-be victim who has something of known value to steal or otherwise compromise. These types of attacks are referred to as *targeted attacks* and are usually much more aggressive and dangerous. Organized crime and even governments commit large amounts of resources to the methodical and ongoing development of intelligence and sophisticated exploits and malware, often specifically designed for the compromise of a specific target.

Attacks vary in their intent in that some attacks are designed to steal information to compromise confidentiality; some are designed to violate the integrity of the information, such as a website defacement attack; and still others are crafted to defeat availability. Information theft and denial of service (DoS) are the two most prevalent goals of attacks.

Denial of service attack

The *DoS attack* is designed to overwhelm a system's resources with bogus requests so that the victim system cannot service legitimate requests for service. Following are several of the classic DoS attacks. The majority of these attack vectors have been rendered obsolete with updates to the protocols that allowed them to function or by establishing controls through vendors' recommended best practices on the configuration of the vulnerable systems.

- **SYN flood**   Systems that use TCP/IP establish a TCP session using a three-way handshake: SYN, SYN/ACK, ACK. With each new inbound request for a TCP session, the system allocates buffer memory to maintain the apparently legitimate session. An attacker spoofs a source IP address and then floods the victim with SYN packets, seemingly requesting many TCP sessions. The TCP session handshakes are never completed, but the victim system has allocated so much buffer memory to these bogus requests that it has no more memory to allocate and now cannot service legitimate inbound requests for TCP session services.

- **Ping of death**   Ping is an application administrators use to test IP connectivity. Ping sends an ICMP echo request to a remote system. When a remote system receives a ping request, it is supposed to respond by copying the payload, usually 32 bytes, back to the source system to verify connectivity between the two systems. Attackers use ping to request an echo greater than 64 KB, which causes a buffer overflow in the target system, causing the target system to crash (lock up).

- **Smurf attack**   The attacker spoofs the target's IP address as the source IP address and then sends a ping (ICMP echo request) with a large payload to a broadcast address. Each recipient of the broadcast then sends an ICMP echo response to the intended target system. This floods the target with responses to the extent that it can no longer process legitimate inbound communications. The Fraggle attack is similar but uses UDP instead of TCP.

- **Teardrop attack**   This attack is also called the Frag or Fragmentation attack. At a router, when a received packet is larger than the next hop network can accept, the router breaks the too-large packet into smaller fragments that will fit on the next hop network. When the fragments arrive at the destination, they are reassembled in the correct order to reconstruct the original payload. This process is called fragmentation and reassembly. As the router breaks up the original, too-large payload into smaller fragments, it identifies the fragment number and the offset from the first byte of the original payload in each fragment header, providing instructions to the destination system on how to reassemble the various fragments upon arrival. Attackers craft and send fragments to target victims with reassembly instructions that cannot be accomplished, preventing the receiving system from processing the fragments. With no programmatic instruction on how to process these fragments, the receiving system simply holds the fragments in memory, eventually consuming all available inbound buffer memory space, leaving no memory to process legitimate inbound packets or fragments.

- **LAND (local area network denial) attack** An attacker crafts packets by using the victim's IP address and open port number as both the source IP address and port number and destination IP address and port number. This causes the victim to reply continuously to itself, consuming its network resources until it cannot service legitimate network requests.

Distributed denial of service attack

As with the denial of service attack, it is the goal of the *DDoS attack* to consume the system resources of the victim to the point of preventing the system from servicing legitimate requests for service. The difference is that instead of there being one attacker, as in the DoS attack, the attacker uses many compromised systems to perform the attack from many systems. The attacker, called the *master* in this model, compromises many systems over time. The individual compromised systems are called *zombies* or *bots*. The collection of zombies is called *an army*. The collection of bots is called a *botnet*.

To isolate herself from the attack, the attacker controls these zombie systems through a layer of intermediate compromised systems called *handlers*. The attacker communicates with her handler systems usually through some anonymous and publicly accessible communication channel such as Internet Relay Chat (IRC). The handler systems monitor a specified chat room watching for a coded message. When the message is received, each handler uses IRC in a similar manner to communicate anonymously with its battalion of zombies and identify the time and target of the DDoS attack. Figure 7-32 shows this DDoS architecture.

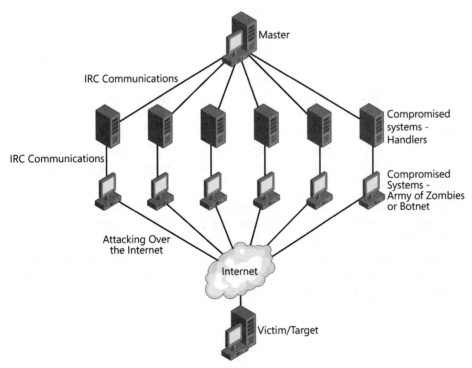

FIGURE 7-32 Architecture of the distributed denial of service attack

Some of the better-known DDoS attacks include the Tribe Flood Network (TFN), TFN2k, Trinoo, and Stacheldraht.

Information theft

Another objective of attackers is the theft of valuable information such as credit card numbers and customers' personally identifiable information (PII). This information can bring tremendous financial benefit to attackers through using the stolen credit card information to make fraudulent purchases, using PII to steal the identities of victims and take out fraudulent loans or forge identities for other purposes, or extort fees from the victim company for "consulting services" to protect the release of the stolen information. Companies and governments might also steal information to gain competitive advantage or for marketing purposes. Following are several types of attacks on a network that are implemented to steal information.

- **Eavesdropping/sniffing**   Whether the network is wireless or wired, a sniffer can capture and record all frames commuting across the network media. The eavesdropping attack is very difficult to detect because the attacker doesn't need to do anything except connect to the network media. On a wired network that uses switches, the attacker must convince the switch to forward all packets to the port the sniffer is connected to. This is usually done by telling the switch that its MAC address is every MAC address; therefore, forward every frame to this port.

- **Traffic analysis**   In critical situations, such as during disagreements between governments and during battles, communications are usually encrypted to keep the contents of the communications secret. However, sometimes, just the nature of the traffic patterns might reveal something about the content. Imagine the communications surrounding an upcoming battle. The defending army cannot understand the messages being transmitted by the attackers, but it can monitor the nature of the traffic. If it identifies a long, encrypted transmission from headquarters to the battalions, followed by short transmissions from each battalion back to headquarters, this might likely be the instructions for the attack followed by acknowledgements from the individual battalions. This could mean that an attack is imminent, providing valuable information to the defending army. A good defense against traffic analysis is to pad the traffic all the time, maintaining a relatively steady level of traffic and burying the legitimate traffic within the garbage padding of traffic.

- **Emanations detection**   As electrons flow through a wire, they emanate an electromagnetic (EM) field around the conductor. This EM field can be detected and deciphered, allowing the attacker to access information he is probably unauthorized to access. Shielding, including the use of a Faraday cage and other Tempest technologies, can reduce the emanations. Fiber optic cabling (which uses photons, not electrons, for signaling) can also defeat emanations detection attacks.

- **Man-in-the-middle (MITM)**   This is a family of attacks in which the attacker spoofs the identity of the remote system to the two legitimate endpoints of a session. If Lulu and BoBo are establishing a session, the attacker pretends to be Lulu to Bobo and BoBo to Lulu. In this manner, the attacker intercepts every communication between the two, allowing her to violate the confidentiality, integrity, availability, or all three, of the information sent between the two. If Lulu and BoBo use VPNs to secure their trans-mission, they are each actually building their VPN with the attacker, thinking she is the correct destination. Strong mutual authentication of the remote endpoints, knowing with certainty that you are connecting to the correct destination endpoint, is the best solution to avoid MITM attacks. Figure 7-33 shows the MITM attack.

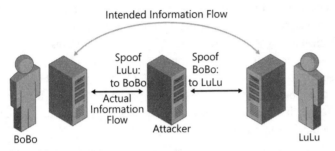

FIGURE 7-33 Man-in-the-middle attack

- **Session hijacking**   This is a family of attacks that typically allow the attacker to inject himself as a man in the middle between two legitimate endpoints of a session, allow-ing him to violate confidentiality, integrity, availability, or all three, of the information flowing between the two legitimate endpoints. Attack methods can include ARP cache poisoning, IP spoofing, or name spoofing.

- **ARP cache poisoning**   Address Resolution Protocol (ARP) is a Layer 2 protocol that resolves destination IP addresses on the local subnet to the host's MAC address to complete the Layer 2 header of an outbound frame. ARP sends out a broadcast query asking, "Whoever is using this IP address, please send me your MAC address." When the querying host receives an ARP reply, the host stores that MAC address informa-tion in a chunk of memory called the ARP cache because it will probably need to use this MAC address for multiple outbound frames. In early implementations of ARP, if an unsolicited ARP reply were received, the system would simply add or update the IP-address-to-MAC-address mapping in the ARP cache. By sending unsolicited ARP replies, an attacker could inject his MAC address as the destination MAC address for outbound frames from the poisoned victim. To implement himself as a man in the middle and hijack the session, an attacker could poison the ARP caches on two systems that have an established session. Newer implementations of ARP reject unsolicited ARP replies, mitigating this attack.

- **Route poisoning** Early implementations of dynamic routing protocols transmitted the route tables among the routers in a network by using unauthenticated transmissions. This vulnerability allowed an attacker to inject bogus updates and routes into legitimate route tables, enabling her to deny service on a network (a DoS attack) or to hijack network communications and steal information. Later implementations of dynamic routing protocols use authenticated transmissions of the route table updates, largely defeating this kind of attack.

- **Trojan horse software** Trojan horse software has some beneficial or enjoyable functionality (like a game) but also contains unknown, malicious code that introduces one or more vulnerabilities into a system. Software that is downloaded from the Internet should always be suspected of being trojaned and should be verified as coming from a trusted source or scanned for known malware infection; however, the software still might contain unknown forms of malicious code. Often, an attacker uses trojaned software to entrench in a system that has been compromised, providing multiple and hidden access channels to the system, enabling the attacker to steal information from the system (pillaging), or enabling the attacker to escalate privilege. Trojaned software is typically identifiable only if it has been previously detected and its signature included in the antivirus definitions used on the system.

- **Backdoor attack** The backdoor attack is a family of attacks in which access can be provided by bypassing standard authentication, enabling the attacker to steal information from the system (pillaging). The backdoor is either a vulnerability that exists in the system natively or it can be inserted by malware or by an attacker who has compromised a system and wants to be able to gain unauthorized access at a later time. Backdoors are often injected into a system by means of a trojaned or virus-infected executable. The backdoor provides access at the level of privilege of the executable that contains the backdoor process. Another way backdoors are produced is through the use of maintenance hooks that are inserted during code development as part of the legitimate development process and then not removed prior to compiling and publishing the code. Backdoors are typically identifiable only if they have been detected previously and their signatures are included in the antivirus definitions used on the system.

- **DNS poisoning** A tool attackers use to steer victims inappropriately to malicious websites is DNS poisoning. Every IP client allocates a piece of memory to storing FQDN-to-IP-address mappings; this memory segment is called the resolver cache. Early implementations allowed the acceptance of unsolicited DNS query responses and would update the resolver cache with the new information. DNS poisoning also occurs on the DNS server itself. When a DNS server forwards a query to another DNS server and receives a response, the DNS server caches the response in its DNS server cache (memory). If an attacker can inject bogus FQDN-to-IP-address mappings into the server cache, as in the resolver cache, users are directed to bogus and potentially malicious websites instead of the legitimate target of their DNS query. By using malware pushed down to victims from the bogus website, the attacker can now compromise the victim system, providing unauthorized access often leading to the theft of information. Updates to the DNS protocols, such as the use of DNSSEC, are improving the security of the DNS systems.

- **Instant Messaging (IM)** IM isn't exactly an attack, but it is a common path to the loss or leakage of sensitive data. This is a communications channel on the Internet that allows relatively anonymous users to share messages and file attachments. Outbound attachments can contain sensitive information, and inbound attachments can contain malicious code, infecting one or more local systems and introducing one or more vulnerabilities into those systems, potentially leading to data leakage.

EXAM TIP

Most attacks on networks target the availability of services (denial of service) or focus on compromising systems to perform data theft, attacking confidentiality.

Attacks on wireless networks

Wireless networks are inherently vulnerable due to their transmission mechanism of electromagnetic emanations propagated into the air. This makes it easy for an attacker to intercept these transmissions without exposing himself to any risk such as needing to penetrate the facility physically to connect to the wired network. An attacker can capture all network traffic while sitting in a legally parked vehicle outside the facility. If the attacker cannot get close to the source of wireless transmissions, a highly focused antenna, such as a Yagi antenna, can detect and transmit signals from and to an AP tens of miles away, only requiring line of sight with the general area of the target AP. An attacker can capture all packets, exposing potentially sensitive information, or exploit the security of the wireless network to gain access to the wired network attached to the AP.

Attackers often map out the APs in an area by driving through the area with a wireless sniffer attached to a global positioning system (GPS). The wireless sniffer, such as AiroMap, Kismit, MacStumbler, WellenReiter, or NetStumbler, senses the APs within range and records all the details the AP presents and the client systems associated with the AP. Later, the attacker simply reviews the map showing all the detected APs and identifies the juiciest targets for attack. This process of traveling an area to map the wireless networks is called *war driving*. Data collected by war driving is often uploaded into a web-accessible database in the Wireless Geographic Logging Engine at WiGLE.net to produce a global map of all logged wireless APs.

After the APs have been mapped, the attacker might decide to mark the building or sidewalk with the details of the wireless network to locate the target easily later on or to provide other wireless attackers information about the wireless networks that are accessible in the area. They use special symbols and markings to provide these coded messages (see Figure 7-34). War chalking is rarely performed these days.

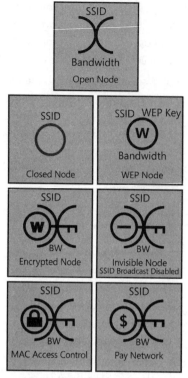

FIGURE 7-34 War chalking symbols

As was described earlier in this chapter, the wireless network security introduced in 802.11, WEP, was loaded with vulnerabilities that easily exposed the WEP key used for authentication of client nodes and for encryption of the wireless traffic. By recording the WEP-protected wireless traffic for a few minutes with a wireless sniffer and then dropping that capture data into a WEP password–cracking tool such as WEPCrack, an attacker can reveal the WEP key, typically in less than one minute. This enabled the attacker to decrypt the WEP-protected wireless traffic and authenticate and associate to the wireless AP as a legitimate and authorized client, often providing access to the wired network behind the AP.

Another type of attack on the wireless network is to attach a rogue wireless AP to the corporate network. This allows an inside attacker to transmit large amounts of stolen data to a counterpart with a wireless laptop computer parked in the parking lot, avoiding the standard corporate network monitoring, logging, and filtering.

Last but not least in the list of attacks on wireless networks is when an attacker intercepts wireless transmissions over a Bluetooth network. This is called *bluejacking*.

Attacks on phone systems and cell phones

Often overlooked in security audits, telephones and telephone systems present security vulnerabilities to organizations. These should be considered when performing a vulnerability assessment or risk assessment and during penetration testing.

Cell phones are often issued to employees, and these devices can be used to store large amounts of data, providing the inside attacker with an easy means to steal data without passing though network monitoring, logging, or content filtering. The cell phones can often be used to tether a computer to the Internet, again allowing unmonitored logged or filtered data transmission or allowing systems to access otherwise blocked websites. Cell phones typically include a still camera or a video camera, which might violate company policy in highly restricted areas of the facility.

Attackers who target phones and phone systems are referred to as *phreakers*. In one form of attack, they might try to steal a legitimate customer's cell phone minutes by *cloning* a legitimate authorization code into their *subscriber identity module (SIM) card*. These authorization codes were formerly transmitted in plaintext to initiate phone calls and during phone calls, but they are now strongly encrypted, defeating the bulk of these types of attacks. Now attackers who want to steal your minutes must perform *SIM code tumbling*, which tumbles to a random code and tests it. If the code works, the attacker will be using stolen minutes until he or she is detected. If the code doesn't work, the attacker simply tumbles the code to another random code, trying over and over again until a good authentication code is found.

Another attack vector phreakers use is through the maintenance modem on the PBX phone system many companies use. Remember that the PBX connects to a T1 or T3, and each channel represents a discrete phone number, or unused channels can be aggregated to provide Internet connectivity bandwidth. Recall that T1 = 23 B channels, a D channel = 24 total channels, and T3 = 672 total channels. The Japanese equivalent is called the J1, with specifications similar to the US T1 (24 channels and 1.544 Mbps). The European variation is the E1 with 32 channels, providing 2.048 Mbps. As a company hires and fires personnel and employees transfer and change offices, the PBX might need to be reconfigured to add phone extensions, remove old extensions, and so on. These configuration changes are typically performed by outside technicians, who often use the maintenance modem to dial into the PBX and implement the configuration changes. The connection on the maintenance modem might or might not use authentication, and if authentication is required, it uses password-based authentication. Technicians often use no password or easy passwords, often the same password for all the systems they work on, to avoid forgetting a password and being locked out of the system. This combination of vulnerabilities lends itself nicely to exploits of the PBX systems. Phreakers can break into the PBXs through these poorly authenticated maintenance modems and eavesdrop on the company's phone calls, disconnect calls, and configure after-hours long-distance dialing codes (when long-distance calls were toll calls, resulting in big monthly expenses for companies). Phreakers can then commit *toll fraud* by selling these long-distance dialing codes to others and pocketing the money while the victim company foots the bill for all the long-distance phone time being stolen.

TELEPHONE SLAMMING

In 1984, shortly after American Telephone and Telegraph (AT&T) was declared a monopoly and broken up, the newly formed smaller phone companies were in heated competition to acquire a bigger slice of the pie. Each phone customer was allowed to choose which long-distance carrier he wanted to use. However, the phone companies developed the controversial practice of independently changing a customer from his chosen long-distance carrier to themselves without the customer's knowledge or consent. This phone company practice of ordering this unauthorized change of a customer's long-distance carrier was called *telephone slamming*.

In addition, phone companies erroneously billed customers for miscellaneous charges and then challenged customers who complained, often winning these disputes (and being paid by customers) simply because the companies seemed willing to argue longer than the customers. This fraudulent practice was called *telephone cramming*.

To stop this telephone fraud by the phone companies, legislative action at the state and federal level in the United States has specifically targeted these crimes against consumers, and these practices are being effectively limited and controlled.

Exercises

In the following exercises, you apply what you've learned in this chapter. The answers for these exercises are located in the "Answers" section at the end of this chapter.

The following scenario applies to all the exercises.

You are planning a network that must include the following components:

- Publicly accessible services: an email server, a web server, an application server, and a name resolution server
- Wired connectivity to provide internal client computers access to internal network resources
- Internet connectivity for employees
- Three security zones: Internal, Administrative, and Confidential
- A persistent connection to the branch office
- Wireless network access for internal clients
- An isolated wireless network, providing Internet connectivity only, for visitors in the lobby
- Prudent security

Exercise 7-1

Draw the network, showing the required components and security systems and functions.

Exercise 7-2

For session management, the publicly accessible application server uses a wide range of port numbers. Describe the configuration of the NAT server to satisfy this requirement plus the previously described required services.

Exercise 7-3

Describe how you would secure the connection from the wireless client computers for the employees.

Chapter summary

Table 7-10 shows a review of the details of the Open Systems Interconnection (OSI) Model by the International Standards Organization (ISO), alongside the TCP/IP model.

TABLE 7-10 A quick review of the OSI Model and the TCP/IP model

Layer	OSI model	Form	Function	Devices	TCP/IP model
7	Application	Data stream	Network access for applications	Gateway function	Application
6	Presentation	Data stream	Data conversion into standard format, encryption, compression		Application
5	Session	Data stream	Inter-host communications, session maintenance		
4	Transport	Segment	End-to-end connection, TCP or UDP; ports		Transport
3	Network	Packet or datagram	IP addressing (logical), routing	Router, packet filter firewall	Internet
2	Data Link	Frame	MAC address, CRC, media access	Bridge, switch, wireless access point	Link
1	Physical	Binary bits	Modulation and encoding, transmission, hardware	NIC, hub, repeater, transmission media, wireless access point	Link

- Emanations can be detected and used to steal information. Media selection can improve the emanations security, from most secure (top) to least secure (bottom):
    - Fiber optic
    - Coax
    - Shielded twisted pair (STP)
    - Unshielded twisted pair (UTP)
    - Wireless
- Media access methods include polling, token passing, Carrier Sense Multiple Access with Collision Avoidance (CSMA/CA) and Carrier Sense Multiple Access with Collision Detection (CSMA/CD).
- The network architecture should include security zones isolated by security devices (such as firewalls) and include perimeter networks when connecting to untrusted networks.
- IP networks use sockets (IP address: port#) to identify the service requested from the remote computer. Virtual private networks (VPNs), such as IPsec and PPTP, usually provide strong confidentiality and can provide authentication and integrity validation.
- Networks vary in their size from personal area networks (PANs) to local area networks (LANs), metropolitan area networks (MANs), and wide area networks (WANs). Different technologies are used within these physical scopes of networks to satisfy the specific needs of the transmissions lengths.
- Wireless networks are inherently insecure and should be configured by using the standards for the Robust Secure Network (RSN), also referred to as Wi-Fi Protected Access version 2 (WPA2). As technology evolves to defeat attacks on networks, attackers find new ways to attack. New protocols increase the attack surface of networks, providing attackers new attack vectors. True cellular networking is nearly a reality and should be included in network security assessments.

Chapter review

Test your knowledge of the information in this chapter by answering these questions. The answers to these questions, and the explanations of why each answer choice is correct or incorrect, are located in the "Answers" section at the end of this chapter.

1. Which of the following devices does NOT operate at Layer 2, the Data Link layer?

   A. Hub

   B. Switch

   C. Wireless access point

   D. Bridge

2. Which organization developed and publishes the OSI Model?

   A. IEEE

   B. ISO

   C. IANA

   D. IETF

3. Which of the following protocols operates at Layer 4, the Transport layer, and provides best-effort, connectionless delivery of segments?

   A. ARP

   B. IGMP

   C. TCP

   D. UDP

4. Data and header information being processed at Layer 3, the Network layer of the OSI Model, is called which of the following?

   A. Packet

   B. Data stream

   C. Frame

   D. Segment

5. Which of the following places the layers of the OSI Model in the correct order when processing inbound data from the network media?

   A. Application, Presentation, Session, Transport, Network, Data Link, Physical

   B. Physical, Transport, Network, Data Link, Presentation, Session, Application

   C. Application, Session, Presentation, Transport, Network, Data Link, Physical

   D. Physical, Data Link, Network, Transport, Session, Presentation, Application

6. Which of the following media types provides the best protection against emanations detection?

   A. Coax

   B. Shielded twisted pair

   C. Unshielded twisted pair

   D. Fiber optic

7. Which of the following media access methods is contention oriented?

   A. Token-passing bus

   B. Carrier Sense Multiple Access with Collision Detection (CSMA/CD)

   C. Token-passing ring

   D. Polling

8. Which of the following is the filter used on firewalls to block packets leaving the private network using a public source IP address?

   A. Ingress filter

   B. Content filter

   C. Egress filter

   D. Stateful filter

9. Which of the following best describes a bastion host?

   A. A system that has been hardened against attack

   B. A system that uses a default deny rule

   C. A system that performs FQDN-to-IP-address resolution

   D. A system that replaces private IP addresses with public IP addresses as the packet exits the private network

10. Which protocol prepends a tag in front of the Layer 2 header of a frame to facilitate its transmission through the protocol-compliant cloud?

    A. Multi-Protocol Label Switching (MPLS)

    B. Network Address Translation (NAT)

    C. Open Shortest Path First (OSPF)

    D. Dynamic Host Configuration Protocol (DHCP)

11. Which of the following allows systems to use multiple and yet-to-be-developed mechanisms to verify the identities of users?

   A. Zero-knowledge proof

   B. Extensible Authentication Protocol (EAP)

   C. Challenge Handshake Authentication Protocol (CHAP)

   D. Synchronous Optical Network (SONET)

12. A wireless access point that uses more than one transmitter, receiver, and antenna is described by which IEEE specification?

   A. 802.11h

   B. 802.11j

   C. 802.11b

   D. 802.11n

13. Which of the following attacks uses an army of zombies?

   A. Ping of death

   B. DDoS attack

   C. LAND attack

   D. SYN flood

Answers

This section contains the answers to the exercises and the "Chapter review" section in this chapter.

Exercise 7-1

The diagram should look similar to the following:

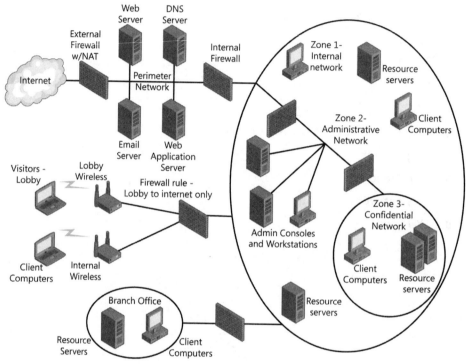

FIGURE 7-35 Exercise 7-1 network diagram

Exercise 7-2

At least two public IP addresses must be used on the public interface of the external firewall/NAT server. One address will be used to provide Internet access for internal users (many to one) and to provide public access to the web server, DNS server, and SMTP server using port forwarding (PAT), mapping port 80 and 443 to the private IP address of the web server, 53 to the private IP address of the DNS server, and 25 to the private IP address of the SMTP server. The other public IP address must be reserved for, and mapped to, the private IP address of the application server and cannot be used for anything else.

Exercise 7-3

Implement the standards and technology described by the Robust Secure Network (RSN) also known as WPA2. This includes the use of 802.1x port-based authentication using EAP, a RADIUS server, an authentication system such as X.500 directory services, and encryption using AES and CCMP over the wireless connection. In addition, require the use of a VPN in the Zone 1, Internal Network area for all wireless, nonvisitor clients.

Chapter review

1. **Correct answer:** A

   A. **Correct:** The hub operates at Layer 1, the Physical layer of the OSI Model.

   B. **Incorrect:** The switch operates at Layer 2, the Data Link layer of the OSI Model.

   C. **Incorrect:** The wireless access point operates at Layer 2, the Data Link layer of the OSI Model.

   D. **Incorrect:** The bridge operates at Layer 2, the Data Link layer of the OSI Model.

2. **Correct answer:** B

   A. **Incorrect:** The IEEE published the 802 specifications describing Layers 1 and 2 of the OSI Model but not the OSI Model itself.

   B. **Correct:** The International Organization for Standardization developed and publishes the OSI Model.

   C. **Incorrect:** The IANA defines port numbers and ranges for protocols, the Top Level Domains, and the DNS root servers and administers the allocation of IP address space.

   D. **Incorrect:** The goal of the IETF is to make the Internet work better by producing high-quality, relevant technical documents that influence the way people design, use, and manage the Internet, but it does not develop and publish the OSI Model.

3. **Correct answer:** D

   A. **Incorrect:** Address Resolution Protocol (ARP) operates at Layer 2, the Data Link layer of the OSI Model. ARP broadcasts the IP address of the destination system and hopes to resolve the destination system's MAC address.

   B. **Incorrect:** Internet Group Management Protocol (IGMP) operates at Layer 3, the Network layer of the OSI Model. IGMP uses a multicast transmission from a single-source server to many destinations systems.

   C. **Incorrect:** Transmission Control Protocol (TCP) operates at Layer 4, the Transport layer of the OSI Model. TCP is a guaranteed-delivery, connection-oriented delivery service that establishes a TCP session with a three-way handshake and uses acknowledgements for each delivered segment.

   D. **Correct:** User Datagram Protocol (UDP) operates at Layer 4, the Transport layer of the OSI Model. UDP is a best-effort, connectionless delivery service.

4. **Correct answer:** A

   A. **Correct:** Data and header information being processed at Layer 3, the Network layer of the OSI Model, is called a packet.

   B. **Incorrect:** Data and header information being processed at Layers 5, 6, and 7, the Session, Presentation, and Application layers of the OSI Model, are called a data stream.

   C. **Incorrect:** Data and header information being processed at Layer 2, the Data Link layer of the OSI Model, is called a frame.

   D. **Incorrect:** Data and header information being processed at Layer 4, the Transport layer of the OSI Model, is called a segment.

5. **Correct answer:** D

   A. **Incorrect:** Answer A (Application, Presentation, Session, Transport, Network, Data Link, Physical) reverses the correct order for processing an inbound frame.

   B. **Incorrect:** In answer B (Physical, Transport, Network, Data Link, Presentation, Session, Application), the transport and Data Link layers are reversed, and the Presentation and Session layers are reversed.

   C. **Incorrect:** Answer C (Application, Session, Presentation, Transport, Network, Data Link, Physical) reverses the Session and Presentation layers.

   D. **Correct:** The correct order of the layers of the OSI Model that process inbound data from the network media is: Physical, Data Link, Network, Transport, Session, Presentation, Application.

6. **Correct answer:** D

   A. **Incorrect:** The order of best emanations security to worst is: fiber optic, coax, shielded twisted pair, unshielded twisted pair, and wireless transmissions.

   B. **Incorrect:** The order of best emanations security to worst is: fiber optic, coax, shielded twisted pair, unshielded twisted pair, and wireless transmissions.

   C. **Incorrect:** The order of best emanations security to worst is: fiber optic, coax, shielded twisted pair, unshielded twisted pair, and wireless transmissions.

   D. **Correct:** The order of best emanations security to worst is: fiber optic, coax, shielded twisted pair, unshielded twisted pair, and wireless transmissions.

7. **Correct answer:** B

   A. **Incorrect:** Only the system holding the token is allowed to transmit, making this a deterministic, contentionless media access method.

   B. **Correct:** Carrier Sense Multiple Access with Collision Detection (CSMA/CD) is a nondeterministic, contention-oriented media access method by which nodes sharing the media contend for transmission time.

C. Incorrect: Only the system holding the token is allowed to transmit, making this a deterministic, contentionless media access method.

D. Incorrect: Only the system being polled by the network moderator (such as the mainframe computer) is allowed to transmit, making this a deterministic, contentionless media access method.

8. **Correct answer:** C

A. Incorrect: The ingress filter is used on firewalls to block packets entering the private network by using a private-source IP address. This is typically an attack on an internal system.

B. Incorrect: The content filter is used on application layer proxy firewalls to block disallowed content such as gambling, games, or pornography entering the private network.

C. Correct: The egress filter is used on firewalls to block packets exiting the private network by using a public-source IP address. This is typically an attack on a public system.

D. Incorrect: The stateful filter records outbound requests from internal clients and dynamically opens ports to allow the stateful responses to those requests.

9. **Correct answer:** A

A. Correct: The bastion host system is hardened against attack by disabling or deleting unnecessary user accounts, services, and applications. It is updated regularly and typically includes antivirus, host-based IDS, and personal firewall protection.

B. Incorrect: Firewalls typically employ a default deny rule.

C. Incorrect: Domain Name System (DNS) servers perform FQDN-to-IP-address resolution.

D. Incorrect: Network Address Translation (NAT) replaces private IP addresses with public IP addresses as the packet exits the private network.

10. **Correct answer:** A

A. Correct: Multiprotocol Label Switching (MPLS) prepends a tag on each frame as it enters the MPLS cloud to facilitate its transmission through the cloud.

B. Incorrect: Network Address Translation (NAT) is used to share a few public IP addresses with many client systems on the private network.

C. Incorrect: Open Shortest Path First (OSPF) is a link-state dynamic routing protocol used on large networks to share route table information with other routers.

D. Incorrect: The Dynamic Host Configuration Protocol (DHCP) assigns IP configuration data automatically to hosts on an IP network.

11. **Correct answer:** B

    A. **Incorrect:** Zero-knowledge proof is a concept of verifying a user's identity without the user ever sharing her password with the authentication service.

    B. **Correct:** The Extensible Authentication Protocol (EAP) is an application programming interface on the authentication engine of an authentication service that enables systems to use multiple and yet-to-be-developed mechanisms to verify the identities of users.

    C. **Incorrect:** The Challenge Handshake Authentication Protocol (CHAP) is an open-standard authentication protocol that is designed to satisfy the concept of zero-knowledge proof.

    D. **Incorrect:** The Synchronous Optical Network (SONET) is a fiber optic MAN and WAN network technology that provides optical carriers at 52 Mbps.

12. **Correct answer:** D

    A. **Incorrect:** 802.11h describes standards in the 5-GHz range to avoid conflicting with satellite communications in Europe.

    B. **Incorrect:** 802.11j describes standards in the 5-GHz range to avoid conflicting with satellite communications in Japan.

    C. **Incorrect:** 802.11b describes standards in the 2.4-GHz range using FHSS and DSSS with data rates up to 11 Mbps.

    D. **Correct:** 802.11n describes standards in both the 2.4-GHz and 5-GHz ranges using multiple-input, multiple-output (MIMO) technologies.

13. **Correct answer:** B

    A. **Incorrect:** The ping of death uses an ICMP echo request with a payload that is too large.

    B. **Correct:** The DDoS attack uses a master (the attacker), a layer of compromised systems called handlers, and a larger layer (army) of compromised systems called zombies.

    C. **Incorrect:** The LAND attack uses IP packets with identical source and destination IP addresses and port numbers.

    D. **Incorrect:** The SYN flood sends many SYN packets to the victim without ever completing the TCP session.

CHAPTER 8

Business continuity and disaster recovery planning

A disaster can be defined as any undesirable and often sudden event that causes great damage, destruction, loss, or hardship and carries the risk of forcing the enterprise to cease operations permanently.

For many enterprises, because most are realistically unprepared, a disaster would mean the end of the business. For the prudently managed enterprise, this notion should be absolutely unacceptable. *Senior management must accept the rigid position that the failure of the enterprise will not be permitted for any reason.* Period.

With this self-imposed mandate, the prudently managed enterprise must:

- Do everything possible *proactively* to avoid the disaster, any disaster, every imaginable disaster.

- For planning purposes, assume that each imaginable disaster is unavoidable. Plan a *reactive* course of action so that, in spite of the unavoidable disaster and the resulting disastrous losses, the enterprise will survive and continue its productive operations for generations into the future.

Today, the requirement for a functional disaster recovery plan (DRP) and a business continuity plan (BCP) is more than ever considered a standard of due care and prudent management. Some enterprises refer to these plans as the Continuance of Operations Plans (COOP). These components of the security program are not only the demonstration of a well-managed enterprise but required by many laws and regulations that apply to various businesses. The absence of a DRP and BCP is likely to be considered negligence on the part of management in a legal sense, and this negligence increases the likelihood of litigation and liability.

The DRP and BCP are an extension of the risk assessment and management program described in Chapter 1, "Information security governance and risk management." However, for the development of the DRP and BCP, the security professional is required to extend his vision to a perhaps bizarre extreme. To develop the DRP and BCP effectively, the security professional must assume that if *anything ever* causes the enterprise to fail, it is because the security professional failed to develop these plans correctly. Although human safety remains, as always, the top priority, the focus of the DRP and BCP is not just to protect people, minimize risk, and avoid losses but to plan and prepare the disaster response so that the company will never go out of business for any reason.

When the development of these plans is complete, and the plans are being maintained properly, the enterprise will enjoy several benefits, including the following:

- Increased safety in the workplace
- Assurance that the enterprise can survive a disaster
- Demonstration of prudent management
- Demonstration of due diligence and due care
- Reduced losses when incidents and disasters occur
- Avoidance of negligence
- Decreased likelihood of litigation
- Decreased liability in case of litigation
- Increased reliability and value for shareholders and stakeholders
- Increased appeal as a business partner
- Reduction in insurance premiums because of less risk and fewer losses to insurers

These two plans are intended to protect human safety, to ensure that the enterprise will never go out of business, and to minimize losses when a disaster strikes by quickly, smoothly, and efficiently returning the enterprise to a state of normal operations.

Exam objectives in this chapter:

8.1   Understand business continuity requirements

    8.1.1   Develop and document project scope and plan

8.2   Conduct business impact analysis

    8.2.1   Identify and prioritize critical business functions

    8.2.2   Determine maximum tolerable downtime and other criteria

    8.2.3   Assess exposure to outages (e.g., local, regional, global)

    8.3.4   Define recovery objectives

8.3   Develop a recovery strategy

    8.3.1   Implement a backup storage strategy (e.g., offsite storage, electronic vaulting, tape rotation)

    8.3.2   Recovery site strategies

8.4   Understand disaster recovery process

    8.4.1   Response

    8.4.2   Personnel

    8.4.3   Communications

    8.4.4   Assessment

Disaster recovery plan and the business continuity plan

 In contrast to risk management, the development of the disaster recovery plan and the business continuity plan is driven primarily by *critical business functions* rather than by the financial value of specific information assets.

The disaster recovery plan

The disaster recovery plan (DRP) is a subset of the overarching business continuity plan. The DRP is a reactive short-term plan and describes the immediate, specific, and sequential actions to be taken after a disaster event to recover the most critical business functions that keep the enterprise solvent, functional, ongoing, alive. The DR process is usually information technology–centric, with the objectives to recover the facility, the information systems, and the business operations. If successful, the DR process helps reduce losses in the short term and in the long term. The DR plans should convey a sense of urgency to the DR team members as they carry out their mission-critical DR activities. During this DR period, quite often, normal business operations are suspended so the safety of personnel can be ensured, and all hands can be put to work recovering the most critical business functions in a timely manner. The DRP provides complete and appropriate documentation of procedures and typically includes preapproved authorization by management to take action if and when the disaster is formally declared.

The DRP is very much like the paramedic at the scene of an accident. By using a prioritizing technique, he identifies the injury that will kill the patient (the enterprise) the soonest and fixes that just well enough to prevent the patient from dying right now. Then he identifies the next injury that will kill the patient the soonest and fixes that, and so on. The paramedic (disaster recovery process) works until he attains some confidence that the patient will survive until she can be delivered to the hospital. This is when the paramedic (the disaster recovery process) stops. At the hospital (the reconstitution phase), the major repairs can be effected over a longer period of time, and the patient can convalesce, recover to a productive and efficient state, and eventually return to a normal state of activities. Like the paramedic, the disaster recovery process must work fast on the most urgent and life-threatening priority to keep the enterprise from going out of business. The process is complete when the survivability of the enterprise is ensured, and all the critical business functions are operational enough to sustain the business. At that point, the recovery process is transitioned into reconstitution, the effort to return the enterprise to a state of normal.

The business continuity plan

The business continuity plan (BCP) is an overarching plan and activity that never stops. Its goal is to ensure the long-term survivability of the enterprise by introducing preventive controls to avoid disasters proactively or to mitigate the severity of an unavoidable disaster by reducing its impact. The business continuity plan also provides guidance during the reconstitution phase, the reactive, long-term recovery to normal operations phase, of a disaster event. Collectively, these measures should reduce losses over the long haul.

Business continuity is accomplished by continuously performing risk assessment, evaluating the vulnerabilities inherent in the enterprise and the local, regional, and global threats that could negatively affect those vulnerabilities. Business continuity then identifies cost-justified countermeasures and presents this risk assessment vision and appropriate countermeasure proposals to management. Based on management's vision and its tolerance for risk, management might approve one or more proposed countermeasures for implementation. This is strictly management's decision. (Try not to be too emotionally attached to the proposals.) Business continuity then implements and maintains those countermeasures as part of the ongoing and routine security program. They become a component of the overall security posture of the organization during its normal operations.

Business continuity planning also helps during a disaster event. After a disaster, when the survivability of the enterprise has been ensured by the efforts of the disaster recovery operations, the BCP provides guidance on how the enterprise will repair itself, convalesce, and recover to a state of normal operations. This might resemble the functions and activities at a hospital, where the patient is stable with minimal risk of death but is injured, having diminished capacity and capability. It will take time for the damages to be repaired, the patient to retool and retrain itself as necessary (as in physical therapy), and no longer need supplemental support to return to normal.

The part of the business continuity plans that address this reconstitution period will initially be higher level, less detailed than disaster recovery plans. The specific details of the reconstitution of the enterprise cannot be known with great precision until the state of the enterprise is assessed and fully understood after the disaster occurs. Initially, this part of the business continuity plan provides some general guidance that addresses, for example, the need for a line of credit until the insurance check is received; recertification and compliance verification as necessary; generalities regarding whether to rebuild the original location or where to relocate; how to deal with and recover lost functionality; and so on. The specific details and actions to be taken for the successful and cost-effective reconstitution must be determined after the disaster event has done its damage and at the earliest possible stages of reconstitution.

The disaster event is not over until all intended repairs are complete, the enterprise has recovered, and the business processes are fully functional and occurring in an efficient manner. Figure 8-1 shows the timeline of the business continuity and disaster recovery process.

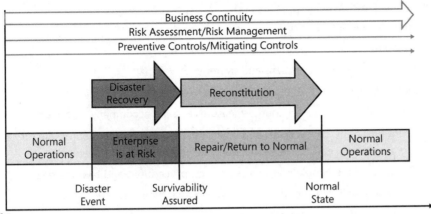

FIGURE 8-1 The timeline of disaster recovery and business continuity

Although a return to a normal state is the goal, recognize that after a disaster, very often, the new normal state might be different from the original normal state, sometimes very different. The new state of normal for the enterprise might be at a reduced capacity and capability due to the injuries and destruction incurred during the disaster. However, the new state of normal for the enterprise might be much more efficient than before by redesigning, retooling, and rebuilding from scratch, trimming off the weak and dead wood. For better or for worse, the goal of the reconstitution phase is to return the enterprise to its new state of normal operations.

Stages of the planning process

Following is an overview of the stages to be completed in the development of the DRP and BCP. Manage this planning process like any other business project.

- Define the need for the DRP and BCP in the enterprise framework for governance.
- Define the planning team leader, the scope, the team, the tools, the budget, and the schedule for developing the plans.
- Perform the business impact analysis (BIA).
  - Identify the business functions, the dependency functions, and the information assets that support those functions.
  - Determine the maximum tolerable downtime (MTD) for each business function.
  - Perform a vulnerability, threat, and risk analysis for the functions and assets that support the functions.

- Develop the plans. Proposals:
    - Identify preventive controls.
    - Develop the business continuity plans (guidelines).
    - Develop disaster recovery plans and strategy.
    - Develop the DRP and BCP team(s) and assign roles and responsibilities.
- Get management approval for countermeasures and the accompanying budget.
- Implement the DR BC components and integrate them in the security program for ongoing monitoring, enforcement, maintenance, testing, and improvement.
- Train the appropriate people on the new policies, procedures, and technologies.
- Test the plans to validate and improve them and train the DR team(s).
- Maintain the plans with (at least) an annual review, and a review with any significant change to the enterprise.

This process is all just talk and paper until management approves the specific plans for implementation as part of the security program for the enterprise. At that point, the activities of implementation, training, monitoring, enforcement, testing, and maintenance of the preventive controls and recovery resources and processes begin and continue indefinitely into the future.

Defining need for DRP and BCP in the enterprise framework

Senior management must drive the initial development and ongoing maintenance of these plans. Senior management must also dogmatically require these plans to be doable and effective. The failure of either of these plans means the death of the enterprise. If the death of the enterprise is not completely unacceptable to management, the shareholders and stakeholders should immediately replace the management.

The requirement for the DRP and BCP should be defined within the framework of governance for the enterprise, the policy documents. These policy documents should map out the assignment of responsibility, the authority, and the budgeting for the planning project. Further, the policy documents should define the required disaster recovery teams, the plan testing, the appropriate personnel training, and the ongoing maintenance of the plans.

Define the planning project leader

The DR and BC planning project requires a strong leader, typically one person with the direct support of and access to senior management. The planning project leader needs an understanding of where and how the operations of the business occur and the resources required to execute those operations. This understanding will be greatly enhanced as the planning project develops. The planning project leader also requires good project management skills and the ability to manage people.

Define the scope of the planning project

Senior management defines the scope of the assignment to the project leader. The scope might be to develop the DRP and BCP for a department, a floor in the building, the entire building, a collection of buildings such as within the campus area, or perhaps the entire enterprise. Whatever the scope of the planning project is, the project leader must not allow that scope to grow beyond the formal assignment from management. This occurs commonly and is called *scope creep*.

Imagine the assigned scope of the planning project is the facilities in Oshkosh. The Oshkosh project leader soon recognizes that operations at Oshkosh rely heavily on regular deliveries from the Schenectady facilities; without those deliveries, the operations at the Oshkosh facilities will cease in a very short time. It becomes a natural extension, therefore, for the DRP and BCP for the Oshkosh facilities to include operations at the Schenectady facilities, and this is the mistake. This is unauthorized and unassigned scope creep.

The proper way to manage scope creep is simply to document the interfaces and the assumptions required for the ongoing operations of the assigned scope. From the previous example, simply document the dependency of regular deliveries from Schenectady (the interface) and the expectation that these deliveries will occur on schedule (the assumption). This information might force management to recognize the need for a DRP and BCP for the operations at the Schenectady facilities, and it might make an assignment for this, but do not assume that a reliance on resources outside the assigned scope means that you must include that external area in the assigned scope.

Management might provide the mission statement, charter, or both for the enterprise to help identify a vision of management's priorities to the planning team.

Define the DRP and BCP planning team

The planning team requires representation from each major facet of the organization within the scope of assignment. It is the goal of the team to understand the business functions within the scope of assignment. This is usually best accomplished by requiring someone with some vision of those functions, such as a department manager or division manager, to be a member on the team. Much research and greater development of these business functions will still be needed, but it is usually better to begin with a pretty good sense of how these functions are accomplished.

In addition to these department leaders or division managers, representation is commonly needed (in some capacity) from:

- The legal department
- Human resources
- Network operations
- Security operations
- Communications

Define the DRP and BCP planning budget and schedule

Senior management must allocate sufficient funds to support the DRP and BCP planning project. A big portion of the required budget is for the hours the team spends performing its research and analysis tasks, taking the members away from other revenue-generating tasks. In addition to the labor costs for this project, the amount of information that this project must develop and organize will be gigantic. This is not a project that can stay organized using bingo cards and pencils. A project of this size will likely require a specialized application to assemble the volume of information and the proper relationships between the various details.

Management also requires a schedule to identify when specific deliverables are expected to be completed. The initial DRP and BCP planning project often takes as long as three years to complete; after the first set of plans is complete, these plans require updating at least once a year.

EXAM TIP

Candidates should be aware that ISC2 estimates it will take an approximately three-year timeframe to complete the *initial* planning for a fully functional BCP and DRP. The annual review and update of both plans should continue after that.

The planning deliverables will include:

- An inventory of business functions that occur within the scope of the project, their dependency functions, and the information assets that support those functions.
- The results from the business impact analysis; the MTD for each business function.
- A vulnerability, threat, and risk analysis for each function and its supporting assets.
- A collection of proposed preventive controls to avoid the disasters that can be avoided and to mitigate the impact of unavoidable disasters.
- A collection of disaster recovery procedures, complete with a list of required hardware, software, services, manpower, and other recovery controls to support the proposed recovery strategies within the maximum tolerable downtime for each function.

This collection of details must be organized and presented in a complete and cohesive manner to management for approval. Management typically approves some but not all the proposed procedures and controls, based on its vision, its tolerance for risk, and, of course, its budgetary concerns. After approval, the DRP and BCP plans can be formalized and completed, and the following deliverables can be expected:

- The acquisition and implementation of proactive preventive controls, including new hardware, software, administrative training, new and updated security program policy documentation, and updated security awareness training for users
- The completed collection of reactive disaster recovery plans and strategies, complete with assignments of roles and responsibilities for the members of the recovery team(s)

- The acquisition and implementation of reactive recovery controls, including new hardware, software, disaster recovery team training, administrative training, new and updated policy documentation, and updated security awareness training for users as appropriate
- The procedures for the ongoing monitoring, enforcement, and maintenance of the new proactive and reactive controls and the inventory of recovery-related components
- Training of DR and BC team members and management
- Testing plans and procedures for the new plans
- Ongoing maintenance plans and procedures for the DRP and BCP

With the leader selected; the scope of the project defined; the team members identified; and the budget, the tools, and the schedule completed, the DRP and BCP planning team is ready to begin work on the development of the plans.

 Quick check

1. What is the primary objective of the DRP and BCP?
2. What is the secondary objective of the DRP and BCP?

Quick check answers

1. Safety
2. The rapid and smooth recovery of the enterprise to a normal state of operations after a disaster strikes

Perform the business impact analysis

The planning team members are chosen because they represent each major facet of the enterprise within the scope of the planning project. Collectively, they provide specific knowledge, skills, and awareness of the operations within that scope and develop greater understanding and documentation of those operations within their area of specialization. For the department or division she represents, the BCP/DRP team member develops the initial draft of the business functions, the dependency functions, and the information assets that support those functions within her area. The team (rather than an individual, usually) then determines the MTD for each business function and performs a vulnerability, threat, and risk analysis for the functions and assets that support the functions.

IDENTIFYING BUSINESS AND DEPENDENCY FUNCTIONS AND SUPPORT

In this phase of the planning process, the team members begin by brainstorming. Without discrimination or prejudgment of the importance or criticality of any of the functions, they must come up with a complete list of every business function that occurs within the scope of the planning project.

The specific business functions in different organizations vary greatly, but examples might include:

- Accounts payable
- Accounts receivable
- Payroll
- General ledger/accounting
- HR management
- Network operations
- Security operations
- Internal communications
- Project and job costing
- Production
- Purchasing
- Order entry
- Inventory control
- Materials flow management
- Transaction analysis
- Intercompany transactions
- Marketing
- Pre-sales support
- Sales
- Shipping
- Return materials authorization
- Customer relationship management
- Partner relationship management

After there is a level of certainty that the list is complete, it can now be organized. Standardize terms for the items on the list and remove any redundancy. Verify completeness of the list again.

Identify all functions the first function on the list requires or depends on. These are referred to as dependency functions. Finally, identify every information asset that is required to support the primary function and its dependency functions. These information assets include human assets (personnel), processes, technologies, data, workspace, and supplies. Figure 8-2 shows an example charting of this series of relationships.

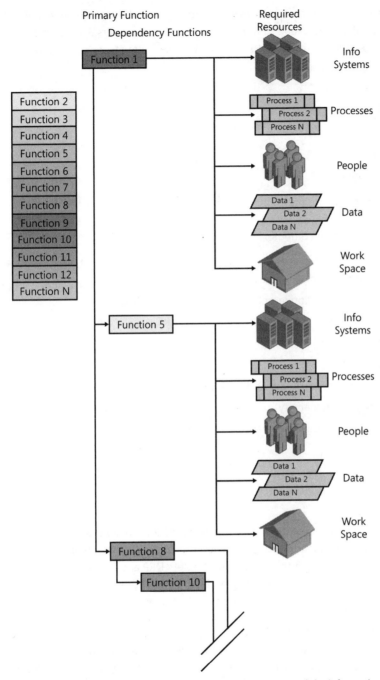

FIGURE 8-2 Business functions, their dependency functions, and the information assets that support those functions

For example, the payroll function requires a weekly summary for each department (within scope) of the workers and their hours logged from the department managers. Further, that information must be successfully transmitted to the payroll department in a timely manner.

Dependency functions might include:

- General ledger/accounting
- HR management
- Network operations
- Security operations
- Internal communications

Assets required to support the primary function (payroll) and its dependency functions might include:

- **IT resource**   A workstation computer
- **IT resource**   The payroll application
- **IT resource**   The general ledger application
- **IT resource**   The HR application (employee information, hourly rate)
- **Supply system**   Stable electrical power
- **IT resource**   Check printer
- **Supplies**   Blank checks
- **Personnel**   Accounting department worker: 4 hours weekly
- **IT resource**   Network connectivity
- **IT resource**   Access to tax payment website
- **Data**   Employee hours
- **Data**   Employee hourly rate
- **Workspace**   A safe, secure, and habitable place for resources and for personnel to work

For each function identified within scope, identify its dependency functions and the assets required to support the primary function and its dependency functions. The gathering and organization of this data are major components of the complete DRP and BCP. A poor job done here is likely to result in a poor job of avoiding and recovering from a disaster. Pursue a complete and accurate picture of the business functions.

DETERMINE MTD FOR EACH BUSINESS FUNCTION

The accurate determination of the BIA for each business function is one of the most important steps in the DRP and BCP planning process. The purpose of the BIA is to identify the level of criticality of each business function. In the BIA, this level of criticality is evaluated as the *maximum tolerable downtime* (MTD) for each function. To accomplish this, assume that some unnamed disaster has just struck (likelihood = 100%) and has caused the failure of the first business function on the list of business functions within the scope of this planning process.

With this in mind, determine how long the company could continue to operate without this function until the company can no longer recover and is destined for failure. At what point in time after the disaster strikes does the company go out of business because this one function is unavailable? This amount of time becomes the MTD for this first function and is the definition of the level of criticality of this function for the enterprise. This period might be hours, days, weeks, or perhaps even months. The shorter the period of the MTD, the more critical the business function. Without this function operating, the business will die soonest. Longer MTDs imply that the function(s) are less critical to the ongoing operations of the enterprise. Table 8-1 lists the terms that describe the level of criticality of the business functions related to the MTD for the business function.

TABLE 8-1 Definitions of maximum tolerable downtimes (MTD)

Level of criticality	Maximum tolerable downtime (MTD)
CRITICAL OR ESSENTIAL	MINUTES TO HOURS
URGENT	UP TO 24 HOURS (1 DAY)
IMPORTANT	UP TO 72 HOURS (3 DAYS)
NORMAL	UP TO 7 DAYS
NONESSENTIAL	UP TO 30 DAYS (OR MORE)

EXAM TIP

Be sure you know the terms that describe the level of criticality for the business functions and the related time periods shown in Table 8-1.

The accurate determination of the MTD for each function is an important component of the DRP and BCP planning process. When a disaster causes a function to cease, the single-minded, dogmatic, unfailing objective of the DRP is to have the plan, the tools, the resources, the skills, the replacement parts, and whatever else it takes to restore that function within its MTD. Otherwise, the enterprise goes out of business. Anything less than a completely doable plan is completely unacceptable and useless as a DRP. Pretense will kill the enterprise. The DRP and the strategies to implement the DRP must work with an exceptional level of certainty.

NOTE WHEN DISASTER STRIKES

The following sentence is so important a concept that it bears repeating: When a disaster causes a critical business function to cease, the single-minded, dogmatic, unfailing objective of the DRP is to have the plan, the tools, the resources, the skills, the replacement parts, and whatever else it takes to restore that function well within its MTD.

Each business function within the scope of the planning process must be accurately evaluated in this manner. After an accurate MTD has been associated with every business function, reorder the list of business functions so that the function with the shortest MTD is at the top of the list and all functions are listed in order from the shortest MTD to the longest. This defines the order of priority for the planning process, the most critical business function first. As the stages of the planning process continue, work from the top of this list down to the least critical functions. The MTD drives the disaster recovery plan for each business function.

The most critical business functions, the ones with the shortest MTD, should be worked first. They should be the best understood operations, have the most detailed recovery plans (with backup plans and perhaps even backup plans for the backup plans), probably have the greatest amount budgeted for the recovery, and be one of the most rehearsed and well-trained roles on the disaster recovery team(s) because the failure of this function will kill the enterprise the fastest.

Recognize that if a function has an MTD of three days, the recovery strategy cannot take three days to accomplish. The recovery strategy must recover the function well within the three-day maximum. Plan for components of the plan to take longer than expected. The plan must accommodate unforeseen perturbations and delays and still achieve success within the MTD, hopefully well within the MTD. Plan for the overnighted replacement part to be delivered to the wrong facility or dead on arrival. It might have the wrong version of firmware or any number of other unpredictable complications. Correcting these problems takes time when the critical functions have no time to spare. Remember that the life of the enterprise relies on this function to work. Figure 8-3 shows the relationship between the MTD of a business function and the recovery strategies occurring well within that MTD, with an indication of the increased costs associated with shorter MDTs and recovery times.

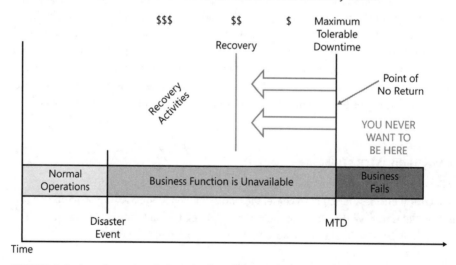

FIGURE 8-3 Business impact analysis evaluation of the maximum tolerable downtime for a business function

PERFORM VULNERABILITY, THREAT, AND RISK ANALYSIS FOR FUNCTIONS AND SUPPORT

For each business function within the assigned scope of the planning project, beginning with the functions with the shortest MTD, identify the weaknesses inherent in that function's systems and processes. Identify the threats that could affect those vulnerabilities or render that system or process unavailable. Identify the level of risk for each vulnerability/threat pair by determining the likelihood and the impact of a successful exploit. This process was described in detail in Chapter 1.

Consider threats from each of the four categories of threats. Any threat that could cause a business function to fail must be included in the analysis. Examples include:

- **Natural** Natural threats are Mother Nature having her way with the world. Natural threats include earthquake, volcanic eruption, tornado, hurricane, tsunami, ice storm, snowstorm, flood, and fire.

- **Human-made** Human-made threats are the actions of people, such as errors and omissions, litigation, theft, sabotage, riot, strike, malicious hacker attack, social engineering attacks, dumpster diving, fraud, an insider with too much privilege, lack of an incident response plan, and political action.

- **Technical** Technical threats are the failings of technology such as a hard disk drive or server failure, data corruption, and damages from a computer virus infection.

- **Supply system** To remain functional, humans and computers need certain supplies. Humans need a habitable workplace and the supplies that keep the workplace habitable, including clean air, heating, ventilation and air conditioning (HVAC), drinkable water, and a sewer system. Computers need a clean supply of electricity and typically require a certain amount of cooling.

In the context of the business continuity planning process, the threats to the supply system extend to a somewhat extreme and, perhaps, even bizarre degree. When it comes to keeping the business operational for decades, threats to the supply system even include the availability of raw materials to produce whatever products the company produces. Consider a manufacturing company that survives on one unique product, for example, some new technology that requires a rare element or, perhaps something as basic as avocados to make your top-selling signature product, avocado-flavored bubble gum. If that rare element suddenly becomes unavailable, or if there is some blight on avocados for one or more growing seasons, these company-sustaining products could not be produced. In the context of the BCP planning process, these possibilities must be considered, and plans must be produced to avoid these supply system disasters from forcing the enterprise out of business.

Also remember from Chapter 1 that, typically, both quantitative analysis (specific documented values such as from receipts) and qualitative analysis should be performed for a complete view of the potential impact of any threat to the enterprise. The qualitative analysis should include the threats and potentially fatal damage to the reputation of the enterprise. The protection and recovery of the goodwill and good reputation that the company has developed with its customers and the public can be as critical to the survival of the enterprise as its data center.

This information is needed to complete the next steps, including identifying preventive controls and the development of the disaster recovery strategies and, again, during the presentation of proposals to management for approval and implementation of preventive and recovery controls.

 Quick check

1. What are the levels of criticality for the business processes defined by the MTD?
2. What are the types of assets that must be recovered to support the critical business processes?

Quick check answers

1. Critical or essential, Urgent, Important, Normal, Nonessential
2. Facilities, technologies, data, personnel.

Develop the plans: Proposals

This stage is still just talk and paper. It is a creative process to determine what proactive and reactive (preventive and recovery) options are available to present to management. After the proposals are completed, at the approval stage, management reviews this collection of proposals and, based on its vision, tolerance for risk, and the impact on the budget, it will approve the proposed components it feels will provide the best balance of protection for the enterprise within an acceptable budget.

The goal of this stage is for the security professional to develop an accurate vision of the controls that could avoid disaster and ensure that the enterprise can survive an unavoidable disaster. Present that well-developed vision to management in terms it can understand so it can make the best possible management decisions and approve the appropriate plans and controls that become part of the ongoing security program.

Identify preventive controls

As an ongoing component of the security program, and included within the business continuity planning process, the process of identifying preventive controls is the same as the risk assessment that was described in Chapter 1. Beginning with the functions with the shortest MTD, identify preventive controls that could prevent the disaster from occurring or reduce the impact of the event to mitigate losses and make recovery easier. These controls must be cost justified, reducing losses more than the cost of the control. Preventive controls are a component of the business continuity program, the long-term protection of the enterprise. If they are approved and implemented, they become a standard component of the security program and the security posture of the enterprise.

Preventive controls for the dependency on relatively unique and single-source raw materials would include identifying second sources, developing relationships with multiple providers, and perhaps buying 10 percent of your raw materials from this second supplier. Identify other consumers of this critical raw material and negotiate some arrangement with them to share these critical resources at critical times. Diversify the product lines to reduce the dependency of the enterprise on a single product. These are supply-system issues that go beyond traditional security professional concerns but must be included in the business continuity planning.

Work through the entire list of business functions in the order of shortest MTD to longest MTD to identify cost-justified preventive controls. Provide a list of multiple preventive controls for each asset and threat to give management a range of options to choose from. Remember that controls should mitigate or eliminate vulnerabilities, threats, likelihood, and impact to the critical business functions. When completed, this information, in the form of proposals, will be presented to senior management for approval.

Develop disaster recovery plans and strategy

Begin with the business function with the shortest MTD and develop the details for a plan to recover that functionality *within the MTD period*. The supporting elements that typically need to be restored to recover the critical business processes include:

- Work space and facilities
- Supply systems
- Technologies
- Data
- Human assets and critical personnel

EXAM TIP

The disaster recovery strategies must successfully recover operations of all the critical business processes before their respective MTD is reached. If the plans do not accomplish this with certainty, the planning team must continue to research and develop plans that satisfy this objective.

Alternative procedures

For each business process, consider the possibility of accomplishing the same results by using alternative procedures. If the old way of performing the business function is destroyed, is there another way to get the same results? If the procedure had been automated, consider whether the procedure could be performed manually or by using some other method of processing. For example, analyze the possibility of converting an available workstation into an application server to recover the destroyed server's functionality, albeit at likely a diminished capacity, but the functionality now exists, and the enterprise survives.

Compliance

As the plans to recover critical business functions after a disaster are being developed, the recovery solutions must meet or exceed the security standards required by laws and regulations, without exception. Law enforcement and regulatory bodies are unconcerned about any particular hardships an organization might endure. The question will be strictly, "Did you comply fully (100%) with the laws and regulations, or did you violate the laws and regulations (anything less than 100% compliance)?" Unfortunately, the enterprise will likely be substantially more vulnerable during a disaster, but the standard of compliance must remain unchanged, before, during, and after a disaster. Company policy, the parts that are not defined by laws and regulations, might include documented exceptions in the case of disaster recovery operations if management is willing to accept those (hopefully well-understood) increased risks.

EXAM TIP

Legal and regulatory compliance requirements must be met 100 percent before, during, and after a disaster, and in most cases, any failure to comply requires reporting the breach to the appropriate authority.

Increased operating costs

Recognize that during a disaster, many resources become scarce, yet more resources will be required to facilitate repair and recovery efforts. With supply low and demand high, prices will increase for just about everything the enterprise needs and uses. These increased costs must be anticipated and factored into the DR plans.

As different recovery options are analyzed, their cost must be balanced with the cost of the ongoing disruption. The ultimate cost is when the MTD is reached without successful recovery, the enterprise ceases operations, all employees are laid off, all revenue-generating activities stop, and the DR and BC processes have failed.

Recovery of the workspace

A place for people to work is required to continue performing the critical business functions that keep the enterprise alive. There are several recovery solutions for the facility, at very different costs and very different recovery times. These costs must be balanced against the losses incurred if the facility is destroyed or becomes uninhabitable. Recovery solutions for the facility include:

- Parallel processing facilities
- Collocations
- Alternate (owned) sites
- Subscription services (leased sites)
  - Hot
  - Warm
  - Cold
- Tertiary sites
- Rolling hot sites
- Reciprocal agreements

To help ensure that the secondary site will actually support the critical business functions, consider compatibility and capacity issues. If the critical business functions require 40 workers, be sure the secondary site has sufficient space for those workers.

Get it settled now

When a disaster strikes, it is quite possible that the disaster has also affected many organizations within some local proximity, such as from a flood or a hurricane. This means that if the secondary site has not already been acquired, there will be much competition for any available space that has not been affected. If you are lucky enough to be the organization that acquires the space, the cost for the space, due to the very high demand and the very low supply, will likely be substantially greater than if the space had been acquired before the disaster. These arrangements should be settled when all is well, before a disaster strikes. Taking a chance on locating and acquiring a facility during a disaster places the enterprise in a position of huge risk.

Although buying or leasing a space and not using it for revenue-generating purposes might seem to be a waste of money, the best possible news, long term, is that you never have to use the secondary facility because the enterprise has successfully avoided all disasters.

EXAM TIP

Firming up possession (owned or leased) of a secondary facility should be accomplished *before a disaster strikes* as part of the business continuity planning and implementation of preventive controls if possible.

Location of secondary facilities

Any secondary facility where critical functions are to be recovered should be far enough away to avoid the disaster that disrupted operations of the primary site. In addition, the secondary facility should be located in a different geographical environment, not farther down the valley where a flood would wipe out both facilities, along the same fault line where an earthquake might easily take out both facilities, or close to the same shoreline and therefore subject to the same tsunami.

Consider the need for skilled workers to commute; the availability of local replacement workers; deliveries to and from the secondary locations; required communications infrastructure; HVAC, water, sewer, electrical supply, and other facilities; and close proximity to trains or airports (as necessary).

Parallel processing facilities

This recovery strategy is a highly preferred solution. Parallel processing facilities perform the same operations at two (or more) remote locations. This means that each location must have all the technology, infrastructure, data, trained personnel, support services, and supply systems to support the required and critical business functions. The redundancy provides fault tolerance, nearly instant disaster recovery, and greater capacity, and it tends to support itself financially by performing revenue-generating operations.

During the initial BCP and DRP planning process for an enterprise with one location, this recovery solution might become a front-runner even if there has been no previous need for multiple locations. If parallel processing facilities exist or can be built into the BCP strategies, the DRP failover process is usually quite simple and fast. If parallel processing facilities do not yet exist, it will be expensive to get it set up initially, but then it begins to pay for itself, and it helps tremendously with the BCP and DRP.

Collocation of processes

This alternate-location DR option targets the automated processes primarily, where the only services required are IT based, such as e-commerce website services. With collocation, instead of having your web-based services hosted at one location and by one hosting company, locate a redundant set of web servers at a different hosting company in a different geographical area. Synchronization processes and failover processes must be developed, but this solution, too, provides system fault tolerance, data redundancy, nearly instant disaster recovery, and greater capacity; it also tends to support itself financially by performing revenue-generating operations.

Alternate (owned) sites

An alternate site is a facility the enterprise owns and is intended to be used only if a disaster strikes, not for routine business operations, which would be a parallel processing site. There are many levels of preparedness of these alternate sites that offer different costs and different recovery periods. They must be designed and assembled in accordance with management's tolerance for risk as designated by its approval of specific BC and DR proposals. Although their level of preparedness might equate to the descriptions of the hot, warm, and cold redundant sites, the terms "hot site," "warm site," and "cold site" typically imply (to ISC2 and on the exam) a leased site from a subscription service, as the following section describes.

Subscription services: Leased sites, hot, warm, and cold

Subscription services are similar to those of alternate sites but are leased rather than owned. The functional objectives of the hot, warm, and cold subscription sites are similar to those of owned alternate sites, but a third party is responsible for providing the space and some or most infrastructure for a fee. Usually, subscription services charge a monthly subscription fee that guarantees the member certain access to the resources but also might charge an activation fee and use fees if the enterprise elects to use the facilities. Following are descriptions of the hot site, the warm site, and the cold site. There is no distinct definition of the time frames for each of these terms, but the concepts are as follows.

HOT SITES

The hot site is ready to occupy and begin operations of the most critical business processes typically within a few hours, perhaps up to a day. To accomplish this, all required infrastructure, systems, communications, devices, software, furniture, supplies, and so on must be in place, compatible, and functional at the hot site. The failover process requires people and access to copies of the most current data, such as backups. The DR team arrives, powers up the facility and systems, restores the data from backup tapes, and starts the critical business operations. Because this facility is owned, practice restores of the backups should occur at the hot site to verify that these systems are operational, and other system tests should be completed on a regular basis. This is the most expensive disaster recovery option for the alternate site.

WARM SITES

The warm site is ready to occupy and begin operations within a few days. To accomplish this, much but not all the required infrastructure, systems, communications, devices, software, furniture, and supplies are in place and mostly compatible at the warm site. The failover process will require additional hardware systems and software, people, and data backups. Periodic system inspections and tests should be performed to verify the operational status of the warm site. This DR strategy is less expensive than the hot site.

COLD SITES

The cold site is ready to occupy and begin operations within a few weeks or longer. It is typically an empty building such as a warehouse. Power, water, sewer, and communications are connected at the building, but the interior of the facility must be built out. Virtually all IT, telephone, security systems must be installed and configured. Furniture must be delivered and set up. Periodic inspections should be performed to verify the status of the cold site. This DR strategy is the least expensive of the three.

Routine office space with standard office requirements such as desks, telephone, Internet connection, photocopying and fax machines, and receptionist are commonly available as a failover hot site for routine office functions. The more unique, specialized, and customized the needs, the more compatibility becomes an issue and the less likely a third party will be prepared as a hot site but might lend itself as a warm or cold site (such as a leased, empty warehouse).

These sites, leased from subscription services, are typically much less expensive than owning and developing the appropriate alternate site. The subscription membership should be established and in place before a disaster occurs and should carry some sort of assurance of access even—especially—after a disaster. There will be a run on these subscription services during and after any type of local disaster, and the availability might be gone at those times. Choose a location that will not be subject to the same disaster that compromised the primary facility.

Tertiary sites

Consider developing a plan for when both the primary and secondary sites are incapacitated. This is a backup plan for the backup plan. This plan would be more likely required if the secondary site must be located close to or in the same geographical area of risk as the primary site for some business-related reason.

Rolling hot sites

The rolling hot site is essentially a data center inside a cargo container or semi-truck. These are typically highly customized and built to satisfy very specific business function needs. Make it mobile so it can be relocated to any of several locations, as needed, or relocated outside the disaster area.

These sites often contain racks of servers and storage, HVAC, wired and wireless external communications (satellite, Internet, VoIP), AC power generators, and space for just a few workers. Roll to the desired location, connect to AC power or locate a nearby source of fuel, establish external communications, and start up the data center. Because they are typically packed with IT infrastructure and resources, these sites tend to be quite expensive but equally capable and versatile.

Reciprocal agreements

The reciprocal agreement might be used instead of maintaining access to a secondary site. These agreements are typically drawn up between businesses with a symbiotic relationship in which both enterprises reap benefit from the other, and each desires to support the other business to keep it alive and functional. This agreement essentially states that if one of the two enterprises suffers the loss of its facility, the other enterprise will provide it space within its facility.

This could satisfy the business needs of the two entities if one of the facilities suffers a disaster. However, if these symbiotic enterprises are located near one another, what happens if they both suffer the same disaster? What happens if, over time, the free space that had been available at the time of signing the reciprocal agreement is no longer available, or the hosting party cannot satisfy business needs?

There are several areas of serious concern when using the reciprocal agreement as part of the DR plan. These agreements are not enforceable, so if company A showed up on company B's doorstep and needed space, as agreed upon in the reciprocal agreement, and company B simply said, "No, sorry," and closed the door, company A cannot force its way into the facility and take over the space. Litigation (a civil suit) could be filed, but the resolution of that civil suit will likely come much too late for the now doomed company A, which has no place to go to initiate disaster recovery operations.

Even if company B did provide the agreed-upon space to company A, the disruptions and disharmony that develops in the now cramped, shared, contentious, limited space will often not support the required business functions.

The reciprocal agreement might look good on paper and enable the enterprise to check off a box on its compliance checklist but, all too often, it will not provide the intended and necessary recovery of the critical business functions during and after a disaster.

Recovery of supply systems

To support the business functions, certain conditions must be satisfied in the workplace. The workplace can't be too cold or too hot. Systems require AC power. Deliveries of raw materials must be received, and deliveries of finished product must be delivered to the paying customers. Disasters affect these components of the enterprise and can cause critical business functions to fail. The recovery of these supply systems must be a considered component of the DRP and the BCP.

HEATING, VENTILATION, AND AIR CONDITIONING

Although the workers will tolerate some limited discomfort for a short period, at some point, if the environment is too warm or too cold, the workers will become less productive and eventually stop working. Data centers (typically) are kept between 61 and 75 degrees Fahrenheit (16 to 24 degrees Celsius) to dissipate the heat generated by all those servers. Humidity controls are also often a concern in data centers. Consider this potential need as well.

Owning a few portable air conditioning units and portable heating units might be a reasonable solution. Remember that these units will need servicing and testing on a periodic basis. If you hope to rent units when needed, consider the likely increased demand. They might not be available when needed. Other enterprises might be experiencing the same type of problem and be looking for the same rental solution.

ELECTRICITY

For most enterprises, when the power goes out, all operations stop. This is unacceptable for those critical business functions. Many power outages affect a single transformer substation that powers a single grid. As a preventive control, having the power company pull redundant power lines from an alternate but nearby power grid is a good option. There is a one-time charge for initially pulling the wires but minimal additional costs thereafter. However, some power problems will affect multiple grids.

The next level of emergency power is that from a power generator, which usually runs on gasoline or diesel fuel. First, be sure the generator can actually supply enough power to run the critical business functions plus some additional margin. More things will always need to be powered than the strictly planned items. These generators must be tested regularly, and the fuel must be maintained regularly. Fuel goes bad over time due to condensation and other contaminants. Consider a store of fuel large enough to run the generators for a planned duration of outage, usually a minimum of several days. Plan the resupply of fuel well within this period and consider the potential disaster state of the environment. Fuel deliveries might be very difficult or impossible, and many other enterprises will be vying for those rare, few fuel deliveries.

Battery-backup uninterruptable power supplies (UPS) are generally not considered components of disaster recovery, except for the large-scale data centers, because the supplemental power they can provide is usually limited to minutes, not hours or days. These UPS devices should be part of the ongoing preventive countermeasures to provide clean power to IT systems; they do help with common, momentary power outages.

DELIVERIES INBOUND AND OUTBOUND

The timely delivery of raw materials falls under the purview of the security professional. In the case of the business continuity plan, it can be considered a responsibility of the security professional. The objective of the BCP is to prevent the enterprise from going out of business for any reason. If the business relies on some noncommodity raw material, the supply of that material might fail, which could lead to the failure of the enterprise. More as a preventive control than a recovery item, consider identifying multiple sources of these materials, establish a relationship with these multiple distributors, even 10 percent to 20 percent of the need, just to develop working processes. Consider product diversification to avoid depending on a single product for the survival of the enterprise.

During and after a disaster, vendors and perhaps customers must be made aware of any changes to the previously routine delivery processes. Whether the original facility now must receive all deliveries and provide all pickups at building 2 instead of building 3, or if the enterprise was forced to relocate to its secondary facility 75 miles away, these inbound raw materials and outbound deliveries to customers must be planned and coordinated to continue.

Recovery of technologies

The disaster recovery process is often quite technology-centric. Although there are many aspects to getting an enterprise up and running, many of the critical business functions rely heavily on information systems and communications.

As wireless networking technology improves, the recovery of basic networking functions becomes easier by eliminating the need for running hard wire to every node on the network. However, much of the network, routers, servers, firewalls, and other equipment will still require hard wiring.

Consider and develop these key aspects of the recovery of technologies in the DRP processes.

DOCUMENTATION

Before you can reproduce the lost IT infrastructure, you must know what was lost. Document the enterprise's networking environment. Document specific device configurations with reasons for the configuration details. This documentation should be part of your policy documents as network and device baselines. These documents should be referred to or included as part of the DRP and BCP documentation provided to management and to the team members. If referred to, consider how to convey the documents to the team members in a disaster. (If the server was lost in the flood, the documentation stored on that server is gone.) If this documentation is included with the plans, consider how to keep it updated properly as changes are made to the IT infrastructure.

DELIVERIES OR IN-HOUSE INVENTORY

The MTD for each business function largely defines whether deliveries or an in-house inventory will be required for the IT assets required to support those functions. If deliveries are the plan to acquire replacement parts, know all details of the parts, know where to acquire them, monitor the inventory of the parts, and know delivery times. Does this sound as if it might be too much to monitor long term?

Service level agreements (*SLA*) might take some of the burden off the in-house resources. By paying a monthly or annual maintenance fee, the SLA provider accepts responsibility for providing replacement parts within guaranteed timeframes. Be sure these timeframes align with the appropriate MTDs for the critical business functions. Keep in mind that the SLA providers likely must also be governed appropriately according to applicable laws, regulations, and policies.

Maintaining an in-house inventory of the parts and systems that support the most critical business functions provides the greatest level of control and certainty, but it comes also with the highest price. Consider what spare parts and systems must be kept and consider how to keep these updated and tested. Another key consideration is where to keep this inventory of spares. If this inventory is wiped out in a disaster, it is useless for the urgently needed recovery processes.

REDUNDANCY AND FAULT TOLERANCE

Identify single points of failure. Include redundancy and fault tolerance in the DRP and BCP proposals to management for each of the points that supports any critical business functions.

Consider:

- Disk mirroring or duplexing—redundant array of independent disks (RAID) 1
- Stripe set with parity—RAID 5
- Cluster servers
- Partial mesh networking topology

- Redundant Internet connections using different ISPs
- Collocation of applications and data to support remote workers
- Parallel processing sites to provide excellent benefits in disaster recovery efforts—two or more facilities far enough apart that they don't both suffer the same disaster but provide the same services and functions. With this setup, the people, the skills, the infrastructure, the applications, and the data are all present and functional in two locations.

> **MORE INFO** **REDUNDANT AND FAULT TOLERANT TECHNOLOGIES**
>
> The various levels of RAID and clustering are covered in Chapter 10, "Operations security." Network topologies and connections to the Internet are covered in Chapter 7, "Telecommunications and network security."

COMPATIBILITY

The redundant or rebuilt IT infrastructure must be compatible with the original IT infrastructure. Compatibility of the hardware, tape backup systems, software, and other systems and equipment should be considered before the plans are implemented and relied on. It is not uncommon for even minor revisions of the same software to be incompatible with one another. Consider updating and upgrading the software at the alternate site with any updating and upgrading of the software at the primary site.

COMMUNICATIONS

The IT infrastructure also includes communications. Inbound, outbound, and internal communications must be established to support the critical business functions. Identify the number and placement of communications devices and services, whether they are VoIP, PSTN, or even cellular, and build this critical functionality into the recovery and continuity plans.

Security standards

The rebuilt IT infrastructure must remain compliant with laws, regulations, and organizational policies. It is not acceptable to violate laws and regulations just because the enterprise is facing some networking problems.

If the original infrastructure had to be certified and accredited, then the rebuilt infrastructure must also be certified and accredited before it can go live. This process often takes days, weeks, or even months to accomplish, and this might be much too long to wait.

Remember to provide permissions by following the principle of least privilege, harden servers appropriately, and regularly update operating systems, applications, and firmware.

Recovery of data

If the disaster has destroyed the primary data set that supports the critical business functions, this data must be recovered. Before it can be recovered, though, a second copy of the data must be produced. Designing an appropriate system to produce this redundant data is based largely on five primary factors:

- Recovery point objective (RPO)
- Recovery time objective (RTO)
- Storage location
- Security requirements
- Cost

RECOVERY POINT OBJECTIVE (RPO)

The recovery point objective (RPO) defines the maximum amount of data the enterprise is willing to lose, or can afford to lose, from some failure or disaster. The RPO defines some point in the past when the most recent redundant data was produced, and it represents the amount of data that would be lost if a disaster struck at this moment. In essence, it defines the time interval between backups of the current data set. If the value of the data is very high, the RPO should be very short to minimize the amount of data (value) lost. If the value of the data is not so high, the RPO could be increased to minimize the cost of producing the redundant data and still risking only the loss of an acceptable amount of data (value).

Some techniques continuously update the redundant copy. These are referred to as *real-time* copies. Technologies that produce real-time copies typically cost more and risk the loss of only a few milliseconds' worth of transactions, maybe one or two transactions, if any at all. Other techniques only periodically produce the redundant copies. These are called *batch* processes. Batch processes are typically much less expensive but will lose all the new data since the last batch job to produce redundant data was executed. These are scheduled daily backups, for example.

The determination of whether to use real-time techniques or batch techniques for producing the redundant data copies is based on the value of the new data. If the enterprise can afford to lose 24 hours' worth of transactions and new data, the batch process of running daily backups is a reasonable and cost-effective solution. In some cases, 24 hours' worth of transactions and new data lost is too much loss, so a batch process should be executed more frequently, perhaps every four hours. If the data set represents a very high value—$1 million per hour—daily backups will not be a satisfactory solution, and real-time backups will likely be required to produce the redundant data.

Different data elements have different values, so it is common for a mix of these technologies to be required within the enterprise.

RECOVERY TIME OBJECTIVE

The recovery time objective (RTO) is a forward-looking value and identifies the amount of time required to recover the redundant data after the loss of the original data. This parameter must be aligned to be well within the MTD for any business process that requires the data being recovered. In some cases, the failover to the redundant data set is instantaneous. Users of the data likely will not even notice the loss of the original data. Other technologies require the acquisition of the backup tapes, then the physical access to the backup server, and then a several-hour restore process. The technologies used and the procedures defined, again, must integrate within the MTD for any business process that requires the data being recovered. Figure 8-4 shows the recovery point objective (RPO) and the recovery time objective (RTO) along a timeline.

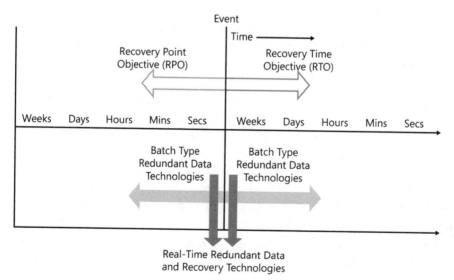

FIGURE 8-4 RPO and RTO

STORAGE LOCATION

Keeping the backup copies of the data close by typically improves the RTO, but keeping it close also puts the redundant data at the same risk of loss as that of the original data set. Keeping the redundant data at a remote location helps ensure its survivability but often delays its recovery. Therefore, a balance of these two aspects is often required. It is not uncommon to keep the critical redundant data in both places. If the enterprise does not have a convenient remote location for the remote storage of the redundant data, professional secure pickup, delivery, and storage services are readily available in most areas and might be mandated by compliance requirements.

SECURITY REQUIREMENTS

The data classification program, part of the overall security program for the organization covered in Chapter 1, defines the required protection measures for the various classifications of data. This same level of protection must also be met for all redundant copies of the data. If different classifications of data are mixed in any particular redundant copy, the redundant copy must be labeled and protected at the highest classification level. Consider designing the backup systems to group the redundant copies of different classifications of data on separate media to optimize the security costs.

Consider the security ramifications of storing the redundant copies at remote locations. These locations must also meet the organization's security requirements for the protection of the data. If the storage location is a subscription service provided by a third party, such as cloud-based storage area network (SAN) services, that third party must be contractually bound and further governed to comply with the applicable laws, regulations, and policy requirements of the enterprise.

EXAM TIP

As the following redundant data technologies are reviewed, note the RPO, RTO, and storage location (onsite versus offsite).

DISK MIRRORING AND DATABASE MIRRORING

Disk mirroring is commonly referred to as RAID1. It is a real-time redundant data technology requiring two hard disk drives in the same computer system. Both disks are labeled the same so that when the operating systems tells the file system to write the data to the disk, the data is actually written to both disks in the mirror set. The recovery point is essentially identical to the current time. The mirror set provides one-disk fault tolerance as well, allowing one of the two disks in the RAID 1 mirror set to fail and still provide access to 100 percent of the data by accessing the other disk without the need to take any action. The recovery time is also essentially zero. System performance is degraded, however, after the failed disk is replaced and is being mirrored with the surviving disk.

In the mirror set, the redundant copy of the data exists on the same server as the original data. If there is data corruption or inappropriate alteration of the data, both copies of the data are affected.

Database mirroring is very similar to disk mirroring except that it mirrors only one or more databases to a second disk in the local computer instead of mirroring the entire file system on a disk.

> **MORE INFO** **RAID**
>
> The various levels of RAID are covered in Chapter 10.

DISK SHADOWING AND DATABASE SHADOWING

Disk shadowing is a real-time, redundant data technology requiring two hard disk drives, but in this case, the disks are installed in two computer systems. Typically, one system provides services to end users, and the second system acquires the redundant data set; it does not support end users. The original system is configured so that when the operating systems tells the file system to write the data to the original disk, it writes the data to the original disk and sends a copy over the network to the shadow disk. The recovery point is essentially identical to the current time. If the original disk or system fails, and the data is lost, the shadow disk contains all of the original data, with the possibility of the loss of typically not more than a few milliseconds' worth of data caused by network latency. The recovery time will vary, depending on the technology and level of preparation on the shadow server. The application might need to be installed, and the data set must be mounted to provide access as necessary.

In the disk shadow, the redundant copy of the data can exist on a nearby server in the same data center but could also be located on a server at a remote data center as long as the network connectivity between the two servers provides sufficient performance.

Database shadowing is very similar to disk mirroring, except that it copies only one or more databases to a second disk in the local computer instead of copying the entire file system from one disk to another.

TRANSACTION JOURNALING

Transaction journaling is a real-time backup technology used on transaction-oriented database applications. The original copy of the database is accessible to users and responds to queries (reads) as well as accepting transactions—changes—to the stored data set (writes). A second copy of the database is stored (usually) on a second computer in the local data center or at a remote data center and is not directly accessible to end users. As a transaction from a user is committed to the original database, that transaction is journaled, copied, and sent over the network to the system holding the second database, where it is committed there as well. This keeps the second copy of the database synchronized in (near) real time, suffering only the few milliseconds' propagation delay between copying the transaction on the original system and sending it successfully to the second database.

If the original database or its hosting server were to fail, the application could mount the second database and expose it to the users, bringing it back online usually within a few minutes. During this failover time, there is no data redundancy. This is a very risky state, so the recovery of the original system is urgent.

Backup strategies and storage

Backups are the most common approach to producing redundant data. Classically, backups are a batch process by which the desired data is copied periodically to magnetic tape. Magnetic tape is used because of its low cost per byte and the ability to remove the tapes (called *removable media*) and store them in a remote location. A backup application produces the *catalog* of data (usually at the file level) to be backed up. The catalog is the list of every file that needs to be backed up. Then on a schedule, the backup application identifies the appropriate files defined in the catalog and writes them on the magnetic tape. These backups are commonly performed when the servers and network are at their lowest level of demand by end users, typically late at night. This provides an RPO of 24 hours.

> **NOTE THE SLOWEST TECHNIQUE FOR RECOVERING DATA**
>
> Tape drives read and write sequentially, one of the slowest techniques for recovering specific data.

Three types of backups are commonly used in combinations to provide the required data redundancy RPO and recoverability RTO:

- The full backup
- The incremental backup
- The differential backup

These three types of backup operate differently on the files defined in the catalog and rely on the *archive bit*, or *A bit*, file attribute. The A bit is set to a binary one (1) when the file is new on the partition or is modified and saved (written) to the partition but has not yet been copied to a full or incremental backup. The full and incremental backups reset the A bit to a binary zero (0) when those backup processes successfully write the file to tape (or whatever the backup media is). The A bit set to 1 indicates that this file (or version of the file) has not yet been copied to tape. The A bit set to 0 indicates that this file (or version of the file) has been copied to tape successfully.

THE FULL BACKUP

The *full backup* copies every file listed in the catalog to tape regardless of the state of the A bit. At the end of the backup process, when every file listed in the catalog has been copied to tape, the full backup resets the A bit of every file in the catalog to 0, indicating that the file in the catalog has been copied to tape successfully. The full backup takes the longest to complete and consumes the most server, network, and tape system resources.

This is the preferred backup type if there are plenty of these resources available every night during the backup process, because the daily full backup is the easiest to restore in case of emergency. However, many enterprises find this demand on resources too high every night, so they run the full backup once a week, perhaps on Sunday morning at 2 A.M., when the information systems are at their lowest demand, and there is plenty of time to complete the full backup.

THE INCREMENTAL BACKUP

The *incremental backup* is used in conjunction with the full backup, typically running the full backup once a week on Sunday morning and running the incremental backups every other night (five or six times weekly). The incremental backup copies only the files listed in the catalog whose A bit is set to 1, those new files or versions of existing files that have not yet been copied to tape. Therefore, if only 20 percent of the A bit files in the catalog are set to 1, only those 20 percent are copied to tape during the incremental backup. At the end of the incremental backup process, when every file listed in the catalog whose A bit is set to 1 has been copied to tape, the incremental backup resets the A bit of all these files to 0, indicating that the 20 percent of new and modified files in the catalog have been copied to tape successfully. By having this incremental backup plus the previously run full backup, every file and the latest version of every file that is listed in the catalog is available on tape for recovery purposes.

Each subsequent night when the incremental backup runs, only the new or modified files from that day are copied to tape, keeping the incremental backups short.

The combination of the weekly full backup and the nightly incremental backups takes the shortest time to complete and consumes the smallest server, network, and tape system resources. This combination is optimized for backing up the critical data. However, it is the most demanding restore process and is not optimized for restoring data when needed. For example, if a disk failure occurs on Saturday, the preceding Sunday full backup and then the following days' backups must be restored to recover the data. Therefore, six tapes must be restored in the correct order to bring the data to its most current state at the time of the most recent backup on Friday night (the RPO).

THE DIFFERENTIAL BACKUP

The *differential backup* is used in conjunction with the full backup. As with the full plus incremental backup combination, administrators typically run the full backup once a week on Sunday morning and run the differential backups every other night (five or six times weekly). The differential backup copies only the files listed in the catalog whose A bit is set to 1, those new files or versions of existing files that have not yet been copied to tape. Therefore, if only 20 percent of the A bit files in the catalog are set to 1, only that 20 percent are copied to tape during the differential backup. At the end of the differential backup process, when every file listed in the catalog whose A bit is set to 1 has been copied to tape, the differential backup *does not* reset the A bit of all these files to 0 but *leaves them set to 1*. This causes the number of files whose A bit is set to 1 to grow daily. By having this differential backup plus the previously run full backup, every file—and the latest version of every file that is listed in the catalog—is available on tape for recovery purposes.

Each subsequent night, the number of new or modified files grows. When the differential backup runs, a larger number of files needs to be backed up, but again, only the new or modified files since the most recent full or incremental backup are copied to tape. This keeps the differential backups shorter than a full backup but makes it longer than an incremental backup.

The combination of the weekly full backup plus the nightly differential backups takes less time than a daily full backup to complete and consumes fewer server, network, and tape system resources than a daily full backup. The combination of the weekly full backup plus the nightly differential backup is somewhat optimized for backing up the critical data. However, it is the most efficient restore process and is optimized for restoring the data when needed.

To build on this example, if a disk failure occurs on Saturday, the preceding Sunday full backup must be restored, and then only the most recent differential backup—the Friday night differential backup's two tapes—must be restored in the correct order to bring the data to its most current state at the time of the most recent backup on Friday night (the RPO).

Figure 8-5 shows how these combinations are chosen to optimize either the backup process or the restore process.

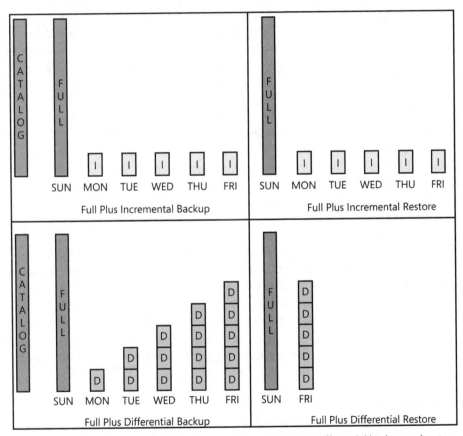

FIGURE 8-5 Full plus incremental backup and restore and full plus differential backup and restore

Most backup applications put all backed-up files into a single backup file. This means that the files can be accessed only by using the backup application to restore the files. Most backup applications can also provide encryption for the backed-up content to provide protection for the data.

It is a common practice to cycle tapes, for example keeping the last week of daily backups on site along with the Sunday full backup for the past four weeks to support the recovery of the most likely data that would be needed. The other tapes are often securely transferred to a remote location for secure storage. This remote content can be retrieved for recovery of data, but it might take a day or longer just to get the tapes back in hand. Policy and procedures should define this tape rotation and the retention period for the backups.

ELECTRONIC VAULTING

Electronic vaulting is a batch process that copies files over the network and writes them to hard disk drives. Content on remote servers can then be backed up over the network to a single backup system. Electronic vaulting is faster than writing the files to tape because hard disk drives perform better than tape drives, and hard disk drives are direct-access read and write devices rather than tapes, which are sequential access. Because electronic vaulting is faster than using tape drives, backups can be scheduled to run more frequently, decreasing the RPO, and restores can be accomplished more rapidly, decreasing the RTO. The downside to electronic vaulting is that hard disk drives are more expensive storage than magnetic tape, and the disks cannot be removed as easily for remote storage.

TAPE VAULTING

Tape vaulting is a batch process that copies files over the network and writes them to tape drives. Content on remote servers can then be backed up over the network to a single tape backup system. Because tape drives are sequential-access devices, this is a relatively slow process, but magnetic tape is less expensive storage than hard disk drives and can be removed from the systems for secure and remote storage.

COLLOCATION OF DATA

Collocation of data allows for one or more remote copies of the data, and each copy of the data set is (typically) accessible like a distributed database. This provides redundancy of data and a higher level of availability. The multiple copies of the data are synchronized through replication processes that might be *synchronous replication* (real-time) processes or *asynchronous replication* (near real-time or batch) processes, depending on the capabilities of the synchronization application, the connectivity between the multiple locations, and the dynamic or static nature of the data, which affects the volume of data to be synchronized over any given period.

PRACTICE RESTORES OF THE DATA

One of the practices enterprises overlook most is the practice restore of the data. Although being great at producing backups of the critical and valuable data is a very good thing, being great at restoring the data from the redundant copy is perhaps more important. When the data can be restored and actually mounted or used, it validates that the backup procedures and technologies are working correctly. Second, it keeps the data custodian rehearsed, well trained in the procedures that will be needed during a disaster, when every second might count.

The practice restore procedures should be carried out in the earlier described hot site secondary facility if it exists. Practice restore procedures should be carried out at the primary facility if the secondary facility is anything less than a hot site.

Recovery of people and critical personnel

Wherever possible, the automated recovery is the preferred approach. It can usually happen without much of a delay and ideally without mistakes. However, it is unlikely that the entire recovery process after a disaster can be completed without people. As soon as the disaster is detected, recognized, and declared by the appropriate personnel in senior management, someone (or several people) should be assigned the responsibility to begin dialing the numbers on the preconfigured, properly ordered call list. Not all members of the call list will need to be called for every type of disaster, so call only those who are appropriate for the specific type of event that is occurring.

- Emergency services: fire, ambulance, police, hazmat; human safety is paramount
- Evacuation and safety personnel as appropriate
- Disaster recovery team members
- Outside professional services and consultants as needed
- Additional senior management members
- Board of directors
- High-level management of the affected area(s)
- Law enforcement, as appropriate, in case the disaster represents a criminal act
- Public media: TV, news, shareholders, stock market traders
- Vendors and customers
- Others as necessary and as directed by management

Consider the need to use out-of-band communications without allowing other company personnel (insiders) to know that some event is occurring in case insiders are cooperating with the attack or the outside attackers can monitor the standard communications channels. If the attackers can learn your approach to the response, they can adjust their attack to continue to maximize the damages and cover their tracks to elude the investigative processes.

Consider having public relations determine and polish what is said to the different entities on the call list. Some of this information might be inappropriate for some of the entities on the call list and leaked to the outside world.

Not all the members of the disaster recovery team will always be available. People will be traveling or on vacation. There will be turnover over time. Individuals might be injured or worse. Individuals might be heading home to take care of family members during the disaster. Anticipating these holes in the disaster recovery team means that all members must be not only well trained in their areas of specific responsibility but also cross-trained in the other team members' areas of responsibility; they must accept the additional responsibilities for those absent during the disaster.

If certain individuals possess specialized, perhaps one-of-a-kind skills only a specific individual is capable of performing, preventive controls dictate that those specialized skills should be duplicated among multiple additional personnel. Skills that specialized are too valuable to leave in the hands of a single individual.

In addition, many companies are built by and achieve continued success because of the strength of the company patriarch or matriarch, a publicly known and recognized figurehead, an individual who, over time, becomes known as the face, the strength, and the reliability of the enterprise.

These individuals, too, are often too valuable to the success of the company. Although he has become known as the icon or trademark representing all the good things of the enterprise, reliance on one individual becomes too risky to the ongoing enterprise in case of sudden death, illness, or even planned retirement. The unexpected loss of this figurehead could severely damage the public's perception of the enterprise's quality, trustworthiness, and reliability and even its ability to continue. The DRP and BCP should include components to plan for this *executive succession* and minimize the associated risks.

When this condition is recognized, the careful and public grooming of a parallel senior manager or replacement for this figurehead should begin and continue over a relatively long period, all in the public eye. This can defuse the critical perceptions if and when the strong leader becomes unavailable for any reason.

Developing the BCP (reconstitution guidelines)

Reconstitution can only begin when management can declare that the disaster recovery plans and the disaster recovery team(s) have been successful, the critical and essential business processes are operational, and the risk of the enterprise failing is now very low. The enterprise is still damaged and may be far from fully functional at a normal state, but the business continuity is essentially ensured.

Specifics of the reconstitution phase of the disaster recovery and business continuity process cannot be precisely documented like the plans and procedures for the disaster recovery phase of the process. It isn't practical to plan the reconstruction of the facility fully because the disaster that strikes might never wipe out the facility. It isn't practical to plan the complete reassembly of the number 2 widget production systems unless or until the number 2 widget production line is declared destroyed and must be rebuilt from scratch. The specific details cannot be planned until the exact status of the enterprise is accurately assessed after a disaster.

It is, however, practical to establish reconstitution guidelines that describe solutions to more general reconstitution concerns. Such proactive measures as establishing a line of credit—before the disaster to keep the enterprise solvent while awaiting reimbursement from the insurance claims—or documenting the source and general requirements of the number 2 widget production systems and the general facility are important precautions. That way, if a disaster strikes and destroys a key element of the enterprise, it is understood what the requirements of the replacement include.

Document the general requirements, function by function or department by department, to help during the reconstitution phase, including:

- Facility requirements
- Safety-related issues and concerns
- Supply system requirements—sources, quantities, and schedules
- Technology requirements and a diagram of the current IT infrastructure
- Data, type, destination location required, volume, restored from what type of redundant copy or media
- Reconstitution team roles and responsibilities
- Financial planning and line of credit
- In-house spare systems and their locations
- General migration plans to repopulate the primary facility moving from the secondary facility
- If–then decision points whose solutions might improve overall performance for the enterprise beyond the current ability to perform

Some specifics that should be included in the BC guidelines include:

- Testing and verification procedures for systems. There might be a need for certification and accreditation of information systems before they can be used.
- Criteria for the termination of the DR and reconstitution phases. The declared new state of normal for the enterprise must be established.
- Disaster review. What lessons were learned, what worked well, what didn't work well, what feedback and recommendations should be given to management?
- Plans for testing the plans should be documented.
- Plans to maintain the plans should be documented.
- Training requirements and sources should be documented.

Presentation to senior management

Remember that at this phase of the planning process, this is only talk and paper, the development of multiple proposals and options for management to choose from during the upcoming review for approval phase.

Senior management will review the deliverables from the planning team and absorb the present state of risk to the enterprise and current security posture. Based on its vision, tolerance for risk, desired resulting security posture, and concerns for the budget, it will begin to recognize what it feels are the appropriate, specific, preventive countermeasures and the appropriate disaster recovery strategies to ensure the ongoing continuity of the business. As it approves specific components of the proposed plans, it is gathering additional details, including the required hardware, software, personnel, training, policy documents, and, perhaps most important, the feasible budget for the implementation of the DRP and the BCP.

At this point, all this work stops being just talk and paper and begins to take true form in implementation.

Because of the size of the disaster recovery and business continuity planning projects, the initial pass will produce numerous discrete plans and procedures, which must integrate with one another to produce an overall, comprehensive, cohesive, enterprise-wide collection of approved plans.

Any aspects of the proposed security, preventive controls, and disaster recovery and business continuity strategies that are not approved should be well secured and well documented. These accepted risks remain vulnerabilities in the security posture of the enterprise, and although they might not be affordable this year, they must be reviewed and understood during the ongoing DRP and BCP maintenance process next year.

 Quick check

1. What are the parameters that describe the time frames to recover data?

2. If critical business processes need to be recovered within 60 minutes after a disaster, what alternate location types might support this?

Quick check answers

1. Recovery point objective and recovery time objective

2. Parallel processing site, collocation site, hot site

Implementing the approved plans

The wide array of plans, function by function, department by department, facility by facility, and division by division, must be properly integrated to produce an overall, comprehensive, cohesive, enterprise-wide BCP and DRP.

The approved preventive countermeasures are implemented and become a standard and routine component of the security posture of the organization. The preparatory actions required to support the approved DRP and BCP must begin to take shape.

Policies, standards, baselines, procedures, and guidelines must be completed to describe the intended functionality, use, maintenance, and benefits accurately of the new security systems. The required hardware and software must be purchased and integrated into the current information systems. Any new personnel required must be hired and trained, and existing administrative personnel must be trained on these new tools. End-user training must be developed and provided so the end users understand the new policy requirements and the proper use of the new systems. Low-level and mid-level management must be trained to identify violations of policy regarding these new controls and in the proper enforcement and remediation procedures.

It takes time, but eventually, the finalized DRP and BCP will be completed. These completed, approved plans must be classified to protect them properly, and they must be managed through formal and strictly followed change control procedures. These are highly sensitive documents that are essentially a map to the jugular vein of the enterprise, documenting where to strike to hurt the enterprise in the most devastating way. Enemies of the enterprise would like very much to find a copy of these plans.

DR and BC team members need copies of these plans. The plans should not just be kept on one of the file servers, but there must be printed copies as well. These printed copies must be distributed, not just in the various offices of the team members but at their homes, in their vehicles, and at the secondary site(s). Wherever they are distributed, they must be carefully protected according to the data classification policies. Copies should be numbered and signed for as they are distributed.

As the plans are maintained over time, earlier copies should be collected and destroyed as the new versions are distributed, again using numbered copies and documentation of who received which copies.

Components of the plans

The completed DRP and BCP documents (probably one or more large binders) should contain components similar to these:

- Overview
- Roles and responsibilities
- Activation of the disaster recovery procedures
- Recovery plans for the critical business functions
- Business continuity guidelines
- Testing of the plans
- Finishing touches
  - Plans for the testing of the plans
  - Maintaining the plans
  - Training
- Appendices

Overview

The overview should include a description of the organization of the plans (how and where to find what) and should convey a sense of urgency to the reader. The overview should also provide a summary of the current state of the enterprise, including the inventory of the business functions (identified in the order of their MTD, shortest MTD at the top of the list) with a mapping of the related critical business functions and the resources that support each function and its dependency functions. This is often referred to as a *statement of operations*.

The overview should also include a current vulnerability, threat, and risk assessment for those functions and information assets that complete the description of the security posture of the organization.

Roles and responsibilities

This section should identify the roles required to implement the various facets of the plans and list the tasks and functions assigned to each role. The role, for most organizations, is actually defined as a team of individuals, so assignments should be defined for the team and then might be further defined for individual activities. An overall DR and BC coordinator role should be defined and described. Each team should be assigned a team lead and an alternate team lead in case the team lead is unavailable for any reason. Specific members of the teams and their assigned position of responsibility on the team are usually listed separately because this aspect can vary the most over time.

Different organizations will need different types of DR and BC teams (roles). Some examples of the types of DR and BC teams include:

- DR and BC coordinator
- Evacuation and safety team
- Damage assessment team
- Various DR teams, often based on the critical business functions to be recovered
- Secondary facility relocation team
- Primary facility restoration team
- Network recovery team
- Telecom team
- Security team
- Salvage team
- Public relations
- Plan maintenance team

Activation of the disaster recovery procedures

Often, a disaster doesn't present itself as a disaster at first. An anomalous event is noticed first. As it is escalated through the incident response process, its severity becomes apparent. This initial assessment and escalation procedure should be described here but follows the Computer Emergency Response Team (CERT) procedures closely. Often, the security professional must present the details of the anomalous event to senior management, and only senior management can escalate the event to incident status for investigation or to disaster status for the activation of the DR plan procedures. This reserves the costly decision to escalate for senior management.

Several senior managers should be assigned the authority to declare the disaster in case one or more are unavailable for any reason. There should also be established criteria that define the threshold of a disaster. These senior managers with the authority to escalate events and declare disasters must be trained so their perceptions and interpretations about the criteria are synchronized.

This becomes a critical turning point for many organizations facing a disaster. Declare a disaster (that isn't a disaster) too soon, and the enterprise is wasting money and increasing its own risks. Declare the real disaster too late, and the losses mount rapidly, bringing the MTD closer every minute the response is inaccurately delayed.

When senior management declares the disaster, the business operations within the scope of the disaster typically cease, and all efforts become focused on the safety of personnel and the urgent recovery of the critical business functions, the DR processes.

As described earlier in this chapter, one or more team members are assigned responsibility for initiating the call list. This list must be prepared in advance, with the entities to be called listed in a specific order and with specific name and current contact information. This information should be verified on a periodic basis because it will change all too frequently.

Meanwhile, one team should be responsible for the initial damage assessment. Much of the next immediate actions will be based on this initial assessment, which must be provided to management for approval to take specific disaster recovery actions. In some organizations, these intermediary approvals within certain specified guidelines are preapproved, and the DR activities can proceed more rapidly.

The security team is required to ensure that the security standards defined by policy, laws, and regulations are not violated (to the best of its ability) throughout this DR phase and the eventual, hopeful, reconstitution phase. Security thresholds must be maintained.

Recovery plans for the critical business functions

As the damage assessment is providing details of the state of operations for the enterprise, various specific DR activities will be triggered to recover the identified lost business functions and should specifically identify the functions with the shortest MTD first. This section in the plans contains the bulk of the planning material and description of recovery activities. First should be an inventory of the business functions within the scope of this set of plans, and the functions should be listed in order of the shortest MTD to the longest MTD. The detailed recovery plans will be stepwise, sequential procedures that describe how to recover every business function quickly within that function's MTD.

These recovery activities will often require coordination and communication between various DR teams. These coordination and communication details and methods must be part of the DR plans, understood, developed, and well documented during the planning stage before the disaster occurs.

Beginning with the business function with the shortest MTD, follow the planned procedures to recover that business functionality within the MTD period. The supporting elements that typically need to be restored to recover the critical business processes include:

- Work space and facilities
- Supply systems
- Technologies
- Data
- People and critical personnel

Criteria for the termination of DR phase and the initiation of the reconstitution phase should be defined. The point when the DR phase should be terminated is when the state of operations and functionality can sustain the enterprise indefinitely. When it can be reasonably ensured with some confidence that although still damaged and operating at a reduced capacity, the enterprise is no longer at risk of failure and will survive while operating at this level of functionality, the DR phase has been completed. This point defines the termination of the DR activities and the initiation of the reconstitution phase. The goal is to maintain this minimum level of operational functionality to effect repairs, continually improve the level of operational functionality, and, as quickly and smoothly as possible, return the enterprise to a state of normal operations.

Business continuity guidelines

The next component of the completed DRP and BCP manuals is the set of guidelines that have been prepared to set general concepts about how to implement reconstitution to a state of normal after a disaster and when the DR process is complete. Many of the components identified in this section will have been put in place prior to any disaster and already become a component of the standard security posture for the organization, but they are documented here to connect the state of operations during the disaster with the prepared resources to assist with the reconstitution of the enterprise.

As stated previously in this chapter, BC guideline documentation includes the general requirements, function by function, or department by department, to help during the reconstitution phase.

Finishing touches

Some additional specifics that are part of the ongoing business continuity of the enterprise include:

- Plans for testing the plans
- Plans to maintain the plans
- Training requirements and sources

These ongoing activities relative to business continuity become part of the standard and routine security program and establish the ongoing security posture for the enterprise.

PLANS FOR TESTING THE PLANS

The DR plans should be tested periodically to validate the accuracy, effectiveness, and completeness of the plans in their current state. ISC2 identifies five (5) levels of testing that begin with a low-cost, low-complexity, low-risk but less-telling test and progresses to higher levels of cost, complexity, and risk but provides a much more realistic view of the ability of the plans, personnel, and strategies.

- **Checklist testing** (also known as unit testing, consistency testing) When performing the checklist test, the DR coordinator sends each team member the sections of the plans that he is responsible for. The team member reviews his section(s) and makes any required additions, deletions, or modifications as necessary and then returns his section(s) to the coordinator. The coordinator then updates the sections as they are returned from the team members and reassembles the complete collection of updated plans. The checklist test is inexpensive, easy, and low risk but not very telling of whether the plans will actually work.

- **Structured walkthrough testing** (also known as table-top testing, integration testing, or validity testing) In the structured walkthrough test, the coordinator calls a meeting of the team members and then describes a disaster scenario. Team members then each describe what his responsibilities, tasks, functions, integration, and communication requirements would be relative to the described scenario. This test is more costly, more complex, riskier (because the personnel are taken away from their daily activities), and more telling of how well the plans will work. Integration issues in the plans will begin to present themselves.

- **Simulation testing** This test begins with the structured walkthrough testing, but instead of just describing their individual activities, the team members actually go and do them, without taking any destructive actions, up to meeting at the secondary facility to review the specific activities the individuals perform.

- **Parallel testing** Begin with the simulation testing, only this time, proceed into the secondary facility, restore data, and initialize systems as required actually to perform a few sample transactions on the systems at the secondary site.

- **Full interruption testing** Begin with parallel testing, but after running a few sample transactions, shut down the primary facility to verify that the secondary site can actually perform the critical business functions at an acceptable level to keep the enterprise alive. This test is the most costly, the most complex, the riskiest, but the most telling of the testing types.

Testing of the DR and BC plans should occur at least annually or any time the enterprise experiences significant changes such as buying or selling a division, adding or dropping a production line, adding a new facility or location, or merging with another enterprise.

EXAM TIP

Be sure you understand the five levels of testing and the activities included in each level.

MAINTAINING THE PLANS

The first implementation of the DRP and BCP will often take up to three years to complete. After that first set of plans is complete, reviewing and updating the plans is considerably simpler. The requirements for the ongoing review and updates should be defined formally in the policy document structure.

The DR and BC plans should be reviewed and updated at least annually or any time the enterprise experiences significant changes as mentioned previously. Changes in the MTD for the business functions and technology, changes in personnel, and identification of an oversight or error in the current plans could all trigger the need to perform an out-of-schedule review and update of these plans. Because these are formal documents within the enterprise, they should follow strict change control procedures as defined in the policy document structure.

An individual or team should be formally assigned to accomplish this plan review and update each year. Senior management should provide oversight to ensure that this review is accomplished appropriately and on a timely basis.

TRAINING

As management begins approving specific preventive controls and disaster recovery techniques and strategies, the specifics of training needs will firm up. Several types of training will be required for the various types and groups of personnel affected by the DRP and BCP. This training must occur once upon completion of the various components of the DR and BC plans and then again at least annually as a refresher and to incorporate all changes to the plans as they are maintained over time.

Additional training will be required after any significant changes to the enterprise; the safety, security, and recovery technologies; or the plans themselves. All new hires must receive the proper training before being provided access to valuable information systems and assets. Supplemental training should be provided for users with heightened privilege levels to bring into focus the increased risk they present and reinforce the enhanced security controls implemented to protect these assets. Remedial training should be provided to any users who violate policy, whether the violation was accidental or willful.

As preventive controls and recovery technologies are acquired and added to the security posture for the organization, the administrators responsible for those systems and technologies must be trained in the proper installation, configuration, use, ongoing maintenance, and recommended best practices for those technologies.

New policies, standards, baselines, procedures, and guidelines (collectively called policy documents) must be written and approved, and then all users must be trained in the new policy documents, new procedures, and use of the new systems and software.

The approved technologies, plans, and strategies must be formalized and compiled into the complete and comprehensive DR and BC manuals. Every member of the DR and BC team must be trained in her specific area of responsibility and cross-trained in additional areas to cover for any missing team members during the disaster recovery process. The various DR and BC team leaders and some high-level management personnel will need comprehensive training to include all their team members' priorities, tasks, and responsibilities and perhaps additional training in project management.

Many laws and regulations require these documents, their annual testing and annual update, and the appropriate training of personnel in these matters.

Appendices

The appendices should include anything that could be helpful that hasn't yet been included in the DR and BC manuals.

- **Contact list, in order, with recently verified phone numbers**   A description of who to call and under what conditions. A description of the type of info to provide to the entity being called should be provided in case there are no active public relations (PR) activities at this point. This list tends to be a bit dynamic as personnel changes jobs and turnover occurs.
- **Safety and emergency medical response information**   Poison control, CPR, automated defibrillator use, fire suppression, and other rescue operations.
- **Hazardous materials**   Lists of hazardous materials present in the workplace, hazmat call lists, handling details, treatment details.
- **Assignments**   Specific names of the team members mapped to the role(s) they have been trained for and are expected to provide during the DR and BC periods. This list tends to be a bit dynamic as personnel changes jobs and turnover occurs.
- **Diagrams**   Facility layout, evacuation plans, flow charts, decision trees, process charts, and so on.
- **Schematics**   For any custom circuitry and wiring.
- **Maps**   Locations of critical assets, facilities, suppliers, resources, and so on.
- **Vendors and suppliers**   Where to get recovery materials and resources, how to contact them, account information, and so on.
- **Alternate plans**   Backup plans when the DR plans won't work or aren't working.

The plans are written function by function, department by department, division by division, and facility by facility and are eventually collected, organized, and integrated into a complete and comprehensive set of DR and BC plans. These components of the completed disaster recovery and business continuity plans must remain secured yet distributed sufficiently to be available even when the facility is no longer accessible. Hard (printed) copies and soft (electronic) copies must be controlled and accounted for. The plans require regular review and updating, and the changes to these formalized documents must be managed using strict change control procedures. Versions must be managed so that during a disaster, someone doesn't pull out the outdated plans from seven years ago and begin working based on those plans. Team members must be trained and cross-trained, and the plans must be tested regularly.

Share the accomplishment with the world?

Often, after the DRP and BCP are completed, management is eager to tell the world and begin to reap the benefits of the newfound state of maturity of the enterprise. It wants to tell the members of the board of directors to show them what a great job it's doing, tell the shareholders to convince them to buy more stock, tell the insurance company so it can reduce the company's premiums, tell the banks so it can get better interest rates and a larger line of credit, and tell potential business partners so they'll be more willing to do more business together.

However, the details that management or anyone else provides to the outside world must be carefully managed and should follow data classification controls. Many details should never be exposed to outsiders. Share the accomplishment of completing the DRP and BCP but not the details or the documents.

 Quick check

1. What type of plan tests relocated business processes in the alternate site and then shuts down the primary site?

2. What part of the business continuity plan becomes a routine component of the security posture of the enterprise and is intended to avoid the disaster altogether?

Quick check answers

1. The full interruption test

2. Preventive countermeasures

Exercises

In the following exercises, you apply what you've learned in this chapter. You can find the answers to these exercises in the "Answers" section at the end of this chapter.

Exercise 8-1

Management has just assigned you to be the DRP planning coordinator for your department, whose scope is your household kitchen. Identify the functions and dependency functions within this scope.

Exercise 8-2

Identify five preventive controls that might help avoid disasters within this scope.

Chapter summary

- Human safety is the primary objective in the DRP and BCP. The rapid and smooth return to a normal state of operations is the secondary objective of the DRP and BCP.

- The BCP is the overarching collection of long-term plans designed to avoid disasters, mitigate the impact of unavoidable disasters, quickly and smoothly return the enterprise to a state of normal operations after a disaster, and assess and manage risk continuously. The IT-centric DRP, a subset of the overarching BCP, is the collection of short-term plans designed to recover the critical business processes within their MTD to keep the enterprise operational. The DRP and BCP planning process must be driven by senior management, formalized within the policy documents, and reviewed and tested initially and annually. Members of the DR and BC teams, administrators, users, and management must all be regularly trained.

- The measure of the criticality for each business function is called the maximum tolerable downtime (MTD), which identifies how long a function can be absent before the enterprise is doomed to failure.

- The terms used to describe the level of criticality for each business function include:

    - **Critical/Essential** Up to a few hours

    - **Urgent** Up to a day

    - **Important** Up to 3 days

    - **Normal** Up to 7 days

    - **Nonessential** Up to 30 days

- The core components that typically must be recovered during the DR process include facilities and workplace, information systems and technologies, data, and personnel.

- Plans for relocation to an alternate (secondary) facility must support recovery of the critical business functons within the MTD and include the parallel processing site, col-location site, hot site, warm site, cold site, subscription services (leased sites), rolling hot site and the reciprical agreement.

- The recovery point objective (RPO) defines the maximum allowable time since the last backup of a data set and limits the amount of data that could be lost in case of disaster. The recovery time objective (RTO) identfies the maximum allowable time to recover the data after a disaster.

- Criteria should be defined to identify a disaster, the end of the disaster recovery phase, and the end of the reconstitution phase. The disaster recovery phase ends when enough critical business functions are operational to sustain the enterprise indefinately after a disaster. The reconstitution phase ends when the enterprise is operating normally.

Chapter review

Test your knowledge of the information in this chapter by answering these questions. The answers to these questions, and the explanations of why each answer choice is correct or incorrect, are located in the "Answers" section at the end of this chapter.

1. Which of the following is the best type of recovery process?

   A. A process that maximizes vulnerabilities and impact

   B. A process that identifies vulnerabilities and impact

   C. A manually implemented process

   D. An automated process

2. Which of the following describes the technology that produces a redundant data set within a single server?

   A. Disk shadowing

   B. Electronic vaulting

   C. Disk mirroring

   D. Collocation

3. A partition on a disk drive that loses its data due to corruption from a hacker attack is what kind of threat?

   A. Natural

   B. Technical

   C. Human-made

   D. Supply system

4. Which of the following is NOT a reason to review and update the DRP and BCP out of schedule?

   A. Changes to the maximum tolerable downtime

   B. Change of the insurance providers

   C. Discontinued business functions

   D. Changes in technologies

5. Which of the following is the primary goal of performing the business impact analysis (BIA)?

   A. To identify the threats to the assets

   B. To identify the risks to the assets

   C. To identify the qualitative value of the business functions

   D. To identify the maximum tolerable downtime (MTD)

6. Which of the following describes the technology that produces a redundant data set at the file level in real time on a remote server?

   A. Disk shadowing

   B. Electronic vaulting

   C. Disk mirroring

   D. Remote journaling

7. What must be done if management is unable to reduce risk to an acceptable level by using the proposed countermeasures?

   A. Identify the threats and threat agents.

   B. Identify and propose additional countermeasures.

   C. Fortify the facility.

   D. Acquire a hot site as a secondary location.

8. Which of the following is the most telling of the testing plans?

   A. Structured walkthrough

   B. Parallel

   C. Full interruption

   D. Simulation

Answers

This section contains the answers to the exercises and the "Chapter review" section in this chapter.

Exercise 8-1

The primary functions in the household kitchen might include the following:

- Storage of consumables
- Preparation of consumables
- Distribution of consumables
- Inventory control
- Storage of, and easy access to, tools
- Cleaning of workspace and tools used in the preparation and distribution of consumables
- Removal of refuse

The dependency functions might include:

- Storage of consumables
  - Ambient temperature storage
  - Refrigerated storage (chilled)
  - Refrigerated storage (frozen)
- Inventory control
  - Acquisition of consumables (materials input required)
  - Storage of refuse
  - Removal of refuse
- Preparation of consumables
- Heating of consumables
- Storage of, and easy access to, tools
- Cleaning of workspace and tools used in the preparation and distribution of consumables
  - Acquisition of cleaning materials
  - Storage of cleaning materials
- Distribution of consumables

Exercise 8-2

- Redundant power lines from a second transformer grid
- Antibacterial cleansers
- Operator training
- Establishment of relationship with multiple suppliers of consumables
- Fire suppression technologies (sprinklers, fire extinguishers)

Chapter review

1. **Correct answer: D**

   A. **Incorrect:** You need to eliminate or minimize vulnerabilities and impact.

   B. **Incorrect:** A process that identifies vulnerabilities and impact is used better as a planning process than as a recovery process.

   C. **Incorrect:** Manually implemented recovery processes rely on humans, who might or might not be available and able to implement the recovery process.

   D. **Correct:** Automated processes are more likely to be implemented than a manually implemented recovery process.

2. **Correct answer: C**

   A. **Incorrect:** A disk shadow produces a redundant data copy on a different computer.

   B. **Incorrect:** Electronic vaulting produces a redundant data copy on a different computer.

   C. **Correct:** A disk mirror produces a redundant data copy on a disk in the same computer as the original.

   D. **Incorrect:** Collocation synchronizes data to a different server in a different location.

3. **Correct answer: C**

   A. **Incorrect:** Natural threats include tornado, hurricane, earthquake, volcano, and tsunami.

   B. **Incorrect:** Technical threats include disk failure and server failure.

   C. **Correct:** The hacker is the human threat agent that implements this threat.

   D. **Incorrect:** Supply system threats include power failure; HVAC failure; and, in the case of BCP, the unavailability of critical raw materials.

4. **Correct answer: B**

   A. **Incorrect:** If the MTD of a business function changes, the recovery plans most likely need to be changed.

   B. **Correct:** Simply changing insurance providers does not require an out of schedule review and update of the DRP and BCP.

   C. **Incorrect:** Eliminating business functions should trigger changes to the DRP and BCP. The enterprise is likely paying for unneeded preventive and recovery controls.

   D. **Incorrect:** As technologies change, more cost-effective and time-effective recovery controls might be available and even eliminate the need for the controls.

5. **Correct answer: D**

   A. **Incorrect:** The BIA assumes some unnamed threat and threat agent has been successful, and the disaster has occurred.

   B. **Incorrect:** The BIA assumes some unnamed risk has unfortunately happened, and the disaster has occurred.

   C. **Incorrect:** The qualitative value of a function is only part of the picture. The BIA identifies how long the business can continue operations without the operation of a specific business function.

   D. **Correct:** The MTD identifies how long the business can continue operations without the operation of a specific business function. It identifies the required recovery time frame of each business function to sustain the business if it fails.

6. **Correct answer: A**

   A. **Correct:** A disk shadow produces a real-time, redundant data copy on a different computer.

   B. **Incorrect:** Electronic vaulting produces a batch-type, redundant data copy on a different computer.

   C. **Incorrect:** A disk mirror produces a real-time, redundant data copy on a disk in the same computer as the original.

   D. **Incorrect:** Remote journaling produces real-time copies of transactions in a database on a different computer. This is not a file-level copy.

7. **Correct answer: B**

   A. **Incorrect:** The identification of threats and threat agents should occur as countermeasures are being identified and considered for proposal before management sees the proposal.

   B. **Correct:** Additional countermeasures must be identified and proposed to satisfy management's need to reduce risk to an acceptable level.

   C. **Incorrect:** Fortifying the facility might be one countermeasure but might not complete the required reduction of risk.

   D. **Incorrect:** Acquiring a secondary hot site might be one countermeasure but might not complete the required reduction of risk.

8. **Correct answer: C**

   A. **Incorrect:** The structured walkthrough test is a tabletop discussion among the key players in the planning process to identify errors, omissions, and overlaps in the plans. Because it does not test the physical logistics and transaction testing at the secondary site, it is not the most telling test.

   B. **Incorrect:** The parallel test requires one or more transactions to be performed at the secondary site but is still not the most telling test.

   C. **Correct:** The full interruption test performs full load testing of transactions with the primary site shut down. This is the most telling test. In ascending order of usefulness, the tests are the checklist, the structured walkthrough, the simulation, the parallel, and, finally, the full interruption test.

   D. **Incorrect:** The simulation test addresses the physical logistics of the plans. Because it does not perform any transaction testing at the secondary site, it is not the most telling test.

CHAPTER 9

Software development security

This chapter builds on Chapter 5, "Security architecture and design," by detailing the software component based on the premise that "subjects use computers and programs (software) to access objects." To secure the valuable information assets properly, the entire path between the subject and the object must be secure, and the path through the computer and applications must be trusted not to be the source of a security breach. If this path cannot be trusted, the breach will likely occur here, and all the other security controls will not help protect the assets.

This chapter describes the ways software introduces vulnerabilities into the information systems, the way applications are developed, and the various techniques that are used in the effort to reduce those vulnerabilities. An overview on database systems and the artificial intelligence tools used to evolve the value of data to higher levels is also explored.

Exam objectives in this chapter:

4.1 Understand and apply security in the software development life cycle

    4.1.1 Development Life Cycle

    4.1.2 Maturity models

    4.1.3 Operation and maintenance

    4.1.4 Change management

4.2 Understand the environment and security controls

    4.2.1 Security of the software environment

    4.2.2 Security issues of programming languages

    4.2.3 Security issues in source code (e.g., buffer overflow, escalation of privilege, backdoor)

    4.2.4 Configuration management

4.3 Assess the effectiveness of software security

The need for improved security in software

Flaws in the software are and have been one of the largest attack surfaces on information systems. It is generally accepted that applications contain an average of 10 to as many as 50 flaws per 1,000 lines of code.

With operating systems containing tens of millions of lines of code, and many applications requiring millions of lines of code, the average computer will have more than a million flaws in the software that it runs. Each of these flaws is a vulnerability that could lead to a complete compromise of the system and its data and is often used as the stepping stone to compromising multiple systems within an enterprise.

Typically, the more mature software development companies produce applications with a more rigid development methodology and operate on the low end of this range of flaws per lines of code; the less mature software companies, such as a startup software vendor, typically produce software on the higher end of the range.

Historically, software developers were trained to develop the application so that it accomplishes the work defined in the requirements quickly and efficiently and to complete the application development and deploy it into production as quickly as possible. Developers were trained in how to find shortcuts that kept their code lean and system performance high. Many of the shortcuts that run the applications more quickly and efficiently are the vulnerabilities that enable attackers to exploit and compromise the information systems.

On contemporary information systems, the data that users need access to typically can be accessed only by way of an application, so the user launches the application (some .exe file), and his access token is bound to the processes the application spawns. (Remember this from Chapter 5?) The application, on behalf of the user, requests access to the data.

Attackers identify the flaws in the application's coding that are exploitable vulnerabilities. When she launches a successful exploit against such a flaw, she has compromised the application, the data the application is accessing, and the access token of the user who launched the application. By having the access token of the authorized user, the attacker can now access anything the authorized user can access on the local machine. Further, if the compromised user account is a domain or realm account with authorized access to network resources, the attacker now can access whatever the authorized user has been granted privilege to over the network, enterprise wide.

Many developers resist the notion of accepting responsibility for the secure coding of applications. The extra code required to tighten security and eliminate vulnerabilities increases the lines of code in their application, a violation of their basic developer training. Besides, it takes too long to write all the extra code that might prevent a security breach. Secure coding also makes the application run slower because the security controls are doing their work, and they might actually, heaven forbid, trigger a warning banner or, worse yet, trigger an error that would prevent the application from continuing (allowing a breach of security to occur). In addition, management is always pressing developers to complete the coding as quickly as possible, for the application to be as small as possible, and for the code to execute as quickly as possible. Many developers shudder at the thought of actually building any type of control into their application that would stop it from doing its intended work, meanwhile ignoring the security breaches they open the doorway for. They become convinced that they must avoid putting those controls in their code.

The application *should* stop performing its work when the work is a breach of security. However, those imposed security features must be reasonably balanced with the need for use of the applications and access to the data. This inertia in the move to write all code with a proper balance of security and access is slowly being overcome. Very slowly. Secure coding guidelines and methodologies are beginning to surface, and the occurrence of code review prior to release is actually included in many IT-related laws and regulations, which will begin to get some traction and drive this programming concept into the mainstream.

Maturity models

To help software development vendors produce better applications, several models have been developed to guide the vendors toward higher levels of maturity in the industry. These models enable vendors to identify where they currently exist on the maturity scale and show them where they might be lacking features, processes, and controls that improve their application's performance, accuracy, security, and even profitability.

The software development life cycle

The software development life cycle (SDLC) describes the sequential phases of the process of developing an application. Although the number of stages and the specific terms might vary depending on the source, in general, the conceptual flow of the software development life cycle includes the following stages:

- Project initiation
- Functional design
- System design
- Software development
- Installation and test
- Operational use and maintenance
- Disposal and end of life

EXAM TIP

Security concerns should permeate every stage of this software development life cycle to integrate security throughout the process. This lends itself to a more cohesive, effective, and efficient security structure within the software rather than adding on some stand-alone, monolithic security filter as an afterthought.

Project initiation

Someone has an idea for an application and proposes the development project. Its cost justification will be reviewed and, ultimately, a decision to reject the proposal or to move forward
with the development project will be made. Security ramifications should be considered at
this stage. Can the application perform its work without degrading the security of the information assets? What security controls might be required? These will bear on the cost justification, and the overall increase in risk to the environment might affect the decision whether to
proceed.

Functional design

This initial design begins to formalize the functional needs of the proposed application and
would include a description of the application architecture to be implemented. Document
the baseline security components for the application and initial plans for testing the security
components of the application.

System design

A finalized and more detailed design document that includes the hardware and software system specifications as well as details of the communications processes for the application is developed. Identify detailed security requirements and the (likely) controls to be used. Formalize
the security testing procedures.

Software development

This is the actual writing of the application's code by the programmer along with detailed
documentation of how and where the code manifests the desired functionality of the design
specification and anywhere the code deviates from the design specification, with explanations. Secure coding practices should be defined and required by company policy and strictly
adhered to during this phase. The programmer develops code and performs initial testing
to verify appropriate functionality and security of the application as defined in the design
specification. The first level of testing by the developer is *unit testing* of smaller chunks of
code, followed by *integration testing* as the various units (or chunks) of code are integrated to
complete the development process.

Installation and testing

When the developer completes the coding, the source code for the proposed finished product is delivered for a secure *code review*, performed by a security professional with programming skills and, quite often, white-hat hacker skills so he can recognize the areas of coding
vulnerability. There are several automated tools to assist with the secure code review, but
ultimately, and often in combination with the secure code review tools, a review by a skilled
human is the best approach.

The code review is usually an iterative process with the reviewer making recommendations and the developer implementing the suggested changes, updating the documentation as necessary and then resubmitting the code to the reviewer. This iterative review process continues until all issues have been resolved.

Historically, a code review was very rare indeed. However, several IT security-related laws and regulations have taken effect in recent years that require the code review prior to the release and use of software, where applicable.

 The next step in the installation and testing is the *quality assurance (QA) review* of the now compiled executable. The QA technician installs and evaluates many aspects of the application, including functionality and security. This, too, is usually an iterative process, with the QA technician identifying functional issues and security issues that deviate from the specification and policy requirements, and the developer implementing the appropriate changes, updating the documentation as necessary and resubmitting the code to the QA technician. Like the code review, this iterative review process continues until all issues have been resolved. After the code review and the QA evaluation are satisfied, and the documentation has been updated, the code is compiled, and the executable is released, usually to a secure software library. Management is notified of the application's completion.

 It is imperative for someone other than the developer to perform these QA tests. This is when *separation of duties* is required. The developer has been working closely with the application and the code, and someone less familiar with those intimate details should perform the QA evaluation of the new application. A well-trained and fresh pair of eyes, not the application developer's, must approach the use of the application from different and unexpected angles and identify bugs and flaws that cause the application to crash or provide an attacker with an angle of attack and exploit.

 Some software is written for internal use only, customized for specific, custom, and dedicated purpose. Other software is developed for sale to the public. For the more custom code, developed for a single client, *acceptance testing* might also occur at this time. This is when the client installs and evaluates the software. If the software does not meet the client's requirements as defined in the specifications, the client provides feedback to the developers with the required changes. When the client is satisfied that the software meets its specifications, it formally accepts the software.

Operation and maintenance

When the QA evaluation is completed successfully, and the application meets both the design specification and company policy, management makes the decision of when to release the software into production for its actual use. When it's released, the software users receive the benefits of the functions built into the application. During this phase of the software's life cycle, the application code will need to be modified. The modified code then must be released to the users, and those users must deploy the updated software.

As the application is used, the users, developers, marketing people, and others identify improvements that could be made to make the application more usable and capable. Modifications to software that improve the capabilities of the software are commonly called *feature enhancements*, which are commonly included in the purchase price of the software for some fixed period but might also be provided through a maintenance agreement between the software vendor and the software purchaser for a fee.

Sometimes, mistakes or flaws in the programming cause unexpected results by the program. These *software bugs* might be discovered by the intended users and by hackers, some with good intent and some with malicious intent. The users and the white-hat hacker typically report the bug to the software developer so it can be corrected. The black-hat hacker often keeps his finding a secret so he can develop his exploitation of this newfound vulnerability.

Attackers take advantage of these flaws to develop exploit code and compromise these vulnerable applications. In some instances, compromising the software simply causes the application to stop operating. In other instances, the exploitation of the flaw provides the attacker access to the compromised system, usually with the credentials of the user account that launched the application. This is how the vast majority of information system security breaches occur.

Many websites track the known and revealed vulnerabilities in software for the purpose of defense. A massive database is kept and is publicly available that stores these *common vulnerabilities and exposures*, identified as *CVEs*. These sources include the National Institute for Standards and Technology (NIST), and the Mitre Corporation.

When (responsible) software developers become aware of flaws in their software, they develop a fix for the flawed code, called an *update*. These updates are then released, usually over the Internet, to the users (the public), who must download and install the updates to fix the flaws. Unfortunately, there are so many flaws in software that regular updates is not just a good idea; it has become a necessity. Many developers have built the process to check for these common and expected updates into their applications. Due to the security ramifications of the flaws in software, most enterprises include regular updating procedures in their policy structure, and most IT-related laws and regulations now place strict requirements on regulated enterprises to implement formalized, timely, and verifiable updating practices. The Payment Card Industry-Data Security Standard (PCI-DSS), for example, requires any security-related updates to be applied to 100 percent of the systems within the scope of compliance within seven (7) days of the release of the security update, and the complete and timely updating of these systems must be verifiable during compliance audits.

Virtually all software has flaws. Recognize that the update is nothing more than another piece of software; although the update corrects the identified flaw in the software, the update is likely to contain new flaws that can be exploited and might need to be updated by yet another piece of flawed software. The cycle continues.

EXAM TIP

Be sure to understand the life cycle of flawed (buggy) software.

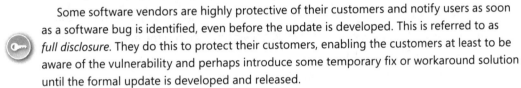

1. Software vendors release flawed software.
2. Hackers and others identify the flaws in the software.
3. Hackers develop exploit code to compromise the flaws in the software.
4. Vendors become aware of the flaws and develop and release updates to fix the flaws.
5. Users download and deploy the updates to fix the flawed software.

Some software vendors are highly protective of their customers and notify users as soon as a software bug is identified, even before the update is developed. This is referred to as *full disclosure*. They do this to protect their customers, enabling the customers at least to be aware of the vulnerability and perhaps introduce some temporary fix or workaround solution until the formal update is developed and released.

However, for several reasons, many software vendors will not release this information. Many users and activists perceive this behavior as less than prudent, even irresponsible or perhaps unethical on the part of the software vendors.

Regression testing

Anytime a new feature enhancement or update is released for software used in production, it should be fully tested before it is deployed to ensure that the update does not break anything or degrade the security of the system below acceptable security baselines. It is not uncommon for an update of one part of the application to cause some software failure in another part. To avoid these unexpected failures, the update should be installed in a test environment, and the application should undergo regression testing to verify that all required functionality remains functional.

Change management

Change management (also called change control) defines formalized procedures for making any alterations to the approved documentation of the enterprise. These documents include the policy documents (policies, procedures, baselines, standards and guidelines), the disaster recovery plan, the business continuity plan, the configuration controls for systems and devices, and, related to this chapter, the software (source code) developed in-house. Any changes to the program code should be strictly controlled and follow the change management policy for the enterprise. This typically requires a methodical procedure to change the application, complete the documentation, and acquire the appropriate approval of the newly released production code. As always, security concerns should permeate every step in this process, which follows.

- Initiate the change with a change request form.
    - Identify the cost and benefit of the proposed change.
    - Identify any impact on security from the proposed change.
    - Identify design considerations for the proposed change.
    - Submit the change request for review and approval (often to the change approval board [CAB]).
- Include (at least) the approvals of the product manager, security team, software development manager, and anyone else the proposed change might affect. Design the proposed change, including which sections of code to modify, deployment plan, rollback procedure, and other design decisions.
- Modify a copy of the software code to implement the proposed change.
- Document the details of the specific new code and its integration with the original code.
- Submit the change request form, the code documentation, and the modified application to QA testing to verify that:
    - The new code meets the approved change request.
    - All prior (desired) functionality remains intact and functional (regression testing).
    - The security of the application has not been degraded below policy standards.

> **NOTE THE QA/DEVELOPER LOOP**
>
> This is an iterative process. QA resubmits the code to the developer(s) until the new code meets these requirements and receives QA approval.

- Document the version changes.
- Release the new software to the software library.
- Return the completed change request form to the CAB with full documentation.

Management will determine when to release the new code into production.

The software library for the developers is usually a secure source code control system that includes features such as distributed authoring and versioning (released or not), version controls (labeling, ownership, permissions), version archive, documentation and configuration details, and a rollback function to undo a change or a series of changes such as to a prior, unreleased developer version.

EXAM TIP

Be sure to understand that change control is a formalized process that includes much documentation and many approvals.

Configuration management

For software to operate as intended, expected, and securely, without introducing unnecessary vulnerabilities, the systems the software is running on must be secure and stable. In the enterprise, this typically requires policy-driven change management and configuration management of the systems, including the mandate to standardize and manage the configuration of systems, the documentation of system configuration in standards and baselines, and procedures to accomplish the standardized configuration of systems. Changes to system configurations should follow policy-based change control as described in the preceding section, complete with approvals and updated documentation.

Configuration management then requires routine and ongoing monitoring of the systems to detect unauthorized changes. Periodic manual auditing of system configuration should also be part of systems management. Each week or month, randomly select some number of systems to spot check and compare their current configurations with the documented standard for their intended, approved, and expected configurations. Deviations from the standards should be investigated. None of the findings from the investigation will be good news. Deviations typically fall in one of three categories:

- Approved change, but documentation was never updated. The responsible party for the documentation should be reprimanded. Documentation should be updated in a timely fashion.

- Accidental misconfiguration. The responsible party should be reprimanded, and additional training should be required. Changes should include independent verification of accuracy. The secondary inspector (verifier, QA) should be reprimanded, and additional training should be required.

- Willful misconfiguration. Attackers often reconfigure systems to introduce vulnerabilities and evade detection. This finding might (should?) trigger an incident response investigation to identify the source of the misconfiguration (who, when, why) and identify any breach of the confidentiality, integrity, or availability of valuable information assets. In addition, identify whether the breach violated any laws or regulations and pursue the findings accordingly.

Disposal and end of life

Typically, after a few years, the needs for the application change, the related technology changes, programming languages or methodologies change, and even laws change. At some point, it is time to begin developing a new version of the application, often recoding it from scratch and providing a new set of features and capabilities. This major revision of the original application is released, and its operational lifetime often overlaps the earlier version. This provides the opportunity to refine the new version and take advantage of feedback from the marketplace and time to prepare the users of the earlier version for the end of its life and the need to purchase the latest version with all its new bells and whistles.

The period of overlap might be just a year or two or up to ten years in some cases. At some point, the software vendor declares an end of life and support for the earlier version. This frees developer resources to focus on the latest version during the operation and maintenance phase of its life cycle.

Uses must be aware that after the end of life for an application, no additional support will be offered, and the vendor will not update newfound vulnerabilities. This leaves the application exceptionally vulnerable to exploit. Users should immediately cease using any applications that have been declared at their end of life and should (typically) replace the application with the latest supported version.

Figure 9-1 shows the software development life cycle.

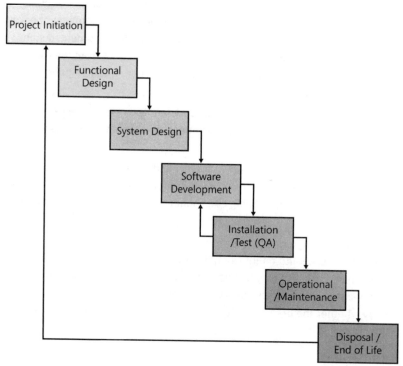

FIGURE 9-1 The software development life cycle (SDLC)

 If source code is being developed to be sold, it is usually proprietary in nature and protected securely so no one can reproduce the intellectual property (the source code) easily. However, some source code, called *open source software*, is developed and freely shared. This allows the public to benefit from the development of the code and enables users to view, understand, modify, and even distribute the code to maximize these benefits. Open source software usually is provided through an open source license that might define specific parameters that must be met to use the software freely, such as that it must be for personal and noncommercial use only.

Separation of duties

Each of the stages of the software development life cycle should be performed by a different person or team to provide a broader vision, optimize specialized skills, and avoid conflicts of interest.

Software Capability Maturity Model Integration

Capability Maturity Model Integration (CMMI) for (in this case) applications is a quality enhancement model intended to improve the process of developing software applications. It was developed largely at the Software Engineering Institute (SEI) at Carnegie Mellon University. The model identifies five major levels of maturity of software development organizations to help their progressive maturity. The five levels are:

- Initial
- Managed
- Defined
- Quantitatively managed
- Optimized

Initial level

This is the level of a typical small startup software development enterprise. This phase is often characterized by heroics of single individuals. Processes are unpredictable, with little or no ability to control them, and priorities and activities are reactive in nature.

Managed level

The enterprise is planning project cost, scheduling, and development processes of projects and is taking advantage of know-how developed on earlier projects, but it is still largely reactive in nature.

Defined level

The enterprise operates on standardized and documented development processes for projects. Projects are reviewed and approved based on their compliance with the approved development processes. The enterprise in now operating in a proactive manner.

Quantitatively managed level

Detailed metrics are collected and reviewed on the approved development processes and are compared to defined quality standards. Subtle process adjustments are made to control and maintain the quality of the project.

Optimized level

The enterprise has evolved into an industry leader by focusing on continuous improvement of the development processes and piloting new ideas, innovations, and technologies.

The five stages of the CMMI are shown in Figure 9-2.

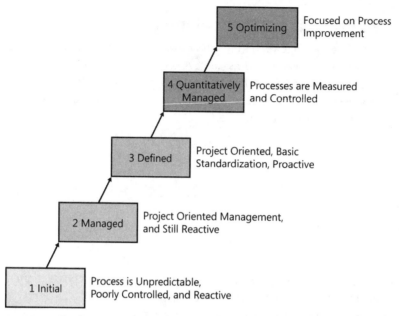

FIGURE 9-2 The five stages of the capability maturity model integration (CMMI) process

The IDEAL model

The SEI at Carnegie Mellon University also introduced the IDEAL model for software process improvement.

- **Initiating**   Define the software process improvement project.
- **Diagnosing**   Identify the baseline of the current software development processes.
- **Establishing**   Define a strategic plan to improve the current software development processes.
- **Acting**   Implement the software process improvement plan.
- **Leveraging**   Maintain and improve the software based on lessons learned.

Software development models

The development of software applications is a project like many other projects, and it requires a project plan. Following are several commonly used software-development project-planning models.

WATERFALL MODEL

The waterfall model is much like a Gantt chart; it identifies sequential stages of the development process and the dependency relationship between the various stages. It provides a
very simple flow for the entire project. The disadvantages are that it is not very flexible. After
a stage is completed, that developed software component cannot be altered or adjusted
in any way, and the upcoming components must use it in that frozen state. The customer is
not involved during the development process and might end up with a software application
that does not do quite what was envisioned at the start of the project. The waterfall model is
shown in Figure 9-3.

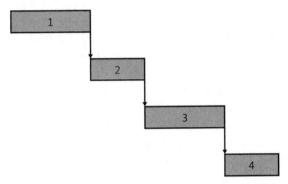

FIGURE 9-3 The waterfall software development model

SPIRAL MODEL

The spiral model maps out one development phase at a time and then develops the software
for that one phase. Then, based on the *level of risk*, the next development phase is defined in
ever widening or increasing phases. These iterative spirals allow flexibility and adjustment as
the development progresses. The spiral model is shown in Figure 9-4.

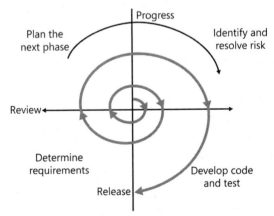

FIGURE 9-4 The spiral software development model

RAPID APPLICATION DEVELOPMENT MODEL

Rapid Application Development (RAD) minimizes the planning and jumps right into the development of prototype code, providing a great deal of flexibility during the development process. Initial stages typically build and present nonfunctional display screens to the prospective users to acquire feedback and additional input, allowing the planning of the programming details to occur during the development. This typically saves time (by not preplanning the application's development) and facilitates the development of a software product that satisfies the users' needs and expectations because they are involved during the application's development.

CLEANROOM MODEL

The goal of the cleanroom development process is to eliminate defects during the development of the software code rather than remove them after the software is released. This development model, too, provides a great deal of flexibility because it produces a small chunk of software code and then measures it against defined quality standards, refining as necessary before developing the next chunk of code.

The basic principles of the cleanroom software development model mandate that the software is developed by using formal methods, the incremental implementation of the application is accomplished while being monitored by using statistical quality controls, and the statistically sound testing of the finished product is performed before release.

Computer-aided software engineering tools

Computer-aided software engineering (CASE) tools establish a software development platform containing a collection of tools to produce high-quality applications with a minimum of defects and vulnerabilities. CASE tools typically include diagramming tools, a library of standard function source code, tools to define application programming interfaces (API), version control tools, code review tools, and project management tools.

Software testing

Various types of testing are performed during the development of software applications and during their use. These testing types include:

- **Unit testing** Testing of small, discrete chunks of code, often to establish a proof of concept.

- **Integration testing** More complete testing of multiple units of code to ensure the proper information flow between the different units of code.

- **Acceptance testing** Testing the end user performs to verify formally the proper functionality and acceptance of the software. This usually identifies the end of the initial development phase and the beginning of the operational phase of the software.

- **Regression testing** Testing of all major functions of an application after some alteration or update to verify that the change(s) have not broken some previously functional process.

- **Verification** Testing to verify that the product meets the design specifications.

- **Validation** Testing to verify that the product satisfies the customer's needs.

- **Operational assurance** Defined in the Orange book described in Chapter 5. These are independently evaluated mechanisms to validate the processes of the application, which include system architecture, system integrity, covert channel analysis, trusted facility management, and trusted recovery. Operational assurance is a subset of Life-cycle assurance that focuses specifically on the operational phase of the life cycle.

- **Life-cycle assurance** Defined in the Orange book described in Chapter 5. These are independently evaluated mechanisms to validate the design, development, distribution, installation, maintenance, and end of life of an application, which include security testing, design specification and verification, configuration management, and trusted system distribution.

Software updating

As stated earlier in this chapter, because the software being released is filled with flaws, the need is constant to check for and then download, test, and install software updates. This is a new facet of the standard enterprise network that is typically required by IT security-related laws and regulations. Updating is now essentially required for not just operating system software but for applications and even device firmware. Because these updates are the (supposed, possible, probable) fixes for security vulnerabilities, there is a required urgency in the time-sensitive process of updating software on IT systems. In addition to these operating system, application, and firmware update processes, antivirus (AV) signatures and intrusion detection system (IDS) signatures also require constant updates.

An enterprise must accomplish these software updates in a timely manner; several types of resources should be allocated to support this effort, including personnel, a test lab, and documented policies and procedures to ensure the prudent and timely completion of systems updates. The update process should follow this sequence:

- **Actively search for new updates** Someone should be formally assigned the responsibility to search for updates for every operating system, application, device firmware, AV application, and IDS system, most likely on a daily basis. This means that these various operating systems, applications, devices, AV applications, and IDS systems must be known and well documented, including their update level.

- **Testing and approval** Each update must be tested for potential conflicts before deployment to the production systems. This requires a lab environment with every operating system, application, device, AV application, and IDS system the enterprise owns in the test lab. The more closely the lab can mirror the production networking environment, the more valid the testing. Testing procedures and the test results must be documented.

- **Rollback procedures**   Before deploying updates to production systems, a rollback procedure should be developed and tested in case a conflict arises. Just because the update passed the lab testing, there is no guarantee that the update will not cause some conflict or failure when deployed to production systems. A plan must be in place to uninstall the updates and return to the prior stable yet not updated state.

- **Change control**   Updates are changes to the systems; therefore, these changes must be processed through the change control procedures. Many organizations preapprove standard and routine updating that falls within some bounds of systems and risk levels. Full testing, rollback procedures, and documentation are still required on these, but the approvals have already been granted. Beyond the definition of standard updates, a formal but timely pass though the change approval board is usually required.

- **Deploy**   After locating, downloading, testing, documenting, and identifying rollback procedures have been performed and approvals have been granted, the updates must be deployed to the appropriate systems. In large enterprises, a staged deployment is common with a carefully chosen, select handful of systems being deployed to first. These might be chosen because of their less significant value to the critical business processes, their proximity to good technical support, or for other reasons, but they act as the test bed for the update. The help desk is monitored to evaluate the level of success with the deployment. If problems are reported, adjustments are made to the deployment processes, and another, smaller deployment is initiated. If all goes well, the update is deployed to a larger and perhaps more valuable or distant set of systems, and deployment is continued to sets of systems, in stages, until all systems have received the update successfully.

- **Documentation**   The documentation of the change control processes must be completed and kept for a specified retention period. This documentation becomes part of the configuration baseline of the systems and may be used for troubleshooting purposes later on or required by IT-related laws and regulations for auditing purposes.

Logging requirements

For monitoring, troubleshooting, compliance, and auditing purposes, operating systems software, applications, and devices are typically required to log many types of events. This logging function must be built into the software and enabled and configured by the end user. Policy, laws, and regulations often specify the level of logging required, and system configuration baselines should include logging configuration details. These should be reviewed or audited for compliance periodically.

The logged events commonly remain on the local system where the logged event occurred for troubleshooting purposes. However, for monitoring, auditing, and compliance purposes, these logged events must be immediately (real time) and securely recorded (copied) to a remote system. The syslog protocol was developed to do this, and many third-party network monitoring systems are available as well.

The recorded event is typically sent to the remote log repository by using a guaranteed delivery protocol over an encrypted channel to protect its integrity. As the event arrives at the log repository, a hash value is calculated at this known-good time, so that the integrity of the logged event can be verified at a later time such as during an audit.

The log repository server is typically a hardened server, a bastion host server, dedicated as a secure log repository server. The log repository usually is a large storage server, often with terabytes of storage, and the store is typically encrypted to control access and protect the integrity of the logged events. Periodically, the events that are recorded in the log repository should be compared to the events logged on the source system to verify that all the required events are actually making it to the log repository system. A good attacker often finds a way to disable some or all logging of a compromised system in an attempt to remain covert for as long as possible.

Administrators who monitor the systems should only ever have read-only access to these legged events to minimize the potential for data corruption and avoid the possibility of insider log tampering. These events are often also processed by security information and event management (SIEM) systems to correlate and identify system misconfigurations, malware outbreaks, and complex attack patterns quickly.

The logs should be securely stored for the required retention period. Typically, at the end of the specified retention period, a secure method should be used to destroy the now un-needed log data. This includes overwriting the entire expired log file data with random bits and then deleting the overwritten file.

The software escrow

Many powerful and sophisticated business management software applications exist and are designed to support most, if not all, the IT needs of a business. An enterprise might spend a hefty price for the base software but then often need to spend five or ten times that amount to have the software customized and fine-tuned to fit its specific and unique needs. The enterprise also often must hire an outside software development company, consultants who specialize in the customization of the basic business management application.

The third-party software development company writes custom code that integrates with the basic business management application to extend its functionality and support the business needs of the enterprise. However, the consulting company doesn't just sell the customized software to the enterprise. Instead, it just leases the use of the customized software and provides updates in the form of compiled (essentially encrypted) executables to the enterprise; it never releases the source code to the enterprise. This way, it is only and ever the consulting company who can troubleshoot and further update this now heavily customized business management application.

As the business application is tuned and functions are enriched and empowered for the specific needs of the enterprise, the enterprise becomes increasingly reliant on the application for its critical business functions. For many enterprises, this reliance is so severe that if the business management application fails, the enterprise is at risk of failure as well—a disaster. Therefore, much effort is exerted to keep the application alive and fully functional.

If the consulting company goes out of business, however, the documentation and expertise for this highly specialized application also go away. This means no ongoing support, no troubleshooting, no more refinement and improvement as the needs of the enterprise evolve further. This risk is unacceptable for most enterprises, and a solution for this risk must be included in the original consulting agreement. That solution is the software escrow.

When an enterprise must rely on a third-party software development company that does not release update source code but provides only the compiled executable updates, the consulting agreement requires the source code for every update to be sent to a neutral escrow agent (usually a lawyer with no prior relationship or bias toward either party) for secure storage. The consulting agreement further requires the escrow agent to release the escrowed source code to the enterprise if the software development company ever ceases its operations. The enterprise then has sufficient documentation to acquire support from another third-party company for its critical business management application. Figure 9-5 shows this source code escrow relationship.

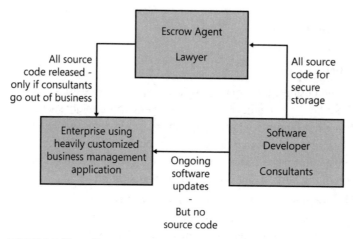

FIGURE 9-5 The software escrow process

Programming concepts

Programs are commonly developed and written as human-readable scripts in one of many programming languages. These scripts must then be converted into a language suitable for the processor that must execute the program. Processors can only understand *machine language*, so the human-readable scripts are converted into machine language by using one of two techniques. Machine language is not human readable.

> **NOTE HUMANS CAN'T READ MACHINE LANGUAGE**
>
> To demonstrate the preceding point, launch the Microsoft WordPad application. Open a small executable (machine language) such as C:\Windows\notepad.exe. What WordPad presents is a representation of machine language. Although some characters and words are readable in the machine language executable, such as menu items and error messages, the processing instructions are quite incomprehensible.

Each processor has an *instruction set*, the specific and limited set of instructions that particular CPU can process, and the scripts must be converted into the proper machine language instructions within that processor's instruction set. Computers that operate using processors such as the DEC Alpha, the Sun SPARC, the PowerPC, and the MIPS processors use the *Reduced Instruction Set Computing (RISC) instruction set* that contains a relatively small set of instructions. The bulk of personal computers and servers that use System 360, VAX, Motorola 68000, and the Intel x86 series processors operate by using the *Complex Instruction Set Computing (CISC) instruction set* that contains a larger set of instructions.

During development, the programmer writes his human-readable scripts and then needs to test the script for proper functionality. After testing this small chunk of code, the programmer makes adjustments to the script and tests again in an iterative manner until the code functions the way the programmer intended. To test the functionality of the script, the script must be converted into machine language by an *interpreter*, a process unique to the scripting language. The interpreter converts the script into machine language at run time and feeds the machine language instructions to the CPU for processing. This leaves the script intact and in human readable form so it can be adjusted and further developed.

When the script finally performs all the necessary functions desired of the program, and the programmer is ready to release the program for QA testing, the script is permanently converted into machine language as an executable, a *.exe file*. This process requires a *compiler*, and like the interpreter, the compiler is unique to the programming language, so the script is compiled into a non–human readable executable, the native language of the CPU, for distribution, often to the public.

Compiling scripts into non–human readable executable files for distribution provides two very valuable functions. First, because the executable is not human readable, the intellectual property (the script) is now essentially encrypted, hidden, confidential, and protected. No one can steal the programmer's work and use it as her own.

Second, because no one can read the underlying script that became the executable, the functions of the executable are essentially locked down and cannot be modified further, so the program cannot be intelligently altered to perform differently by someone with access to only the compiled, machine language, executable.

The generations of programming languages

Programming languages have evolved over the past 70 years since digital computers were first produced, and there are predictions about the future evolution of these languages. Following is a list of the generally recognized generations of programming languages:

- **First-generation language**   Machine language. The language the CPU understands and requires based on its instruction set, but it is not human readable.

- **Second-generation language**   Assembly language. Somewhat human readable (with training), crude and cumbersome and written in hexadecimal. Must be converted into machine language by an assembler application. Not used commonly today except, perhaps, as a training tool for computer science students.

- **Third-generation language**   High-level language. Programs are written in human-readable scripts. The scripts must be converted into machine language at run time by an interpreter or converted permanently by a compiler. This is the state of programming languages today.

- **Fourth-generation language**   Very high-level language. Some advancement over today's programming languages, a generic and nonspecific middle ground between where technology is today and the ultimate desired programming technology of tomorrow.

- **Fifth-generation language**   Natural or spoken language. Relies on artificial intelligence; tells the computer what information is needed, and the system, dynamically and in real time, produces its own program code to complete the requested task. Some say that the Siri function in the Apple iOS 6 has achieved this fifth-generation language functionality, but only within specific limits. Siri cannot complete a tax filing, for example.

Object-oriented programming

The front-running programming approach to writing programs is called object-oriented programming. It differs from the historic and traditional procedural programming techniques. *Procedural programming* is a script of sequential processing steps to perform a transformation of data and achieve the desired output. Object-oriented programming is a newer programming paradigm that offers the ability to *reuse* a great deal of code that has already been developed, with variables built in to afford flexibility. The objects are *modular* and allow easy development of programs in a very *natural*, rational, and linear manner. Some examples of object-oriented programming (OOP) languages include C++, Java, C#, Microsoft Visual Basic .NET, Python, JavaScript, ACTOR, and Eiffel.

In object-oriented programming, the *object* is a program component, and that object uses data as *attributes* that act as variables within the object. The object manipulates or processes that data by using program code called *methods*. The methods of an object produce the behavior of the object—how the object manipulates, uses, processes, or transforms the attributes.

Series of objects are linked and interact within a program to take input (data), process that data by using the methods within the specific objects, and produce the desired output data. The data, as it flows into, between, or out of objects, is called a *message*. Figure 9-6 shows this object–method–message relationship.

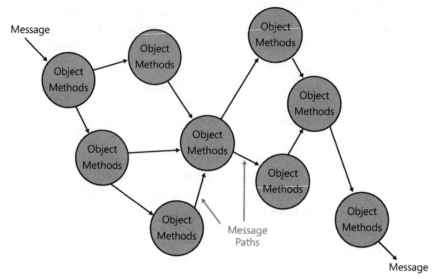

FIGURE 9-6 Object-oriented application architecture

A large library of object code is available for programmers to choose from for use within new programs. When object code exists in this library, before it is used within a program and is nothing more than ink on paper, like the recipe for a cake, it is called a *class*. When a programmer copies the class (the object code) into a program being developed, the programmer is *instantiating* the class into an object, like when a baker instantiates the recipe (class) as an actual cake (object) that can be consumed.

The class, and its instantiated object, contain data fields that can be filled with data dynamically as input from any number of sources, such as from a table in a database, from user input on a keyboard, or as a message from an adjacent object. This flow of messages into, out of, and between objects can be defined and locked down as the program is compiled so messages always flow in the same paths, called *static binding*. Alternatively, the paths can remain flexible based on the current needs and state of the program and be defined at run time; this is called *dynamic binding*.

Objects are encapsulated, isolated from one another. This *encapsulation* provides modularity and helps protect the intellectual property of the method(s) hidden and contained within the object. Classes are developed in a hierarchical manner, so that a child class inherits many characteristics (structure and methods) from its parent class and does not require additional programming. The *inheritance* feature of objects allows easy extension of the classes and supports increased reusability. Another characteristic of classes and objects is called *polymorphism*, the ability of an object to alter its behavior based on numerous variables that become known only at the time of execution, its run time. Therefore, based on some external or internal data, the object can produce different results. A classic example would be the shape of a mouse pointer changing as its position on the display is changed by moving the mouse.

Whereas the encapsulation of objects supports their modularity, abstraction from one another, and provides protection of intellectual property (the code) and data within the object, objects require data flow by means of the messages into and out of the object. Well-designed objects manifest two characteristics in this regard: high *cohesiveness* and low *coupling*.

- **High cohesiveness** Cohesiveness of objects refers to the degree the methods within a single object belong together. The methods work on a more narrow collection of data types and perform similar tasks. This supports the modularity and reusability of object code. An example of *low* cohesiveness would be a grocery store because it contains diverse types of products; an example of *high* cohesiveness would be a liquor store because it contains a much more narrow type of products.

- **Low coupling** Coupling of objects refers to the object's reliance on external resources such as data and methods. Imagine an object that requires 100 data inputs to be satisfied before its methods could begin their work (high coupling: high reliance on external resources) in contrast to an object that requires one or two data inputs before its methods could begin their work (low coupling: low reliance on external resources). The latter object is much more likely to be able to operate more often and more easily than the first object, making it a better designed and higher-quality object.

EXAM TIP

These terms might also be described as tight and loose or strong and weak instead of high and low:

- tight cohesion = strong cohesion = high cohesion
- loose cohesion = weak cohesion = low cohesion
- tight coupling = strong coupling = high coupling
- loose coupling = weak coupling = low coupling

Distributed computing

Although it is not uncommon for a user to work on a single computer that contains all the data, programs, and processing power needed, it is more common for one or more of these elements of computing to be provided by one or more remote systems across a network in a distributed computing architecture. The distribution and sharing of processes and data must be carefully managed to ensure appropriate protection of the confidentiality, integrity, and availability of valuable information assets and full compliance with company policy and applicable laws and regulations.

Distributed computing architectures exist on many levels and in many combinations. The technologies that support and manage distributed computing often fall in the category of *middleware*, not the client-side application and not the server-side application but software that manages the flow of information between the two. Following are several of the commonly used technologies that support distributed computing.

Processes sharing data on a single computer

In the early days of computing, on a single system, operating systems provided a shared memory space. Any running process had direct access to the other processes in memory and to all the data stored in memory. This was recognized as a very insecure design, and the requirement for process isolation was formalized in the Trusted Computing System Evaluation Criteria (TCSEC) in the Orange Book. Therefore, operating systems such as UNIX, Linux, OSX, VMS, and Windows NT 3.1 began to isolate processes and their data from one another. However, there is a definite need, from time to time, for applications to share processes and data.

Several technologies were developed to support the controlled, secure sharing of processes and data. On a stand-alone computer, for OOP applications, Microsoft introduced the *Component Object Model* (*COM*). The OOP applications must be written to the COM standard, but then one COM application can access the exposed objects and methods (processes) and data of another COM-compliant application on the same computer. The access request is handled through a secure channel, and authentication and permissions are managed by the security kernel and the security reference monitor, so sharing processes and data by COM-compliant applications on a single computer remain secure. Figure 9-7 shows how applications written to the COM standard share and access processes and data from other COM-compliant applications.

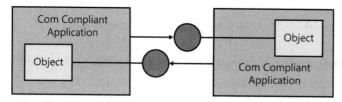

FIGURE 9-7 COM-compliant applications sharing objects (processes) and data

COM operates within the application, and the user is generally unaware of its activities. However, when this process and data sharing is required at the user level, an extension of COM, called *Object Linking and Embedding* (*OLE*) is used, as when a user copies a series of cells from an Excel spreadsheet and pastes them into a Word document. COM is strictly a Microsoft technology, technically supported only on the Windows platform.

Processes sharing data and processes on multiple computers across a network

To extend the controlled, secure sharing of processes and data over the network on multiple computers, Microsoft extended COM and introduced the *Distributed Component Object Model* (*DCOM*). Now a DCOM process on one computer can request and, if permissions allow, receive access to processes and data on one or more remote computers. DCOM is COM across the network. It is strictly a Microsoft technology, technically supported only on the Windows platform.

This process and data sharing across the network capability is supported by two other *platform-independent* and *application-independent* technologies to maximize interoperability in distributed computing systems. Applications written to the *object request broker* (*ORB*) standard can issue and receive *remote procedure calls* (*RPC*) to share and gain access to processes and data across the network. ORB processes expose their existence to be readily located in a distributed computing system. ORBs can also operate within a single system.

An extension of ORB is the *common object request broker architecture* (*CORBA*). It operates on multiple platforms (operating systems), applications from different vendors, and applications written in different programming languages on a single computer or across a network in a distributed computing system. CORBA is an application development standard defined by the *Object Management Group* (*OMG*) in 1991. OMG is an international consortium to improve object-oriented programming standards.

Client and server applications

Client and server application architecture was developed by Xerox during the 1970s and has become the dominant distributed computing architecture. In this model, a relatively small, light-duty application is installed on client computers. This client application typically provides an interface to the user for submitting queries and presenting results and for communicating across a network to a heavier, server-side application. The client-side application, often called the front-end application, typically does very little, if any, client-side data processing. The client computer initiates communications with the server computer.

The server-side application is usually installed on a much more powerful computer and, very often, a computer that holds or has direct access to the large and common data store. The server-side application, often called the back-end application, performs most, if not all the data retrieval, processing, and distribution.

Classic examples of client server applications are web browsers and web servers, email clients and email servers, and client operating systems that connect to file and print servers. Figure 9-8 shows the application architecture used commonly in distributed computing environments.

> **NOTE** **OTHER TYPES OF DISTRIBUTED COMPUTING**
> Cloud computing and grid computing are also types of distributed computing. These topics were covered in Chapter 5.

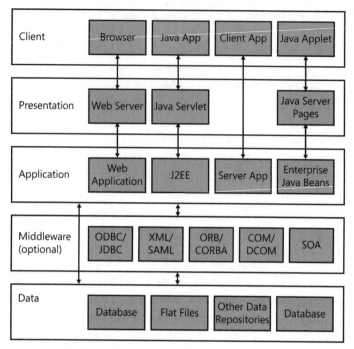

FIGURE 9-8 Application architecture

Web applications

Historically, an application had to be written for a specific operating system, which limited its usability. It was difficult and costly to port the application to additional operating systems, often requiring approximately a full rewrite of the source code for the application. Often, the functions within the application operated differently, and the output from the applications running on the different operating systems would be formatted differently, frustrating end users.

In the past five years or so, web-based applications have become popular and help resolve the interoperability problems of the past. Web applications are becoming a standard way of delivering data services to end users, across the Internet, and even on the intranet. Web applications are written for the operating system of the web server, and then clients use a web browser to access the web application. The client-side browser can be running on any operating system, making the web application essentially compatible with any operating system. Although there are variations in the ways browsers render the web content, this is typically in the presentation (formatting) of the output from the web application and not in the heavy lifting of the server-side web application that processes the data. Designing the output from the application to adjust its HTML and other data formatting based on the browser type that the client is running requires some extra development work during the development of the web application, but much of the web application, often considered the hard part of the application, operates correctly.

Single sign on for web-based applications

As described in Chapter 2, "Access control," a common requirement or objective for enterprises is to allow a user to authenticate once and then gain access to every object the user is authorized to access enterprise wide. This, again, is called single sign on (SSO) and is desired for web-based applications. In this case, the authentication process is channeled through the client browser to the web server. Recall that cookies were originally commonly used to store authentication data until cookies were recognized as much too exposed and vulnerable to store such sensitive information. The *Security Assertion Markup Language* (*SAML*) was developed by the *Organization for the Advancement of Structured Information Standards* (*OASIS*) to help satisfy this objective. SAML is an extension to the Extensible Markup Language (XML) and is currently on version 2.0.

SAML provides authentication and authorization communications services and uses three components: the principal (the user), the service provider (the SAML-compliant web application), and the identity provider (the SAML-compliant authentication service). The principal uses his web browser to access the web application and authenticate. When the principal attempts to access the web application, the service provider requests an assertion from the identity provider regarding the identity of the principal. The identity provider prompts the principal for proof of identity, typically a user name and password or, in some cases, a multi-factor authentication, or it might even back end into a directory service. When the principal successfully authenticates to the identity provider through the browser and web server, the identity provider submits a security assertion to the service provider regarding the trusted identity of the principal. The service provider then identifies the authorization level of the principal and provides the appropriate level of access.

One identity provider can submit assertions to many SAML service providers, and a service provider can be configured to accept and trust the assertions of many SAML identity providers. SAML can take advantage of the *Simple Object Access Protocol* (*SOAP*) to support and help secure the assertion processes. SOAP is a versatile web application messaging framework. The SAML assertions can be sent as SOAP messages to support the use of various transport protocols and programming languages.

The open web application security project (OWASP)

The *open web application security project* (OWASP) was introduced in 2001 and is a world-wide, vendor-neutral, nonprofit, open-source consortium whose intent is to improve the security of web applications. OWASP publishes standards on the various aspects of the development of secure web-based applications. This area of software development probably leads all others relative to the security awareness of the software developers because of OWASP. OWASP has published or is developing recommended code, practices, and tools to help developers secure their web applications, including:

- OWASP Application security verification standard
- OWASP Development guide
- OWASP Testing guide

- OWASP Code review guide
- OWASP Top ten web application security risks
- OWASP Software assurance maturity model
- OWASP Secure Coding Practices: Quick Reference Guide
- OWASP Zed attack proxy project: Penetration testing toolkit for targeting web-based servers and applications
- OWASP Webgoat: A sample vulnerable web application for testing and training purposes

Mobile code

Mobile code is the collection of software that is pushed down from web servers to the clients' web browser for local execution. Because this mobile code is executed on the client system, it has become the most popular approach to distribution and delivery of malware to the public masses. The client-side web browser is designed to trigger the execution of these downloaded executables automatically to provide a feature-rich, enhanced, browsing experience to the end user—in essence, for good cause. However, the bad guys also use this to infect many client computers with very little effort. Mobile code includes:

- **Executables** Compiled, machine-language executables (.exe files). These must be compiled for the appropriate CPU.
- **Java applets** Mobile code written in Java Bytecode. Runs in a Java sandbox or Java virtual machine to provide platform independence and some level of isolation between the potentially malicious mobile code and the host operating system. For several years, it was claimed that a Java applet could not break out of the sandbox or virtual machine, but that was eventually proven incorrect.
- **ActiveX controls** Mobile code written to the Microsoft COM and OLE standards, usable in Internet Explorer (and now others). Microsoft introduced Authenticode, the digital signing of ActiveX controls that are released by trusted developers.
- **Scripts** Can be written in one of many scripting languages as long as the appropriate interpreter is installed on the client system.

To secure the client browser, much of the mobile code has to be disabled, causing a reduction in the feature-rich, enhanced, browsing experience of the end user.

Executable email attachments can sometimes be referred to as mobile code as well because of its transmission by the email systems, but this is only loosely accurate. The client's email application typically does not automatically initiate the execution of these attachments. Attackers rely on the lack of security awareness of the end user, anticipating that some number of end users will attempt to launch the malicious executable attachment. Many organizations filter these inbound and outbound executable email attachments and never let them reach the end user.

Database systems

Databases were introduced in computer technology in the 1960s. A database is a repository or store of data that organizes the data in a meaningful way so that the data can be easily input, processed, and retrieved. The database is intelligently structured to support the organization of the data, typically by using rows and columns of data fields, the location to store a single *data element* or piece of data. These rows and columns of data fields build a *table* in the database, and databases typically have many tables. Each table in a database holds different types of data, but the tables and the data they hold typically interrelate with one another.

> **NOTE   DATA FIELD OR CELL?**
> The data field can also be called a cell in the table and is a storage location in the table; the data element is the data or information that is stored in the data field.

In layman's terms, the row in a table that holds a series of related data elements is referred to as a record. In more technical terms, this record is called a *tuple*. This term implies some number of related data elements, such as a single data element, a pair of data elements, a triple, quadruple, quintuple, sextuple, or some number *n*, *n*-tuple.

The columns in a table are called attributes and describe the nature of the type of data to be held in this column of data fields. Putting these together, a record might be information about a single customer and his account at the business. The fields in a record (series of related data elements) might be:

- Account number
- Customer name
- Street address 1
- Street address 2
- City

- State
- ZIP or postal code
- Phone number 1
- Phone number 2

where the data elements for a single row, record, or tuple relate to this one customer account with your business. Multiple customers mean multiple rows, and the rows of related data about the customers collectively become the table. An example of this is shown in Figure 9-9.

Attribute

Customers Table

Account Number	Customer Name	Street Address 1	Street Address 2	City	State	Zip Code	Phone Number 1	Phone Number 2
09771	David Ahs	123 Any Street		Woodgrove	HI	17884	555-123-4567	555-765-4321
09772	Jim Hance	456 Some Ave.	Apt. 309	Coho	HI	17867	555-456-7890	555-098-7654
09773	Lori Penor	789 Other Dr.	Building 6	Woodgrove	HI	17887	555-246-8101	
09774	Mike Ray	100 Heretoo Ave.		Lucerne	HI	17843	555-135-7811	

Tuple

FIGURE 9-9 A database table, showing data fields, data elements, attributes, and tuples

The amount of data stored in a database can become very large. To help manage this potentially giant volume of data, restrictions can be applied to each field (column) that will limit the type of data that can be input. For example, a restriction might be placed on the postal code field that will only allow numeric data because all postal codes are numbers only. Limits are also typically assigned for each field to control the number of characters the field can hold. There is no benefit to allowing several million characters if the postal code will only ever be nine numbers, so limit the field to nine (numeric only) characters.

The number of fields in a record, the type of attribute each field is intended to hold, the character restrictions, and the manner in which the tables relate to one another define the structure of the database. The details that define the structure of the database are called the *schema* of the database. The schemas of databases are usually different, even when the data the databases hold might be very similar. This becomes important to understand as the need to share data with other databases develops and is discussed in the "Accessing databases" section later in this chapter.

Many database software vendors provide a core collection of tools used to build, populate, maintain, and query the database and present the query results in customizable report forms. This collection of tools used to administer the database is called the *database management system* (*DBMS*). The DBMS can also be custom developed by using a third-party programming language typically providing a much higher level of capability. The DBMS often provides the ability to establish a security structure for user accounts or roles and then the assignment of specific access privileges within the database. The DBMS can also provide encryption, integrity protection and integrity verification, concurrency controls (described later in this chapter), and backup and restore services for data redundancy and recovery.

Quite often, application developers write custom code by using third-party programming languages to support the data input, processing, data retrieval, and reporting processes. The database and the DBMS operate on back-end application servers, and front-end database applications operate on client systems.

Well-known databases and database management systems include Oracle, MySQL, Sybase, Foxpro, Microsoft Access, Microsoft SQL, and others.

EXAM TIP

The exam requires only a basic understanding of the differences between the different database models.

Database models

Databases have evolved over time as technology and needs have changed. They originally started as flat, two-dimensional databases, just rows and columns in tables. They later evolved into three-dimensional databases in which the tables can have very complex relationships and link with tables in external databases and files. The major differences between database types are the manner in which the relationships are constructed between tables.

Hierarchical databases

The first database model, called the *hierarchical database*, was developed by IBM in the 1960s. It resembles a tree-like structure with a major group at the root and one or more series of subgroups that branch off the root, much like the structure of most file systems. This structure supports a very simple parent–child relationship between tables. A parent can spawn multiple child objects (table), but a child object can only ever have one parent object, as shown in Figure 9-10.

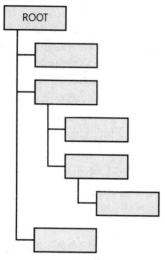

FIGURE 9-10 A hierarchical database

A disadvantage of this architecture is that a table on one branch cannot ever connect or relate to a table in another branch directly but must connect to the other table by tracking the hierarchical path back to the root of the tree and then out the adjacent branch to the target table.

Network databases

The network database model added a level of increased complexity and flexibility. In this model, a parent can spawn multiple children, and a child can have multiple parents, as shown in Figure 9-11. This allows more direct communication paths between tables because the tables in different branches can now connect to one another directly.

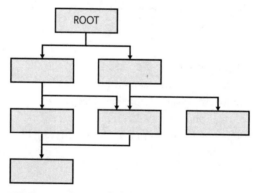

FIGURE 9-11 A network database

Relational databases

The relational database was introduced in 1969 by Edgar Codd. This model enables the relationships between tables to be declared in any manner needed rather than be governed by a pre-specified structure. This was considered the first three-dimensional database because of this lack of a defined two-dimensional (flat) structure like the hierarchical and network database models.

Relationships are declared between tables through a unique value representing each record (tuple) called the *primary key* for each record in a table. That primary key value for a record can be used in a different table to represent all the data in the record. When used in this manner, the primary key from one table, which is being used on a different table to establish the relationship or link between the tables, is called a *foreign key* in the second, now-related table. An example of this is shown in Figure 9-12.

CPUs

Primary Key	Description	Speed	QTY	Unit Cost	BIN #
A237	CPU 13	2.3G	10	168.00	D4
A255	CPU 15	2.3G	4	210.00	D78
L53	CPU 17	3.3G	20	250.00	E1
T192	CPU 13	1.6G	8	92.00	E3

Motherboard
Assemblies   Foreign Key

Primary Key	CPU	L2 Cache	EEPROM	Video	Total Cost
M203	A237	C28-1	ROM44	NV601	292.00
M205	A255	C28-1	ROM46	NV601	378.00
M205-4	A255	C28-3	ROM46	NV603	404.00
M205-11	A255	C504	ROM46	NV702	460.00
M207	L53	C67	ROM3	SB27	552.00

FIGURE 9-12 A relational database, showing the primary key–foreign key relationship

Two types of integrity validation checks were required to ensure the proper functioning of the relational database.

- **Entity integrity validation**   A primary key value must exist (cannot be null) for every tuple, and that primary key value must be unique within that table.

- **Referential integrity validation**   If a primary key value is referenced as a foreign key in a table, the primary key and its record must exist in the related table.

Object-oriented databases

An *object-oriented database* extends the functionality of each of the preceding database models by supporting the storage of nontextual data such as audio and video data but, most important, like machine language code, executable program code. This allows the storage of the programs that process the data to be maintained inside the database itself and eliminates the need to use third-party programming languages and an external executable application for the database application. This extension to databases can apply to hierarchical, network, or relational databases to produce object hierarchical, object network, or object relational databases.

Accessing databases

It is common for an enterprise to use more than one database and more than one type of database. Often, an application is designed to draw on data sets that exist in different databases. To make best use of these collections of data, the data must be able to flow freely between the various databases. However, the structures of the different databases often differ and are rarely the same. This makes it difficult to flow this data as needed without the risk of losing data. Losing data would be a violation of data integrity requirements.

Imagine a database with a name field and a control that allows only 30 characters. Next, imagine a database with a name field and a control that allows only 20 characters. If all records had to flow from the first database to the second database, the records with more than 20 characters could not be imported into the target database because of the 20-character limit on the name field. The import function would simply not import those records. Again, a violation of integrity requirements.

Therefore, because the data is required to flow between different databases with different structures somehow, the application developer must ensure that every record and data element that is required to flow actually does flow and is imported into the target database as needed to maintain proper data integrity.

In the early days of databases, a manual approach was often used. You export the source data into a file with each field in the record delimited with a tab or a comma. These were called *tab-separated value (.tsv)* files or *comma-separated value (.csv)* files. Then you open the .csv file in a spreadsheet and adjust all the data elements as necessary until all data fits in the target database schema. In the preceding example, locate all records that have more than 20 characters in the name field. Then truncate those excess characters, or cut then and paste them into some other field that can take them like a free-form type of Notes field. Then the import could proceed and, assuming all schema conflicts were resolved properly, all records would flow properly. This was a manual and time-consuming process.

Open database connectivity drivers

A programmatic approach to solving this schema conflict issue with databases is to use an *open database connectivity (ODBC) driver*, a piece of middleware that operates between the two databases, understands the schema of the source and destination databases, understands the conflict areas with the two schemas, and then programmatically adjusts any data elements that would violate the schema in the target database. The ODBC driver is open because it is generic in nature and not particularly specialized for any particular type of database until it is customized for the specific needs of an enterprise.

Figure 9-13 shows the placement of the ODBC driver so it can normalize the data from three databases having different schemas and drop the now normalized data into the database application the enterprise uses. This ensures that all records and data that should be presented by the application can be extracted from whatever database it resides in, no matter what its original structure, formatting, or syntax might be.

Data Repository

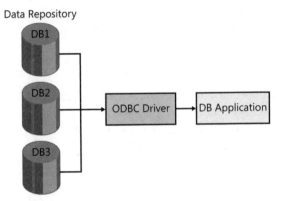

FIGURE 9-13 The open database connectivity (ODBC) driver

In this example, the database application acts as the data *consumer*, and the collection of databases in the data repository acts as the data *provider*. The ODBC driver is a piece of software called middleware that provides the standardization—more accurately, the normalization—of the data from the providers to the consumer. The ODBC driver also converts the data formatting, as necessary, when writing data to the databases in compliance with their specific and typically different formatting requirements as defined by the schema of the individual database.

There are more-specialized types of these database connectivity drivers, and one example is the very popular *Java database connectivity (JDBC) driver* that is optimized for use with Java database applications. COM-based applications accomplish this normalization of data from differing schemas in their *Object Linking and Embedding Database (OLE DB)* and the *ActiveX Data Objects (ADO)*. The OLE DB provides access to the data, and the ADO to manipulate the data as necessary.

The new kid on the block is the use of the *Extensible Markup Language* (*XML*). XML is both human readable and machine readable. It exports textual data in a standardized, well-formed format, following a collection of syntax rules and documenting the constraints on the data (such as schema). The importing XML-compatible database can validate the schema definition of the exporting database and then can properly adjust the data as necessary to accommodate schema differences and accurately accept or import all of the inbound data.

Constrained view

For the database application to operate correctly, all records must be able to flow into, out of, and between the various databases with their differing schemas and flow into and out of the application itself. However, although integrity requirements demand every record that matches the query to be presented—otherwise, the completeness of information is violated—the system must still comply with access controls appropriate for the user submitting the query to the application. Even if a query to the database returns 100 records that match the query, a filter, called a *constrained view* or a *database view*, must remove the nonauthorized records before presenting the results set to the user if he is authorized to view only 10 of them.

Polyinstantiation

 Polyinstantiation means the creation of multiple (poly) instances (instantiation). Relative to databases, polyinstantiation is used to protect the confidentiality of sensitive data, typically in the stronger mandatory access control (MAC) environments. Remember that MAC is used primarily in government and military information systems and uses labels to identify different levels of access privilege. In the United States, the government labels are:

- TOP SECRET
- SECRET
- CONFIDENTIAL
- SENSITIVE BUT UNCLASSIFIED
- UNCLASSIFIED

The subjects with TOP SECRET clearance are allowed greater access to information, and the lower levels are provided less access to sensitive information, so secrets are known at the top levels that cannot be shared with or known by the lower levels. If a piece of information cannot be shared with lower levels, a vulnerability to the aggregation and inference attack exists that polyinstantiation is designed to mitigate.

Imagine the following scenario:

Robert works at a navy base and has a CONFIDENTIAL clearance. He is allowed to know some things, the things with a CONFIDENTIAL (or lower) classification. He is not allowed to know other things such as those with a SECRET or TOP SECRET classification. Every day, as Robert walks from the parking area to his office, he walks past several docks where ships are tied up. Over a period of several weeks, he notices a particular ship that intrigues him. The ship has a great deal of activity around it and on it. Painting, grinding, hammering, loading, unloading, all sorts of noises, people with clipboards of papers, people who are pointing and shouting, people going onboard, and people disembarking the ship. The existence of the ship, the ship's present location, and the general activities about the ship are all pieces of information Robert is authorized to know.

One day, as Robert is walking from the parking area to his office, he notices much more water and sky than before and that the bigger water and sky are where the ship had been. The ship has left the dock. Robert is a little disappointed that the ship and all the activity is gone, and he wonders about the adventure the ship must be participating in. However, the details of the mission of the ship are above Robert's clearance, and he is not allowed to know them. There is now a hole in Robert's knowledge, and if that absence of information remains, Robert's mind is compelled to fill that void, to figure out where his favorite ship is. Whether the pursuit of an answer is willful and conscious or accidental and subconscious, for the satisfaction of curiosity and the pleasure and entertainment of envisioning the adventure, or whether the analysis is to be used for malicious intent, Robert is very likely to aggregate information he is authorized to know and use it to infer an answer that he is not authorized to know. This is an *aggregation and inference attack*.

Now Robert might just aggregate and infer an incorrect answer, perhaps multiple incorrect answers, like misguided theories. Maybe no harm is done. Nevertheless, Robert could get dumb lucky and infer correctly, accidentally concluding accurate answers that he is not authorized to know. This is classically and formally a breach of security! Robert now knows something he is not authorized to know. This is a violation of the required confidentiality of the information of the ship's mission. Security professionals (you) are required to anticipate and defeat this breach before there is ever a chance of being successful.

The breach occurred because of not providing data where data is expected. The absence of information incited the natural human compulsion to fill the void and infer satisfactory information. So what could mitigate this risk? Robert cannot be told the truth of the mission of the ship. He is not authorized. So management (or the database application in this case) must tell the unauthorized subjects plausible lies to fill that void of information and defeat, or at least mitigate, the unintentional or willful aggregation and inference attack that leads to the breach of security.

The plausible lies that must be told to unauthorized subjects are variations of the truth or, to put it into context, multiple (poly) instances (instantiation) of the truth based on the different clearances of the subjects.

In relational databases, *polyinstantiation* is supported by adding the classification level of the individual instances of the truth (lies) to the primary key (PK) of the record to keep the primary key for each record unique. Table 9-1 shows the primary key (SHIP #) value appended with the classification label of the various instances of the status record for a ship.

TABLE 9-1 Relational database table of ship status showing polyinstantiation

Ship # (PK)	Ship name	Location	Destination	Cargo	Departure	Arrival
U731 TS	LULU	MANILA	SOUTH KOREA	WEAPONS	JAN 13	JAN 17
U731 S	LULU	MANILA	SOUTH KOREA	FOOD	JAN 13	JAN 17
U731 C	LULU	MANILA	NEW ZEALAND	FOOD	JAN 13	JAN 27
U731 U	LULU	MANILA	NEW ZEALAND	FOOD	JAN 13	JAN 27
U404 TS	TREY	SIDNEY	KOREA	WEAPONS	JAN 15	JAN 20
U404 C	TREY	SIDNEY	PERTH	FOOD	JAN 15	JAN 28

TS=TOP SECRET; S=SECRET; C=CONFIDENTIAL; U=UNCLASSIFIED

Transaction processing

Because databases are powerful software tools that can accept input, store, process, and output large amounts of data, enterprises have come to rely heavily on them. Many users can simultaneously access data within a database, and this produces a certain risk to the integrity of the data. What if two users were simultaneously accessing the same record in a database? Not a problem, yet. But what if they were both modifying the data in the same field simultaneously? Here is a potential problem. If one user modifies the data and saves his changes while a different user is modifying data in the same field and then saves her data a few seconds after the first user, the second user's write to the database would overwrite the first user's data, and the first user's data would be lost. The second user is unaware of the newly lost data from the first user. Losing data would be a lack of completeness of the data, a violation of data integrity requirements. The management of transactions with regard to this nature of error condition is called *concurrency control*: disallowing conflicting concurrent transactions.

 A common approach to resolving the conflicts and violations of integrity is called *record locking*. When the first user accesses the record to make changes to the data (in read/write mode), lock the record so that no one else may write to the record. A second user could still read the data (read-only mode) but could not modify and write new data. After the first user saves the changes to the record and closes the record, many database applications notify the second user that the record is now available for editing. If the second user switches to read/write mode, the database updates the second user's display with the new data so the second user becomes aware of the recent changes to the record and can adjust the data as necessary, following company policy.

In another transaction-processing example requiring concurrency controls, imagine a database that holds the seats to be sold for an upcoming concert. User1 browses the list of available seats, selects seats 101 and 102, and adds them to the shopping cart but has not yet made payment to complete the transaction. Without proper controls, User2 would be allowed also to select seats 101 and 102 and add them to his shopping cart because the seats have not yet been purchased. Now two sets of tickets might be sold for the same seats, a violation of integrity.

In the concert ticket example, when User1 places seats 101 and 102 in the shopping cart, the two seats should immediately be removed from the inventory of available seats to defend against concurrency errors. However, what if User1 never submits payment for the seats to complete the purchase? Seats 101 and 102 have been removed from inventory and will go unsold. This doesn't maximize profits. The proper concurrency control for this type of transaction processing error is called the *rollback*. The rollback transaction processing concurrency control operates like this:

- User1 selects two seats and places them in the shopping cart.

- The database program includes a *begin transaction* marker, and a timer begins.

- A series of programmatic steps begin to complete the purchase of the two tickets, for example, regarding payment type, payment card information, customer information, delivery options, and the purchase approval by the payment card company.

- Following the programmatic step that completes the payment, when User1 has actually purchased the two tickets, another marker, called *end transaction*, exists. (This is also commonly referred to as the *commit* statement, when the transaction is now complete: Commit these changes [the sale of the two seats in this case] to the database.)

- After triggering the begin-transaction timer, if the end-transaction marker is not reached in a timely manner, all changes of the data are rolled back to the point just prior to the begin-transaction marker as if nothing happened. Therefore, if User1 does not complete the purchase of the two tickets in, let's say, 5 minutes, seats 101 and 102 return to inventory, making them available for purchase by someone else, and User1's shopping cart session expires. If, after the 5-minute time-out, User1 attempts to complete the purchase transaction, an apology message is displayed describing the shopping cart session time-out, and instructs User1 to begin shopping for tickets again.

The order of the transaction is as follows.

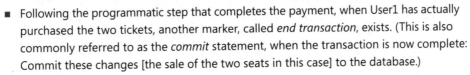

| 1. Items placed in shopping cart: begin transaction |
| 2. Remove items from inventory. |
| 3. Complete customer data. |
| 4. Complete delivery data. |
| 5. Complete payment data. |
| 6. Request and receive payment approval. |
| 7. Commit data: end transaction. |

Roll Back

Some database processes might take a very long time. For example, the DES cracker system used to crack DES keys, described in Chapter 3, "Cryptography," took months to complete its transaction. Imagine getting five months into the transaction processing and, just hours before the DES key would be revealed, some glitch occurs and interrupts the process. Starting from the beginning would be painful and costly. For long-running transactions, the transaction processing database application places checkpoints periodically in the data. The *checkpoint* is a marker in the transaction processing timeline; it takes a snapshot of the process and its data at that instance. If the transaction is interrupted, it can simply roll back to the nearest checkpoint and begin processing from that point rather than starting at the beginning. All too often, during a large FTP download and when using the wrong FTP client, at 990 MB downloaded on a 1 GB file transfer, the FTP session is reset, and the download must begin again with the first byte. A good FTP client places checkpoints in the data periodically, and if the FTP session is reset, the (worthy) FTP client application resumes the download at the nearest checkpoint.

The *two-phase commit* is another approach to ensuring data integrity during transaction processing. In this protocol, the two parties attempting to complete the transaction, called *cohorts*, are managed by a *coordinator*. The coordinator queries each cohort and asks whether the cohort is prepared to commit to the transaction. The two cohorts vote yes to proceed or no to abort the transaction. This is phase 1 of the two-phase commit. If the coordinator receives two yes votes, the coordinator instructs the cohorts to commit their new data, the completion of the transaction. The cohorts report their successful commit of the data to the coordinator as a second yes vote. This is phase 2 of the two-phase commit. If either cohort votes no, the coordinator instructs both cohorts to abort the transaction and roll back to phase 1. This process is summarized in the following timeline.

- Begin transaction
- Phase 1
    - Coordinator to cohort 1: Are you ready to commit?
    - Cohort 1 to coordinator: Yes
    - Coordinator to cohort 2: Are you ready to commit?
    - Cohort 2 to coordinator: Yes
- Phase 2
    - Coordinator to cohort 1: Commit
    - Cohort 1 to coordinator: Yes
    - Coordinator to cohort 2: Commit
    - Cohort 2 to coordinator: Yes
- End transaction

The ACID test for the development of transactions

Well-written transaction code has several characteristics. When developers are writing transaction code, these four traits should be evaluated, and the code should be adjusted to provide these features adequately:

- **Atomicity**   The transaction should be atomic in its nature, meaning that the transaction must be implemented in its entirety, or it must be completely rolled back to the state prior to its initiation, as if no transaction ever occurred. The transaction cannot ever be partially implemented.

- **Consistency** The results of a transaction must be of high integrity; the data must be consistent with internal and external reality.

- **Isolation** Do not present mid-transaction information to the users, only the before-transaction data and the after-transaction data.

- **Durability** After a transaction has been committed, it is a fact in history and cannot be deleted or removed. If the transaction was an error, introduce a second transaction to correct the first transaction, but once committed, the transactions must remain in the transaction logs and the data adjusted accordingly.

NOTE THE DEFINITION OF *ATOMIC*

Interestingly, the definition of the term *atomic* as it is used in this case—having either a complete transaction or no part of a transaction—is technically inaccurate. When the meaning for the term was defined, it was thought that the atom was the smallest possible unit of matter and could not be subdivided. It was thought that a portion of an atom could not exist independently of the whole atom. There is either one whole atom, a binary 1, or there is no atom, a binary 0; anything in between was an impossibility. It has since been well established that the atom can be subdivided into smaller, subatomic particles such as protons, neutrons, electrons, quarks, bosons, and so on.

Online transaction processing

Many databases are high performance and high capacity, taking many transactions per second as on an ecommerce website. These online transaction processing (OLTP) databases require real-time processing. They are often accessed by a cluster of application servers (web servers in the ecommerce example) and might even be supported by different companies, requiring middleware brokering software between the database servers and interaction with the database application. The database application must support concurrency controls, such as record locking and rollback, and often implement transaction journaling as described in Chapter 8, "Business continuity and disaster recovery planning."

 Because of the high volume of transactions and the very rapidly changing dataset, *online analytical processing*, a form of artificial intelligence, is often applied to these databases to identify rapidly developing trends and patterns in the transactions. Recognizing these trends and patterns early on in this very dynamic database can greatly increase revenue and profits.

Distributed databases

Distributed databases are examples of *distributed computing* and *distributed data processing*, in which there is not only client-to-server communications and data flow but, often, server-to-server data flow as well. There are two modes of distributed databases in a distributed computing system. In one model, the environment maintains multiple databases residing on different database servers. Each database holds different data, but the computing environment needs access to multiple data sets, so the clients communicate with multiple database servers. Figure 9-14 shows the communications flow between a client and multiple database servers that hold different data.

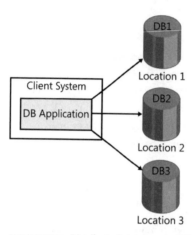

FIGURE 9-14 Distributed databases, different data

In the second distributed database model, the environment maintains multiple copies of the same database residing on different database servers. The database servers are often geographically dispersed to provide local access to the data, and there might be multiple copies of the same database in a single location to increase capacity and availability. The computing environment needs access to these single data sets, and the clients communicate with (typically) a single, local database server. In this model, these copies of the same database must be synchronized to ensure data integrity (accuracy, completeness, and consistency). To support this requirement, server-to-server synchronization (replication) processes must continually communicate changes to all other copies of the database. An example of this type of distributed database is the active directory database used in Active Directory (domain) environments. The domain controllers are (somewhat specialized) database servers that must remain synchronized. Figure 9-15 shows the communications flow between clients and multiple database servers that store the same data, and the synchronization of the data between the servers.

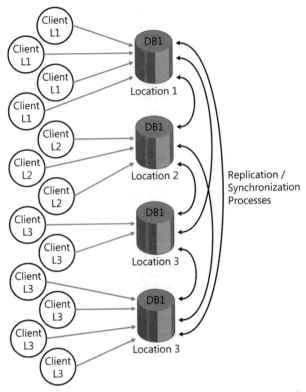

FIGURE 9-15 Distributed databases—same data requiring synchronization

Increasing the value of data

Individual databases can be quite large, holding vast amounts of data. As connectivity improves, storage prices continue to decrease, and technologies advance, specifically artificial intelligence, it becomes easier for enterprises to gain access to increasing amounts of data, and the opportunities to increase the value of data continue to grow.

Many software development companies are building features into their software products that report statistics and events from the installed base of customers back to the company in efforts to improve the overall quality of the software products. This collection of data from the customers becomes a valuable resource, not just to the collecting enterprise but, perhaps, to other vendors and eventually to humankind. Some enterprises acquire databases and other data repositories from other enterprises, often assembling giant stores of databases of almost any kind and holding data of virtually any type. The data, whatever its format, must be organized in a way that is machine readable and allows programmatic inferencing. *Data aggregation* is rapidly becoming a powerful tool, holding tremendous potential wealth, if it can only be mined properly to reveal hidden trends and patterns. However, these databases also present tremendous risks when the bad guys can mine them with malicious intent.

The collection of many databases and other data formats from many sources is called a *data warehouse*. Some data warehouses are now exceeding the petabyte (more than 1,000,000,000,000,000 bytes) size. To access all this data, several issues must be resolved. First, these databases almost always use relational databases to provide a workable structure and improve versatility and efficiency. Next, some form of ODBC driver must be used to enable information to flow between the databases with differing schemas. Then, a process called *data normalization* must be performed.

Two of the primary functions of data normalization are:

- **Refer to data types in a consistent manner**   When looking at the STATE field in a large database, the reference to the state of California might include CA, ca, Ca, Cal, CAL, Cali, California, Califormia (misspelled), and many other variations intending to communicate the same information. Refer to the data "California" in a consistent manner such as CA. So for every record that implies California in the STATE field, change its data to CA, change all Pennsylvania references to PA, Florida to FL, and so on.

- **Eliminate redundancy of the data**   Store the data in only one place. If a data element is required in multiple places, define a primary source, delete all other copies of that data, and insert a pointer to the one copy at the primary source. This way, if the data, such as an address field, ever must be changed, it needs to be changed in only one place, and all other references to that data will present the correct information by pointing to the only copy of the data, the updated copy.

The next component of preparing a large dataset for efficient use in a data warehouse is to sanitize the data to eliminate any data that should not be accessed, perhaps to comply with a law or regulatory mandate, perhaps by company policy, or for other (usually risk-driven) reasons. When the data is compliant, secondary sanitization processes will likely be required during the post-processing of queries and analysis, when considering the authorization level of the subject being provided the output data. (Remember the database view?) Therefore, two rounds of sanitization are often required: one to satisfy compliance requirements and one to satisfy authorization requirements.

To use the data warehouse for the purpose of increasing the value of the data, analytical processes are applied to the data to reveal hidden or previously unrecognized trends or patterns that lend themselves to increased insight, intelligence, awareness, and, ultimately, revenue generation. This process of evolving raw data into information, then knowledge, and eventually wisdom is referred to as *data mining* or *knowledge discovery*.

The analytical processes often involve applying different levels and forms of *artificial intelligence* to the target dataset, a varying array of artificial neural networks, expert systems, fuzzy logic, machine learning, statistical analysis, inference, interestingness metrics, business intelligence, and other disciplines and technologies. The resulting data output from the analysis, hopefully the data with increased value, is called *metadata*. Metadata is not the data being analyzed; it is data about the data being analyzed.

Applying these analytical and complex processes on petabytes of data is impractical, so data mining targets smaller subsets of the data warehouse called a *data mart*: a collection of databases selected for a specific data-mining process and often for a specific data-mining objective.

To pull this all together, imagine a data mart containing databases on the following topics:

- Male shoppers
- Diapers
- Beer

The first level of data mining might reveal that, 86 percent of the time, when male shoppers buy diapers, they also buy beer. The rationale that might explain this previously unnoticed pattern is that the dad was loafing all day watching sports on the TV. The mom was cooking and taking care of the kids and eventually orders dad to "help with something. Anything. Fine. Go get some diapers for the baby." The dad reluctantly heads down to the local convenience store to purchase the diapers and, while there and feeling sorry for himself, decides to do something to feel better. What could be better than an ice-cold six pack of beer?

The next level of analysis might produce the metadata beneficial to store owners: To sell more beer, always place the diapers on a shelf in direct view of the beer to remind the dad that he deserves a treat for himself. Another piece of metadata to store owners might be not to put diapers on sale if beer is on sale, too. Make some profit on one product or the other.

Remember, when post processing, sanitize the data. If the client who is paying for this increased-value metadata hasn't paid for the more evolved and valuable metadata, implement a database view to show only the metadata of the "86% of male shoppers who buy diapers also buy beer" statistic. Don't allow the client to access the second level of analysis metadata that reveals the more valuable metadata about maximizing profits.

> **NOTE IDENTIFYING TRENDS AND PATTERNS**
>
> Although it is likely that this particular data-mining scenario would be discarded because of its low rating in its interestingness metrics, it is an example of the potential increase in value of the low-value, raw data held in previously disconnected and unassociated databases by identifying previously unidentified trends and patterns.

Artificial intelligence

In a strict sense, artificial intelligence (AI) is defined as a (nonhuman) system that perceives its operational environment and makes decisions (and possibly takes action) to maximize its chances for success, however success is defined for the system. As it applies to knowledge discovery within information systems, success is defined as increasing the value of data by producing metadata, the previously undetected trends and patterns that exist, hidden in the mountains of low-value, raw data in the data warehouse.

Below the level of data is noise, meaningless gibberish or static, which has little or no value. By adding content to the noise, data is produced. This is typically what is held in the data warehouse. The data in the data warehouse has been refined through formatting to allow inferencing and make it machine readable; it has also been normalized to provide standard referencing and remove redundancy (along with other normalizing functions). It sounds like the data has been worked pretty hard already, but at this level, it is still considered very close to the lowest level of value, raw data. However, there has been an increase, perhaps ever so slight, in the value of this data. This would be like processing to produce the first level of metadata. By adding context to data, information is produced, increasing its value. Add meaning to the information, and knowledge is produced, another increase in value. Add insight to the knowledge, and wisdom is produced. This is defined as the highest level of processing and value for the metadata, now called wisdom. This describes the *knowledge pyramid*, also known as the DIKW (data, information, knowledge, wisdom) pyramid, the knowledge hierarchy, or the information hierarchy. This process of escalating the value of the data is shown in Figure 9-16.

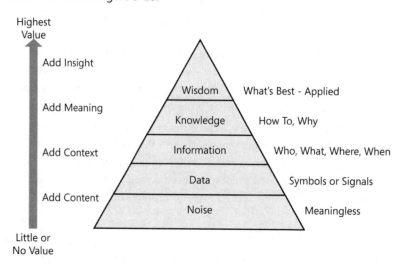

FIGURE 9-16 The knowledge pyramid

To accomplish this increase of value from the data, a much smaller subset of the data warehouse, a data mart, is selected. The massive volume of data in the warehouse would take too much time to process, and the selection of specific topics of data from the warehouse provide context. Then various forms of artificial intelligence are applied to the data mart to produce the first level of metadata, the once refined data about the data. This metadata is now information. Apply the correct artificial intelligence algorithms to the information, and the resulting metadata is knowledge. Apply the correct artificial intelligence algorithms to the knowledge, and the resulting metadata is (hopefully) wisdom.

Fuzzy logic

Fuzzy logic is considered a lower form of artificial intelligence and is based on approximate reasoning instead of attempting to reach an exact or absolute answer. It operates by assigning a level of truth, implying the ability to have a partial truth that exists between being completely false (zero percent true) and completely true (100 percent true). Fuzzy logic applications use an inference engine on these ambiguous variables, called *fuzzy data*, to reach its conclusions and recommendations.

An example is a 1 GB USB flash memory drive that holds 400 MB of data. A completely empty drive is 0 percent full and 100 percent empty, but this drive is 40 percent full and 60 percent empty. Fuzzy logic will provide a better answer to the more binary-type question of "Is the flash memory drive empty or full?" than absolute logic that might only answer "empty" or "full." Fuzzy logic can conclude that it is 40 percent true that the disk is full.

Expert systems

The expert system is a form of artificial intelligence that mimics how experts in a given field reach their conclusions by applying *if-then reasoning* to the presented information. Experts from a given field of knowledge, such as medical doctors, are surveyed with if-then type questions such as, "If a patient presents with a sore throat and a pain in her lower-right abdomen, what is the diagnosis (what then)?" The responses by a number of experts are then analyzed to identify statistical agreement. If a statistical agreement exists in the answers, the information is entered in the *knowledge base*, also called the *rule base*.

An *inference engine* provides the reasoning power that works on the knowledge base. A user is offered a series of symptoms, perhaps as check boxes. When the user has selected the one or more symptoms he is experiencing, the inference engine compares these symptoms to the if-then rules in the knowledge base to produce its conclusion, in this case, the diagnosis and perhaps even the prescribed remedy.

Expert systems perform *forward chaining* when symptoms are input by a user, and a diagnosis is output by the expert system. Expert systems perform *backward or reverse chaining* as a validation of a theory or conclusion. A diagnosis is input by a user, and the collection of symptoms associated with that condition is output and verified by the expert system with the user to validate the diagnosis.

Expert systems are limited to the base of human knowledge. The survey can only contain questions humans can think of to ask based on existing knowledge. The expert responses can only come from the responses that are already known. Expert systems are very good at aggregating, accessing, and regurgitating the body of already known knowledge and can identify contradictions in presented information, but they are not great at extending human knowledge. The expert system is only ever as good as humans already are, both on the knowledge base and on the inference engine (the programmed, reasoning logic). Therefore, the expert system is considered low to mid-level artificial intelligence.

Artificial neural network

The *artificial neural network* (*ANN*) is built by assembling processing elements, such as CPU chips, in layers to resemble layers of neurons in the human brain, as shown in Figure 9-17. More layers of processing elements means more-complex processing capabilities.

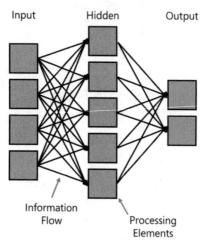

FIGURE 9-17 The connectivity of a three-layer (input, hidden, output) artificial neural network

This is the most powerful form of artificial intelligence constructed to date because it can learn from a set of observations (input data, scenarios). In other words, the ANN can extend human knowledge by recognizing complex relationships and patterns between data elements. The network alters its structure during its learning phase and then adjusts again as it shifts into its activation phase, when it produces output. A weight is assigned to data inputs (the significance of the data element) and interconnections (connection strength) between processing elements. Then the network processes the data to develop a set of solutions while optimizing cost, with the lowest cost solution (typically) being the output.

 Quick check

1. What is used in relational databases to relate one table to another table?

2. What is the term that refers to the structure of the database?

Quick check answers

1. A primary key and a foreign key

2. Schema

Attacks on applications

Many of the vulnerabilities inherent in the enterprise are borne in the less than secure coding of applications. Several of the primary reasons software is inherently insecure are:

- Lack of validating and filtering data input
- Failure to release memory securely
- Residual maintenance hooks
- Unintended (covert) communications channels
- Race conditions

Further, software, such as viruses, worms, Trojan horse applications, backdoors, rootkits, and exploit code, is used to commit attacks on systems.

Lack of validating and filtering data input

 The *buffer overflow attack* and the *SQL injection attack* are two of the most prevalent attacks on software. These could both be reduced to a very low frequency, if not completely eliminated as vulnerabilities, if secure coding practices were used to develop applications, specifically the validation and filtering of data input into the applications. The buffer overflow attack is described in Chapter 5.

In the SQL injection attack, the lack of verifying and filtering the user data could allow the attacker to input SQL statements that break out of normal SQL input for the SQL engine, which it processes directly. Instead of filling an address field on an input form with address data, the attacker enters escape characters or SELECT statements. The developer should program code to validate the user input, and if the address data doesn't look like address data, the program should reject the data and prompt the user for address data. More specifically, if the data contains escape characters or the syntax for a SELECT statement, plus the many other forms of SQL attacks, for example, the program should reject the data and prompt the user for address data.

Typically, the types of filters include:

- **Number of characters**   If the expected data should be only 20 characters, for example, truncate all characters past 20 or reject the data with an error message.
- **Type of data**   If the data expected is a phone number or a postal code, reject anything except numbers. Names rarely contain numbers, so accept only alphabetic characters in name fields.
- **Special syntax characters and character strings**   Different applications can have different characters or strings that can be interpreted by the application engine or by the operating system directly instead of as data within the application code itself.

In addition to these input controls, additional controls should be in place to deny direct access to the database, allowing access only through the intended database front-end application, and all access to the database must be logged locally on the database server and to a secure, remote log repository.

Failure to release memory securely

When a process is issued buffer memory by the memory manager of the operating system, the process should return that memory when the process has completed its work. However, to avoid leaving potentially sensitive data and intellectual property unprotected in system memory (remember remnants?), the secure way to release memory is first to overwrite the entire buffer with random bits and then release that overwritten buffer memory space back to the memory manager. This return of unneeded memory to the memory manager of the operating system is referred to as *garbage collection*.

Automatic garbage collection is built in to some newer programming languages; unfortunately, it is not always accurate or successful in securely overwriting the entire buffer or in returning all unneeded memory to the system. The software developer should add code as necessary to ensure that all unneeded buffer space is overwritten first and then released, even if the programming language (theoretically) performs this function automatically.

Some processes in some applications inconsistently or never release the buffer memory back to the operating system when the process has completed its work. Each time the faulty process executes, it requests its required amount of RAM from the memory manager but retains it. At some point, the faulty process still holds so much memory that the operating system becomes starved for RAM, and the performance degrades from the increasing reliance on virtual memory. (Remember that virtual memory is approximately one million times slower than RAM.) When one or more processes in applications fail to return memory to the operating system, the application has a *memory leak*.

Residual maintenance hooks

Maintenance hooks are entryways to software that bypass the standard security controls and processing order. They are inserted into code during development to enable the software developer to test iterations of code quickly while debugging and testing. The maintenance hooks should all be removed before the source code in scripting language is compiled into machine language. When attackers can locate a residual maintenance hook in the program, they have found a free *backdoor* into the application. Some CASE tools include the automated search and removal of residual maintenance hooks just prior to compiling the source code into the machine language executable.

Unintended (covert) communications channels

An obvious and intended communications channel is referred to as overt. A hidden or unintended communications channel is covert. Applications and systems very often, unfortunately, have both types of communication channels. When found, these covert communications channels are used mostly for breaches of confidentiality but could also be used to violate the integrity and availability of valuable information assets. Developers should identify and eliminate potential covert channels during software design. There are primarily two types of covert communications channels. The covert storage channel

Information is placed in a location for later retrieval. In an application, this might be data legitimately placed in a buffer that isn't cleaned up after the processes are complete. A moment later, a second process, perhaps a utility specifically written to exploit the vulnerability in the software, scans the RAM for remnants and collects whatever it can locate. In the physical world, a *covert storage channel* might be an attacker marking a specific telephone pole with an X at a specific height from the ground to signal a fellow attacker to meet at 4 P.M. for a data pickup at the coffee shop. The telephone pole was never intended to store data for these two to use, and no one else understands (or even notices) the marking except these two attackers.

The covert timing channel

When a *covert timing channel* is used, information is communicated by oscillating some system component. For example, a sender would toggle the CAPS LOCK on and off on a remote system to signal the recipient by using either Morse code or binary data. Another example would be for the recipient to monitor a specific file located on a specific network share at a specific time. The sender would use a program to alter the file size every two seconds to either zero (0) bytes or one (1) kilobyte to communicate in binary. The recipient would use a utility to record the file size and decode the message.

Race conditions

Race conditions are a family of *timing attacks* to strike during the one brief moment when the system (or software) is in a vulnerable state. An attacker might even manipulate the system to cause the vulnerability and increase the window of opportunity by delaying some following process that might eliminate or reduce the vulnerability. An example of a race condition existed with the first-generation firewalls, the packet-filtering firewall. This security system was essentially a router that had an application added to its functionality. This application monitored source and destination IP addresses and port numbers within packets and would filter based on a set of allow and deny rules (called the rule base). Attackers figured out that if they could crash the filtering application and cause it to restart itself while the packet-filtering firewall was restarting the filtering application, the device operated as a router with no filtering functionality. As the filtering application restarted and reloaded its rule base, the device began working as a firewall once again, but for a few brief moments, the attacker could pass anything through the recovering firewall—a race condition. Packet-filtering firewalls from several vendors had this same vulnerability.

Another race condition is the *Time of Check/Time of Use (TOC/TOU) attack*. This attack targets the moment a subject requests access to an object. As described in Chapter 5, the security kernel for the operating system provides an isolation boundary between the subject and the object. Subjects submit requests to the kernel for access to objects. The security kernel calls the security reference monitor to read the access control list (ACL) bound to the object and then compares the ACL with the request from the subject to determine whether the request for access is approved or denied. This is the moment of the Time of Check (TOC) and the beginning of the race condition. If an attacker could replace the requested object (the ACL with an allow privilege for the subject) with a different object (that the subject had no access privileges to) between when the kernel approves the request and the subject actually uses the object (the moment of TOU), the subject could gain unauthorized access to objects. The goal is to slow the system down and provide enough time to make the object substitution between the Time of Check and the Time of Use. This TOC/TOU attack falls in a family of attacks known as *asynchronous attacks* because it performs an asynchronous (simultaneous or parallel) alteration to the data while the synchronous (sequential) process is being executed.

Malware

Malware is a large family of types of malicious software, software specifically written to exploit vulnerabilities and compromise systems and data. When malware is successful, the program or operating system behaves in an unexpected and unintended manner. Applications and systems being affected by malware is usually considered a breach or incident and commonly results in *unauthorized system* or *unauthorized data access, arbitrary code execution, command and control* of systems, *unauthorized escalation of privilege*, or *denial of service (DoS)*.

Malware can be designed to exploit targets of opportunity automatically, affecting whoever in the masses is vulnerable (shotgun, grazing, or spray and pray attacks), or it can be human initiated and driven (by the attacker), very focused and targeted, to compromise a single, targeted entity.

When malware is successful in affecting a system, it gains access to the access token, the credentials, and therefore the privilege level of the user who launched the compromised application or operating system component. Whatever that authorized user has access to, the malware now has access to. This is one of the reasons access should always be granted by following the *principle of least privilege*. It is with this level of privilege that the malicious payload of the malware can inflict its damages.

The following sections describe common examples of malware.

Exploit code

Exploit code is malware program code that targets and exploits vulnerabilities identified in program code. Automated worms, viruses, and hacker activities use exploit code to accomplish their dirty work. When previously unseen exploit code is released, it is referred to as a *zero-day exploit*, which implies that the vulnerability it affects was previously unknown, and there is no antivirus or intrusion detection system signature to identify the exploit code yet. Often, security system vendors can develop and distribute signatures within a few days of the recognition of a zero-day exploit. Software updates to mitigate the vulnerabilities usually take a little longer to be released.

Virus

A virus is malicious code that requires a *host executable* to replicate and deliver its payload. Typically, when the infected host executable is launched and loads into memory, the virus also loads into memory. It is only while in memory that the virus can replicate (by infecting other executables in memory) and deliver its often malicious payload. *Transient viruses* exit memory when the host exits memory. *Resident viruses* remain behind in memory even after the host executable exits memory.

Viruses use several techniques to remain stealthy and avoid detection on a system. Some mutate or garble their own code with each replication in the hopes of altering their signature over time so the antivirus detection methods fail. *Encrypting viruses* encrypt their malicious code and then decrypt when it is time to deliver its payload. *Polymorphic viruses* are encrypting viruses that also alter the decryption engine and decryption key, so it is different with every replicated copy of itself. A *metamorphic virus* rewrites the entire virus with each replicated copy but requires a fairly large and complex metamorphic engine to accomplish this.

The European Institute for Computer Antivirus Research (EICAR) has assembled a collection of nonmalicious virus files commonly called the EICAR Test Files that can be downloaded for the purposes of testing antivirus tools. When the executable eicar.com file is exposed to the antivirus software running on the test system, the file should be quarantined or whatever the antivirus application is configured to do with virus files. EICAR includes a zipped eicar.com file and a double-zipped eicar.com file to test the zip file–scanning capabilities of the antivirus software. Users should NOT download these files to enterprise systems. These should be used in the enterprise by only authorized administrators who need to evaluate the effectiveness of antivirus applications.

Worm

The worm is much like a virus in its ability to deliver a malicious payload to a remote system, but the worm does not require a host executable to infect. The worm is *self-replicating* exploit code that targets and affects one or more vulnerabilities in running program code on the target systems and then delivers its payload. Worms usually target zero-day vulnerabilities and commonly spread rapidly. The payload is often to find new targets by network connections, by email address lists, and so on and then dispatch copies of itself to those new targets. If the new targets have the exploited vulnerabilities, those systems are now infected by the worm.

The worm was initially developed to perform good deeds on computer networks but were quickly converted into malicious software. The Morris worm was written and released as a proof of concept by Robert T. Morris at MIT and is considered the first worm released over the Internet (11/02/88). Other examples of worms include MyDoom, Blaster, Code Red, I LOVE YOU, Melissa, Nimda, Sassir, Sober, Sobig, SQL Slammer, and the more recent Stuxnet, Duqu, and Flame.

Trojan horse

A Trojan horse is an application that has some apparent beneficial use and is distributed because users want to benefit from that functionality, but the application also contains hidden malicious code. Trojan horse malware does not replicate other than by unwary users making copies of the seemingly beneficial application, often referred to as *drive-by downloads*.

Rootkits

Rootkits are a collection of malware that attackers covertly install (implant) on a compromised system to entrench, retain their (unauthorized) access, hide their tracks, and essentially take full control of the compromised system. They are called rootkits because the attacker who controls the *rooted* system usually has the access and privilege level of the system root, the most privileged entity on a Linux or UNIX system. *Kernel-mode rootkits* are usually installed as Trojaned device drivers and run in the more powerful kernel mode. Well-designed and implanted kernel mode rootkits can be very difficult to detect. *User-mode rootkits* are more common. They run in the weaker user mode, must make requests for access, and typically run in Trojaned applications.

Examples of rootkits include NTRootkit, HackerDefender, and the Sony BMG rootkit.

Backdoors

Backdoors are a system or program entry point that bypasses standard and intended security controls such as authentication and authorization. Some backdoors are simply the developer's maintenance hooks that were legitimately inserted in the program code during the development of the application but were never removed as they should have been. Other backdoors are implanted as Trojaned system executables so they launch automatically in a compromised system and allow the attacker continued unauthorized access. The attacker will often implant multiple backdoors in case one or more fail or are replaced. If the attacker is good, the backdoor will use the attacker's authentication so another attacker can't use the backdoor if found. The backdoor can also be called a trapdoor.

Adware

Adware is advertising-supported malware that propagates (usually unwanted) advertisements on the computer display of the victims. Adware is often delivered as Trojan horse software, by shareware, or by website drive-by downloads.

Spyware

Spyware is malware that is intended to collect information about the victim covertly, often on his Internet use activities so they can be targeted better for adware and email spam campaigns. Like adware, spyware is often delivered as Trojan horse software, by shareware, or by website drive-by downloads.

Ransomware

Ransomware is a class of malware that prevents access to critical system files unless a virus clean-up fee (the ransom) is paid. Like adware and spyware, ransomware is often delivered as Trojan horse software, by shareware, or by website drive-by downloads.

Keystroke loggers

Keystroke logger software records all keyboard activity and stores it for later retrieval or delivers it automatically by way of email. These are commonly used to steal user names and passwords. Keystroke loggers are often installed within Trojaned operating system files so they run any time the computer is operational. There are also hardware keystroke loggers that do not rely on Trojaned system files but are devices that connect between the keyboard and the computer hardware.

Meme

Although not exactly malware, the *meme* is a hoax, the rumor of a vulnerability or exploit that spreads among system administrators, causing a loss to the affected enterprises in wasted time and effort. Occasionally, the rumor will include instructions on the detection and eradication of the nonexistent malware, and the prescribed recovery procedures may actually introduce vulnerabilities in the system to empower a real exploit. Because the meme relies on a host process, such as an over-trusting administrator, to perform its malicious actions, many consider the meme to operate like a virus.

Traffic analysis

Often, the attacker can infer sensitive information from data in transit even when she cannot directly understand the data (due to encryption). Patterns in the volume, source, destination, or types of traffic (protocol used) will tell the attacker more than is desired. Because it is difficult to detect an eavesdropper—someone running a sniffer, for example—the attacker can monitor the traffic for a long time. With a satisfactory sample of normal traffic, the attacker can identify unusual or abnormal traffic and might be able to infer or deduce conclusions that could cause the enterprise damages.

In high-risk environments, a common solution to this problem is to pad the traffic by constantly transmitting a stable level of traffic. Whatever is not actual legitimate data flow is supplemental garbage traffic, or noise on the network, to shield the levels, source and destination information, and the protocols being used.

Attacking web-based applications

Because of global public access, often poorly managed web servers, and vulnerabilities in web applications and operating systems, there are many threats to be aware of in this specific area of applications. Web browsing is a client–server type of application, and vulnerabilities exist on both ends. Compromised web servers are commonly used for the distribution of malware. Client-side browser applications are designed to run mobile code automatically that is downloaded from websites. Users are often unaware of the risks they take as they poke around on websites.

Following are several types of threats that are prevalent on the Internet.

Cross-site scripting attacks

Cross-site scripting (XSS) attacks are a large array of attacks based on the browser/web server application platform. There are many variations of the XXS attacks, but the three primary types differ in where the malware resides.

THE NONPERSISTENT CROSS-SITE SCRIPTING ATTACK

This attack is based on a poorly configured web server and a successful social engineering attack on an unsuspecting, unaware end user. To perform the nonpersistent XSS attack, the attacker must locate a web server that uses the default error pages. When most web servers receive requests from client browsers that contain strings or variables the web server doesn't understand, most servers simply copy the incorrect parameters from the submitted uniform resource locator (URL), place that incorrect information on a default error page, and send the error page back to the user. This shows the user what part of the URL needs to be corrected so an appropriate request can be resubmitted to the web server.

Next, the attacker writes a malicious script and then embeds that script in a URL to the aforementioned web server. Then the attacker uses one of many ways to trick users into clicking the hyperlink with the embedded script. This might be a phishing attack or a compromised web pop-up, but the trick is to get the user to click the hyperlink.

When the user clicks the hyperlink with the embedded script, the URL is sent to the web server. The web server parses the URL and errors when it gets to the embedded script. Therefore, following its default error processing, it copies the malicious script to an error page and returns the error page to the user, requesting a correction for this part of the URL.

As the client browser receives the error page that contains the malicious script, the browser executes the script in the intended process of rendering the webpage for the user's feature-rich and enhanced browsing experience. The user's system just became infected and compromised.

In the case of the nonpersistent XSS attack, the malware doesn't reside anywhere persistently but is sent to the user as a variable parameter in a hyperlink. When the hyperlink is clicked, the malware is reflected off the web server and is sent back to the user's browser where it is processed.

This process is shown in Figure 9-18.

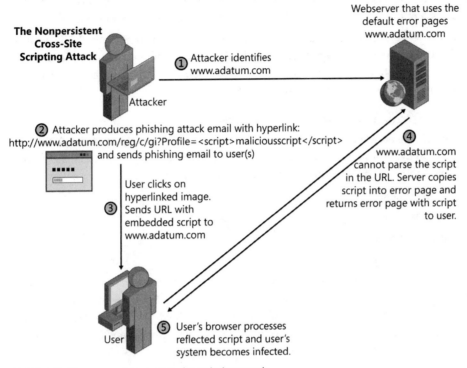

FIGURE 9-18 The nonpersistent cross-site scripting attack

The web server should not copy information from the inbound URL and paste it into the error page being returned to the user (use custom error pages and responses), and the user should know better than to click hyperlinks from unknown and untrusted sources.

THE PERSISTENT CROSS-SITE SCRIPTING (XSS) ATTACK

This attack is based on a compromised or poorly configured web server and on an unsuspecting, unaware end user. If the web server can be directly compromised, the malicious code can be added to any or all webpages and sent to any visitors of the site. If the web server hosts a blog or comment page that is not moderated, the poorly managed website simply receives textual input from users and programmatically posts that comment without inspection or filtering.

An attacker identifies this poorly managed web server and submits a comment that includes a malicious script. The comment and the script are posted.

When a user is reading the comments on the website and clicks the comment with the malicious script, the script is sent to the user, and the user's browser processes the script, infecting the user's system.

In the case of the persistent XSS attack, the malware resides persistently on the web server, often in a comment posted on the unmoderated website. When the comment is clicked, the malware is sent from the web server to the user's browser, where it is processed.

The web server should be hardened and monitored so it is not compromised. The website should not post comments without reviewing them first. All comments should be sent to a blind drop box (write only), and the site administrator should review all uploaded comments and post only the comments that are appropriate.

THE DOM-BASED CROSS-SITE SCRIPTING (XSS) ATTACK

In this attack, the attacker writes malicious code into the *Document Object Model* (*DOM*) environment on the user's system, for example by using a malicious hyperlink. Examples of the vulnerable and misused DOM environment parameters include:

- document.location
- document.URL
- document.referer
- document.cookie

Then, using the DOM functionality in the user's browser when a web server triggers the DOM function, the browser executes the malware placed in the DOM environment on the client system, and the user's system is now infected. In the DOM-based XSS attack, the malware is executed on the client computer within the DOM environment and is triggered by a website that uses the DOM functionality of the browser.

Web cache poisoning

The web cache is a store usually kept on a proxy firewall to improve the firewall's performance. Because of the deep inspection capabilities of the proxy firewall, they tend to slow Internet browsing to a sometimes painful pace. To try to overcome this, many proxy firewalls include the ability to store web content after it has been requested and inspected. Some web-caching servers can be configured proactively to download, inspect, and cache web content regularly that might be commonly needed within an enterprise.

When a user launches his browser and enters a URL, if the web caching server does not have the content already stored in its cache, the proxy firewall retrieves the web content and filters it based on its rule base. If the web content is acceptable, the content is forwarded to the requesting user and copied in the web cache. If another user requests the same content, instead of retrieving another copy from the Internet and then filtering the downloaded content, the web-caching server simply sends the second user the already inspected content it has stored in the web cache. The hits from the web cache are substantially faster than fetching and inspecting another copy.

If an attacker can inject malware into the web cache (poison the web cache), the proxy firewall and its web-caching server provide the storage and distribution of the malware, and end users are typically completely unaware because the web content is supplied to them from a trusted infrastructure system.

A second place cached web content is stored is on the client system in the temporary Internet files store. This client-side cached web content is, again, placed here to improve the performance of the browser. If the attacker can poison this cache, any hits from the cache will infect the client system. By poisoning this cache, an attacker will only compromise one system at best. By poisoning the web cache on the proxy firewall, the attacker could compromise the entire enterprise, a much better return on the investment.

Hijacking webpages

By using an active software tool that crawls websites, called a *web crawler,* an *Internet bot,* or *spider,* attackers copy one or more webpages from a legitimate website and then poison those copied pages with malware. The attacker then publishes the malicious, cloned webpages. Next, using one of many techniques, such as phishing or manipulating search engines, the attacker tricks users into accessing these hijacked and poisoned pages; the user believes she is connected to the legitimate website. Attackers often use similar but slightly different domain names as the legitimate sites they are spoofing.

This technique can be used simply to infect and compromise the client systems or perhaps to steal the data, such as logon credentials and financial account information, that the user enters in the seemingly legitimate webpages.

The defense against users accessing hijacked webpages begins with security awareness training. Users should learn not to trust hyperlinks and to enter URLs manually anytime there is any question about the source of the link. The next line of defense is through aggressive

filtering on the firewalls, disallowing access to known *Internet dark space* (*darknet, bogon*) and malicious web servers. Several sources of lists of known malicious domains and web servers include regular updates and formats that could be imported into firewalls and other filtering systems.

> **NOTE** **INTERNET DARK SPACE**
>
> *Internet dark space, darknet,* and *bogon* describe public IP addresses that cannot be legitimate because the address has not yet been allocated by the Regional Internet Registries (RIR). Attackers set up malicious web servers by using these unallocated addresses and inject routing information into the routing system of the Internet. Any traffic to or from this dark address space should be rejected, and an inspection of the local system with the other, legitimate IP address should be initiated in case the system has already been compromised. Somehow, that system came to be communicating with the darknet. The term *bogon* comes from hacker jargon because the IP addresses from the Internet dark space are ultimately bogus.

Directory transversal attacks

Successful *directory transversal attacks* enable the attacker to access content on a web server other than the intended web content. Directory traversal is implemented by injecting the syntax to traverse to the parent directory. On a UNIX system, the . . / (dot dot slash) command accomplishes this. On a Windows system, the . . \ (dot dot backslash) command accomplishes this. There are many variations of the character strings that might be successful at traversing the directory structure on the web server, but these are the most common. By sending these commands to the web server, it is possible for the attacker to gain access to these higher-level directories on the web server. This attack requires permissions on the directories for the user or the compromised credentials being used to attempt the attack on the web server.

For example, an attacker could submit a series of . . / commands to reach the root of the directory tree; if followed by /etc/passwd, this could allow the attacker access to the password file on the UNIX or Linux web server.

The web server should validate all user input and filter on and reject the risky (. . / or . . \) character strings. Further, the web server should filter on and reject the various encodings (Unicode Character Set Transformation Format-8 bit [*UTF-8*] and *percent encoding*) of these character strings.

UTF-8 for . . / = 002e 002e 002f
Percent encoding for . . / = %2e%2e%2f
UTF-8 for . . \ = 002e 002e 005c
Percent encoding for . . \ = %2e%2e%5c
And the variations: 002e 002e /
                             . . 002f
                             002e 002e \
                             . . 005c
                             %2e%2e/
                             . . %2f
                             %2e%2e\
                             . . %5c

Sensitive data retrieval

Websites and web servers commonly present too much information. Server banners provide operating system version and sometimes update-level information as well as service type, version, and update-level information. Error response webpages from the web server often provide these details and even actual source code on occasion. Attackers can assemble a vulnerability profile of the server with this information. Often, the HTML of any given webpage presents too much information regarding hard-coded path statements, the intellectual property of the code used on a page, or even user names and passwords. Review all published web content for the enterprise and remove or obscure anything that might be considered sensitive.

Cookies

Cookies are ASCII-based text files that websites write to the client systems to enable session-related features and functions. They provide good benefit, such as storing the contents of the shopping cart on ecommerce websites, identifying whether the user has successfully authenticated, and personalizing characteristics on various websites. Cookies cannot host viruses or install malware, but they often hold too much information. Cookies track browsing habits and store personal information such as names, addresses, and perhaps even payment card or other financial information.

Website developers should recognize the storage of sensitive information in the cookies they write and find a way to eliminate the need to store sensitive information in the cookies or introduce encryption and obfuscation techniques to protect the sensitive information.

 Session cookies are stored temporarily on the client computer and are (in theory) deleted by the browser typically when the browser application is closed. *Persistent cookies* remain on the client computer for longer periods and often track the user on the website that wrote the cookie; they could be used to track the user's browsing habits across all websites. This raises privacy concerns for many, and in 2011, the United States and European Union enacted laws requiring explicit consent to track users and enabling users to specify Do Not Track.

 Third-party cookies are written by the visited website but link to some third-party domain, usually an advertiser on the visited website. These cookies are often used as the persistent tracking cookies that introduce the privacy concerns. It could be said that the third-party tracking cookie is evidence of the visited website selling the privacy of its visitors. Most browsers can block these third-party cookies, and they can be manually deleted.

Malware detection mechanisms

There are several ways to detect malicious software, but no one detection method identifies all types of malicious software. It is reasonable and perhaps prudent to use multiple detection methods simultaneously.

Signature-based detection

 Signature-based detection is the most commonly used detection method. When a new piece of malware is identified, the antimalware vendors produce a signature or fingerprint of the malware and then distribute that signature to all their customers. Now their scanning engines check each executable for the signatures of known malware. Signature-based detection is one of the most certain detection methods, but it can only be used to identify malware that has already been seen, captured, and fingerprinted, and then the signatures must be distributed.

Polymorphic viruses and metamorphic viruses alter their code, hoping to change enough that the recorded signature no longer applies, and the now morphed virus can break out in the wild once again. Zero-day or new viruses have not been fingerprinted yet, so these can also run wild until captured and fingerprinted and the signatures distributed and installed.

Of course, these signatures must be regularly updated by connecting to the vendor's website, downloading the new signatures, and installing them in the signature database on the monitoring systems.

Heuristic-based detection

Heuristic-based detection relies on a more generic, less specific signature. Because many viruses are variants of earlier viruses, heuristics fingerprints the commonalities within the family of variants and can detect any member of the family. These often operate by analyzing the code in executables and identifying various and often dispersed functions commonly used in malicious software. Another approach is to emulate the execution of the suspicious code in an isolated sandbox (virtual environment) and monitor what the code is accomplishing.

Heuristic-based detection is much better at detecting new malware than signature-based detection but can trigger false positive alerts and quarantine.

Behavior-based detection

Behavior based detection techniques monitor processes that are running and identify those that behave in a risky or abnormal manner. Notepad.exe should not open a network listener, and MSPaint.exe should not produce a compiled executable and write it to the file system.

Behavior-based detection is also much better at detecting new malware than signature-based detection but, like heuristic-based detection methods, can trigger false positive alerts and quarantine.

Integrity validation

Malware often alters the configuration of the compromised system or replaces legitimate system files with Trojaned system files. Validating the integrity of these parameters on systems is a commonly used method to detect post-infection indicators. Some systems scan daily and compare today's details with the details from yesterday, assuming that yesterday's details were valid, safe, and trusted. The system would then report any differences in the scanned configuration parameters and systems files.

Another technique compares the scanned system with a gold-standard system having a valid, safe, and trusted configuration and set of system files, once again reporting any differences in the scanned configuration parameters and systems files. The relatively new trusted platform module (TPM) integrated circuit chip can perform the latter of these two integrity validation scanning techniques.

Integrity validation detection techniques can identify various forms of malware, new and old, based on the malware's impact on the system configuration and system files.

Quick check

1. What type of cross-site scripting (XSS) attack reflects the malware off the poorly managed web server?

2. What should the program do to a buffer before returning it to the memory manager?

Quick check answers

1. The nonpersistent XSS attack

2. Overwrite the buffer with random bits to remove any sensitive data.

Exercises

In the following exercises, you apply what you've learned in this chapter. You can find the answers to these questions in the "Answers" section at the end of this chapter.

Exercise 9-1

Investigate and describe the security features provided by the web browser application.

Exercise 9-2

Review the store of cookies and identify an approximate ratio of first-party cookies (websites you willfully visited) to third-party cookies (typically, advertisers on the websites you visited).

Internet Explorer: C:\Users\%UserName%\AppData\Roaming\Microsoft\Windows\Cookies

Ubuntu Firefox: In Firefox, Preferences>Privacy>Show cookies or Preferences>Privacy>remove individual cookies

Chapter summary

- Security should permeate every phase of the software development life cycle (SLDC). The SDLC phases include project initiation, functional design, system design, software development, installation/test, operational maintenance, and disposal/end of life.

- Change control and configuration management help stabilize the software development environment.

- Separation of duties to avoid conflicts of interest should be implemented within the software development environment.

- Component Object Model (COM) and Distributed Component Object Model (DCOM) allow processes to share processes and data in Microsoft applications. Object request brokers (ORB) and common object request brokers architecture (CORBA) allow processes to share processes and data in applications on various operating systems and in different programming languages.

- Database types include hierarchical, network, and relational. Object-oriented databases, an extension of the three database types, can hold nontextual data such as audio, video, photographs and, most important, program code.

- Transaction processing often requires concurrency controls and rollback capabilities.

- Artificial intelligence techniques include fuzzy logic, the expert system, and the artificial neural network.

- Design software following secure coding standards and best practices (public) and security policies and standards (internal), including:

  - Qualifying all user and data input to prevent buffer overflow, SQL injection, and directory traversal attacks.

  - Securely returning memory (garbage collection).

  - Removing all maintenance hooks (backdoors).

  - Identifying and removing covert channels and race conditions.

  - Avoiding the use of known vulnerable functions.

  - Heeding compiler warnings.

  - Sanitizing output data appropriate for intended recipient.

  - Minimizing information available to unauthenticated and unauthorized users, such as banners, errors, and HTML code.

  - Performing a secure code review and security testing for all new code.

  - Securing the environment (defense in depth).

Chapter review

Test your knowledge of the information in this chapter by answering these questions. The answers to these questions, and the explanations of why each answer choice is correct or incorrect, are located in the "Answers" section at the end of this chapter.

1. The software escrow is intended to mitigate which of the following risks?

    A. In case the software vendor performs poorly

    B. In case the software developer goes out of business

    C. In case the original source code becomes infected or corrupted

    D. In case a transaction fails, and the system must roll back to a known good state

2. Which of the following describes the preferred characteristics of an object in OOP?

   A. Tight COM and loose CORBA

   B. Loose acceptance testing and tight regression testing

   C. Tight methods and loose messages

   D. Loose coupling and tight cohesion

3. Which of the following is designed to support data sharing in Microsoft databases?

   A. The ACID test

   B. ADO

   C. SAML

   D. The IDEAL model

4. Dot dot slash is the syntax used to commit what type of attack?

   A. A race condition attack

   B. A DOM cross-site scripting attack

   C. A directory traversal attack

   D. A buffer overflow attack

5. At which stage of the software development life cycle (SDLC) should security concerns first be analyzed?

   A. System design

   B. Functional design

   C. Testing

   D. Project initiation

6. When does an application developer need to implement middleware in the application?

   A. When using primary and foreign keys between two tables in a database

   B. When using multiple databases

   C. When artificial intelligence is being implemented

   D. When performing the garbage collection process

7. Which of the following best describes the reason to use artificial intelligence on data?

   A. To produce metadata

   B. To increase the value of the application

   C. To increase the value of the data

   D. To manage real-time concurrency controls

8. Which of the following is commonly used to defend against the threat of an aggregation and inference attack?

   A. Polyinstantiation

   B. Static binding of messages

   C. Polymorphism

   D. Regression testing

Answers

This section contains the answers to the exercises and the "Chapter review" section in this chapter.

Exercise 9-1

Because of the large attack surface, most browsers support numerous security features, including (but not limited to):

- Warning of potentially dangerous downloads
- Filtering and disallowing active content and mobile code
- Filtering and disallowing suspicious websites
- Disabling online tracking
- Recognizing cross-site scripting attacks
- Disabling recording browsing-session details
- Deleting browsing history on exit
- Disallowing SSL-secured sites with certificate errors
- Disallowing submission of cleartext form data
- Blocking pop-ups
- Disallowing website redirects
- Blocking third-party cookies
- Blocking all cookies
- Parental controls: Allowing lists for children using the browser
- Content controls: Managing objectionable content
- Connecting through a proxy firewall
- Disabling DOM storage
- Disabling SSL 2.0 (vulnerable protocol)

Exercise 9-2

On Internet Explorer: C:\Users\%UserName%\AppData\Roaming\Microsoft\Windows\Cookies

On Ubuntu Firefox: In Firefox, Preferences>Privacy>Show cookies or Preferences>Privacy> remove individual cookies

Open the cookie file and identify the referenced domain such as yahoo.com or microsoft.com. There are often multiple cookies for different purposes from the same website that reference the first-party website, the website willfully visited. Ignoring those duplicate first-party cookies, it is not uncommon for the ratio of first-party cookies to third-party cookies to approach 1:5, but often, it is closer to 1:2.

Answers to the chapter review

1. **Correct answer: B**

   A. **Incorrect:** A software escrow does not protect the enterprise (customer) when the enterprise is dissatisfied.

   B. **Correct:** If the software developer goes out of business, the customer is provided with the source code from the software escrow.

   C. **Incorrect:** Typically, it is compiled executables that become infected, not source code.

   D. **Incorrect:** The rollback is an integrity-protection design feature in transaction processing and has nothing to do with software escrow.

2. **Correct answer: D**

   A. **Incorrect:** The Component Object Model (COM) and the common object request broker architecture are OOP design standards that allow sharing of processes and data. Being tight or loose is irrelevant in these standards.

   B. **Incorrect:** Acceptance testing and regression testing are performed on the completed application after being released. They have nothing to do with discrete objects.

   C. **Incorrect:** Methods are the processes within an object, and messages are the communications flowing into, out of, and between objects. Being tight or loose is irrelevant to these terms.

   D. **Correct:** Loose coupling implies a low reliance on other objects to perform the methods of an object. Tight cohesion implies that the methods within an object work well together, are similar to one another, and naturally belong together. These are two beneficial characteristics of objects.

3. **Correct answer: B**

   A. **Incorrect:** The ACID test (Atomic, Consistent, Isolate, Durable) are design objectives for transaction design in transaction processing.

   B. **Correct:** ActiveX Data Objects (ADOs) are Microsoft COM-based objects used to access data sources.

   C. **Incorrect:** The Security Assertion Markup Language (SAML) is an extension of the Extensible Markup Language (XML) and is designed to support authentication and authorization in a web-based, single-sign-on (SSO) environment.

   D. **Incorrect:** The IDEAL model (Initiating, Diagnosing, Establishing, Acting, Leveraging) by the Software Engineering Institute (SEI) at Carnegie Mellon University is a model designed to drive an effective software process improvement program in software development organizations.

4. **Correct answer: C**

   A. **Incorrect:** A race condition is a timing attack with a small window of vulnerability and opportunity for the attacker.

   B. **Incorrect:** The document object model (DOM) cross-site scripting attack is based on planting malware on the client computer and then triggering its execution by using the DOM framework within browsers.

   C. **Correct:** The . . / (dot dot slash) syntax is used to traverse to the parent directory in a UNIX or Linux operating system. On a Windows system, the syntax is . . \ (dot dot backslash).

   D. **Incorrect:** The buffer overflow attack relies on unqualified user input fields, and the attacker overflows the data buffer.

5. **Correct answer: D**

   A. **Incorrect:** Security should permeate each phase of the SDLC. System design is not the earliest phase in the answer set.

   B. **Incorrect:** Functional design follows the project initiation.

   C. **Incorrect:** The testing phase is too late in the SDLC to begin considering security ramifications of the design.

   D. **Correct:** Project initiation is the first phase of the SDLC, and security concerns related to the project should be considered at this early phase.

6. **Correct answer: B**

  A. **Incorrect:** When using primary and foreign keys, entity integrity and referential integrity validation checks should be implemented, not middleware.

  B. **Correct:** Because different databases likely use different schemas, the data from the databases might be incompatible with the needs of the application or the importing database. Middleware puts data (of differing formats) into a standard format so it can be imported and processed properly.

  C. **Incorrect:** AI is commonly used to increase the value of data and occurs after the data has been standardized and normalized.

  D. **Incorrect:** Garbage collection deals with secure disposal of data remnants in RAM and returning the RAM to the memory manager. It does not require middleware to accomplish this.

7. **Correct answer: C**

  A. **Incorrect:** Although metadata is the output of AI, the objective of AI is to increase the value of the data, not just produce metadata.

  B. **Incorrect:** The objective of AI is to increase the value of the data, not the application.

  C. **Correct:** The objective of AI is to increase the value of the data from noise to data to information to knowledge, and, ultimately, to wisdom.

  D. **Incorrect:** Concurrency controls in transaction processing are implemented to protect the integrity of the data and typically do not require artificial intelligence to accomplish this.

8. **Correct answer: A**

  A. **Correct:** Multiple instances, or polyinstantiation, of the truth for the various clearances of the users helps defend against the aggregation and inference attack.

  B. **Incorrect:** Static binding of messages, used in OOP, locks down the message flow between objects when the program is compiled so this flow will occur every time. Dynamic binding establishes this flow relationship at run time when the program is executed.

  C. **Incorrect:** Polymorphism (multiple forms) enables a class to be instantiated as objects, but the objects can demonstrate different behaviors.

  D. **Incorrect:** Regression testing verifies that changes to application code in one area do not break the application's overall operation.

CHAPTER 10

Operations security

This chapter looks at the daily activities of the operations of an enterprise and identifies where vulnerabilities are often created and exist. One area of vulnerability in the enterprise that has been largely absent in the preceding chapters is that of availability. Almost all other chapters primarily address the vulnerabilities and protections of the confidentiality and integrity of the valuable information assets. This domain still handles those issues but also discusses availability to complete the confidentiality, integrity, and availability (CIA) triad. This chapter also looks at the potential countermeasures that are commonly implemented to reduce the risks inherent in the daily operations of the enterprise.

Finally, this chapter reviews many kinds of attacks on the enterprise and its information systems, including a review of the penetration testing process and the anatomy of a targeted attack.

Exam objectives in this chapter:

7.1 Understand security operations concepts

    7.1.1 Need-to-know/least privilege

    7.1.2 Separation of duties and responsibilities

    7.1.3 Monitor special privileges (e.g., operators, administrators)

    7.1.4 Job rotation

    7.1.5 Marking, handling, storing and destroying of sensitive information

    7.1.6 Record retention

7.2 Employ resource protection

    7.2.1 Media management

    7.2.2 Asset management (e.g., equipment life cycle, software licensing)

7.3 Manage incident response

    7.3.1 Detection

    7.3.2 Response

    7.3.3 Reporting

    7.3.4 Recovery

    7.3.5 Remediation and review (e.g., root cause analysis)

7.4 Implement preventative measures against attacks (e.g., malicious code, zero-day exploit, denial of service)

7.5 Implement and support patch and vulnerability management

7.6 Understand change and configuration management (e.g., versioning, base lining)

7.7 Understand system resilience and fault tolerance requirements

The activities of operations

The operations department is primarily responsible for supporting the networking and information systems operations of the enterprise. The team members are typically technical and management personnel, often with technical expertise and experience, having hands on the hardware and configuration consoles of the various IT infrastructure systems and services, servers, and client systems.

Operations must implement and maintain the information technology systems to support the needs of the business, and it must do so in a manner that protects the IT resources, reduces risk, and complies with the policies of the enterprise. Following is a sample list of tasks commonly performed by the operations team:

- **IT hardware installation** Infrastructure, servers, client systems, security systems
- **IT system configuration** Compliance with policy, standards, baselines
- **IT system monitoring** Anomaly detection, variance detection, failure detection
- **IT system maintenance** Repairs, planned and unplanned, to maintain availability
- **System recovery planning** Integration with disaster recovery plan (DRP)
- **Software installation** Deployment of approved software/applications
- **Software updates** Operating system, applications, firmware
- **Signature updates** Antivirus, antispyware, intrusion detection systems, firewall blacklists
- **User provisioning** User accounts, permissions
- **Remote access** Remote users, remote administration
- **Connectivity management** Availability maintenance, including intranet, Internet, virtual private network (VPN), remote locations, branch office, partner
- **IT security infrastructure** Deployment, maintenance, validation
- **Helpdesk and IT support** Resolve standard types of user issues and assist administrators as needed

- **Data management**   Ensure data remains available, classify data, and implement and maintain appropriate physical and technical access controls
- **Data redundancy and recovery**   Availability maintenance, including backups, mirroring, shadowing, journaling
- **Incident response support**   Hands-on team
- **Media management**   Data at rest, retention, removable media, secure destruction, object reuse
- **Configuration management**   Document approved system configuration, identify and submit needed configuration change requests, implement approved configuration changes, update configuration documentation, and verify/ monitor/audit system configuration changes
- **Security, vulnerability, and penetration assessments**   Assist with and perform assessments as needed, report vulnerabilities and proposed controls to management, and improve breach recognition and response skills
- **Software license management**   Maintain software license and use information, assist with the requisition of needed software licenses, and identify and remedy the use of unlicensed software

Roles in information technology

The various roles that interact with the information systems vary greatly with regard to their required access requirements, the risks they introduce to the enterprise, and the countermeasures used to manage that risk. Typically, the more access a user needs, the more risk he presents to the enterprise. The access level is defined by the productive work the user is to perform but must be balanced with proper controls to avoid introducing unnecessary losses through errors and omissions, data disclosure, data destruction, loss of availability of IT assets, system misconfiguration, fraud, and other forms of theft.

The operations roles that interact with the information systems include:

- The data owner
- The manager
- The data custodian
- The system custodian
- The user

The data owner

Although it is true that senior management is ultimately responsible for everything within the enterprise, senior management delegates that responsibility to top-level managers who are often responsible for divisions, product lines, or larger departments within the organization. These top-level managers are the business owners of the major facets of the enterprise. They are also the data owners for all the data and supporting infrastructure within their respective facet, division, product line, or department. They become the party responsible for compliance with policy, laws, and regulations and the protection of the valuable information assets within their areas.

The data owner identifies priorities, provides oversight, and approves budgets and proposals to accomplish the required business functions. She should be a required signature (often delegated) on new hires; privilege escalations; relevant policy changes; and significant system, process, or program changes within the scope of her responsibility.

The data owner, of course, delegates responsibility downhill to mid-level managers, further dividing the organizational structure, where the nature of the tasks and responsibilities become increasingly granular. Eventually, the delegated tasks settle on the shoulders of the custodians, the administrators who actually perform the bulk of the tasks through technical skills and hands-on activities in the IT systems and assets.

The manager

The manager is delegated one or more areas of responsibility to support the needs of the higher-level business owner or data owner. The manager identifies priorities, provides oversight, and typically proposes budgets and projects or activities to accomplish the required business functions within his division. He supervises subordinates; proposes hiring, termination, and privilege provisioning needs; develops schedules; and remediates and reprimands as necessary. The manager is the policy enforcer.

Mid-level and low-level managers can be identified as custodians with regard to their area of responsibility, but they typically delegate the technical, hands-on tasks to the nonmanagement personnel with the specialized skill sets.

The data custodian

Data custodians are privileged users. They have heightened privileges to support the administrative tasks of managing and handling the data assets of the enterprise. They often have specialized technical skills related to operating systems, file systems, implementation of permissions, encryption tools and techniques, backup and recovery systems and technologies, monitoring technologies, the IT systems within their scope of responsibility, and, often, the enterprise-wide IT system. They perform their tasks by following the policies, procedures, standards, baselines, and guidelines of the enterprise closely. Their activities administering the data assets are driven mostly by well-documented and approved change requests.

> **NOTE CHANGE CONTROL AND CONFIGURATION MANAGEMENT**
>
> Change control and configuration management are described in Chapter 9, "Software development security."

The system custodian

System custodians are also privileged users. They have heightened privileges to support the administrative tasks of implementing, maintaining, and repairing the IT hardware and connectivity of the enterprise. The IT hardware includes infrastructure systems, application-providing and resource-providing systems, and client systems such as the following:

- Infrastructure systems (hardened systems and bastion host configuration)
  - Firewalls
  - Routers
  - Switches
  - Authentication servers (directory services servers, domain controllers)
  - Domain Name System (DNS) servers
  - Dynamic Host Configuration Protocol (DHCP) servers
  - Network Address Translation (NAT) servers
  - Port Address Translation (PAT) servers
  - Remote access systems (Remote Authentication Dial-In User Service (RADIUS), Terminal Access Controller Access Control System (TACACS+), Diameter, 802.1x port-based authentication)
  - Wireless access points
  - Virtual private network (VPN) concentrators
  - Load balancers
  - Storage area networks (SAN)
  - Cloud systems (usually virtual machine host systems)
  - Virtual desktop infrastructure (VDI) support systems
  - Security systems (intrusion detection systems, intrusion prevention systems, log repositories, security information and event management [SIEM] systems, and so on)

- Application-providing and resource-providing systems (hardened servers and bastion host configuration)
    - Email servers
    - Database servers
    - File and print servers
    - Application servers
    - Web servers
    - File Transfer Protocol (FTP) servers
- Client systems
    - Desktop operating systems
    - Client applications
    - Client connectivity
    - Bring your own device (BYOD) connectivity and security
    - Endpoint security systems
    - Help desk

The operations personnel often have specialized technical skills related to network operating systems, operating systems, file systems, applications, encryption tools and techniques, fault-tolerant and redundancy systems and technologies, monitoring technologies, vendor-specific hardware, the IT systems within their scope of responsibility, and often, again, the enterprise-wide IT system. Like all personnel, they perform their tasks following the policies, procedures, standards, baselines, and guidelines of the enterprise closely. Their activities are mostly driven by well-documented and approved change requests.

The user

The user is the person who needs access to the valuable information assets to perform her work and increase the value of the enterprise (revenue, profits) through her productivity. She is the consumer of the IT resources. Security awareness training, monitoring, and enforcement are essential components of prudently managed users. Technical controls can help manage unauthorized access, but the users are authorized to access the sensitive content, so the administrative controls are intended to mitigate risk when the user must access the valuable content. There are many more users than there are data owners, managers, and custodians, so their immediate supervisor (manager) becomes the most granular monitor and enforcer of policy.

Collectively, the managers and the custodians perform asset management, including change control and configuration management. They document system configurations, system connectivity, and the inventory of assets. They are privileged users, so increased monitoring and careful separation of duties should be implemented to avoid conflicts of interest and reduce the risk of fraud.

Remote access

Many users need access to the enterprise network and IT resources while away from the office. They might work from home as telecommuters, they might be traveling, as some district managers and sales people must, but they must be able to connect to the corporate network from outside the physical facility or without a hard-wired connection, such as over the Internet, over a wireless connection, or perhaps (more historically) over a dial-up connection.

These types of connections introduce a heightened level of risk. Because the user is not necessarily within the facility, physical controls are not effective on these users. If a user must enter and move about the interior of the facility and eventually use an Ethernet cable plugged into a wall jack to establish a network connection in this physical space, there are many opportunities to verify his identity. However, when the network connection comes in over a telephone line, through a VPN over the Internet, or through a wireless access point, such physical opportunities to authenticate the user do not exist. The connections over public networks (Internet, wireless, dial-up) should be considered hostile.

Therefore, it is quite common for remote user connections to be more strongly authenticated, such as by using multifactor authentication and mutual authentication, as described in Chapter 2, "Access control." Further, information assets are flowing over public networks, where security cannot be ensured. To top this off, another area of risk and vulnerability exists on these remote connections. Because the remote computer is not within the control of the enterprise, it is difficult to know or trust the level of security of that remote system. It might be loaded with malware and lead to an enterprise-wide breach if a connection is allowed. Figure 10-1 shows a sample network diagram with multiple remote access connections from the Internet and from wireless clients.

The security solution should include strong authentication and monitoring and require a VPN to protect the data in transit over public wires and air waves (wireless). Some form of control and validation of the security posture of the remote system should be implemented such as strongly taught and enforced acceptable use policy, an approved software policy on remote systems (if company owned), and network access control (NAC). VPNs and NAC were described in Chapter 7, "Telecommunications and network security."

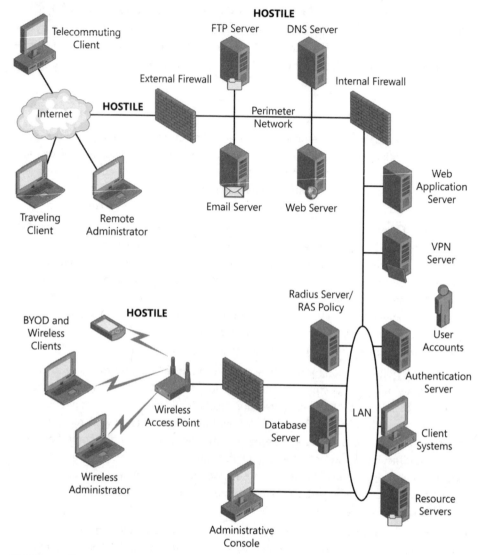

FIGURE 10-1 Remote access connections

Remote administration

Administrators are responsible for configuration, ongoing maintenance, and configuration adjustments to servers and infrastructure systems. They can usually log on to the system locally and perform necessary tasks but, very often, connect to those systems from a remote administrative console or workstation on the enterprise network. It is also not uncommon for the administrator to be completely remote and connect to the enterprise network from some remote location to perform these administrative tasks. Like all remote connections, these should be more strongly authenticated and require secure connectivity such as a VPN. Because the users are administrators, it is more likely that policies will be an effective control in maintaining the proper security posture for their client remote systems, but NAC always provides stronger security if it can be cost justified.

Availability

The primary mentality of operations is almost always "Availability at all cost!" To a large extent, this is not too far off target. Keeping the information system services available is an important aspect of the daily activities of the operations team. Remember the CIA triad, confidentiality, integrity, and availability? The howls and screams will be heard up on the mountain if the network or some portion of it goes down. Users will be frustrated and angry, and operations personnel will be yelled at. So yes, availability is a very important part of their jobs.

At a slightly higher level of vision, though, that availability must be balanced with security. Uncontrolled or even too much availability causes increased losses and could put the enterprise out of business more quickly than a periodic network outage. The somewhat different, if not contradictory perspective of the security professional is, "If the asset is not secure, disconnect it. After that, availability is the next priority." Disconnecting the IT asset means it is no longer available, a concept that is diametrically opposed to the goal of the operations team.

If management and policy support the security aspects properly, the operations team must do its best to ensure the highest possible level of availability to the users of the enterprise assets within that framework of governance. To accomplish this, and in parallel (and perhaps in harmony) with the efforts of the risk assessment team and the business continuity and disaster recovery planning (BCP/DRP) team, operations analyzes the information system overall and identifies *single points of failure*. Initially, this is done as a brainstorming list. It is then distilled and prioritized based on the severity (losses) of an outage caused by the single device, connection, or process becoming unavailable for any reason.

After the prioritized list is completed, countermeasures are considered and evaluated based on their respective cost justification details. Don't spend $100,000 on countermeasures to defend against a potential $10,000 loss. The type of countermeasure against single points of failure falls largely into two categories: *fault tolerance* and *redundancy*. Fault tolerance is the ability of a device, system, or process to experience one failure but still provide its services and resources functionally. Often, performance or capacity can degrade, but the services and resources remain available for use. Redundancy is provided when a second device, system, process, connection, or data set exists and can provide availability if the first one fails or goes offline. These might sound like the same thing, and the two terms are often conflated, but they are different. Fault tolerance does not ensure a second anything, such as a second copy of the data. Redundancy does.

Various fault-tolerant and redundant technologies and techniques are described in detail in the "Single points of failure" section later in this chapter.

User provisioning

The operations team is typically responsible for provisioning user accounts and the permissions assigned to those users. These activities are driven by a formal procedure that includes documentation and approvals, and after all these pieces are in place, the assignment lands on the operations department to perform the defined and approved provisioning work. It should be followed up with independent verification, documentation of provisioning accomplished, and completion of the provisioning request form to be returned to management and archival.

Provisioning the user accounts typically includes the creation of accounts, disabling accounts when appropriate, and the eventual removal of user accounts. Permissions provisioning in mandatory access control (MAC) environments typically includes the requested clearance level of the user along with the need-to-know labels and other more specific access controls. Permissions provisioning in discretionary access control (DAC) environments typically includes the requested role or security groups to be assigned to.

The provisioning request is often initiated by the human relations (HR) department when a new employee is hired, or it is initiated by a manager of the user. The role (or perhaps the more detailed job description) of the worker should be included along with the start date and the various resource access privileges requested. This provisioning request document should be approved by:

- HR
- The manager of the user
- The security department, to weigh in on any conflicts of interest, separation-of-duty issues, privilege excess, and so on
- The business owner for final approval because he is responsible for all things within the division

You may have others to add to this list, as appropriate and (hopefully) defined by policy.

Permissions should always be requested, approved, and assigned following the principle of least privilege and a need to know. The request for elevated privileges, such as for administrator or root-level permissions or access to highly valued information assets, should require additional or more stringent review and approvals along with elevated monitoring and auditing defined by policy. More access should equate to more review, approvals, and monitoring.

If the provisioning request is related to an existing user but is a permissions adjustment, such as for a job transfer or promotion, the documentation should include all the previously mentioned details and the permissions to remove from the user. It is all too common for additional permissions to be granted as appropriate but left-over and unneeded permissions to remain, violating the principle of least privilege. This is referred to as *authorization creep* or *authorization aggregation*. Although a carefully documented and followed procedure tends to minimize authorization creep, periodic and randomized auditing of permissions by the operations team should be mandated by the policy documentation to detect and manage it.

User provisioning also includes periodic disabling or locking of user accounts, such as when a user takes time off work for an extended vacation or sabbatical, and the removal of access, privilege, and user accounts, but not monitoring, after a termination event. Again, the details of these procedures should all be defined within the policy documents, and the operations personnel should follow them carefully.

EXAM TIP

Be sure to understand the user provisioning life cycle:

- **New user account request**
- **Creation**
- **Privileging**
- **Adjusting privilege (adding/revoking)**
- **Auditing user's privilege**
- **Disabling**
- **Deleting**

Fraud protection

Fraud is the criminal act of intentionally deceiving a person or enterprise for the purpose of the theft of property, money, or other valuables or for implementing some other form of damage. In some cases, fraud can also be a violation of civil law. A recent study by the Association of Certified Fraud Examiners (ACFE) shows that on average, an enterprise loses 5 percent of its annual revenue to fraud, and fraud is most often committed by managers and subordinate workers but is also committed by owners and senior management.

Fraud is implemented in many forms, including:

- Mail fraud (postal service)
- Wire fraud (telegraph, radio, television)
- Internet fraud (phishing attacks, gaining unauthorized access, identity theft)
- Tax fraud
- Bank fraud
- Falsifying business records (cooking the books, willful integrity violations)
- Unauthorized disclosure (willful confidentiality violations)
- Extortion

Within the enterprise, fraud is most commonly committed by inappropriately altering data. Occasionally an external attacker, acting as an unauthorized user, might compromise one or more systems and alter the data of the enterprise to commit fraud, perhaps by adding a vendor and scheduled monthly payment to that vendor or by marking a customer account paid. However, most of the time, fraud is committed by an authorized insider committing fraud through a misuse of privilege.

Of course, it is better to deter fraud if possible, to dissuade the potential attacker from committing the fraud. This is mostly accomplished through awareness training and prudent hiring practices. The next best situation is to prevent fraud by implementing physical and technical access controls. The fallback position is to detect the fraud as early as possible to minimize the losses through awareness training, integrity verification mechanisms, monitoring and auditing, separation of duties, job rotation, and mandatory vacations. Most fraudulent activities are detected because of a tip from a coworker.

The controls used to deter, prevent, and detect fraud include the following measures.

Administrative controls

Administrative controls that are intended to deter, prevent, and detect fraud rely on the user's awareness of policies and laws that carry penalties for violation and by reinforcing in the minds of potential violators that the enterprise is aware of the potential for fraud; it is monitoring and responsive to any perceived violations. Security awareness training should identify the telltale signs of fraud and the obligation of users to report any anomalies.

- **Policies** Including monitoring procedures, auditing requirements, integrity protection requirements, integrity verification procedures, hiring practices
- **Security awareness training of the users and management** Including fraud-related training
- **Prudent hiring practices** Background checks, references checking, work history verification, criminal background checking, drug screening, polygraph testing, and other practices.
- **Integrity verification procedures** Manually verifying inventory, regular third-party accounting reviews

SEPARATION OF DUTIES

Don't grant any user enough privilege to commit fraud independently. If a role has the potential to accomplish this, break the tasks of the role up and assign those tasks separately to several people. For example, if a worker is assigned the roles of purchasing, accounts payable, and inventory control, the worker could order 100 widgets, pay for 100 widgets, and alter the data to show that only 50 widgets were purchased. Then when the widgets arrive, the same worker could steal 50 widgets and sell them online over the weekend. The worker has too much authority, can commit the fraud singlehandedly, and continue the fraud undetected for a long time, maximizing losses to the enterprise. This is, of course, a bad thing. With proper separation of duties in place, multiple employees would need to agree to work together to commit fraud. This is called collusion, which is a bad thing. First, separating duties forces the workers to collude to commit fraud. Second, it acts as a deterrent and makes the detection of the fraud substantially easier. Collusion is the position you want the workers to be in if there might be any ideas or opportunities for the workers to commit fraud.

- *Static separation of duties* defines specific tasks a specific worker or role may perform and those the worker may not perform. For example, a bank teller may provide cash out to a banking customer up to $1,000 without authorization by a bank supervisor. For any cash out in excess of $1,000, a bank supervisor must approve and sign the cash request.

- *Dynamic separation of duties* defines a set of specific tasks a specific worker or role may perform and under what specific conditions those tasks may and may not be performed. For example, a bank teller may provide cash out to a banking customer up to $1,000 without additional authorization, or that same bank teller may authorize cash out in excess of $1,000 but never both in the same transaction. You may be one role or the other, but never both on the same transaction.

JOB ROTATION

Require the workers to rotate to a different job within the enterprise periodically because, over time, as workers get to know one another and become friends, the barrier introduced by separation of duties erodes. It becomes easier for a worker to introduce the proposal to commit fraud against the enterprise. Job rotation disrupts this comfort zone among the workers because a new and unknown worker takes over the tasks of each individual participating in a vulnerable process. Further, if collusion and fraud are being committed, placing a new worker in the job role of the workers committing the fraud significantly increases the chance of identifying anomalies and fraudulent activities in those compromised job processes and data.

Although not directly related to fraud protection, job rotation also provides the benefit of cross training the employees, which can help minimize losses during vacations, incident response, and disaster response situations.

MANDATORY VACATIONS

Mandatory vacations provide a function similar to job rotation. If a worker is aware of the mandatory vacation, he knows that while he is on vacation, someone else is performing his tasks and overseeing processes in which data has been altered and no longer balances correctly without data manipulation. The replacement worker is very likely to identify the anomalies and report them, triggering an in-depth investigation. The fraud will be exposed, and the attacker will be punished, perhaps even jailed. Financial institutions and companies commonly use mandatory vacations for this purpose.

DUAL CONTROL

Dual control is commonly implemented when a single task carries a great deal of vulnerability and risk. If the asset is very valuable, perhaps no one person can be trusted to access it independently. However, by requiring more than one (often several) person for any access, again, collusion would be required to commit a breach, theft, or other form of fraud. Consider, for example, the archive of private keys from a public key infrastructure (PKI) environment. The archive is required so that any of the enterprise's PKI-encrypted information assets could be recovered if the data were encrypted with a user's public key. However, the recovery of any one private key, if recovered for malicious intent, could be a devastating loss to the enterprise. The recovery of these PKI private keys is usually too much authority for any one person to be trusted with, so the recovery techniques might require three (M) of six (N) authorized people to come together and recover the key(s). This M-of-N dual control function is implemented because very often one or more people will be out of the office for various reasons, so you need several to be authorized to recover keys but also a few of those people to participate in the recovery. This tends to substantiate only legitimate reasons for key recovery and reduces the likelihood that a key recovery procedure could be performed for illegitimate reasons.

EXAM TIP

Recognize the relationship among separation of duties, collusion, and job rotation as they relate to deterring and detecting fraud.

Physical access controls

If the potential attacker cannot get to the books, she cannot cook the books. These controls provide confidentiality and integrity protection. Physical access controls used to defend the enterprise against fraud include, among others:

- Fences
- Controlled entry
- Locked doors

Technical access controls

Technical access controls are programmatic functions and processes to keep the attacker away from data. These controls provide confidentiality and integrity protection. Technical access controls used to defend the enterprise against fraud include:

- Permissions implemented following the principle of least privilege
- Encryption
- Firewall rules
- Intrusion prevention rules

Technical detective controls

Technical detective controls are programmatic functions that typically identify changes or alterations of the data and perform integrity verification of the data. Technical controls used to detect fraud include:

- Monitoring and auditing users and their activities
- Integrity verification technologies
- Statistical analysis techniques applied to user activities, system logs, and transaction records
- Artificial intelligence applied to user activities, system logs, and transaction records

Vulnerability assessments

A vulnerability assessment is a subset of a security assessment. It is an analysis of the vulnerabilities inherent in the enterprise and might be limited to the information systems for the Certified Information Systems Security Professional (CISSP) and operations team. The vulnerability assessment is part of the business impact analysis of the DRP and BCP and a risk assessment. Periodic audits or inspections identify vulnerabilities, but several types of vulnerabilities should be monitored continuously.

Many laws and regulations require ongoing and periodic vulnerability assessments, often with very specific targets, tests, schedules, and reporting requirements. Vulnerability assessments are routinely carried out by internal operations personnel but often must also be performed periodically by approved third-party service providers.

Vulnerability scanning

Many organizations perform regular (some daily) automated vulnerability scans on critical information assets, often required by laws and regulations. These scans inspect the target systems for known vulnerabilities, usually known operating system, protocol, and application software vulnerabilities, and can identify configuration changes (part of change management) that might indicate a system misconfiguration, whether accidental or intentional. System misconfigurations violate policy and often increase the attack surface of systems, increasing the risk of a successful attack and resulting breach.

Some vulnerability scans compare the system configuration today with the system configuration from yesterday and then identify any differences. Another type of vulnerability scan compares the system configuration today with an established *gold standard system* that is a representation of the approved system configuration. These differences are then aligned with approved change requests. Any system configuration changes that do not align with approved change requests, or with the gold standard system, warrant an investigation.

Some examples of vulnerability scanning tools and services include Nessus, Open VAS, Qualys, Metasploit, and SAINT.

The list of known software vulnerabilities identified on a system are often rated by the level of criticality of the vulnerability and the level of confidence that the vulnerability is actually present on the system. Some of the vulnerabilities cannot be confirmed without additional credentials or testing. The vulnerability scan report typically includes the nature of the vulnerability, the nature of the possible exploit, the correction or update for the vulnerability if one exists, and a workaround procedure if the solution does not yet exist, but a known workaround does exist.

The list of known software vulnerabilities is maintained in a *common vulnerabilities and exposures (CVE) database* available on the Internet. Vulnerability-scanner software vendors usually maintain their own database but might merge their proprietary list with the publicly available CVE list, which can be accessed at *http://nvd.nist.gov/* and *http://cve.mitre.org/*.

Privileged users

Privileged users represent another type of vulnerability to the enterprise. These users require heightened access privileges to accomplish their assigned work. That heightened level of access could enable those users to violate security controls willfully or, if their systems become compromised, allow an external attacker heightened access to valuable information assets. Privileged users can include users with:

- Access to the more valuable information, physical, or financial assets
- Administrator-level or root-level system access to workstations, servers, or infrastructure systems
- The ability to carry or transmit valuable information outside the physically controlled confines of the facility, such as on laptops
- The physical, technical, or administrative ability to bypass security or monitoring controls
- The ability to approve an exception to policy and thus willfully violate a policy

A complete and regularly updated list of privileged users and their heightened privileges should be maintained. Privileged users should be required to take supplemental privileged-user security awareness training on at least an annual basis and following any violation of policy or breach related to their activities. These users require additional and specially targeted routine monitoring along with the more frequent spot check type of auditing of activities. These users should also be monitored for authorization creep more frequently than the less-privileged users are.

Penetration testing

Penetration testing is a subset of vulnerability assessment. The penetration testing team takes an adversarial position to the enterprise; its intent is to reveal the enterprise's effective security posture. The penetration testing team's objective is to identify vulnerabilities and covertly exploit those vulnerabilities. In addition to identifying existing vulnerabilities (some known, some previously unknown), the penetration test also tests the effectiveness of the monitoring and response mechanisms in place within the enterprise. Do the mechanisms identify the abnormal activities and breaches, how effectively, and do the monitoring and response teams recognize the nature and severity of the identified incidents?

Penetration testing (pen testing) typically targets the exploitation opportunities present on the enterprise network but might also include physical pen testing (Can an unauthorized person bypass physical security controls and penetrate the facility?) and social engineering testing (Can authorized users be tricked into providing unauthorized physical or network access to data?). Many IT-related laws and regulations require periodic penetration testing by internal or third-party teams and might define specific objectives and targets of the penetration test.

EXAM TIP

Understand the hierarchical nature of the highest level of evaluation, called security assessment, its subset, called vulnerability assessment, and the subset of vulnerability assessment, called penetration testing.

THE PENETRATION TESTING AGREEMENT

The nature of the pen test must be clearly defined in the agreement between senior management and the pen testing team. Some of the activities of a pen test could be perceived as criminal actions if the actions were not requested and authorized by someone, typically in senior management, with the authority to approve the tests. The signed document describing the requested activities might just become the "Get out of jail free" card if the penetration tester is caught in the act. The details to document in the agreement typically include the following:

- Target company
- Terms of engagement
- IT system penetration testing (network)
- Facility penetration testing (facility)
- Social engineering testing (personnel)
- Systems, areas, personnel to target
- Systems, areas, personnel to avoid targeting
- Start and stop date
- Attacker position (Internet [outsider], standard user [insider])
- Level of disclosure prior to and during the penetration testing
- Minimizing collateral damage statement
- Hold harmless clause
- Points of contact (typically senior management in case of emergency)
- Reporting requirements
- Confidentiality and nondisclosure clause
- Data protection requirements
- Payment terms (if external penetration testing team)
- Authorized signatures

TESTING SYSTEMS

Management should identify specific IT systems it wants or needs tested and the specific IT systems that should not be tested. The decision of which systems must be tested is usually driven by legal or regulatory compliance requirements, such as the systems within the scope of Payment Card Industry-Data Security Standard (PCI-DSS) compliance. Certain systems are critical to the ongoing activities of the enterprise, and management should identify these systems as ones not to be tested.

The process of exploiting software vulnerabilities in the operating system, applications, and firmware very often cause the target system to lock up or even restart. The attacker is trying to make the target system respond in a manner that was not designed or intended, so the systems often become unstable or fail during the exploitation phase of the attack. Usually, demonstrating a successful denial-of-service (DoS) attack is not the objective of the penetration test; the objective is to compromise the system covertly, pillage the information assets, leave innocuous markers (a nonmalicious file with predefined text) to prove access later, and then use that compromised system to penetrate deeper into the IT environment. Although the pen testing team is not trying to break systems, system crashes are often a byproduct of the testing process. For the systems that are critical to the business operations, this might not be acceptable, and the penetration testing team must be advised of these requirements.

A clear definition should be provided in the pen testing agreement, indicating "Target these systems" and "Do not target those systems."

TESTING FACILITIES

Pen testers might be requested to penetrate the facility to test the physical access controls. Usually by using social engineering tactics, the penetration testing team attempts to enter restricted areas such as data centers, wiring closets, and perhaps even the offices of senior management without proper authorization. Some penetration testing teams have a small card or adhesive decal printed to be planted wherever unauthorized access has been accomplished, once again as proof of the level of penetration into the facility.

A penetration tester dressed in overalls, a little sweaty and a little dirty, with a tool belt, a ladder, and a yellow sheet of paper that might just be a work order, looking a little frustrated and determined, brushes past a secretary, muttering under his breath about "everybody needing their stuff right now, darn it!" might just bypass the access control and enter the facility. Another approach is to call an authorized user to a meeting and then present some product or service (which doesn't even have to be real) to gain a level of access. When inside, the tester sees how much further access can be gained. Again, management might identify specific areas to attempt penetrating and other areas to avoid testing.

Often included in this physical portion of the pen testing is *dumpster diving*. Dumpster diving is the process of rummaging through the contents of the trash containers of the enterprise, the documents and other content that are thrown away, collecting and then inspecting the collected content for sensitive information. Of course, all sensitive content should be effectively destroyed when it is disposed of, but it often is not destroyed first. If a dumpster diver enters private property and is caught there, she might be charged with trespassing, but taking content from a Dumpster is not usually illegal or prosecutable. In most places, when anything is placed in a container for collection by the trash company, the ownership of the item is abandoned. Effectively, nobody owns it at that point, so the contents can't be declared stolen. The trespasser might have to pay a fine to the county, but he is likely to keep anything he takes. Dumpster diving identifies the effectiveness, awareness, compliance level, and mechanisms of the secure disposal policies.

TESTING PERSONNEL

 The *social engineer* impersonates or masquerades as someone who should be trusted by the authorized user and then uses that misplaced trust to manipulate the authorized user and gain unauthorized access to information, resources (sometimes financial), or controlled locations. Although there are many angles on social engineering, in the corporate world, they usually rely on one of the following premises:

- **Position of authority**   A phone call from (supposedly) one of the members of the board of directors requiring access.

- **By association**   A phone call stating that "Your boss asked me to call you and get [something]," or "My father, Mr. Soandso on the board of directors, needs his password reset."

- **In need of help**   Hands full and needing help with a door or "Can you show me how to connect to the file server?"

- **Providing help**   A call from the help desk trying to correct a problem (that doesn't exist) and needs your password to complete the repair or the busy and dirty repairman described earlier.

- **Inciting curiosity or greed**   Dropping a few USB thumb drives in the parking lot, the lobby, or the restrooms. The thumb drives contain exploit content that executes automatically when they are mounted by the file system, compromising the victim's computer or "You've won a prize! Click here to claim your valuable prize!"

- **Combinations thereof**   The phishing email describing the $12.5 million tied up in a secret account of the now deceased husband or politician in a bank in Nigeria. The person needs someone honest—like you, for example—to help her recover the money. She is willing to split the money with you if you would only help.

In the noncorporate world, in addition to these angles, many of the social engineering attacks elicit response by offering the classic "sex, drugs, or rock and roll" by promoting websites for pornography, Viagra, or free MP3 music and song lyrics. The website from which the goodies can be acquired also contains malicious content to compromise the computer of the target. The unfortunate part of social engineering as part of penetration testing is that, if successful, the compromised target can face professional repercussions, a regrettable aspect. However, if personnel are not properly trained and always on guard against social engineering, the entire enterprise can be easily, successfully, and completely compromised. Vulnerabilities in this area must be identified so that remedial training requirements can be identified and performed to mitigate or eliminate these vulnerabilities to manipulation and compromise through social engineering.

THE STARTING POSITION OF THE ATTACKER

The objective of some penetration tests might be to identify the vulnerabilities the enterprise manifests from the perspective of the Internet. In this case, the penetration testing team might be provided with the URL of the web servers for the enterprise. The pen testers must study the target and begin their attack from this position, with little or no knowledge of the target company. This will identify the security posture as seen by the outsider, the competitor, or hacker with access limited to connectivity over the Internet and only through (at least initially) the publicly exposed servers (web servers, FTP servers, DNS servers, and so on).

In other cases, a member of the pen testing team might be provided with a standard user account and physical access to the office, a desk, and a standard corporate computer. This would identify the vulnerabilities available to compromise from the insider's perspective. Management might explain the presence of the new worker simply as a temporary contractor working on a special project.

THE LEVEL OF DISCLOSURE

Three teams are directly involved in the penetration test. The *white team* comprises the senior managers, often with additional advisors that establish the rules of engagement and then monitor the pen testing activities, perhaps even requiring adjustments in the tactics, targets, and other factors during the penetration testing. The white team might define and document metrics and develop the post assessment report to management. The *blue team* includes the security operations team (if one exists), the incident response team, and the operations team who are there to monitor, detect incidents, and defend the information systems in case of an incident. Finally, the *red team* comprises the penetration testers who are assigned the task of attempting to violate the security of the information systems and environment. Historically, the red team was also known as the tiger team.

The white team defines, within the pen testing agreement, how much information about the pen test is made available to the blue team and the red team.

If the blue team is unaware that a penetration test is underway, and the red team is provided only the URL of the target enterprise, this is referred to as *no disclosure, double blind testing*, meaning neither team has an information advantage over the opponent. This type of testing provides a more realistic picture of the security posture of the enterprise but often either requires more time to run the penetration tests (and the accompanying increased costs and risks) or provides only a small amount of data. This is because with little or no information about the target, the red team must do much more homework and move more slowly and carefully.

The next level of testing is called *partial disclosure, blind* (sometimes *single blind),* or *grey box testing.* Either the blue team or the red team is provided with information but not both, placing that informed team at an information advantage over the opposing team. Management might advise the blue team that penetration testing will be performed during some specified time period. This helps ensure diligent monitoring and incident response and a heightened level of defense and resistance, enabling that team to exercise its skills and improve its abilities. Alternatively, management might provide the red team with network diagrams and a standard user account with access to the network but not tell the blue team anything is going on.

When the attacking (red) team is specifically not provided any insight into the internal workings of the networking and computing environment of the enterprise, it is more specifically referred to as *black box testing.* Black box testing shows the enterprise what a skilled *outsider attacker* might be able to exploit successfully as well as a more realistic assessment of the vulnerabilities, the damages, and the losses that could occur from such an attack, based on the current security posture of the enterprise. In this case, the black box testing team must move covertly and, like the double blind testing, might take longer, cost more, and reveal fewer vulnerabilities.

The third level of disclosure is *full disclosure,* or *white box testing,* when both the red team and the blue team are provided information about the penetration testing activities and the IT environment. This is the most efficient penetration testing because it can happen more quickly, reducing costs, but might not represent the true, normal security posture of the enterprise accurately. White box testing shows the enterprise what a skilled *insider attacker* might be able to exploit successfully and what the maximum damages and losses might be from such a pervasive attack, based on the current security posture of the enterprise with no increase in the defenses or resistance. In this case, the white box penetration testing team might not be required to move covertly and will be well informed of how and where they should move, so it is a more efficient testing technique and typically shows higher levels of penetration, potential damage, and potential losses to the enterprise.

If the pen testing is driven by legal or regulatory compliance requirements, the level of disclosure might be mandated by those testing requirements.

HOLD HARMLESS

Although it will be clearly identified as an objective by the white team, and best efforts will be ensured by the red team, the nature of an exploit (the activities requested and required in a pen test) is to misuse the system and make it behave in a manner that was not planned or intended. When an exploit is launched at a target system, unexpected results can often occur. Systems lock up, databases and other data might become corrupt, and occasionally, operating systems crash and reboot in their attempt at trusted recovery.

In addition, the white team will identify systems that the pen testing team is not to attack, so these do-not-target critical systems remain online to support the critical business functions. However, information systems are quite interconnected. It is not uncommon for an attack on an OK-to-target-system to cause it to malfunction and, by its communication with a do-not-target-system, cause the do-not-target-system to have problems.

These damages introduce losses to the enterprise and incur recovery costs. It must be clearly identified that the red team will apply serious effort to avoid breaking any systems or processes and introducing any losses to the enterprise during the execution of the pen test. However, because of the unpredictable nature of penetration testing, the enterprise must hold the penetration testing team and company harmless for any liability or damages resulting from the penetration testing.

CONFIDENTIALITY

The white team requires the pen testing team to keep secret any information it might be provided or acquire during the testing process. This is usually implemented through a *confidentiality agreement* (*nondisclosure agreement*) as part of the pen testing agreement.

The pen testing team typically documents every tactic used, successful or not, and the results of that exploit attempt. When successful, the nature of the successful attack is sensitive. (If the real bad guys were to learn this information, they would attack the enterprise successfully!) The penetration testing team might reveal and collect sensitive data. It must be recognized how critically sensitive all the data the pen testing team is aggregating is and how strongly the pen testing team must protect that sensitive information. If this information were to leak somehow, the damages to the enterprise might be catastrophic. The penetration testing team must strongly exercise every protective measure to ensure that the data collected and the eventual reports and data supplied to management remain confidential.

Reporting

The white team typically assigns specific start and stop dates to penetration testing activities. When such activities are complete, the pen testing team organizes and compiles the results into a report it presents to management. In most cases, the reporting requirements are defined during the initial negotiations and agreement phase. The reporting details might even be defined by the laws and regulations that apply to the enterprise. The report typically contains two major sections: the executive summary and the technical report.

THE EXECUTIVE SUMMARY

The executive summary describes the objectives of the test and the high-level findings. To establish the objectives of the test, the background of the penetration testing activities is detailed, including the nature of the testing (network, facility, personnel), the specific targets and objectives, the start and stop dates, the disclosure level, and the starting point of the attackers. A summary of the overall security posture of the enterprise identifies the nature of the significant security issues found and the level of risk, the potential impact the enterprise faces in its present state of security. This is usually followed by the general findings broken down by metrics showing the effectiveness of the current security structure and the causes of the vulnerabilities, such as missing updates, vulnerable software, weak passwords, and network architectural design flaws.

The executive summary should also include specific remediation recommendations and operational task plans for the immediate future (up to 3 months), tactical task plans for the near future (3 to 12 months), and strategic task plans for long-term and ongoing improvements in the security posture of the enterprise. This section tells management what things to fix and provides some level of guidance and instruction on how to fix them.

THE TECHNICAL REPORT

The technical report describes in detail the methods, tactics, and attack paths used during the pen testing activities. Typically, the pen testing team records or otherwise documents every action taken during the pen test. From this volume of information, the successful exploits will be included in some level of detail in the technical report. The unsuccessful exploits will also be listed as an indicator of effective controls that are in place. The penetration testing activities typically include every phase of an attack, stopping just short of malicious and damaging activities. The anatomy of an attack is described in detail in the "Anatomy of a targeted attack" section later in this chapter.

Typically, the pen testing team provides all documentation to the management and securely purges and destroys any copies to avoid potential exposure or leak of such sensitive information. Therefore, at the completion of the presentation of the report, management has the only copy of the information collected during the penetration test. Management must securely archive this information because this report and supporting information is usually the starting point for next year's penetration testing activities. This is to verify that the vulnerabilities identified last year have been successfully eliminated or mitigated in accordance with those findings and recommendations.

A penetration test is a snapshot in time, and the activities are limited in duration, so the snapshot is a summary of what could be identified during the (usually too small) time window for testing. Given more time, the pen testers will likely identify more vulnerabilities and attack vectors. Moreover, in the weeks and months following the pen test, new vulnerabilities will manifest that affect the security posture of the enterprise.

EXAM TIP

Understand the details to be included in the penetration testing agreement:

- Nondisclosure and confidentiality
- Scope
    - Specific targets and tests
    - Hands-off targets
    - Testing timeframe
    - Disclosure level
    - Full or white box testing
    - Partial, blind, or grey box testing
    - Black box testing
    - No disclosure, double blind
    - Hold harmless: not my fault, the oops factor
    - Reporting requirements

Incident response

The operations team is usually responsible for assisting with incident response activities. They provide the hands-on support. As the incident response team identifies specific containment, corrective, eradication, and recovery techniques, the operations team usually performs the prescribed work to accomplish those objectives. The incident response process is described in detail in Chapter 6, "Legal, regulations, investigations, and compliance."

 Quick check

1. What are the roles relative to operations security?
2. What techniques are used to deter and detect fraud?

Quick check answers

1. Data owner, manager, custodian, user
2. Principle of least privilege, separation of duties, job rotation, mandatory vacations, dual control, auditing, integrity protection, integrity validation

Data management

Policies define how data is to be managed and protected in the enterprise. The operations department is typically responsible for the implementation of the technologies and procedures to satisfy the required management of the data in compliance with those policies, procedures, standards, baselines, and guidelines.

Data management includes:

- The secure storage and transmission of data
- Media management (including removable media)
- Maintaining the systems that store and transmit the data
- Ensuring the availability of the data
- Implementing data redundancy for recovery purposes
- Maintaining the data retention store (archive)
- Secure destruction of unneeded data
- Securely wiping data when media is to be reused
- Protecting faxed data

Data classification

Data classification is described in detail in Chapter 1, "Information security and risk management." However, at a high level, data classification involves the following activities:

- Defining data classification as a requirement along with procedures for the enterprise within policy documents
- Producing an inventory of the data elements
- Establishing a value (sensitivity level) for each data element
- Defining classification levels and appropriate protective controls for each classification
- Classifying each data element based on its value
- Labeling each data element (and removable media) based on its classification
- Implementing the required protective controls for each data element based on its classification and defined by the policy documents
- Training all users on the data classification policies and procedures
- Monitoring the information system environment to verify that the required protective measures are being consistently and effectively implemented by all users and administrators (members of the operations department)

The operations team is typically responsible for some labeling of the data and for the implementation of the various and specific technical and physical controls required by policy to protect the data at its classification level. Those controls include the implementation of permissions, encryption for data at rest, and encryption for data in transit.

Media management

Media store data and include hard disk drives (internal), optical disks, backup tapes, USB flash drives, and external hard disk drives. Internal hard disk drives are typically well protected and aren't moved around much. The removable media presents a special security concern because of its portability. The use of removable media by users must be addressed in the corporate policy documents, presented in security awareness training, and then monitored and policy enforced to control the potential disclosure risks and potential risk of malware infection. Through a combination of administrative policies, technical controls, and physical controls, some enterprises actually do not allow users to connect external disks and other forms of removable media to the corporate systems. For example, in November 2008, several branches of the US Department of Defense (DoD) declared that "effective immediately all USB thumb drives, memory sticks/cards and camera flash cards are PROHIBITED from use on any . . . Network (NIPR or SIPR) until further notice."

The members of the operations department perform some of their work as standard users, so those same standard user rules and controls apply, but the members of the operations department also operate as data and systems custodians and administrators, so another set of policies and controls apply under those conditions.

Operations is commonly responsible for the production and secure handling of backup tapes. Proper data classification labeling of the tapes is essential. Secure transportation and storage of the tapes is also essential. Some enterprises use armed guards and armored trucks to transport their backup tapes to secure, offsite storage locations. Regular pickups of the backup tapes are scheduled, and tape retrieval within specified delivery time limits, in case of recovery needs, are contractually defined.

Internal disks and authorized external, removable disks should be wiped securely before reusing them on different systems or by different users. If third-party service providers will be replacing hard disk drives, these providers must be properly governed to remain in compliance with the policies of the enterprise, including in their training, awareness, monitoring, auditing, and enforcement of the policy details.

The operations department and third-party service providers are also commonly responsible for the secure destruction of internal disk drives and removable media when the media are no longer needed or useful to the enterprise.

The media library

Many of the more developed enterprises implement a media library, a central point for the management of software, media, and software licenses within the organization. Operations is often responsible for this media library, which becomes the chokepoint for access to all approved and installable software on servers and client systems and approved, properly labeled, and securely wiped removable media. This library is often held accountable for the proper maintenance and monitoring of the owned and consumed software licenses.

Maintaining the systems that support the data

The operations department is responsible for the ongoing maintenance of the systems that support the data assets. From the planned replacement of older parts and systems to the emergency repair of failed components, a primary function of the operations team is to maintain the availability of those information systems, services, and data.

Ongoing risk assessment and risk management activities should be performed to identify areas of vulnerability, threat, and risk. Cost-justified preventive countermeasures should be proposed to management for approval and implementation. The risk assessment should identify *single points of failure* that could cost the enterprise the availability of its valuable and critical information assets and should also identify planned replacement schedules for aging hardware.

Mean time between failures (MTBF)

Many devices and systems an enterprise needs and uses within its information systems are provided with a statistical appraisal of the estimated functional lifetime of the device or system. This estimate is called the *mean time between failures (MTBF)* and should be used to plan and schedule the proactive replacement of components as they approach the end of their expected functional lifetime. This proactive planning helps with budgeting, purchasing, and the coordinated scheduling of downtime for these devices to perform the replacements. The absence of this proactive planned and scheduled replacement of parts leads to the emergency replacement or even disaster recovery near the time the MTBF is reached, when the device actually fails.

Generally speaking, the more complex a component or system, the shorter the MTBF is for the device or system. Having many more parts in a device increases the odds that one of those parts could fail today.

An associated term is the *mean time to repair (MTTR)*. This is a statistical appraisal of how long it should take to repair or replace a device or system. It is also commonly used in planning these scheduled and proactive replacement of aging parts and becomes a critical factor within the DRP if and when the components fail unexpectedly, creating a potential disaster situation for the enterprise. The MTTR must be reduced to a time well below the maximum tolerable downtime (MTD) for the systems that support the critical functions. The DRP and the MTD are described in detail in Chapter 8, "Business continuity and disaster recovery planning."

Single points of failure

Because one of the primary concerns of the operations department is to ensure availability of the information systems and data, one angle of the ongoing risk assessment is to identify single points of failure when if only one component of the system fails, the availability of that system also fails. The objective is to reduce or eliminate these vulnerabilities and the associated risks. This is usually accomplished by increasing the system resilience through improving the system *fault tolerance* and by providing device, system, and data *redundancy*.

Fault tolerance implies that a system or device can fail, yet the data and services the system or device supports remain functional and available. Redundancy provides at least two of the specified system, device, or copies of the data.

Redundant Array of Independent Disks (RAID)

Historically, data was written to discrete, nonintegrated hard disk drives, often referred to as *just a bunch of disks* (*JBOD*). To improve disk drive performance, fault tolerance, and data redundancy, hard disk drives can be assembled in various arrays. Redundant Array of Independent Disks (RAID) levels 0, 1, and 5, and combinations thereof, are the most commonly used RAID arrays.

EXAM TIP

Over many years, some vendors have produced proprietary versions of RAID arrays that use the same labels but are different from those described here, so some discrepancy in the various RAID designations might occur. Although it is unlikely, if the exam targets one of these ambiguous RAID levels, read the question and answer set carefully and proceed confidently by choosing the answer that seems most accurate based on your knowledge of the levels of RAID.

- **RAID 0: Stripe Set** RAID 0 is the best performing of all the RAID arrays. It requires a minimum of two disk drives, and the maximum number of disks is usually capped by software drivers or hardware capacity. A maximum of 32 disks in a stripe set is not uncommon.

  The two or more disks are logically aggregated in a single volume, and the data is striped across all the disks in the RAID 0 array. Because the disks can be written to and read from (input/output operations, or I/O) simultaneously, the performance is improved as disks are increased in the array. The formula for read and write time is $T = 1/N$, where T equals the time it takes to complete the I/O operation, and N equals the number of disks used in the RAID 0 array.

  If a file takes 1 second to write to a single disk drive, that same file would take $1/N$ time to write on the RAID 0 array. If using 32 disks in the RAID 0 array, that same file would take about 0.030 seconds (1 second/32) to write. Figure 10-2 shows a three-disk RAID 0 array in which data (four files labeled, A, B, C, and D) are striped across each of the three disks in the array.

  The RAID 0 array provides no fault tolerance or data redundancy. If any one disk fails in the RAID 0 array, all data stored on the array are lost. As a matter of fact, the RAID 0 array is more likely to lose all data stored on the array than if the data were stored on a single disk drive. This is because by increasing the number of disks in the array, there is a greater chance of any one of the many disks in the RAID 0 array failing today than the chance of the failure of a single disk when the data is written to one disk.

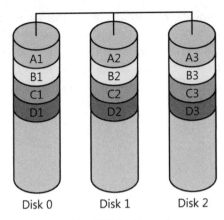

FIGURE 10-2 The RAID 0 stripe set

- **RAID 1 disk mirroring** The RAID 1 disk array requires two disks, typically of approximately the same size (and usually performance level). Each disk receives a copy of the same data, providing one-disk fault tolerance and data redundancy. If either disk fails, the other disk contains a full copy of the data and can be accessed. The two disks are both labeled with the same volume label so that when the operating system and file system performs a read or write function to the volume, both disks respond. The RAID 1 array provides no performance boost or degradation, but because it provides the one-disk fault tolerance and the data redundancy, it is one of the most secure disk arrays to ensure availability. The RAID 1 disk array has the greatest overhead, however, at 50 percent. If two 1 TB disks are used in the RAID 1 array, there is only 1 TB of usable space because two copies of everything are written. Figure 10-3 shows the RAID 1 disk mirror array.

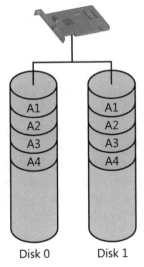

FIGURE 10-3 The RAID 1 disk mirror

- **Disk duplex** This is a hardware enhancement for the RAID 1 disk mirror. An additional disk controller is installed so that each disk has its own independent disk controller. This makes the disk controller redundant and fault tolerant. With the additional disk controller installed, if either disk controller or either hard disk drive fails, the other controller and disk remain available. Figure 10-4 shows the disk duplex, the redundant disk controller hardware enhancement to the RAID 0 disk mirror array.

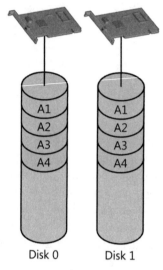

Disk 0   Disk 1

FIGURE 10-4 The disk duplex, a hardware enhancement to the RAID 1 disk mirror

- **RAID 2** This is a rarely used bit-level parity stripe set. It used hamming code to produce bit-level parity on 7 parity disks and striped the data across 32 data disks, requiring 39 disks total.

- **RAID 3** A rarely used byte-level parity stripe set. It produced byte-level parity on 1 parity disk and striped the data across some number of (2 minimum) data disks, requiring 3 disks minimum.

- **RAID 4** A rarely used block-level parity stripe set. It produced block-level parity on 1 parity disk and striped the data across some number of (2 minimum) data disks, requiring 3 disks minimum.

- **RAID 5 stripe set with parity** RAID 5 arrays provide block level parity with data and parity striped across all disks. This provides good performance and one-disk fault tolerance but no data redundancy. The RAID 5 array requires a minimum of 3 disk drives and, like several others, has a maximum capacity limited by the software and hardware capacity of the vendor who provides the array. Figure 10-5 shows the RAID 5 stripe set with parity array.

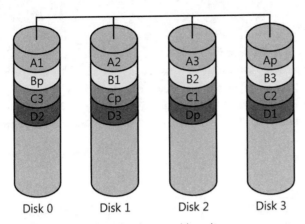

Disk 0   Disk 1   Disk 2   Disk 3

FIGURE 10-5 The RAID 5 stripe set with parity

The read/write performance benefit of the RAID 5 array is $T = 1/(N - 1)$ where T equals the time it takes to complete the I/O operation, and N equals the number of disks used in the RAID 5 array. This is because one disk on each stripe in the array has parity information written to it, not actual data. If a file takes 1 second to write to a single disk drive, that same file would take $1/(N - 1)$ time to write on the RAID 5 array. When using 4 disks in the RAID 5 array, that same file would take about 0.33 seconds (1 second/3) to write. When using 32 disks in the RAID 5 array, that same file would take about 0.032 seconds (1 second/31) to write—just a little slower than the RAID 0 array. The overhead of the RAID 5 array is equivalent to one disk drive. That volume is used to store the parity information that is interleaved across all disks but totals the size of one disk in the array.

- **RAID 10**   This is a mirrored (RAID 1) pair of stripe sets (RAID 0), the best-performing array that includes disk fault tolerance and data redundancy. Build two stripe sets and then mirror those stripe sets. This array provides single-disk fault; the data remains online and fully available and could provide multiple-disk fault tolerance as long as the multiple disks fail in the same stripe set (not something you want to rely on, though).

- **RAID 15**   This is a mirrored (RAID 1) pair of stripe sets with parity (RAID 5). This is a very well-performing array that includes multiple-disk fault tolerance and data redundancy. Build two stripe sets with parity and then mirror those stripe sets with parity. This array provides multiple disk fault tolerance, tolerating one-disk failure in each stripe set with parity plus one additional disk failure in either stripe set with parity, and the data remains online and fully available.

Parity

The parity used on the RAID 5 array (and several other RAID arrays) is a one-bit hash calculation that allows one bit of data to be lost or destroyed and then logically recovered. There are several implementations of parity. In the following 4-disk RAID 5 array example, even parity is used. The data to be protected by the even parity in this RAID 5 example will be 011010000111100.

Stripe the first three data bits across disks 0, 1, and 2, respectively. Add a fourth parity bit, either a 0 or a 1, so that when adding all 4 bits in the stripe (the 3 data bits plus the 1 parity bit), the answer is an even number (0, 2, 4). In this first stripe, the parity bit will be a 0. The parity bit is written on disk 3 and will be designated in Table 10-1 with the *P* on each stripe. 011 Parity bit = 0.

Shift over one disk and stripe next the three data bits across disks 1, 2, and 3, respectively. The parity bit will be written on disk 0. Shifting to the next disk causes the parity information to be interleaved across all disks for a small performance benefit. Add a fourth parity bit, either a 0 or a 1, so that when adding all 4 bits in the second stripe, the answer is an even number (0, 2, 4). In this second stripe, the parity bit will be a 1. The parity bit is written on disk 0 in this second stripe and is designated in the table with the *P*. 010 Parity bit = 1.

This striping, calculating parity, and interleaving parity information is shown in Table 10-1.

TABLE 10-1 Data and parity information (P), striped and interleaved across 4 disk drives in a RAID 5 array

Bit on disk 0	Bit on disk1	Bit on disk 2	Bit on disk 3
0	1	1	0 P
1 P	0	1	0
0	0 P	0	0
1	1	1 P	1
1	0	0	1 P

Complete the shifting over one disk and striping three bits across three hard disk drives and then add the correct parity bit for each stripe on the fourth disk.

- First stripe of data: 011 Parity bit = 0
- Second stripe of data: 010 Parity bit = 1
- Third stripe of data: 000 Parity bit = 0
- Fourth stripe of data: 111 Parity bit = 1
- Fifth stripe of data: 100 Parity bit = 1

With this accomplished during the write function for all data on the RAID 5 array, any one disk can fail, and the data the failed disk held can be logically calculated during any read I/O operations. Cover any column in Table 10-1, and by calculating the even parity (used in this example), the missing data bits are easily determined. The parity information does not need to be calculated for the missing disk during the read functions because it isn't part of the real data and can be ignored.

Redundant Array of Independent Tapes (RAIT)

This technology takes advantage of the performance benefits and the fault tolerance and redundancy benefits of the RAID arrays but applies them to tape backups. The tapes are much less expensive, much slower, sequentially written to and read from, and removable for remote storage. Tapes are usually used for offline data archives but can be directly attached for slow, large storage and always available access.

Storage area networks (SAN)

The storage area network (SAN) is a network-attached, large collection of data storage services provided to the users of the information systems. SAN systems are quite expensive and are sometimes privately owned or might be leased from public SAN operators, with the latter often being referred to as *cloud storage services*, or *storage as a service (SaaS)*, a sub-component of *infrastructure as a service (IaaS)*.

SAN systems commonly include hard disk drive arrays, optical disk (CD/DVD) jukeboxes, and libraries of tapes used to establish a comprehensive *hierarchical storage management (HSM)* solution, moving the less used data to slower, cheaper, and larger-volume storage systems. Connectivity of the SAN to its supported users is most often accomplished over high-speed and long-distance connections such as *high-speed fiber channel*. Users are typically unaware of the remoteness of the data at the SAN. Figure 10-6 shows a typical SAN network architecture.

The SAN typically includes multiple layers of disk I/O performance improvements, fault tolerance, redundancy, and remote storage capabilities. Further, the SAN operators are typically responsible for providing high availability of the data and for all data recovery and disaster recovery technologies and activities.

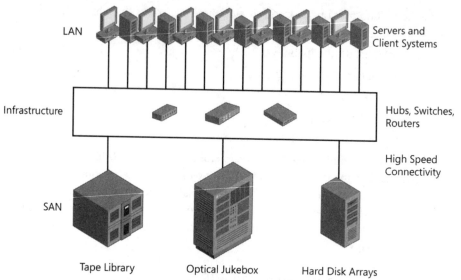

FIGURE 10-6 A typical storage area network (SAN) architecture

SAN systems provide *block-level storage* of data, in contrast to the *network attached storage (NAS)* systems that use *file-level storage* such as *network file system (NFS)*, *server message blocks (SMB)*, or the *common Internet file system (CIFS)* used on standard Windows—or Linux-based computers and servers.

Massive array of inactive disks (MAID)

The massive array of inactive disks (MAID) is a relatively new technology most often used in large SAN storage. This technology spreads the data files over many hard disk drives, incorporating hundreds or even thousands of drives. Then, if the files on a specific disk are not being accessed, that disk can spin down. This saves on power consumption and cooling requirements and extends the life of the disks in the MAID array. This array can also be referred to as a massive array of idle disks (MAID).

Because the disks are not arrayed for improved performance, fault tolerance, or redundancy benefits, these behave similarly to the JBOD storage systems described earlier in this section, but with power management features included. Because the spin-down and spin-up functions tend to wear standard consumer-level PATA and SATA disks, disk drives used in the MAID are designed for frequent speed changes, costing more and performing worse than the more standard disk drives.

Hierarchical storage management

Typically, the more current, useful, and valuable the data is to the users of the enterprise, the more accessible it must be. As that currency, usefulness, and value are reduced over time, that data should be moved to less expensive storage but, ideally, remain available online just in case someone might need a historical review. This is the concept behind the hierarchical storage

management (HSM) system. Move the data from the fast, very accessible, and relatively expensive hard disk drives to slower and less expensive optical disks and then on to slower and
least expensive tape libraries. Although it might take a few minutes to get a file off the optical
disks or tape because the content remains online, the user can locate and request the content
for (eventual) delivery and access.

Server redundancy

Servers are typically the higher-powered, greater-capacity, always-online systems that provide many of the networking and data services in the enterprise. These include data storage
systems such as file servers and database servers, application servers that perform the data
manipulation and processing services, and infrastructure servers that provide authentication,
IP address assignments, and name resolution services. These server class systems are often
located together to simplify administration and provide appropriate and common physical
access and security control. This location is commonly called the data center but can also be
called the *server farm*.

To improve performance and increase capacity and high availability, these critical systems
are often assembled in a manner to support clustering of the critical services the servers
provide. Clustering services places the server applications on more than one server and then
establishes communications between the multiple instances of the server application called
the *heartbeat*. The heartbeat is sent to the servers in the cluster typically once per second.
Although each discrete server is assigned a unique IP address, the cluster service shared by
the multiple systems is assigned a common IP address itself. Clients access the cluster service
by using the *cluster IP address*, not the server's IP addresses.

Some server applications are stateless, meaning that the application does not need to
track discrete user sessions. These *stateless applications* include web services (HTTP) and DNS,
for example, where the communications are unauthenticated and simple queries from the client with simple responses from the server. A user submits a request for service, and the server
provides the information. End of story.

In contrast to the stateless applications and services, a *stateful application* must remember
each client session and at what stage each client currently is within the process or transaction of the stateful application. Stateful applications commonly include transaction-oriented
database applications, authenticated processes and transactions, and applications in which
the data processing might take many sequential steps.

Stateless applications can be clustered by using simple load balancing. In this case, the
cluster heartbeat simply lets the other members of the *load balanced cluster* know which
clustered servers are still awake and functioning so proper load balancing can occur. Stateless
applications often access static types of data such as HTTP content, so it is not uncommon for
each server offering the stateless service to store its own copy of the static content. As a new
request for service arrives at the cluster IP address (an IP address common across all servers
in the load balanced cluster), the system with the lowest load (typically) is assigned that client
request. When a server goes offline, other servers do not hear its heartbeat and therefore
cannot be assigned any new client requests, so the servers load balance inbound requests

for that service among the remaining available load balanced cluster servers. The heartbeat contains a small amount of data and is often sent over the client network by using the same network interfaces on the servers where client requests arrive.

Stateful applications are typically much more dynamic in nature, running longer processes and performing multistep transaction processing. These systems often access a single, shared data repository to manage concurrency, consistency, and latency issues. Stateful applications operating in a *failover cluster* must share the state of every client session each server is maintaining. This is much more information communicated within the heartbeat, so the stateful, failover cluster servers usually require a dedicated, private network for the heartbeat. The heartbeat includes the pulse from the server notifying the other servers that it is awake and functional, and the heartbeat from each server includes the current state of each client session the server is servicing. These requirements typically make the stateful, failover cluster more complex and expensive than the simpler, load balanced cluster server array. Figure 10-7 shows a typical stateful, failover cluster of SQL servers with shared storage.

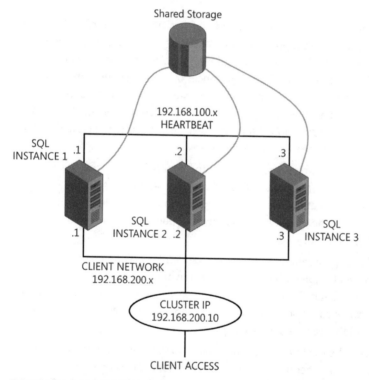

FIGURE 10-7 A typical SQL cluster

Collocation

As a business continuity protection measure to provide some distance between multiple systems providing information services, systems are placed at multiple locations; this is called collocation. Collocation is used with stateless applications and the less-dynamic type of data to avoid concurrency, consistency, and latency issues with client sessions and between data sets. Often, space, server hardware, and operating systems in a remote data center are leased, and the enterprise simply installs the necessary applications and copies of the required (usually static) data. Leasing these components usually helps hold down the cost of the collocation system. Load balancing is usually used between the multiple collocation sites, and some form of redirection is required if and when a location becomes unavailable.

The larger distance between locations minimizes the risk of multiple locations being affected by a single disaster event.

Service-level agreements (SLAs)

As stated previously, the primary mission of operations is to maintain availability (of course, properly peppered with security). Many organizations outsource some of the challenges of maintaining availability by paying a third party to provide service and replacement parts as needed within specified time frames. These contracts are called service-level agreements (SLA). These agreements are usually established by paying the third-party service provider a monthly or annual fee as a retainer and can include stipulations for some level of labor hours and replacement parts. Additional hours and parts are often provided for additional fees.

The response and repair time limits must satisfy business needs and must definitely satisfy the MTD defined by the business impact analysis (BIA)—as described in Chapter 8—if the SLA is used as part of the DRP. Shorter response and repair times, of course, typically translate to higher SLA contract costs.

Data backups

Data backups are a routine procedure for virtually every enterprise. The classic data backup produces a second copy of all the critical data of the enterprise on magnetic tapes. These tapes are then securely transported to a secure offsite location to protect them in case of the destruction of the facility. Tapes provide a large removable storage volume and are slow and inexpensive. Most backup systems place the flagged file content in a proprietary format on the tape and usually provide compression and encryption. These same applications are used then to perform any necessary data restore.

The administrator of the backup system identifies all content intended for the backup by adding it to the *catalog* for the backup procedure. This selection of valuable content is defined by policy through data classification and the resulting required protection procedures. Next, because data backups are a batch process occurring only periodically, a *backup schedule* is defined. It is also defined by policy and data classification and is the result of the *recovery point objective* (RPO). The RPO identifies how much data the enterprise is willing to lose in case of disk drive or other forms of device failure resulting in data loss. This is balanced against the costs of performing the backups, which includes the tape itself, the degradation on the servers, and the degradation of performance of the network. When losing any record of transactions or other data collection and processing becomes too expensive, shorten the time interval between backup jobs. Shorter time intervals between backups increase those costs.

 There are primarily three types of backups: the *full backup,* an *incremental backup,* and a *differential backup.* Most enterprises perform a full backup once a week and then either an incremental backup (full plus incremental) or a differential backup (full plus differential) each weeknight.

 These different backups use a file attribute called the *archive bit,* or the *A bit.* (Remember the Read-only, Archive, System, and Hidden [RASH] attributes?) The archive bit is a binary bit (either a 0 or a 1) and is set to 1 on a file as it is added to a volume or when it is modified and saved (written) to the volume. This indicates that the contents of the new or modified file do not yet reside on any backup tape. Archive bits of files that have been copied to tape by using the full or incremental backups are set to 0, indicating that the data resides on a backup tape. The A bit remains 0 until the file is opened, modified, and then saved to the volume, when the archive is switched to a 1 to indicate that this version of the file and its new data do not yet exist on tape.

THE FULL BACKUP

The full backup reads the list of files on the catalog and copies every one of them to the tape. At the end of the full backup, when every file listed in the catalog has been copied to the tape, the full backup resets the A bit of every file in the catalog to 0, indicating that these files now reside on a backup tape. The full backup is the single most complete backup, and it would be best if every backup could be a full backup for recovery purposes. However, the full backup is expensive and typically takes too much time, tape, server, and network resources to perform every night. Full backups are usually performed when the information systems and network are most quiet, late night on Saturday or very early Sunday morning.

THE FULL PLUS INCREMENTAL BACKUP

In this example, the incremental backup would be executed each weeknight (M–F) when the network and servers are at their quietest, often firing off somewhere between 11 P.M. and 3 A.M. The incremental backup begins by reading the list of files in the catalog. Then the incremental backup copies every file listed in the catalog whose archive bit is set to 1 onto tape, ignoring all the files listed in the catalog whose archive bit is set to 0. Remember that the files whose archive bit is set to 1 have just been added to a volume or modified and saved (written) to the volume since the most recent full or incremental backup, indicating that the contents of the new or modified file do not yet reside on any backup tape. Those files whose archive bit is set to 0 have already been copied to a backup tape. By only copying those files whose A bit are 1 to tape, the backup is fast and consumes less tape and fewer server and network resources.

At the end of the incremental backup, the incremental backup resets the A bit of each file it has copied to tape to a 0, indicating that the contents of the new or modified file have been copied to a backup tape. Every file listed in the catalog now has been copied to tape, and its bit has been set to 0.

Each weekday, workers add and modify files. Each weeknight, the incremental backup executes the same procedures with short and efficient backups, resetting each A bit to 0. This keeps the weeknight backup routines very efficient and less demanding on resources.

However, if a restore process is required, the full plus incremental backup strategy is more demanding. For example, if a disk fails on Saturday morning—the worst possible case—first the Sunday night full backup must be restored, and then the Monday night backup, the Tuesday night backup, the Wednesday night backup, the Thursday night backup, and finally, the Friday night backup must be restored to bring the data set to the point of the most recent backup. These six tapes must be restored in the correct order, or older files will overwrite newer, modified files, and the newer data will be lost. During a disaster situation, when data recovery is critical, the recovery processes of the full plus incremental backup strategy are quite demanding.

As with any batch process backup procedures, any new files or modified and saved files since the Friday night backup (the RPO) will be lost.

Figure 10-8 shows the full plus incremental backup and restore strategy.

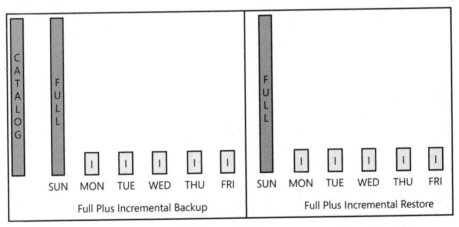

FIGURE 10-8 The full plus incremental backup and restore

THE FULL PLUS DIFFERENTIAL BACKUP

In this example, the differential backup would be executed each weeknight (M–F) when the network and servers are at their quietest, often firing off sometime between 11 P.M. and 3 A.M., just like the full plus incremental backup strategy. The differential backup begins by reading the list of files in the catalog. The differential backup copies to tape every file listed in the catalog whose archive bit is set to 1, ignoring all the files in the catalog whose archive bit is set to 0, just as in the incremental backup. By copying to tape only those files whose A bits are 1, the backup is fast and consumes less tape and fewer server and network resources.

At the end of the differential backup, the differential backup *does not* reset the A bit of each file it has copied to tape but leaves it set to 1. At the end of the differential backup, the new or modified files still have their A bit set to 1, and the balance of the files' A bits are still set to 0 (from the most recent full backup, typically on Sunday).

Each weekday, workers add files and modify files. Each weeknight, the differential backup executes the same procedures with its relatively short but growing backups, without resetting the A bit of each file in the catalog. This keeps the weeknight differential backup routines relatively efficient and less demanding on resources than a full backup but more demanding than an incremental backup.

If a restore process is required, the full plus differential backup strategy is more efficient. If, for example, a disk fails on Saturday morning, first the Sunday night full backup must be restored, and then only the Friday night backup must be restored to bring the data set to the point of the most recent backup. These two tapes must be restored in the correct order, or older files will overwrite newer, modified files, and the newer data will be lost. During a disaster situation, when data recovery is critical, the recovery processes of the full plus differential backup strategy are notably faster and more efficient.

As with any batch process backup procedures, any new files or modified and saved files since the RPO will be lost.

Figure 10-9 shows the full plus differential backup and restore strategy.

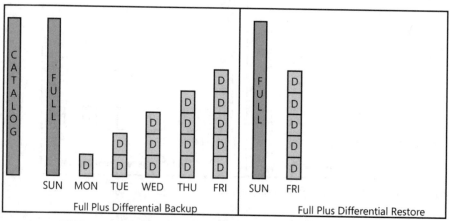

FIGURE 10-9 The full plus differential backup and restore

PRACTICE RESTORES

Although it is very important to be very good and well-rehearsed with the backup procedures, it is substantially more important to be very good and well-rehearsed at performing the restore from the backups. During an emergency restore, time is critical, and profits are lost every minute the data is unavailable.

Be very good at performing the backups.

Be great at performing the restore.

In addition, only by performing a restore from backup can you validate the proper functioning and completeness of the backup. Restore the data from a backup and actually mount the databases or open and read the files to prove that the data has been properly backed up and that recovery of the viable, readable, usable data is truly possible. Practice restores should be completed on a regular basis, weekly or at least monthly. It is a bad thing to learn that all the backup efforts for the past six months or year were wasted, and there is no data to recover after some disaster or disk failure.

Related to the disaster recovery process, the practice restore should be completed at the hot site if one exists. If the enterprise has anything less than a hot site, the practice restore should be completed at the primary site, usually within a testing lab and not directly accessible by the production network users.

EXAM TIP

Be able to identify where a specific file would reside when given a file creation date and a calendar of when full, incremental, and differential backups were performed.

Data retention

When data no longer has value for business purposes, it is either securely archived, or it should be destroyed. Most laws and regulations have specific data retention requirements for the data within the scope of compliance. Senior management, and usually the legal department, have specific opinions and demands regarding how long to retain data after its usefulness and value to the business have been eliminated. These data retention requirements should be clearly outlined in the policy documents and supported with the appropriate secure storage equipment and technologies. Operations is usually responsible for the ongoing maintenance of the data retention repository.

Data that must be retained is often securely spooled off onto the HSM, described earlier in this chapter, to remain online and accessible to authorized users. If this more costly, permanently online HSM technique is not a requirement, the tapes may be cycled offsite to a secure storage location, following a specified rotation procedure. Many tape rotation strategies exist, but an example might be to keep 1 week of daily backups on site for quick and current recovery requirements and rotate the 13 (one quarter) prior weeks' Sunday full backups to the offsite secure storage location. In addition, it is common for a monthly and a year-end full backup to be permanently archived for auditing purposes. This should, as stated before, be defined in a data retention policy and supported by specific procedures in the policy documents.

Each Monday, return the oldest cycled Sunday full backup to the facility for wiping and reuse and rotate the week-old Sunday tape to the offsite secure storage location. It is not uncommon for armed guards and an armored truck to be hired to perform this secure tape rotation and retrieval.

The backup types and intervals, tape cycling, tape retrieval, and data restore times must be considered during the incident response recovery planning and the disaster recovery planning to satisfy the RPO, the RTO, and the MTD for the data resources being recovered. These topics are covered in Chapter 8.

Secure deletion

On most file systems, the data contained within a file is stored in blocks or clusters on the hard disk drives. A table of contents, often called the file allocation table (FAT) or the master file table (MFT), is kept to record the file name and the handful of file attributes (such as RASH, create time, access time, modify time, the file's access control list, and the file's audit list, called the system access control list). The table of contents also records where on the hard disk the first block of the file is written.

When a file is deleted by using standard deletion techniques, most file systems simply edit the table of contents for the disk by replacing the first character of the file name with a question mark. This tells the file system that the disk space previously occupied by the file is now free space and is available for reuse. The actual data remains intact as nonvolatile magnetic impulses on the hard disk platter. This residual, but now unnamed data is referred to as *remnants*.

Remnants can be reclaimed by using built-in tools, such as the recycle bin in Windows, or by using one of the many other more specialized reclaiming and recovery tools such as Linux Foremost and UndeletePlus for Windows (to name a couple). The recycle bin is usable only if 100 percent of the file remnants are available. The other more specialized tools can usually recover file fragments even if some of the blocks used by the original deleted file have been overwritten by new content.

If users are using only the standard deletion processes built into the file systems to delete files, much of the sensitive data that these files held remains on the disk drives and recoverable. Sensitive files must be securely deleted to avoid leaving sensitive and recoverable remnants on the disk drives.

There are two common techniques to delete files securely. The first approach is simply to overwrite all the data within the file with random bits and no data and then save the file. Then delete the file. The remnants contain random bits and no recoverable data. The second approach is to use symmetric key cryptography (because it is fast) to encrypt the file and then save the file. Then delete the encrypted file. The symmetric encryption key, the one key that could be used for decryption, is used this one time in RAM and is then destroyed. The remnants contain encrypted ciphertext, unreadable by humans if it were to be recovered. In these two examples, the file remnants remain on the hard disk, but the file remnants do not contain any readable sensitive data. These types of tools are readily available and are included in numerous security-related applications such as the Microsoft SDelete utility and PGP's shred utility.

Now, just when it seems it is all figured out, there is still a wrinkle. Many applications create and write temporary files to the hard disks. Most autosave functions operate this way. Some journaling file systems automatically store a file in multiple locations for disaster recovery purposes. The point is that sensitive data within a file might commonly be written in multiple locations on the hard disk, and the secure deletion techniques described will only overwrite and protect the one original file.

One solution is to use the Microsoft cipher /w command-line utility or something similar. This nondestructive utility overwrites all the free blocks first with 0s, then with 1s, and then with a pattern of 1s and 0s. This eliminates the sensitive data created by the temporary files. Cipher does not overwrite any blocks that contain file data. Cipher must be executed manually and exercises (wears out?) hard disk drives. System performance is usually quite poor while the overwriting processes are running, but the remnants in free blocks will be eliminated.

Secure deletion and the regular wiping of free space should be defined by policy. Secure deletion and wiping requirements, tools, and procedures should be part of the security awareness training that all users are required to take annually. Management should enforce these policies and procedures.

Object reuse

Often, as systems are decommissioned from one task, the system and its parts can be tasked for other purposes. Some organizations simply clean up obvious file and profile debris from the first use or user and then assign the system or media for its next use or user. This is very likely to leave sensitive information tucked into less-obvious directories, in temporary file stores and caches, and in remnants in the free space. This could easily violate the data classification and protection policy and lead to a breach of sensitive information.

Any storage media that is re-tasked, especially magnetic media, such as hard disk drives, flash memory drives (USB drives), and magnetic tape media, should be carefully wiped or degaussed before being reissued for other purposes. Wiping overwrites the entire volume one or more times. Two free tools to perform secure media overwrite are HDDErase, available from the University of California, San Diego (UCSD), and Darik's Boot and Nuke (DBAN). These tools are completely destructive of all data on the target media. Be sure the media have nothing of value and that the correct media are selected before running either of these tools.

If the final overwrite is all binary zeros, this is called zeroization. Another method of zeroizing magnetic media is by using a degaussing system that introduces a strong positive and then negative magnetic field on the media, ringing down the magnetic field over time to eliminate any magnetic impulses completely on the media.

Rewritable optical disks should be included in this collection of potentially reusable media whose contents must be properly purged before reusing.

The wiping of re-tasked media should be documented and the documentation retained, including date, time, who performed the wiping, completion status, and where the media was eventually reissued. All media should be properly labeled (needs wiping or wiped) and stored securely, often in the previously described media library. The issuance of the media should be tracked.

When whole systems are being re-tasked, such as servers, desktops, or laptops, the operating system should be reinstalled from scratch or reimaged from trusted source images.

Secure destruction

Remnants aren't the only way data leaks out of the enterprise. Business materials headed for the trash often contain sensitive data. In many locations, when an owner places content in a receptacle for trash pickup, he is literally giving up ownership of the items. Until the garbage truck comes by and collects the trash, the items in the trash bin have no owner. If anyone picks them up, it is not theft. In many cases, it is not a crime to take things out of a trash bin (dumpster diving) when the trash bin is in a position to be collected.

Printed documents, optical disks, tape media, flash drives, and hard disk drives that are being disposed of must be physically destroyed. A paper shredder should cut the pages not just in strips (which can be reassembled) but crosscut into small squares or diamond shapes. Most commercial grade shredders include chippers to destroy optical disks. Some larger companies and commercial secure-destruction businesses certify the physical destruction of bulk materials, including printed documents, optical disks, tape media, flash drives, and hard disk drives.

Secure destruction should be defined and managed by policy. The requirements and procedures should be part of the security awareness training that all users are required to take annually. Management should enforce these policies and procedures.

Fax security

Fax machines present another risk to the exposure of sensitive information. Many of them print the inbound messages and eject the printed copy into a common output bin. If the fax machine is not physically secure, unauthorized people have access to data they are unauthorized to see. By physically securing the fax machine, it becomes dedicated to a specific clearance, classification, or privilege level of use.

Another method of securing inbound fax content is to integrate the fax system with the email system. This technique forwards the inbound fax to the intended recipient's email mailbox, which, of course, requires appropriate authentication to gain access. Inbound faxes that cannot be directed to the proper destination email mailbox must be delivered to a default mailbox, and someone with the proper clearance or privilege level must be assigned to assess these faxes securely and manually forward them on to the proper recipient email box.

 Another aspect of fax security is in the transmission of sensitive faxes. An add-on to fax machines is a *fax line encryption* device. These typically are placed inline on the telephone line and are programmed with the fax numbers to which sensitive information may be sent or received from. These inbound and outbound numbers then trigger the encryption and decryption process and the appropriate symmetric key to complete the encryption and decryption process as necessary. A fax-line encryption device is required at each end of the transmission line, and symmetric keys must be exchanged securely between these endpoints. Numbers that are different from these pre-identified, sensitive locations do not trigger the encryption and decryption process and are sent and received in plaintext.

 Quick check

1. What are the RAID levels that provide data redundancy?
2. Why is it necessary to overwrite or encrypt a file and then save it before deleting it?

Quick check answers

1. RAID 1, RAID 10, RAID 15, all containing a mirror set
2. To remove any valuable data that will become a remnant

Attacks on operations

The operations department and team are responsible for the ongoing operation and maintenance of the information systems. Their daily activities are driven and controlled by policies, standards, procedures, baselines, and guidelines. These policy documents are infused with the security intentions and controls that have been identified and implemented by legal and regulatory compliance requirements, by risk assessment and risk management, disaster recovery and business continuity, and the data classification components of the security program. Although operations is instrumental in the proper maintenance of the security of the information systems of the enterprise, its focus is usually on maintaining the availability of the information resources. The confidentiality and integrity components are usually baked into the procedures the operations team must follow, but operations must keep its eyes open for newly created or discovered vulnerabilities and threats. It must also diligently watch for violations and anomalies that might be an indication of a breach of security.

Preventive measures

The best way to avoid losses is to prevent the loss event from happening at all. Following are many of the components enterprises use consistently in their attempt to prevent bad things from happening. These high-level topics and their interrelationships have been described throughout this book.

- Senior management's vision on inherent vulnerabilities and threats, tolerance for risk, and ethical standards
- Applicable laws and regulations
- Due diligence, due care, and prudent management
- Risk assessment and risk management

- The business impact analysis
- Disaster recovery planning
- Business continuity planning
- Administrative, physical, and technical controls
- Policies, standards, procedures, baselines, and guidelines structured following accepted standards, recommendations, and best practices
- Configuration management and change control
- Third-party governance
- A trusted path as subjects use computers and programs to access objects
- Strong authentication
- Strong physical security
- Strong network security
- Access granted at least privilege
- Separation of duties, job rotation, dual control
- Ongoing monitoring and auditing
- Hiring and termination practices
- Security awareness training with reminders and enforcement
- Safety training
- Social engineering awareness training
- Consistent enforcement of policy

By keeping this high-level vision of security and safety part of the daily operations, an enterprise is more likely to identify and avoid accidents, injuries, errors and omissions, theft, fraud, exploit and compromise, and, in general, breaches of the confidentiality, integrity, and availability of its valuable information assets.

Common attacks and losses

Following is a list of many of the types of attacks that cause potentially avoidable losses to the enterprise. These attacks have been described throughout this book.

- Unauthorized use
- Misuse of privilege
- Password cracking/guessing/sharing
- Key cracking
- Emanations detection
- Social engineering
- Dumpster diving
- Aggregation and inference

- Traffic analysis
- Errors and omissions
- Accidents and injuries
- Fraud
- Theft
- Employee sabotage
- Keyboard loggers
- Hacking (black hat)
- Penetration testing (white hat)
- Random/browsing/spray and pray/opportunistic attack
- Targeted attack/advanced persistent threat (APT)
- Malicious code/malware/virus/worm
- Zero-day attack
- Denial of service (DoS)
- Distributed denial of service (DDoS)/botnet/army of zombies

Anatomy of a targeted attack

Opportunistic attacks, also called shotgun attacks, grazing attacks, going after the low-hanging fruit, or the spray and pray attacks, include a few of the same steps as the targeted attack but are based on exposure to many potential targets, with the expectation that some can be successfully exploited. In contrast to the more common opportunistic attacks that spread their hooks and malware everywhere they can, as fast as they can (before the attack is identified and defenses are installed) hoping to affect a small percentage of vulnerable systems and unwitting users, the targeted attack is often slow and stealthy, with a specifically chosen target and usually for a specifically chosen valuable information asset. The relatively new APT falls into this category.

Following are the major steps of the targeted attack.

- Target selection
- Passive reconnaissance
- Active reconnaissance
- Exploit
- Escalate privilege
- Entrench
- Cover tracks
- Pillage
- Pivot and attack

EXAM TIP

Be sure to understand phases and the order of the targeted attack and that these phases and this order are used in the advanced persistent attack.

Target selection

The targeted attack begins with a carefully selected target. Sometimes this target is chosen because of a grudge or a political or philosophical position (called hacktivism), but the distinct and growing trend in cyber-attacks is that the target is chosen so the attacker can take something of value for financial benefit. This is often the theft of financial account information so credit card fraud can be committed or bank accounts emptied. Sometimes, that financial benefit is obtained by renting out the attacker's botnet (also called army of zombies) to someone who wants to harm the victim. (Remember that the victim is the owner of the targeted system.) In this case, the botnet renter identifies the target enterprise to be attacked.

Also growing as a key motive for target selection is governmental cyber-espionage, which some are equating to cyber-warfare. In March 2013, the US Senate Intelligence Committee declared that cyber-attacks and cyber-espionage have become the top security threat, over terrorism, facing the United States.

Passive reconnaissance

Passive reconnaissance is information gathering about the target and victim in a manner that cannot be detected. So much information is freely available in the public domain about just about everyone that simple Google or Bing searches reveal many insights to vulnerabilities and tools for social engineering attacks. If the company is publicly held, its quarterly and annual tax filings are public, senior management and the members of the board of directors are published details, financial holdings and future plans are revealed. The Electronic Data Gathering, Analysis, and Retrieval (*EDGAR*) database is a publicly accessible and free collection of the Securities and Exchange Commission (SEC) filings of every publicly held foreign and domestic company. These types of information gathering are anonymous and beneath the radar of the target and victim.

Getting closer to the victim, but still anonymous and beneath the radar are reconnaissance techniques such as viewing the source HTML on all webpages of the target enterprise. Most websites and their content can be copied by automated spider-bots or robots that crawl the links and download content. Then offline, the attacker can review and study this content for code comments, hard-coded network paths, version documentation, and other superfluous information that provide clues to the application and network architecture and, sometimes, even user names and passwords.

By using a Telnet client, an attacker can telnet to various well-known ports on a target server to perform *banner grabbing* anonymously. The active services on a server respond with the service banner that presents enough information about the server and the service to begin to map out the public areas of the network architecture of the enterprise in the perimeter network along with operating system and application versions and update levels of the identified systems. Although this process actively probes the server, the process is anonymous and is therefore usually considered passive reconnaissance.

 Because most enterprises are adding fast and easy wireless networks, an attacker can be within a few yards or a few miles of the target and begin to sniff the wireless network covertly for details and vulnerabilities. This falls into the category of *war driving*, by which a tool such as Netstumbler (for Windows) or Kismit (for Linux) maps out many details of the wireless access points in the area of the target enterprise.

 EXAM TIP

When the details of a wireless access point are discovered, attackers often use a form of substitution cipher cryptography called war chalking and paint symbols on the building or sidewalks nearby to enable them and others, with understanding of the substitution characters, to access the wireless network at a later time.

These and other forms of passive reconnaissance are undetectable by the target when done carefully and correctly.

Active reconnaissance

Active reconnaissance provides the attacker more directly related and tangible information about the target but is the first point in this anatomy of an attack where the attacker can be noticed and detected as the bad guy he is—if the target enterprise is monitoring and knows what, how, and where to look for it.

 In this phase of the attack, the attacker is using scanning and probing software tools first to *footprint* the target network and nodes to develop an overview of the exposed network architecture. Network scanning tools, sniffers (also called network analyzers or protocol analyzers), ping sweeps, and variations thereof can identify active nodes in the publicly exposed perimeter network and might begin to reveal some of the attributes of the active nodes.

 Footprinting can also include *war dialing*, by which the list of phone numbers the company uses are dialed by a computer with a modem, and the computer then identifies and logs all numbers that electronic devices answer. By using the AT commands, nearly 300 telephone device commands, the war dialer can very often document the type of answering device (answering machine, fax machine, computer modem, PBX, and so on) along with the vendor, model number, and firmware version number. Many of these war dialer databases include the default remote codes to gain access to the phone line–attached devices that might facilitate an easy break-in.

 As this network layout begins to develop more, specific nodes, targets of interest and opportunity begin to present themselves. The second half of this phase includes the usually more aggressive, informative, and revealing *fingerprinting* of specific nodes that have been identified on the network. By learning about specific traffic patterns and protocols used, one or more identified systems attract the attention of the attacker. Perhaps a relatively new vulnerability was recently identified in Secure Sockets Layer (SSL). SSL traffic to a server makes this server more interesting because of its potential and, perhaps, likely vulnerabilities and ease of exploitation. Nevertheless, for one or more reasons, identified nodes begin to grab the interest of the attacker.

 These interesting nodes will now be targeted for more detail analysis, usually by means of *port scanning*, or identifying open ports where networking services are listening for service requests. (Remember the well-known server side ports and the ephemeral port at Layer 4 of the OSI model?) By identifying the *network listeners*, also known as *server services*, with the open ports, usually the operating system, network services, and applications can be identified, very often along with their version, service pack, and update levels. By gathering this much detail about a system, the attacker can now identify the list of known and potential vulnerabilities on this system that can be exploited.

 Vulnerability databases are a collection of all the known vulnerabilities of operating systems, protocols, infrastructure systems and services, and applications. They are used for good cause to help system administrators (such as the operations team members) recognize the vulnerabilities and mitigate or eliminate them in their systems and software. Vulnerability databases are used for malicious purposes by attackers to identify the weaknesses that can be exploited.

 This phase can also include some noninvasive forms of social engineering for information gathering and intelligence purposes, such as when the trash is taken to the Dumpster and then later collected (for dumpster diving opportunities later on), shift schedules, personnel in targeted roles in the enterprise, and so on.

Exploit

This is the phase in which the attacker is fully exposed, but again, it is only risky to the attacker if the target enterprise is watching and knows what to watch for. Now that the attacker has a good idea what systems are interesting and potentially valuable targets (for a number of reasons) and knows the operating system, network services, and applications, including versions and update levels, he knows the vulnerabilities and usually has a database of exploits for a large number of the identified probable vulnerabilities. The attacker begins to execute the exploits that target these vulnerabilities. The exploits are various types of executables, scripts, and other types of *attack code* that complete the violation of the application or system. With the large number of software vulnerabilities on systems, sooner or later, one of the exploits is likely to be successful.

Many *exploit databases* are available that link exploit code with the vulnerabilities in the operating systems and applications. These are used, again, for good intent, for penetration testing of systems to verify strength or weakness in the information systems, or for malicious intent by attackers to break in and compromise one or more systems and violate the confidentiality, integrity, or availability of valuable information assets. Some of these exploit database sources even offer *zero-day exploits* for sale. Zero-day exploits target vulnerabilities that are previously unknown and unpublished, and the exploit code is therefore very likely to affect successfully every system running the vulnerable software that the code is used against. Because the exploit code has never been seen before in the wild, the antivirus signature databases do not contain a signature for the exploit code, and the code can run undetected and unstoppable, often spreading very fast, compromising many systems, and causing a great deal of loss to enterprises.

Privilege escalation

The attacker needs enough privilege on the compromised system to install applications and adjust configuration settings for her malicious purposes. Because of the recent (and appropriate) trend of granting access following the principle of least privilege, very often the attacker does not have sufficient privilege level to entrench and pillage to the fullest extent after the first successful exploit on a system. The attacker, now with her limited level of privilege and access to the newly compromised system, must find a way to increase her privilege level to support the entrenching activities and pillage of the assets that drew her here. Often, a second and third successful exploit are required for the attacker to achieve the desired level of privilege on a system, ideally a local administrator, a domain administrator, or root.

Remember that legitimate users are first authenticated before any access to computer resources is allowed. Because the now authenticated user wishes to run programs and access information system resources, the user's access token or Kerberos ticket is bound to each access request and process the user's activities spawn. The security reference monitor at the requested resource (object) validates the user's (subject's) privilege level and, when the privileges assigned to the user on the object match the request, the security kernel allows the subject to access the object. This authorization process the security reference monitor controls is described in Chapter 5, "Security architecture and design."

The applications and their processes are executed with the privilege level of the user who launched the application. It is the vulnerabilities in the running applications (that have the access token of the user who launched the application bound to it) that are exploited. When an exploit is successful at compromising a vulnerability in running software on a target system, the attacker gains access to the system at the privilege level of the user who launched the exploited code. The attacker, who now can use this compromised application and system, has the same privilege level as the legitimate user who ran the now compromised application.

Historically, users were granted plenty of privilege so they could do their required work without running into security boundaries that slow down the user's productivity. In many enterprises, all users were granted administrator privileges, often at the network level, and almost always on their local workstation system.

As the number of compromises increased and drew enough attention, it became clear that this heightened level of privilege was more than what was required to perform users' work. The principle of least privilege came into focus and became more of a standard than an abstract concept. Even administrators who require heightened levels of privilege are commonly provided two user accounts, one that has been granted the heightened root or administrator privileges and one with much lower levels of privilege like that of a standard user. These system custodians are trained to use their standard user accounts routinely for their daily computer use and use their root or administrator accounts only when required to accomplish the tasks that require this heightened level of privilege. This minimizes the number of applications and processes that run with heightened levels of privilege on the administrators' systems. When an attacker can exploit an application, it is more likely that he will have the lower level of privilege on the system and need to find some way to escalate that privilege to entrench and pillage fully.

With a standard user level of privilege, the attacker has some level of trusted access on the compromised system. Using that level of access, the attacker performs reconnaissance on the system to identify potential paths of least resistance to escalate his level of privilege.

Attackers use several techniques to escalate privilege. Many local and network resources will be available to them. Stored user names and passwords, like those offered in the browser on website logon pages, might be accessible. The user's local data files might also be available to the attacker. Some users list their various account information in data files on the local system. On a Windows system, the local *Security Accounts Manager* (*SAM*) *database* can be accessed. On a Linux system, the *passwd file* and the *shadow file* can be accessed. The attacker can access other forms of *cached credentials* offline. These stored and cached credentials are typically protected by encryption or by being double hashed but can now be extensively probed and analyzed, perhaps compared to the rainbow tables for reverse lookup of the plaintext passwords.

Other techniques trigger the startup of one or more services on the compromised system. Services are nothing more than applications (remember applications are software, and all software contains vulnerabilities) that are configured to launch automatically at system startup or later on as needed to support user activities. Services are typically configured with user account (in this case, called *service account*) credentials that have been granted privileges sufficient to perform the functions the service is intended to do. By exploiting and compromising the code that is the service, the attacker can often gain increased privilege on the now twice compromised system.

Still another approach is to search the system logs for failed logon attempts. A common mistake users make is to enter their user name and password in the user name field accidentally by missing the tab button in between. Then, believing their credentials are typed in correctly, they press Enter to submit their credentials for logon. Because the mistyped user name (actually, the user name and password together) is unrecognized, and the submitted password is blank, the logon request fails and is logged. The details of the logged event include the user name (actually, the user name and password together), which presents the user's password in cleartext. Users should be trained to recognize this exposure of their password, and policy should require that in this case, the user must immediately change her password.

Attackers also study the accessible content on a system and gain insight for use in many forms of social engineering attacks to gain deep and highly privileged unauthorized access to the valuable information assets of the enterprise.

Entrench

With sufficient privilege acquired through successful privilege escalation processes, the attacker downloads one or usually more types of malware to the compromised system. This malware is often pulled from Internet locations in forms that evade detection by antivirus software and intrusion detection system (IDS) or intrusion prevention system (IPS) sensors. The malware might be encrypted in transit and then decrypted on the local, compromised system. It might be pulled in small, unrecognizable chunks and then assembled in the effective malware on the local, compromised system.

The malware often includes one or more (usually many) Trojaned executables, often operating system files and dynamically linked libraries (DLL) that the operating system uses. This increases the likelihood that the malware will be executed and functioning anytime the system is running. Some of these Trojaned executables provide a backdoor to the attacker, allowing him to access the system remotely and covertly. Key loggers record the keystrokes of the user(s) on the system. This provides perhaps multiple sets of logon credentials to further the attacker's access to this system, to the networked system across the enterprise, and to systems on the Internet.

The first major objective of entrenching is to reconfigure the system and download and execute enough malware and hacker types of tools for the attacker to gain certain remote access and full control and maintain that access and control as if she were a root, local, or domain administrator. This collection of malware is called a *rootkit*. When successfully deployed on a compromised system, the system is said to be *rooted*. There are user-mode rootkits and kernel-mode root kits. As described in Chapter 9, kernel-mode rootkits are usually installed as Trojaned device drivers and run in the more powerful kernel mode. Well-designed and implanted kernel-mode rootkits can be very difficult to detect. User-mode rootkits are more common. They run in the weaker user mode, must make requests for access, and typically run in Trojaned applications.

Examples of rootkits include NTRootkit, HackerDefender, and the Sony BMG rootkit. Rootkits can be used to compromise operating systems, applications, and firmware. Most antivirus software can detect the known and previously used rootkits, but new rootkits are regularly discovered, such as Stuxnet, Duqu, and Flamer.

The second major objective of entrenching is to harden the now rooted system against compromise from some other attacker. At this point, the attacker has invested much time and effort to take covert and complete ownership of the compromised system, and he intends to retain this level of ownership, so he strengthens the security of the system by patching, adjusting the firewall, updating antivirus, antispyware, IDS and IPS signatures, and so on while keeping covert and unauthorized access channels and processes intact.

Cover tracks

Although listed as a separate phase, covering the tracks of the compromise, the privilege escalation, and the entrenching is closely related to entrenching. The attacker must hide the downloaded malware, hacker tools, and malicious processes and defeat the alerting, logging, and reporting of the malicious activities.

The attacker will create a covert storage location to keep the store of malware and tools and sometimes use as a staging area while extracting valuable information assets of the enterprise. If the compromise is intended to support the distribution of illegal content, such as child pornography, *hidden partitions*, or the use of streams, can be used for this larger hidden store. *Streams* is a technique that buries content inside legitimate and innocent-looking files. Renaming file extensions, such as from .exe to .txt, is a basic technique for hiding malware.

The attacker removes entries in the various logs that report the events of the compromise, escalation, and entrenching. This is called *scrubbing the logs*. This is why the more developed security structure requires real-time journaling of all logs to a remote and secure log repository system.

An extension of scrubbing the logs is to disrupt the alerting and reporting of malicious processes and activities. The well-entrenched attacker disables the processes anywhere that these malicious events could be presented or reported to legitimate users and administrators.

The attacker might reconfigure antivirus and host intrusion detection and prevention software so the malware and malicious processes go undetected, unreported, and unimpeded. Often, this is a solid indicator of a compromised system, especially if the updates to the security software become nonfunctional. Further, the attacker often disables or breaks the updating processes of these security applications as well as the operating system and applications to help remain stealthy on the compromised systems.

To control users' and administrators' activities to detect, scan, or research anything related to the security of the system, the attacker often modifies the local hosts file and reconfigures the IP configuration parameters for the system's DNS servers. By controlling the name resolution processes, the attacker can redirect the users of the compromised systems to any servers the attacker desires. For example, the user or administrator will think he is connecting to the antivirus (AV) definition update Web server but is actually connecting to a spoofed AV webpage that spoofs the AV signature update process and ensures that the attacker's malware remains undetected.

This technique of hijacking the name resolution processes is also used to break the updating processes described earlier and might even cause additional malware downloads to occur on the compromised system.

Pillage

With the successful compromise, escalation of privilege, entrenching, and tracks covering completed, the attacker is now solidly in charge of this system and has minimized any likelihood of being detected. She is now free to take whatever looks interesting or valuable. She copies and uploads all available file content on the local system and anywhere the compromised user accounts have access enterprise-wide.

 By investigating the *most recently used* (*MRU*) shortcuts, files, and network connections, the attacker discovers the most current and potentially valuable assets accessible to the compromised user accounts.

She simply has her way with the compromised system, confident that the activities will go undetected.

Pivot and attack

After the attacker has pillaged the accessible assets to the fullest level of satisfaction, she uses this trusted user credential and vantage point as the attack system to penetrate deeper in the enterprise to compromise more systems and violate the confidentiality, integrity, and perhaps availability of an ever-growing collection of valuable information assets.

The process will repeat, beginning with the active reconnaissance phase of the anatomy of the attack, and continue through to the pillage, pivot, and attack phases. The bad guy now owns the information assets of the enterprise.

✔ **Quick check**

1. What type of reconnaissance uses a wireless sniffer to document the wireless access points in a specific geographic area?
2. What attacker process has led to the network requirement to journal-log events in a remote, secure log repository?

Quick check answers

1. War driving
2. Scrubbing the logs

Exercises

In the following exercises, you apply what you've learned in this chapter. The answers for these exercises are located in the "Answers" section at the end of this chapter.

Exercise 10-1

A four-disk RAID 5 array is being used to store important information. In Table 10-2, the Disk 1 data is missing from the RAID 5 array due to a disk failure. Using even parity, calculate the missing data by adding the missing bit for Disk 1, either a 0 or a 1, so that when adding all 4 bits on each stripe (horizontal), the answer is an even number (0, 2, 4). Note that the missing parity information on Disk 1 is in the third stripe and does not need to be calculated during the read function.

TABLE 10-2 Data and parity information (P)

Bit on disk 0	Bit on disk 1	Bit on disk 2	Bit on disk 3
0		1	0 P
1 P		1	0
0		0	0
1		1 P	1
1		0	1 P

Exercise 10-2

Create a new user standard account on the local computer running Windows Vista or later.

Recognize the option to create a standard user account with reduced privileges and an administrator account with heightened privilege.

Set a strong password on the new account.

After creating the standard user account, recognize the ability to change the privilege level from standard user to administrator.

Chapter summary

- The roles of people in the operations department are data owner, manager, custodian, and user. Operations is typically responsible for system installation and maintenance, configuration management, system availability, data management, user provisioning, fraud protection and detection, vulnerability assessment, and assistance during incident response.Data classification, labeling, and handling instructions are provided in the policy documents of the enterprise.

- Single points of failure must be identified and eliminated where possible by using fault-tolerant and redundancy techniques. Fault tolerance allows for one component failure while all related data and services remain available. Redundancy provides two or more components or data copies so that if any component fails or is destroyed, such as by data corruption, the second component or copy remains available. RAID level 0 does not provide disk fault tolerance or data redundancy and actually increases the likelihood of data loss, but provides enhanced performance. RAID 1, 10 and 15 provide (at least) one disk fault tolerance and data redundancy. RAID 1, 2, 3, 4, 5, 10 and 15 provide (at least) one disk fault tolerance. Storage area networks (SANs) are high-performance, high-capacity, high-availability data storage environments that typically provide all the fault tolerance and data redundancy required. Data backups should be performed regularly by every enterprise with valuable information assets. Full plus incremental backups optimize the backup process but complicate the restore process. Full plus differential backups complicate the backup process but optimize the restore process. Unneeded data on magnetic media must be securely deleted by overwriting or zeroization processes to eliminate data remnants. Fax systems often present the opportunity for data breaches but can be managed by integrating the fax system with the email system and using fax-line encryption devices.

- The phases of a targeted attack are target selection, passive reconnaissance, active reconnaissance, exploit, escalate privilege, entrench, cover tracks, pillage, and pivot and attack.

Chapter review

Test your knowledge of the information in this chapter by answering these questions. The answers to these questions, and the explanations of why each answer choice is correct or incorrect, are located in the "Answers" section at the end of this chapter.

1. Which of the following is not commonly used to eliminate single points of failure?

   A. RAID 0

   B. RAID 1

   C. A second connection to the Internet by using a different ISP

   D. Load balanced cluster server array

2. In black box penetration testing, what information is provided to the red team about the target environment?

   A. The targets and testing time frame

   B. Everything

   C. Nothing

   D. The IP subnet architecture of the enterprise

3. What term describes the statistical appraisal of the functional lifetime of a system or device?

   A. Maximum tolerable downtime (MTD)

   B. Statistical deviation

   C. Mean time to repair (MTTR)

   D. Mean time between failures (MTBF)

4. A device used to return all bits on magnetic media to a neutral state is performing what function?

   A. Active reconnaissance

   B. Zeroization

   C. Zero-day attack

   D. Passive reconnaissance

5. Hierarchical storage management (HSM) is best described by which of the following?

   A. The way files and directories are stored on a disk drive

   B. The way tapes are rotated offsite by armed guards in armored trucks

   C. The way files are migrated away from expensive and fast storage onto cheaper and slower storage

   D. The way disk drives are spun down to reduce power consumption and heat and prolong the life of the disks when the files they hold are not needed.

6. Using a sniffer would be used first during which phase of the targeted attack?

   A. Active reconnaissance

   B. Passive reconnaissance

   C. Pillaging

   D. Fingerprinting

7. Which of the following describes the cause of collusion and the best defense against collusion?

   A. A well-defined penetration testing agreement

   B. Separation of duties and job rotation

   C. Software vulnerabilities and regular operating system and application updating

   D. Data redundancy and fault tolerant technologies

8. When Nicole gets a transfer to a different department and role, why would an administrator need to remove her privileges?

   A. To eliminate single points of failure

   B. To avoid sequential access processes

   C. To reset the archive bit

   D. To avoid authorization creep

Answers

This section contains the answers to the exercises and the "Chapter review" section in this chapter.

Exercise 10-1

The missing bits are 1, 0, 0 P, 1, and 0 from top to bottom.

Exercise 10-2

Click Start | Control Panel | User Accounts and Family Safety | User Accounts | Manage Accounts | Create New Account.

Figure 10-10 shows the dialog box to create a new standard user account with a lower level of privilege, or an Administrator account with a heightened level of privilege.

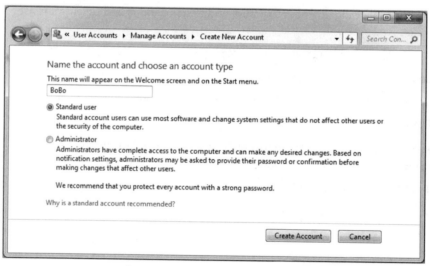

FIGURE 10-10 The Create New User dialog box

Enter a user name, leave Standard User selected, and then click the Create Account button.

In Control Panel, click the new standard user account and then click Create A Password. Figure 10-11 shows the dialog box to create a password for the new standard user account.

Notice that you must enter the password twice, and the option to set a password hint is offered in case the user forgets the password.

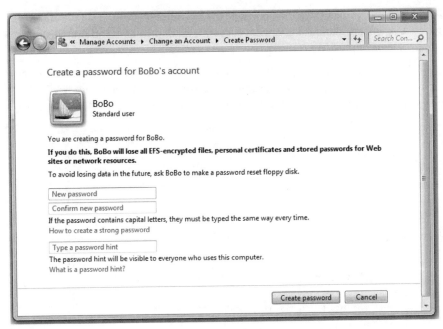

FIGURE 10-11 Setting a password for the new standard user account

Next, select Change The Account Type in the Change An Account dialog box, shown in Figure 10-12.

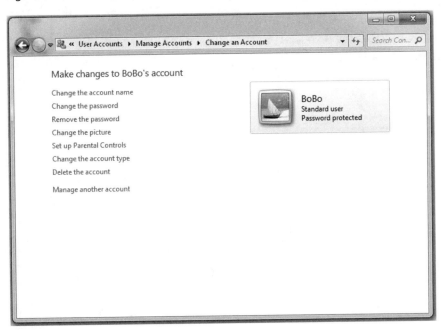

FIGURE 10-12 Managing a user account

This option presents the dialog box to choose a new account type for the standard user. The options, once again, are standard user, with a lower level of privilege, and Administrator, with a heightened level of privilege.

Select the Administrator account type and then click the Change Account Type button, as shown in Figure 10-13. If this option is unavailable, the current account might not have sufficient privilege to increase the privilege level of the new user account to Administrator level.

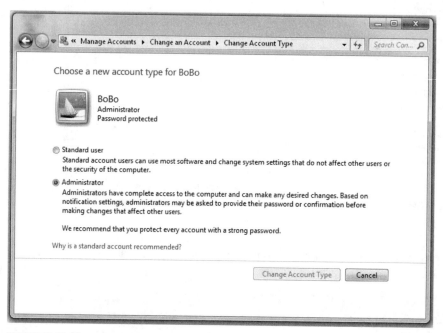

FIGURE 10-13 Managing a user account

Chapter review

1. **Correct answer: A**

   A. **Correct:** RAID 0, a stripe set, provides improved performance but no fault tolerance or redundancy.

   B. **Incorrect:** RAID 1, a mirror set, provides one-disk fault tolerance and a second full copy of the data.

   C. **Incorrect:** A second connection to the Internet and using a different ISP provide fault tolerance and a redundant connection to the Internet.

   D. **Incorrect:** A load balanced cluster server array provides fault tolerance and redundancy of the server hardware and the server applications. Further, this configuration usually includes a redundant data set on each server in the cluster array.

2. **Correct answer: C**

   A. **Incorrect:** Black box testing does not provide the targets of the test to the pen testing team (the red team).

   B. **Incorrect:** Black box testing does not provide any or all the details of the test to the pen testing team (the red team).

   C. **Correct:** Black box testing provides no information to the testing team (the red team).

   D. **Incorrect:** Black box testing does not provide the IP subnet architecture of the enterprise to the penetration testing team (the red team).

3. **Correct answer: D**

   A. **Incorrect:** The maximum tolerable downtime (MTD) is the time a business function can be absent before the business is doomed to failure.

   B. **Incorrect:** Statistical deviation is a term that identifies the variance in a product or process, usually in quality, during a specific period or production run.

   C. **Incorrect:** Mean time to repair (MTTR) is the average or estimated time to repair a specific system or component.

   D. **Correct:** Mean time between failures (MTBF) is the statistical appraisal of the functional lifetime of a system or device.

4. **Correct answer: B**

   A. **Incorrect:** Active reconnaissance is polling or scanning systems for footprinting or fingerprinting potential targets for attack.

   B. **Correct:** Degaussing or overwriting all bits with zeros returns all magnetic impulses that represent bits on magnetic media to a neutral state. This process is called zeroization.

   C. **Incorrect:** A zero-day attack targets previously unknown vulnerabilities, and they are typically very successful. Because the exploit code has never been seen before, the signature-based detection mechanisms cannot detect the attack.

   D. **Incorrect:** Passive reconnaissance is researching a potential target by using public and anonymous techniques and might include eavesdropping and sniffing network traffic; it is fully undetectable.

5. **Correct answer: C**

   A. **Incorrect:** Files and directories are stored on disks in a hierarchical manner, but that is not hierarchical storage management (HSM).

   B. **Incorrect:** Tape rotation to secure offsite locations might be a small part of the HSM but is not itself the HSM process.

   C. **Correct:** In HSM, files are migrated away from expensive and fast storage onto cheaper and slower storage as the data becomes less current and or useful to users. Typically, in an HSM environment, the data remains online but with longer access times.

   D. **Incorrect:** This describes a massive array of inactive disks (MAID), used to reduce power consumption and heat and prolong the life of the disks.

6. **Correct answer: B**

   A. **Incorrect:** Sniffers are typically undetectable on networks and therefore perform passive reconnaissance, not active. In addition, passive reconnaissance occurs before active reconnaissance.

   B. **Correct:** Sniffers are typically undetectable on networks and therefore perform passive reconnaissance.

   C. **Incorrect:** Although a sniffer could be used for pillaging network data, passive reconnaissance occurs before pillaging.

   D. **Incorrect:** Fingerprinting is an active reconnaissance process.

7. **Correct answer: B**

   A. **Incorrect:** Collusion is committed by authorized users of the IT systems, not by penetration testing team members.

   B. **Correct:** Separation of duties is a primary line of defense against fraud, which prevents a single employee from successfully and completely committing a fraudulent act, forcing multiple employees to collude to commit a fraudulent act successfully. Job rotation cycles different employees into critical roles to detect fraud if it is being committed and, if separation of duties is appropriately enacted, the only way fraud could be accomplished is through collusion.

   C. **Incorrect:** Software vulnerabilities and updating are not directly related to collusion.

   D. **Incorrect:** Data redundancy and fault-tolerant technologies are not directly related to collusion; they are used to provide high availability.

8. **Correct answer: D**

   A. **Incorrect:** Eliminating single points of failure is performed to improve availability, not to maintain the principle of least privilege and avoid authorization creep.

   B. **Incorrect:** Sequential access is a technique for accessing data, usually on paper or magnetic tape storage systems (in contrast to direct access), not to maintain the principle of least privilege and avoid authorization creep.

   C. **Incorrect:** Resetting the archive bit is used to identify new files and modified files that need to be backed up, not to maintain the principle of least privilege and avoid authorization creep.

   D. **Correct:** To maintain the principle of least privilege and avoid authorization creep, also known as authorization aggregation, an administrator would remove the now unneeded permissions related to Nicole's old position and grant additional permissions appropriate for Nicole's new position.

Additional resources

The following is a listing of Internet-based resources that provide additional information beneficial to your studies as you prepare for the CISSP exam. This list in no way officially endorses the information presented on these sites, nor does it represent any recommendation of any products or vendors; it's provided solely to demonstrate the wealth of information available on information security topics on the Internet from other sources.

Additional resources available from (ISC)2

- **CISSP Website**   *https://www.isc2.org/cissp/default.aspx*
- **CISSP Candidate Information Bulletin**   *https://www.isc2.org/cib/default.aspx*
- **CISSP Exam Schedule**   *https://webportal.isc2.org/Custom/ExamsSearch.aspx*
- **CISSP Candidate Endorsement Form**   *https://www.isc2.org/endorsement.aspx*
- **Code of Ethics**   *https://www.isc2.org/ethics/default.aspx*
- **Continuing Professional Education Point Guidelines**   *https://www.isc2.org/about-isc2-credentials.aspx*
- **Fact Sheet on DoD Directive 8570.1 regarding required security certifications**   *https://www.isc2.org/dod-fact-sheet.aspx*

Miscellaneous additional resources

- **Shon Harris's Website: Resources and Quiz**   *http://www.logicalsecurity.com/*
- **CISSP Resources and Quiz**   *http://www.cccure.org/*
- **NIST Computer Security Resource Center - Special Publication Series 800**   *http://csrc.nist.gov/publications/PubsSPs.html*
- **SANS Information Security Reading Room**   *http://www.sans.org/reading_room/*

Chapter 1: Information security governance and risk management

- **SANS Information Security Policy Templates** *http://www.sans.org/security-resources/policies/*
- **How to Develop a Risk Management Plan** *http://www.wikihow.com/Develop-a-Risk-Management-Plan*
- **Committee Of Sponsoring Organizations (COSO) of the Treadway Commission** *http://www.coso.org/*
- **COSO Enterprise Risk Management** *http://www.coso.org/documents/COSO_ERM_ExecutiveSummary.pdf*
- **COBIT Framework for IT Governance and Control** *http://www.isaca.org/Knowledge-Center/COBIT/Pages/Overview.aspx*

Chapter 2: Access control

- **Kerberos: The Network Authentication Protocol** *http://web.mit.edu/kerberos/*
- **SESAME: Secure European System for Applications in a Multivendor Environment** *https://www.cosic.esat.kuleuven.be/sesame/*
- **X.500** *http://www.x500standard.com/*
- **RADIUS** *http://portmasters.com/marketing/whitepapers/radius_paper.html*
- **Diameter** *http://www.ibm.com/developerworks/library/wi-diameter/index.html*
- **IDS/IPS** *http://www.sans.org/reading_room/whitepapers/detection/understanding-ips-ids-ips-ids-defense-in-depth_1381*
- **Honeyd Honeypot** *http://www.honeyd.org/*

Chapter 3: Cryptography

- **An Overview of Cryptography** *http://www.garykessler.net/library/crypto.html*
- **NIST Cryptographic Toolkit** *http://csrc.nist.gov/groups/ST/toolkit/index.html*
- **Ron Rivest's Crypto Links** *http://people.csail.mit.edu/rivest/crypto-security.html*
- **Diffie-Hellman(-Merkle)** *http://www.sans.org/reading_room/whitepapers/vpns/review-diffie-hellman-algorithm-secure-internet-protocols_751*
- **Symmetric Key Algorithms** *http://www.encryptionanddecryption.com/encryption/symmetric_encryption.html*

- **Asymmetric Key Algorithms** *http://www.encryptionanddecryption.com/encryption/ asymmetric_encryption.html*
- **X.509 Digital Certificates** *http://www.ietf.org/rfc/rfc2459.txt*
- **Trust Models and Management in PKI** *ftp://ftp.rsa.com/pub/pdfs/PKIPaper.pdf*
- **NIST Federal Information Processing Standards Publications** *http://itl.nist.gov/ fipspubs/*
- **MIT's Introduction to Algorithms** *http://ocw.mit.edu/courses/electrical-engineering-and-computer-science/6-046j-introduction-to-algorithms-sma-5503-fall-2005/index.htm*
- **Attacks on Cryptosystems** *http://www.encryptionanddecryption.com/encryption/ types_of_attacks.html*

Chapter 4: Physical (environmental) security

- **U.S. DoJ: Using Crime Prevention Through Environmental Design in Problem-Solving** *http://www.cops.usdoj.gov/files/ric/publications/e0807391.pdf*
- **Data Center Physical Security Checklist** *http://www.sans.org/reading_room/white-papers/awareness/data-center-physical-security-checklist_416*
- **Uninterruptable Power Supply** *http://en.wikipedia.org/wiki/ Uninterruptible_power_supply*
- **An Introduction to Fire Detection, Alarm, and Automatic Fire Sprinklers** *http://www.nedcc.org/free-resources/preservation-leaflets/3.-emergency-management/ 3.2-an-introduction-to-fire-detection,-alarm,-and-automatic-fire-sprinklers*
- **Fire Extinguishers** *http://www.fire-extinguisher101.com/*

Chapter 5: Security architecture and design

- **Intel Microprocessor Quick Reference Guide** *http://www.intel.com/pressroom/kits/ quickrefyr.htm*
- **Anatomy of a Digital Computer** *http://download.nos.org/srsec330/330L1.pdf*
- **Microsoft History of the Windows Operating System** *http://windows.microsoft. com/en-US/windows/history*
- **History of Linux** *http://ragibhasan.com/linux/*
- **Virtual Machines** *http://en.wikipedia.org/wiki/Virtual_machine*
- **Security Models and Information Flow** *http://citeseer.ist.psu.edu/viewdoc/ summary?doi=10.1.1.35.1103*
- **Trusted Computer System Evaluation Criteria** *http://csrc.nist.gov/publications/his-tory/dod85.pdf*

- **Rainbow Series** *http://csrc.nist.gov/publications/secpubs/rainbow/index.html*
- **Information Technology Security Evaluation Criteria** *http://www.iwar.org.uk/comsec/resources/standards/itsec.htm*
- **Common Criteria** *http://www.commoncriteriaportal.org/*
- **International Organization for Standardization (ISO)** *http://www.iso.org/*

Chapter 6: Legal, regulations, investigations and compliance

- **Internet Crime Complaint Center (IC3) 2010 Cybercrime Report** *http://www.ic3.gov/media/annualreport/2010_IC3Report.pdf*
- **Privacy Rights Clearing House: Chronology of Data Breaches** *http://www.privacyrights.org/data-breach*
- **Intellectual Property Law** *http://www.intelproplaw.com/*
- **United States Department of Justice Intellectual Property Policy and Programs** *http://www.justice.gov/criminal/cybercrime/ippolicy.html*
- **United States Patent and Trademark Office** *http://www.uspto.gov/about/index.jsp*
- **U.S Copyright Office** *http://www.copyright.gov/*
- **Carnegie Mellon Handbook for Computer Incident Response Teams** *http://www.sei.cmu.edu/library/abstracts/reports/03hb002.cfm*
- **Incident Response** *http://www.ussecurityawareness.org/highres/incident-response.html* and *http://www.cio.com/article/218084/Incident_Response_When_Bad_Things_Happen_to_Good_Companies*
- **4th Amendment: Unreasonable Searches and Seizures** *http://www.lectlaw.com/def/f081.htm*
- **Chain of Custody** *http://pdfserver.amlaw.com/legaltechnology/Merrill_Chain_of_Custody_White_Paper.pdf*
- **Forensic Discovery Book** *http://www.porcupine.org/forensics/forensic-discovery/*
- **Order of Volatility** *http://www.porcupine.org/forensics/forensic-discovery/appendixB.html*
- **International Organization on Computer Evidence: IOCE** *http://www.ioce.org/fileadmin/user_upload/2002/ioce_bp_exam_digit_tech.html*
- **ISC2 Code of Ethics** *https://www.isc2.org/ethics/default.aspx*
- **Computer Ethics Institute** *http://computerethicsinstitute.org/*
- **Internet Architecture Board** *http://www.iab.org/*

Chapter 7: Telecommunications and network security

- **International Organization for Standardization** *http://www.iso.org/iso/*
- **OSI Model** *http://en.wikipedia.org/wiki/Open_Systems_Interconnection*
- **Modulation and Encoding** *web.cs.wpi.edu/~rek/Undergrad_Nets/B04/ Data_Encoding.ppt*
- **CSMA/CD - 802.3** *http://standards.ieee.org/about/get/802/802.3.html*
- **TCP/IP Introduction** *http://www.w3schools.com/tcpip/tcpip_intro.asp* and *http://en.wikipedia.org/wiki/Internet_Protocol_Suite*
- **IPv6** *http://ipv6.com/articles/general/ipv6-the-next-generation-internet.htm* and *http://archive.icann.org/en/meetings/saopaulo/presentation-ipv6-tutorial-basics-03dec06.pdf*
- **Firewalls** *http://www.cs.unm.edu/~moore/tr/02-12/firewall.pdf*
- **VPN** *http://en.wikipedia.org/wiki/Virtual_private_network*
- **802.11** *http://en.wikipedia.org/wiki/IEEE_802.11*
- **Wi-Fi Alliance** *http://www.wi-fi.org/*
- **WPA / WPA2** *http://www.wi-fi.org/knowledge_center/wpa2*
- **Defending your Network** *http://www.giac.org/certified-professionals/directory/ latest-papers*

Chapter 8: Business continuity and disaster recovery planning

- **DRP and BCP Planning Templates** *http://www.disasterrecovery.org/*
- **BIA Sample** *http://www.scribd.com/doc/37608733/Sample-BIA-Report*
- **Mobile Hot Site** *http://www2.wwt.com/content/fast-mobile-data-center*

Chapter 9: Software development security

- **Software Development Life Cycle (SDLC)** *http://en.wikipedia.org/wiki/Software_ development_process*
- **Capability Maturity Model Integration (CMMI) Software Engineering Institute (SEI)** *http://www.sei.cmu.edu/cmmi/start/faq/models-faq.cfm*
- **Source Code Escrow** *http://en.wikipedia.org/wiki/Source_code_escrow*

- **Change Management Template** *http://www2.cdc.gov/cdcup/library/templates/ CDC_UP_Change_Management_Plan_Template.doc*
- **Generations of Programming Languages** *http://en.wikipedia.org/wiki/ Programming_language_generations*
- **Object Oriented Programming** *http://en.wikipedia.org/wiki/Object-oriented_ programming*
- **DBMS** *http://en.wikipedia.org/wiki/Database_management_system*
- **Artificial Intelligence** *http://www.aihorizon.com/*
- **Open Web Application Security Project (OWASP)** *https://www.owasp.org/index. php/Main_Page*
- **Secure Code Review** *http://www.homeport.org/~adam/review.html; http://msdn.microsoft.com/en-us/library/ff649315.aspx;* and *http://silverstr.ufies.org/blog/msdn-webcast-code-review.pdf*

Chapter 10: Operations security

- **Configuration management** *http://www.icmhq.com/*
- **Vulnerability Assessment** *http://www.sans.org/reading-room/whitepapers/basics/ vulnerability-assessment-421?show=vulnerability-assessment-421* and *http://iac.dtic.mil/csiac/download/vulnerability_assessment.pdf*
- **Penetration Testing** *http://www.pentest-standard.org/index.php/FAQ; http://www.penetration-testing.com/;* and *http://www.sans.org/reading_room/ whitepapers/testing/*
- **Fraud Management** *http://www.utica.edu/academic/institutes/ecii/publications/ articles/BA309CD2-01B6-DA6B-5F1DD7850BF6EE22.pdf* and *http://www.tofmi.com/*
- **Social Engineering** *http://www.symantec.com/connect/articles/social-engineering- fundamentals-part-i-hacker-tactics; http://www.social-engineer.org/;* and *http://www.sans.org/reading_room/whitepapers/engineering/*

Index

Symbols

B

O

W

About the author

 **DAVID R. MILLER** has been a consultant, instructor, and author since the early 1980s and has specialized in information security, enterprise architecture, network engineering, legal and regulatory compliance, forensics investigation, and security program development. He performs as a security lead and forensic investigator on numerous enterprise-wide IT design and implementation projects for *Fortune* 500 companies, providing compliance, security, technology, and architectural recommendations and guidance. His projects include Active Directory enterprise designs, Security Information and Event Management (SIEM) systems, intrusion detection and protection systems (IDS/IPS), endpoint protection systems, data leakage solutions, vulnerability management and incident response, and more.

David is an author, a lecturer, and a technical editor of books, curriculum, certification exams, and computer-based training videos. He is a principal author of the information systems security book, *Security Information and Event Management (SIEM) Implementation* (McGraw-Hill, 2011). David has coauthored three books for Microsoft Press, on Microsoft Windows Server 2008, Windows Server 2008 R2, and Exchange Server 2007, and two books on Windows Vista for Que Publishing. David has also coauthored three books for Sybex and Wiley Publishing: *Security Administrator Street Smarts*, first, second, and third editions. This *CISSP Training Kit* is David's tenth book.

David is regularly invited to perform as a Microsoft Subject Matter Expert (SME) on product lines, including Windows Server 2012, Windows Server 2008, Exchange Server 2007, Windows 7, and Windows Vista. David has written curriculum and performed instruction for computer-based training videos on Windows Server 2008 and IT security courses such as CISSP, SSCP, Security+, CWSP, Data Loss Prevention (DLP), Information Rights Management (IRM), digital watermarking, and the Microsoft Certified Solutions Expert (MCSE) certification. David has lectured on network engineering and information systems security to prestigious groups, including the Smithsonian Institution; the US Military Academy at West Point; the US Army Advanced Battle Command; the US Department of the Interior; Cisco Systems, Inc.; Oracle Corporation; JP Morgan Chase & Co. Global Financial Services; Symantec Corporation; the Hewlett-Packard Company; and more.

David has earned the following certifications: CISSP; SANS GISP; PCI QSA; SME; MCT; MCITPro Windows Server 2008 Enterprise Administrator; MCSE Windows Server 2003: Security; MCSE Windows 2000; MCSE Windows NT 4.0; LPT; ECSA; CEH; CWNA; CCNA; CNE; Security+; A+; and Network+.

How to download your ebook

To download your eBook, go to http://aka.ms/PressEbook and follow the instructions.

Please note: You will be asked to create a free online account and enter the access code below.

ACCESS CODE:

LDGXJZN

CISSP Training Kit

Your PDF eBook allows you to:

- search the full text
- print
- copy and paste

Best yet, you will be notified about free updates to your eBook.

If you ever lose your eBook file, you can download it again just by logging in to your account.

Need help? Please contact: **msinput@microsoft.com**

NOTE: This access code is non-transferable and is void if altered or revised in any way. It may not be sold or redeemed for cash, credit, or refund.

Now that you've read the book...

Tell us what you think!

Was it useful?
Did it teach you what you wanted to learn?
Was there room for improvement?

Let us know at http://aka.ms/tellpress

Your feedback goes directly to the staff at Microsoft Press,
and we read every one of your responses. Thanks in advance!